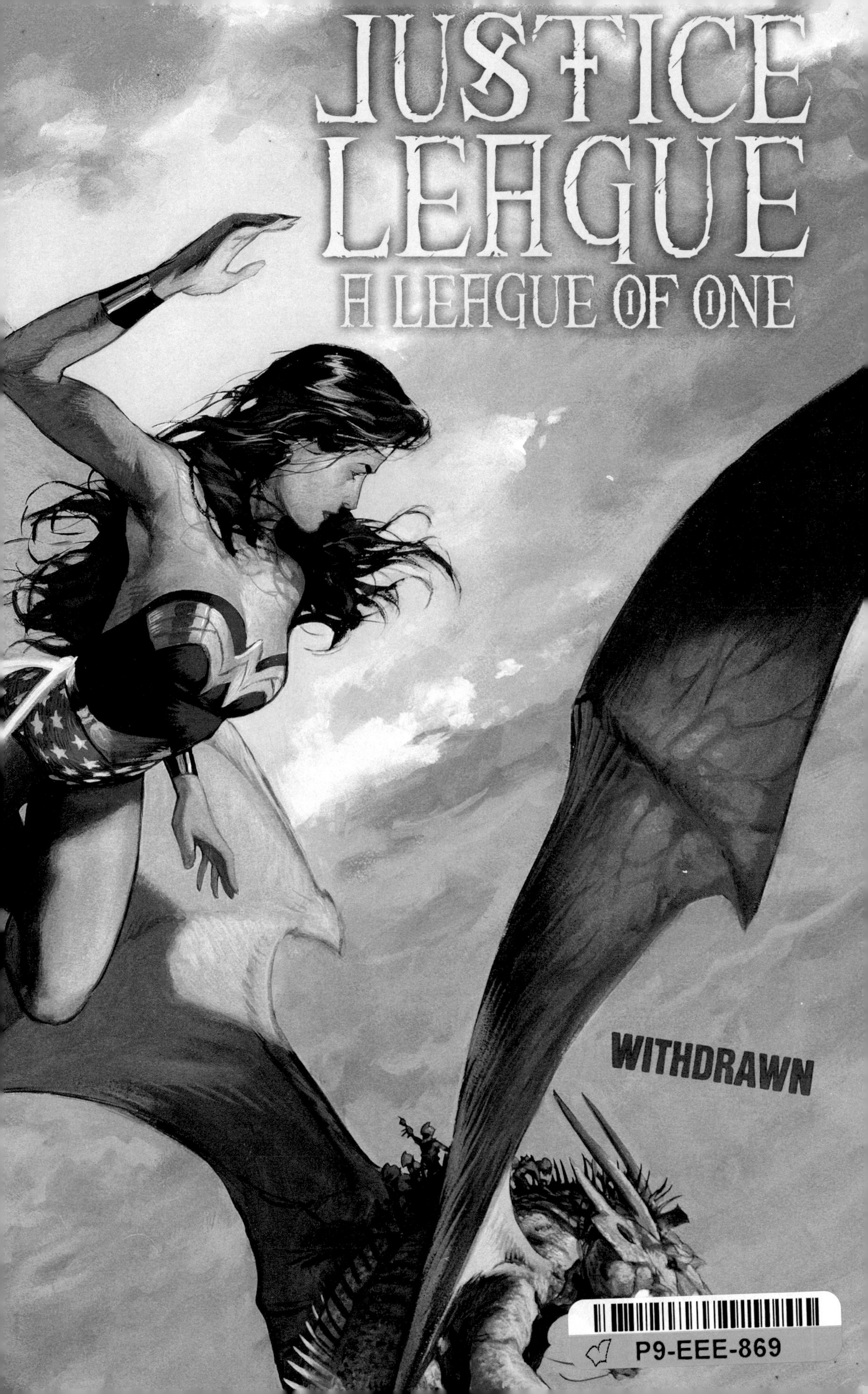
JUSTICE LEAGUE
A LEAGUE OF ONE

MIKE CARLIN DAN RASPLER Editors – Original Series
TOM PALMER JR TONY BEDARD Associate Editors – Original Series
JEB WOODARD Group Editor – Collected Editions
LIZ ERICKSON Editor – Collected Edition
DAMIAN RYLAND Publication Design

BOB HARRAS Senior VP – Editor-in-Chief, DC Comics

DIANE NELSON President
DAN DIDIO and JIM LEE Co-Publishers
GEOFF JOHNS Chief Creative Officer
AMIT DESAI Senior VP – Marketing & Global Franchise Management
NAIRI GARDINER Senior VP – Finance
SAM ADES VP – Digital Marketing
BOBBIE CHASE VP – Talent Development
MARK CHIARELLO Senior VP – Art, Design & Collected Editions
JOHN CUNNINGHAM VP – Content Strategy
ANNE DEPIES VP – Strategy Planning & Reporting
DON FALLETTI VP – Manufacturing Operations
LAWRENCE GANEM VP – Editorial Administration & Talent Relations
ALISON GILL Senior VP – Manufacturing & Operations
HANK KANALZ Senior VP – Editorial Strategy & Administration
JAY KOGAN VP – Legal Affairs
DEREK MADDALENA Senior VP – Sales & Business Development
JACK MAHAN VP – Business Affairs
DAN MIRON VP – Sales Planning & Trade Development
NICK NAPOLITANO VP – Manufacturing Administration
CAROL ROEDER VP – Marketing
EDDIE SCANNELL VP – Mass Account & Digital Sales
COURTNEY SIMMONS Senior VP – Publicity & Communications
JIM (SKI) SOKOLOWSKI VP – Comic Book Specialty & Newsstand Sales
SANDY YI Senior VP – Global Franchise Management

JUSTICE LEAGUE: A LEAGUE OF ONE

DC Comics, 4000 Warner Blvd., Burbank, CA 91522
A Warner Bros. Entertainment Company.
Printed by RR Donnelley, Salem, VA USA. 9/18/15
ISBN: 978-1-4012-5823-8
First Printing.

Library of Congress Cataloging-in-Publication Data

Moeller, Christopher, author, illustrator.
   Justice League : a League of One / Christopher Moeller.
      pages cm
   ISBN 978-1-4012-5823-8 (paperback)
1. Graphic novels. I. Title.
   PN6728.J87M63 2015
   741.5'973—dc23
                    2015014165

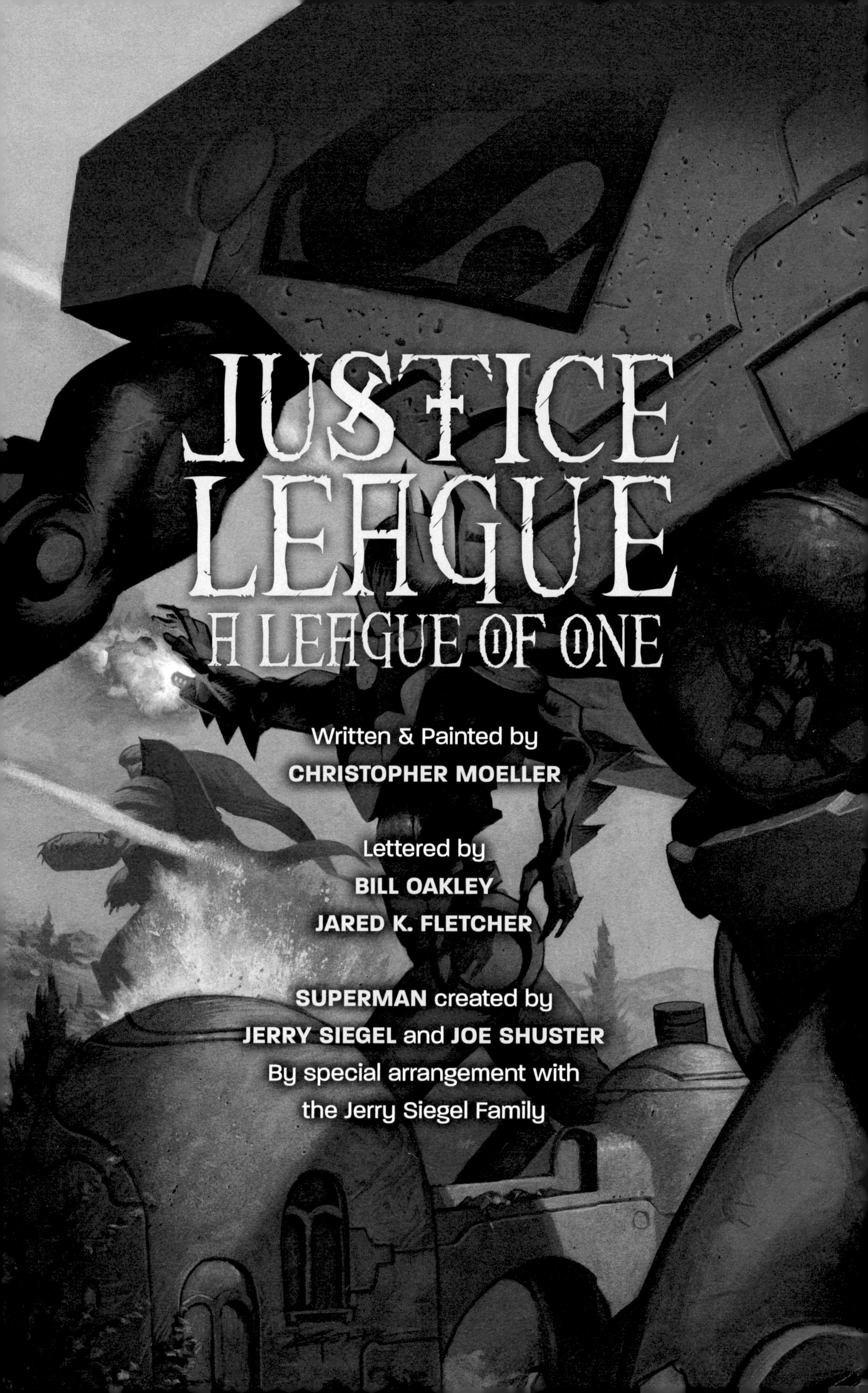

JUSTICE LEAGUE
A LEAGUE OF ONE

Written & Painted by
CHRISTOPHER MOELLER

Lettered by
BILL OAKLEY
JARED K. FLETCHER

SUPERMAN created by
JERRY SIEGEL and **JOE SHUSTER**
By special arrangement with
the Jerry Siegel Family

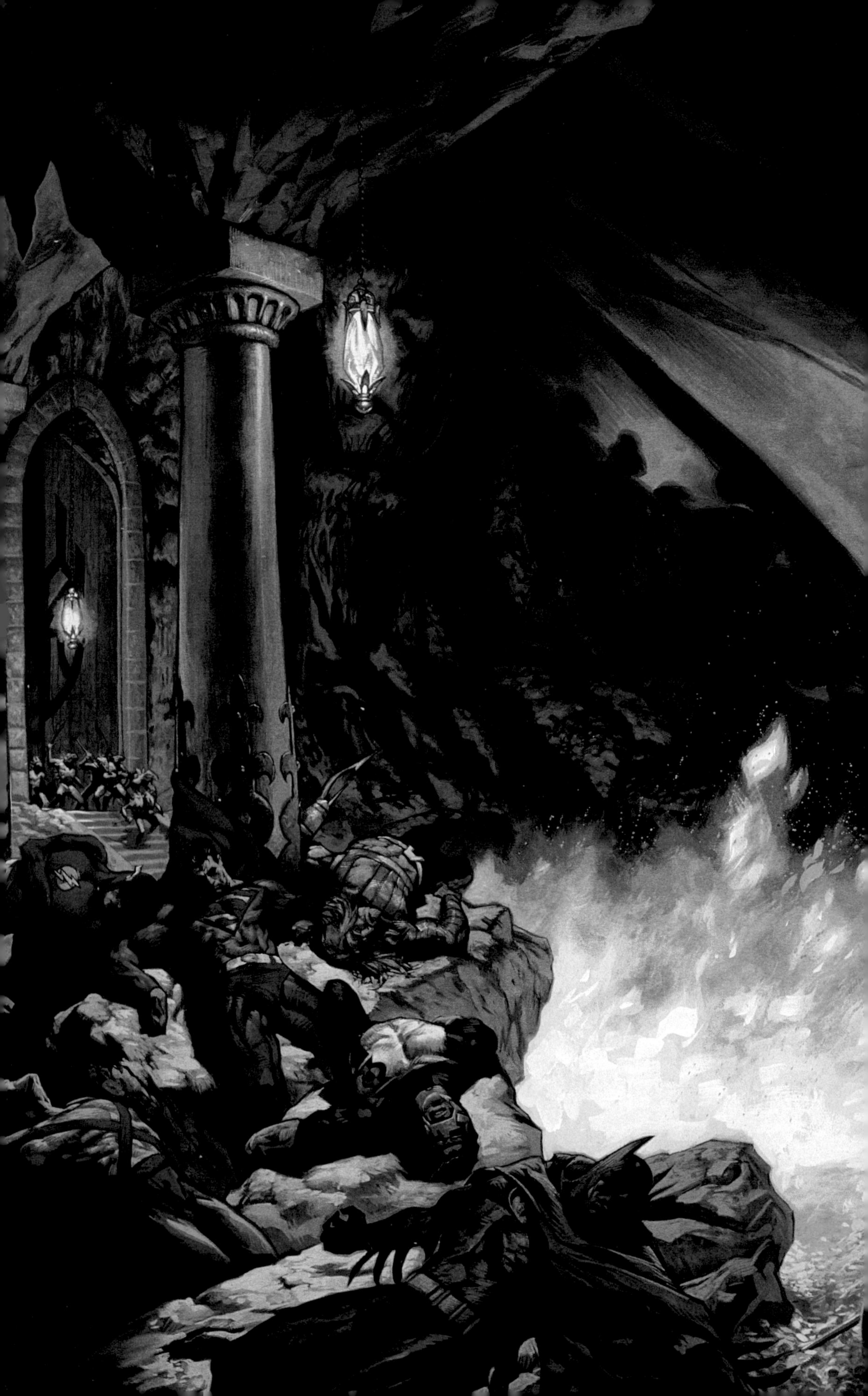

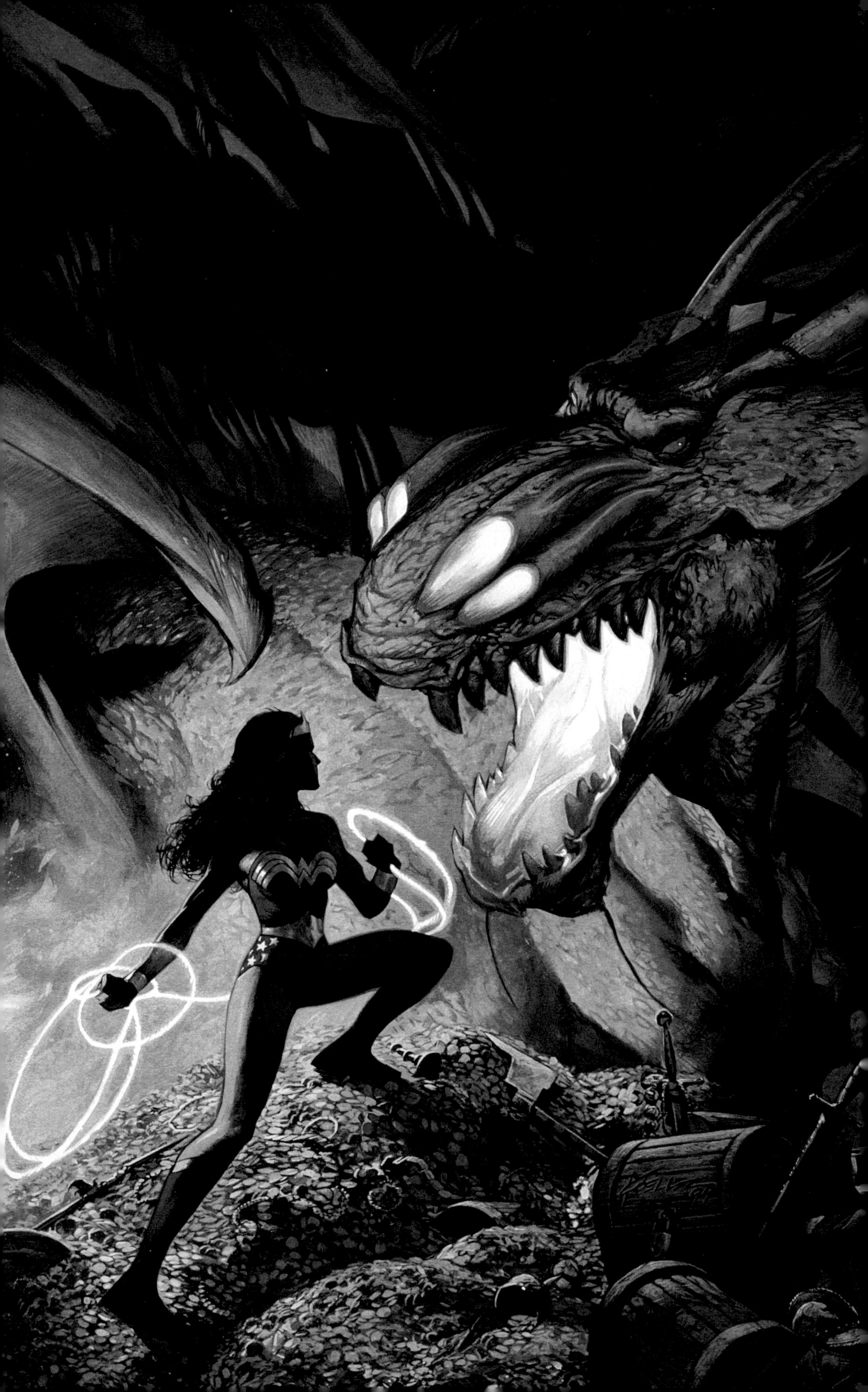

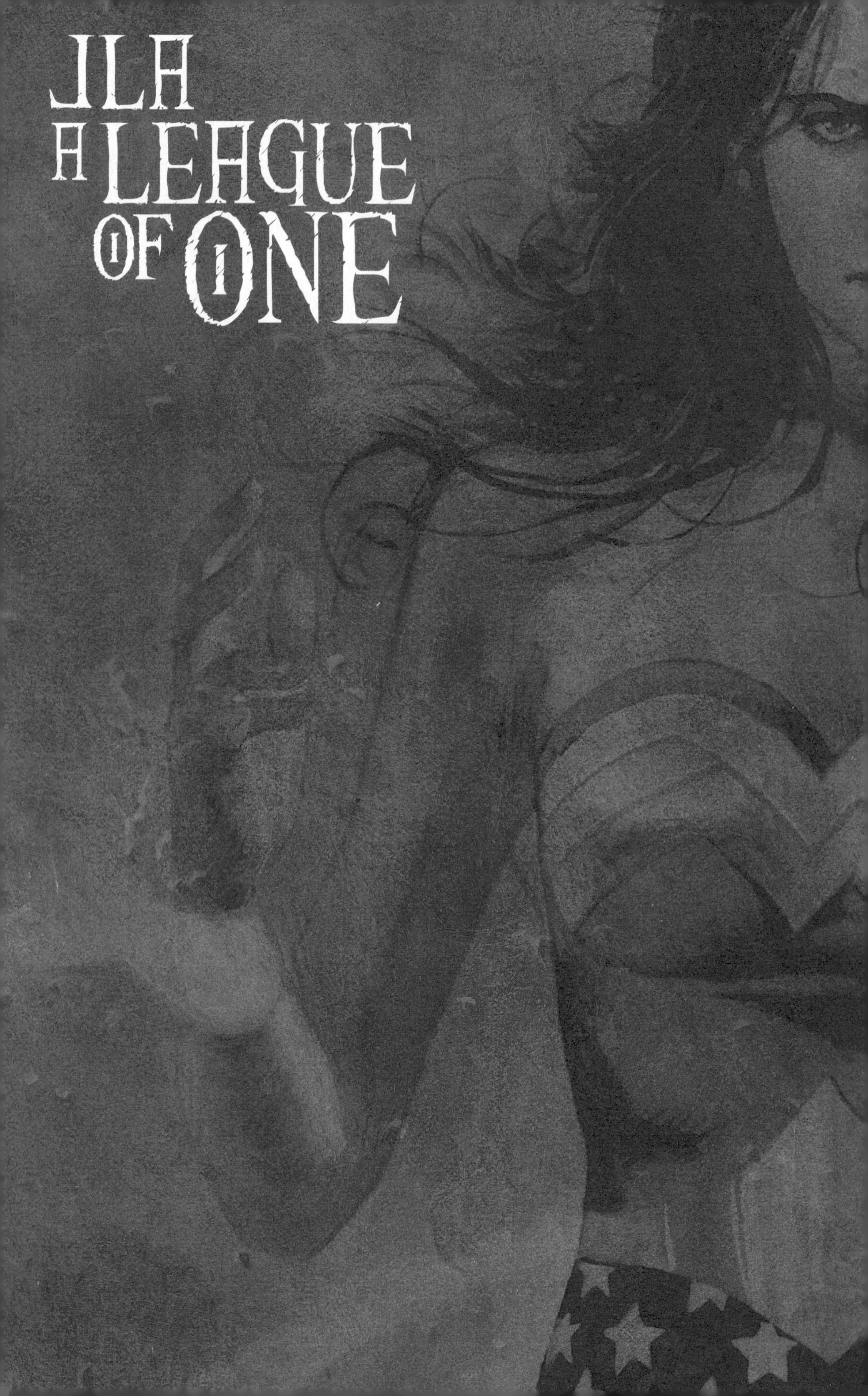
JLA
A LEAGUE OF ONE

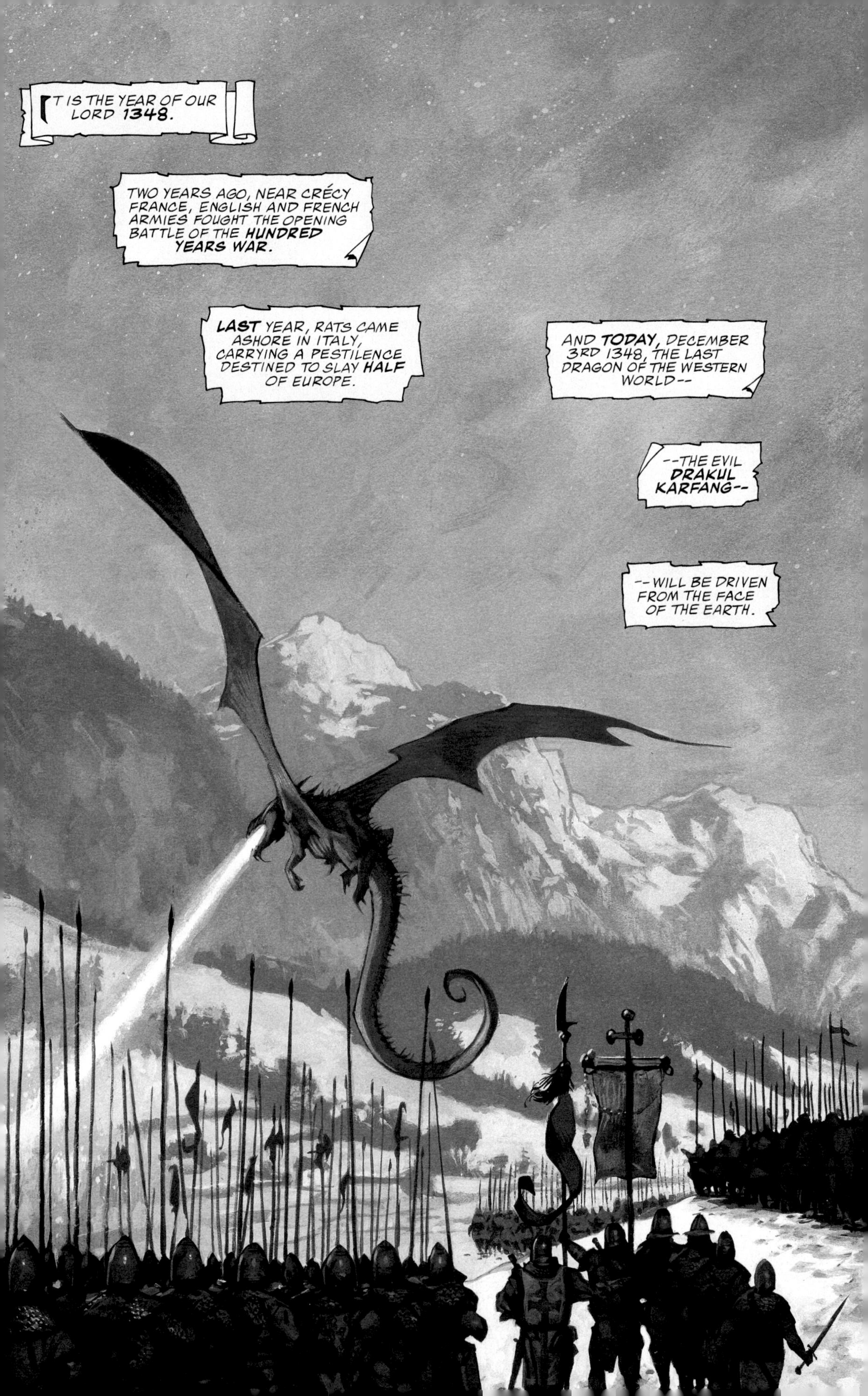
IT IS THE YEAR OF OUR LORD 1348.
TWO YEARS AGO, NEAR CRÉCY FRANCE, ENGLISH AND FRENCH ARMIES FOUGHT THE OPENING BATTLE OF THE HUNDRED YEARS WAR.
LAST YEAR, RATS CAME ASHORE IN ITALY, CARRYING A PESTILENCE DESTINED TO SLAY HALF OF EUROPE.
AND TODAY, DECEMBER 3RD 1348, THE LAST DRAGON OF THE WESTERN WORLD--
--THE EVIL DRAKUL KARFANG--
--WILL BE DRIVEN FROM THE FACE OF THE EARTH.

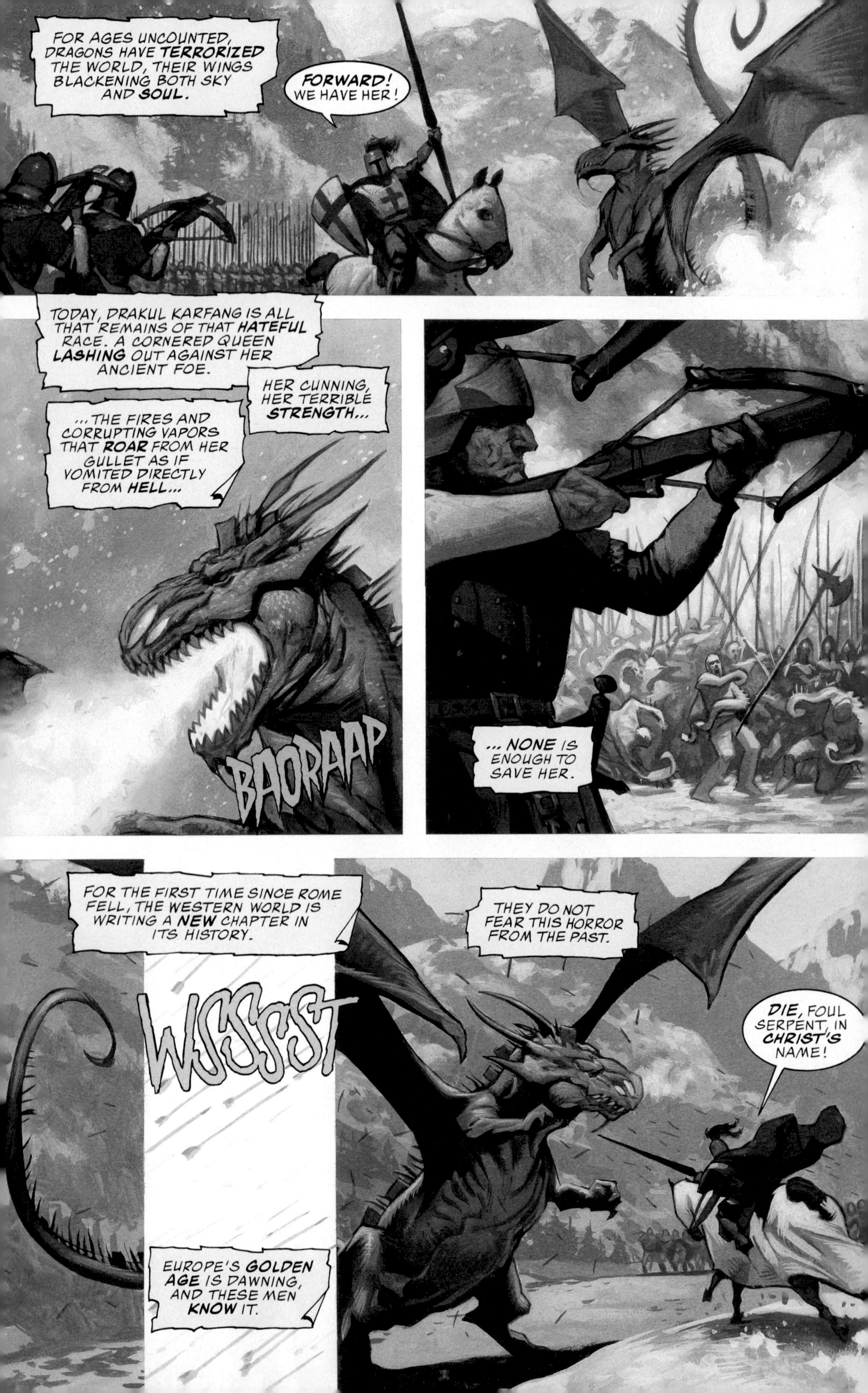
FOR AGES UNCOUNTED, DRAGONS HAVE TERRORIZED THE WORLD, THEIR WINGS BLACKENING BOTH SKY AND SOUL.
FORWARD! WE HAVE HER!
TODAY, DRAKUL KARFANG IS ALL THAT REMAINS OF THAT HATEFUL RACE. A CORNERED QUEEN LASHING OUT AGAINST HER ANCIENT FOE.
HER CUNNING, HER TERRIBLE STRENGTH...
...THE FIRES AND CORRUPTING VAPORS THAT ROAR FROM HER GULLET AS IF VOMITED DIRECTLY FROM HELL...
BAORAAP
...NONE IS ENOUGH TO SAVE HER.
FOR THE FIRST TIME SINCE ROME FELL, THE WESTERN WORLD IS WRITING A NEW CHAPTER IN ITS HISTORY.
THEY DO NOT FEAR THIS HORROR FROM THE PAST.
WSSSST
DIE, FOUL SERPENT, IN CHRIST'S NAME!
EUROPE'S GOLDEN AGE IS DAWNING, AND THESE MEN KNOW IT.

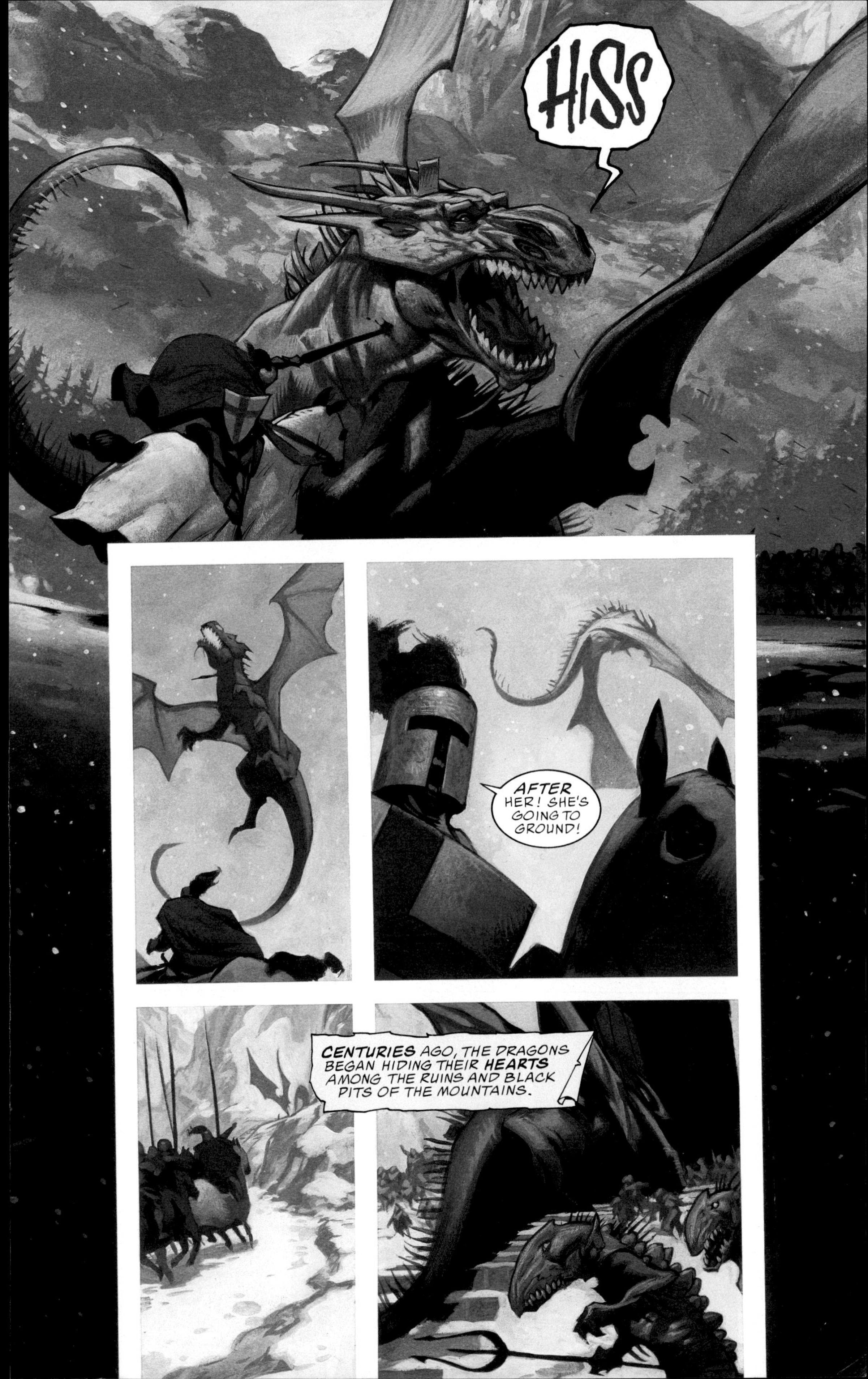
HISS
AFTER HER! SHE'S GOING TO GROUND!
CENTURIES AGO, THE DRAGONS BEGAN HIDING THEIR HEARTS AMONG THE RUINS AND BLACK PITS OF THE MOUNTAINS.

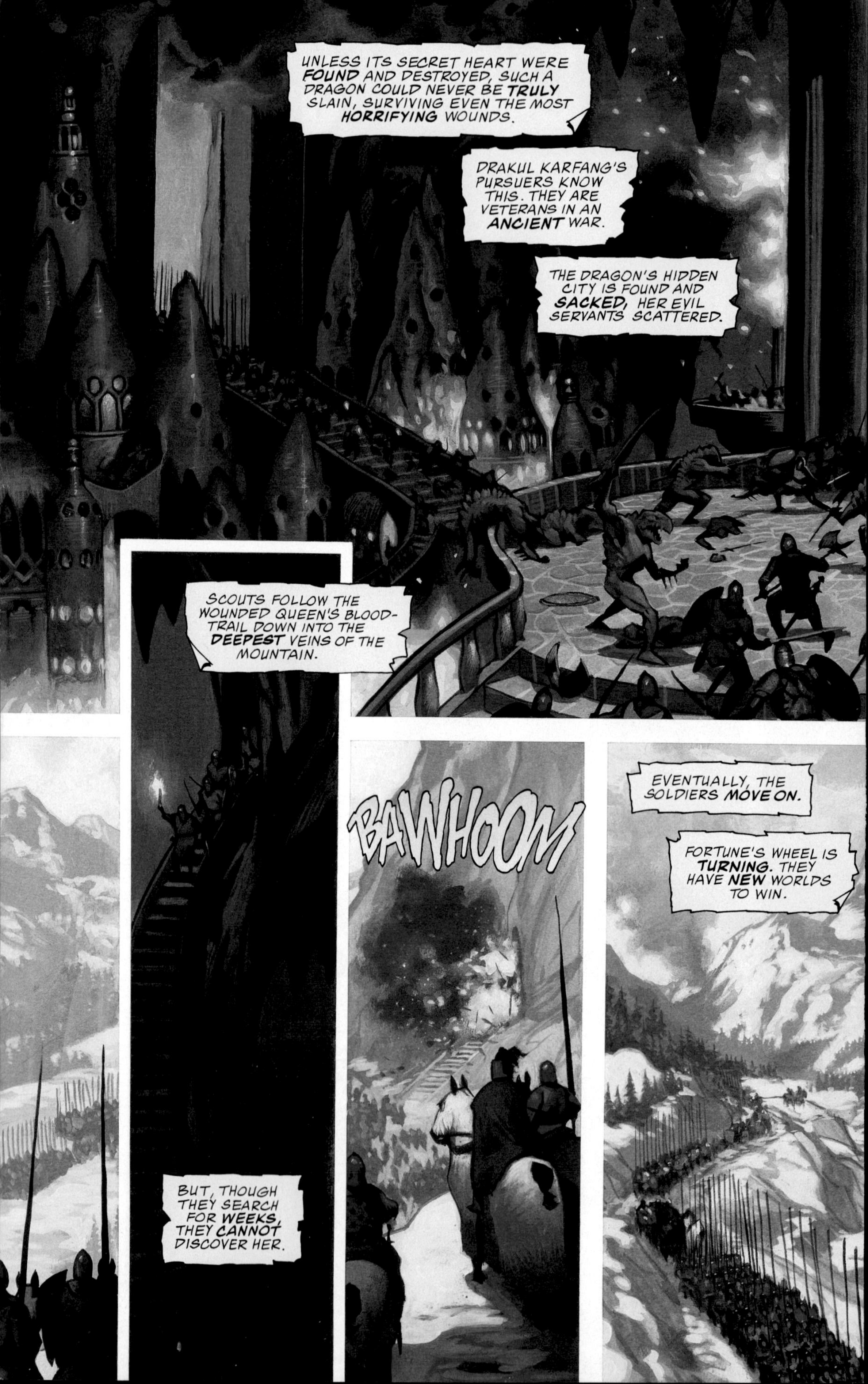
UNLESS ITS SECRET HEART WERE FOUND AND DESTROYED, SUCH A DRAGON COULD NEVER BE TRULY SLAIN, SURVIVING EVEN THE MOST HORRIFYING WOUNDS.
DRAKUL KARFANG'S PURSUERS KNOW THIS. THEY ARE VETERANS IN AN ANCIENT WAR.
THE DRAGON'S HIDDEN CITY IS FOUND AND SACKED, HER EVIL SERVANTS SCATTERED.
SCOUTS FOLLOW THE WOUNDED QUEEN'S BLOOD-TRAIL DOWN INTO THE DEEPEST VEINS OF THE MOUNTAIN.
BUT, THOUGH THEY SEARCH FOR WEEKS, THEY CANNOT DISCOVER HER.
BAWHOOM
EVENTUALLY, THE SOLDIERS MOVE ON.
FORTUNE'S WHEEL IS TURNING. THEY HAVE NEW WORLDS TO WIN.

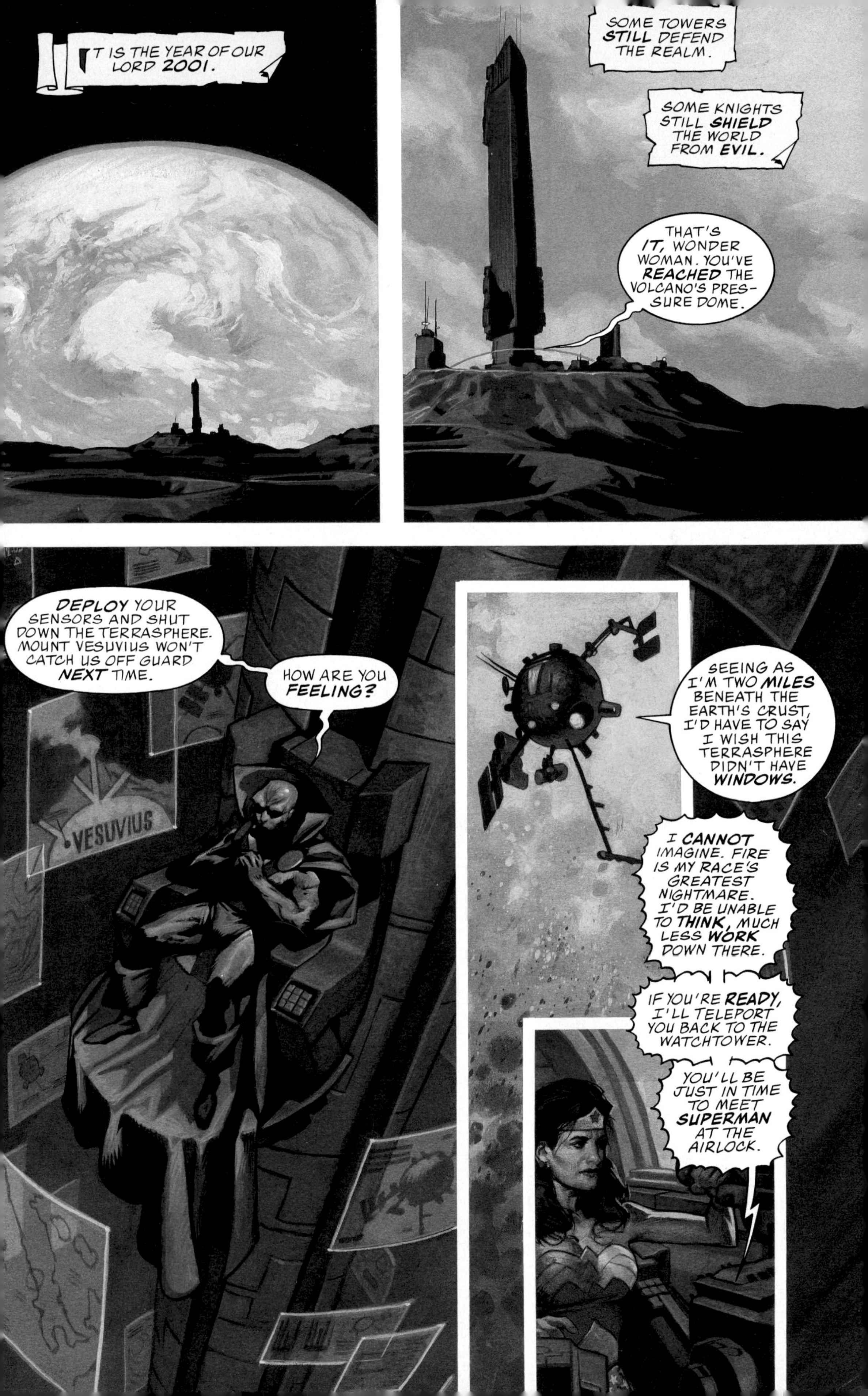
IT IS THE YEAR OF OUR LORD 2001.
SOME TOWERS STILL DEFEND THE REALM.
SOME KNIGHTS STILL SHIELD THE WORLD FROM EVIL.
THAT'S IT, WONDER WOMAN. YOU'VE REACHED THE VOLCANO'S PRES-SURE DOME.
DEPLOY YOUR SENSORS AND SHUT DOWN THE TERRASPHERE. MOUNT VESUVIUS WON'T CATCH US OFF GUARD NEXT TIME.
HOW ARE YOU FEELING?
SEEING AS I'M TWO MILES BENEATH THE EARTH'S CRUST, I'D HAVE TO SAY I WISH THIS TERRASPHERE DIDN'T HAVE WINDOWS.
I CANNOT IMAGINE. FIRE IS MY RACE'S GREATEST NIGHTMARE. I'D BE UNABLE TO THINK, MUCH LESS WORK DOWN THERE.
IF YOU'RE READY, I'LL TELEPORT YOU BACK TO THE WATCHTOWER.
YOU'LL BE JUST IN TIME TO MEET SUPERMAN AT THE AIRLOCK.
VESUVIUS

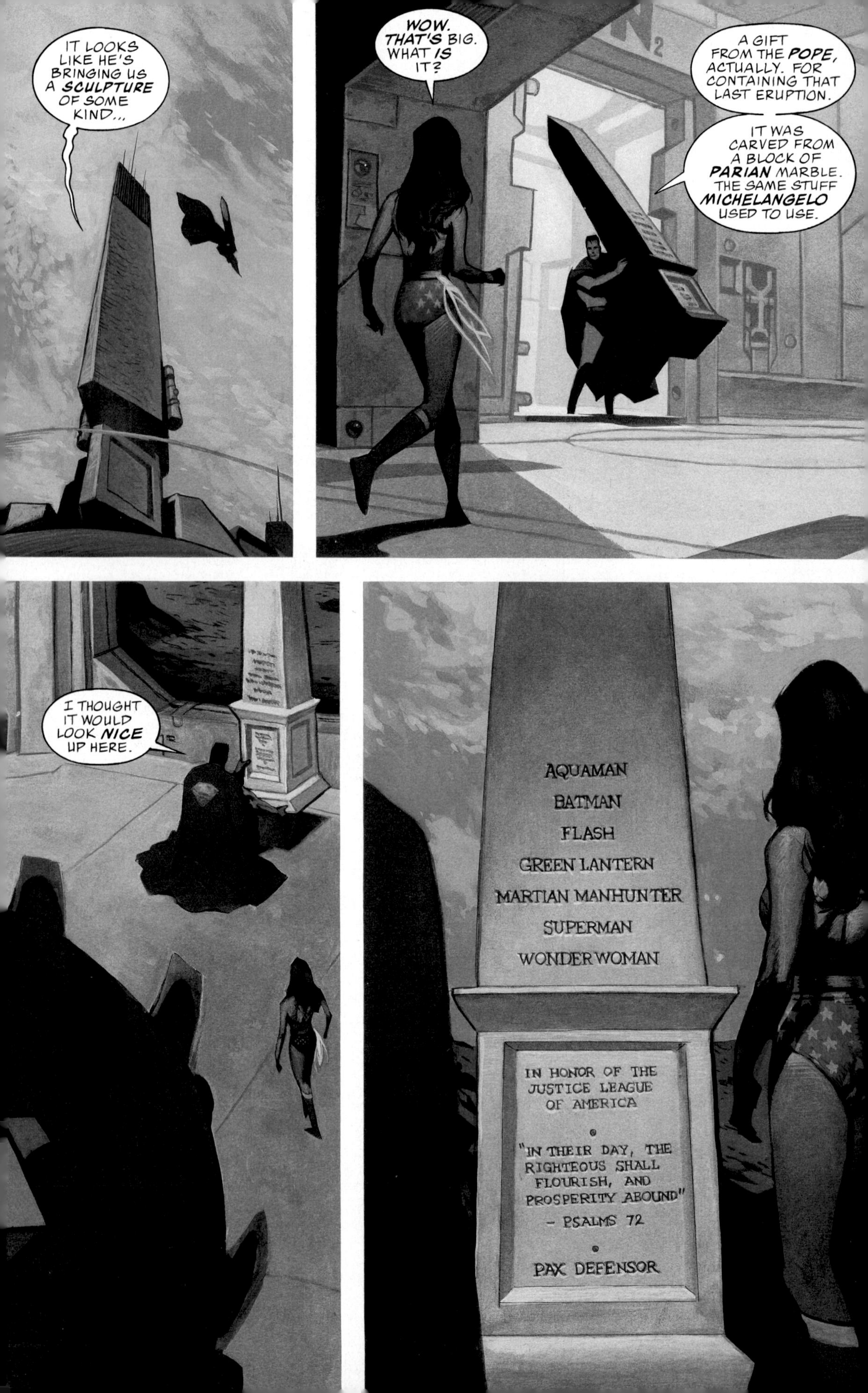
IT LOOKS LIKE HE'S BRINGING US A SCULPTURE OF SOME KIND...
WOW. THAT'S BIG. WHAT IS IT?
A GIFT FROM THE POPE, ACTUALLY. FOR CONTAINING THAT LAST ERUPTION.
IT WAS CARVED FROM A BLOCK OF PARIAN MARBLE. THE SAME STUFF MICHELANGELO USED TO USE.
I THOUGHT IT WOULD LOOK NICE UP HERE.
AQUAMAN
BATMAN
FLASH
GREEN LANTERN
MARTIAN MANHUNTER
SUPERMAN
WONDER WOMAN
IN HONOR OF THE JUSTICE LEAGUE OF AMERICA
"IN THEIR DAY, THE RIGHTEOUS SHALL FLOURISH, AND PROSPERITY ABOUND"
- PSALMS 72
PAX DEFENSOR

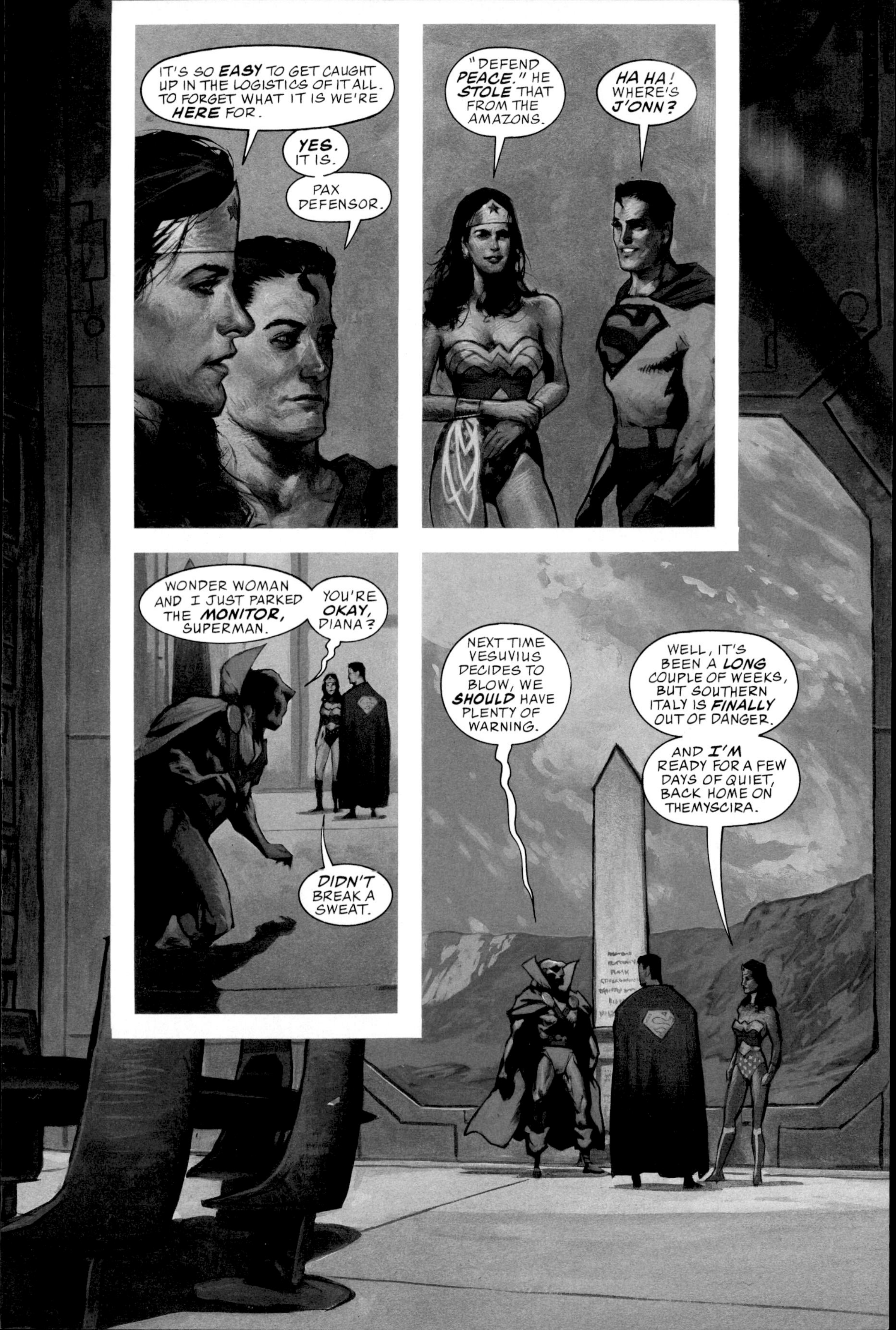

IT'S SO EASY TO GET CAUGHT UP IN THE LOGISTICS OF IT ALL. TO FORGET WHAT IT IS WE'RE HERE FOR.
YES. IT IS.
PAX DEFENSOR.
"DEFEND PEACE." HE STOLE THAT FROM THE AMAZONS.
HA HA! WHERE'S J'ONN?
WONDER WOMAN AND I JUST PARKED THE MONITOR, SUPERMAN.
YOU'RE OKAY, DIANA?
DIDN'T BREAK A SWEAT.
NEXT TIME VESUVIUS DECIDES TO BLOW, WE SHOULD HAVE PLENTY OF WARNING.
WELL, IT'S BEEN A LONG COUPLE OF WEEKS, BUT SOUTHERN ITALY IS FINALLY OUT OF DANGER.
AND I'M READY FOR A FEW DAYS OF QUIET, BACK HOME ON THEMYSCIRA.

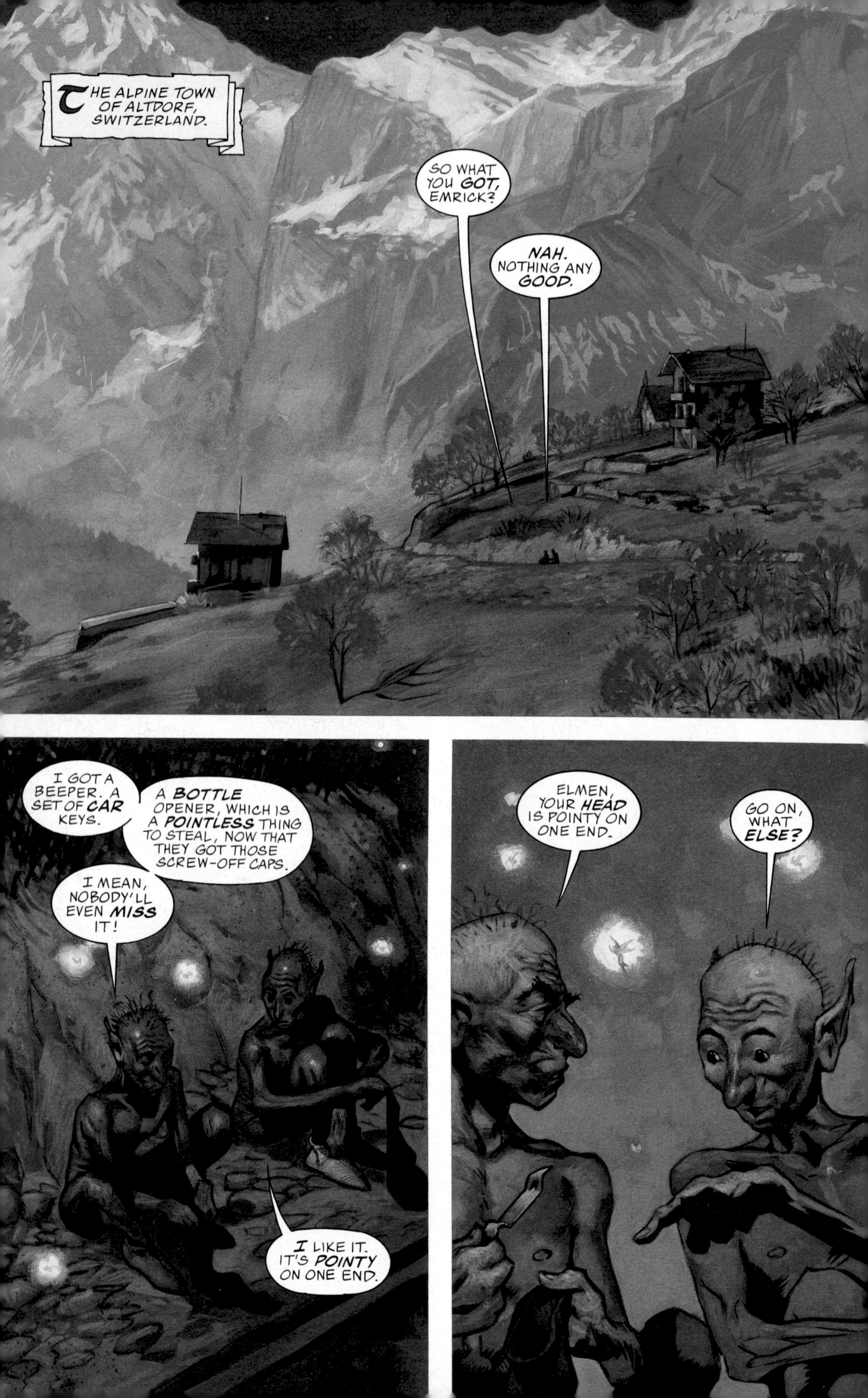
THE ALPINE TOWN OF ALTDORF, SWITZERLAND.
SO WHAT YOU GOT, EMRICK?
NAH. NOTHING ANY GOOD.
I GOT A BEEPER. A SET OF CAR KEYS.
A BOTTLE OPENER, WHICH IS A POINTLESS THING TO STEAL, NOW THAT THEY GOT THOSE SCREW-OFF CAPS.
I MEAN, NOBODY'LL EVEN MISS IT!
I LIKE IT. IT'S POINTY ON ONE END.
ELMEN, YOUR HEAD IS POINTY ON ONE END.
GO ON, WHAT ELSE?

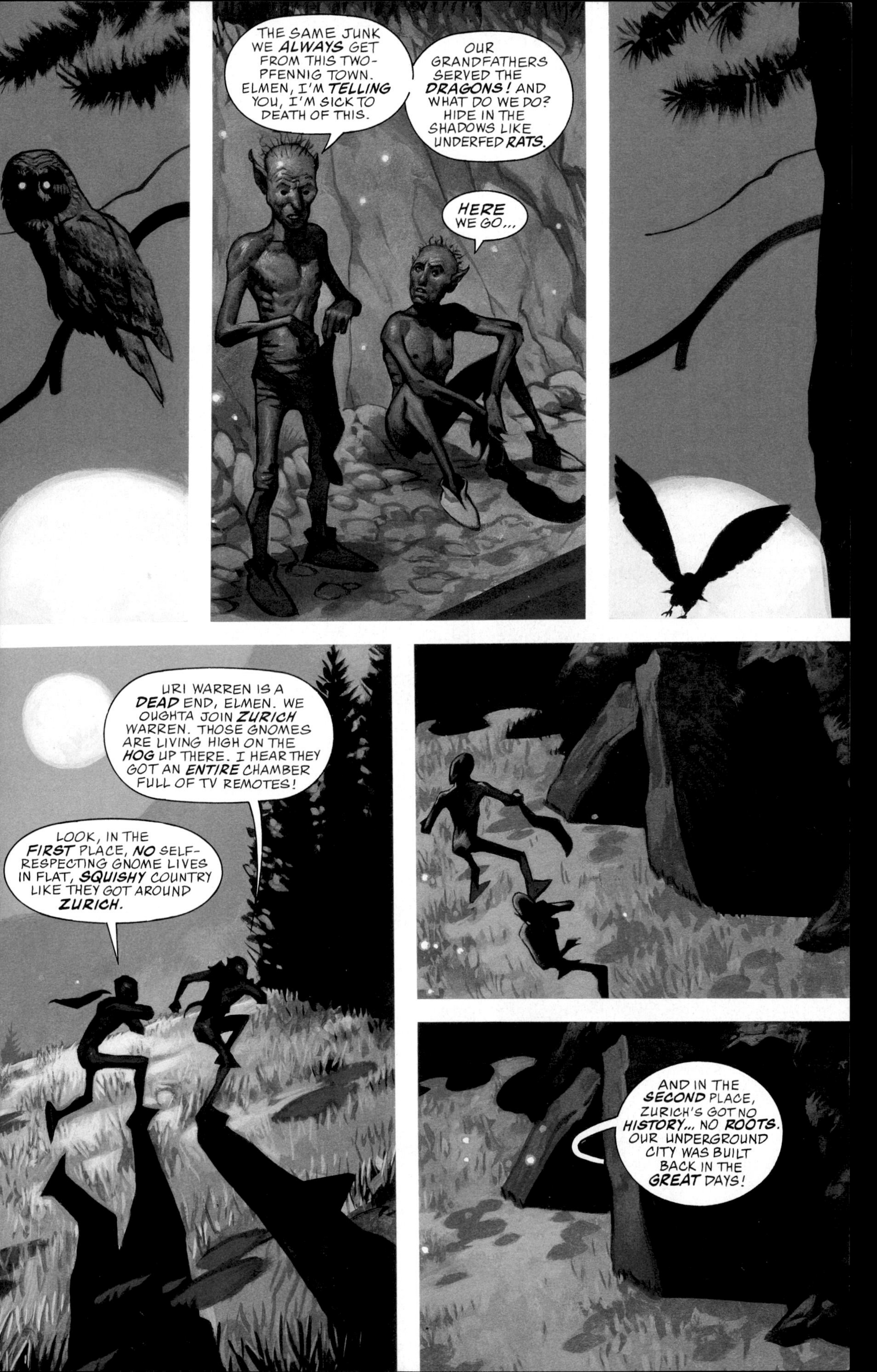
THE SAME JUNK WE ALWAYS GET FROM THIS TWO-PFENNIG TOWN. ELMEN, I'M TELLING YOU, I'M SICK TO DEATH OF THIS.
OUR GRANDFATHERS SERVED THE DRAGONS! AND WHAT DO WE DO? HIDE IN THE SHADOWS LIKE UNDERFED RATS.
HERE WE GO...
URI WARREN IS A DEAD END, ELMEN. WE OUGHTA JOIN ZURICH WARREN. THOSE GNOMES ARE LIVING HIGH ON THE HOG UP THERE. I HEAR THEY GOT AN ENTIRE CHAMBER FULL OF TV REMOTES!
LOOK, IN THE FIRST PLACE, NO SELF-RESPECTING GNOME LIVES IN FLAT, SQUISHY COUNTRY LIKE THEY GOT AROUND ZURICH.
AND IN THE SECOND PLACE, ZURICH'S GOT NO HISTORY... NO ROOTS. OUR UNDERGROUND CITY WAS BUILT BACK IN THE GREAT DAYS!

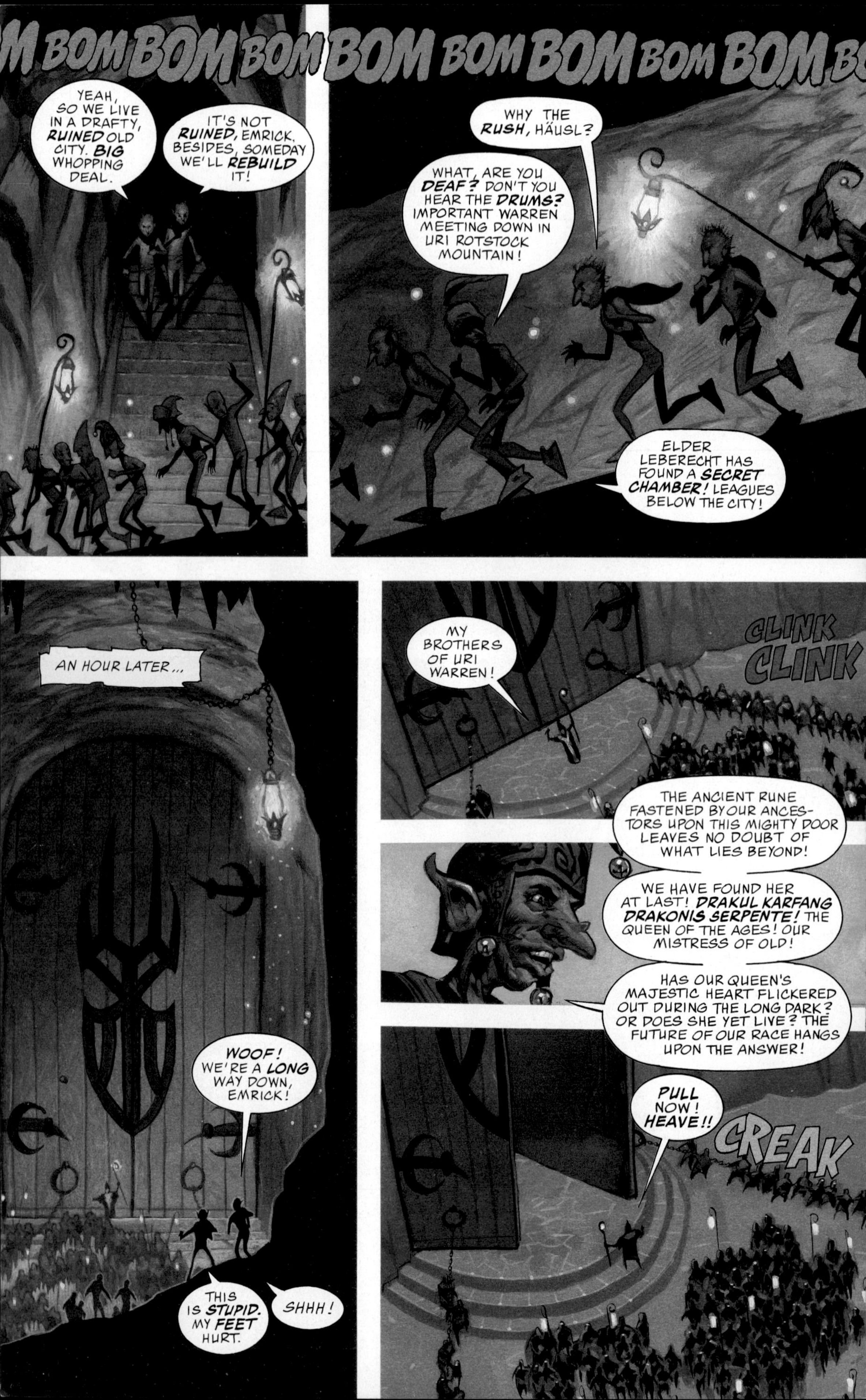
BOM BOM BOM bom BOM bom BOM bom BOM
YEAH, SO WE LIVE IN A DRAFTY, RUINED OLD CITY. BIG WHOPPING DEAL.
IT'S NOT RUINED, EMRICK. BESIDES, SOMEDAY WE'LL REBUILD IT!
WHY THE RUSH, HÄUSL?
WHAT, ARE YOU DEAF? DON'T YOU HEAR THE DRUMS? IMPORTANT WARREN MEETING DOWN IN URI ROTSTOCK MOUNTAIN!
ELDER LEBERECHT HAS FOUND A SECRET CHAMBER! LEAGUES BELOW THE CITY!
AN HOUR LATER...
WOOF! WE'RE A LONG WAY DOWN, EMRICK!
THIS IS STUPID. MY FEET HURT.
SHHH!
MY BROTHERS OF URI WARREN!
CLINK CLINK
THE ANCIENT RUNE FASTENED BY OUR ANCESTORS UPON THIS MIGHTY DOOR LEAVES NO DOUBT OF WHAT LIES BEYOND!
WE HAVE FOUND HER AT LAST! DRAKUL KARFANG DRAKONIS SERPENTE! THE QUEEN OF THE AGES! OUR MISTRESS OF OLD!
HAS OUR QUEEN'S MAJESTIC HEART FLICKERED OUT DURING THE LONG DARK? OR DOES SHE YET LIVE? THE FUTURE OF OUR RACE HANGS UPON THE ANSWER!
PULL NOW! HEAVE!!
CREAK

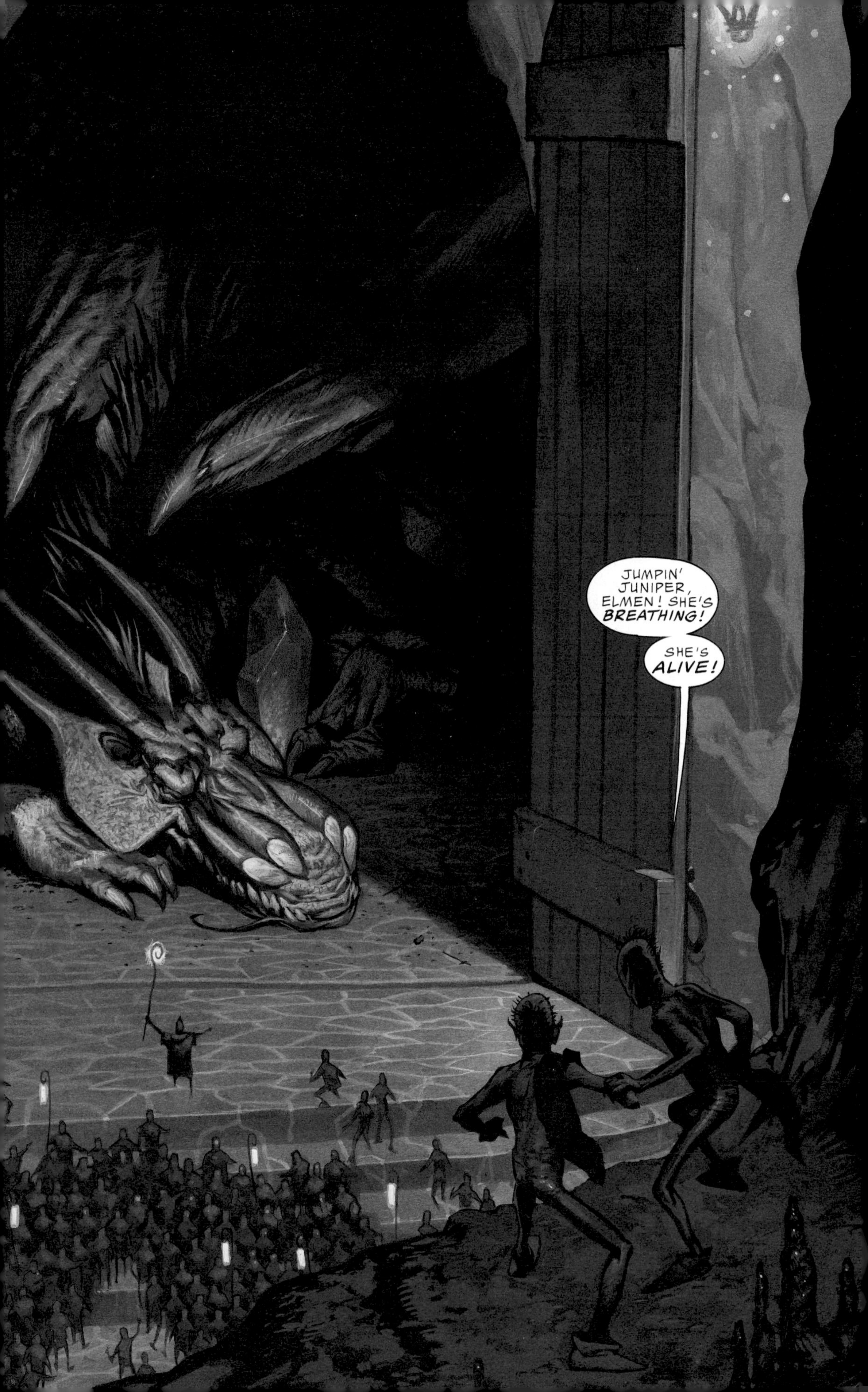
JUMPIN' JUNIPER, ELMEN! SHE'S BREATHING!
SHE'S ALIVE!

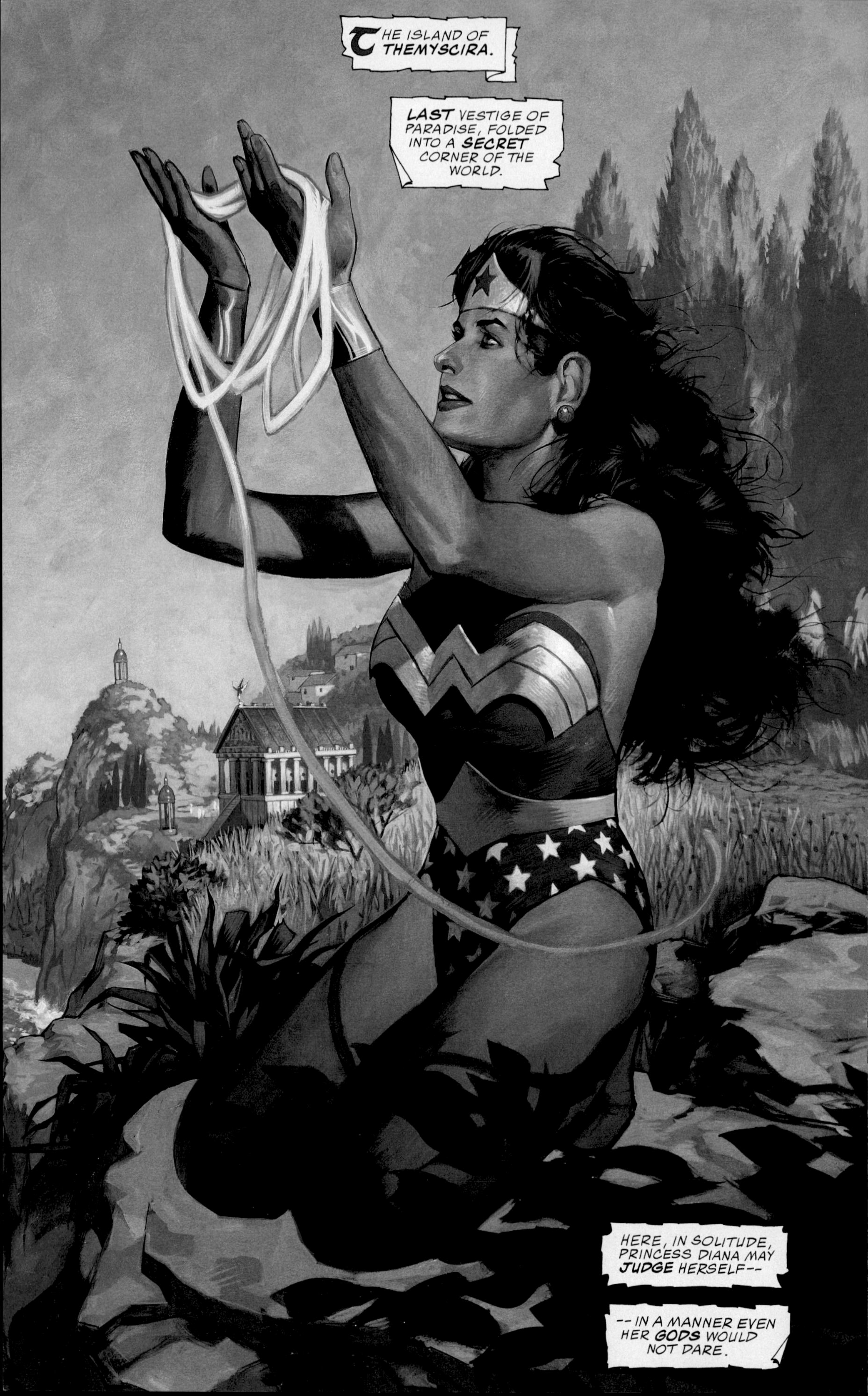
THE ISLAND OF THEMYSCIRA.
LAST VESTIGE OF PARADISE, FOLDED INTO A SECRET CORNER OF THE WORLD.
HERE, IN SOLITUDE, PRINCESS DIANA MAY JUDGE HERSELF--
-- IN A MANNER EVEN HER GODS WOULD NOT DARE.

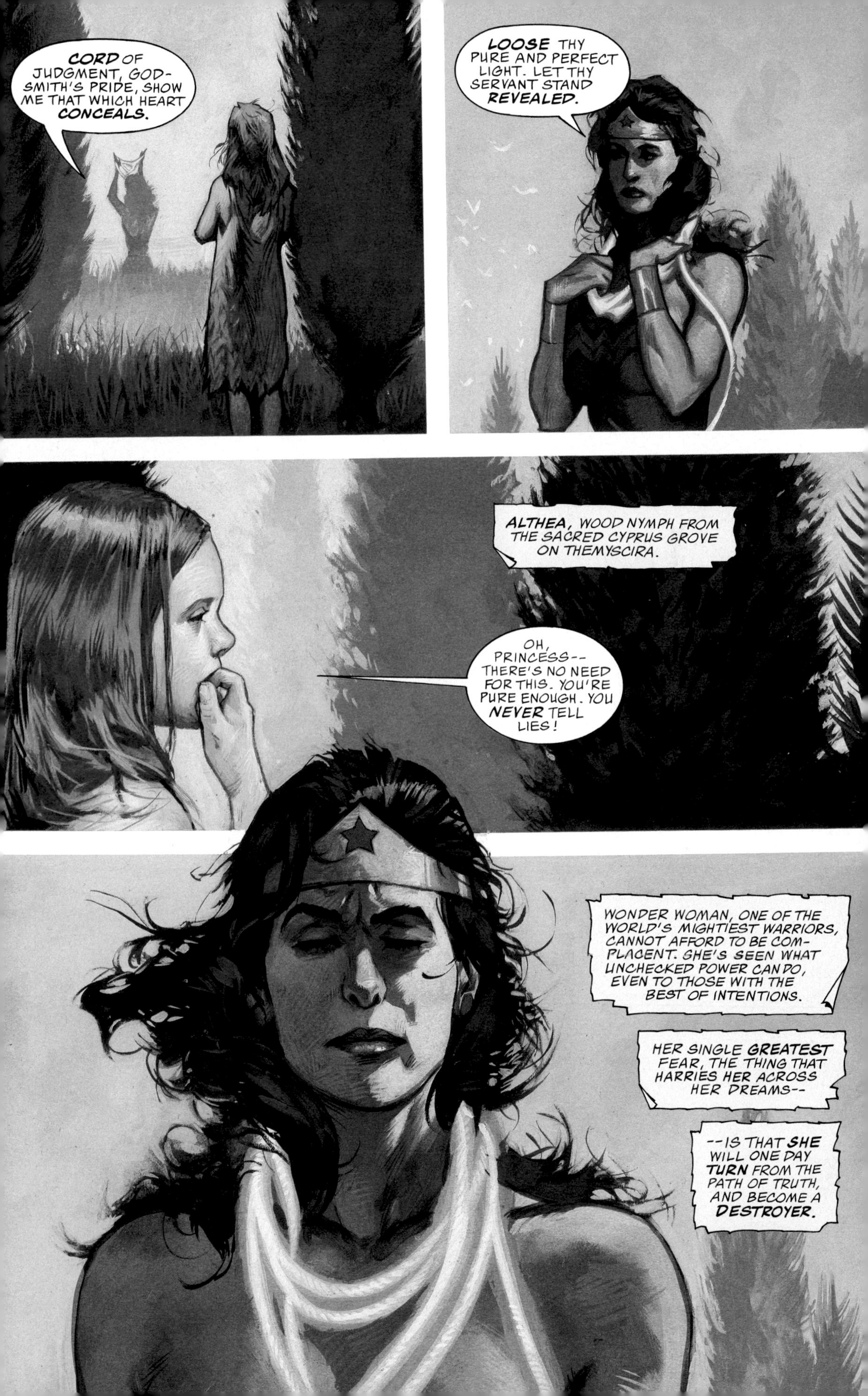
CORD OF JUDGMENT, GOD-SMITH'S PRIDE, SHOW ME THAT WHICH HEART CONCEALS.
LOOSE THY PURE AND PERFECT LIGHT. LET THY SERVANT STAND REVEALED.
ALTHEA, WOOD NYMPH FROM THE SACRED CYPRUS GROVE ON THEMYSCIRA.
OH, PRINCESS-- THERE'S NO NEED FOR THIS. YOU'RE PURE ENOUGH. YOU NEVER TELL LIES!
WONDER WOMAN, ONE OF THE WORLD'S MIGHTIEST WARRIORS, CANNOT AFFORD TO BE COM-PLACENT. SHE'S SEEN WHAT UNCHECKED POWER CAN DO, EVEN TO THOSE WITH THE BEST OF INTENTIONS.
HER SINGLE GREATEST FEAR, THE THING THAT HARRIES HER ACROSS HER DREAMS--
--IS THAT SHE WILL ONE DAY TURN FROM THE PATH OF TRUTH, AND BECOME A DESTROYER.

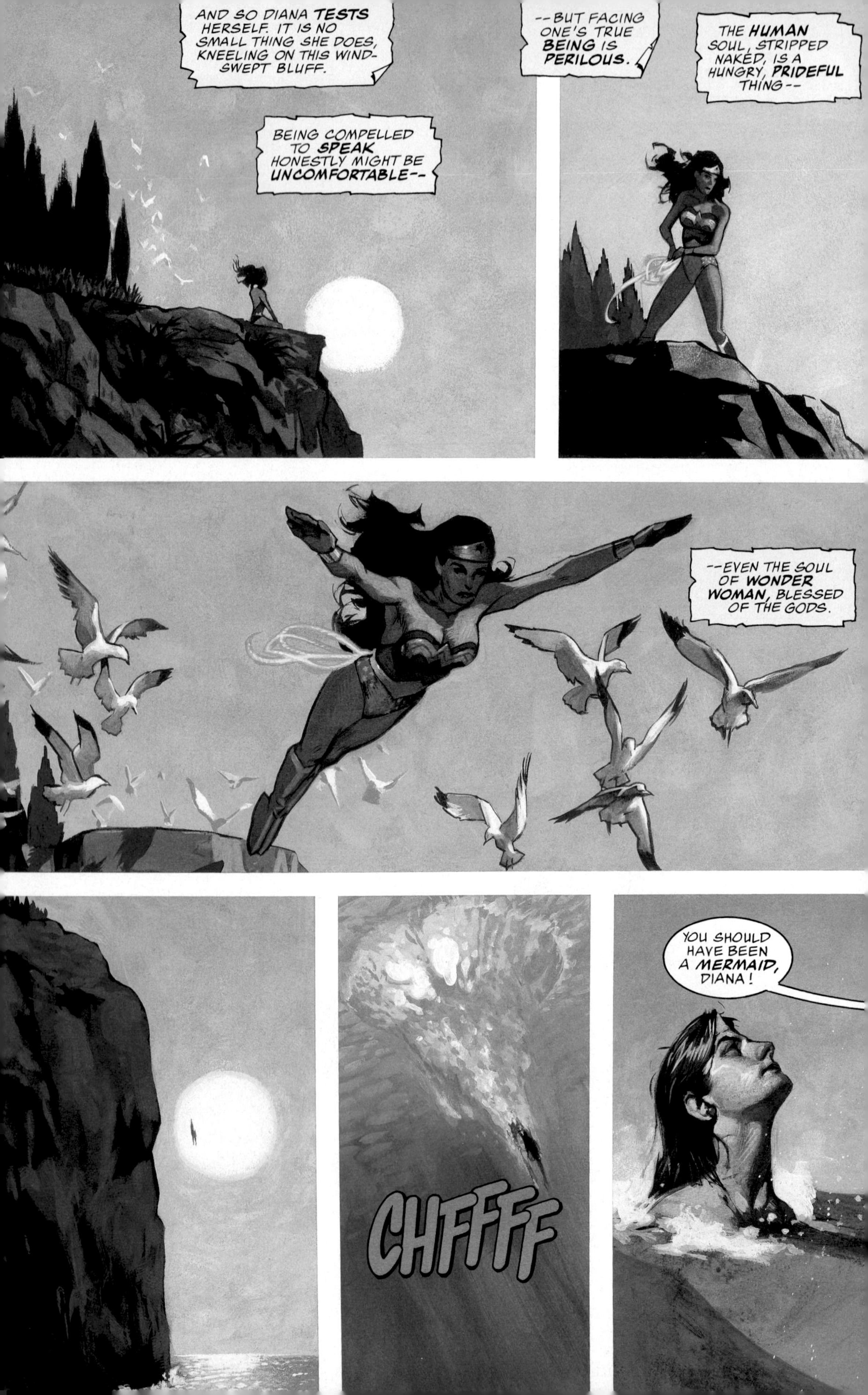
AND SO DIANA TESTS HERSELF. IT IS NO SMALL THING SHE DOES, KNEELING ON THIS WIND-SWEPT BLUFF.
BEING COMPELLED TO SPEAK HONESTLY MIGHT BE UNCOMFORTABLE--
--BUT FACING ONE'S TRUE BEING IS PERILOUS.
THE HUMAN SOUL, STRIPPED NAKED, IS A HUNGRY, PRIDEFUL THING--
--EVEN THE SOUL OF WONDER WOMAN, BLESSED OF THE GODS.
CHFFFF
YOU SHOULD HAVE BEEN A MERMAID, DIANA!

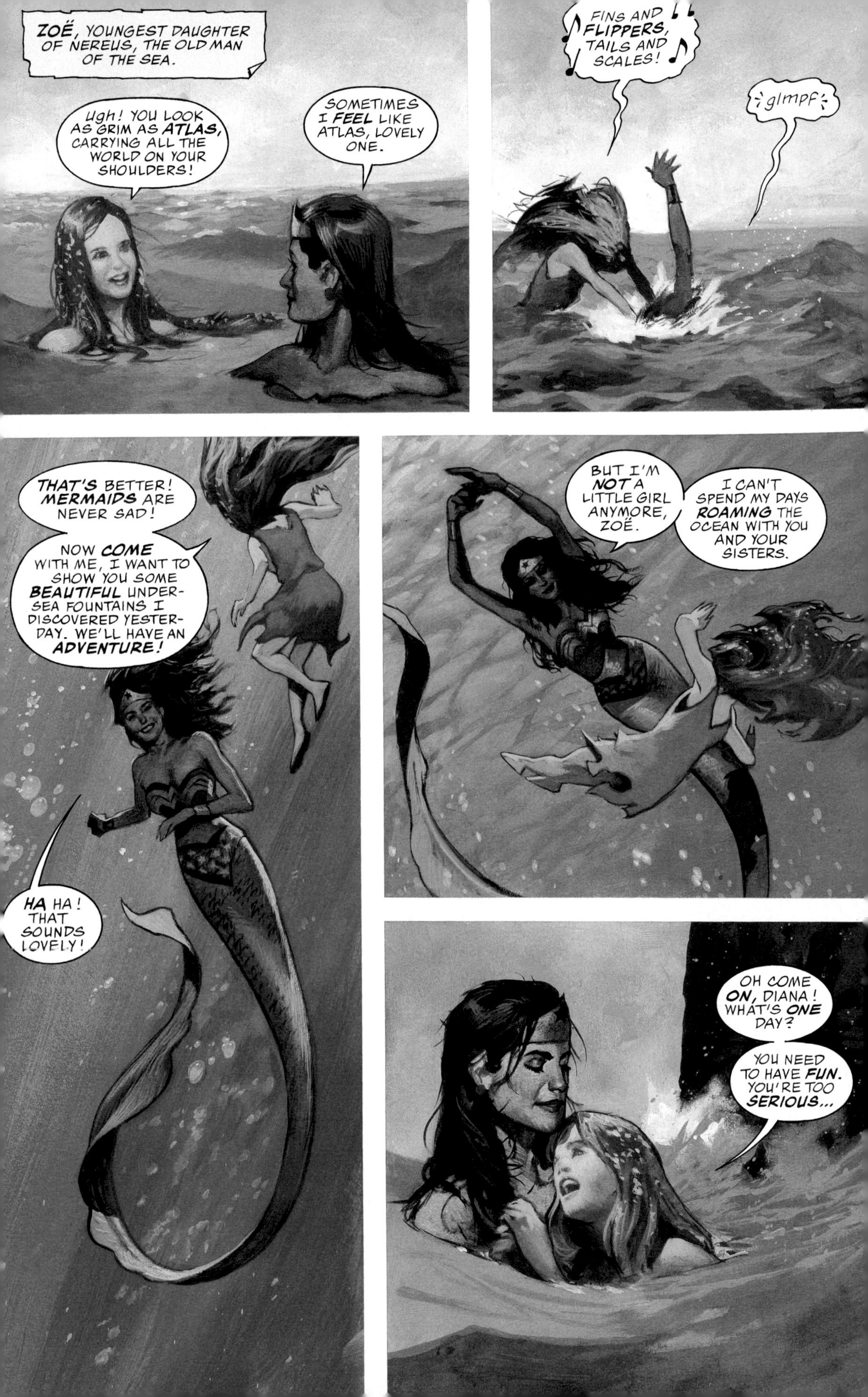

ZOË, YOUNGEST DAUGHTER OF NEREUS, THE OLD MAN OF THE SEA.
Ugh! YOU LOOK AS GRIM AS ATLAS, CARRYING ALL THE WORLD ON YOUR SHOULDERS!
SOMETIMES I FEEL LIKE ATLAS, LOVELY ONE.
FINS AND FLIPPERS, TAILS AND SCALES!
glmpf
THAT'S BETTER! MERMAIDS ARE NEVER SAD!
NOW COME WITH ME, I WANT TO SHOW YOU SOME BEAUTIFUL UNDER-SEA FOUNTAINS I DISCOVERED YESTER-DAY. WE'LL HAVE AN ADVENTURE!
HA HA! THAT SOUNDS LOVELY!
BUT I'M NOT A LITTLE GIRL ANYMORE, ZOË.
I CAN'T SPEND MY DAYS ROAMING THE OCEAN WITH YOU AND YOUR SISTERS.
OH COME ON, DIANA! WHAT'S ONE DAY?
YOU NEED TO HAVE FUN. YOU'RE TOO SERIOUS...

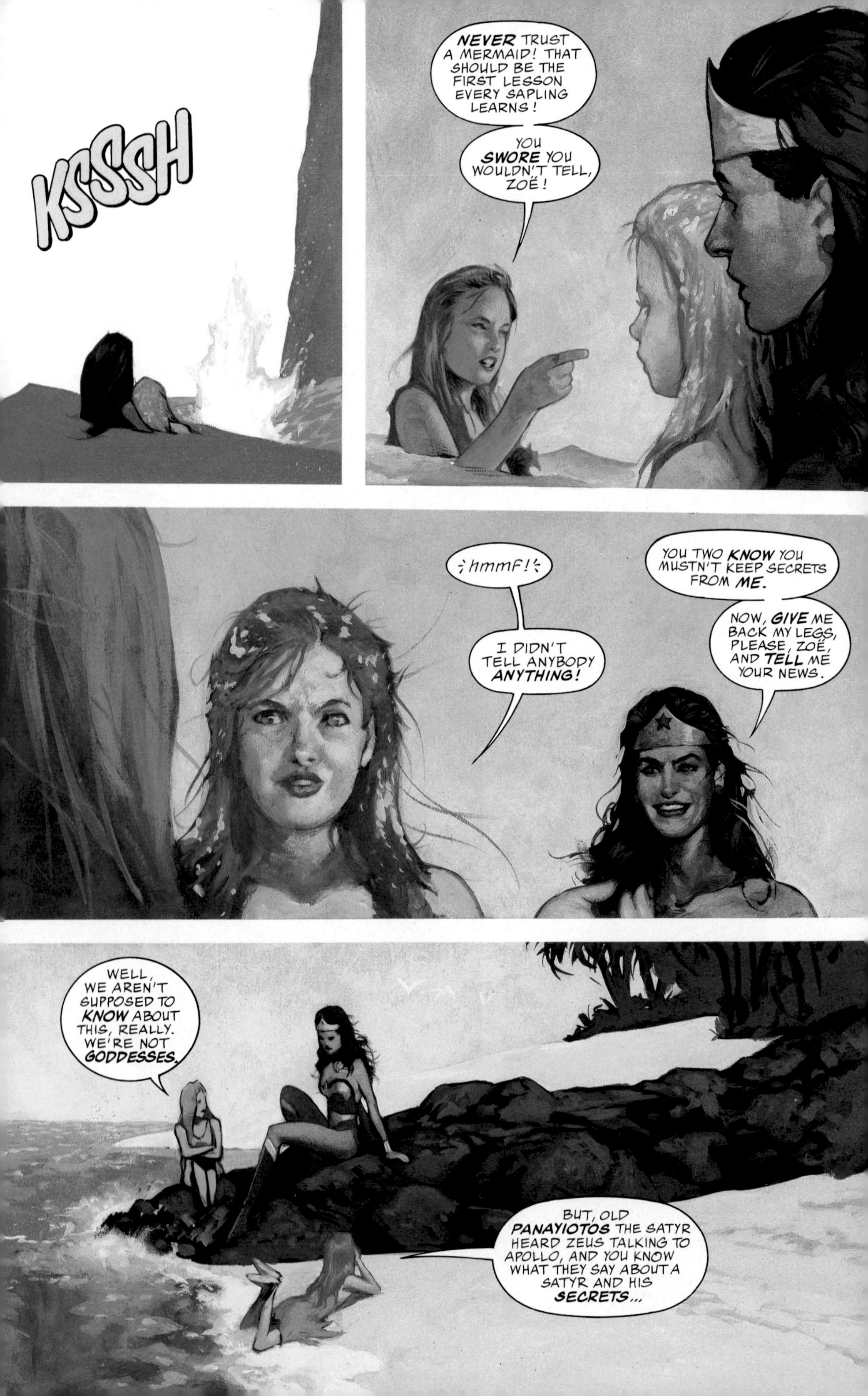
KSSSH
NEVER TRUST A MERMAID! THAT SHOULD BE THE FIRST LESSON EVERY SAPLING LEARNS!
YOU SWORE YOU WOULDN'T TELL, ZOË!
hmmf!
I DIDN'T TELL ANYBODY ANYTHING!
YOU TWO KNOW YOU MUSTN'T KEEP SECRETS FROM ME.
NOW, GIVE ME BACK MY LEGS, PLEASE, ZOË, AND TELL ME YOUR NEWS.
WELL, WE AREN'T SUPPOSED TO KNOW ABOUT THIS, REALLY. WE'RE NOT GODDESSES.
BUT, OLD PANAYIOTOS THE SATYR HEARD ZEUS TALKING TO APOLLO, AND YOU KNOW WHAT THEY SAY ABOUT A SATYR AND HIS SECRETS...

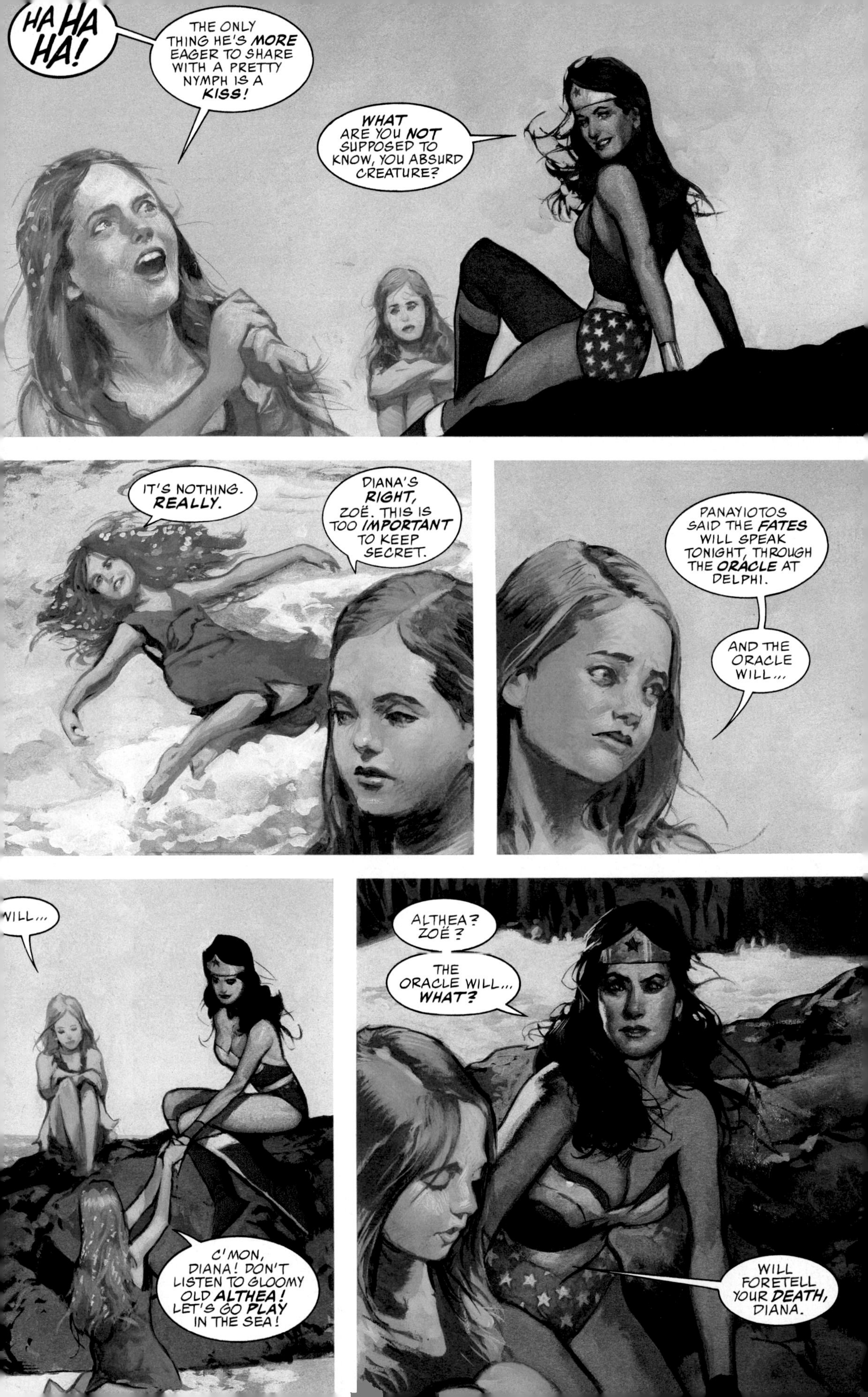
HA HA HA!
THE ONLY THING HE'S MORE EAGER TO SHARE WITH A PRETTY NYMPH IS A KISS!
WHAT ARE YOU NOT SUPPOSED TO KNOW, YOU ABSURD CREATURE?
IT'S NOTHING. REALLY.
DIANA'S RIGHT, ZOË. THIS IS TOO IMPORTANT TO KEEP SECRET.
PANAYIOTOS SAID THE FATES WILL SPEAK TONIGHT, THROUGH THE ORACLE AT DELPHI.
AND THE ORACLE WILL...
WILL...
C'MON, DIANA! DON'T LISTEN TO GLOOMY OLD ALTHEA! LET'S GO PLAY IN THE SEA!
ALTHEA? ZOË?
THE ORACLE WILL... WHAT?
WILL FORETELL YOUR DEATH, DIANA.

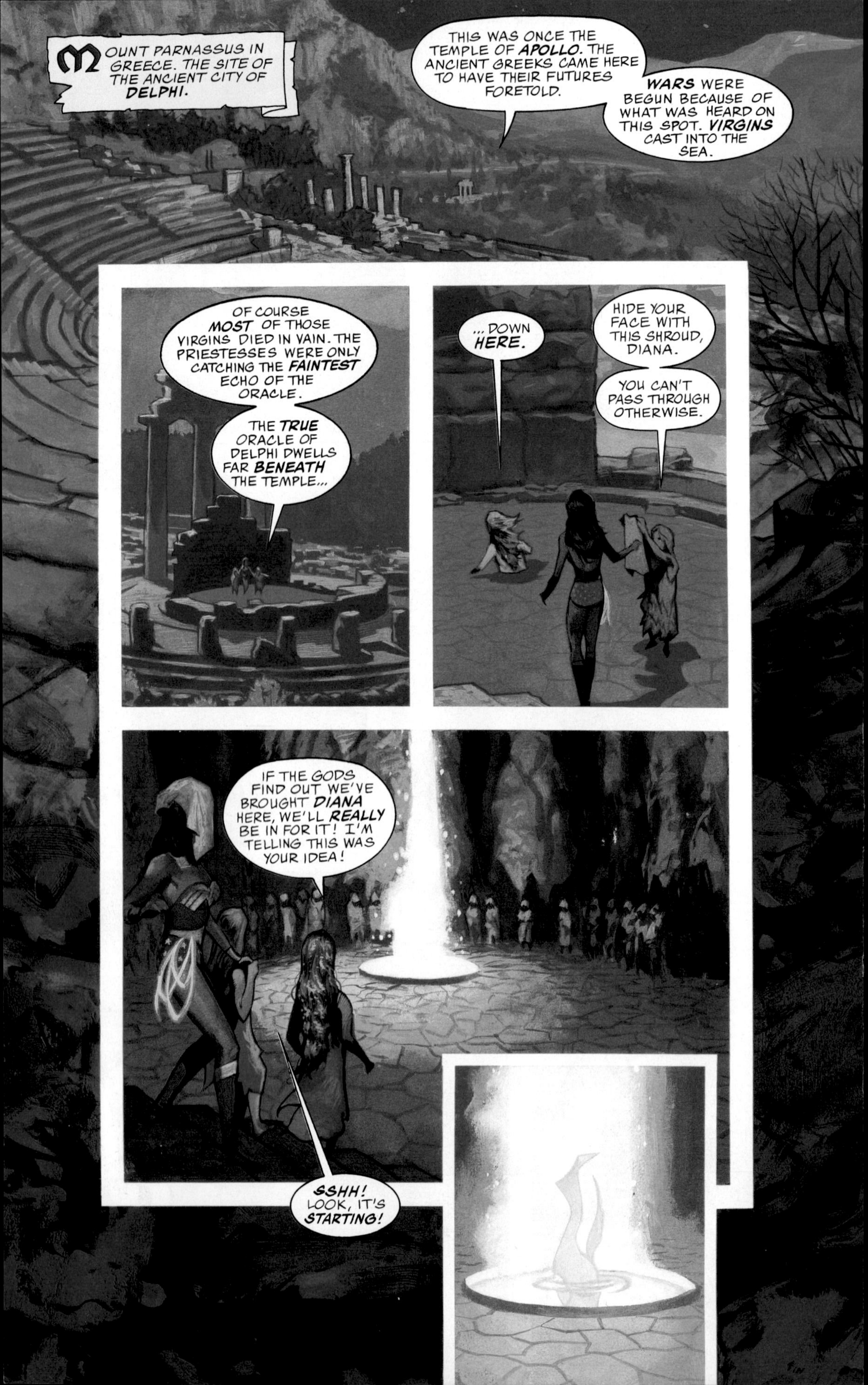
MOUNT PARNASSUS IN GREECE. THE SITE OF THE ANCIENT CITY OF DELPHI.
THIS WAS ONCE THE TEMPLE OF APOLLO. THE ANCIENT GREEKS CAME HERE TO HAVE THEIR FUTURES FORETOLD.
WARS WERE BEGUN BECAUSE OF WHAT WAS HEARD ON THIS SPOT. VIRGINS CAST INTO THE SEA.
OF COURSE MOST OF THOSE VIRGINS DIED IN VAIN. THE PRIESTESSES WERE ONLY CATCHING THE FAINTEST ECHO OF THE ORACLE.
THE TRUE ORACLE OF DELPHI DWELLS FAR BENEATH THE TEMPLE...
...DOWN HERE.
HIDE YOUR FACE WITH THIS SHROUD, DIANA.
YOU CAN'T PASS THROUGH OTHERWISE.
IF THE GODS FIND OUT WE'VE BROUGHT DIANA HERE, WE'LL REALLY BE IN FOR IT! I'M TELLING THIS WAS YOUR IDEA!
SSHH! LOOK, IT'S STARTING!

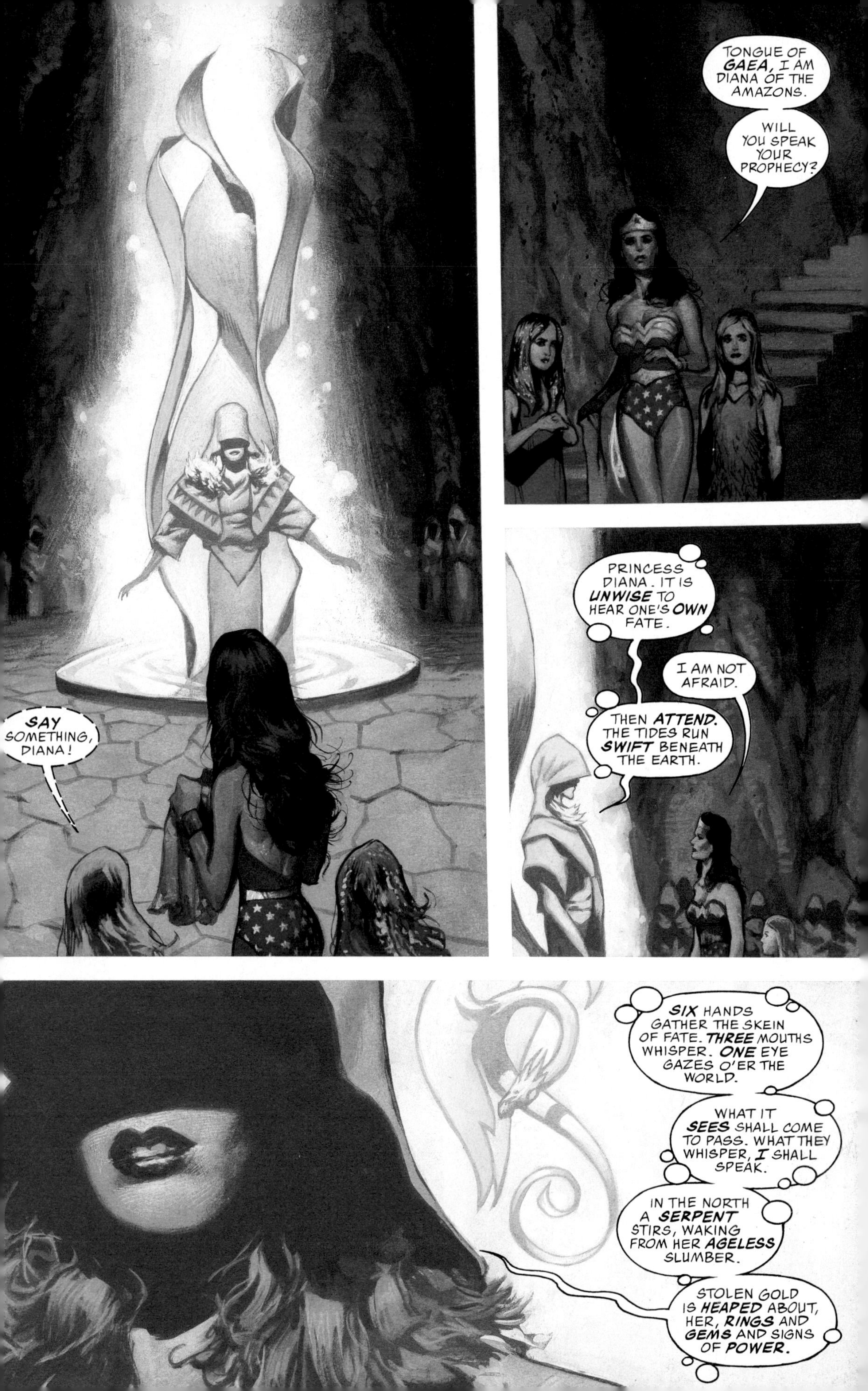

TONGUE OF GAEA, I AM DIANA OF THE AMAZONS.
WILL YOU SPEAK YOUR PROPHECY?
SAY SOMETHING, DIANA!
PRINCESS DIANA. IT IS UNWISE TO HEAR ONE'S OWN FATE.
I AM NOT AFRAID.
THEN ATTEND. THE TIDES RUN SWIFT BENEATH THE EARTH.
SIX HANDS GATHER THE SKEIN OF FATE. THREE MOUTHS WHISPER. ONE EYE GAZES O'ER THE WORLD.
WHAT IT SEES SHALL COME TO PASS. WHAT THEY WHISPER, I SHALL SPEAK.
IN THE NORTH A SERPENT STIRS, WAKING FROM HER AGELESS SLUMBER.
STOLEN GOLD IS HEAPED ABOUT HER, RINGS AND GEMS AND SIGNS OF POWER.

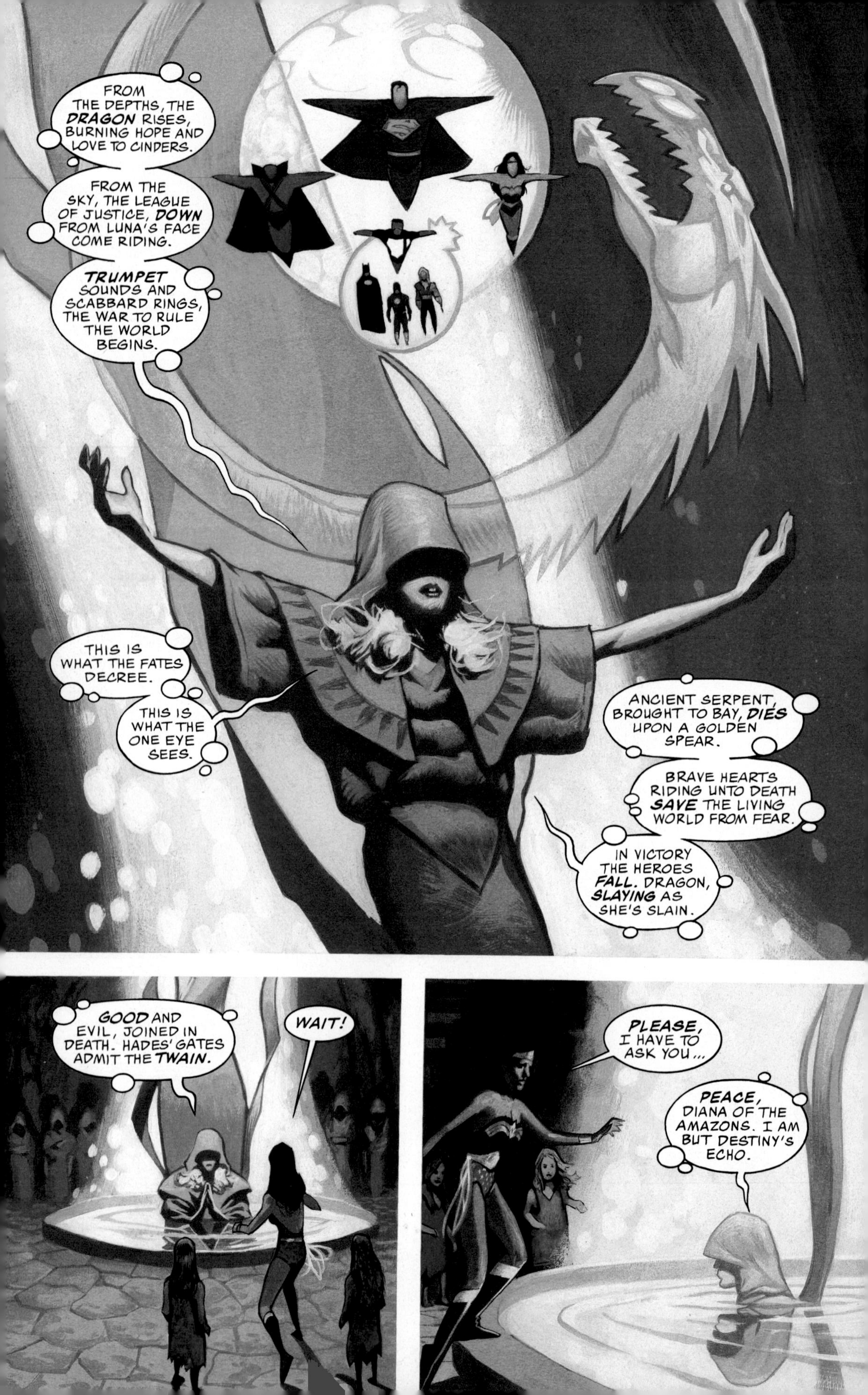
FROM THE DEPTHS, THE DRAGON RISES, BURNING HOPE AND LOVE TO CINDERS.
FROM THE SKY, THE LEAGUE OF JUSTICE, DOWN FROM LUNA'S FACE COME RIDING.
TRUMPET SOUNDS AND SCABBARD RINGS, THE WAR TO RULE THE WORLD BEGINS.
THIS IS WHAT THE FATES DECREE.
THIS IS WHAT THE ONE EYE SEES.
ANCIENT SERPENT, BROUGHT TO BAY, DIES UPON A GOLDEN SPEAR.
BRAVE HEARTS RIDING UNTO DEATH SAVE THE LIVING WORLD FROM FEAR.
IN VICTORY THE HEROES FALL. DRAGON, SLAYING AS SHE'S SLAIN.
GOOD AND EVIL, JOINED IN DEATH. HADES' GATES ADMIT THE TWAIN.
WAIT!
PLEASE, I HAVE TO ASK YOU...
PEACE, DIANA OF THE AMAZONS. I AM BUT DESTINY'S ECHO.

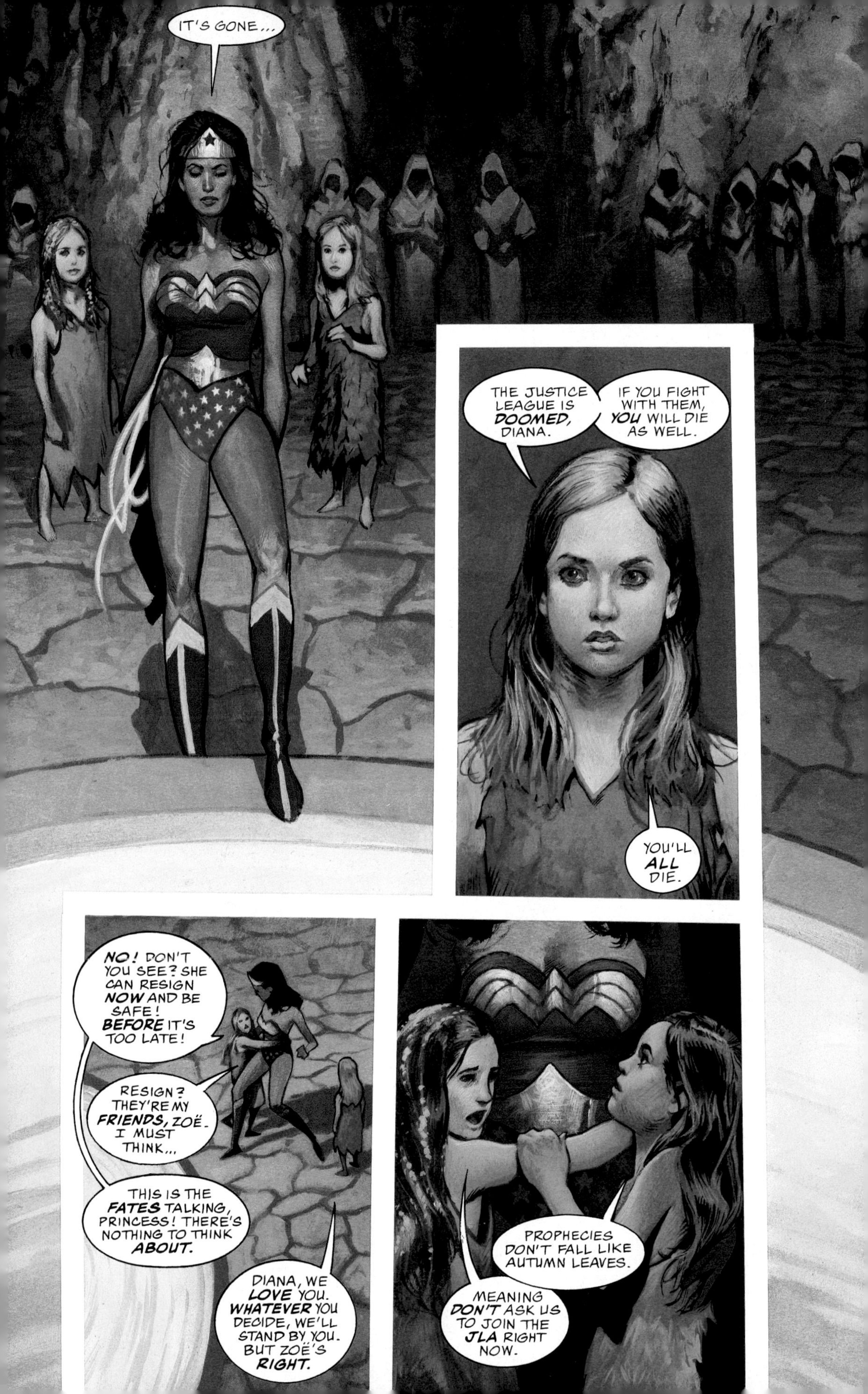
IT'S GONE...
THE JUSTICE LEAGUE IS DOOMED, DIANA.
IF YOU FIGHT WITH THEM, YOU WILL DIE AS WELL.
YOU'LL ALL DIE.
NO! DON'T YOU SEE? SHE CAN RESIGN NOW AND BE SAFE! BEFORE IT'S TOO LATE!
RESIGN? THEY'RE MY FRIENDS, ZOË. I MUST THINK...
THIS IS THE FATES TALKING, PRINCESS! THERE'S NOTHING TO THINK ABOUT.
DIANA, WE LOVE YOU. WHATEVER YOU DECIDE, WE'LL STAND BY YOU. BUT ZOË'S RIGHT.
PROPHECIES DON'T FALL LIKE AUTUMN LEAVES.
MEANING DON'T ASK US TO JOIN THE JLA RIGHT NOW.

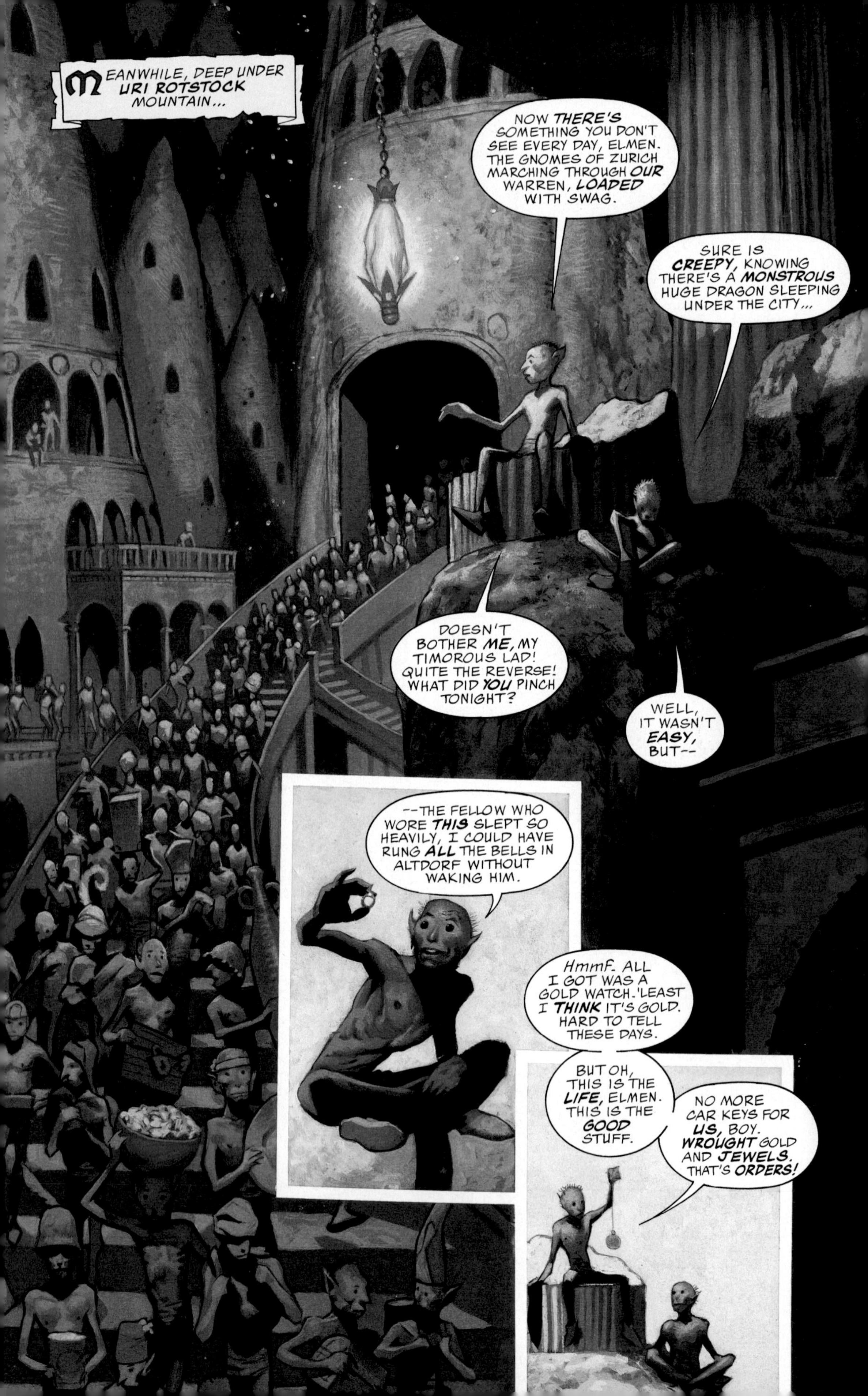
MEANWHILE, DEEP UNDER URI ROTSTOCK MOUNTAIN...
NOW THERE'S SOMETHING YOU DON'T SEE EVERY DAY, ELMEN. THE GNOMES OF ZURICH MARCHING THROUGH OUR WARREN, LOADED WITH SWAG.
SURE IS CREEPY, KNOWING THERE'S A MONSTROUS HUGE DRAGON SLEEPING UNDER THE CITY...
DOESN'T BOTHER ME, MY TIMOROUS LAD! QUITE THE REVERSE! WHAT DID YOU PINCH TONIGHT?
WELL, IT WASN'T EASY, BUT--
--THE FELLOW WHO WORE THIS SLEPT SO HEAVILY, I COULD HAVE RUNG ALL THE BELLS IN ALTDORF WITHOUT WAKING HIM.
HmmF. ALL I GOT WAS A GOLD WATCH. 'LEAST I THINK IT'S GOLD. HARD TO TELL THESE DAYS.
BUT OH, THIS IS THE LIFE, ELMEN. THIS IS THE GOOD STUFF.
NO MORE CAR KEYS FOR US, BOY. WROUGHT GOLD AND JEWELS. THAT'S ORDERS!

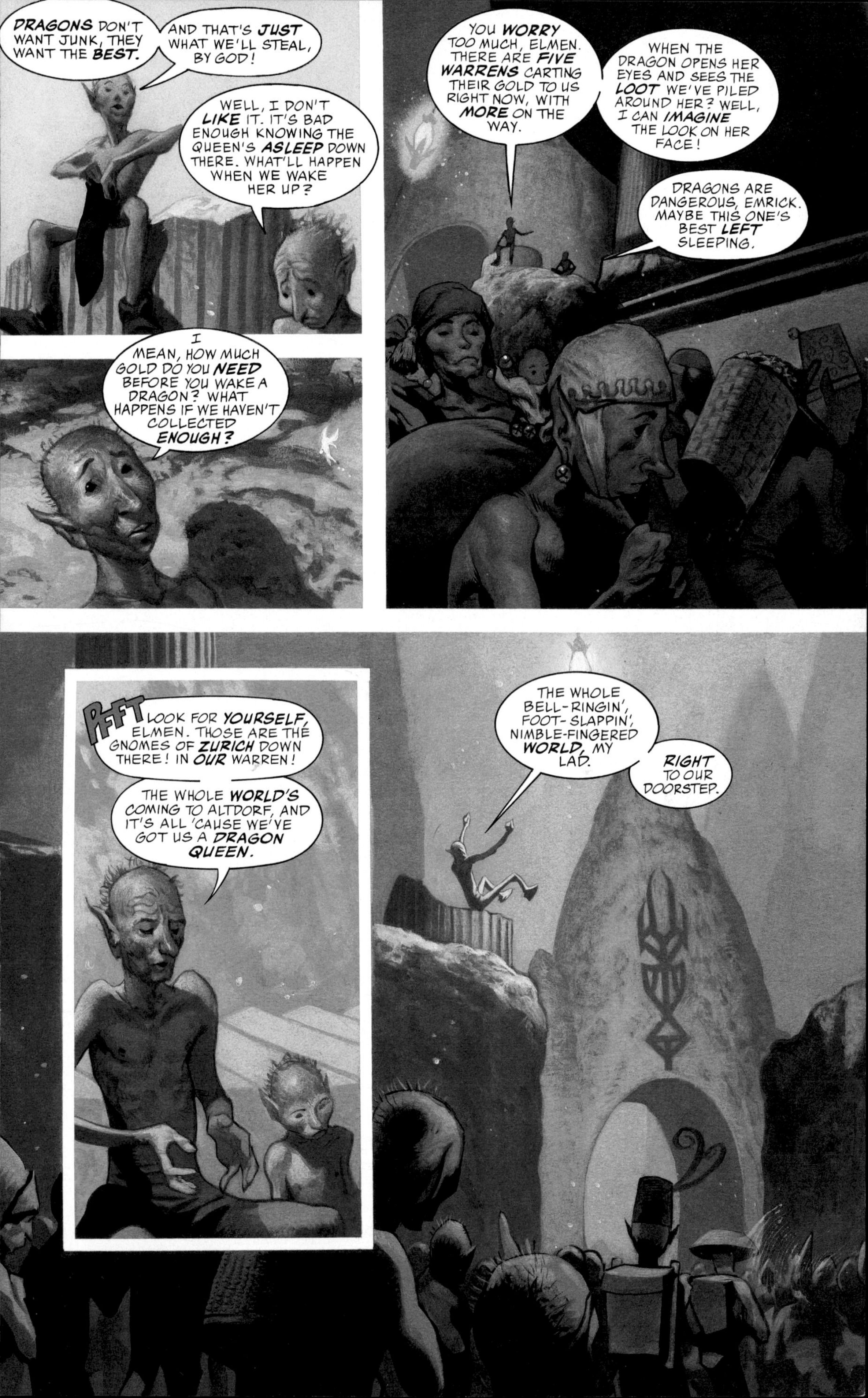
DRAGONS DON'T WANT JUNK, THEY WANT THE BEST.
AND THAT'S JUST WHAT WE'LL STEAL, BY GOD!
WELL, I DON'T LIKE IT. IT'S BAD ENOUGH KNOWING THE QUEEN'S ASLEEP DOWN THERE. WHAT'LL HAPPEN WHEN WE WAKE HER UP?
I MEAN, HOW MUCH GOLD DO YOU NEED BEFORE YOU WAKE A DRAGON? WHAT HAPPENS IF WE HAVEN'T COLLECTED ENOUGH?
YOU WORRY TOO MUCH, ELMEN. THERE ARE FIVE WARRENS CARTING THEIR GOLD TO US RIGHT NOW, WITH MORE ON THE WAY.
WHEN THE DRAGON OPENS HER EYES AND SEES THE LOOT WE'VE PILED AROUND HER? WELL, I CAN IMAGINE THE LOOK ON HER FACE!
DRAGONS ARE DANGEROUS, EMRICK. MAYBE THIS ONE'S BEST LEFT SLEEPING.
PFFT
LOOK FOR YOURSELF, ELMEN. THOSE ARE THE GNOMES OF ZURICH DOWN THERE! IN OUR WARREN!
THE WHOLE WORLD'S COMING TO ALTDORF, AND IT'S ALL 'CAUSE WE'VE GOT US A DRAGON QUEEN.
THE WHOLE BELL-RINGIN', FOOT-SLAPPIN', NIMBLE-FINGERED WORLD, MY LAD.
RIGHT TO OUR DOORSTEP.

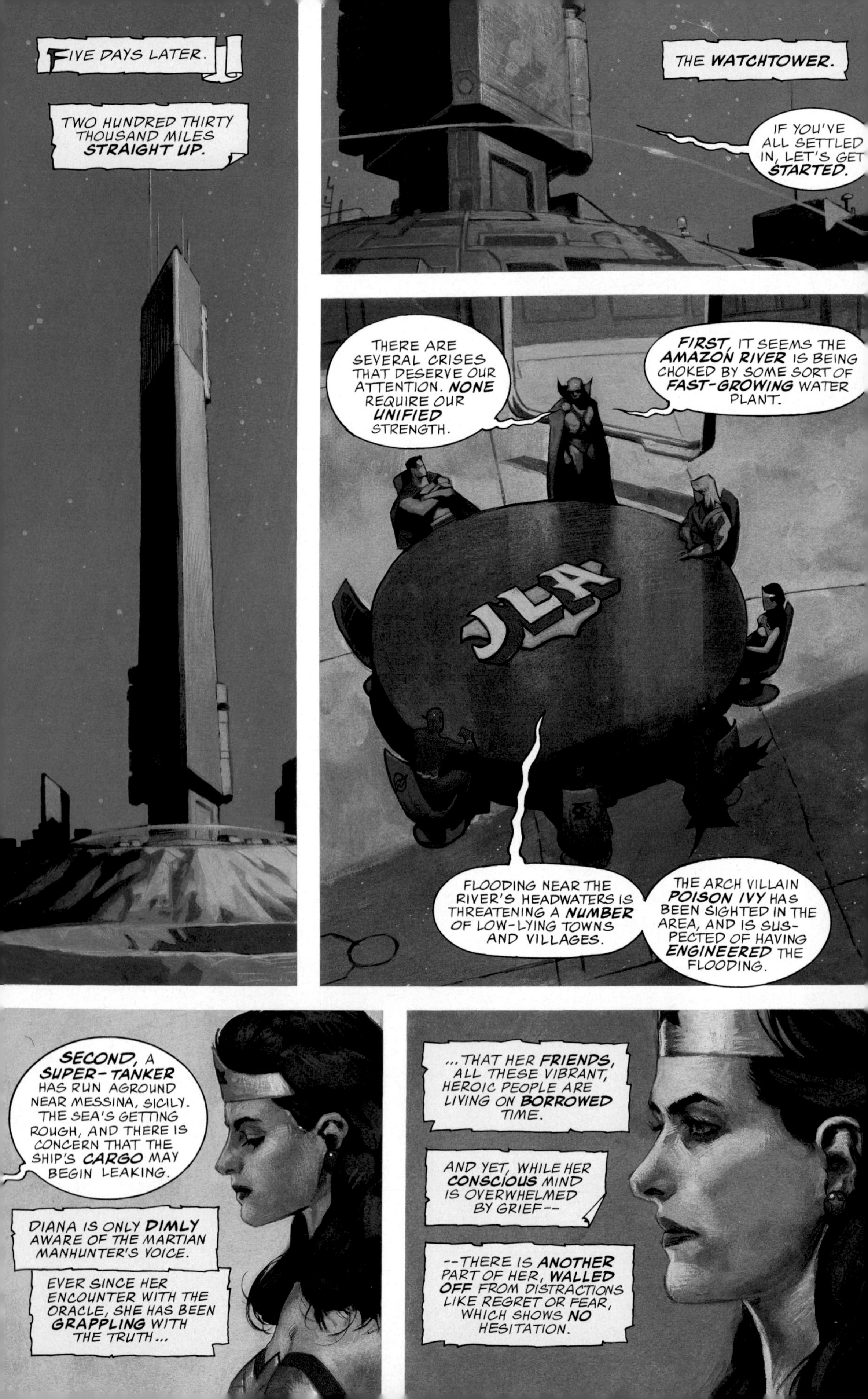
FIVE DAYS LATER.
TWO HUNDRED THIRTY THOUSAND MILES STRAIGHT UP.
THE WATCHTOWER.
IF YOU'VE ALL SETTLED IN, LET'S GET STARTED.
THERE ARE SEVERAL CRISES THAT DESERVE OUR ATTENTION. NONE REQUIRE OUR UNIFIED STRENGTH.
FIRST, IT SEEMS THE AMAZON RIVER IS BEING CHOKED BY SOME SORT OF FAST-GROWING WATER PLANT.
FLOODING NEAR THE RIVER'S HEADWATERS IS THREATENING A NUMBER OF LOW-LYING TOWNS AND VILLAGES.
THE ARCH VILLAIN POISON IVY HAS BEEN SIGHTED IN THE AREA, AND IS SUSPECTED OF HAVING ENGINEERED THE FLOODING.
SECOND, A SUPER-TANKER HAS RUN AGROUND NEAR MESSINA, SICILY. THE SEA'S GETTING ROUGH, AND THERE IS CONCERN THAT THE SHIP'S CARGO MAY BEGIN LEAKING.
DIANA IS ONLY DIMLY AWARE OF THE MARTIAN MANHUNTER'S VOICE.
EVER SINCE HER ENCOUNTER WITH THE ORACLE, SHE HAS BEEN GRAPPLING WITH THE TRUTH...
...THAT HER FRIENDS, ALL THESE VIBRANT, HEROIC PEOPLE ARE LIVING ON BORROWED TIME.
AND YET, WHILE HER CONSCIOUS MIND IS OVERWHELMED BY GRIEF--
--THERE IS ANOTHER PART OF HER, WALLED OFF FROM DISTRACTIONS LIKE REGRET OR FEAR, WHICH SHOWS NO HESITATION.

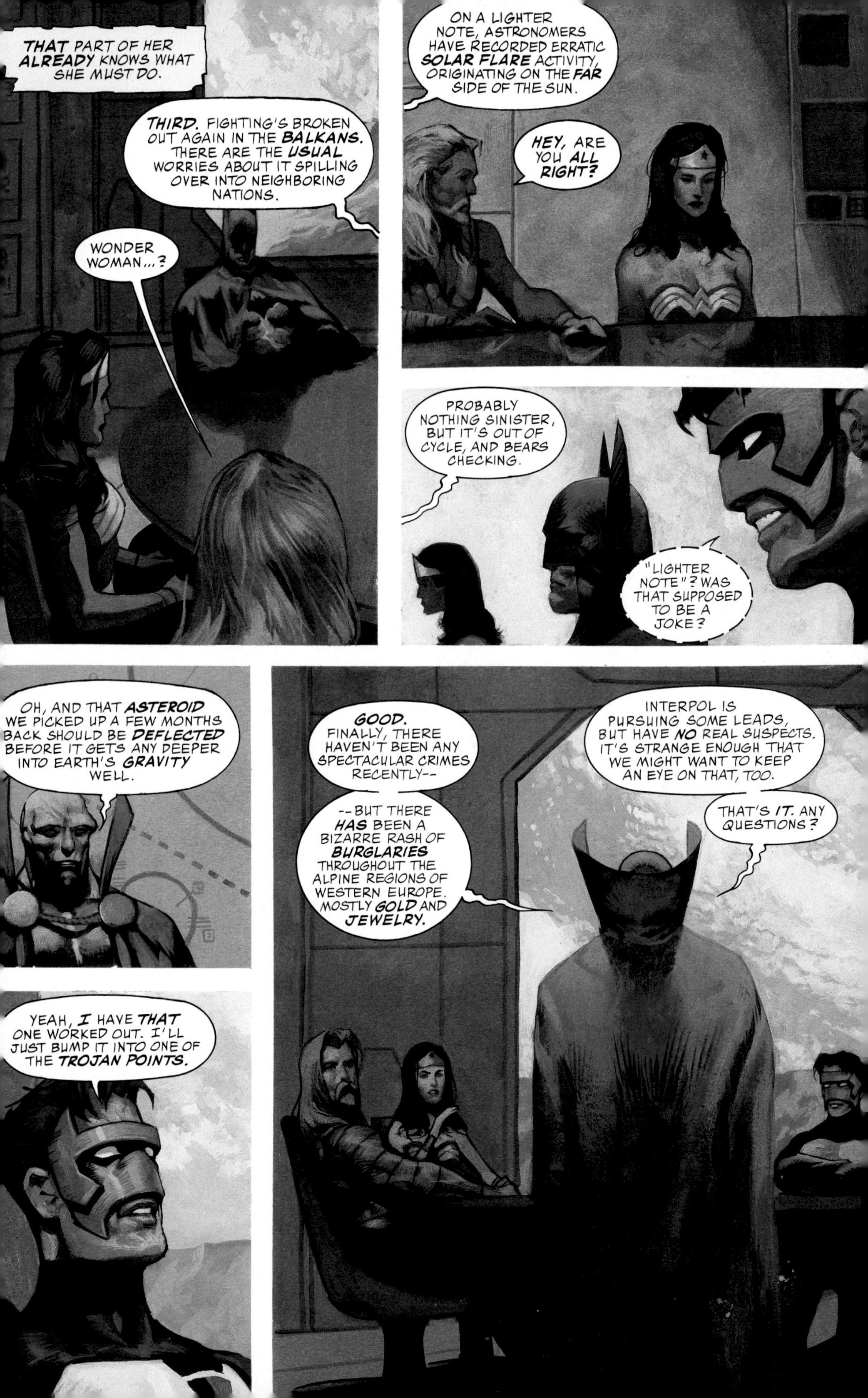
THAT PART OF HER ALREADY KNOWS WHAT SHE MUST DO.
THIRD. FIGHTING'S BROKEN OUT AGAIN IN THE BALKANS. THERE ARE THE USUAL WORRIES ABOUT IT SPILLING OVER INTO NEIGHBORING NATIONS.
WONDER WOMAN...?
ON A LIGHTER NOTE, ASTRONOMERS HAVE RECORDED ERRATIC SOLAR FLARE ACTIVITY, ORIGINATING ON THE FAR SIDE OF THE SUN.
HEY, ARE YOU ALL RIGHT?
PROBABLY NOTHING SINISTER, BUT IT'S OUT OF CYCLE, AND BEARS CHECKING.
"LIGHTER NOTE"? WAS THAT SUPPOSED TO BE A JOKE?
OH, AND THAT ASTEROID WE PICKED UP A FEW MONTHS BACK SHOULD BE DEFLECTED BEFORE IT GETS ANY DEEPER INTO EARTH'S GRAVITY WELL.
YEAH, I HAVE THAT ONE WORKED OUT. I'LL JUST BUMP IT INTO ONE OF THE TROJAN POINTS.
GOOD. FINALLY, THERE HAVEN'T BEEN ANY SPECTACULAR CRIMES RECENTLY--
--BUT THERE HAS BEEN A BIZARRE RASH OF BURGLARIES THROUGHOUT THE ALPINE REGIONS OF WESTERN EUROPE. MOSTLY GOLD AND JEWELRY.
INTERPOL IS PURSUING SOME LEADS, BUT HAVE NO REAL SUSPECTS. IT'S STRANGE ENOUGH THAT WE MIGHT WANT TO KEEP AN EYE ON THAT, TOO.
THAT'S IT. ANY QUESTIONS?

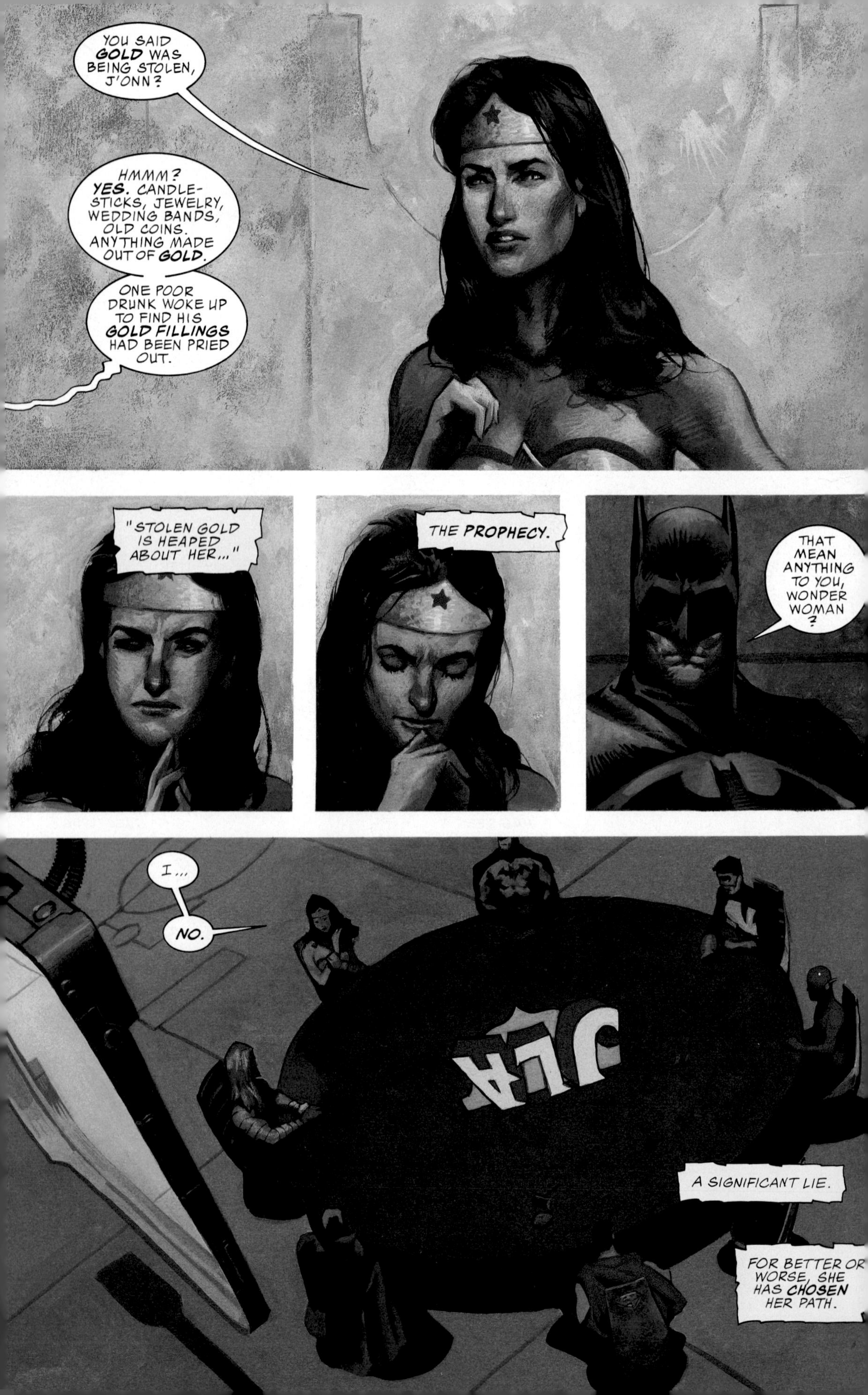
YOU SAID GOLD WAS BEING STOLEN, J'ONN?
HMMM? YES. CANDLE-STICKS, JEWELRY, WEDDING BANDS, OLD COINS. ANYTHING MADE OUT OF GOLD.
ONE POOR DRUNK WOKE UP TO FIND HIS GOLD FILLINGS HAD BEEN PRIED OUT.
"STOLEN GOLD IS HEAPED ABOUT HER..."
THE PROPHECY.
THAT MEAN ANYTHING TO YOU, WONDER WOMAN?
I...
NO.
JLA
A SIGNIFICANT LIE.
FOR BETTER OR WORSE, SHE HAS CHOSEN HER PATH.

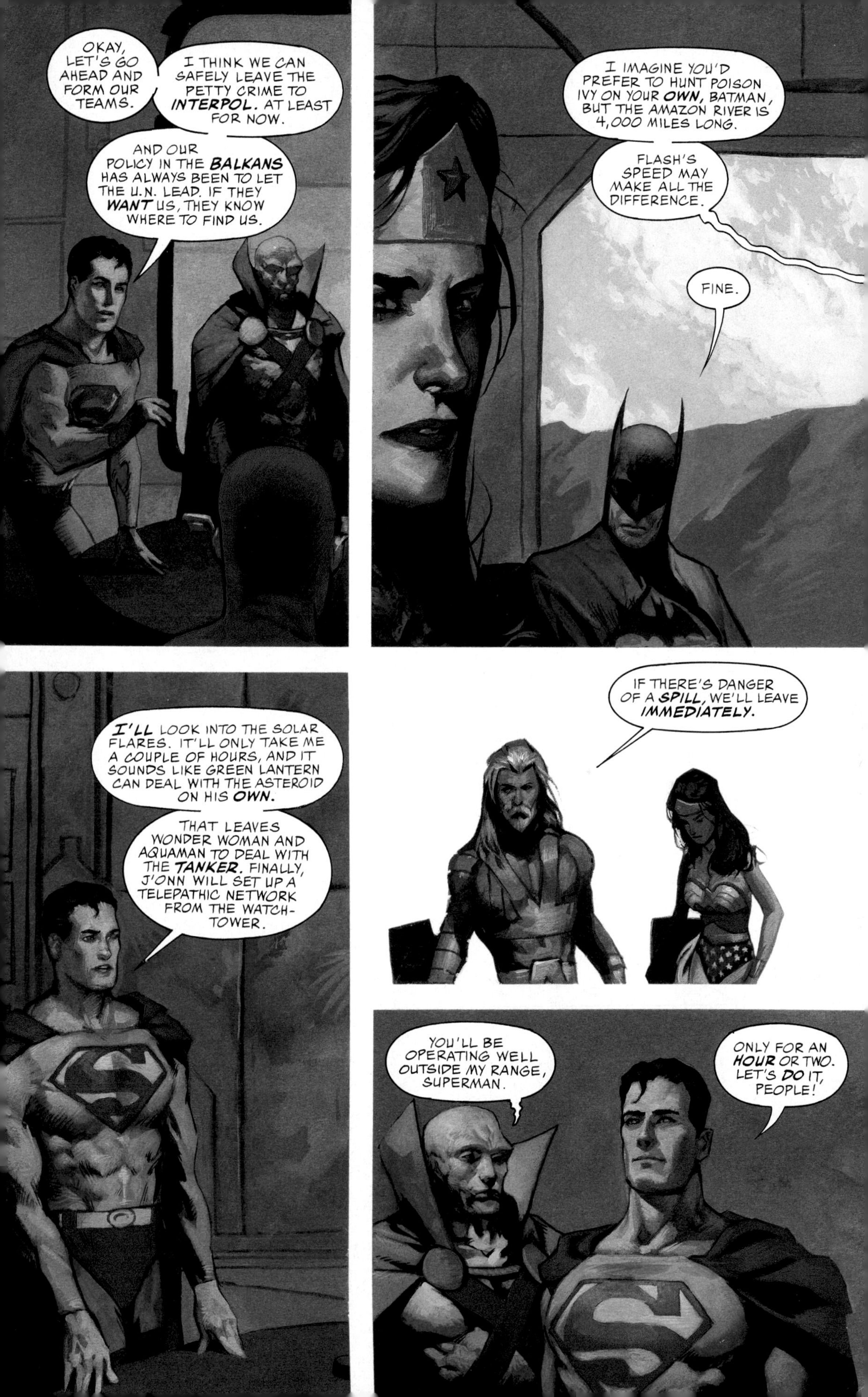
OKAY, LET'S GO AHEAD AND FORM OUR TEAMS.
I THINK WE CAN SAFELY LEAVE THE PETTY CRIME TO INTERPOL. AT LEAST FOR NOW.
AND OUR POLICY IN THE BALKANS HAS ALWAYS BEEN TO LET THE U.N. LEAD. IF THEY WANT US, THEY KNOW WHERE TO FIND US.
I IMAGINE YOU'D PREFER TO HUNT POISON IVY ON YOUR OWN, BATMAN, BUT THE AMAZON RIVER IS 4,000 MILES LONG.
FLASH'S SPEED MAY MAKE ALL THE DIFFERENCE.
FINE.
I'LL LOOK INTO THE SOLAR FLARES. IT'LL ONLY TAKE ME A COUPLE OF HOURS, AND IT SOUNDS LIKE GREEN LANTERN CAN DEAL WITH THE ASTEROID ON HIS OWN.
THAT LEAVES WONDER WOMAN AND AQUAMAN TO DEAL WITH THE TANKER. FINALLY, J'ONN WILL SET UP A TELEPATHIC NETWORK FROM THE WATCH-TOWER.
IF THERE'S DANGER OF A SPILL, WE'LL LEAVE IMMEDIATELY.
YOU'LL BE OPERATING WELL OUTSIDE MY RANGE, SUPERMAN.
ONLY FOR AN HOUR OR TWO. LET'S DO IT, PEOPLE!

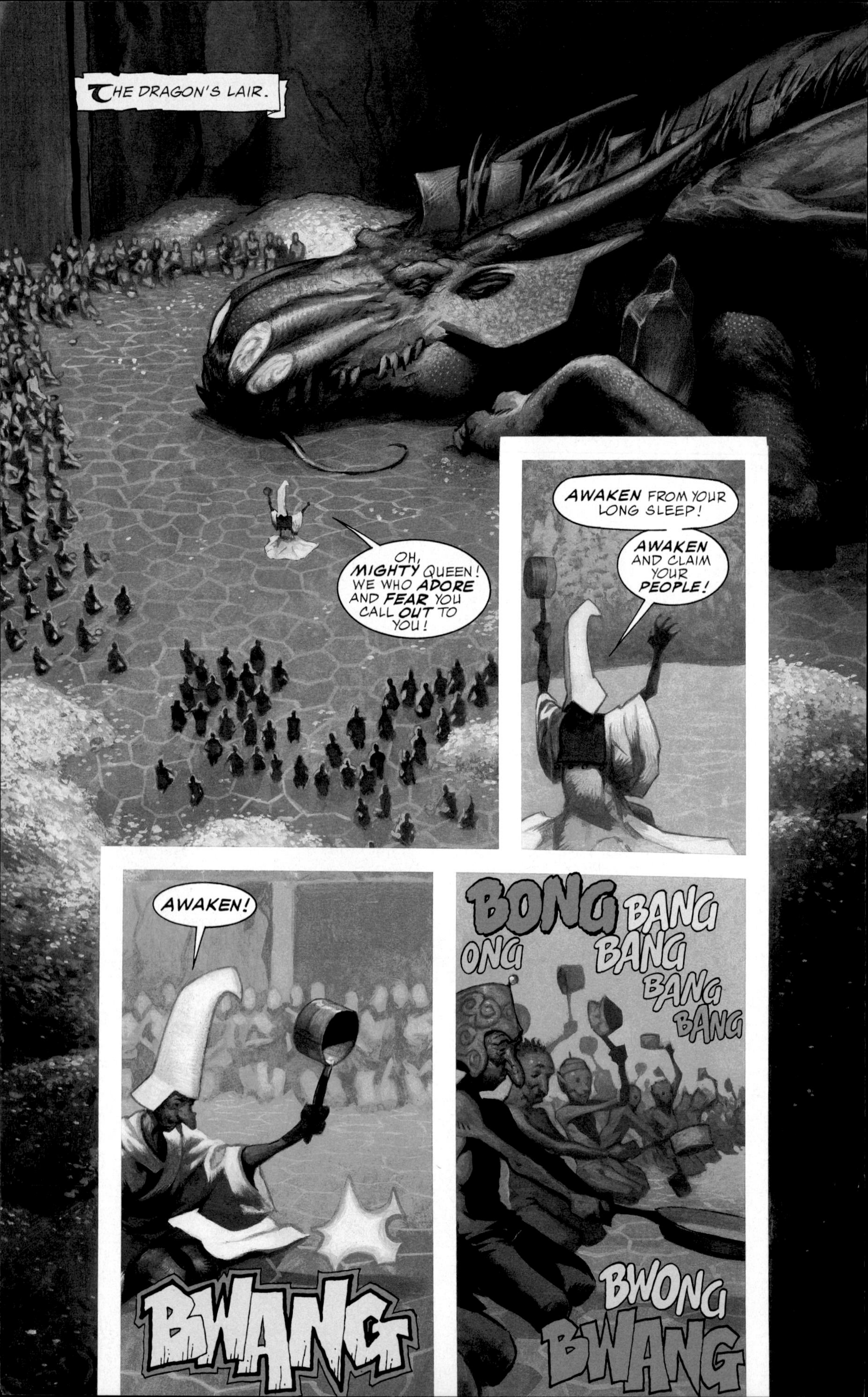
THE DRAGON'S LAIR.
OH, MIGHTY QUEEN! WE WHO ADORE AND FEAR YOU CALL OUT TO YOU!
AWAKEN FROM YOUR LONG SLEEP!
AWAKEN AND CLAIM YOUR PEOPLE!
AWAKEN!
BWANG
BONG
ONG
BANG
BANG
BANG
BANG
BWONG
BWANG

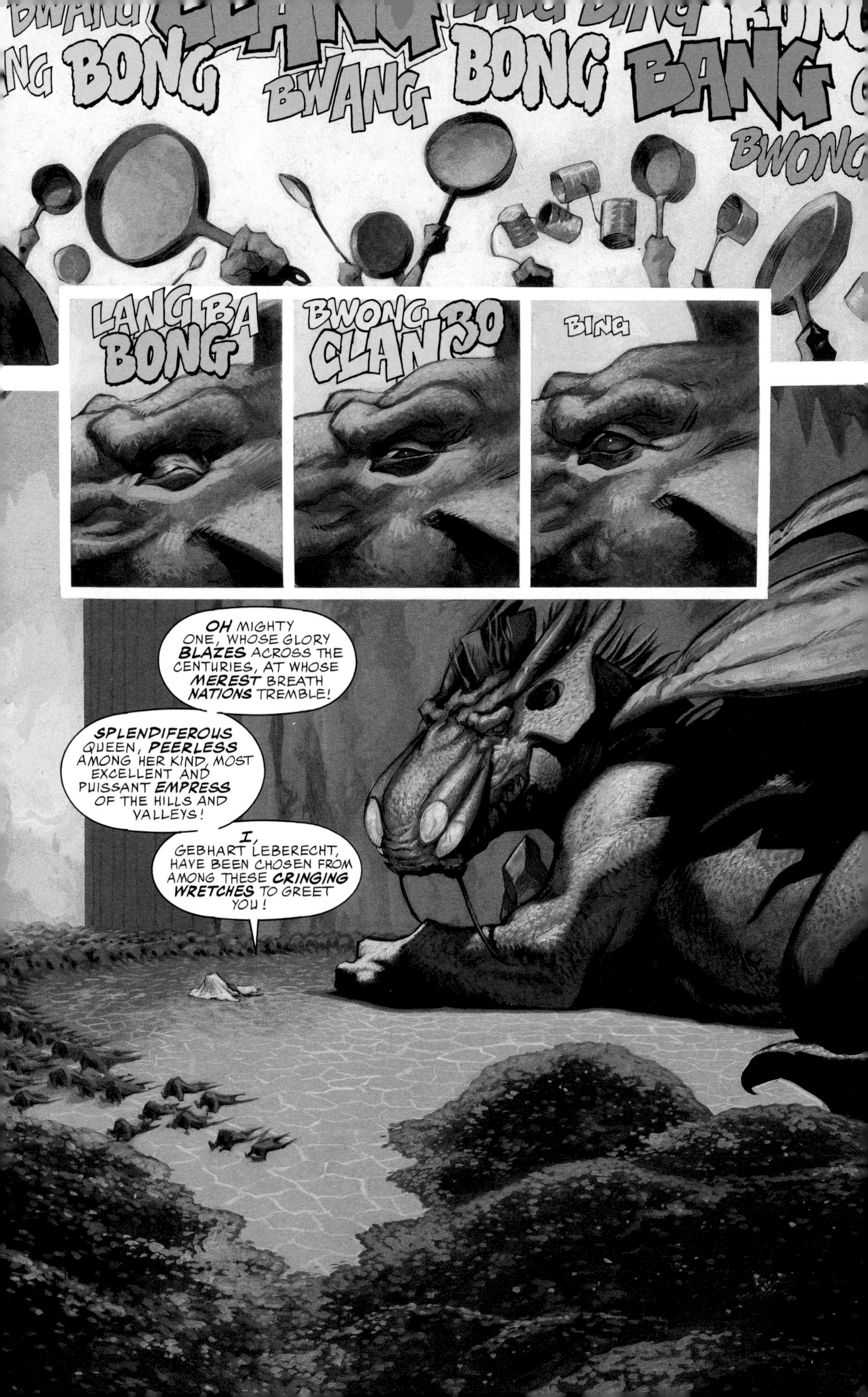
BWANG
BONG
BWANG
BONG
BANG
BWONG
BONG
BWONG
BING
OH MIGHTY ONE, WHOSE GLORY BLAZES ACROSS THE CENTURIES, AT WHOSE MEREST BREATH NATIONS TREMBLE!
SPLENDIFEROUS QUEEN, PEERLESS AMONG HER KIND, MOST EXCELLENT AND PUISSANT EMPRESS OF THE HILLS AND VALLEYS!
I, GEBHART LEBERECHT, HAVE BEEN CHOSEN FROM AMONG THESE CRINGING WRETCHES TO GREET YOU!

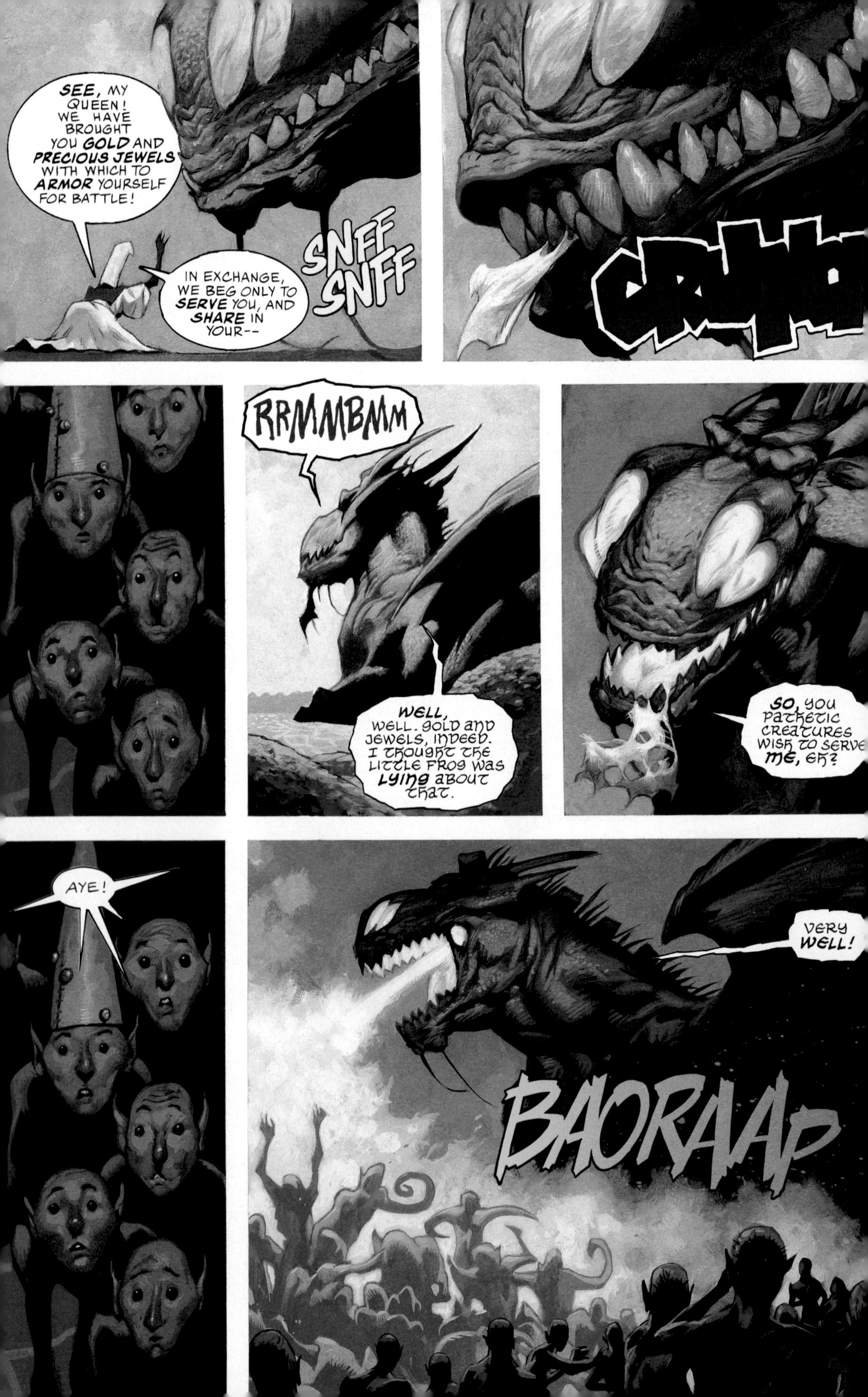
SEE, MY QUEEN! WE HAVE BROUGHT YOU GOLD AND PRECIOUS JEWELS WITH WHICH TO ARMOR YOURSELF FOR BATTLE!
IN EXCHANGE, WE BEG ONLY TO SERVE YOU, AND SHARE IN YOUR--
SNFF SNFF
RRMMBMM
WELL, WELL. GOLD AND JEWELS, INDEED. I THOUGHT THE LITTLE FROG WAS LYING ABOUT THAT.
SO, YOU PATHETIC CREATURES WISH TO SERVE ME, EH?
AYE!
VERY WELL!
BAORAAP

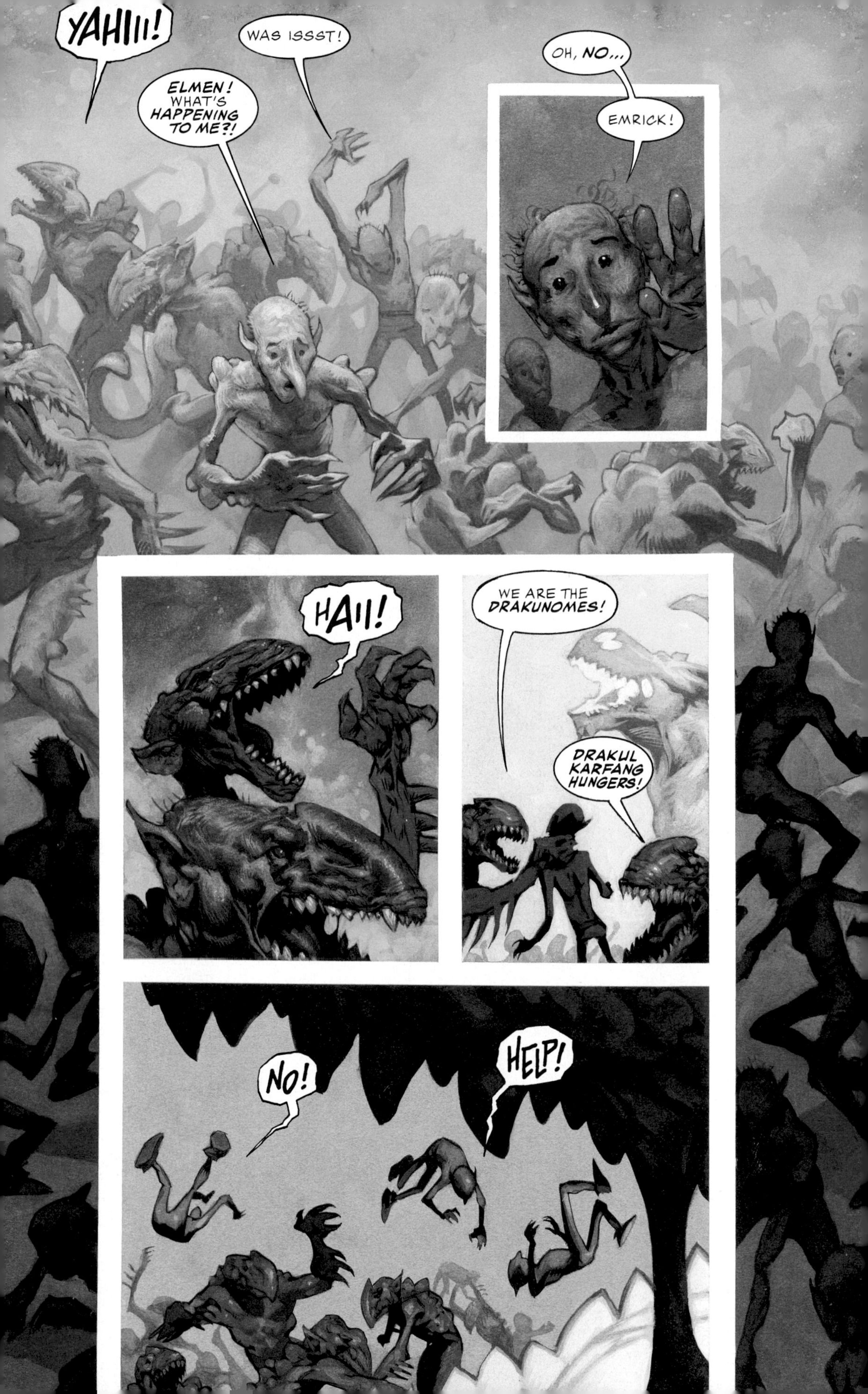
YAHIII!
ELMEN! WHAT'S HAPPENING TO ME?!
WAS ISSST!
OH, NO...
EMRICK!
HAII!
WE ARE THE DRAKUNOMES!
DRAKUL KARFANG HUNGERS!
NO!
HELP!

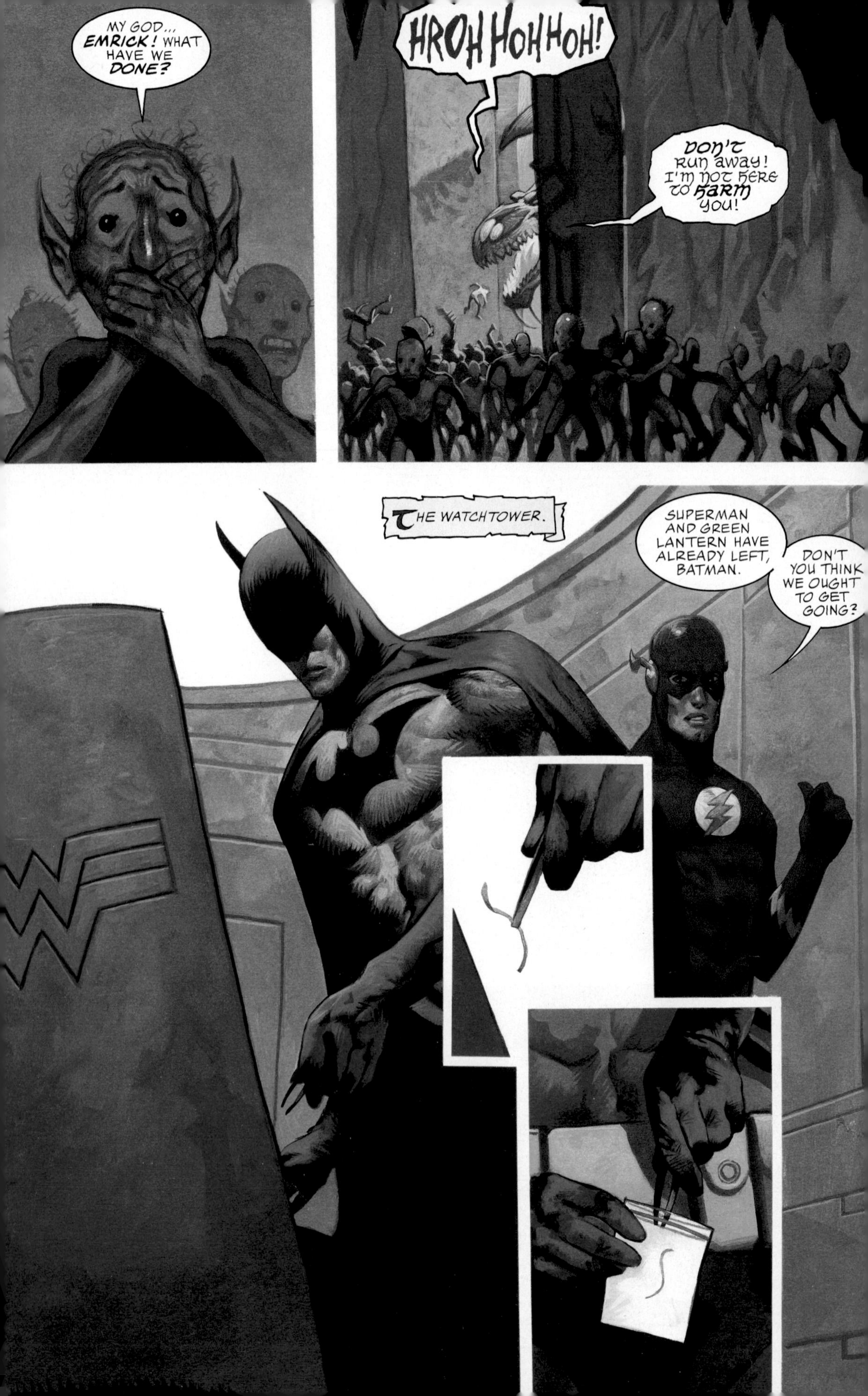
MY GOD... EMRICK! WHAT HAVE WE DONE?
HROH HOH HOH!
DON'T RUN AWAY! I'M NOT HERE TO HARM YOU!
THE WATCHTOWER.
SUPERMAN AND GREEN LANTERN HAVE ALREADY LEFT, BATMAN.
DON'T YOU THINK WE OUGHT TO GET GOING?

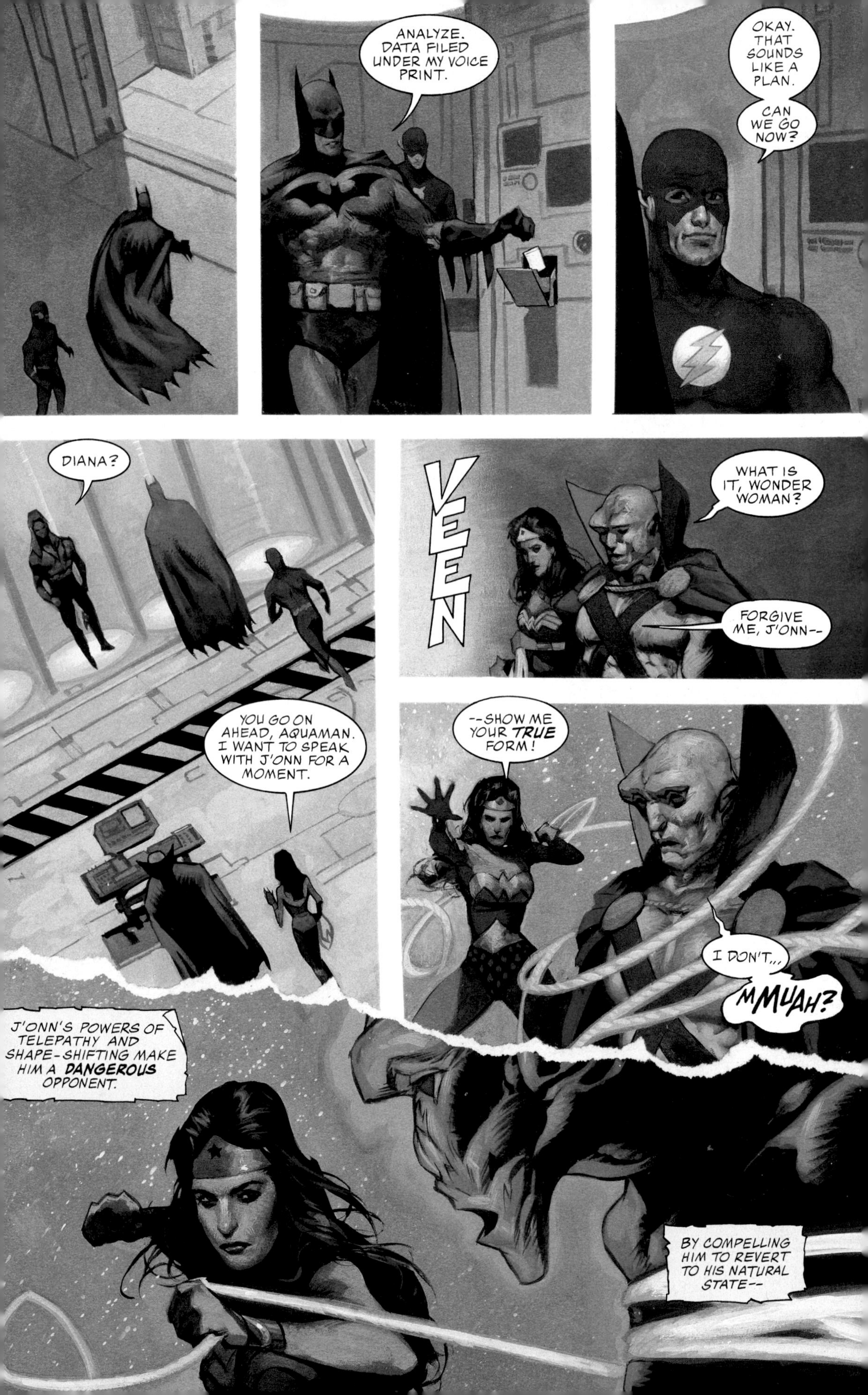
ANALYZE. DATA FILED UNDER MY VOICE PRINT.
OKAY. THAT SOUNDS LIKE A PLAN.
CAN WE GO NOW?
DIANA?
YOU GO ON AHEAD, AQUAMAN. I WANT TO SPEAK WITH J'ONN FOR A MOMENT.
VEEN
WHAT IS IT, WONDER WOMAN?
FORGIVE ME, J'ONN--
--SHOW ME YOUR TRUE FORM!
I DON'T...
MMUAH?
J'ONN'S POWERS OF TELEPATHY AND SHAPE-SHIFTING MAKE HIM A DANGEROUS OPPONENT.
BY COMPELLING HIM TO REVERT TO HIS NATURAL STATE--

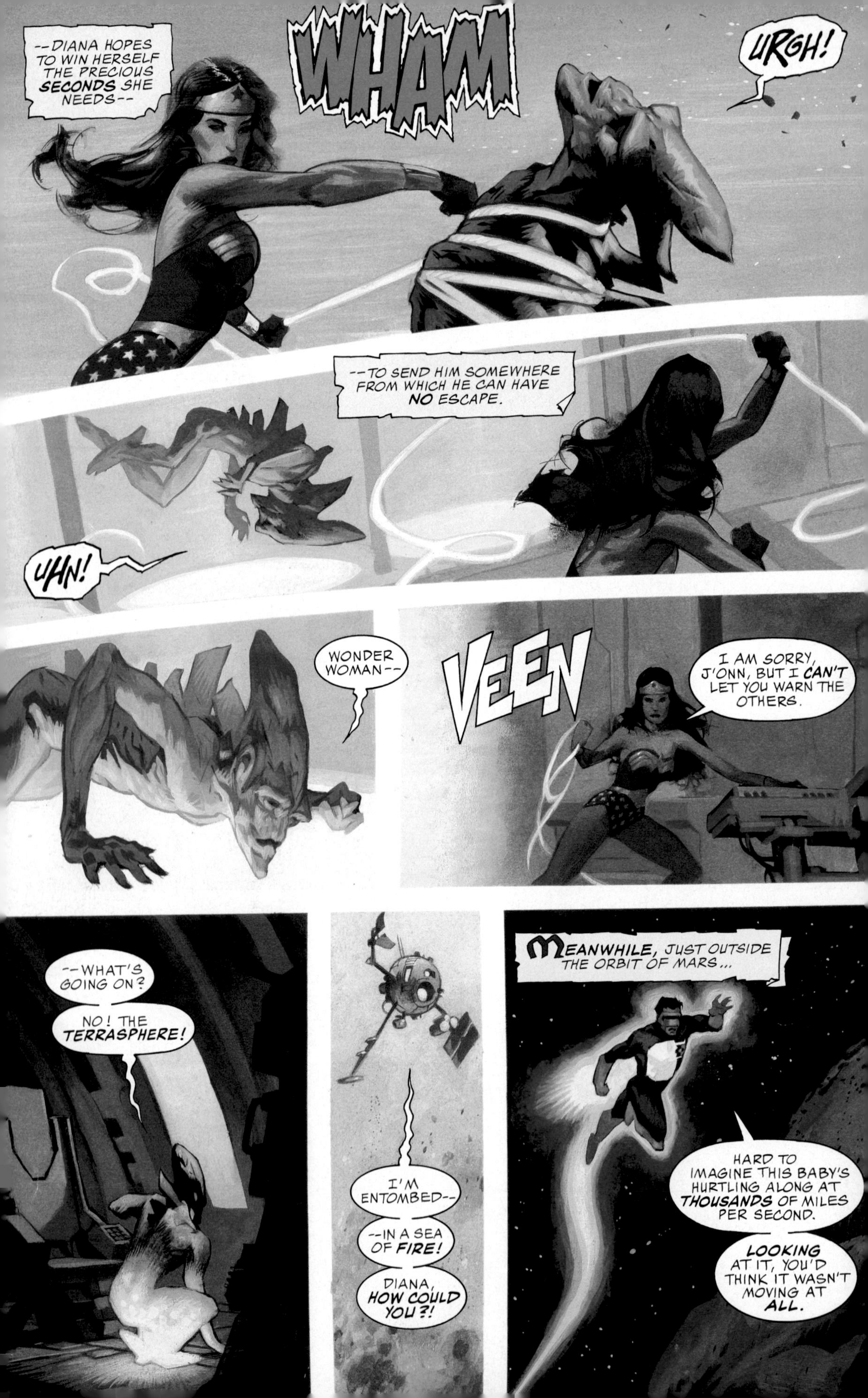
--DIANA HOPES TO WIN HERSELF THE PRECIOUS SECONDS SHE NEEDS--
WHAM
URGH!
--TO SEND HIM SOMEWHERE FROM WHICH HE CAN HAVE NO ESCAPE.
UHN!
WONDER WOMAN--
VEEN
I AM SORRY, J'ONN, BUT I CAN'T LET YOU WARN THE OTHERS.
--WHAT'S GOING ON?
NO! THE TERRASPHERE!
I'M ENTOMBED--
--IN A SEA OF FIRE!
DIANA, HOW COULD YOU?!
MEANWHILE, JUST OUTSIDE THE ORBIT OF MARS...
HARD TO IMAGINE THIS BABY'S HURTLING ALONG AT THOUSANDS OF MILES PER SECOND.
LOOKING AT IT, YOU'D THINK IT WASN'T MOVING AT ALL.

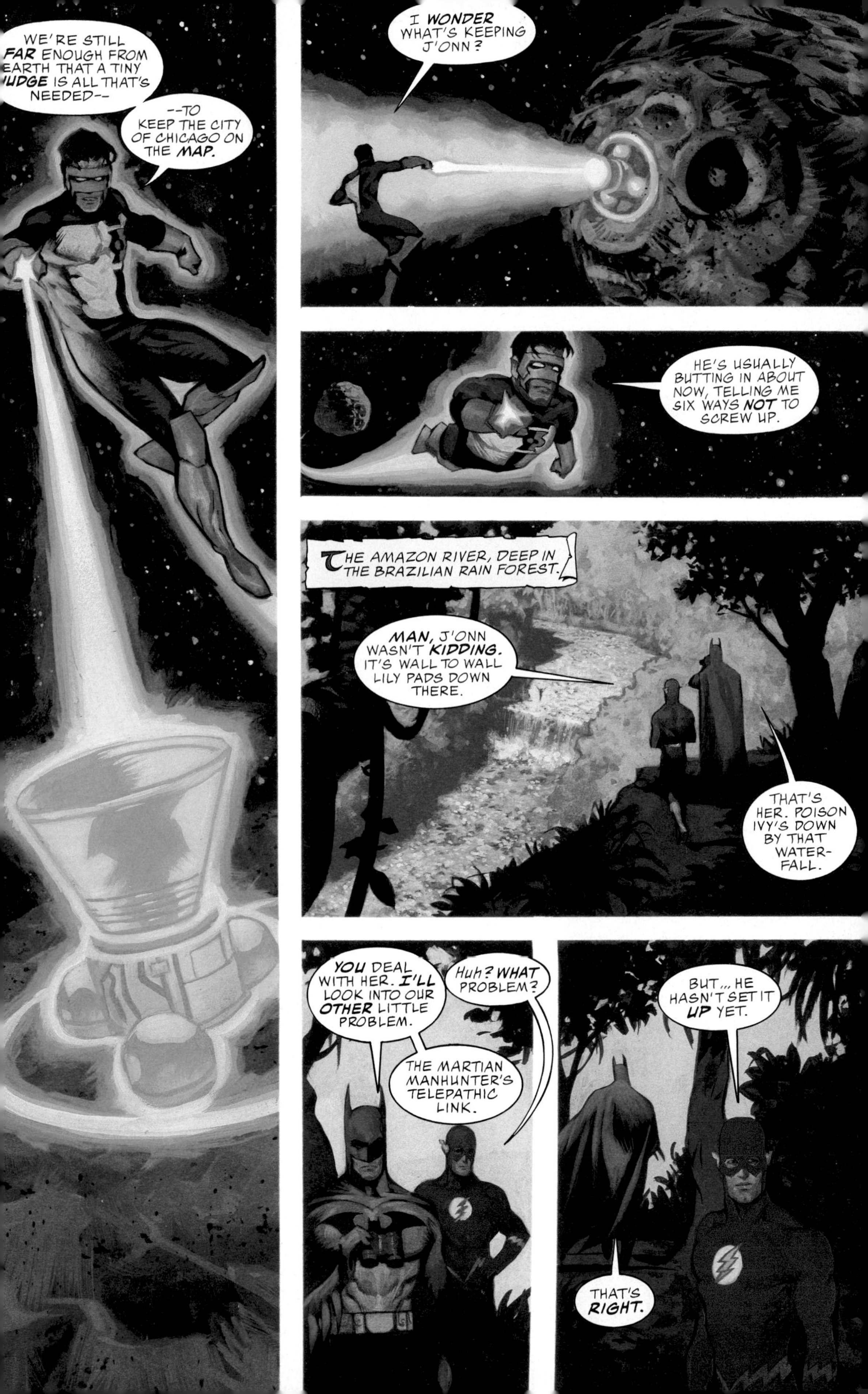
WE'RE STILL FAR ENOUGH FROM EARTH THAT A TINY NUDGE IS ALL THAT'S NEEDED--
--TO KEEP THE CITY OF CHICAGO ON THE MAP.
I WONDER WHAT'S KEEPING J'ONN?
HE'S USUALLY BUTTING IN ABOUT NOW, TELLING ME SIX WAYS NOT TO SCREW UP.
THE AMAZON RIVER, DEEP IN THE BRAZILIAN RAIN FOREST.
MAN, J'ONN WASN'T KIDDING. IT'S WALL TO WALL LILY PADS DOWN THERE.
THAT'S HER. POISON IVY'S DOWN BY THAT WATER-FALL.
YOU DEAL WITH HER. I'LL LOOK INTO OUR OTHER LITTLE PROBLEM.
Huh? WHAT PROBLEM?
THE MARTIAN MANHUNTER'S TELEPATHIC LINK.
BUT... HE HASN'T SET IT UP YET.
THAT'S RIGHT.

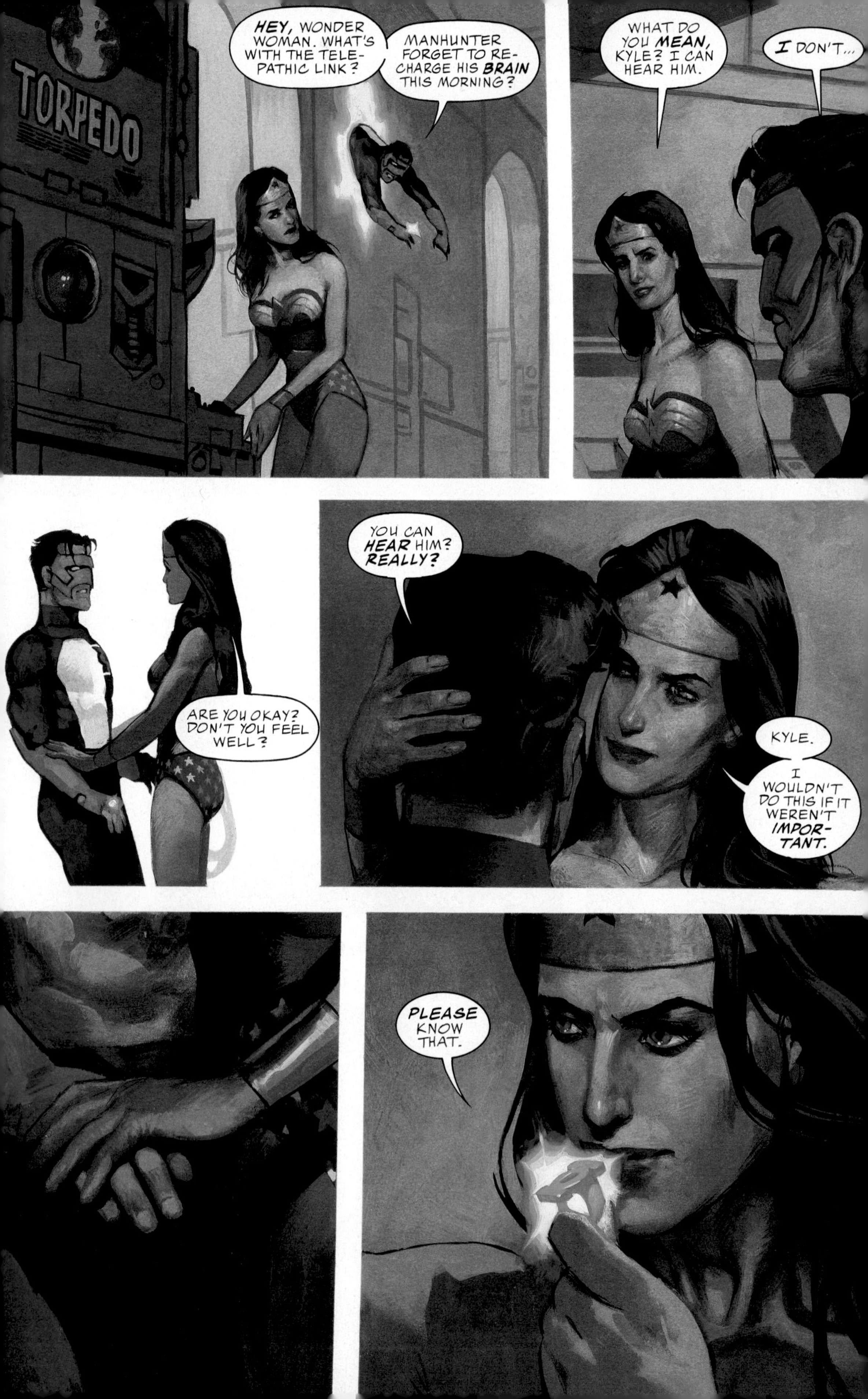
TORPEDO
HEY, WONDER WOMAN. WHAT'S WITH THE TELE-PATHIC LINK?
MANHUNTER FORGET TO RE-CHARGE HIS BRAIN THIS MORNING?
WHAT DO YOU MEAN, KYLE? I CAN HEAR HIM.
I DON'T...
ARE YOU OKAY? DON'T YOU FEEL WELL?
YOU CAN HEAR HIM? REALLY?
KYLE.
I WOULDN'T DO THIS IF IT WEREN'T IMPOR-TANT.
PLEASE KNOW THAT.

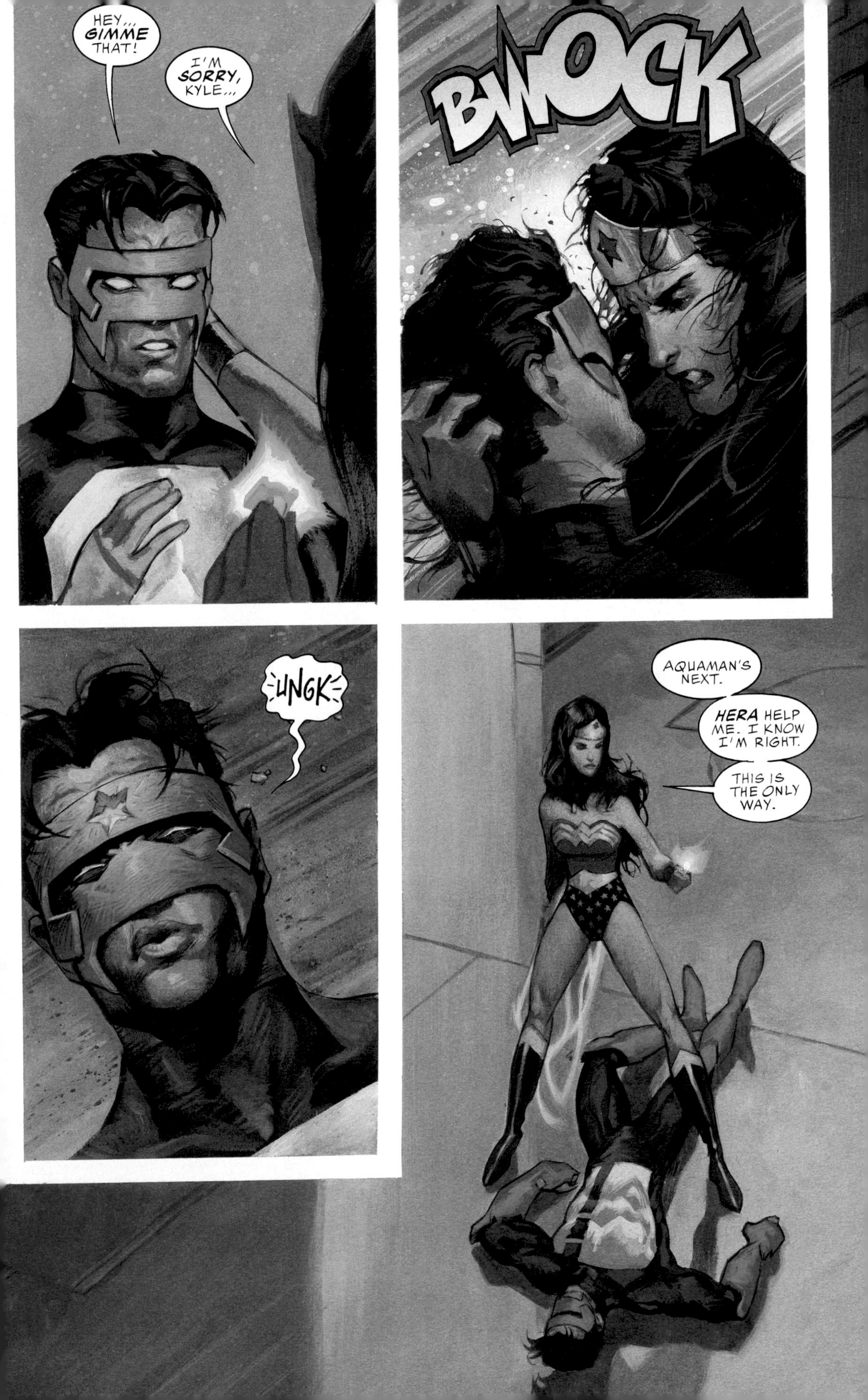
HEY... GIMME THAT!
I'M SORRY, KYLE...
BWOCK
UNGK
AQUAMAN'S NEXT.
HERA HELP ME. I KNOW I'M RIGHT.
THIS IS THE ONLY WAY.

TWO MILES OFF THE COAST OF SICILY.

TAKE THEM TO SHORE SLOWLY, MY FRIENDS. THEY'RE EXHAUSTED.

WHERE IS SHE...

VEEN

WONDER-WOMAN, THANK GOODNESS! THE TANKER!

YOU MUST GET HER OFF THE ROCKS BEFORE SHE BREAKS UP!

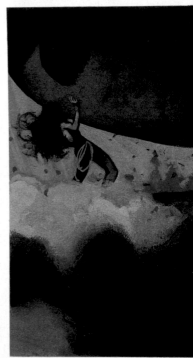

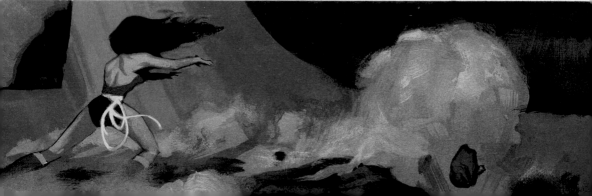

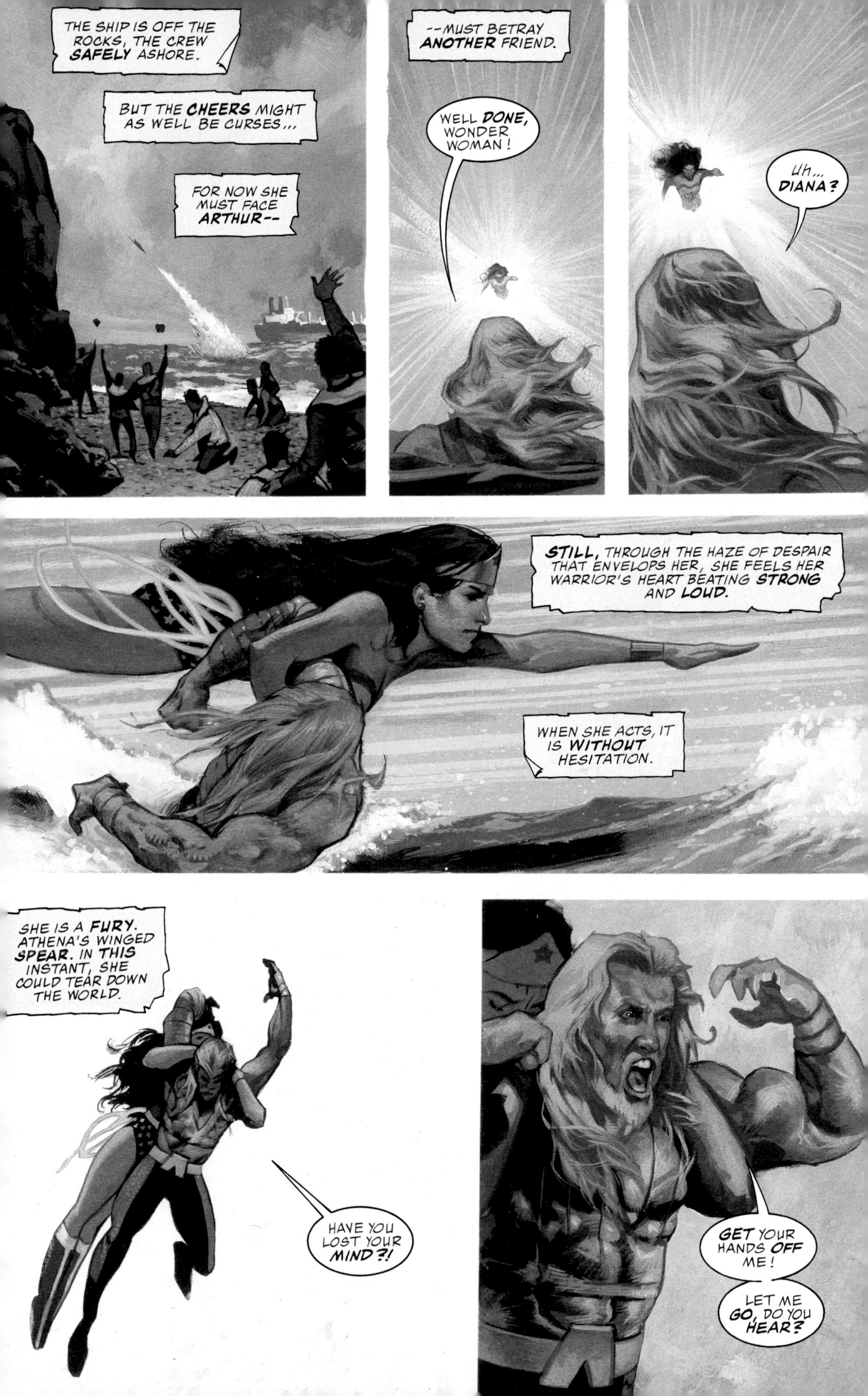
THE SHIP IS OFF THE ROCKS, THE CREW SAFELY ASHORE.
BUT THE CHEERS MIGHT AS WELL BE CURSES...
FOR NOW SHE MUST FACE ARTHUR--
--MUST BETRAY ANOTHER FRIEND.
WELL DONE, WONDER WOMAN!
UH... DIANA?
STILL, THROUGH THE HAZE OF DESPAIR THAT ENVELOPS HER, SHE FEELS HER WARRIOR'S HEART BEATING STRONG AND LOUD.
WHEN SHE ACTS, IT IS WITHOUT HESITATION.
SHE IS A FURY. ATHENA'S WINGED SPEAR. IN THIS INSTANT, SHE COULD TEAR DOWN THE WORLD.
HAVE YOU LOST YOUR MIND?!
GET YOUR HANDS OFF ME!
LET ME GO, DO YOU HEAR?

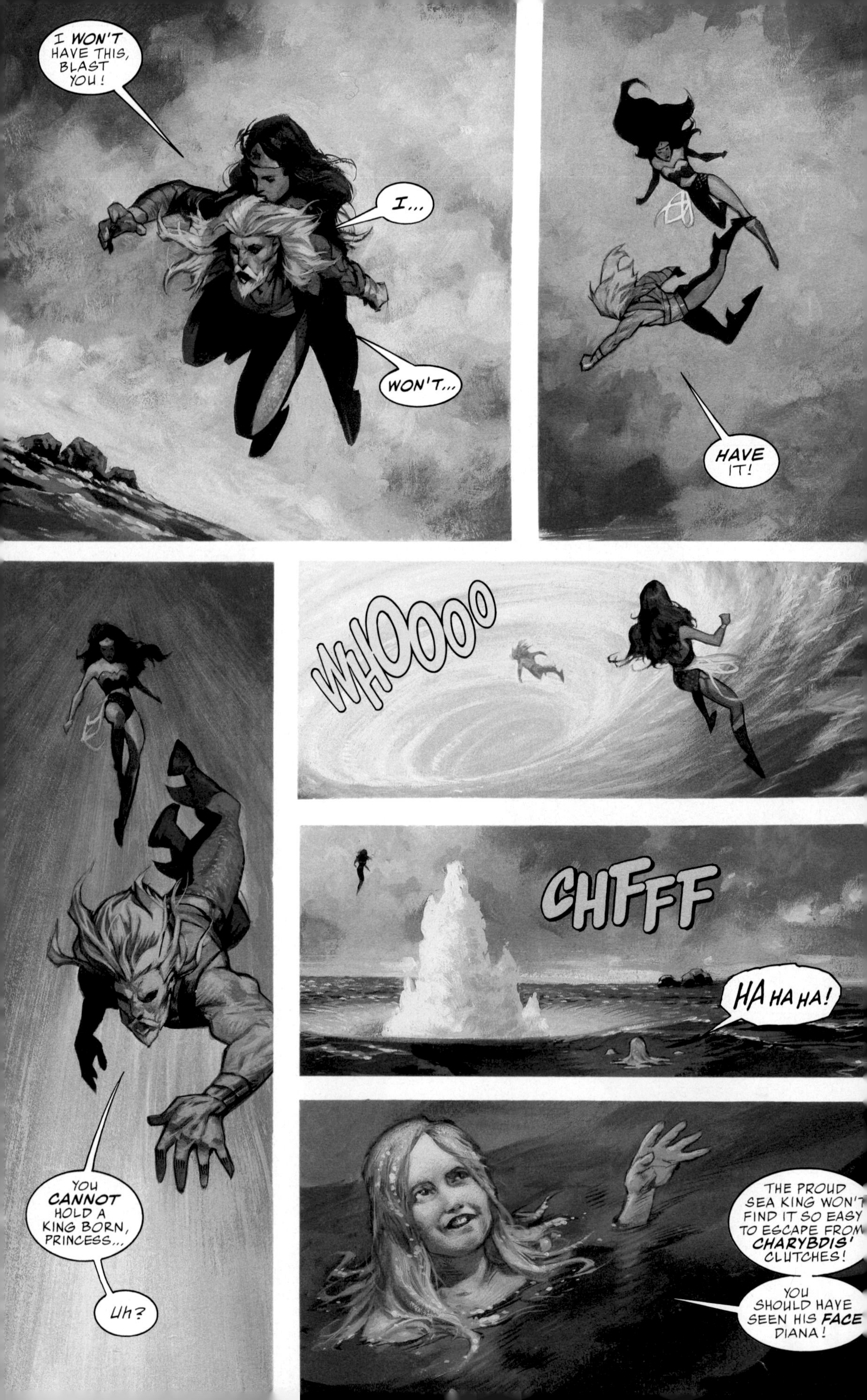
I WON'T HAVE THIS, BLAST YOU!
I...
WON'T...
HAVE IT!
WHOOOO
YOU CANNOT HOLD A KING BORN, PRINCESS...
Uh?
CHFFF
HA HA HA!
THE PROUD SEA KING WON'T FIND IT SO EASY TO ESCAPE FROM CHARYBDIS' CLUTCHES!
YOU SHOULD HAVE SEEN HIS FACE DIANA!

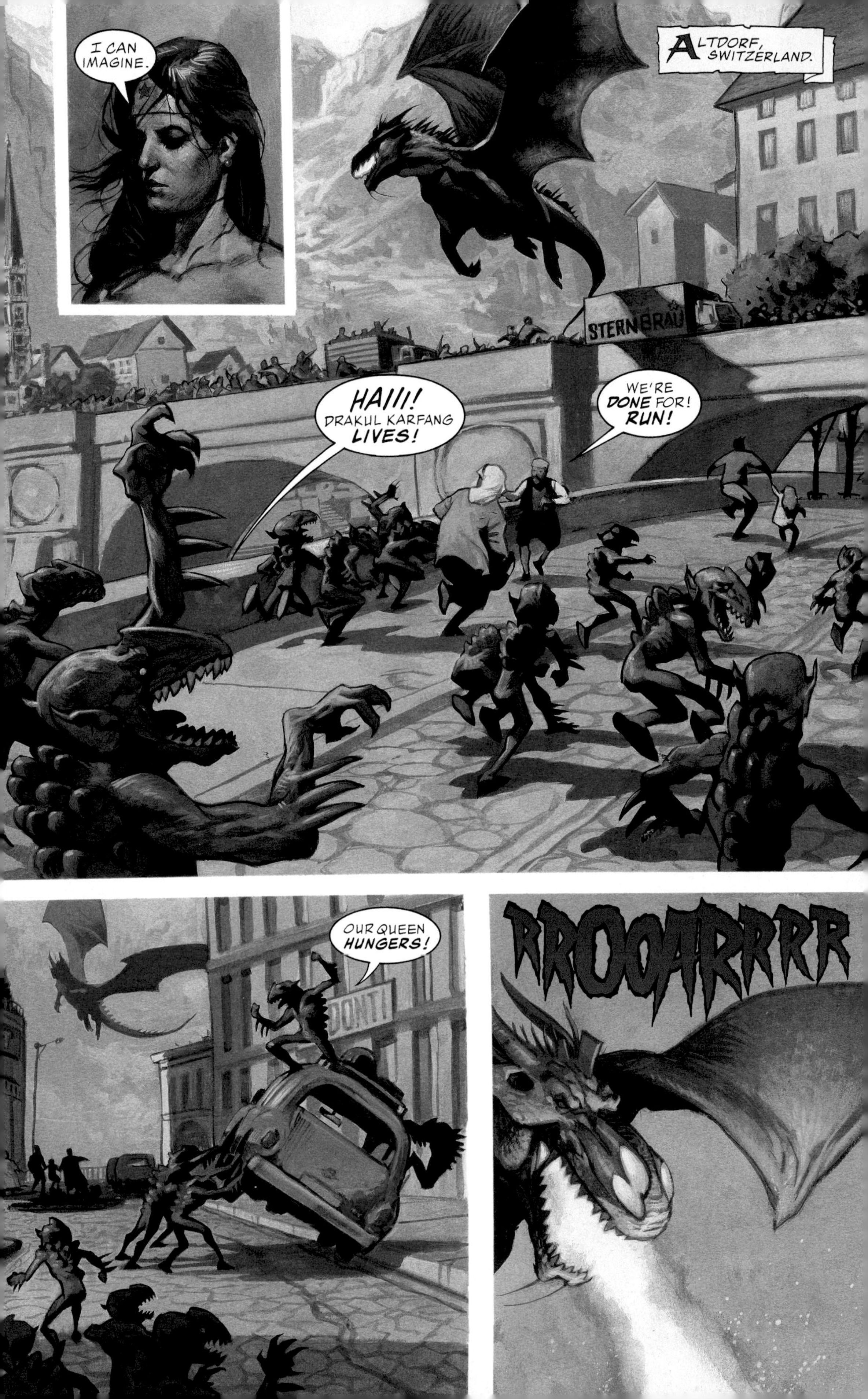
I CAN IMAGINE.
ALTDORF, SWITZERLAND.
STERNBRÄU
HAIII! DRAKUL KARFANG LIVES!
WE'RE DONE FOR! RUN!
OUR QUEEN HUNGERS!
RROOARRRR

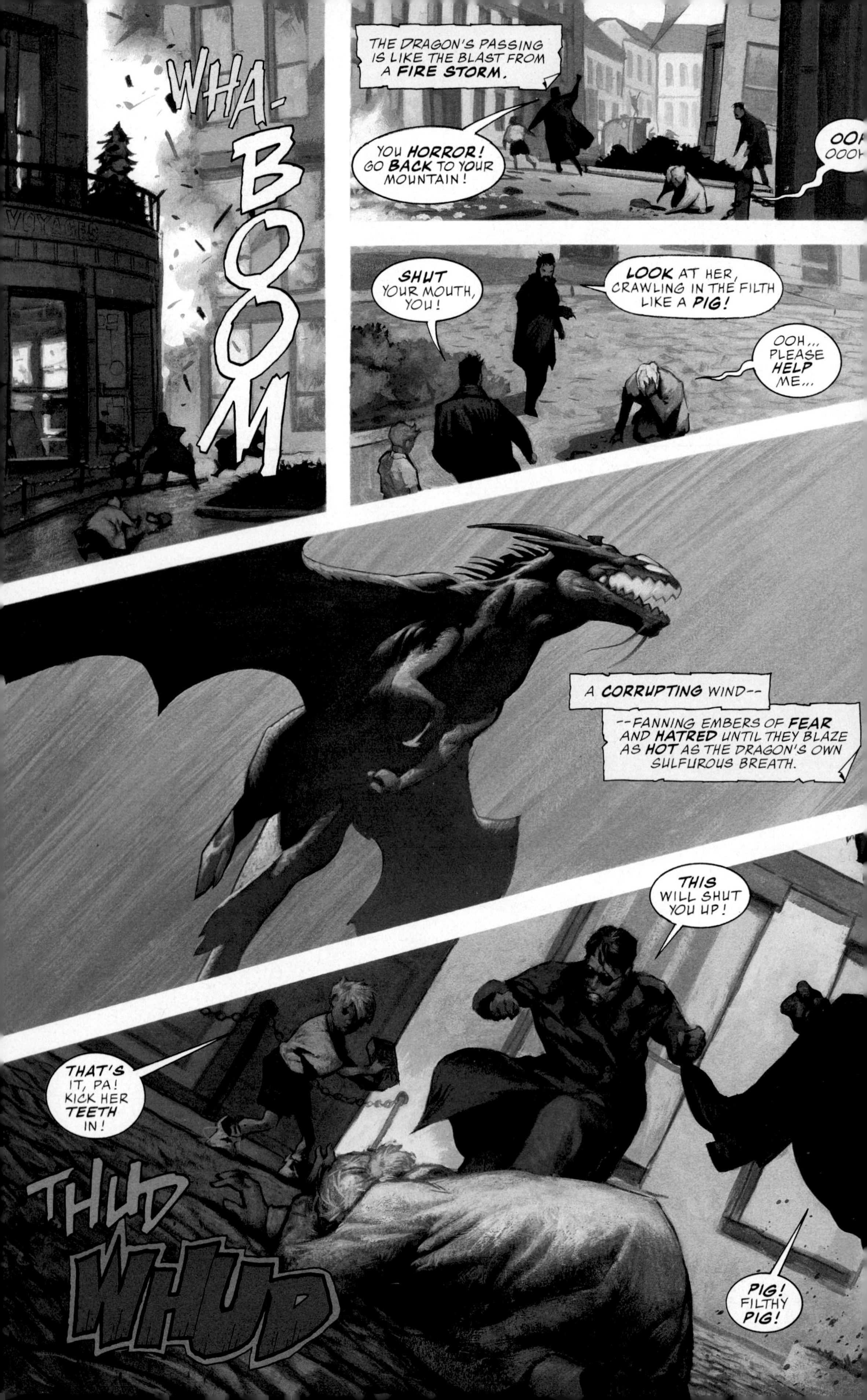
WHA-BOOM
THE DRAGON'S PASSING IS LIKE THE BLAST FROM A FIRE STORM.
YOU HORROR! GO BACK TO YOUR MOUNTAIN!
SHUT YOUR MOUTH, YOU!
LOOK AT HER, CRAWLING IN THE FILTH LIKE A PIG!
OOH... PLEASE HELP ME...
A CORRUPTING WIND--
--FANNING EMBERS OF FEAR AND HATRED UNTIL THEY BLAZE AS HOT AS THE DRAGON'S OWN SULFUROUS BREATH.
THIS WILL SHUT YOU UP!
THAT'S IT, PA! KICK HER TEETH IN!
THUD
WHUD
PIG! FILTHY PIG!

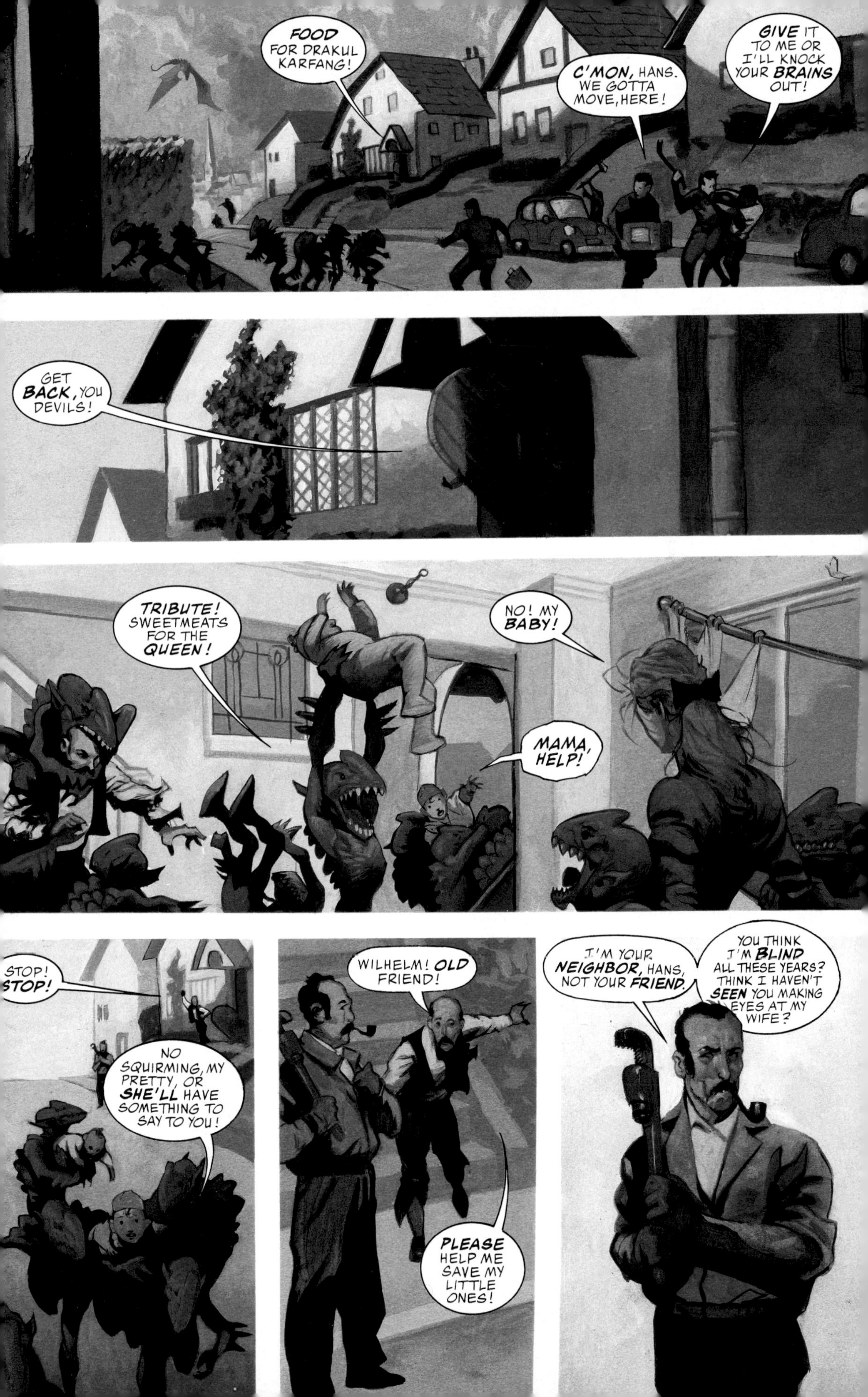
FOOD FOR DRAKUL KARFANG!
C'MON, HANS. WE GOTTA MOVE, HERE!
GIVE IT TO ME OR I'LL KNOCK YOUR BRAINS OUT!
GET BACK, YOU DEVILS!
TRIBUTE! SWEETMEATS FOR THE QUEEN!
NO! MY BABY!
MAMA, HELP!
STOP! STOP!
NO SQUIRMING, MY PRETTY, OR SHE'LL HAVE SOMETHING TO SAY TO YOU!
WILHELM! OLD FRIEND!
PLEASE HELP ME SAVE MY LITTLE ONES!
I'M YOUR NEIGHBOR, HANS, NOT YOUR FRIEND.
YOU THINK I'M BLIND ALL THESE YEARS? THINK I HAVEN'T SEEN YOU MAKING EYES AT MY WIFE?

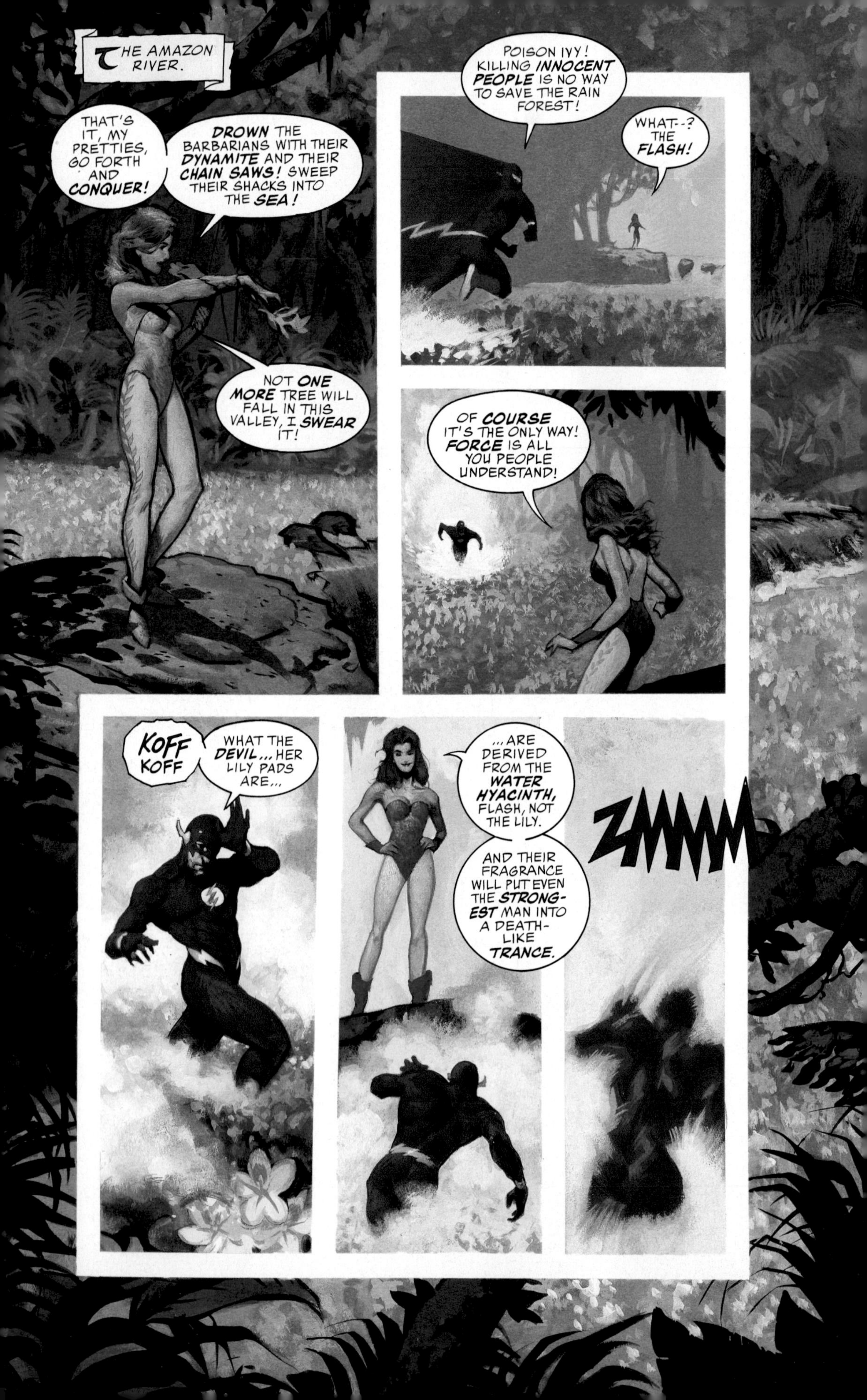
THE AMAZON RIVER.
THAT'S IT, MY PRETTIES, GO FORTH AND CONQUER!
DROWN THE BARBARIANS WITH THEIR DYNAMITE AND THEIR CHAIN SAWS! SWEEP THEIR SHACKS INTO THE SEA!
NOT ONE MORE TREE WILL FALL IN THIS VALLEY, I SWEAR IT!
POISON IVY! KILLING INNOCENT PEOPLE IS NO WAY TO SAVE THE RAIN FOREST!
WHAT--? THE FLASH!
OF COURSE IT'S THE ONLY WAY! FORCE IS ALL YOU PEOPLE UNDERSTAND!
KOFF KOFF
WHAT THE DEVIL... HER LILY PADS ARE...
...ARE DERIVED FROM THE WATER HYACINTH, FLASH, NOT THE LILY.
AND THEIR FRAGRANCE WILL PUT EVEN THE STRONGEST MAN INTO A DEATH-LIKE TRANCE.
ZMMMM

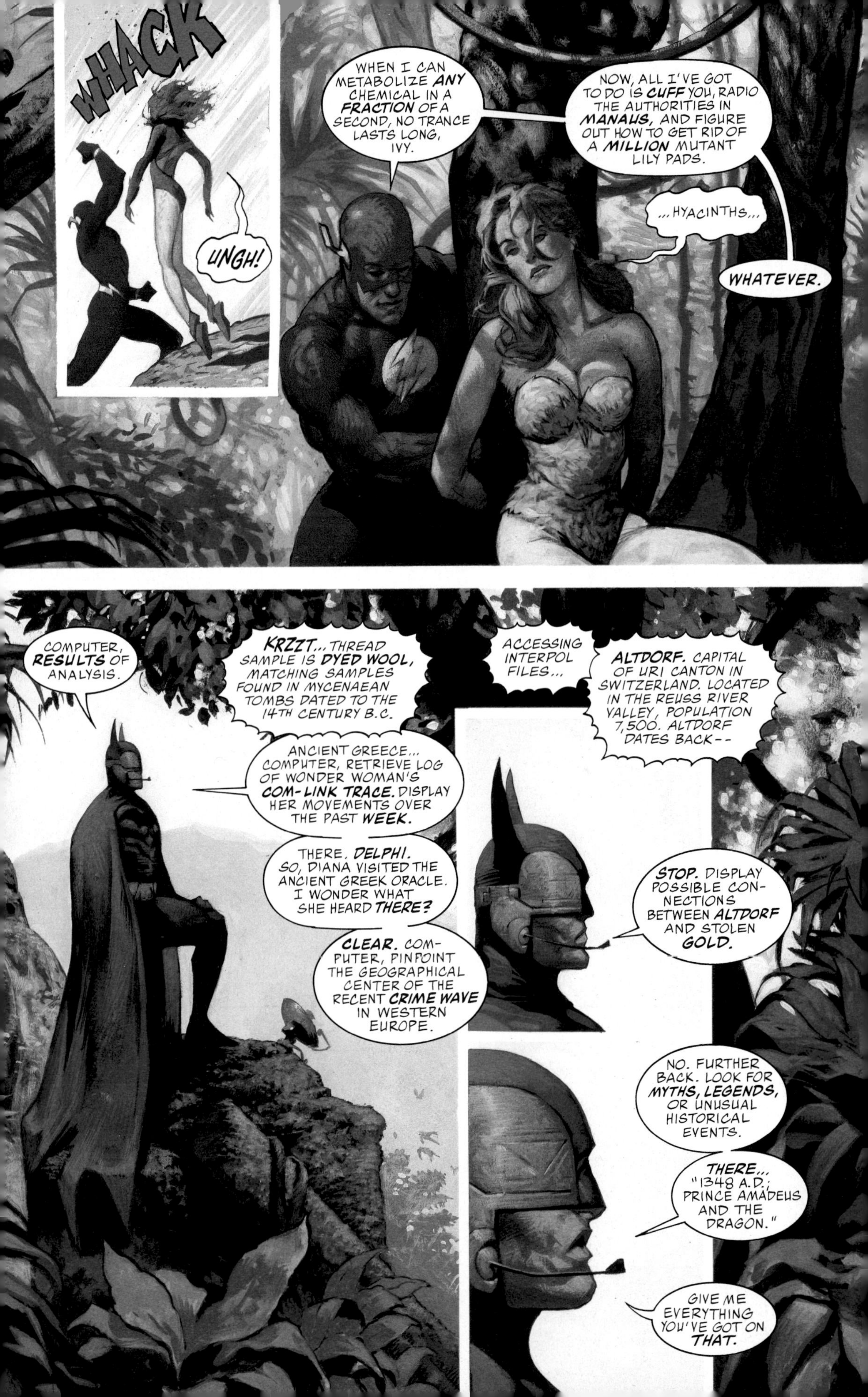
WHACK
UNGH!
WHEN I CAN METABOLIZE ANY CHEMICAL IN A FRACTION OF A SECOND, NO TRANCE LASTS LONG, IVY.
NOW, ALL I'VE GOT TO DO IS CUFF YOU, RADIO THE AUTHORITIES IN MANAUS, AND FIGURE OUT HOW TO GET RID OF A MILLION MUTANT LILY PADS.
...HYACINTHS...
WHATEVER.
COMPUTER, RESULTS OF ANALYSIS.
KRZZT... THREAD SAMPLE IS DYED WOOL, MATCHING SAMPLES FOUND IN MYCENAEAN TOMBS DATED TO THE 14TH CENTURY B.C.
ANCIENT GREECE... COMPUTER, RETRIEVE LOG OF WONDER WOMAN'S COM-LINK TRACE. DISPLAY HER MOVEMENTS OVER THE PAST WEEK.
THERE. DELPHI. SO, DIANA VISITED THE ANCIENT GREEK ORACLE. I WONDER WHAT SHE HEARD THERE?
CLEAR. COM-PUTER, PINPOINT THE GEOGRAPHICAL CENTER OF THE RECENT CRIME WAVE IN WESTERN EUROPE.
ACCESSING INTERPOL FILES...
ALTDORF. CAPITAL OF URI CANTON IN SWITZERLAND. LOCATED IN THE REUSS RIVER VALLEY, POPULATION 7,500. ALTDORF DATES BACK--
STOP. DISPLAY POSSIBLE CON-NECTIONS BETWEEN ALTDORF AND STOLEN GOLD.
NO. FURTHER BACK. LOOK FOR MYTHS, LEGENDS, OR UNUSUAL HISTORICAL EVENTS.
THERE... "1348 A.D.; PRINCE AMADEUS AND THE DRAGON."
GIVE ME EVERYTHING YOU'VE GOT ON THAT.

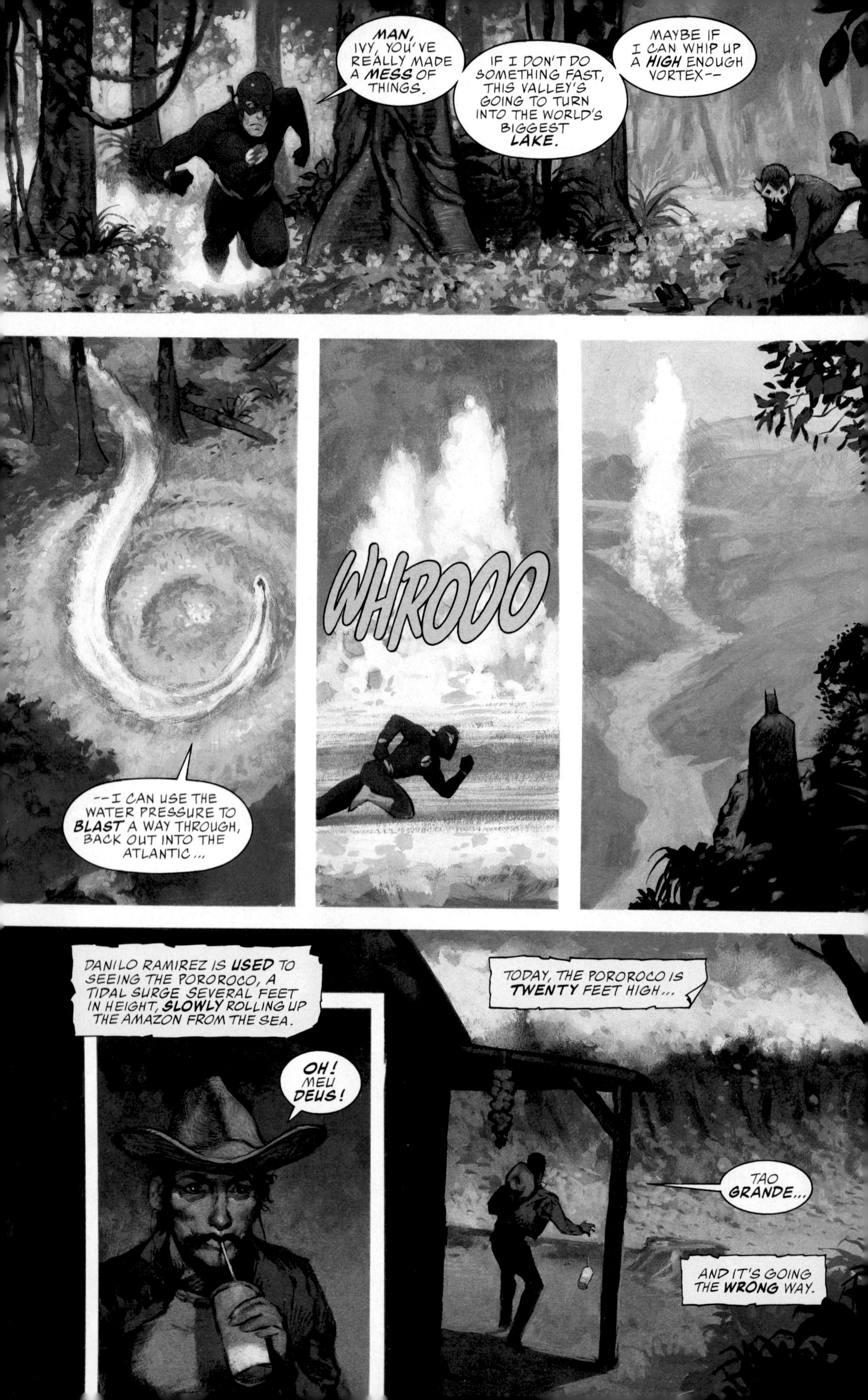
MAN, IVY, YOU'VE REALLY MADE A MESS OF THINGS.
IF I DON'T DO SOMETHING FAST, THIS VALLEY'S GOING TO TURN INTO THE WORLD'S BIGGEST LAKE.
MAYBE IF I CAN WHIP UP A HIGH ENOUGH VORTEX--
--I CAN USE THE WATER PRESSURE TO BLAST A WAY THROUGH, BACK OUT INTO THE ATLANTIC...
WHROOO
DANILO RAMIREZ IS USED TO SEEING THE POROROCO, A TIDAL SURGE SEVERAL FEET IN HEIGHT, SLOWLY ROLLING UP THE AMAZON FROM THE SEA.
OH! MEU DEUS!
TODAY, THE POROROCO IS TWENTY FEET HIGH...
TAO GRANDE...
AND IT'S GOING THE WRONG WAY.

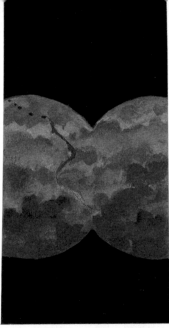

ONE LAST SWEEP BEFORE I RENDEZVOUS WITH BATMAN. MAKE SURE I HAVEN'T *MISSED* ANY--

--THING!

KRRSH

GAAH!

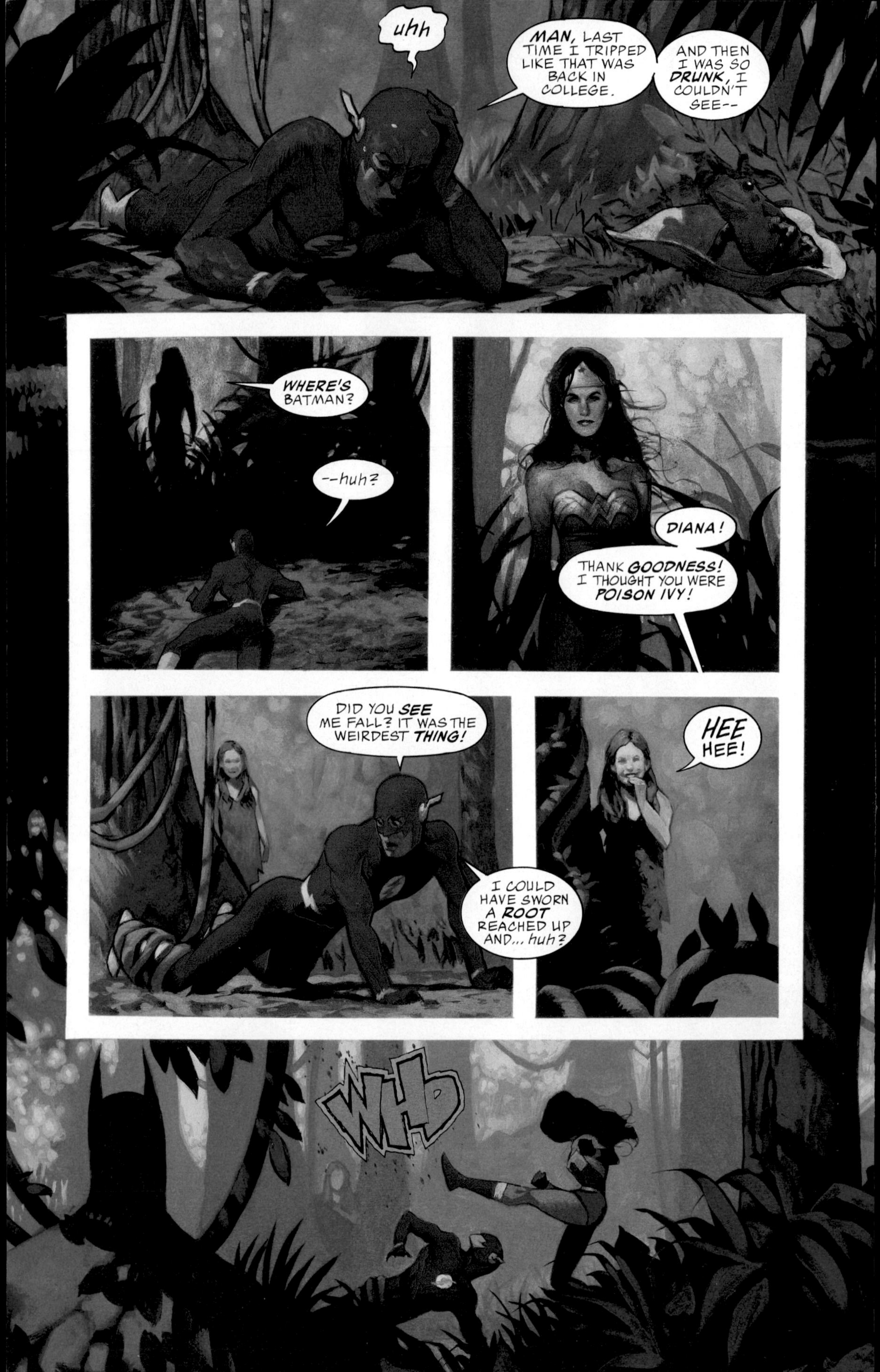
uhh
MAN, LAST TIME I TRIPPED LIKE THAT WAS BACK IN COLLEGE.
AND THEN I WAS SO DRUNK, I COULDN'T SEE--
WHERE'S BATMAN?
--huh?
DIANA!
THANK GOODNESS! I THOUGHT YOU WERE POISON IVY!
DID YOU SEE ME FALL? IT WAS THE WEIRDEST THING!
I COULD HAVE SWORN A ROOT REACHED UP AND... huh?
HEE HEE!
WHD

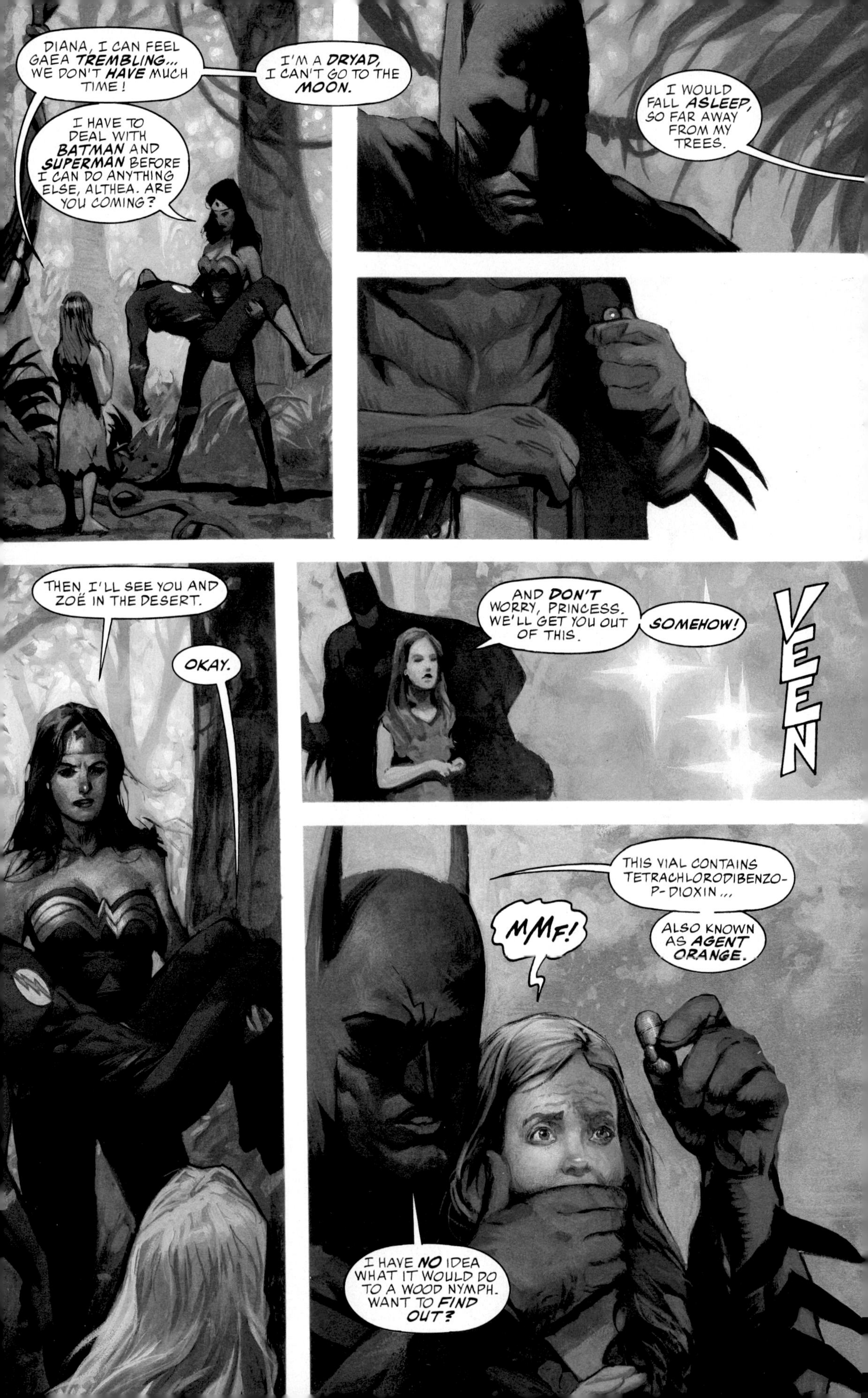
DIANA, I CAN FEEL GAEA TREMBLING... WE DON'T HAVE MUCH TIME!
I'M A DRYAD, I CAN'T GO TO THE MOON.
I HAVE TO DEAL WITH BATMAN AND SUPERMAN BEFORE I CAN DO ANYTHING ELSE, ALTHEA. ARE YOU COMING?
I WOULD FALL ASLEEP, SO FAR AWAY FROM MY TREES.
THEN I'LL SEE YOU AND ZOË IN THE DESERT.
OKAY.
AND DON'T WORRY, PRINCESS. WE'LL GET YOU OUT OF THIS.
SOMEHOW!
VEEN
THIS VIAL CONTAINS TETRACHLORODIBENZO-P-DIOXIN...
ALSO KNOWN AS AGENT ORANGE.
MMF!
I HAVE NO IDEA WHAT IT WOULD DO TO A WOOD NYMPH. WANT TO FIND OUT?

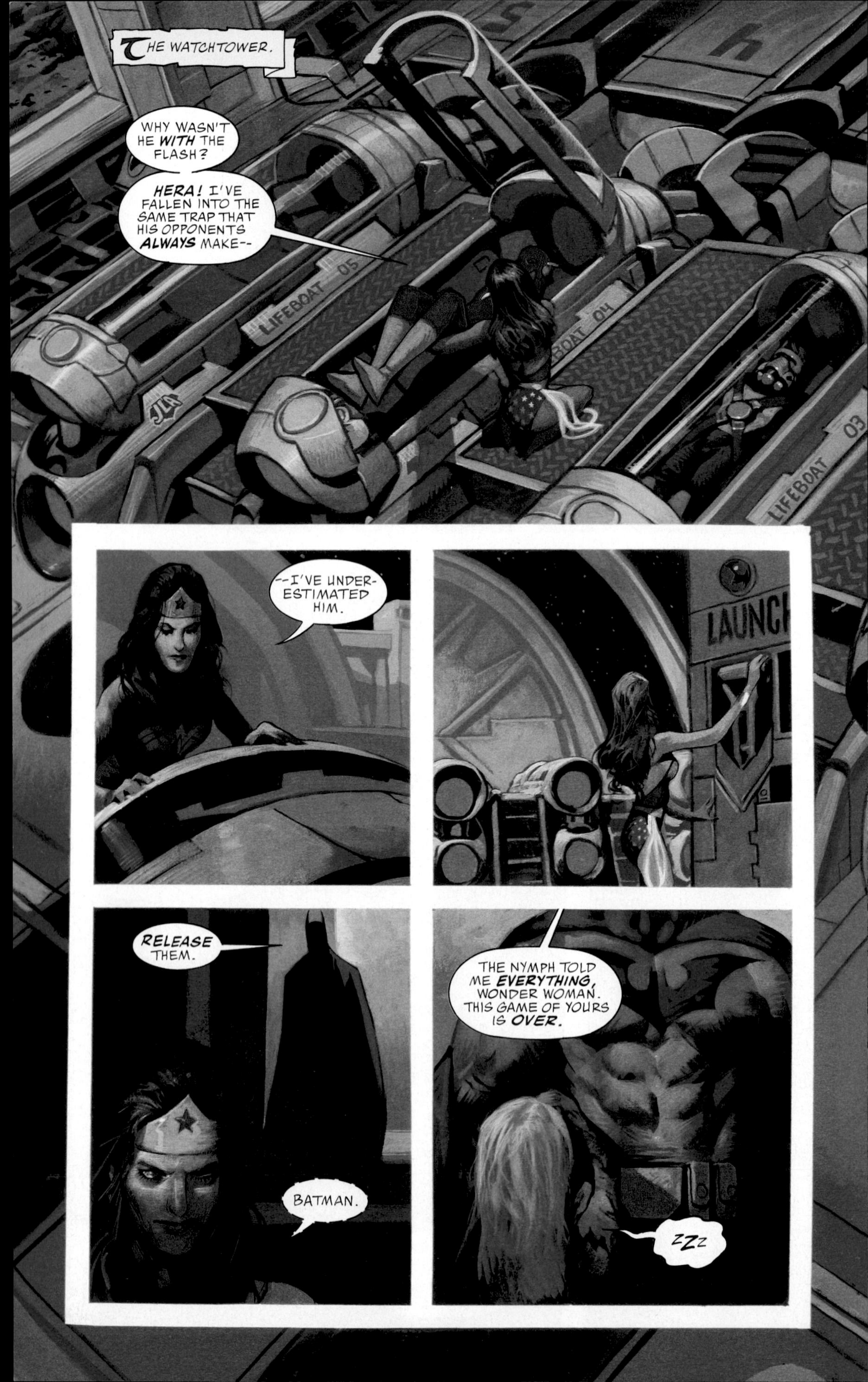
THE WATCHTOWER.
WHY WASN'T HE WITH THE FLASH?
HERA! I'VE FALLEN INTO THE SAME TRAP THAT HIS OPPONENTS ALWAYS MAKE--
LIFEBOAT 05
BOAT 04
LIFEBOAT 03
--I'VE UNDER-ESTIMATED HIM.
LAUNCH
RELEASE THEM.
BATMAN.
THE NYMPH TOLD ME EVERYTHING, WONDER WOMAN. THIS GAME OF YOURS IS OVER.
ZZZ

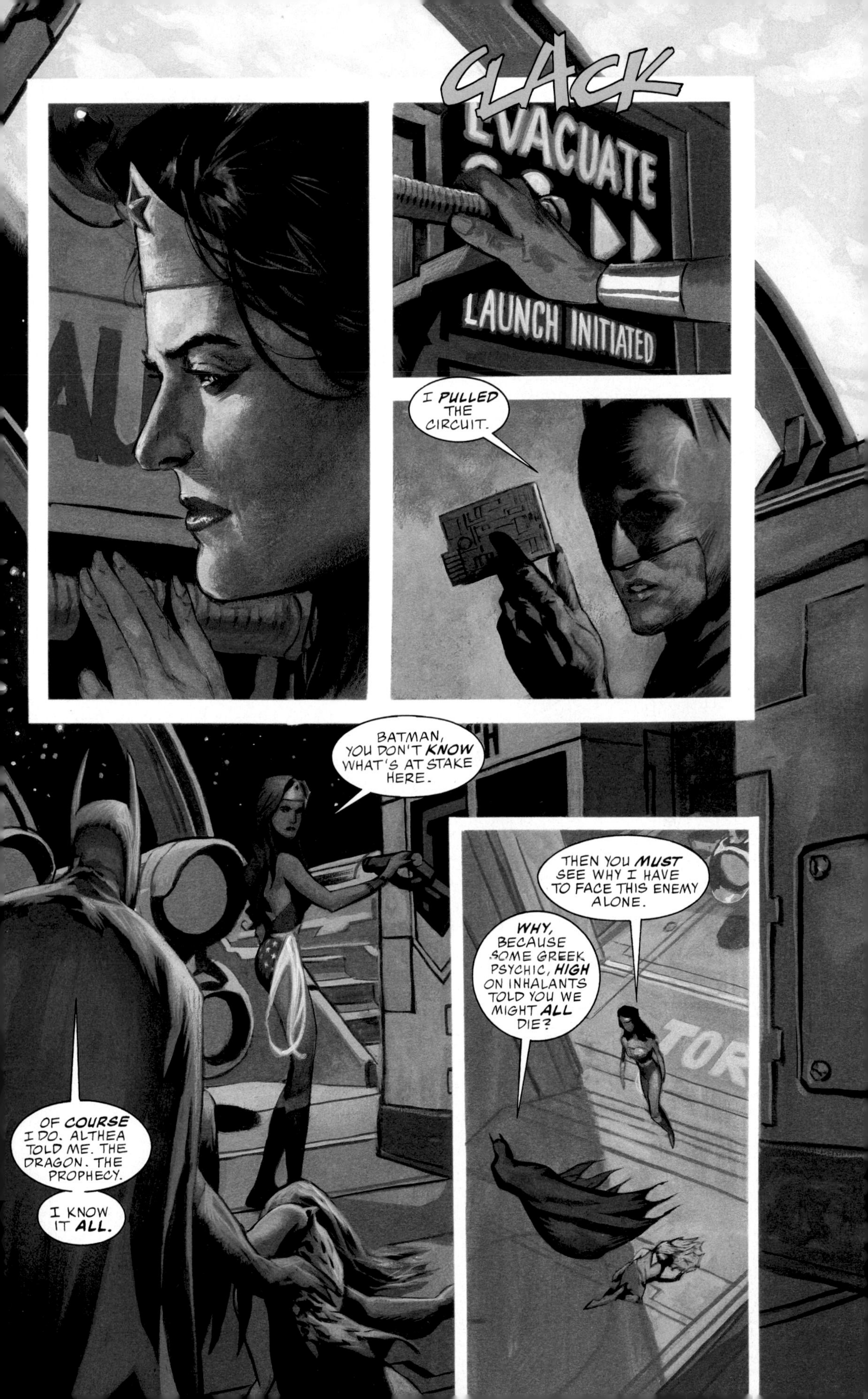
CLACK
EVACUATE
LAUNCH INITIATED
I PULLED THE CIRCUIT.
BATMAN, YOU DON'T KNOW WHAT'S AT STAKE HERE.
OF COURSE I DO. ALTHEA TOLD ME. THE DRAGON. THE PROPHECY.
I KNOW IT ALL.
THEN YOU MUST SEE WHY I HAVE TO FACE THIS ENEMY ALONE.
WHY, BECAUSE SOME GREEK PSYCHIC, HIGH ON INHALANTS TOLD YOU WE MIGHT ALL DIE?

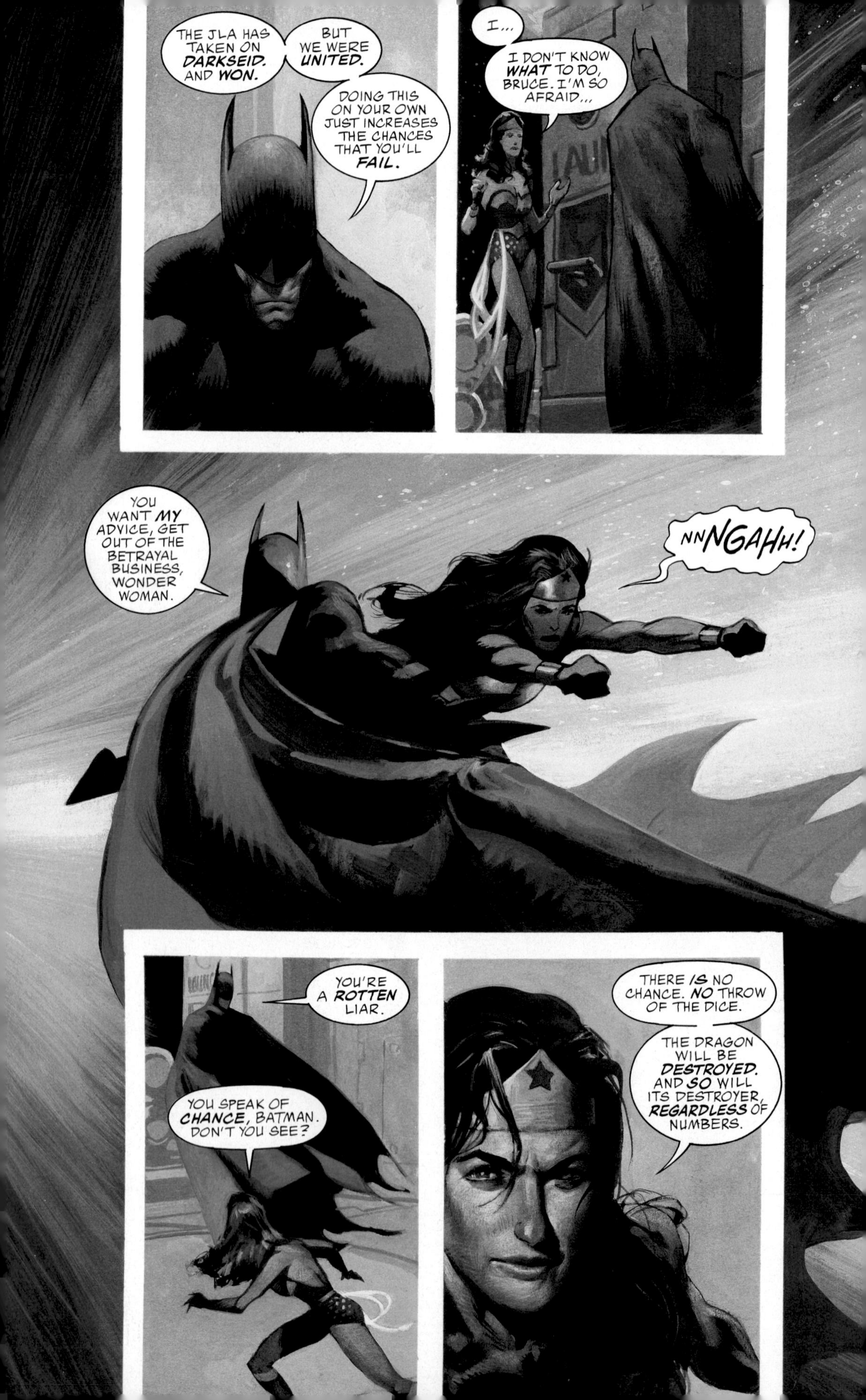
THE JLA HAS TAKEN ON DARKSEID. AND WON.
BUT WE WERE UNITED.
DOING THIS ON YOUR OWN JUST INCREASES THE CHANCES THAT YOU'LL FAIL.
I...
I DON'T KNOW WHAT TO DO, BRUCE. I'M SO AFRAID...
YOU WANT MY ADVICE, GET OUT OF THE BETRAYAL BUSINESS, WONDER WOMAN.
NNNGAHH!
YOU'RE A ROTTEN LIAR.
YOU SPEAK OF CHANCE, BATMAN. DON'T YOU SEE?
THERE IS NO CHANCE. NO THROW OF THE DICE.
THE DRAGON WILL BE DESTROYED. AND SO WILL ITS DESTROYER, REGARDLESS OF NUMBERS.

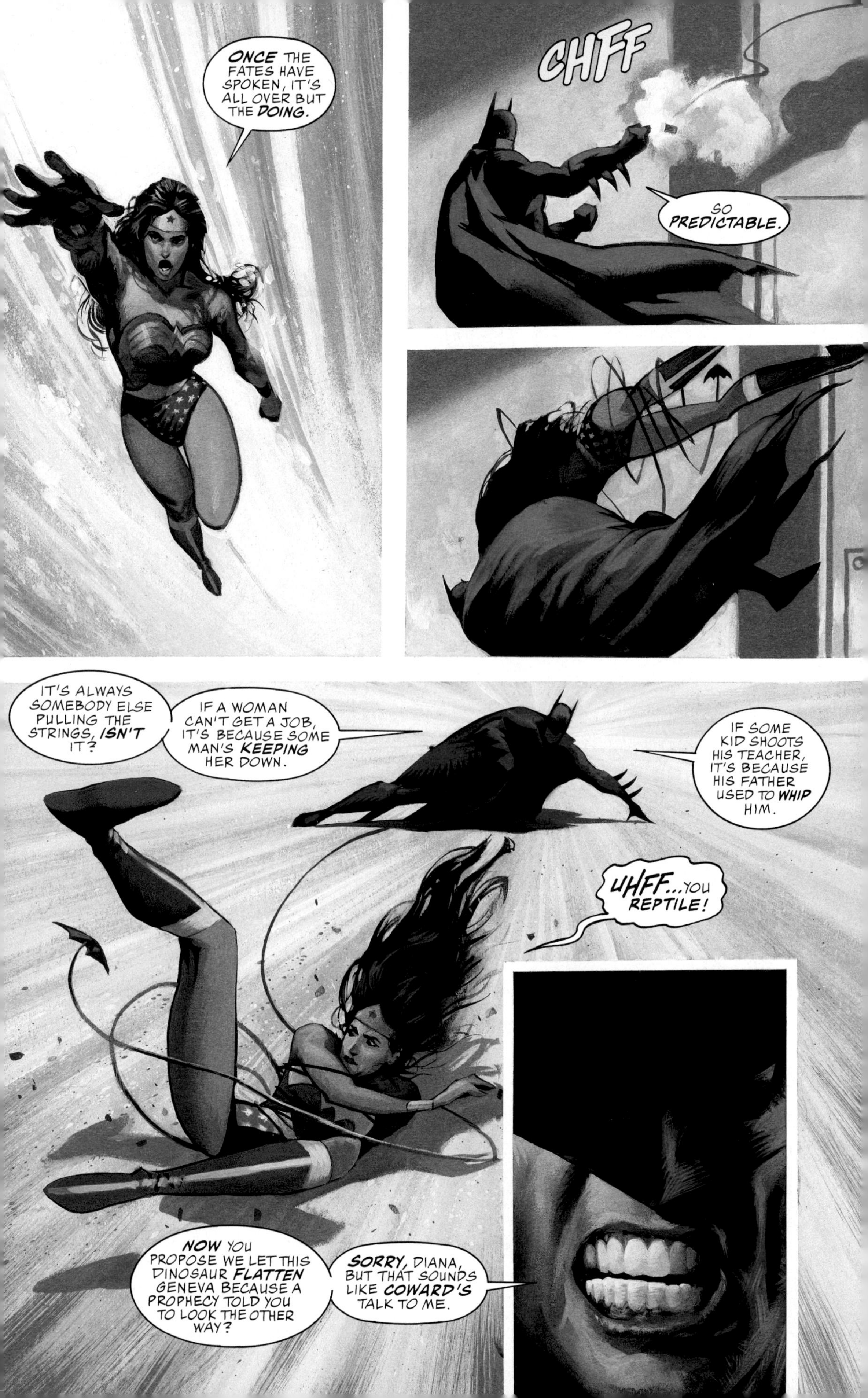
ONCE THE FATES HAVE SPOKEN, IT'S ALL OVER BUT THE DOING.
CHFF
SO PREDICTABLE.
IT'S ALWAYS SOMEBODY ELSE PULLING THE STRINGS, ISN'T IT?
IF A WOMAN CAN'T GET A JOB, IT'S BECAUSE SOME MAN'S KEEPING HER DOWN.
IF SOME KID SHOOTS HIS TEACHER, IT'S BECAUSE HIS FATHER USED TO WHIP HIM.
UHFF...YOU REPTILE!
NOW YOU PROPOSE WE LET THIS DINOSAUR FLATTEN GENEVA BECAUSE A PROPHECY TOLD YOU TO LOOK THE OTHER WAY?
SORRY, DIANA, BUT THAT SOUNDS LIKE COWARD'S TALK TO ME.

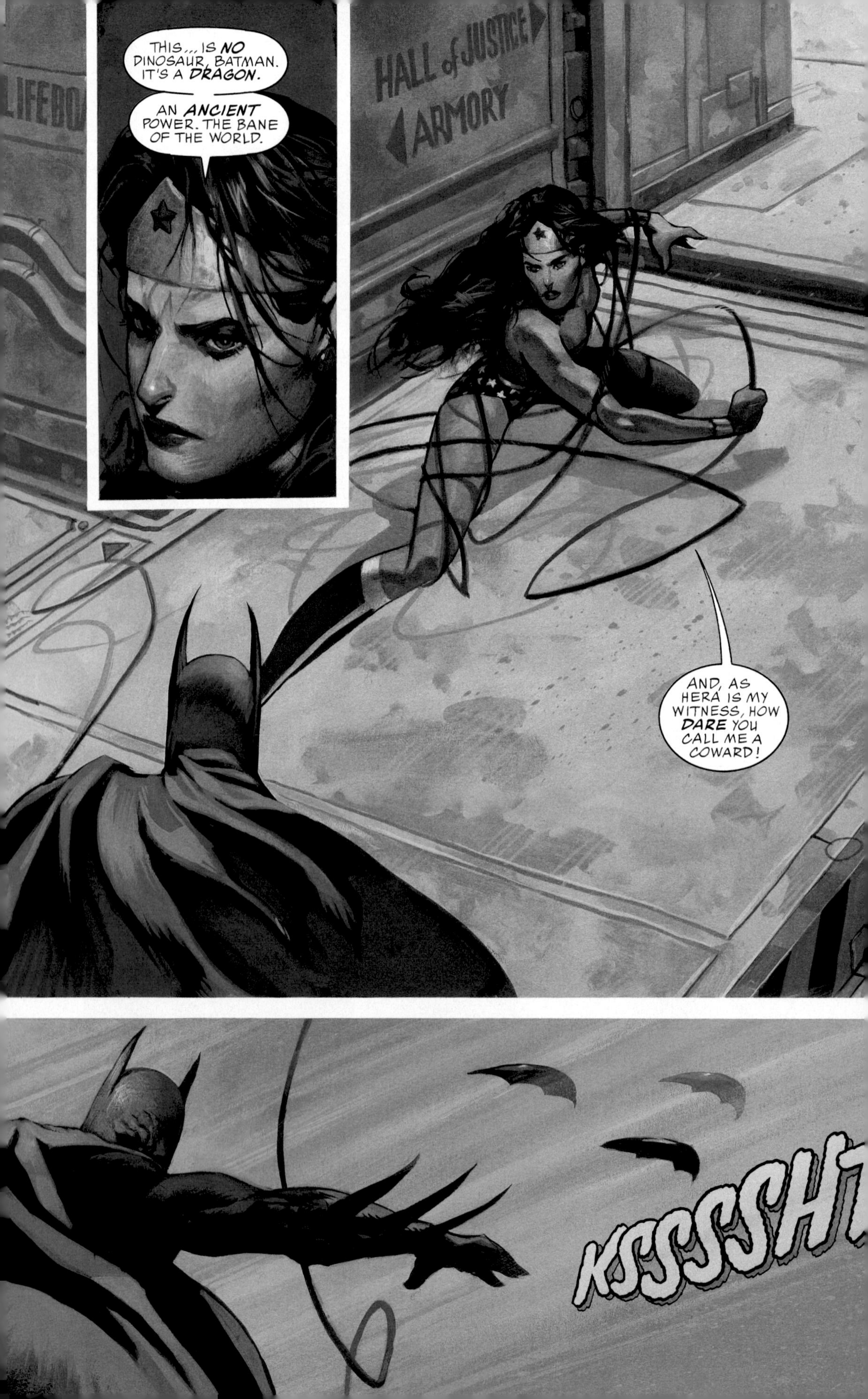
THIS... IS NO DINOSAUR, BATMAN. IT'S A DRAGON.
AN ANCIENT POWER. THE BANE OF THE WORLD.
HALL of JUSTICE
ARMORY
AND, AS HERA IS MY WITNESS, HOW DARE YOU CALL ME A COWARD!
KSSSSH

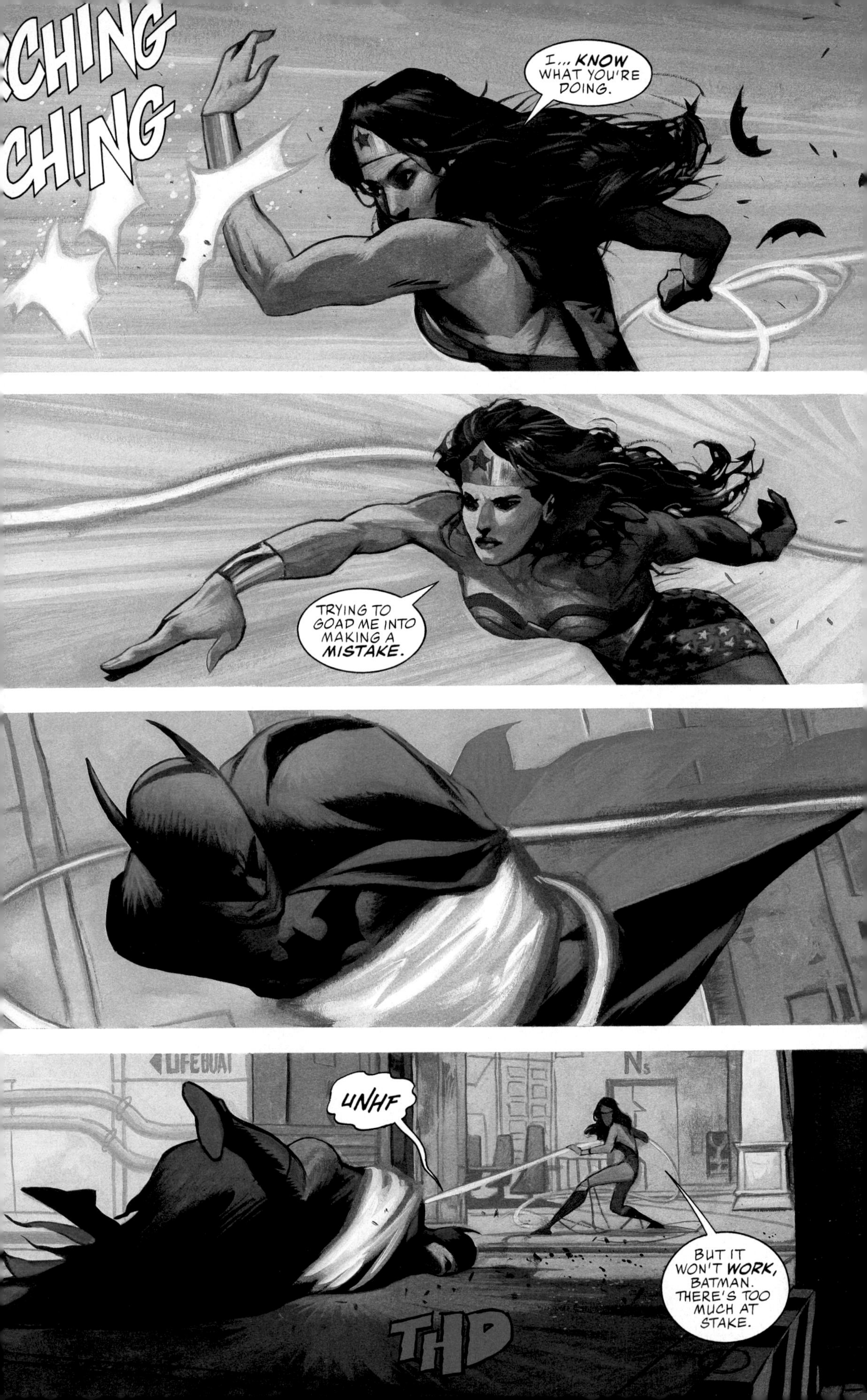
CHING
CHING
I... KNOW WHAT YOU'RE DOING.
TRYING TO GOAD ME INTO MAKING A MISTAKE.
LIFEBOAT
UNHF
BUT IT WON'T WORK, BATMAN. THERE'S TOO MUCH AT STAKE.
THD

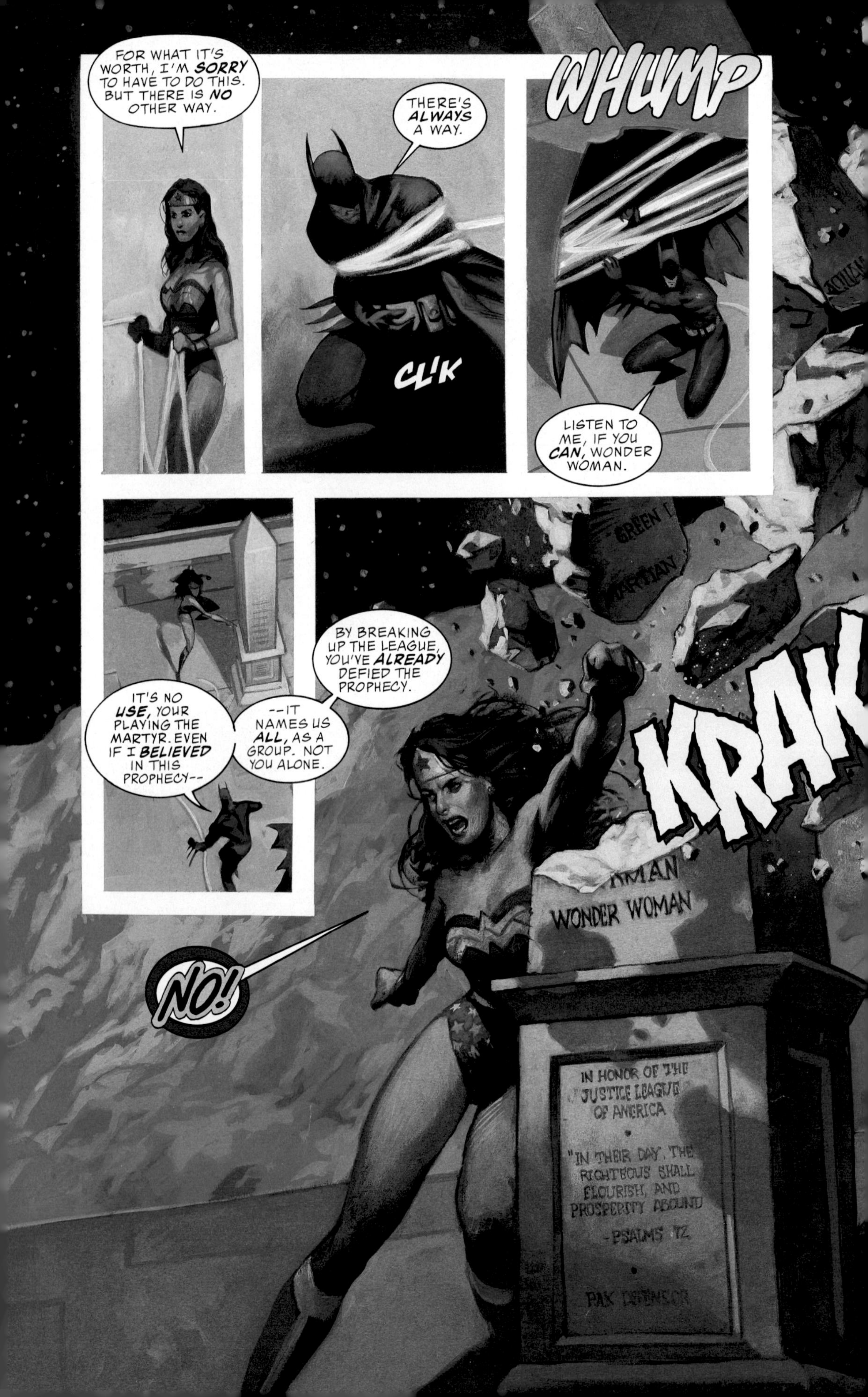
FOR WHAT IT'S WORTH, I'M SORRY TO HAVE TO DO THIS. BUT THERE IS NO OTHER WAY.
THERE'S ALWAYS A WAY.
CL!K
WHUMP
LISTEN TO ME, IF YOU CAN, WONDER WOMAN.
IT'S NO USE, YOUR PLAYING THE MARTYR. EVEN IF I BELIEVED IN THIS PROPHECY--
--IT NAMES US ALL, AS A GROUP. NOT YOU ALONE.
BY BREAKING UP THE LEAGUE, YOU'VE ALREADY DEFIED THE PROPHECY.
KRAK
NO!
WONDER WOMAN
IN HONOR OF THE JUSTICE LEAGUE OF AMERICA
"IN THEIR DAY, THE RIGHTEOUS SHALL FLOURISH, AND PROSPERITY ABOUND
-PSALMS 72

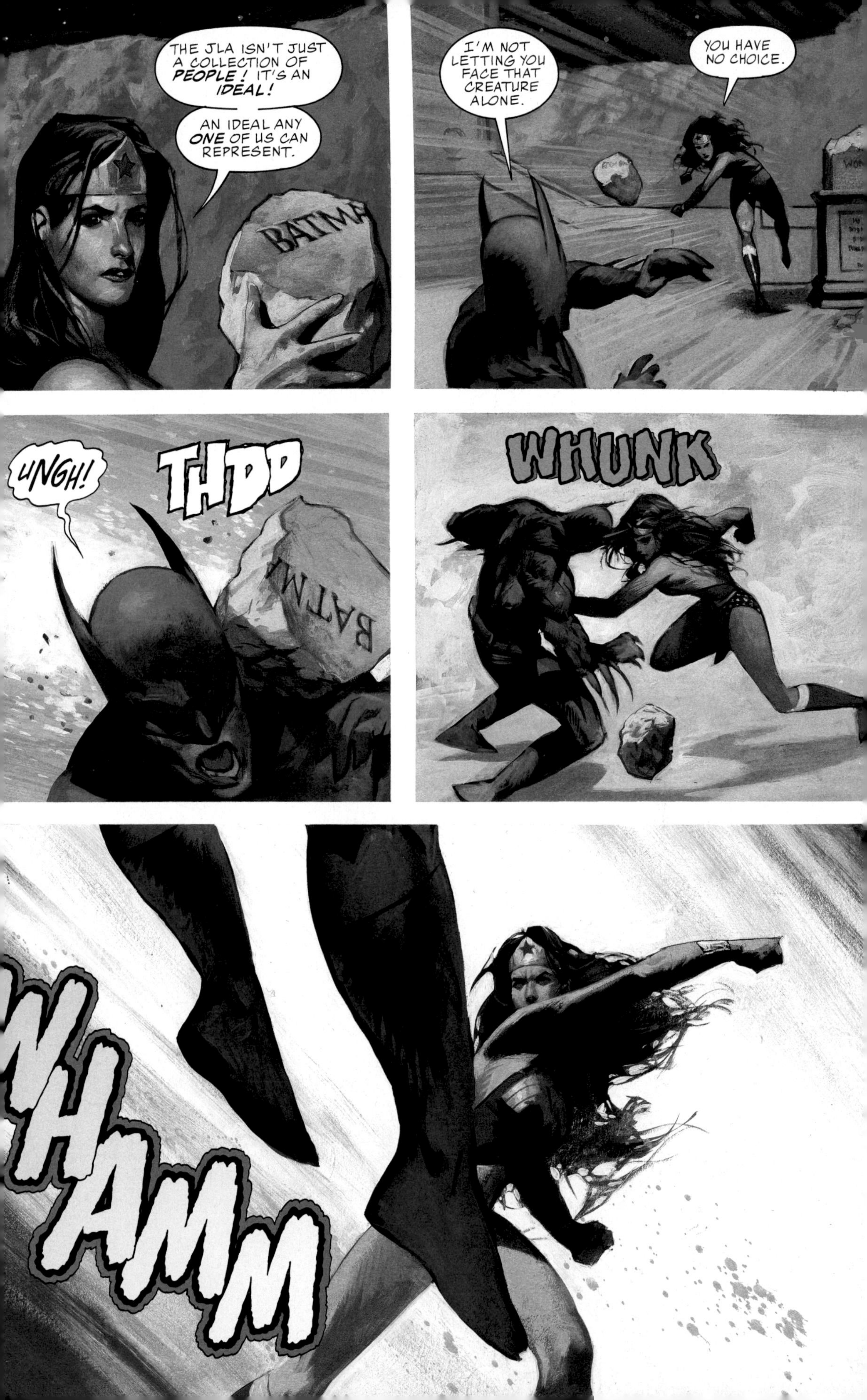
THE JLA ISN'T JUST A COLLECTION OF PEOPLE! IT'S AN IDEAL!
AN IDEAL ANY ONE OF US CAN REPRESENT.
I'M NOT LETTING YOU FACE THAT CREATURE ALONE.
YOU HAVE NO CHOICE.
UNGH!
THDD
WHUNK
WHAMM

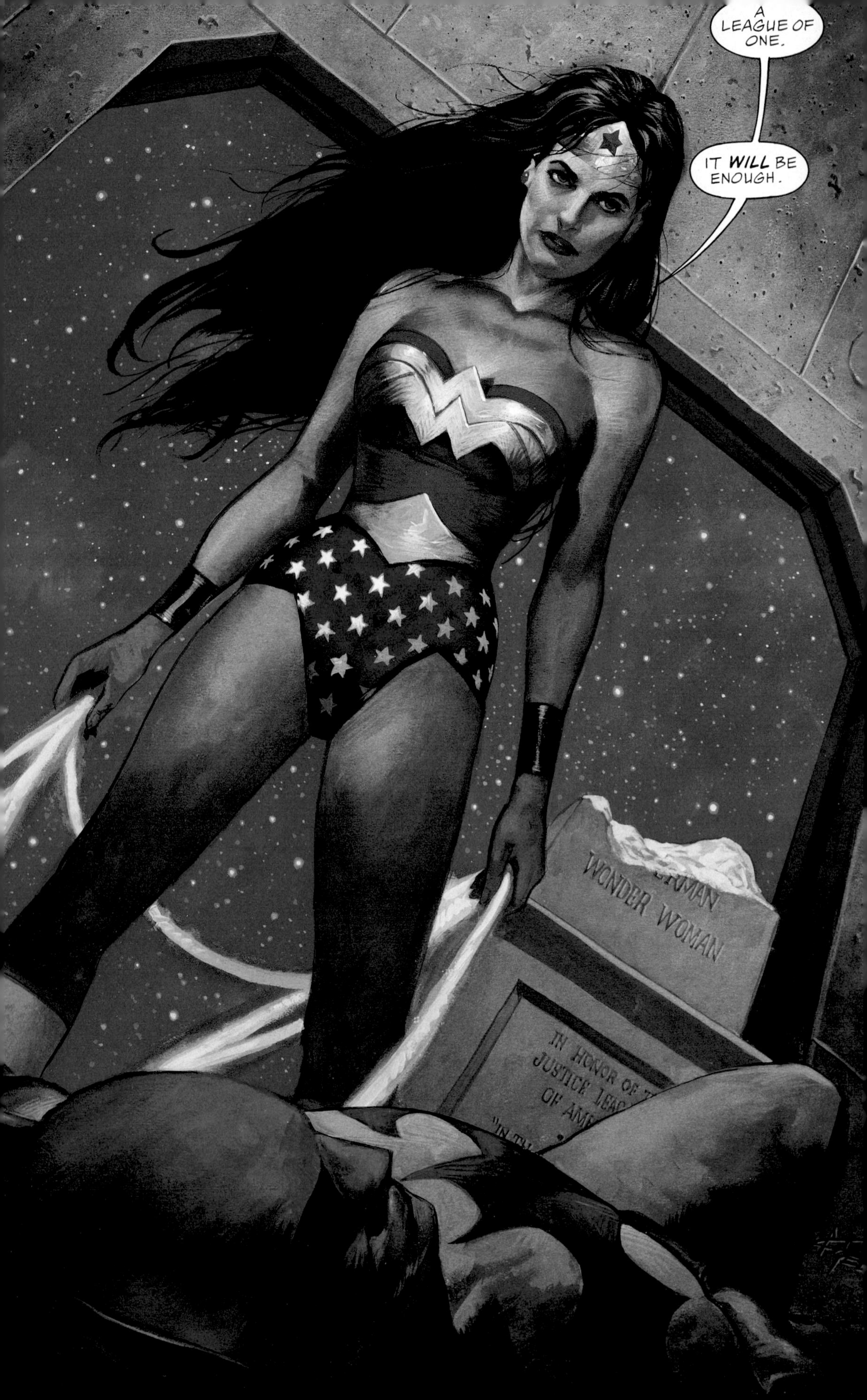
A LEAGUE OF ONE.
IT **WILL** BE ENOUGH.
WONDER WOMAN
IN HONOR OF

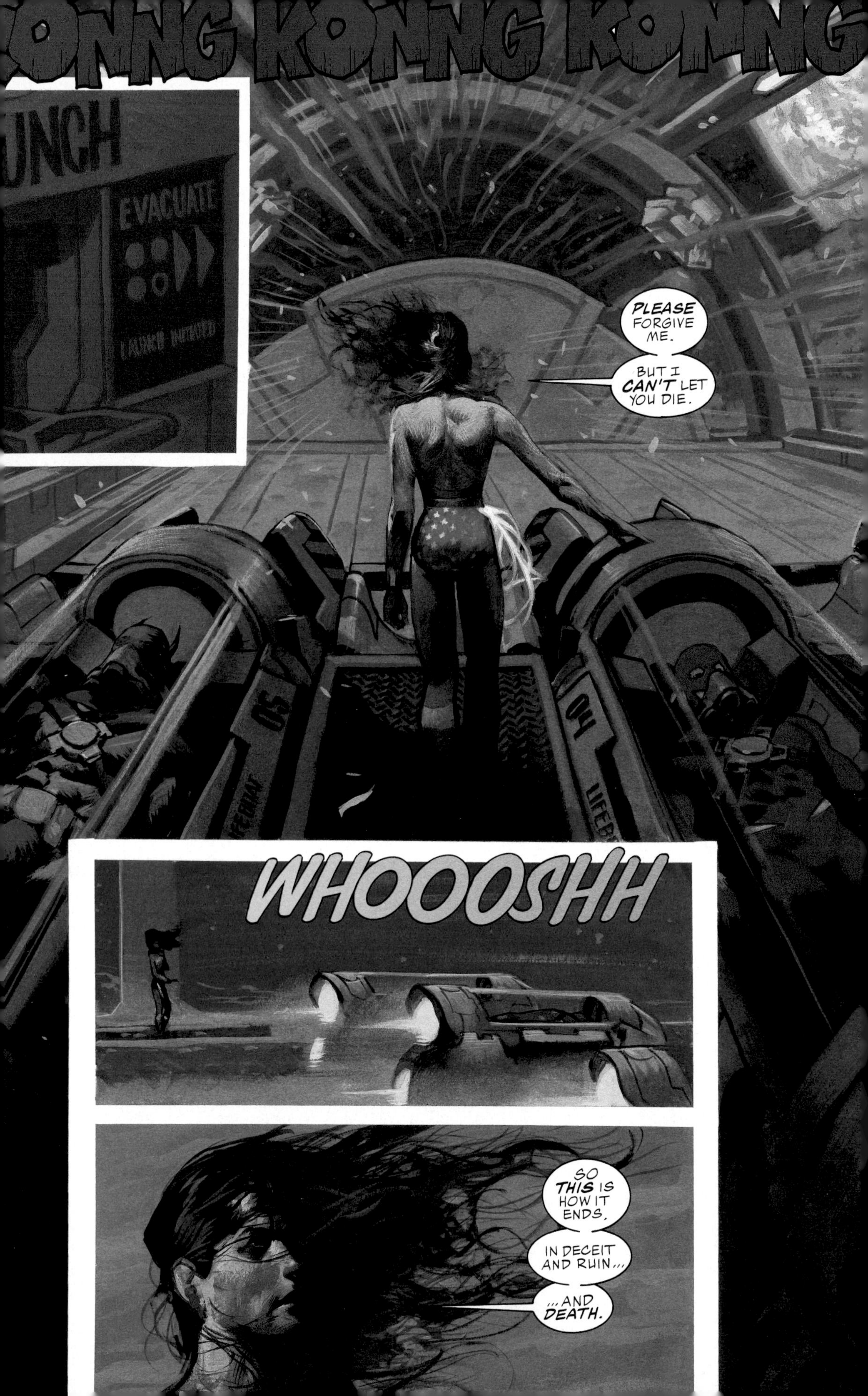
KONNG KONNG KONNG
UNCH
EVACUATE
LAUNCH INITIATED
PLEASE FORGIVE ME.
BUT I CAN'T LET YOU DIE.
05
04
WHOOOSHH
SO THIS IS HOW IT ENDS.
IN DECEIT AND RUIN...
...AND DEATH.

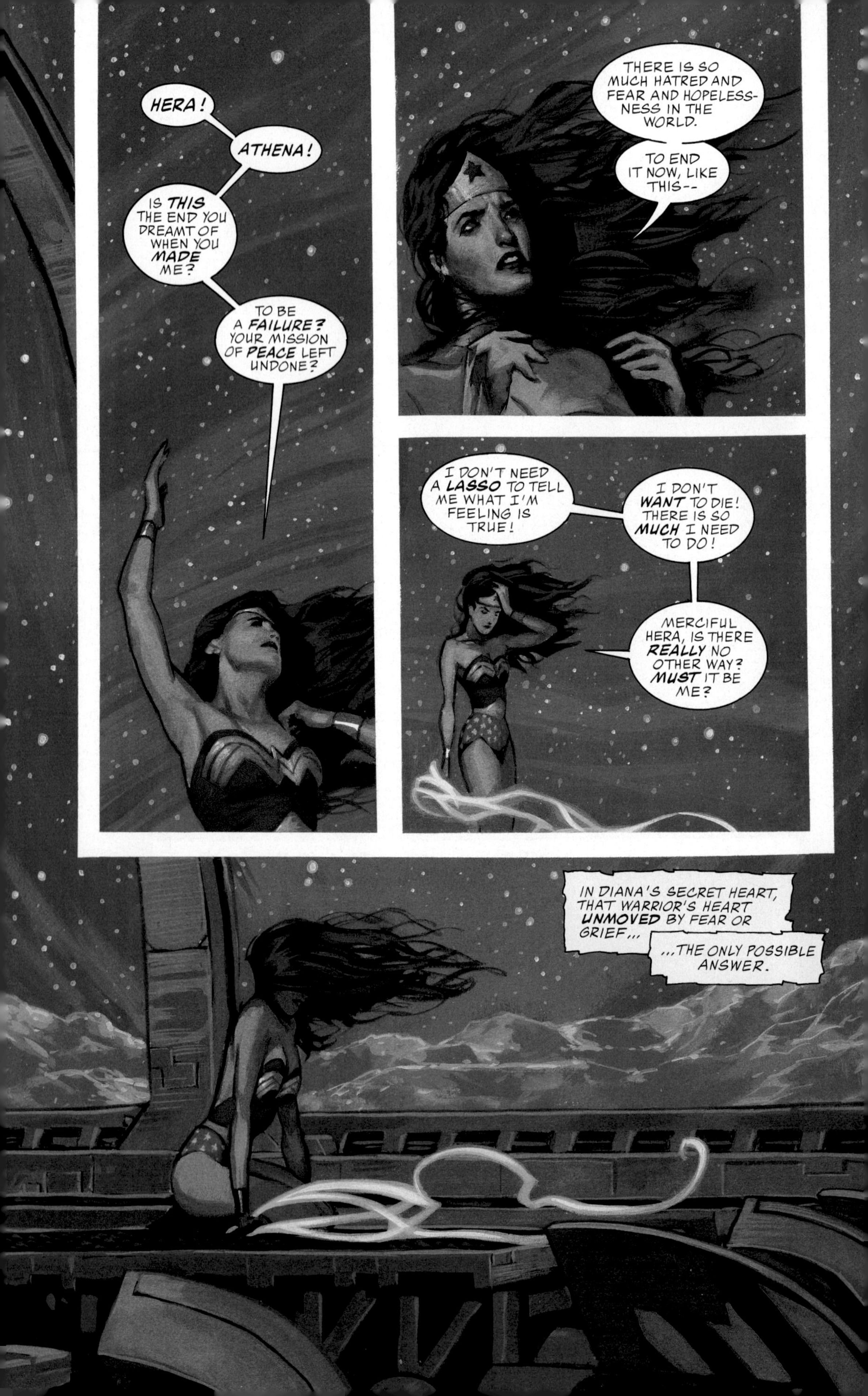
HERA!
ATHENA!
IS THIS THE END YOU DREAMT OF WHEN YOU MADE ME?
TO BE A FAILURE? YOUR MISSION OF PEACE LEFT UNDONE?
THERE IS SO MUCH HATRED AND FEAR AND HOPELESS-NESS IN THE WORLD.
TO END IT NOW, LIKE THIS--
I DON'T NEED A LASSO TO TELL ME WHAT I'M FEELING IS TRUE!
I DON'T WANT TO DIE! THERE IS SO MUCH I NEED TO DO!
MERCIFUL HERA, IS THERE REALLY NO OTHER WAY? MUST IT BE ME?
IN DIANA'S SECRET HEART, THAT WARRIOR'S HEART UNMOVED BY FEAR OR GRIEF...
...THE ONLY POSSIBLE ANSWER.

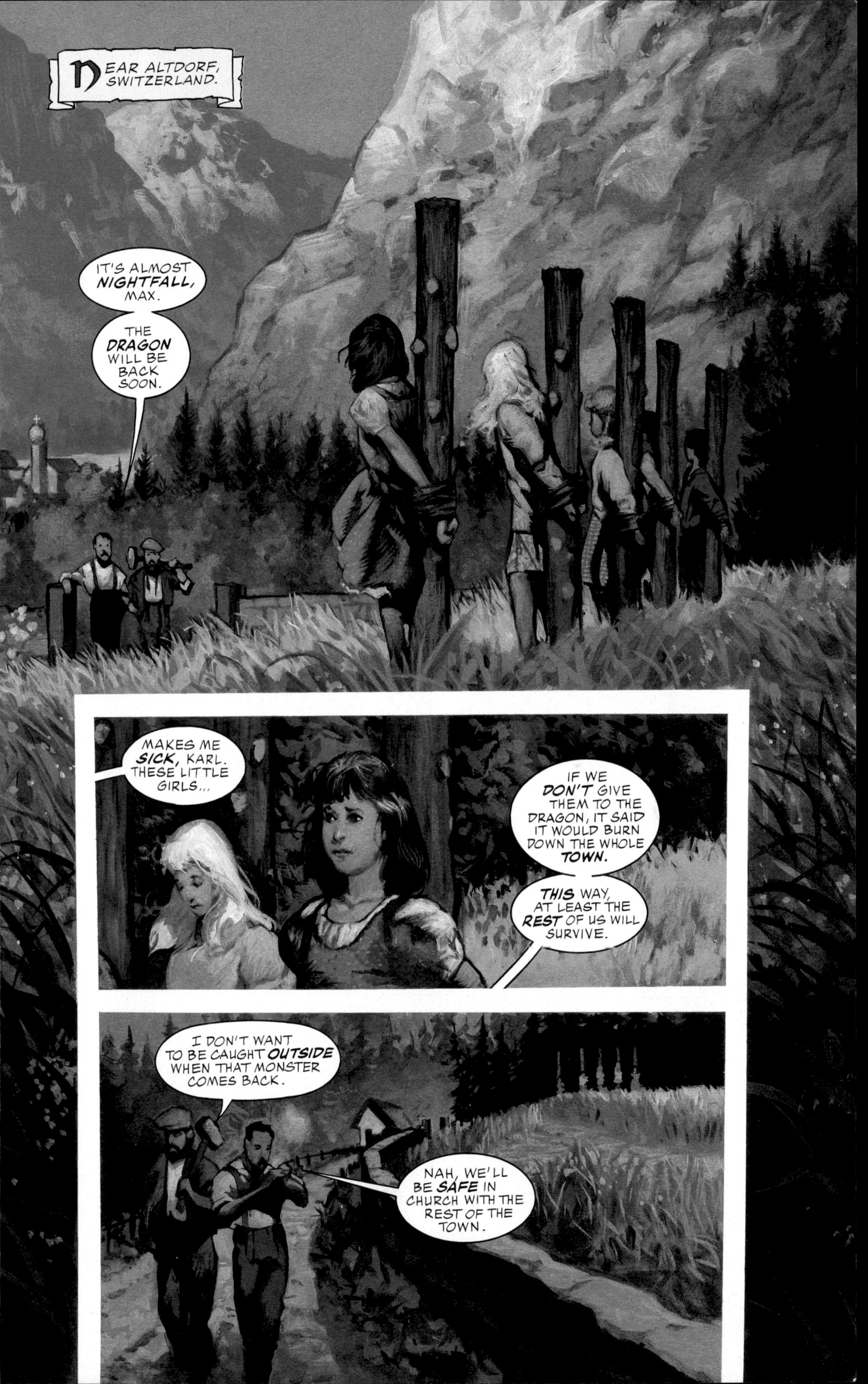
NEAR ALTDORF, SWITZERLAND.
IT'S ALMOST NIGHTFALL, MAX.
THE DRAGON WILL BE BACK SOON.
MAKES ME SICK, KARL. THESE LITTLE GIRLS...
IF WE DON'T GIVE THEM TO THE DRAGON, IT SAID IT WOULD BURN DOWN THE WHOLE TOWN.
THIS WAY, AT LEAST THE REST OF US WILL SURVIVE.
I DON'T WANT TO BE CAUGHT OUTSIDE WHEN THAT MONSTER COMES BACK.
NAH, WE'LL BE SAFE IN CHURCH WITH THE REST OF THE TOWN.

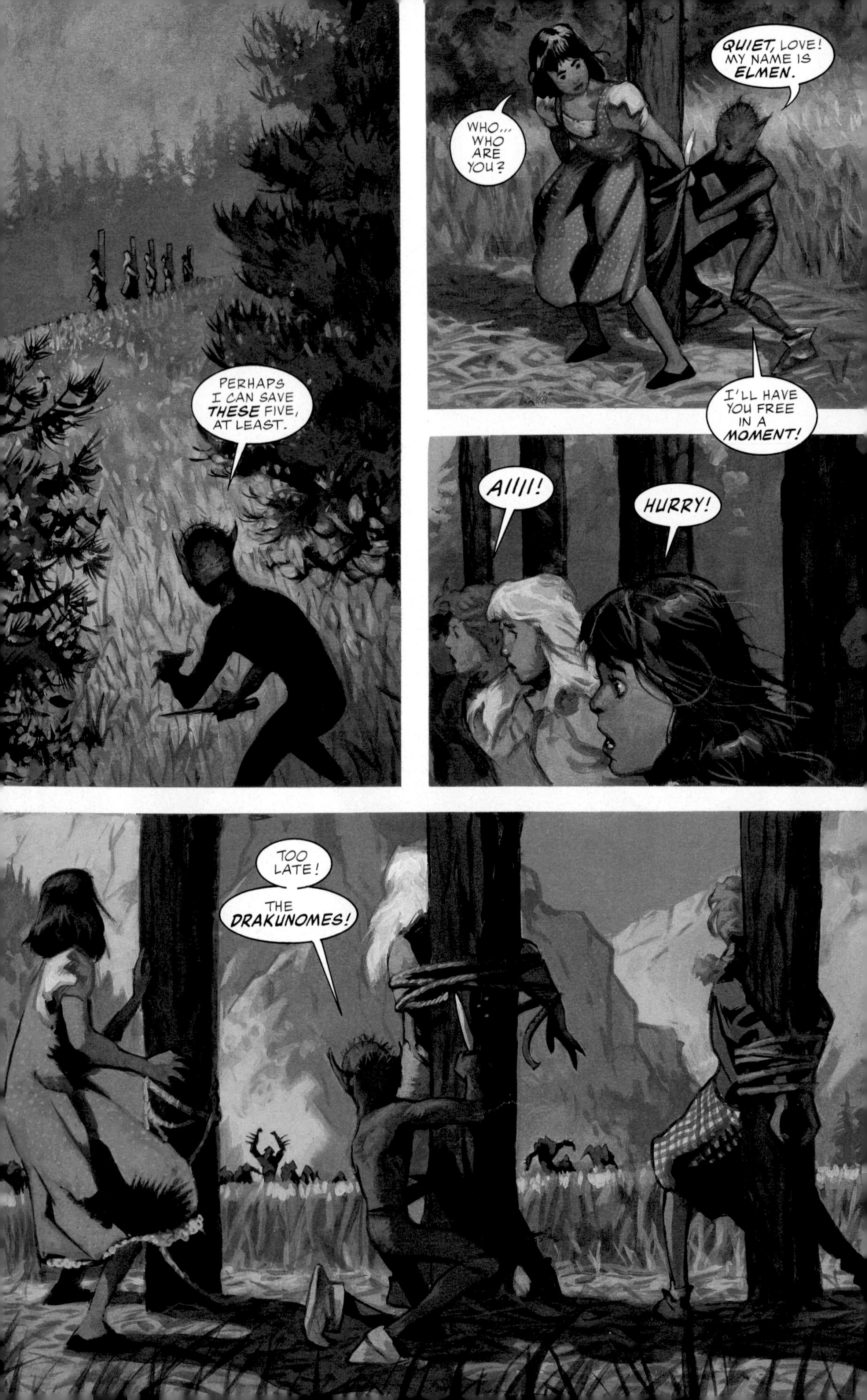
PERHAPS I CAN SAVE THESE FIVE, AT LEAST.
WHO... WHO ARE YOU?
QUIET, LOVE! MY NAME IS ELMEN.
I'LL HAVE YOU FREE IN A MOMENT!
AIIII!
HURRY!
TOO LATE!
THE DRAKUNOMES!

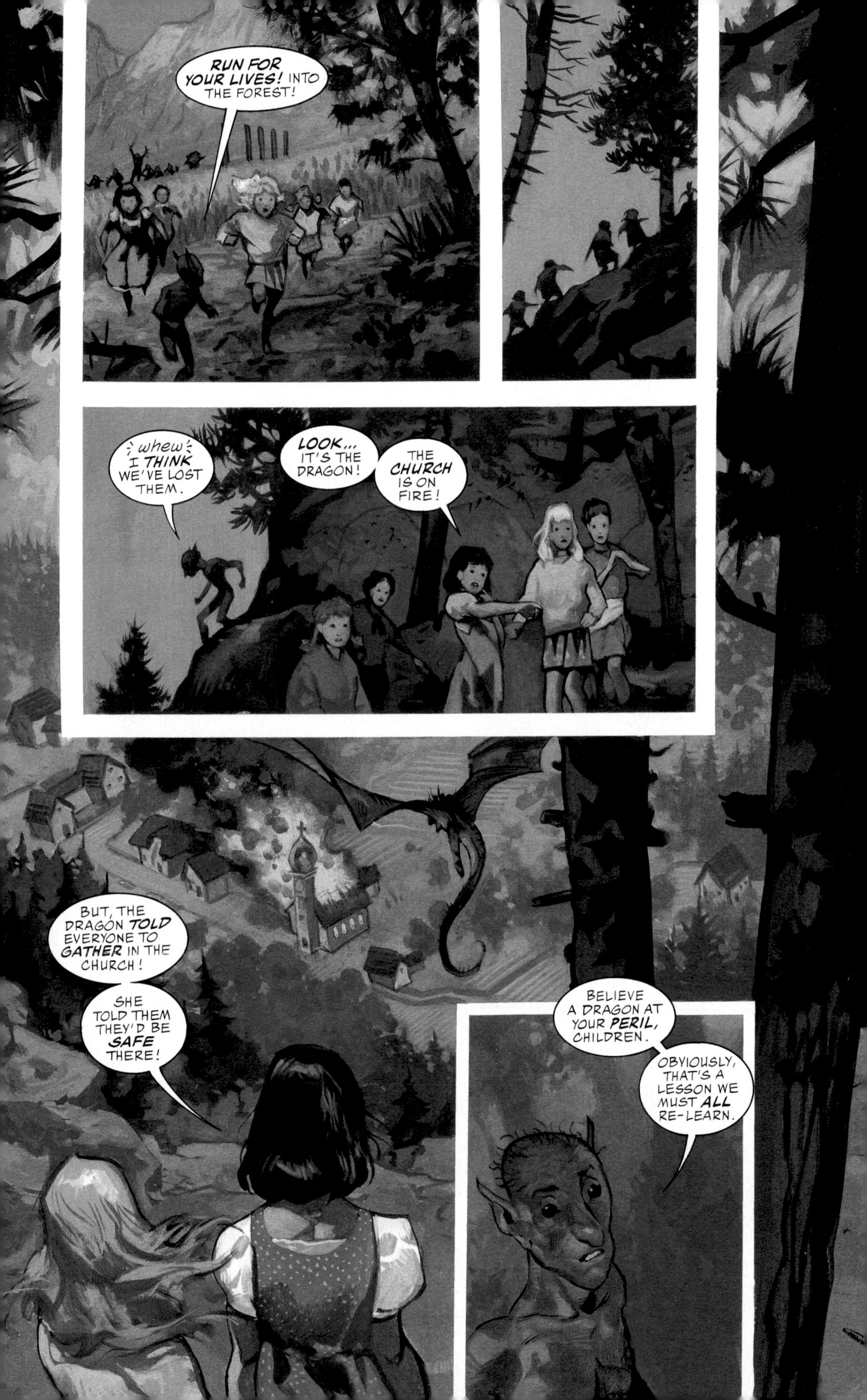
RUN FOR YOUR LIVES! INTO THE FOREST!
whew I THINK WE'VE LOST THEM.
LOOK... IT'S THE DRAGON!
THE CHURCH IS ON FIRE!
BUT, THE DRAGON TOLD EVERYONE TO GATHER IN THE CHURCH!
SHE TOLD THEM THEY'D BE SAFE THERE!
BELIEVE A DRAGON AT YOUR PERIL, CHILDREN.
OBVIOUSLY, THAT'S A LESSON WE MUST ALL RE-LEARN.

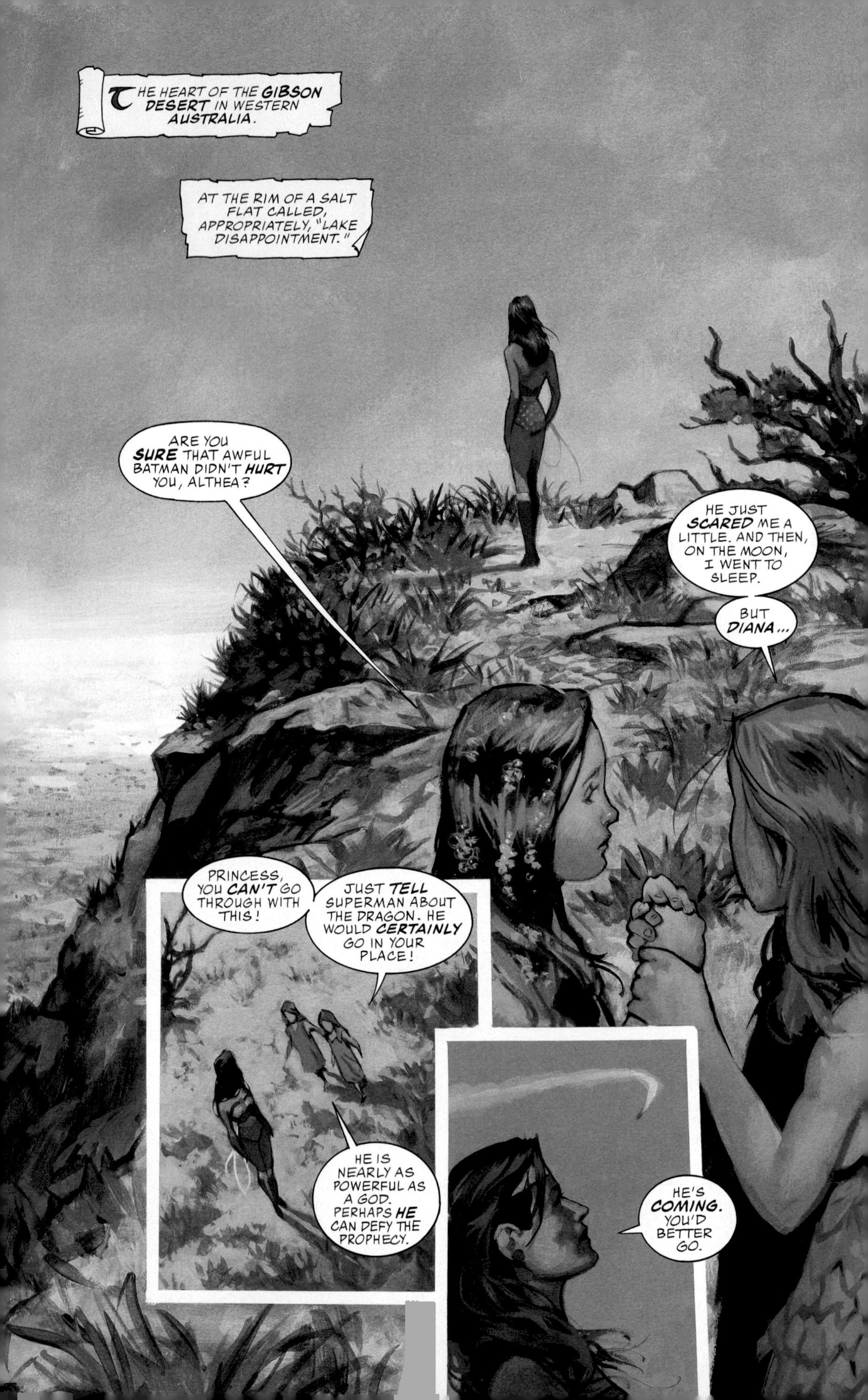
THE HEART OF THE GIBSON DESERT IN WESTERN AUSTRALIA.
AT THE RIM OF A SALT FLAT CALLED, APPROPRIATELY, "LAKE DISAPPOINTMENT."
ARE YOU SURE THAT AWFUL BATMAN DIDN'T HURT YOU, ALTHEA?
HE JUST SCARED ME A LITTLE. AND THEN, ON THE MOON, I WENT TO SLEEP.
BUT DIANA...
PRINCESS, YOU CAN'T GO THROUGH WITH THIS!
JUST TELL SUPERMAN ABOUT THE DRAGON. HE WOULD CERTAINLY GO IN YOUR PLACE!
HE IS NEARLY AS POWERFUL AS A GOD. PERHAPS HE CAN DEFY THE PROPHECY.
HE'S COMING. YOU'D BETTER GO.

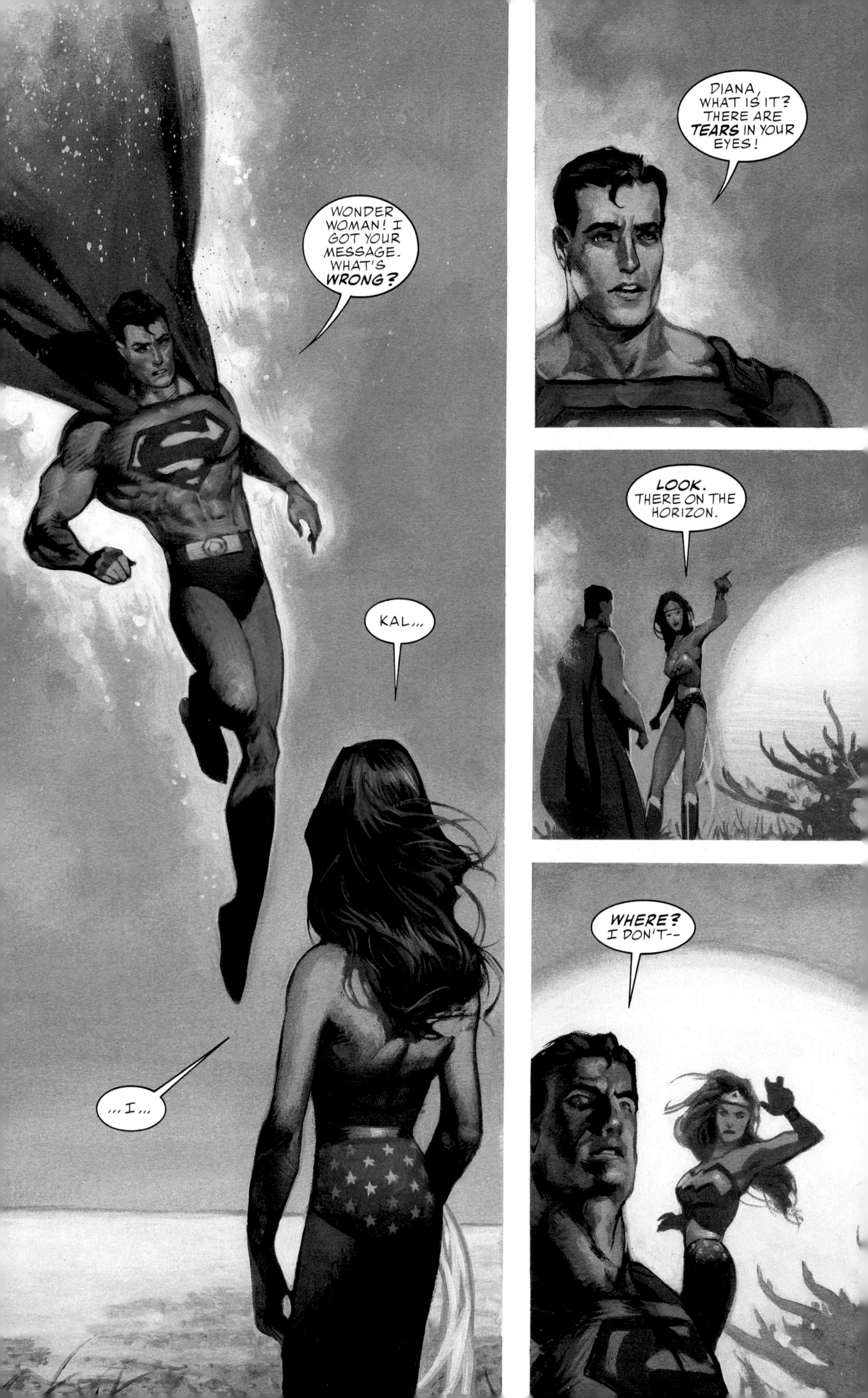
WONDER WOMAN! I GOT YOUR MESSAGE. WHAT'S **WRONG?**
KAL...
...I...
DIANA, WHAT IS IT? THERE ARE **TEARS** IN YOUR EYES!
LOOK. THERE ON THE HORIZON.
WHERE? I DON'T--

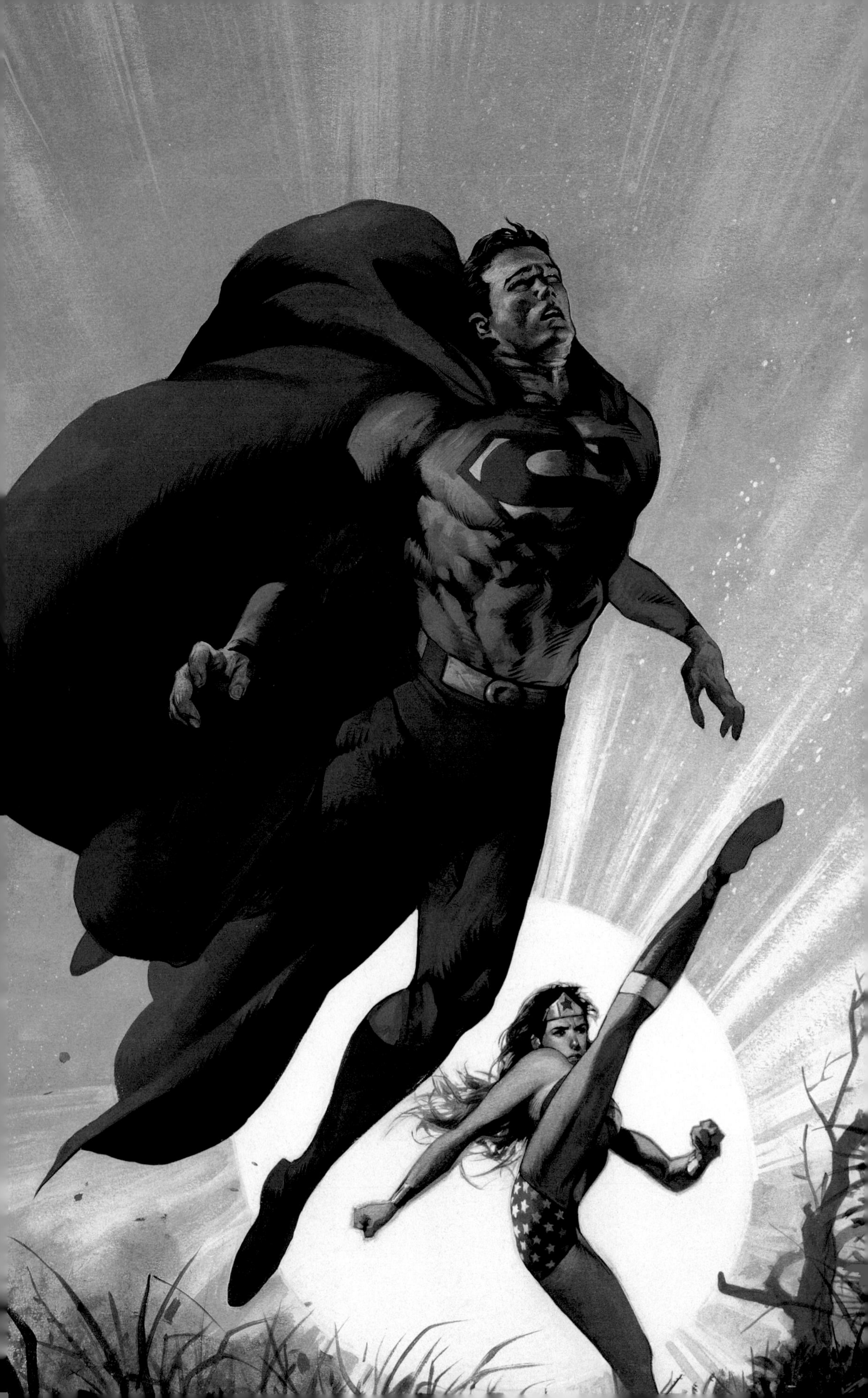

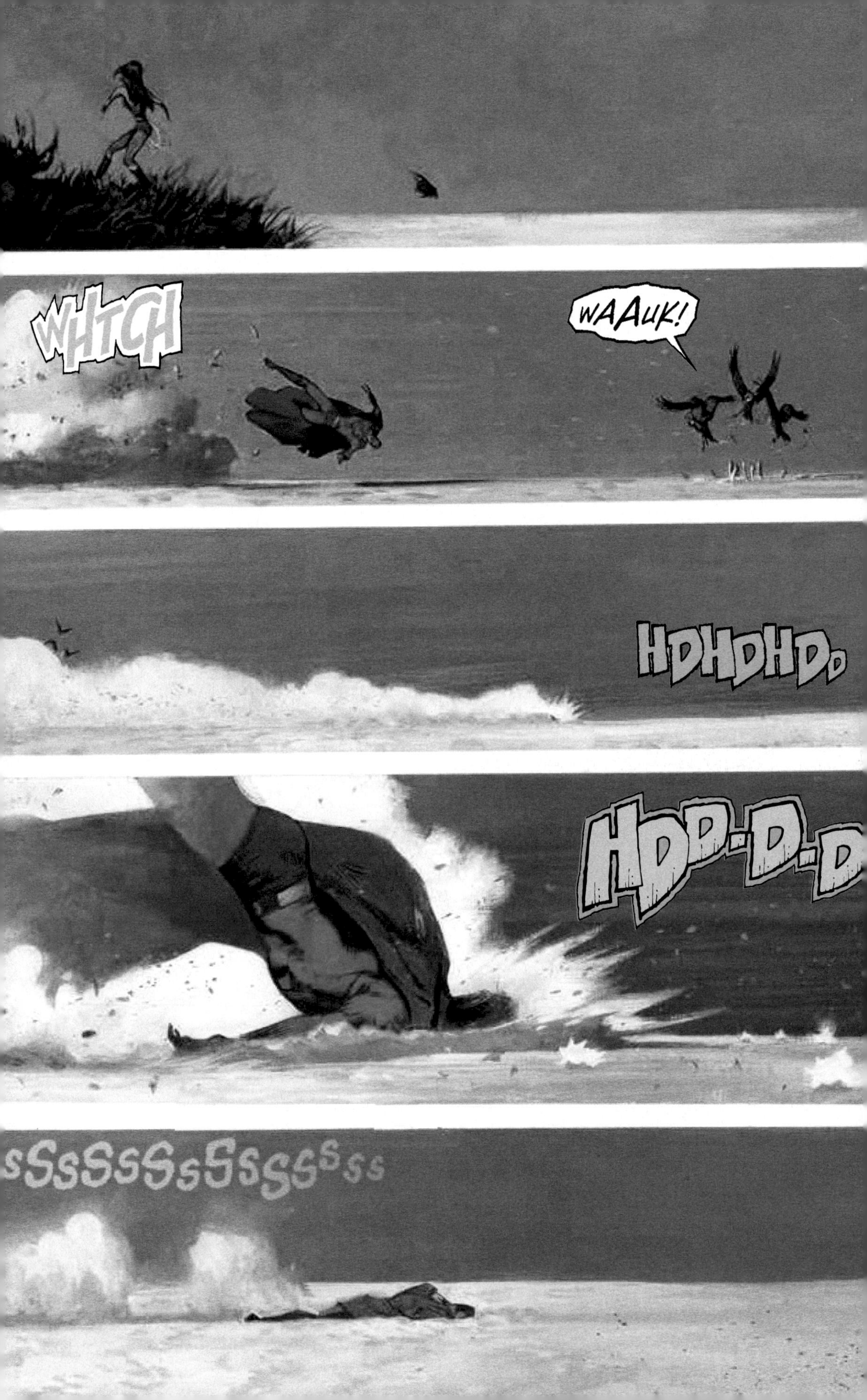
WHTCH
WAAUK!
HDHDHDD
HDD-D-D
sSsSSSsSSsSSsss

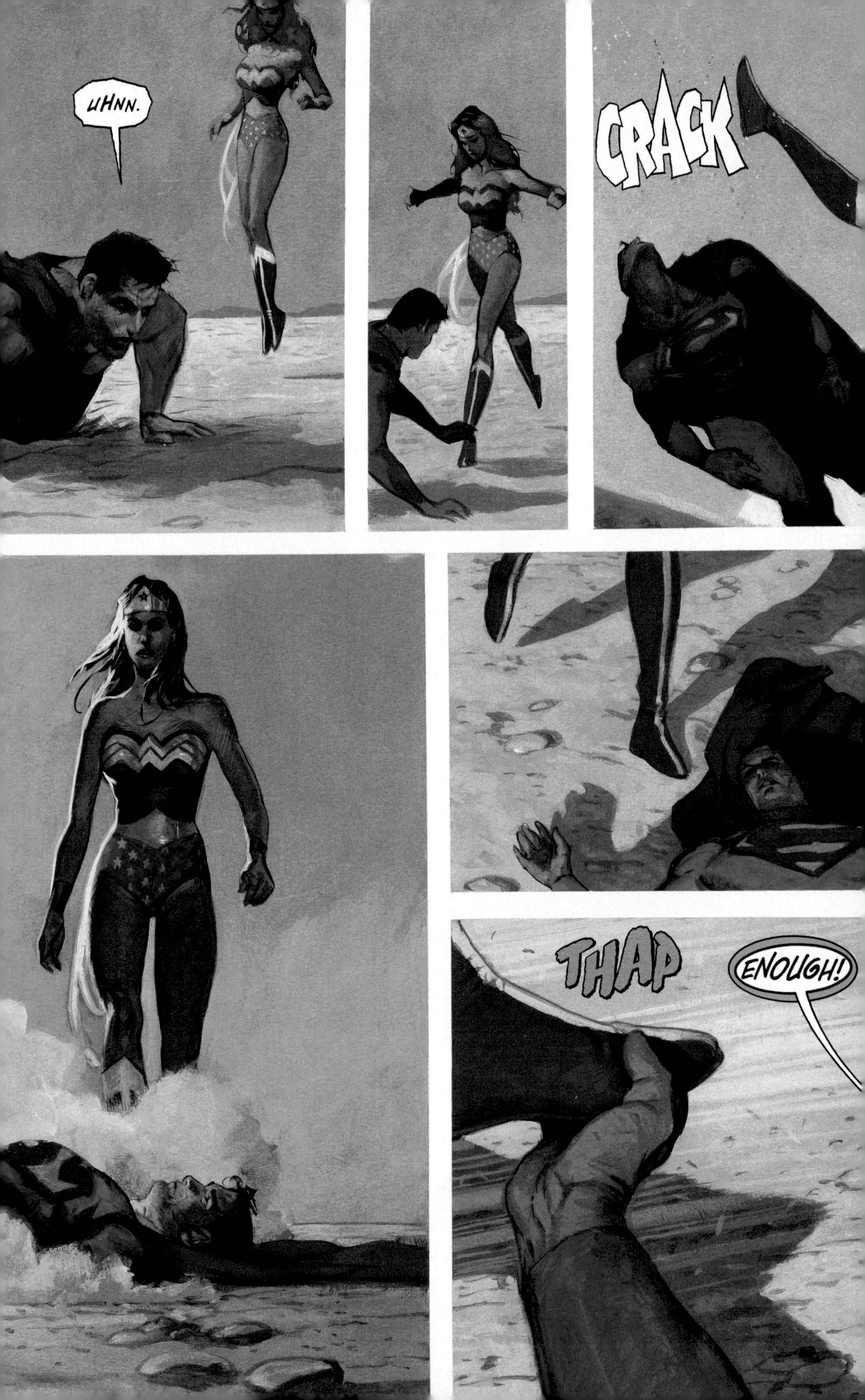
UHNN.
CRACK
THAP
ENOUGH!

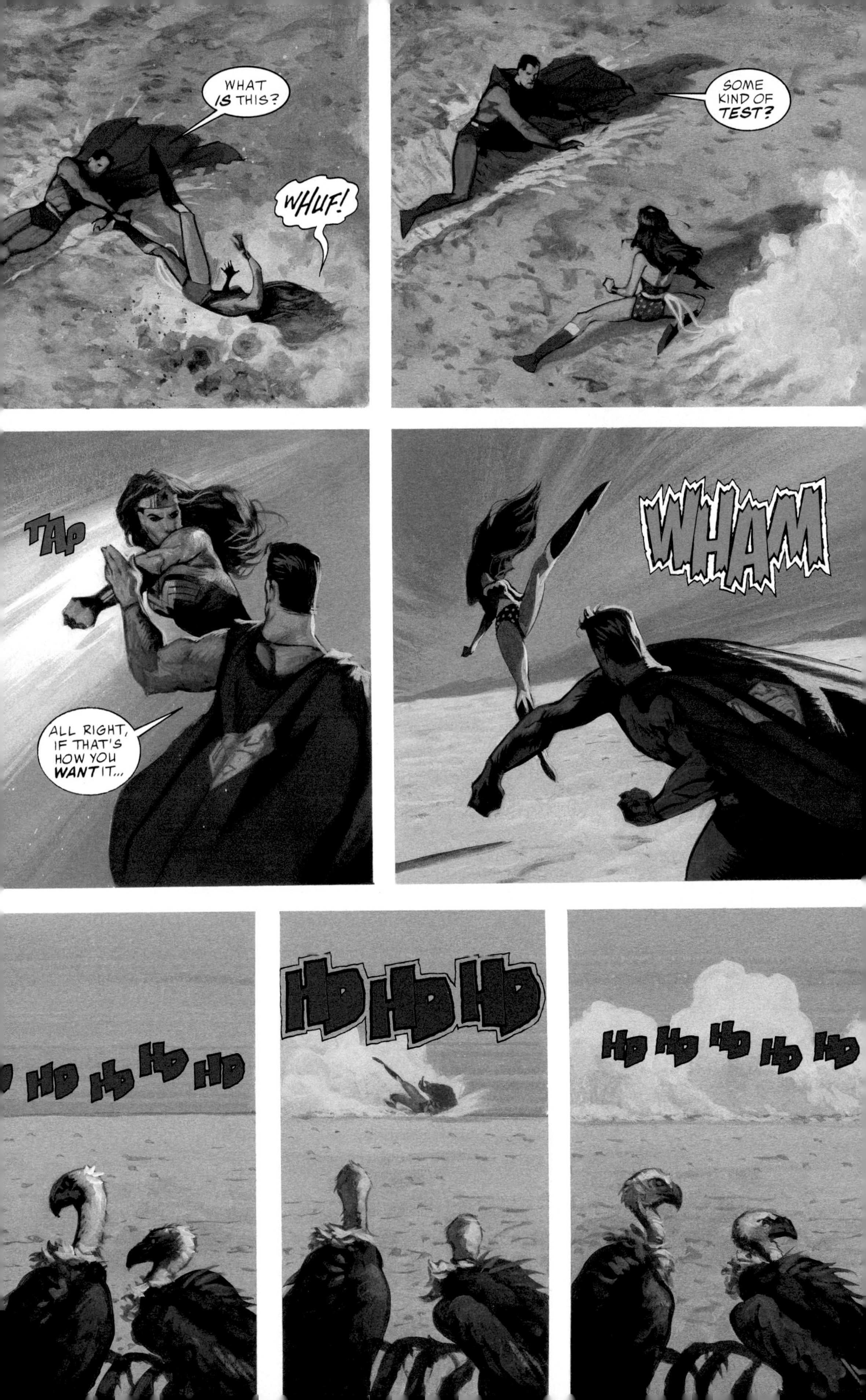
WHAT IS THIS?
WHUF!
SOME KIND OF TEST?
TAP
ALL RIGHT, IF THAT'S HOW YOU WANT IT...
WHAM
HO HO HO HO HO
HO HO HO
HO HO HO HO HO

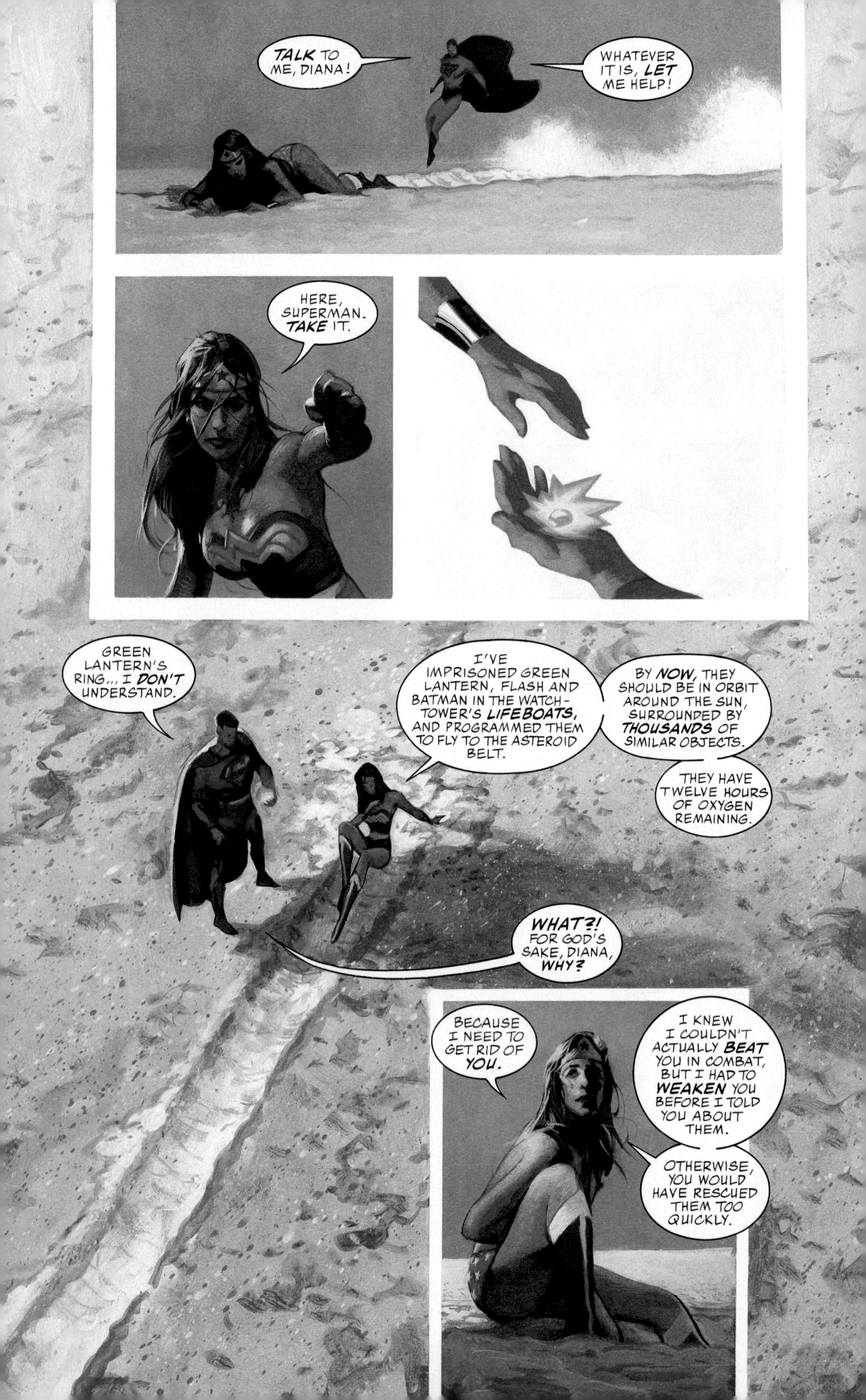
TALK TO ME, DIANA!
WHATEVER IT IS, LET ME HELP!
HERE, SUPERMAN. TAKE IT.
GREEN LANTERN'S RING... I DON'T UNDERSTAND.
I'VE IMPRISONED GREEN LANTERN, FLASH AND BATMAN IN THE WATCH-TOWER'S LIFEBOATS, AND PROGRAMMED THEM TO FLY TO THE ASTEROID BELT.
BY NOW, THEY SHOULD BE IN ORBIT AROUND THE SUN, SURROUNDED BY THOUSANDS OF SIMILAR OBJECTS.
THEY HAVE TWELVE HOURS OF OXYGEN REMAINING.
WHAT?! FOR GOD'S SAKE, DIANA, WHY?
BECAUSE I NEED TO GET RID OF YOU.
I KNEW I COULDN'T ACTUALLY BEAT YOU IN COMBAT, BUT I HAD TO WEAKEN YOU BEFORE I TOLD YOU ABOUT THEM.
OTHERWISE, YOU WOULD HAVE RESCUED THEM TOO QUICKLY.

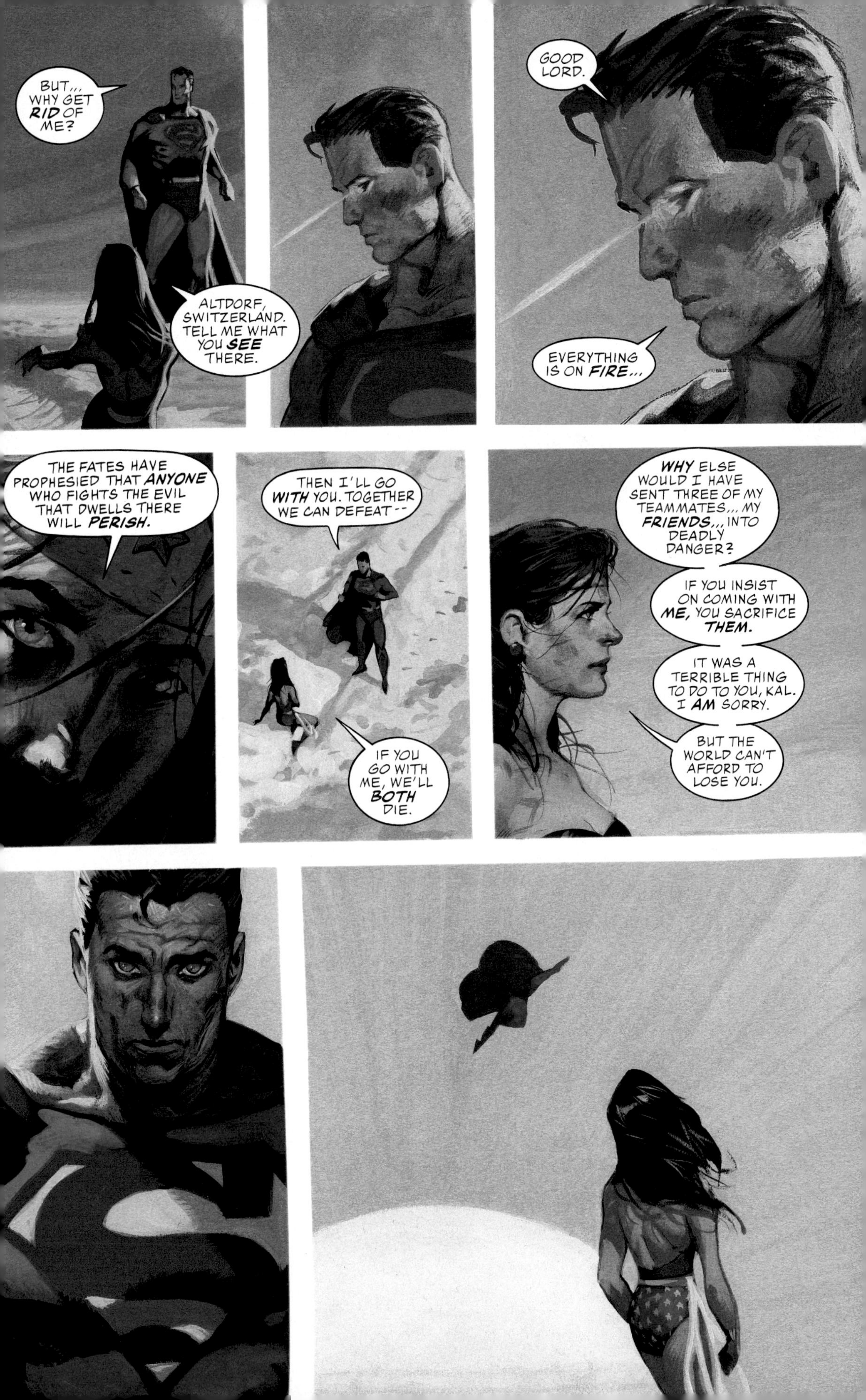
BUT... WHY GET RID OF ME?
ALTDORF, SWITZERLAND. TELL ME WHAT YOU SEE THERE.
GOOD LORD.
EVERYTHING IS ON FIRE...
THE FATES HAVE PROPHESIED THAT ANYONE WHO FIGHTS THE EVIL THAT DWELLS THERE WILL PERISH.
THEN I'LL GO WITH YOU. TOGETHER WE CAN DEFEAT--
IF YOU GO WITH ME, WE'LL BOTH DIE.
WHY ELSE WOULD I HAVE SENT THREE OF MY TEAMMATES... MY FRIENDS... INTO DEADLY DANGER?
IF YOU INSIST ON COMING WITH ME, YOU SACRIFICE THEM.
IT WAS A TERRIBLE THING TO DO TO YOU, KAL. I AM SORRY.
BUT THE WORLD CAN'T AFFORD TO LOSE YOU.

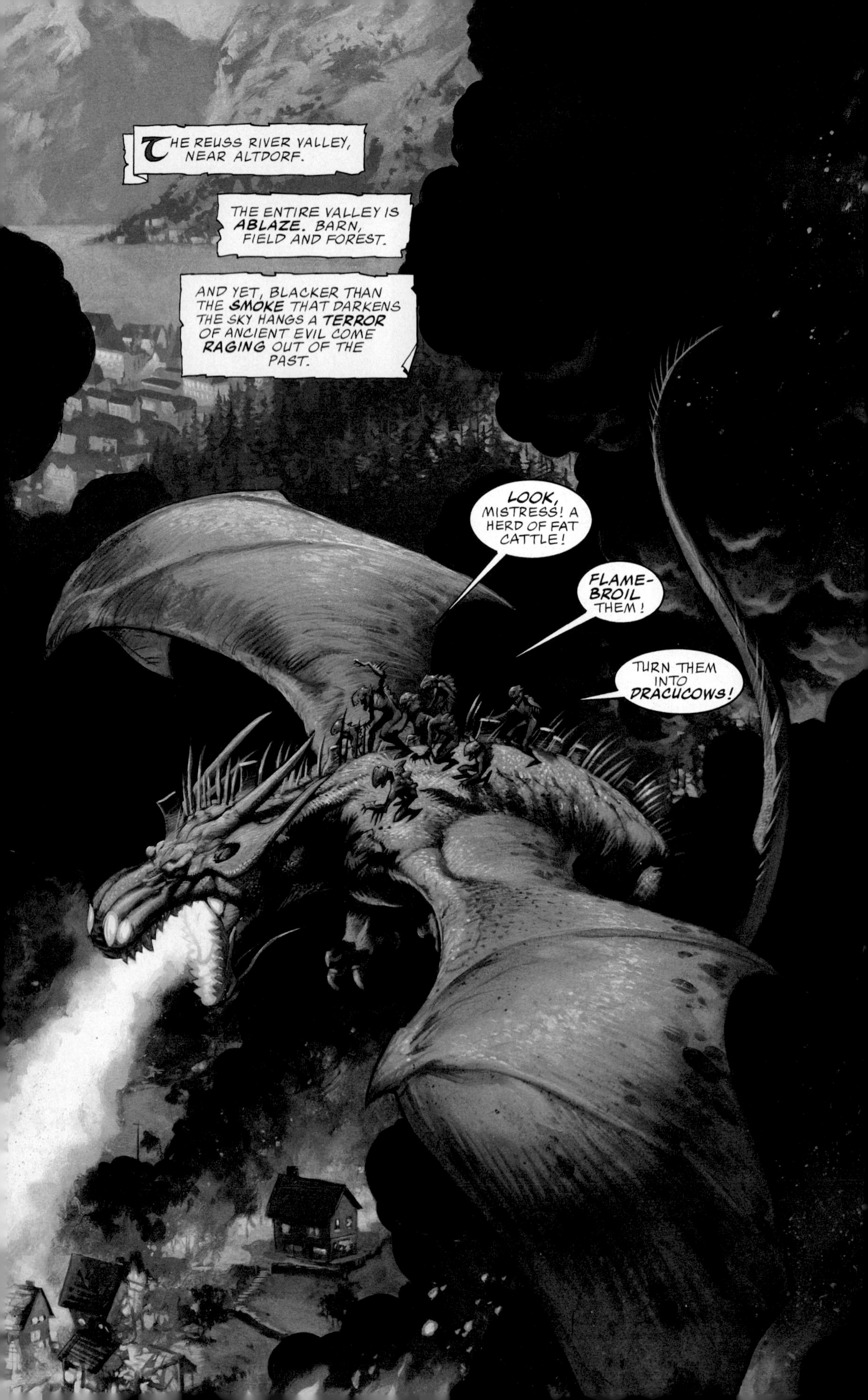
THE REUSS RIVER VALLEY, NEAR ALTDORF.
THE ENTIRE VALLEY IS ABLAZE. BARN, FIELD AND FOREST.
AND YET, BLACKER THAN THE SMOKE THAT DARKENS THE SKY HANGS A TERROR OF ANCIENT EVIL COME RAGING OUT OF THE PAST.
LOOK, MISTRESS! A HERD OF FAT CATTLE!
FLAME-BROIL THEM!
TURN THEM INTO DRACUCOWS!

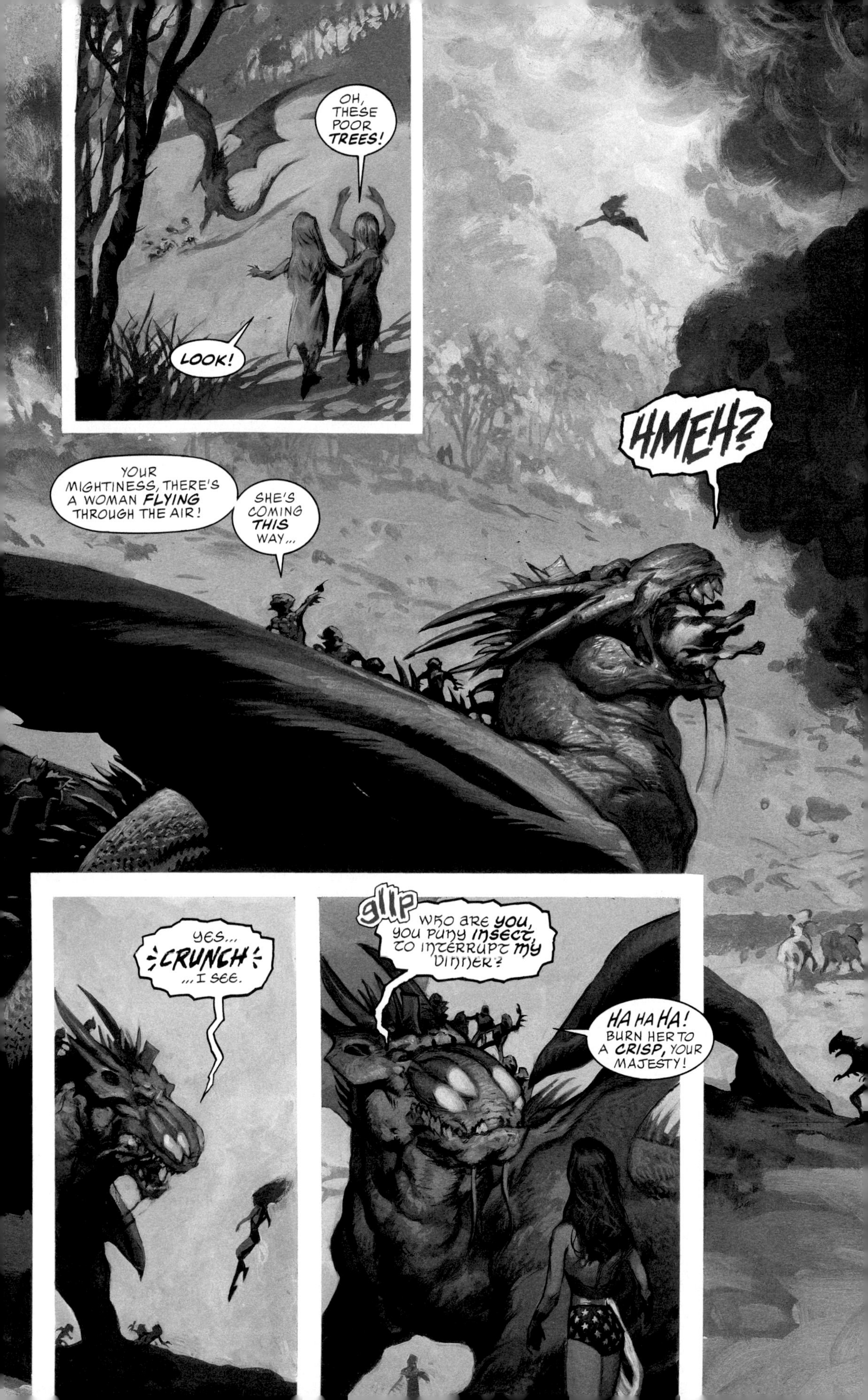
OH, THESE POOR TREES!
LOOK!
YOUR MIGHTINESS, THERE'S A WOMAN FLYING THROUGH THE AIR!
SHE'S COMING THIS WAY...
HMEH?
YES... CRUNCH ...I SEE.
GLLP
WHO ARE YOU, YOU PUNY INSECT, TO INTERRUPT MY DINNER?
HA HA HA! BURN HER TO A CRISP, YOUR MAJESTY!

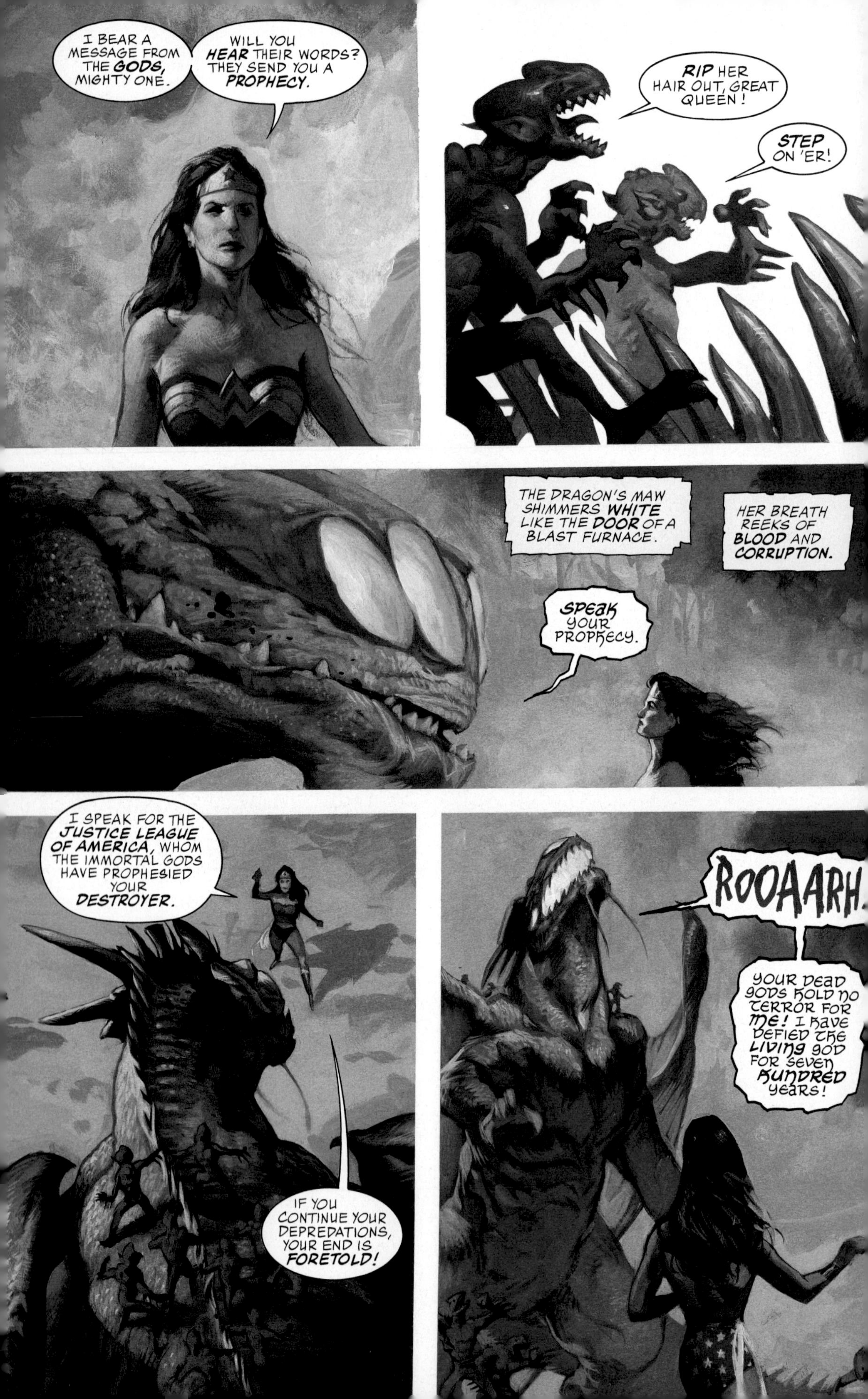
I BEAR A MESSAGE FROM THE GODS, MIGHTY ONE.
WILL YOU HEAR THEIR WORDS? THEY SEND YOU A PROPHECY.
RIP HER HAIR OUT, GREAT QUEEN!
STEP ON 'ER!
THE DRAGON'S MAW SHIMMERS WHITE LIKE THE DOOR OF A BLAST FURNACE.
HER BREATH REEKS OF BLOOD AND CORRUPTION.
SPEAK YOUR PROPHECY.
I SPEAK FOR THE JUSTICE LEAGUE OF AMERICA, WHOM THE IMMORTAL GODS HAVE PROPHESIED YOUR DESTROYER.
IF YOU CONTINUE YOUR DEPREDATIONS, YOUR END IS FORETOLD!
ROOAARH
YOUR DEAD GODS HOLD NO TERROR FOR ME! I HAVE DEFIED THE LIVING GOD FOR SEVEN HUNDRED YEARS!

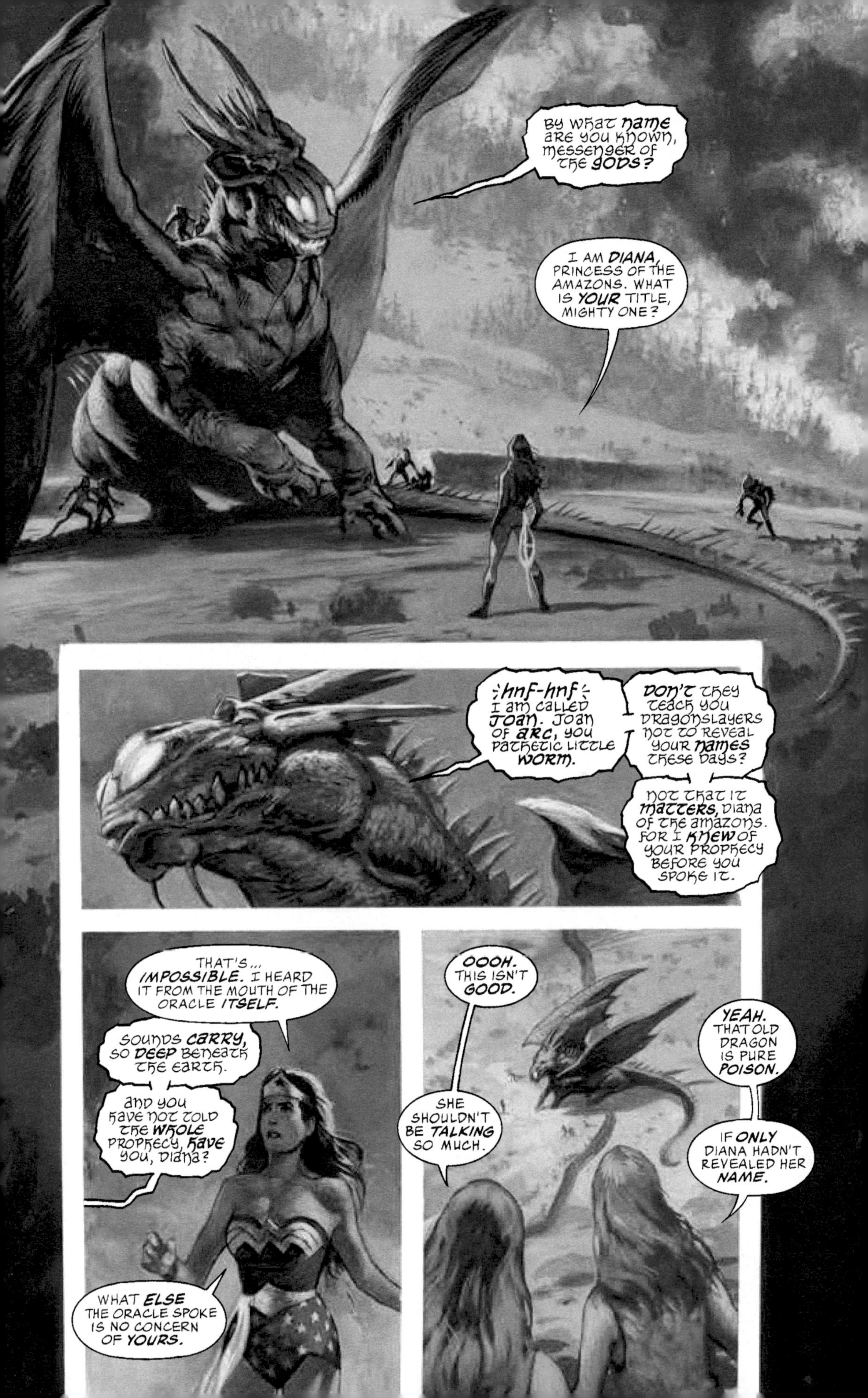
BY WHAT NAME ARE YOU KNOWN, MESSENGER OF THE GODS?
I AM DIANA, PRINCESS OF THE AMAZONS. WHAT IS YOUR TITLE, MIGHTY ONE?
hnf-hnf I AM CALLED JOAN. JOAN OF ARC, YOU PATHETIC LITTLE WORM.
DON'T THEY TEACH YOU DRAGONSLAYERS NOT TO REVEAL YOUR NAMES THESE DAYS?
NOT THAT IT MATTERS, DIANA OF THE AMAZONS. FOR I KNEW OF YOUR PROPHECY BEFORE YOU SPOKE IT.
THAT'S... IMPOSSIBLE. I HEARD IT FROM THE MOUTH OF THE ORACLE ITSELF.
SOUNDS CARRY, SO DEEP BENEATH THE EARTH.
AND YOU HAVE NOT TOLD THE WHOLE PROPHECY, HAVE YOU, DIANA?
WHAT ELSE THE ORACLE SPOKE IS NO CONCERN OF YOURS.
OOOH. THIS ISN'T GOOD.
SHE SHOULDN'T BE TALKING SO MUCH.
YEAH. THAT OLD DRAGON IS PURE POISON.
IF ONLY DIANA HADN'T REVEALED HER NAME.

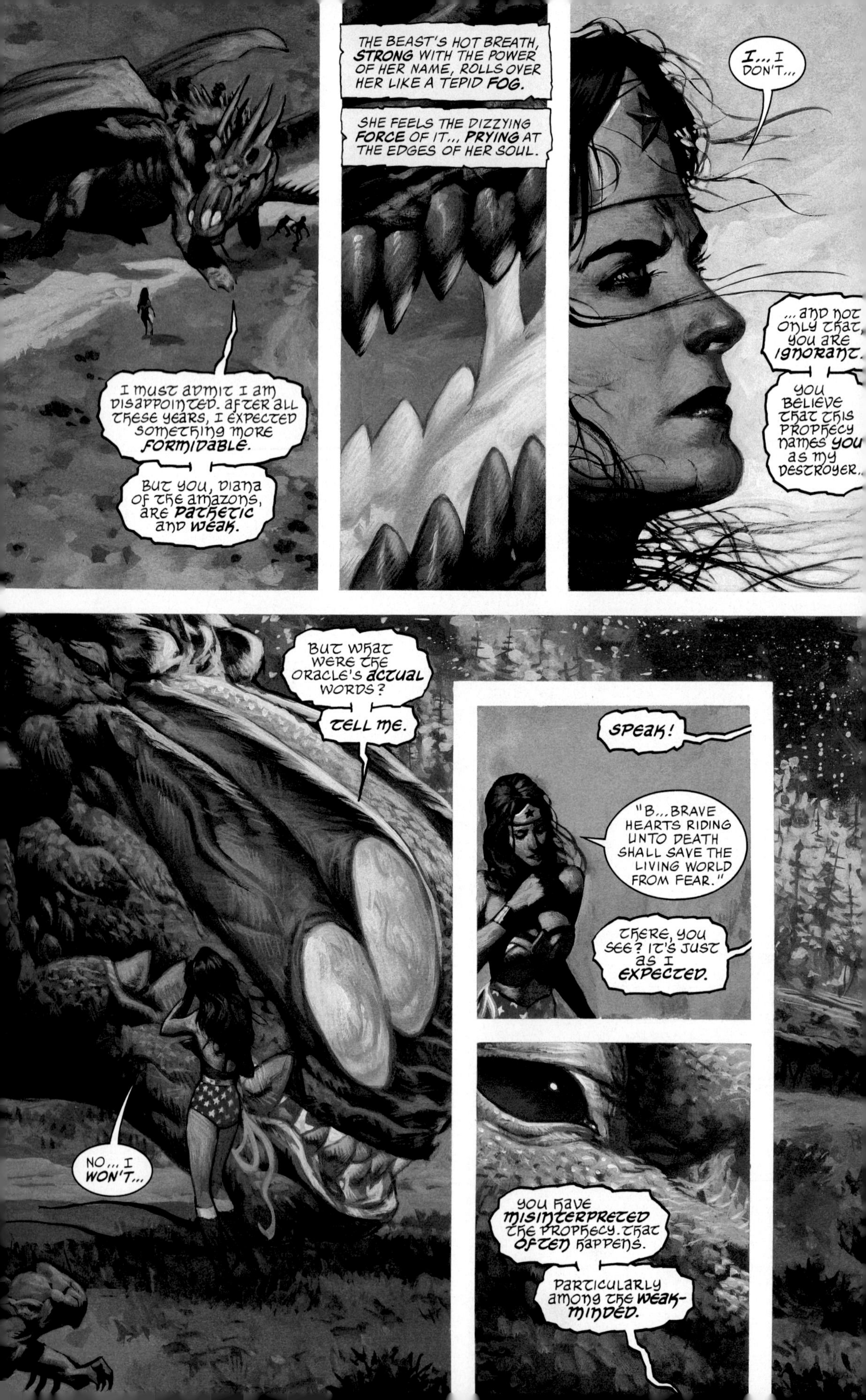
I MUST ADMIT I AM DISAPPOINTED. AFTER ALL THESE YEARS, I EXPECTED SOMETHING MORE FORMIDABLE.
BUT YOU, DIANA OF THE AMAZONS, ARE PATHETIC AND WEAK.
THE BEAST'S HOT BREATH, STRONG WITH THE POWER OF HER NAME, ROLLS OVER HER LIKE A TEPID FOG.
SHE FEELS THE DIZZYING FORCE OF IT... PRYING AT THE EDGES OF HER SOUL.
I... I DON'T...
...AND NOT ONLY THAT, YOU ARE IGNORANT.
YOU BELIEVE THAT THIS PROPHECY NAMES YOU AS MY DESTROYER...
BUT WHAT WERE THE ORACLE'S ACTUAL WORDS?
TELL ME.
NO... I WON'T...
SPEAK!
"B... BRAVE HEARTS RIDING UNTO DEATH SHALL SAVE THE LIVING WORLD FROM FEAR."
THERE, YOU SEE? IT'S JUST AS I EXPECTED.
YOU HAVE MISINTERPRETED THE PROPHECY. THAT OFTEN HAPPENS.
PARTICULARLY AMONG THE WEAK-MINDED.

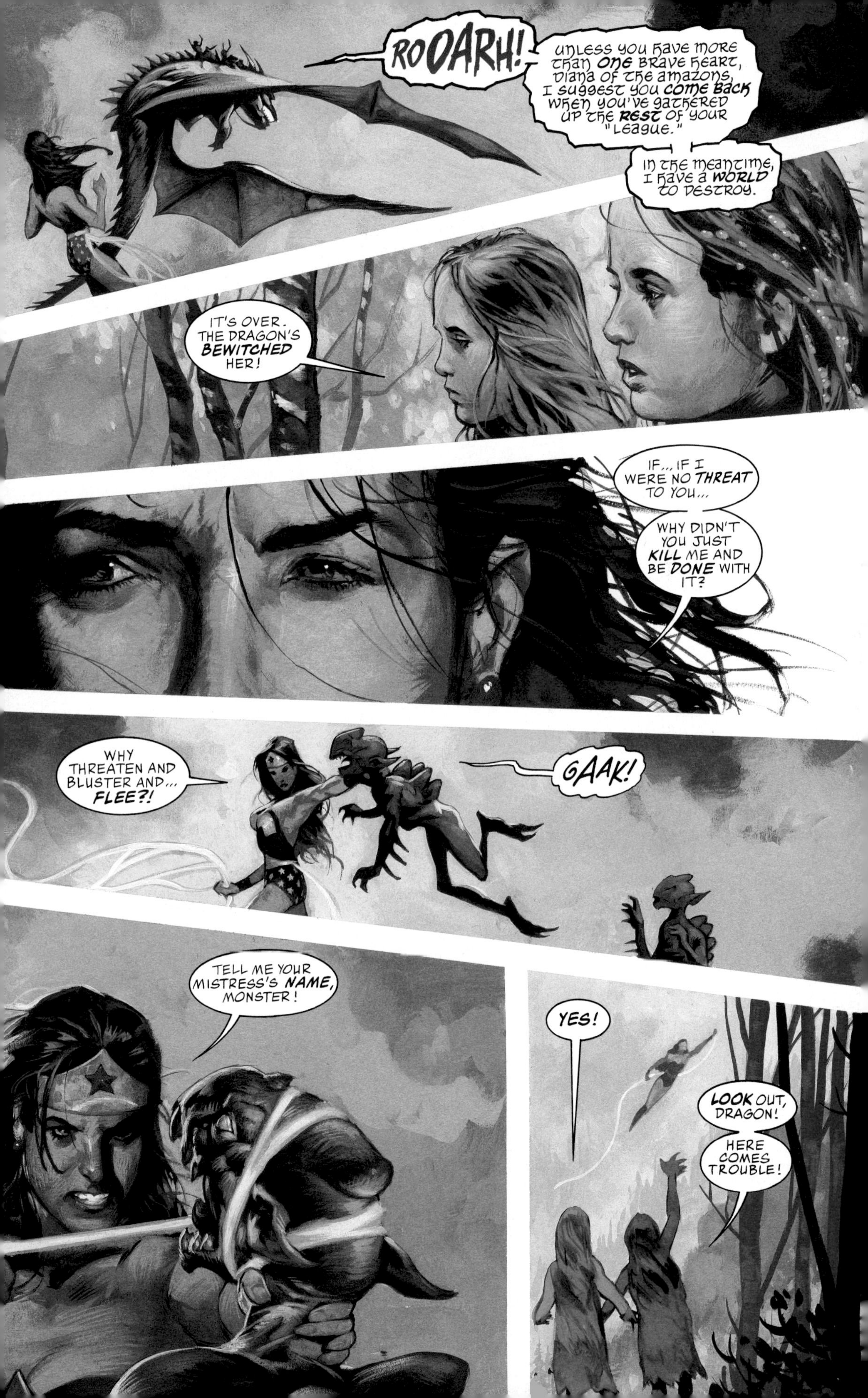
ROOARH!
UNLESS YOU HAVE MORE THAN ONE BRAVE HEART, DIANA OF THE AMAZONS, I SUGGEST YOU COME BACK WHEN YOU'VE GATHERED UP THE REST OF YOUR "LEAGUE."
IN THE MEANTIME, I HAVE A WORLD TO DESTROY.
IT'S OVER. THE DRAGON'S BEWITCHED HER!
IF... IF I WERE NO THREAT TO YOU...
WHY DIDN'T YOU JUST KILL ME AND BE DONE WITH IT?
WHY THREATEN AND BLUSTER AND... FLEE?!
GAAK!
TELL ME YOUR MISTRESS'S NAME, MONSTER!
YES!
LOOK OUT, DRAGON!
HERE COMES TROUBLE!

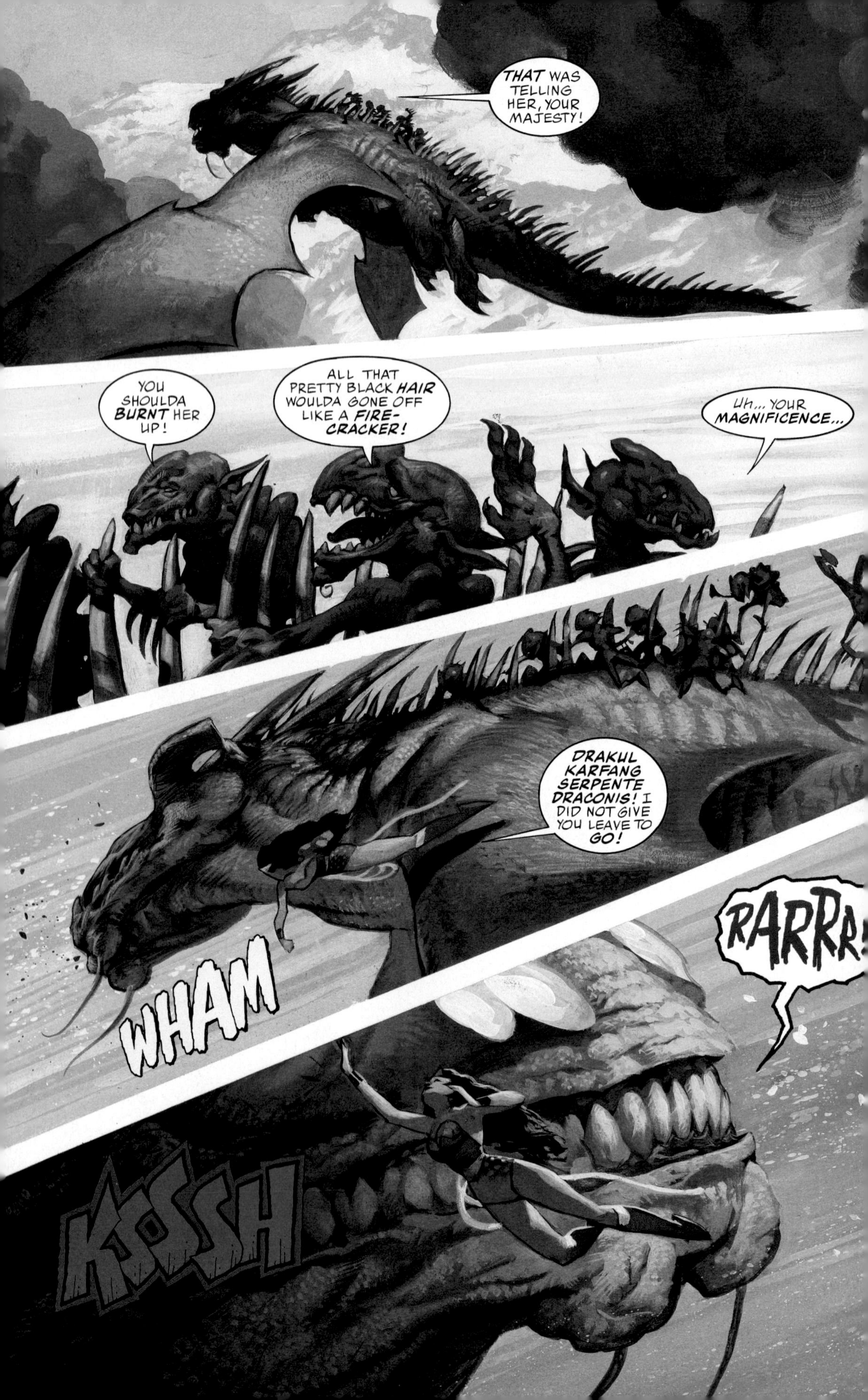
THAT WAS TELLING HER, YOUR MAJESTY!
YOU SHOULDA BURNT HER UP!
ALL THAT PRETTY BLACK HAIR WOULDA GONE OFF LIKE A FIRE-CRACKER!
UH... YOUR MAGNIFICENCE...
DRAKUL KARFANG SERPENTE DRACONIS! I DID NOT GIVE YOU LEAVE TO GO!
WHAM
RARRR!
KSSH

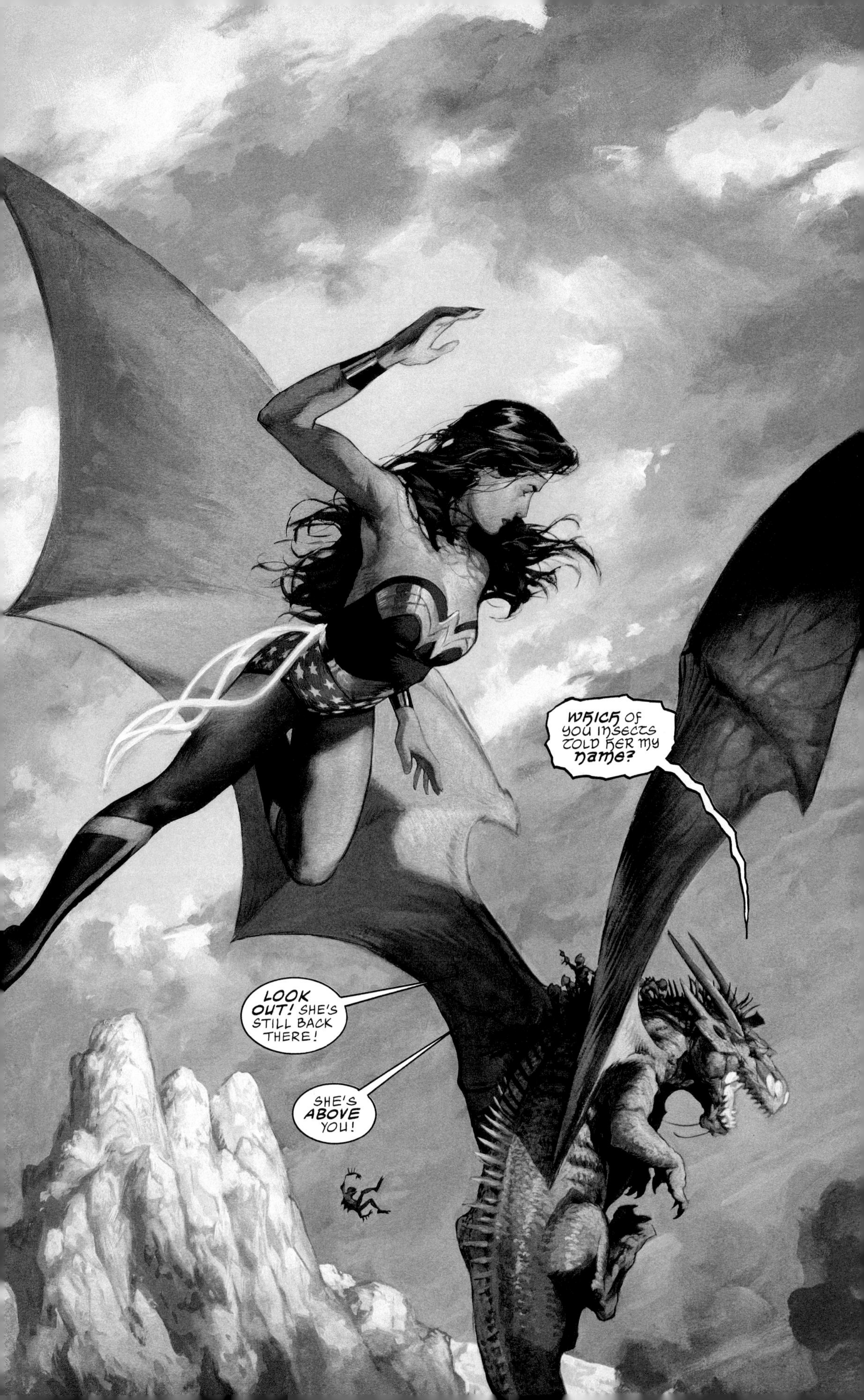

WHICH OF YOU INSECTS TOLD HER MY NAME?
LOOK OUT! SHE'S STILL BACK THERE!
SHE'S ABOVE YOU!

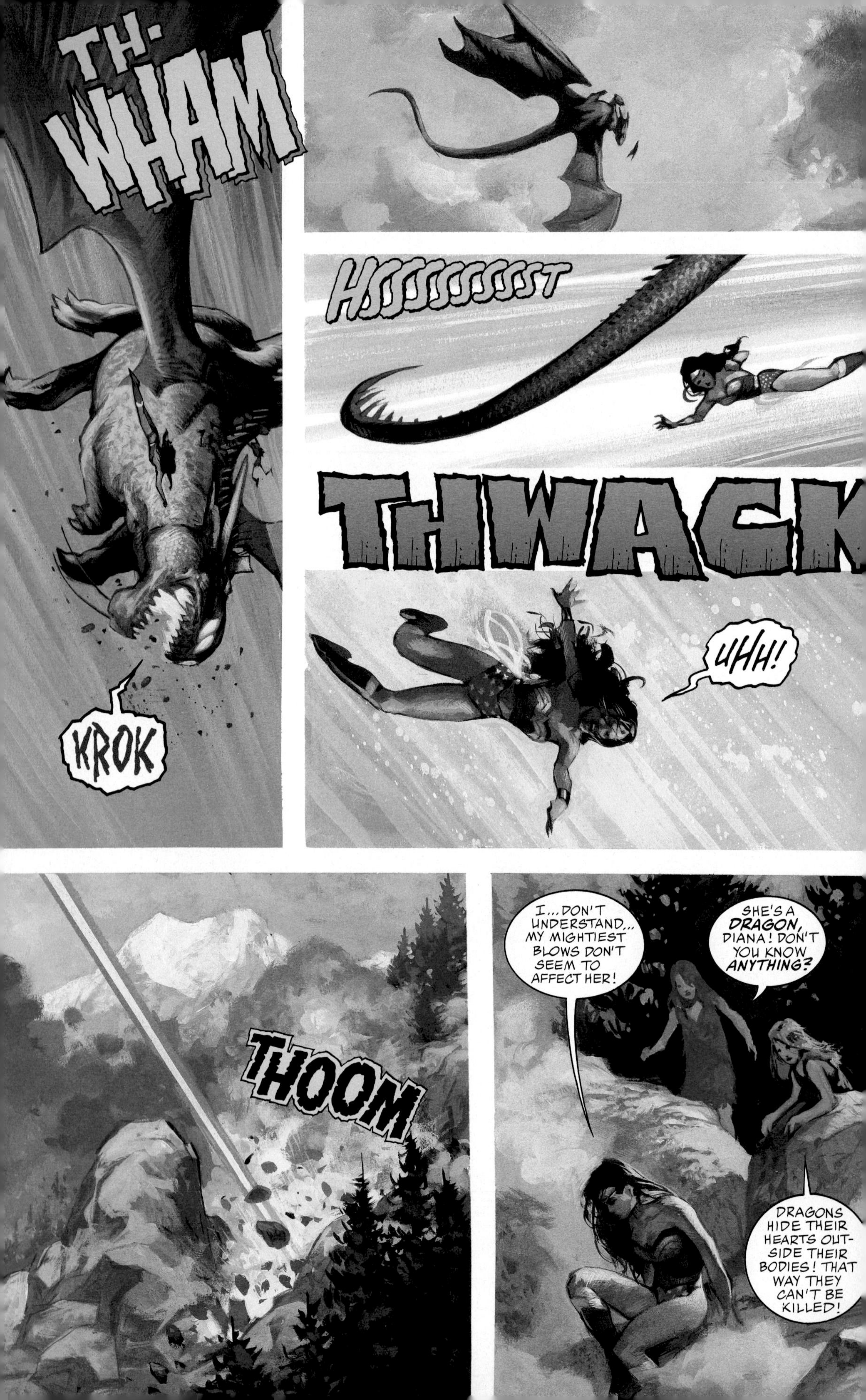
TH-WHAM
KROK
HSSSSSSSST
THWACK
UHH!
THOOM
I... DON'T UNDERSTAND... MY MIGHTIEST BLOWS DON'T SEEM TO AFFECT HER!
SHE'S A DRAGON, DIANA! DON'T YOU KNOW ANYTHING?
DRAGONS HIDE THEIR HEARTS OUT-SIDE THEIR BODIES! THAT WAY THEY CAN'T BE KILLED!

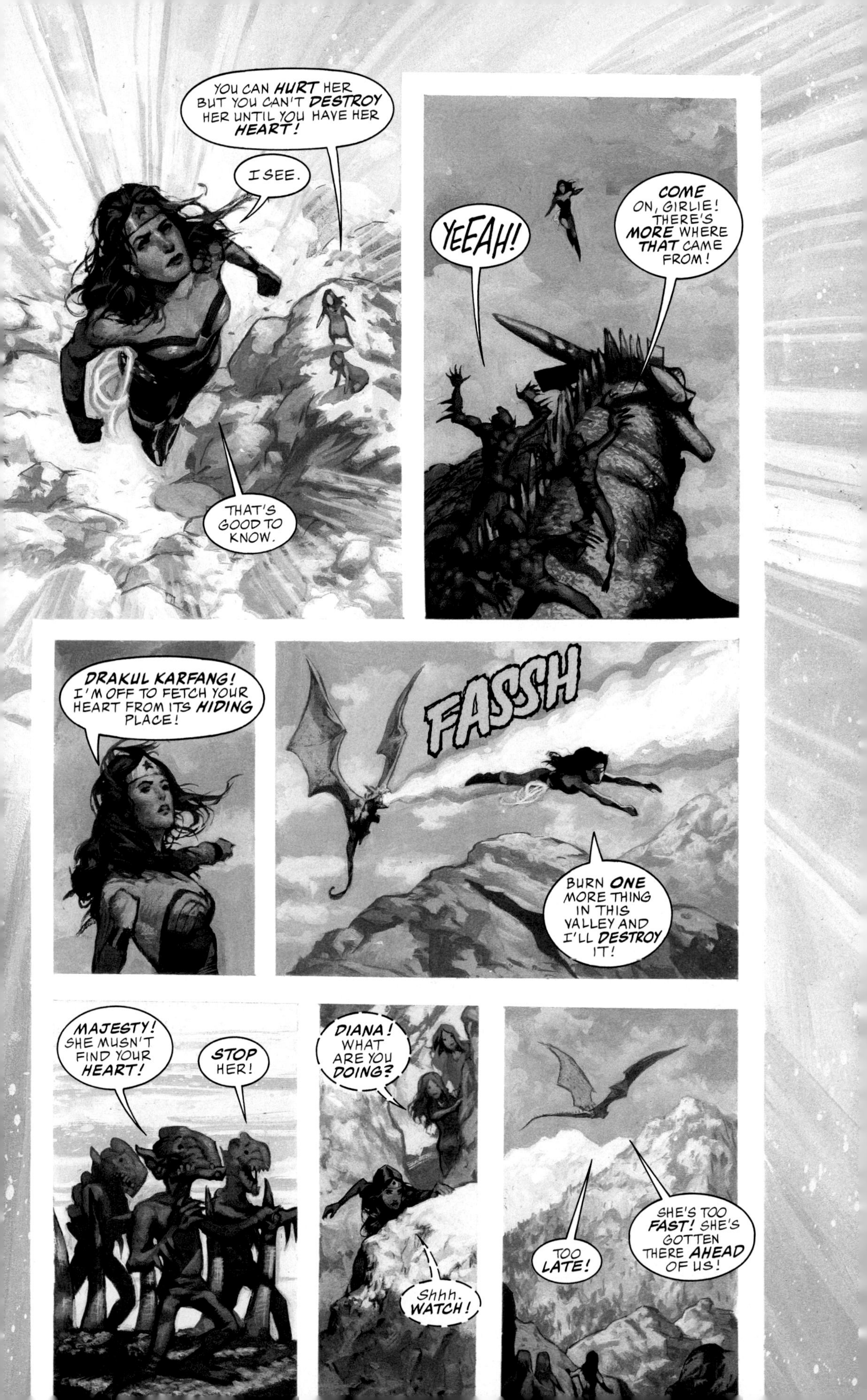
YOU CAN HURT HER BUT YOU CAN'T DESTROY HER UNTIL YOU HAVE HER HEART!
I SEE.
THAT'S GOOD TO KNOW.
YEEAH!
COME ON, GIRLIE! THERE'S MORE WHERE THAT CAME FROM!
DRAKUL KARFANG! I'M OFF TO FETCH YOUR HEART FROM ITS HIDING PLACE!
FASSH
BURN ONE MORE THING IN THIS VALLEY AND I'LL DESTROY IT!
MAJESTY! SHE MUSN'T FIND YOUR HEART!
STOP HER!
DIANA! WHAT ARE YOU DOING?
Shhh. WATCH!
TOO LATE!
SHE'S TOO FAST! SHE'S GOTTEN THERE AHEAD OF US!

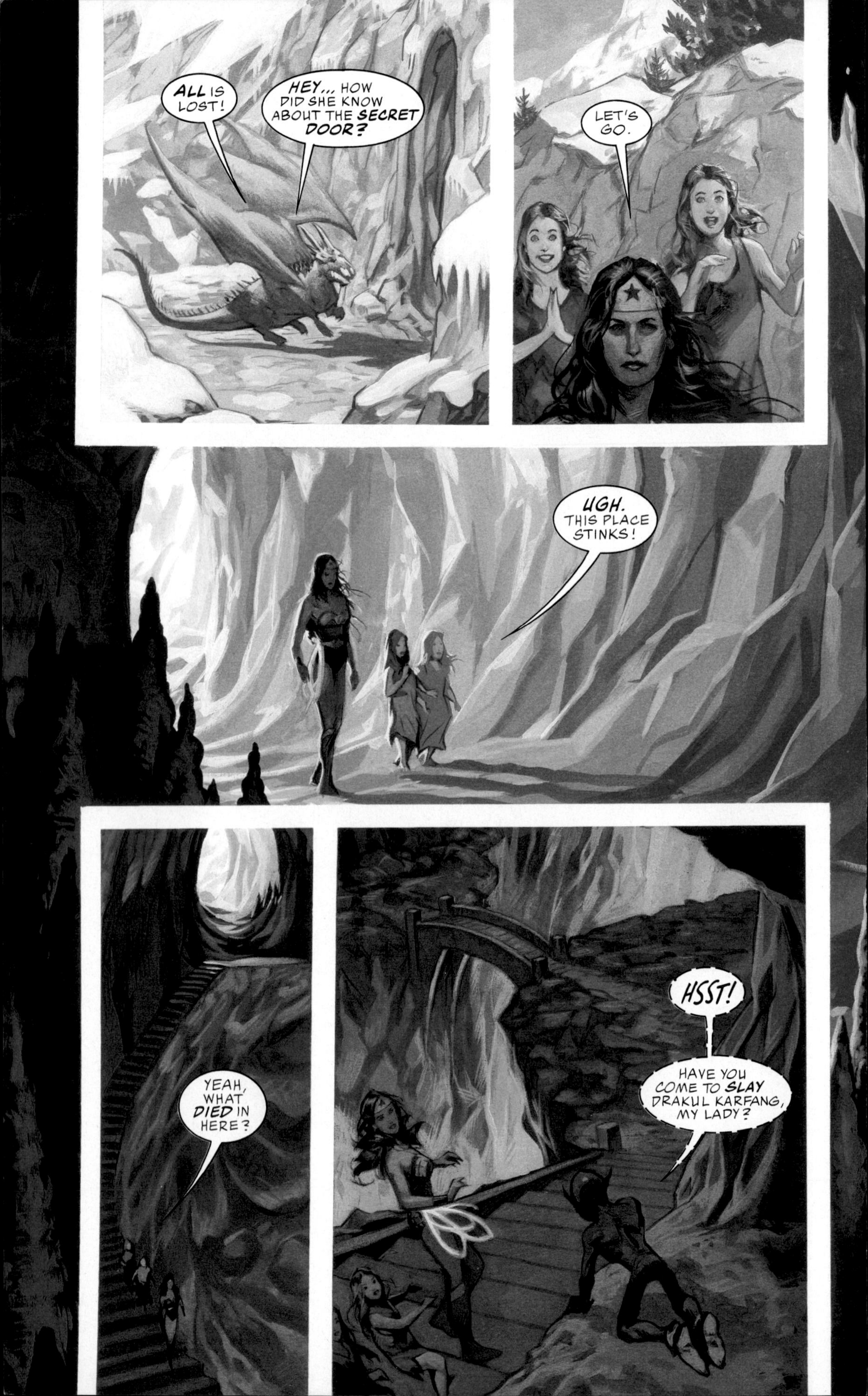
ALL IS LOST!
HEY... HOW DID SHE KNOW ABOUT THE SECRET DOOR?
LET'S GO.
UGH. THIS PLACE STINKS!
YEAH, WHAT DIED IN HERE?
HSST!
HAVE YOU COME TO SLAY DRAKUL KARFANG, MY LADY?

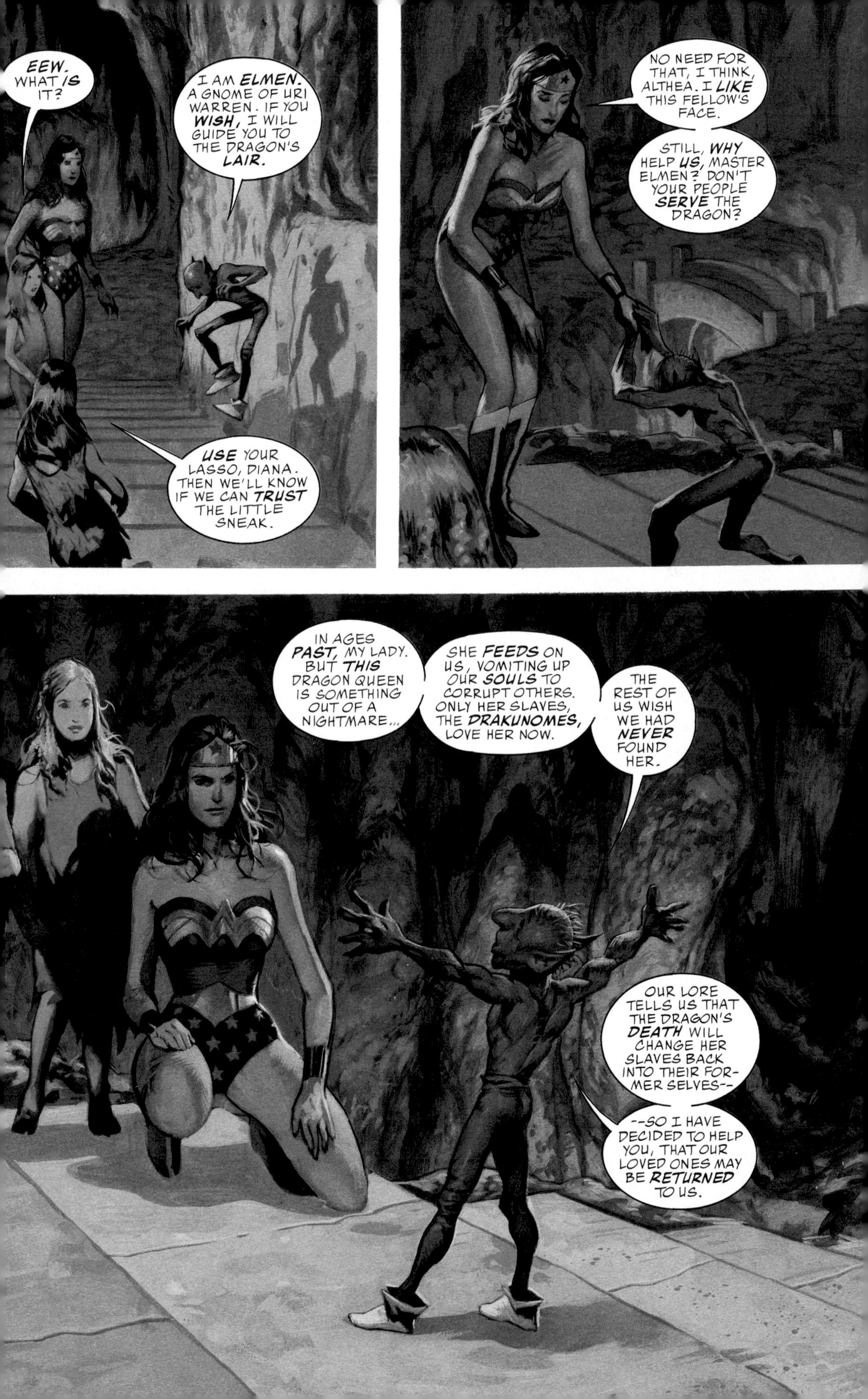
EEW. WHAT IS IT?
I AM ELMEN. A GNOME OF URI WARREN. IF YOU WISH, I WILL GUIDE YOU TO THE DRAGON'S LAIR.
USE YOUR LASSO, DIANA. THEN WE'LL KNOW IF WE CAN TRUST THE LITTLE SNEAK.
NO NEED FOR THAT, I THINK, ALTHEA. I LIKE THIS FELLOW'S FACE.
STILL, WHY HELP US, MASTER ELMEN? DON'T YOUR PEOPLE SERVE THE DRAGON?
IN AGES PAST, MY LADY. BUT THIS DRAGON QUEEN IS SOMETHING OUT OF A NIGHTMARE...
SHE FEEDS ON US, VOMITING UP OUR SOULS TO CORRUPT OTHERS. ONLY HER SLAVES, THE DRAKUNOMES, LOVE HER NOW.
THE REST OF US WISH WE HAD NEVER FOUND HER.
OUR LORE TELLS US THAT THE DRAGON'S DEATH WILL CHANGE HER SLAVES BACK INTO THEIR FORMER SELVES--
--SO I HAVE DECIDED TO HELP YOU, THAT OUR LOVED ONES MAY BE RETURNED TO US.

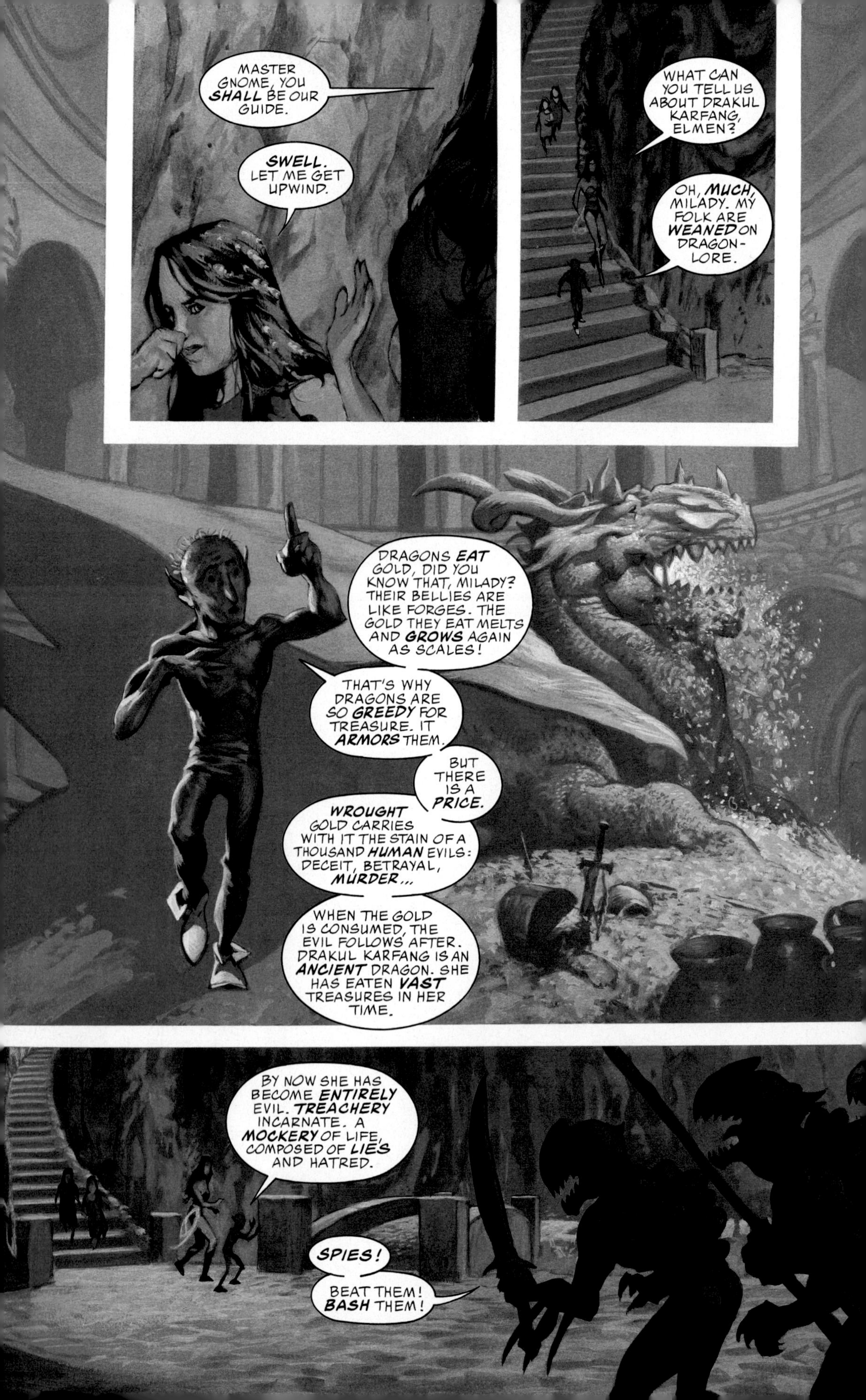
MASTER GNOME, YOU SHALL BE OUR GUIDE.
SWELL. LET ME GET UPWIND.
WHAT CAN YOU TELL US ABOUT DRAKUL KARFANG, ELMEN?
OH, MUCH, MILADY. MY FOLK ARE WEANED ON DRAGON-LORE.
DRAGONS EAT GOLD, DID YOU KNOW THAT, MILADY? THEIR BELLIES ARE LIKE FORGES. THE GOLD THEY EAT MELTS AND GROWS AGAIN AS SCALES!
THAT'S WHY DRAGONS ARE SO GREEDY FOR TREASURE. IT ARMORS THEM.
BUT THERE IS A PRICE.
WROUGHT GOLD CARRIES WITH IT THE STAIN OF A THOUSAND HUMAN EVILS: DECEIT, BETRAYAL, MURDER...
WHEN THE GOLD IS CONSUMED, THE EVIL FOLLOWS AFTER. DRAKUL KARFANG IS AN ANCIENT DRAGON. SHE HAS EATEN VAST TREASURES IN HER TIME.
BY NOW SHE HAS BECOME ENTIRELY EVIL. TREACHERY INCARNATE. A MOCKERY OF LIFE, COMPOSED OF LIES AND HATRED.
SPIES!
BEAT THEM! BASH THEM!

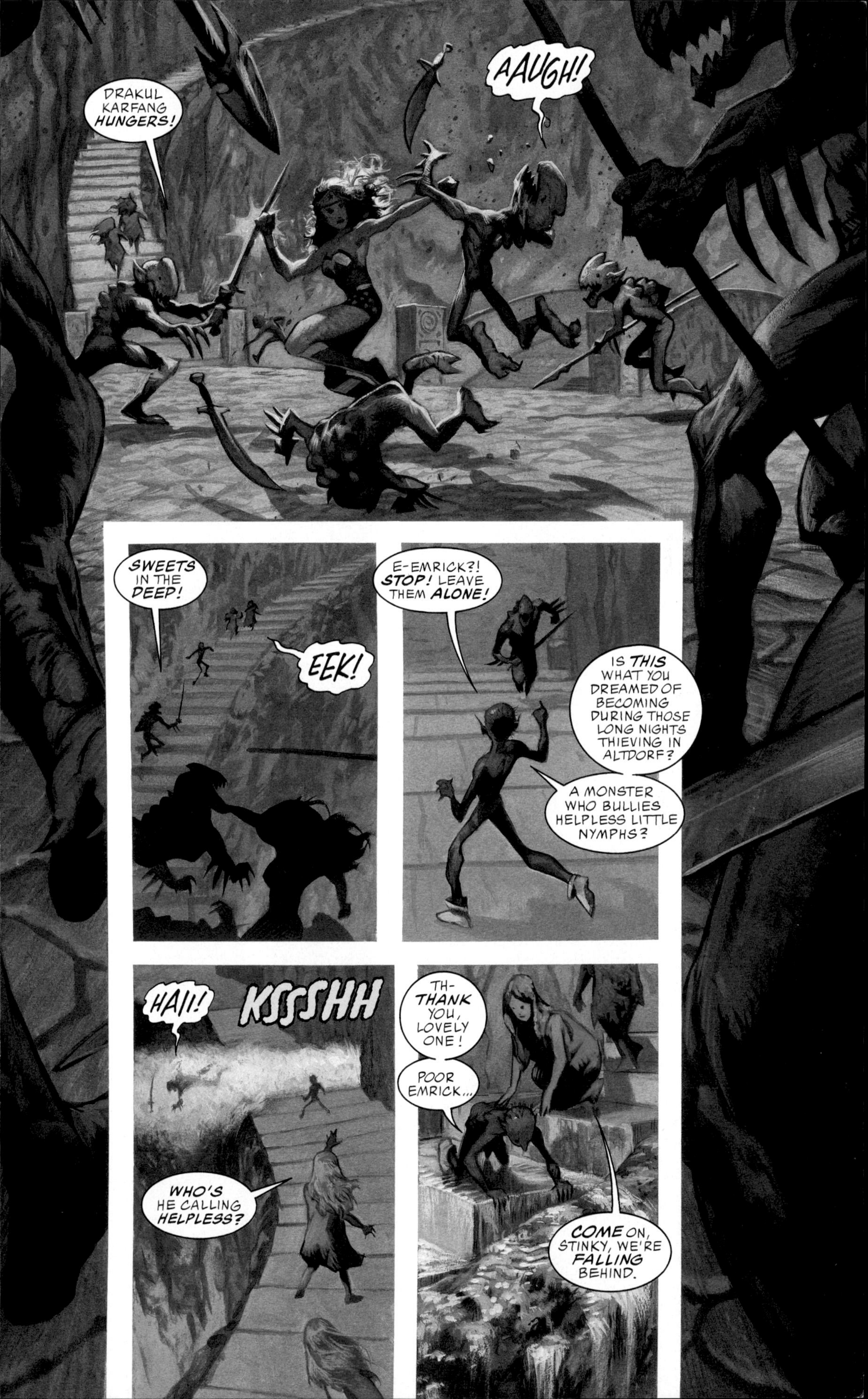
DRAKUL KARFANG HUNGERS!
AAUGH!
SWEETS IN THE DEEP!
EEK!
E-EMRICK?! STOP! LEAVE THEM ALONE!
IS THIS WHAT YOU DREAMED OF BECOMING DURING THOSE LONG NIGHTS THIEVING IN ALTDORF?
A MONSTER WHO BULLIES HELPLESS LITTLE NYMPHS?
HAII!
KSSSHH
WHO'S HE CALLING HELPLESS?
TH-THANK YOU, LOVELY ONE!
POOR EMRICK...
COME ON, STINKY, WE'RE FALLING BEHIND.

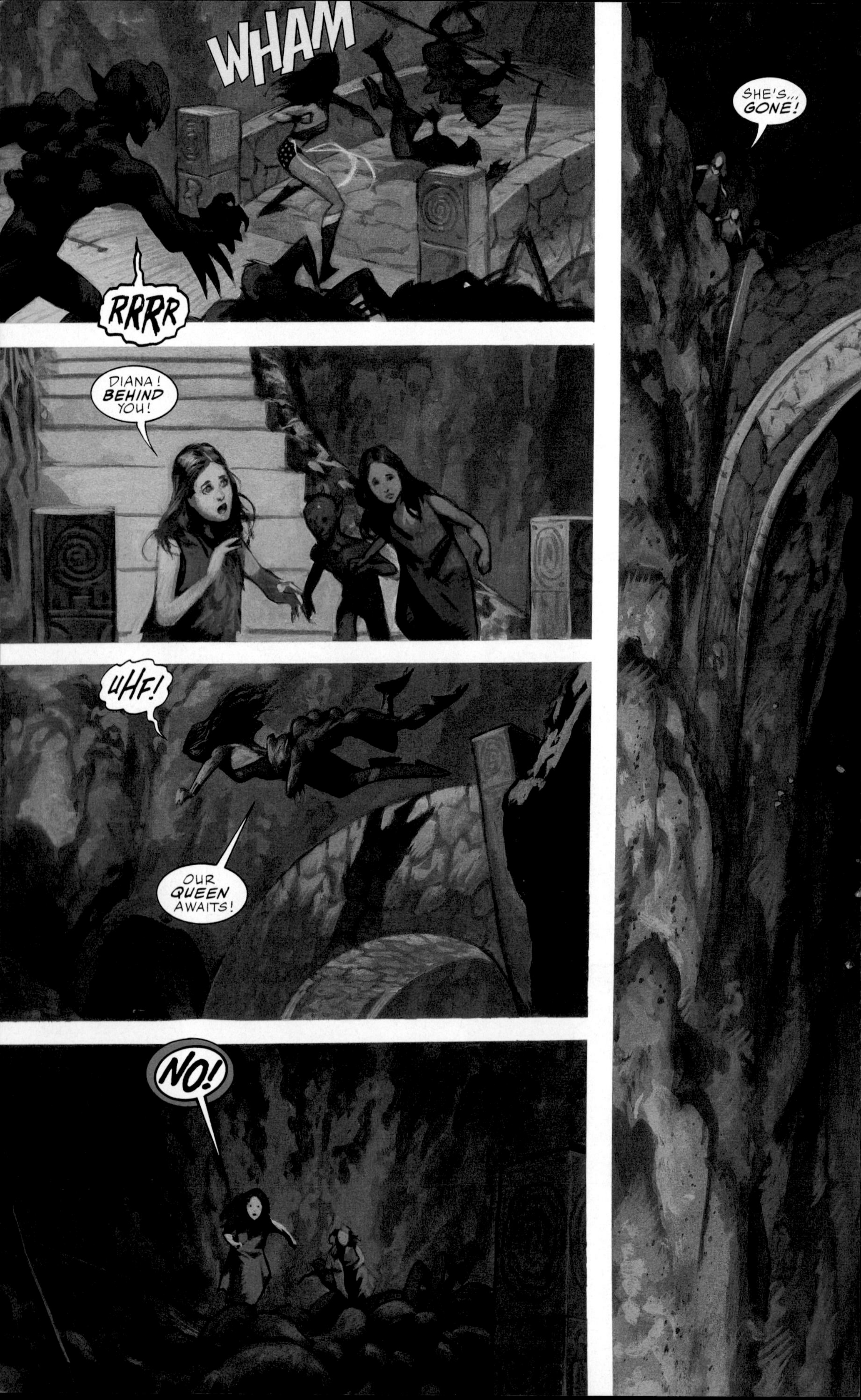
WHAM
RRRR
DIANA! BEHIND YOU!
UHF!
OUR QUEEN AWAITS!
NO!
SHE'S... GONE!

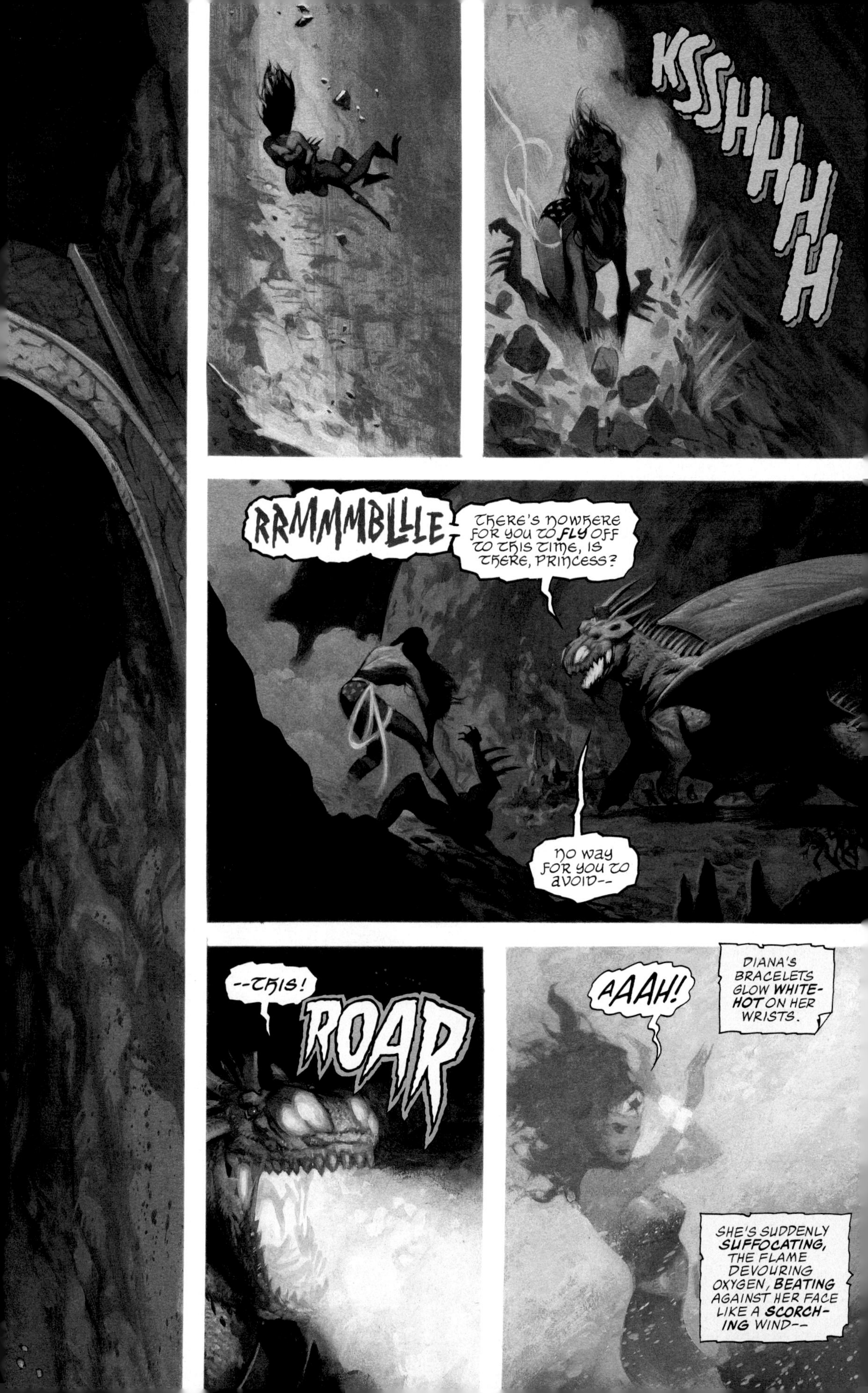
KSSHHHHH
RRMMMBLLLE
THERE'S NOWHERE FOR YOU TO FLY OFF TO THIS TIME, IS THERE, PRINCESS?
NO WAY FOR YOU TO AVOID--
--THIS!
ROAR
AAAH!
DIANA'S BRACELETS GLOW WHITE-HOT ON HER WRISTS.
SHE'S SUDDENLY SUFFOCATING, THE FLAME DEVOURING OXYGEN, BEATING AGAINST HER FACE LIKE A SCORCH-ING WIND--

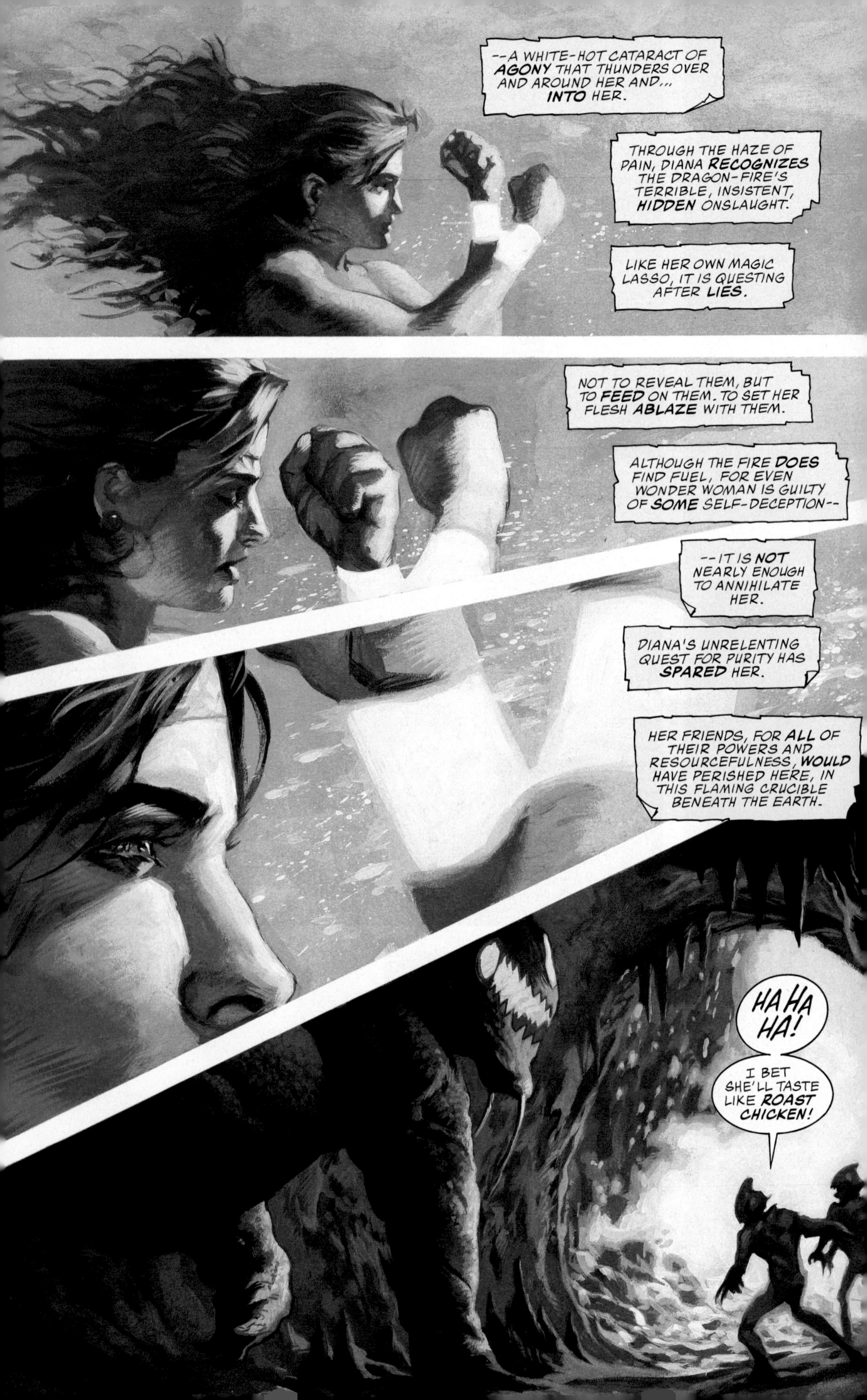
--A WHITE-HOT CATARACT OF AGONY THAT THUNDERS OVER AND AROUND HER AND... INTO HER.
THROUGH THE HAZE OF PAIN, DIANA RECOGNIZES THE DRAGON-FIRE'S TERRIBLE, INSISTENT, HIDDEN ONSLAUGHT.
LIKE HER OWN MAGIC LASSO, IT IS QUESTING AFTER LIES.
NOT TO REVEAL THEM, BUT TO FEED ON THEM. TO SET HER FLESH ABLAZE WITH THEM.
ALTHOUGH THE FIRE DOES FIND FUEL, FOR EVEN WONDER WOMAN IS GUILTY OF SOME SELF-DECEPTION--
--IT IS NOT NEARLY ENOUGH TO ANNIHILATE HER.
DIANA'S UNRELENTING QUEST FOR PURITY HAS SPARED HER.
HER FRIENDS, FOR ALL OF THEIR POWERS AND RESOURCEFULNESS, WOULD HAVE PERISHED HERE, IN THIS FLAMING CRUCIBLE BENEATH THE EARTH.
HA HA HA!
I BET SHE'LL TASTE LIKE ROAST CHICKEN!

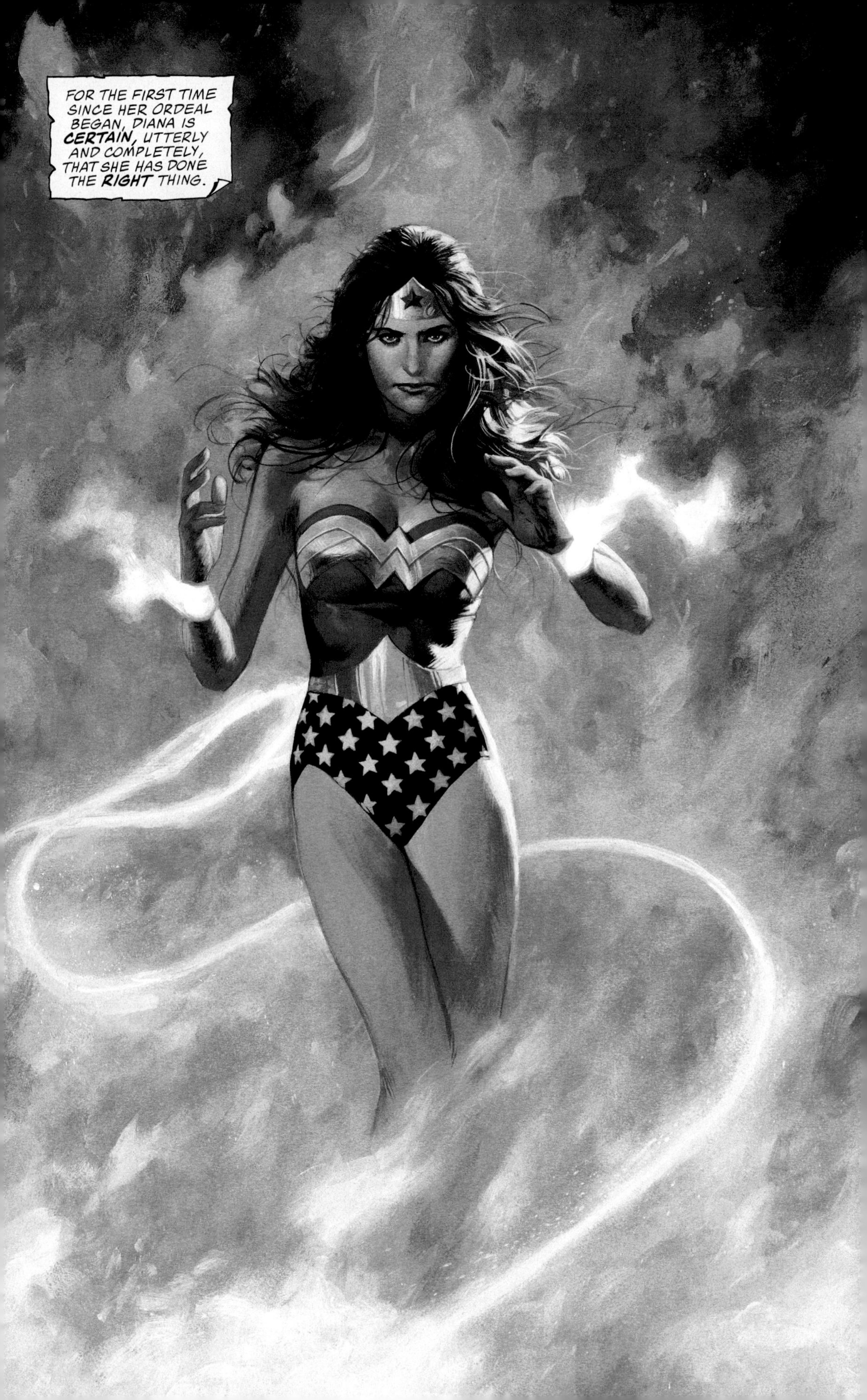
FOR THE FIRST TIME SINCE HER ORDEAL BEGAN, DIANA IS **CERTAIN,** UTTERLY AND COMPLETELY, THAT SHE HAS DONE THE **RIGHT** THING.

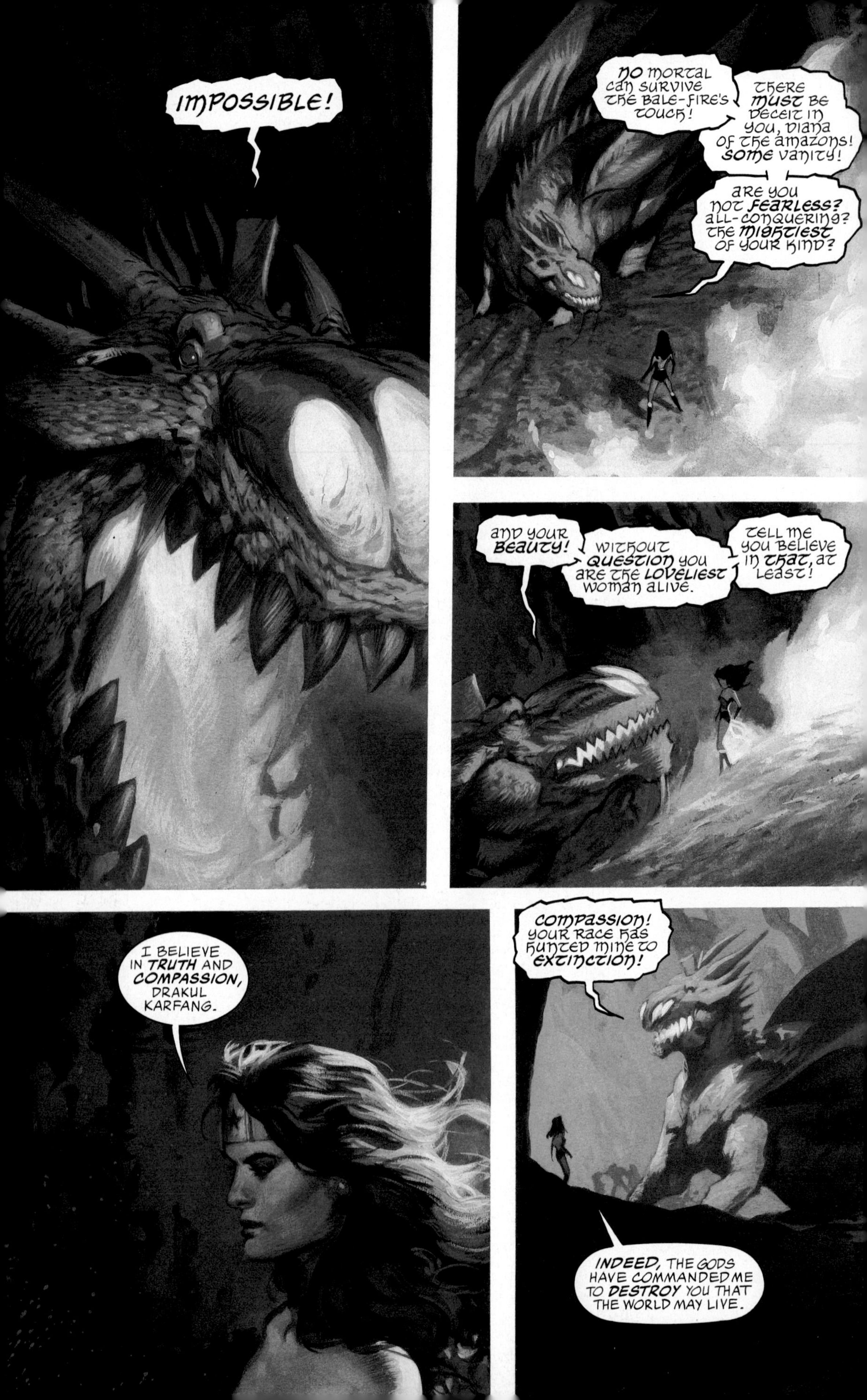
IMPOSSIBLE!
NO MORTAL CAN SURVIVE THE BALE-FIRE'S TOUCH!
THERE MUST BE DECEIT IN YOU, DIANA OF THE AMAZONS! SOME VANITY!
ARE YOU NOT FEARLESS? ALL-CONQUERING? THE MIGHTIEST OF YOUR KIND?
AND YOUR BEAUTY!
WITHOUT QUESTION YOU ARE THE LOVELIEST WOMAN ALIVE.
TELL ME YOU BELIEVE IN THAT, AT LEAST!
I BELIEVE IN TRUTH AND COMPASSION, DRAKUL KARFANG.
COMPASSION! YOUR RACE HAS HUNTED MINE TO EXTINCTION!
INDEED, THE GODS HAVE COMMANDED ME TO DESTROY YOU THAT THE WORLD MAY LIVE.

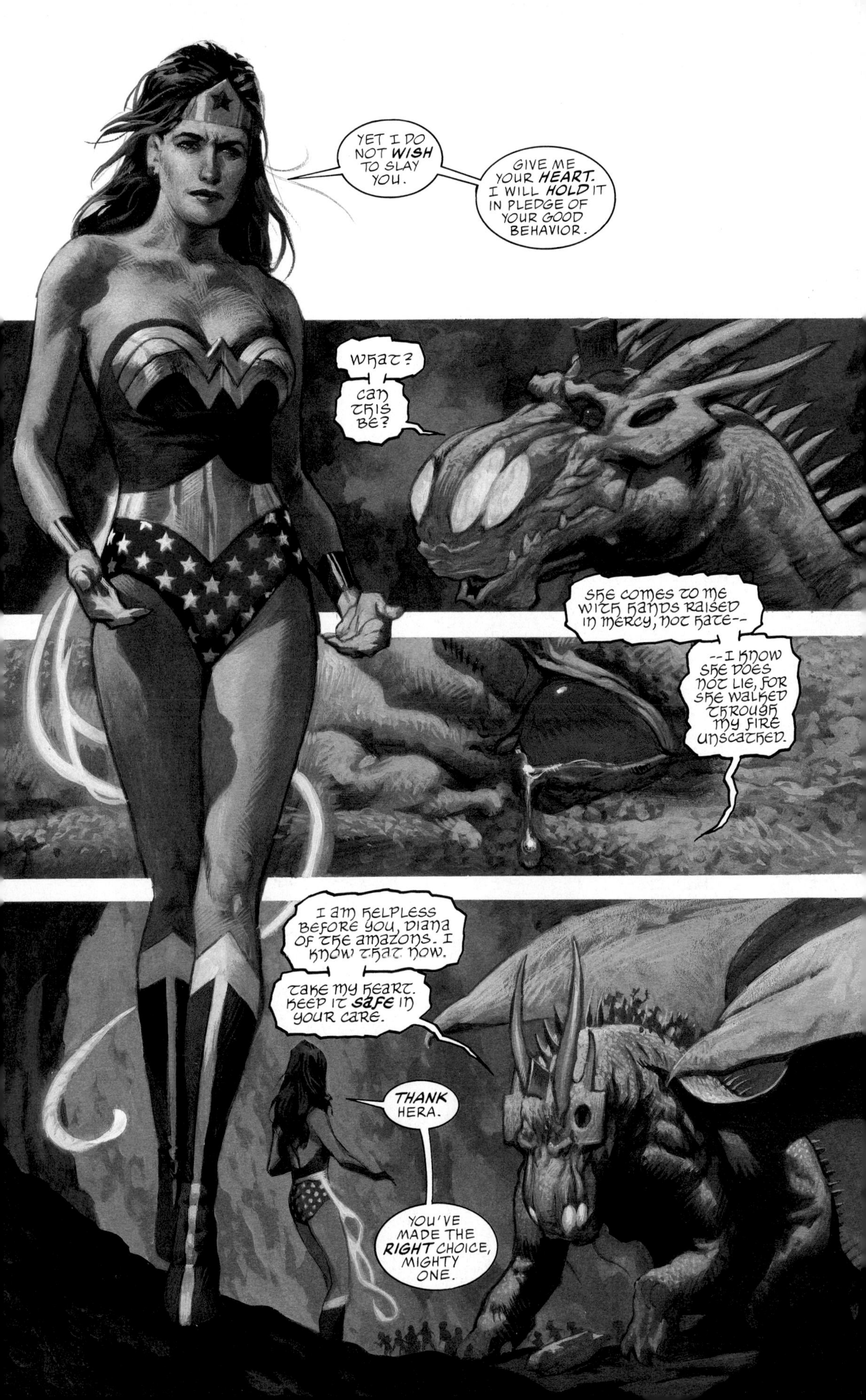
YET I DO NOT WISH TO SLAY YOU.
GIVE ME YOUR HEART. I WILL HOLD IT IN PLEDGE OF YOUR GOOD BEHAVIOR.
WHAT?
CAN THIS BE?
SHE COMES TO ME WITH HANDS RAISED IN MERCY, NOT HATE--
--I KNOW SHE DOES NOT LIE, FOR SHE WALKED THROUGH MY FIRE UNSCATHED.
I AM HELPLESS BEFORE YOU, DIANA OF THE AMAZONS. I KNOW THAT NOW.
TAKE MY HEART. KEEP IT SAFE IN YOUR CARE.
THANK HERA.
YOU'VE MADE THE RIGHT CHOICE, MIGHTY ONE.

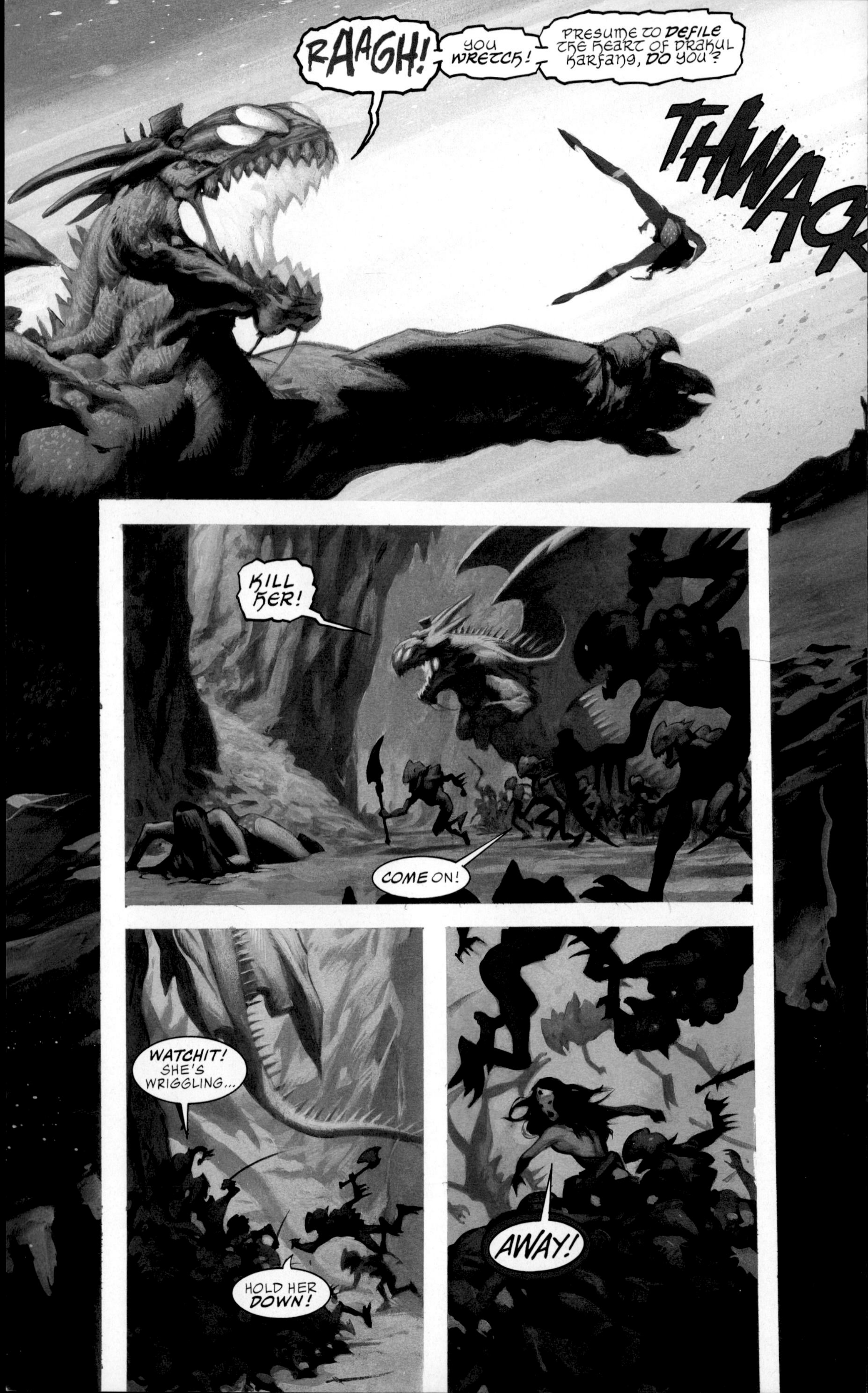
RAAGH!
YOU WRETCH!
PRESUME TO DEFILE THE HEART OF DRAKUL KARFANG, DO YOU?
THWACK
KILL HER!
COME ON!
WATCHIT! SHE'S WRIGGLING...
HOLD HER DOWN!
AWAY!

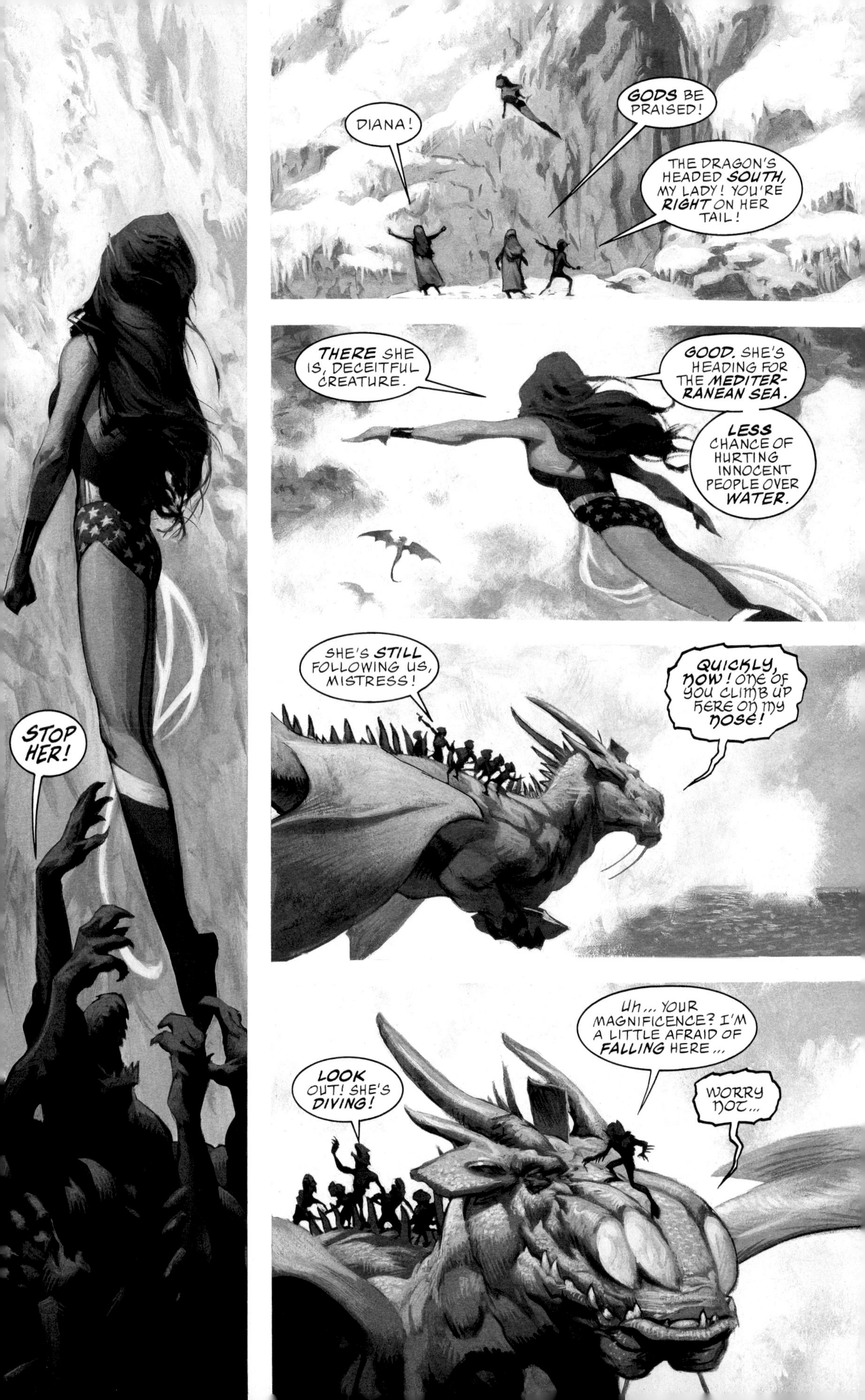
STOP HER!
DIANA!
GODS BE PRAISED!
THE DRAGON'S HEADED SOUTH, MY LADY! YOU'RE RIGHT ON HER TAIL!
THERE SHE IS, DECEITFUL CREATURE.
GOOD. SHE'S HEADING FOR THE MEDITERRANEAN SEA.
LESS CHANCE OF HURTING INNOCENT PEOPLE OVER WATER.
SHE'S STILL FOLLOWING US, MISTRESS!
QUICKLY, NOW! ONE OF YOU CLIMB UP HERE ON MY NOSE!
UH... YOUR MAGNIFICENCE? I'M A LITTLE AFRAID OF FALLING HERE...
LOOK OUT! SHE'S DIVING!
WORRY NOT...

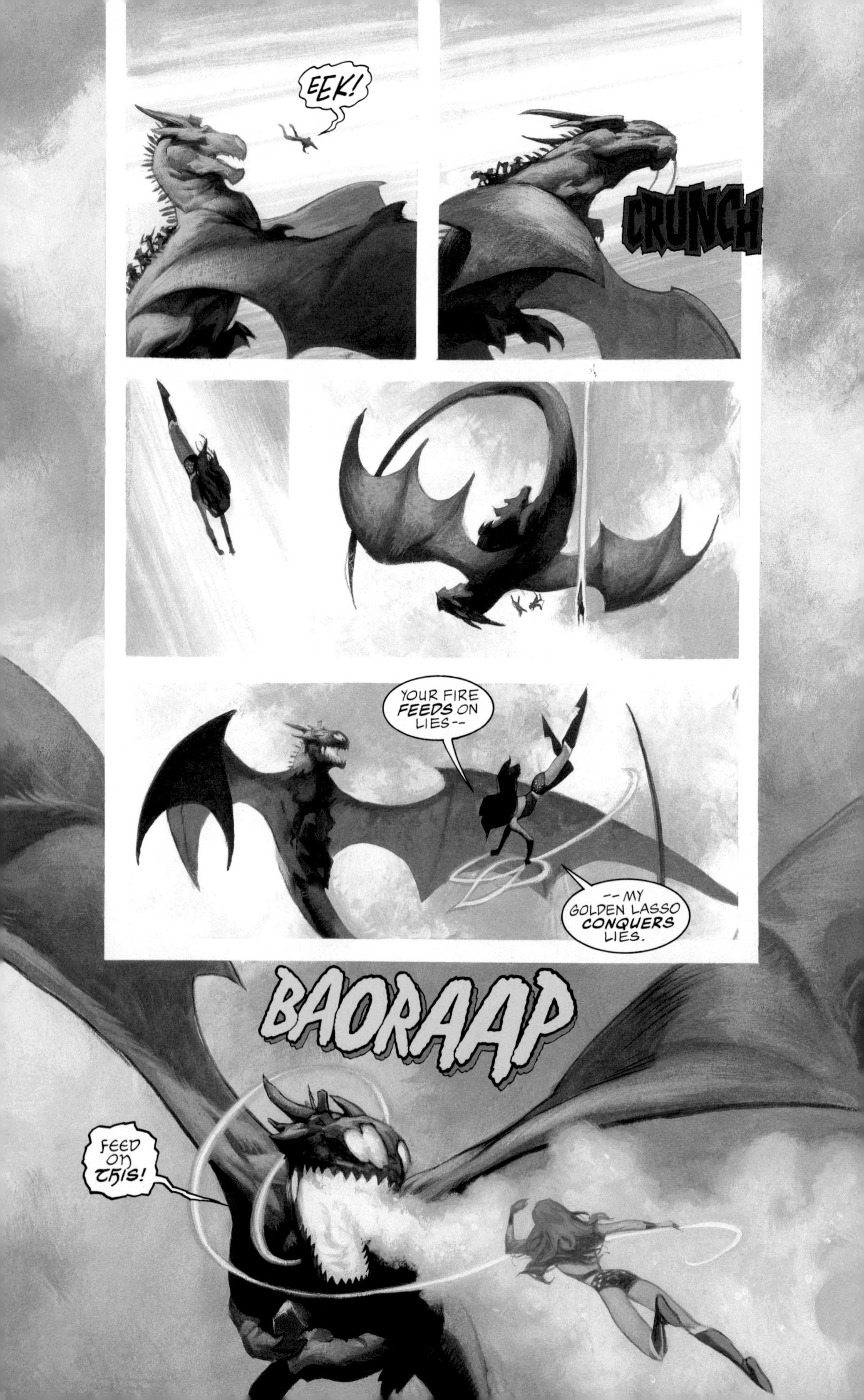
EEK!
CRUNCH
YOUR FIRE FEEDS ON LIES--
--MY GOLDEN LASSO CONQUERS LIES.
BAORAAP
FEED ON THIS!

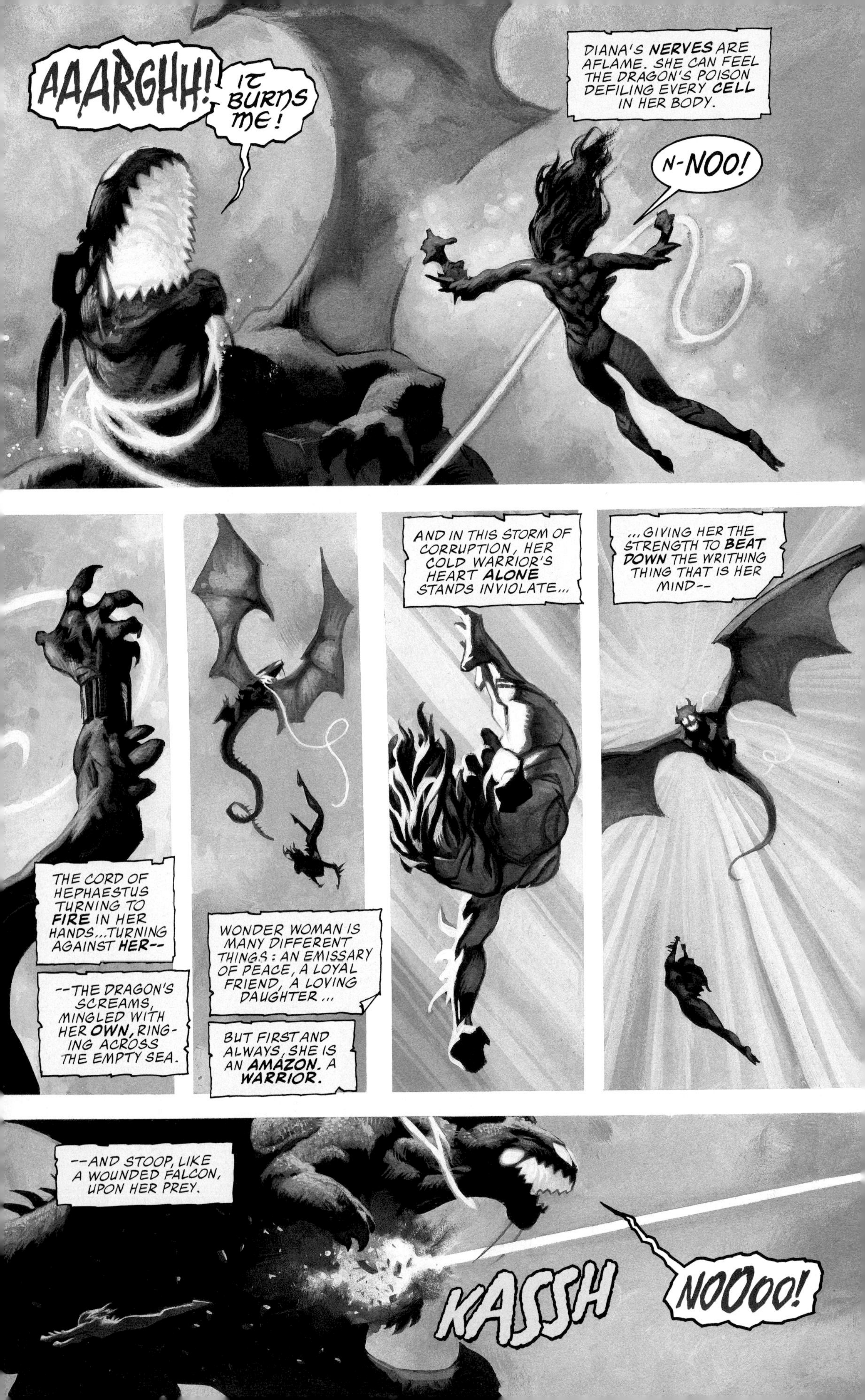

AAARGHH!
IT BURNS ME!
DIANA'S **NERVES** ARE AFLAME. SHE CAN FEEL THE DRAGON'S POISON DEFILING EVERY **CELL** IN HER BODY.
N-NOO!
THE CORD OF HEPHAESTUS TURNING TO **FIRE** IN HER HANDS...TURNING AGAINST **HER**--
--THE DRAGON'S SCREAMS, MINGLED WITH HER **OWN,** RING-ING ACROSS THE EMPTY SEA.
WONDER WOMAN IS MANY DIFFERENT THINGS: AN EMISSARY OF PEACE, A LOYAL FRIEND, A LOVING DAUGHTER...
BUT FIRST AND ALWAYS, SHE IS AN **AMAZON.** A **WARRIOR.**
AND IN THIS STORM OF CORRUPTION, HER COLD WARRIOR'S HEART **ALONE** STANDS INVIOLATE...
...GIVING HER THE STRENGTH TO **BEAT DOWN** THE WRITHING THING THAT IS HER MIND--
--AND STOOP, LIKE A WOUNDED FALCON, UPON HER PREY.
KASSH
NOOOO!

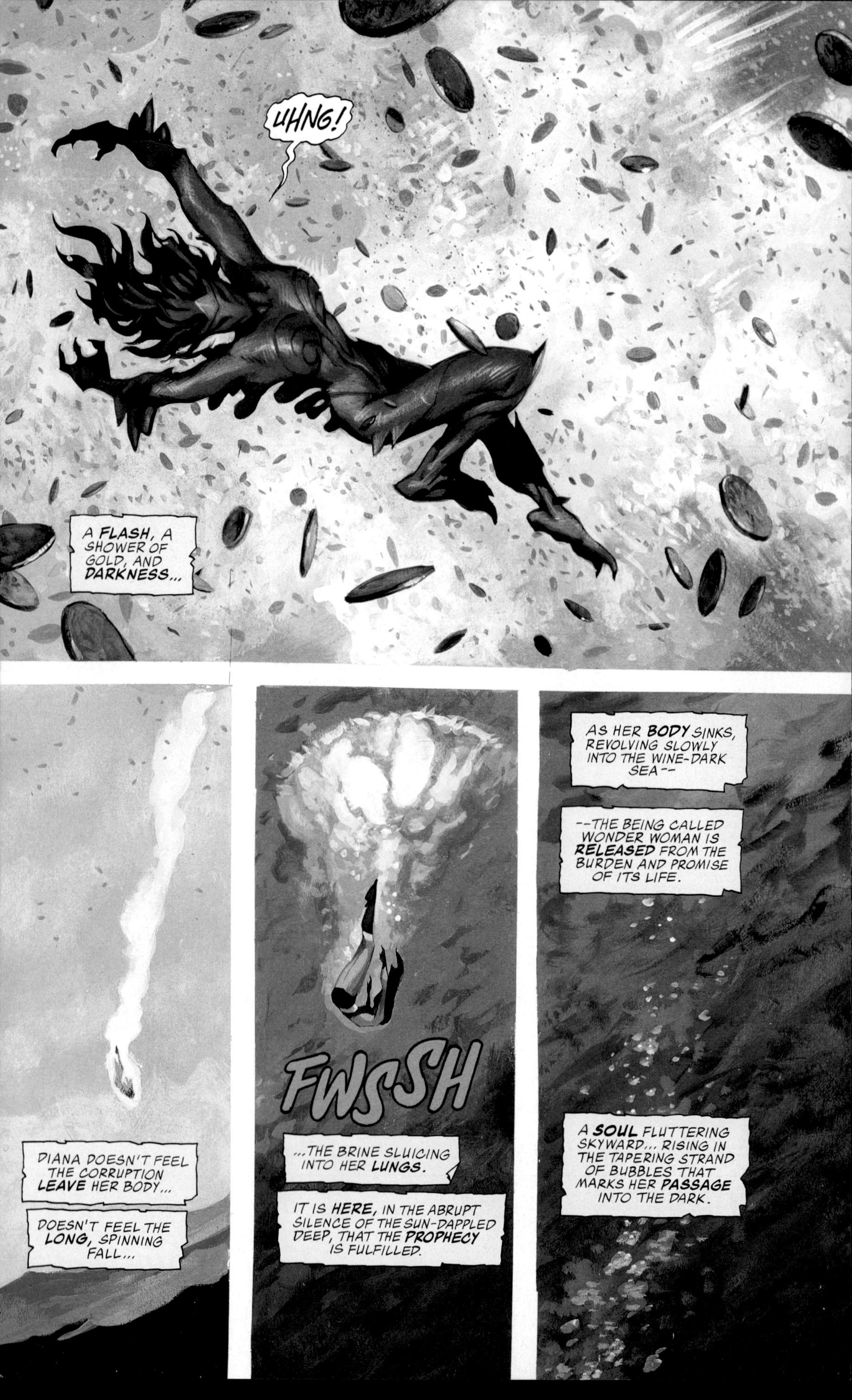
UHNG!
A FLASH, A SHOWER OF GOLD, AND DARKNESS...
DIANA DOESN'T FEEL THE CORRUPTION LEAVE HER BODY...
DOESN'T FEEL THE LONG, SPINNING FALL...
FWSSH
...THE BRINE SLUICING INTO HER LUNGS.
IT IS HERE, IN THE ABRUPT SILENCE OF THE SUN-DAPPLED DEEP, THAT THE PROPHECY IS FULFILLED.
AS HER BODY SINKS, REVOLVING SLOWLY INTO THE WINE-DARK SEA--
--THE BEING CALLED WONDER WOMAN IS RELEASED FROM THE BURDEN AND PROMISE OF ITS LIFE.
A SOUL FLUTTERING SKYWARD... RISING IN THE TAPERING STRAND OF BUBBLES THAT MARKS HER PASSAGE INTO THE DARK.

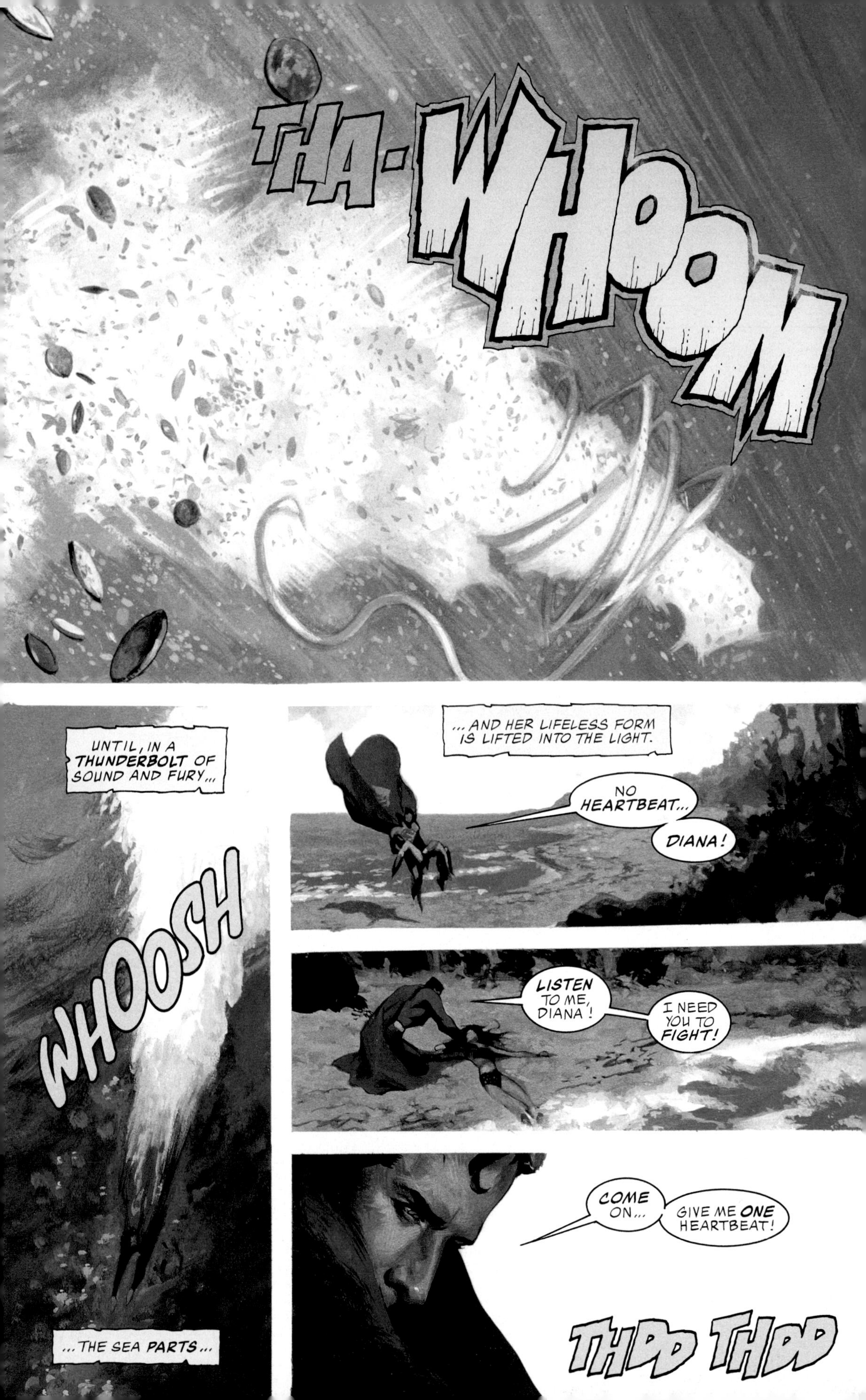
THA-WHOOOM
UNTIL, IN A THUNDERBOLT OF SOUND AND FURY...
WHOOSH
...THE SEA PARTS...
...AND HER LIFELESS FORM IS LIFTED INTO THE LIGHT.
NO HEARTBEAT...
DIANA!
LISTEN TO ME, DIANA!
I NEED YOU TO FIGHT!
COME ON...
GIVE ME ONE HEARTBEAT!
THDD THDD

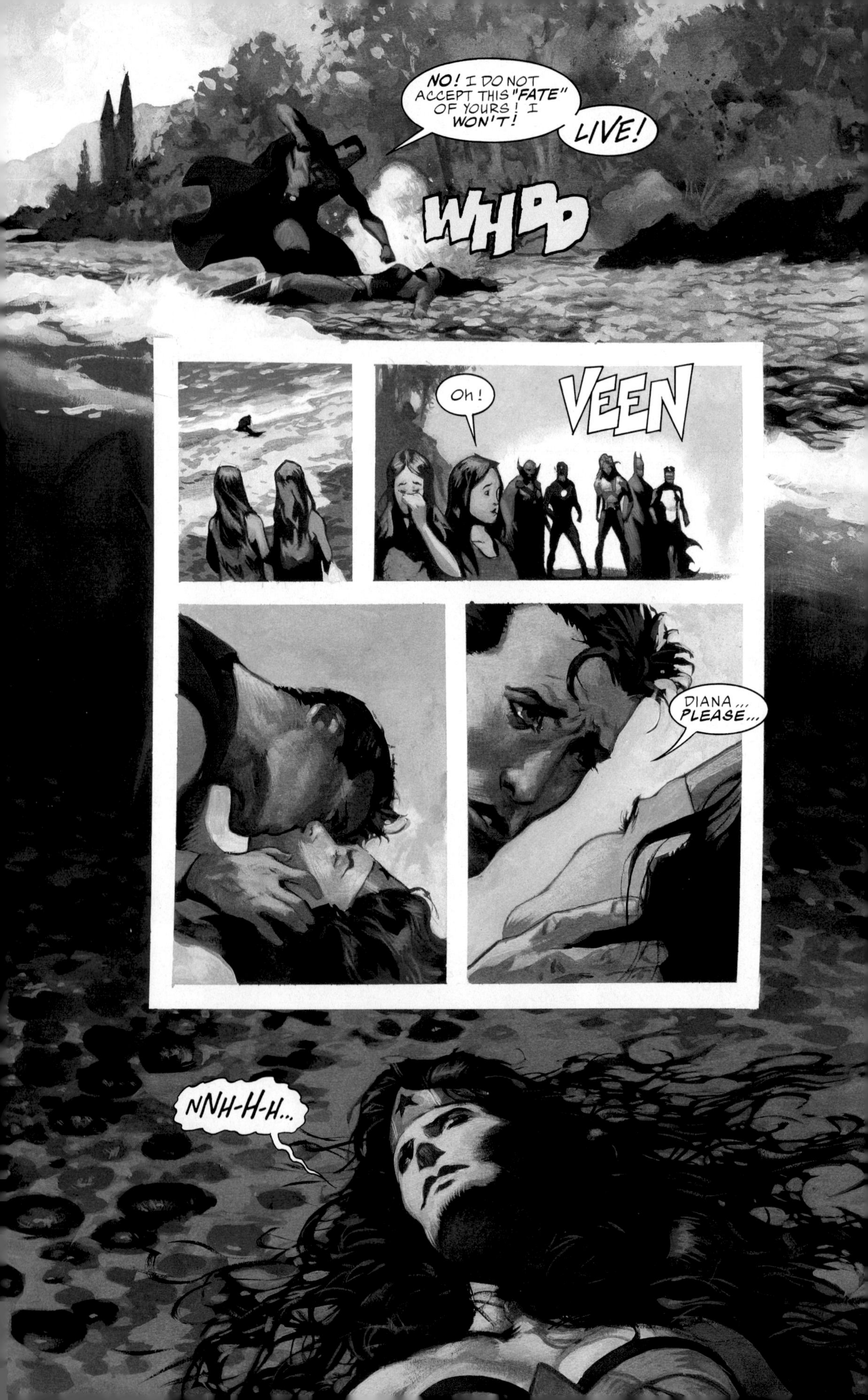
NO! I DO NOT ACCEPT THIS "FATE" OF YOURS! I WON'T!
LIVE!
WHDD
Oh!
VEEN
DIANA... PLEASE...
NNH-H-H...

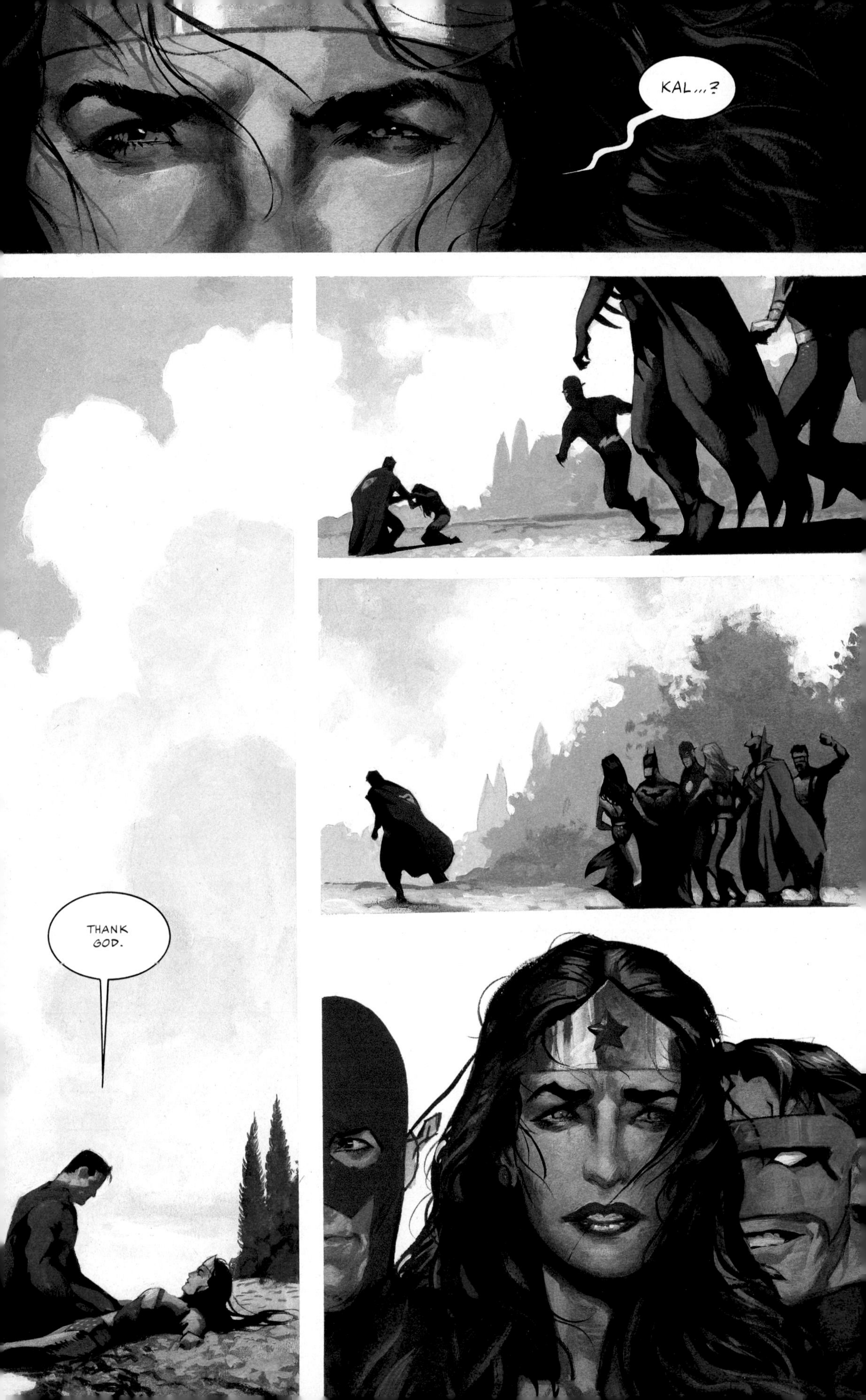
KAL...?
THANK GOD.

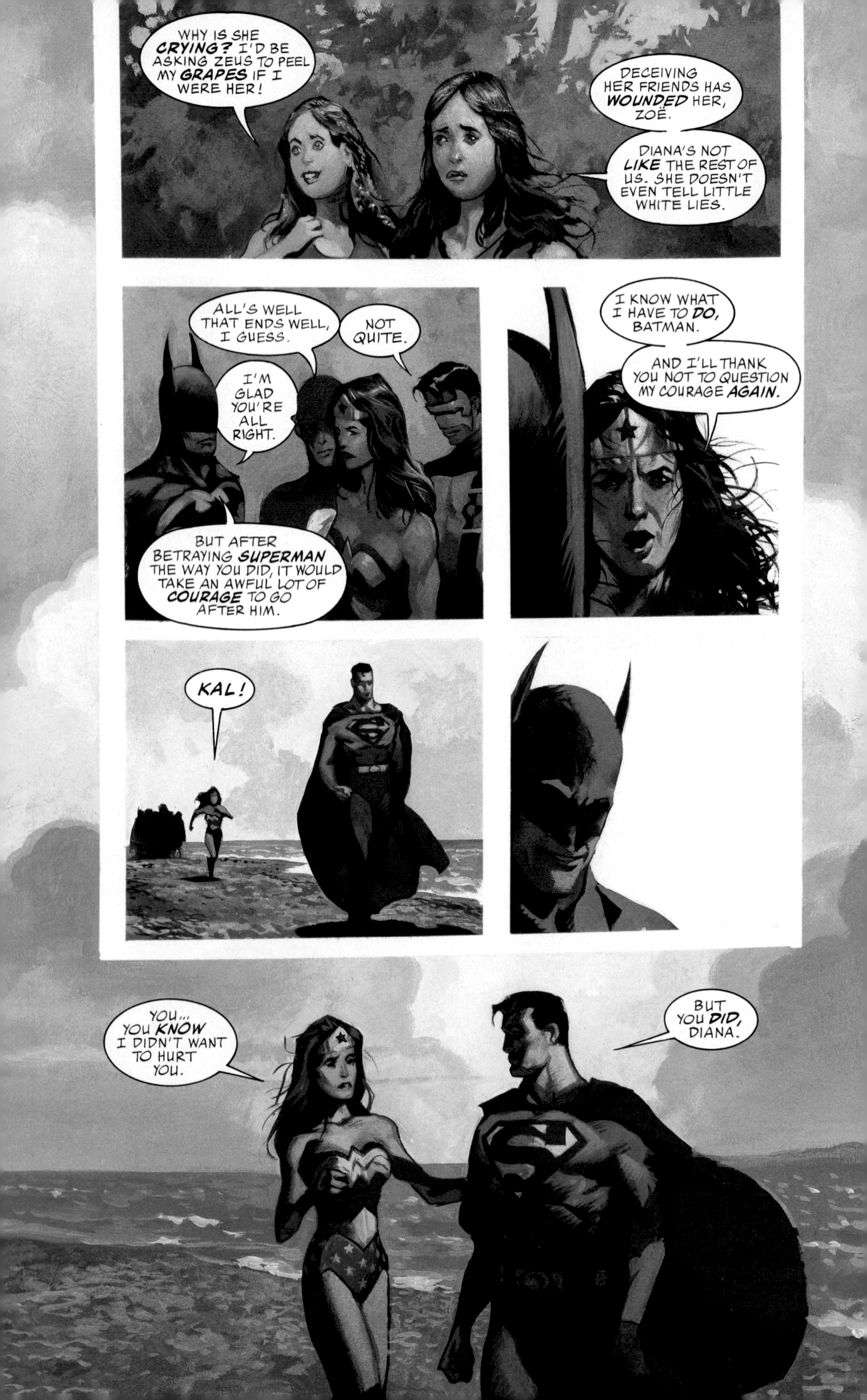

WHY IS SHE CRYING? I'D BE ASKING ZEUS TO PEEL MY GRAPES IF I WERE HER!
DECEIVING HER FRIENDS HAS WOUNDED HER, ZOË.
DIANA'S NOT LIKE THE REST OF US. SHE DOESN'T EVEN TELL LITTLE WHITE LIES.
ALL'S WELL THAT ENDS WELL, I GUESS.
NOT QUITE.
I'M GLAD YOU'RE ALL RIGHT.
BUT AFTER BETRAYING SUPERMAN THE WAY YOU DID, IT WOULD TAKE AN AWFUL LOT OF COURAGE TO GO AFTER HIM.
I KNOW WHAT I HAVE TO DO, BATMAN.
AND I'LL THANK YOU NOT TO QUESTION MY COURAGE AGAIN.
KAL!
YOU... YOU KNOW I DIDN'T WANT TO HURT YOU.
BUT YOU DID, DIANA.

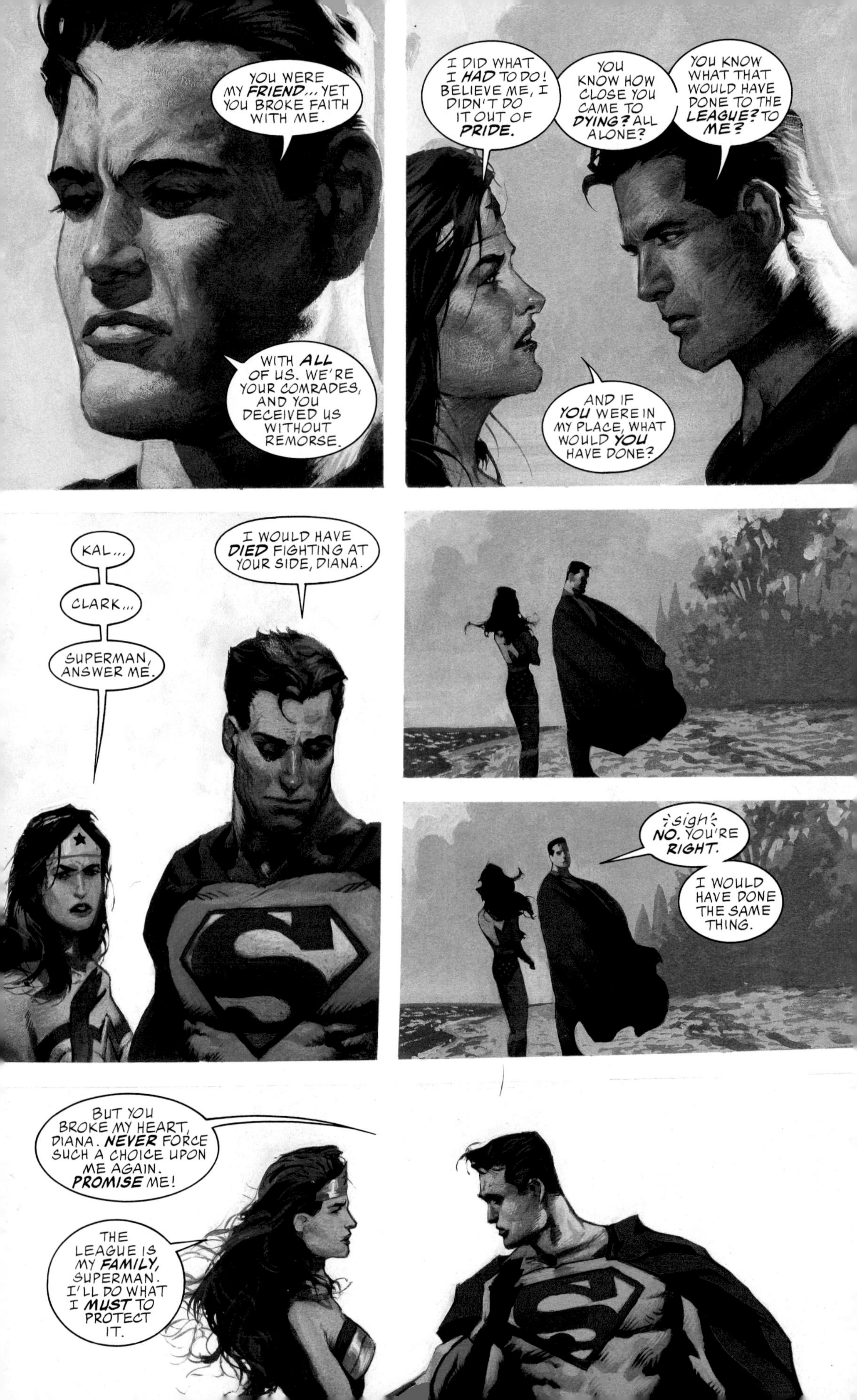
YOU WERE MY FRIEND... YET YOU BROKE FAITH WITH ME.
WITH ALL OF US. WE'RE YOUR COMRADES, AND YOU DECEIVED US WITHOUT REMORSE.
I DID WHAT I HAD TO DO! BELIEVE ME, I DIDN'T DO IT OUT OF PRIDE.
YOU KNOW HOW CLOSE YOU CAME TO DYING? ALL ALONE?
YOU KNOW WHAT THAT WOULD HAVE DONE TO THE LEAGUE? TO ME?
AND IF YOU WERE IN MY PLACE, WHAT WOULD YOU HAVE DONE?
KAL...
CLARK...
SUPERMAN, ANSWER ME.
I WOULD HAVE DIED FIGHTING AT YOUR SIDE, DIANA.
sigh NO. YOU'RE RIGHT.
I WOULD HAVE DONE THE SAME THING.
BUT YOU BROKE MY HEART, DIANA. NEVER FORCE SUCH A CHOICE UPON ME AGAIN. PROMISE ME!
THE LEAGUE IS MY FAMILY, SUPERMAN. I'LL DO WHAT I MUST TO PROTECT IT.

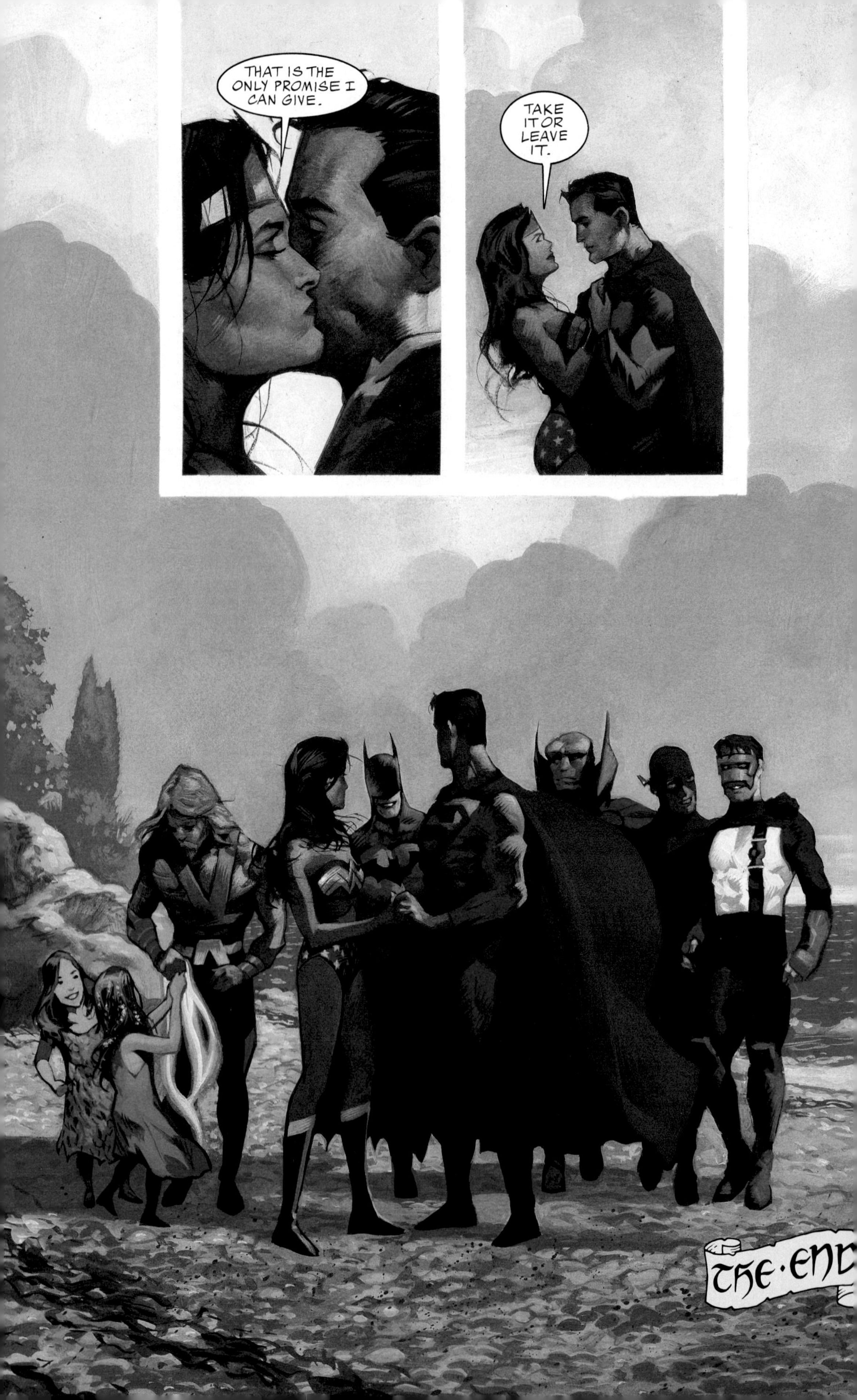
THAT IS THE ONLY PROMISE I CAN GIVE.
TAKE IT OR LEAVE IT.
THE·END

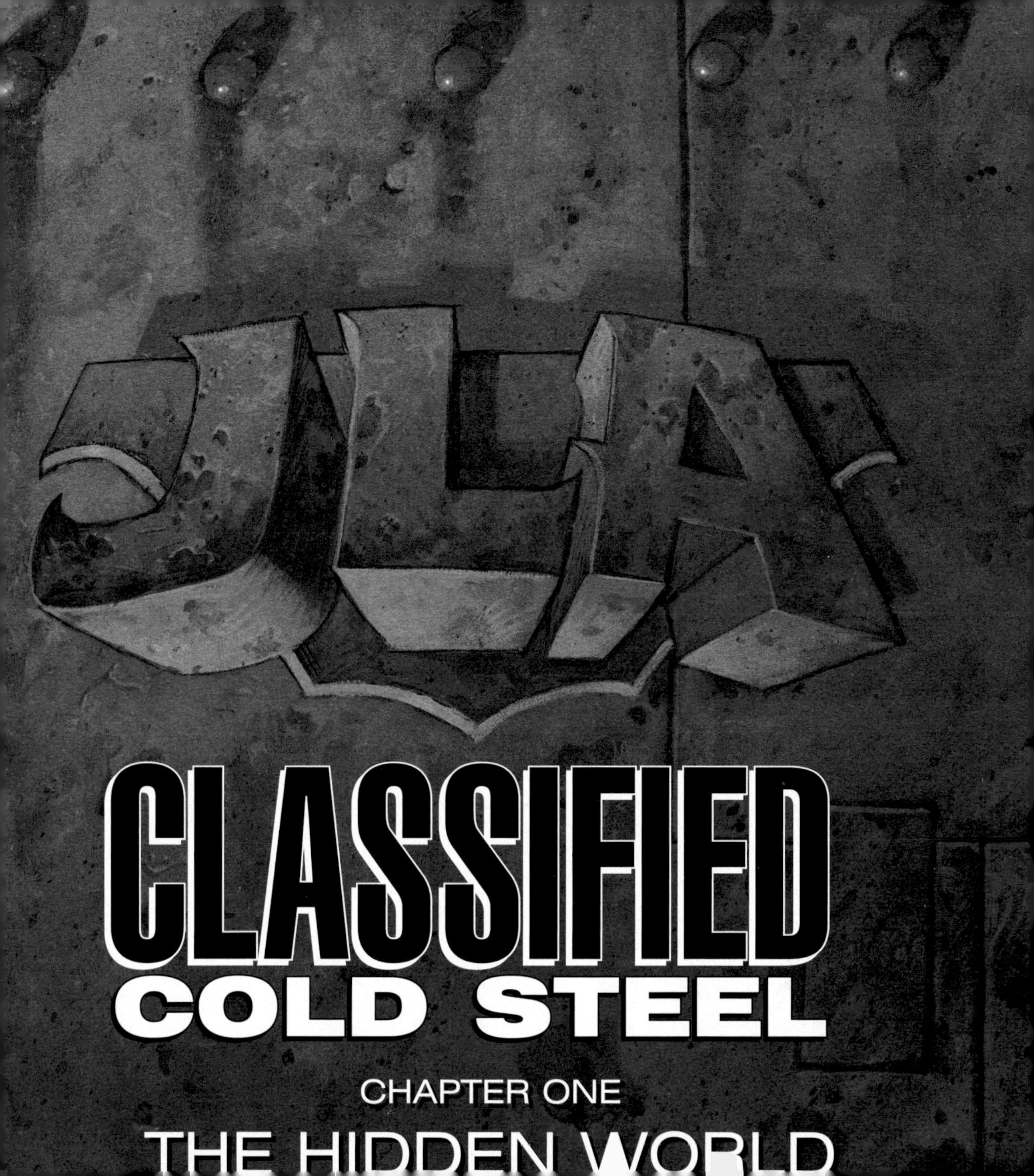
JLA
CLASSIFIED
COLD STEEL
CHAPTER ONE
THE HIDDEN WORLD

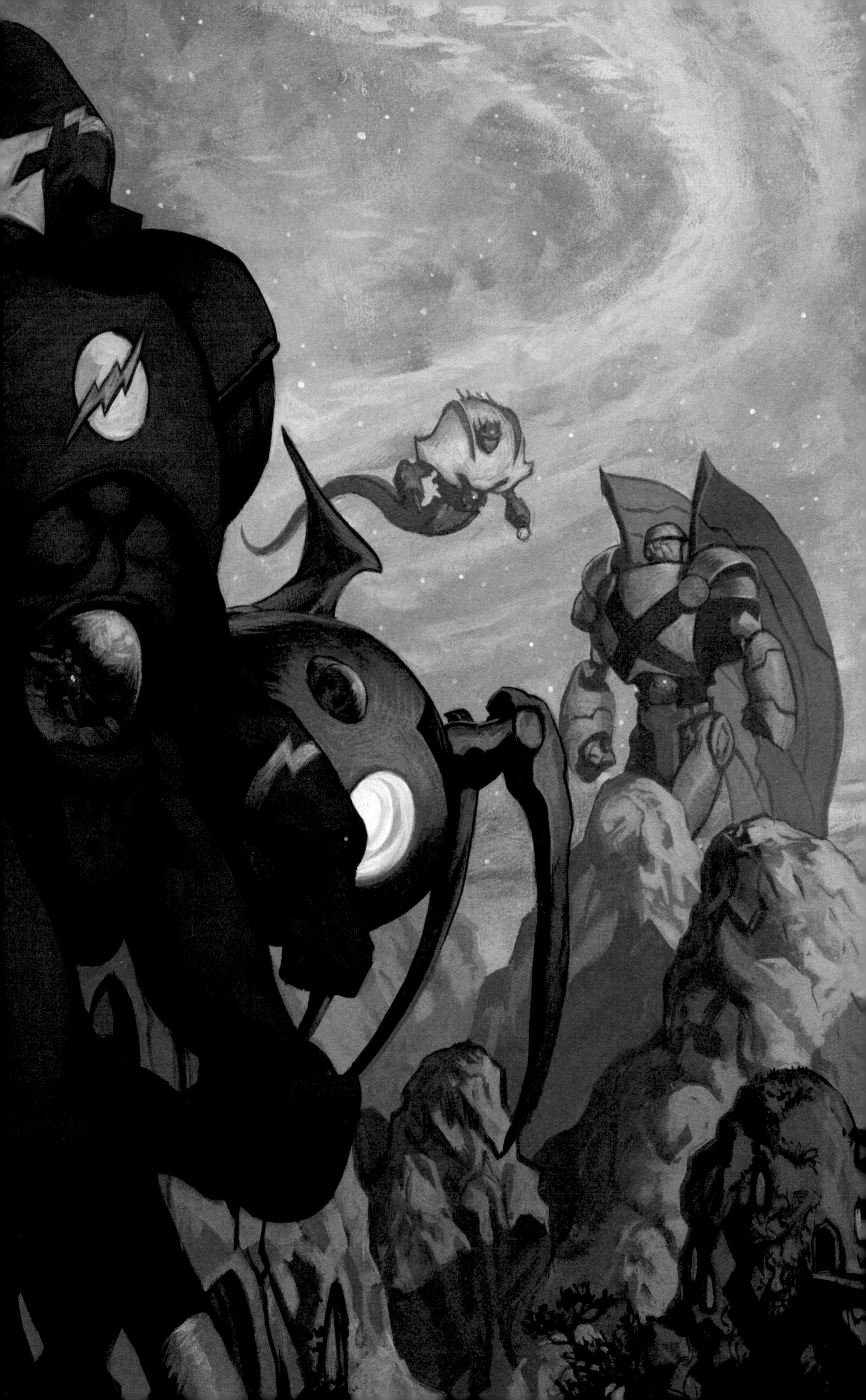

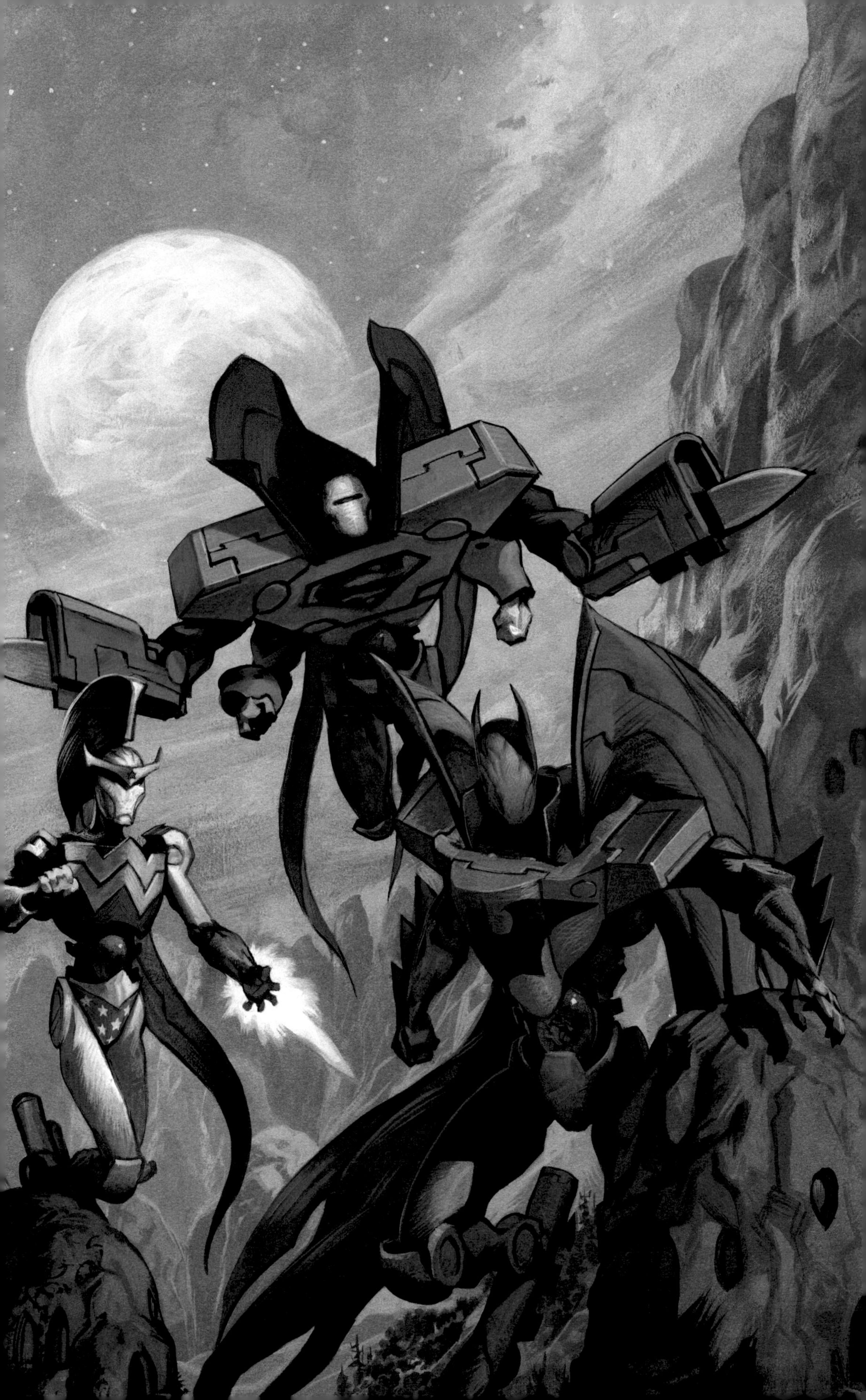

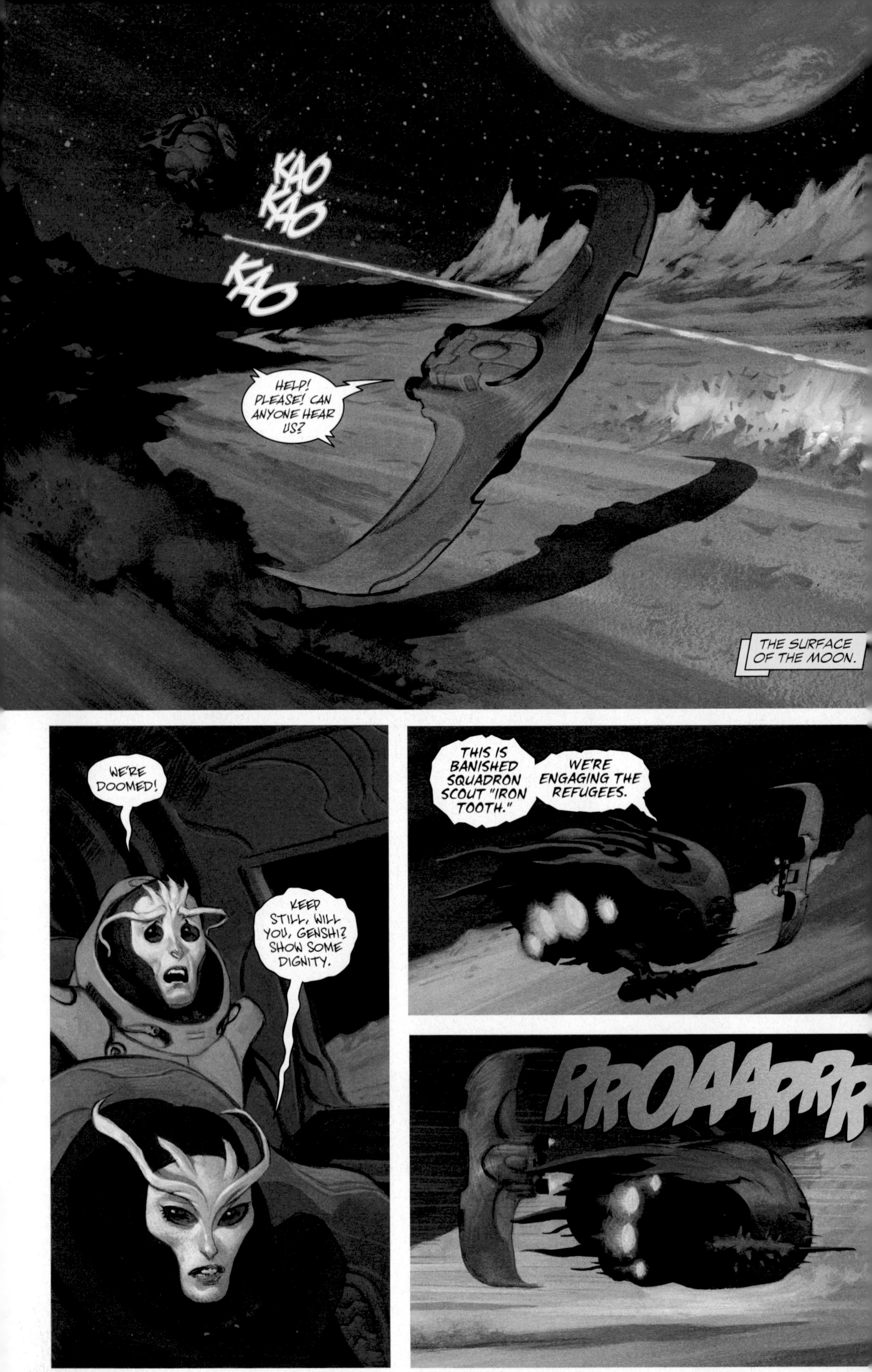
KAO
KAO
KAO
HELP! PLEASE! CAN ANYONE HEAR US?
THE SURFACE OF THE MOON.
WE'RE DOOMED!
KEEP STILL, WILL YOU, GENSHI? SHOW SOME DIGNITY.
THIS IS BANISHED SQUADRON SCOUT "IRON TOOTH."
WE'RE ENGAGING THE REFUGEES.
RROAARRR

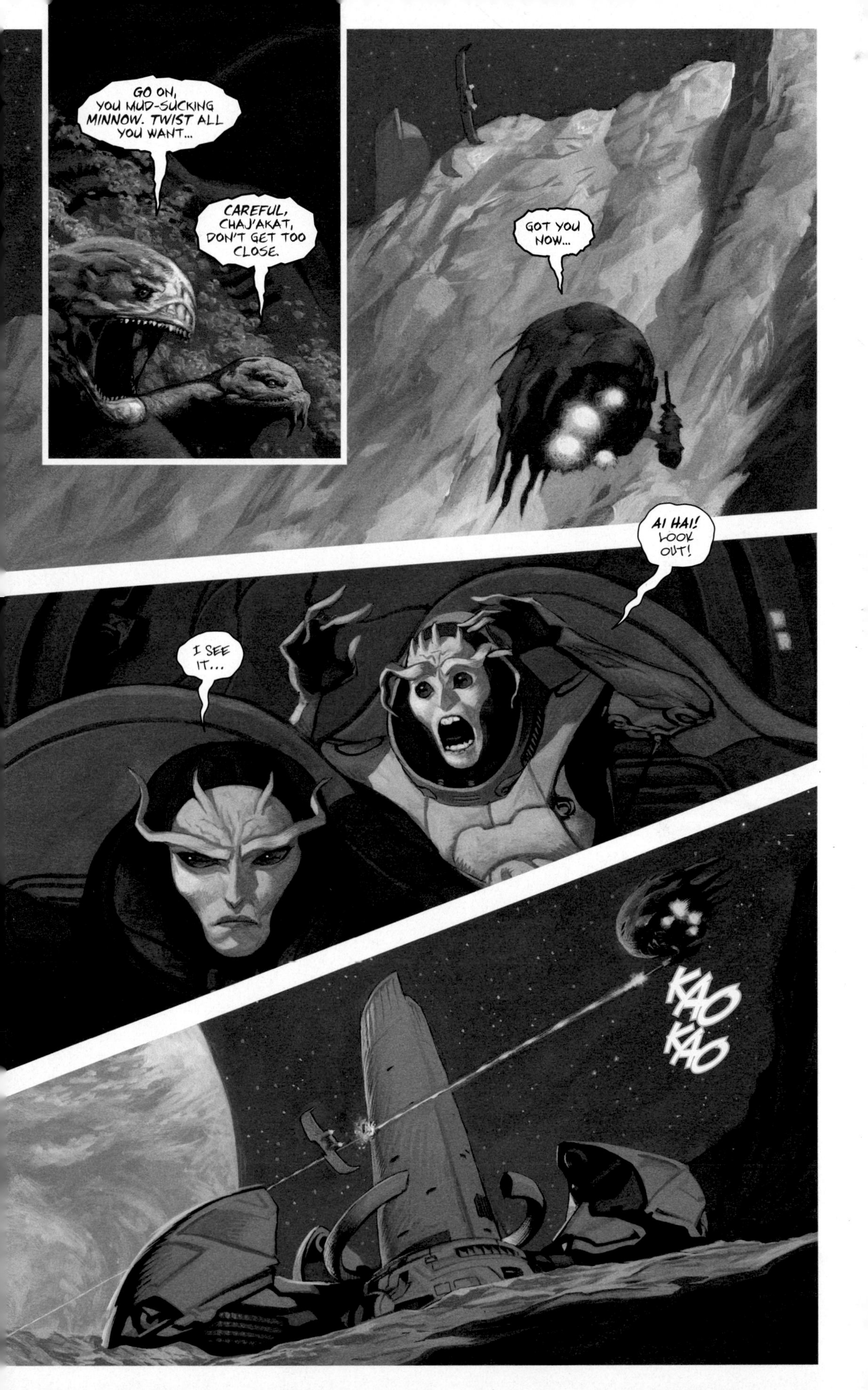
GO ON, YOU MUD-SUCKING MINNOW. TWIST ALL YOU WANT...
CAREFUL, CHAJ'AKAT, DON'T GET TOO CLOSE.
GOT YOU NOW...
AI HAI! LOOK OUT!
I SEE IT...
KAO KAO

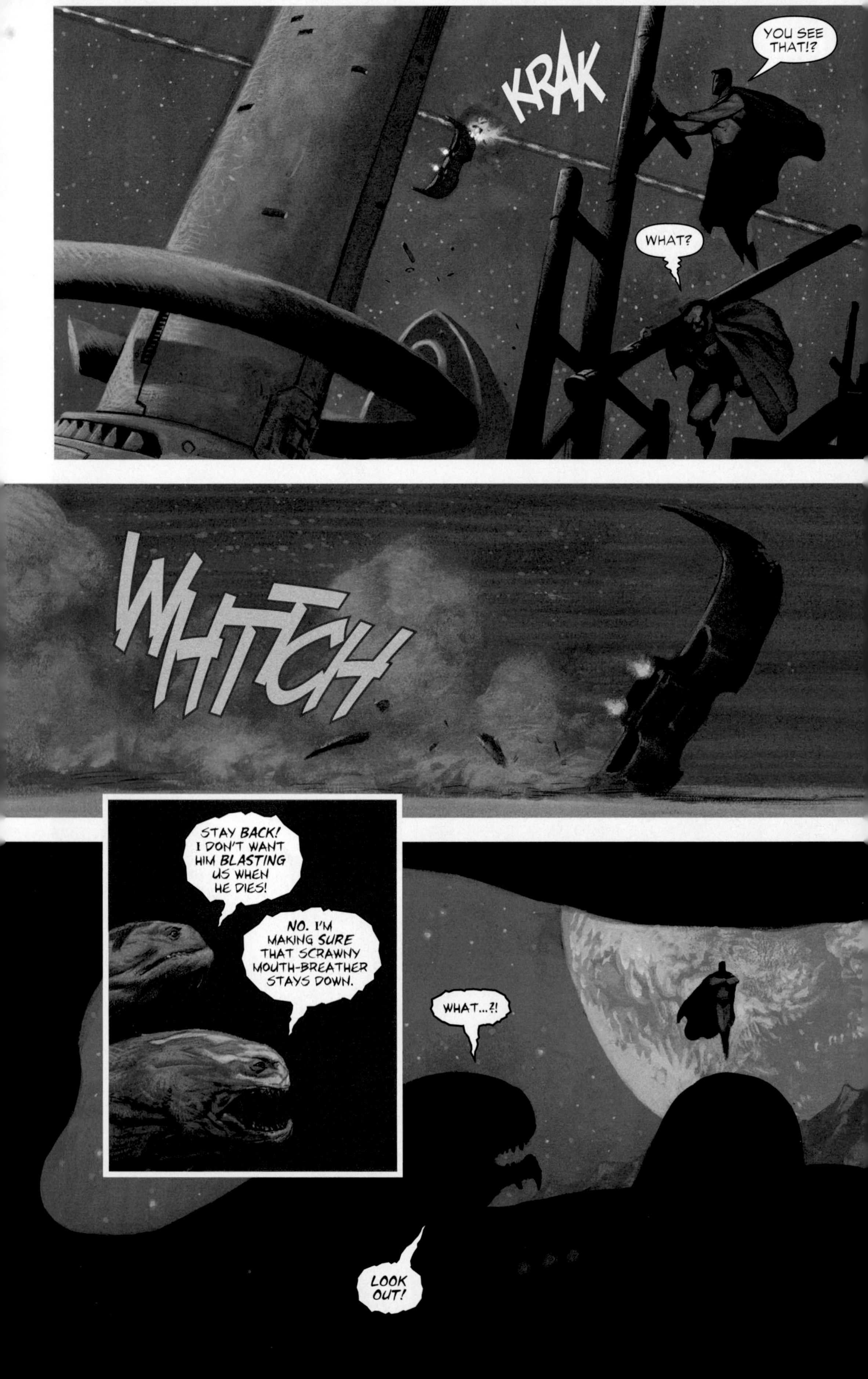
KRAK
YOU SEE THAT!?
WHAT?
WHITCH
STAY BACK! I DON'T WANT HIM BLASTING US WHEN HE DIES!
NO. I'M MAKING SURE THAT SCRAWNY MOUTH-BREATHER STAYS DOWN.
WHAT...?!
LOOK OUT!

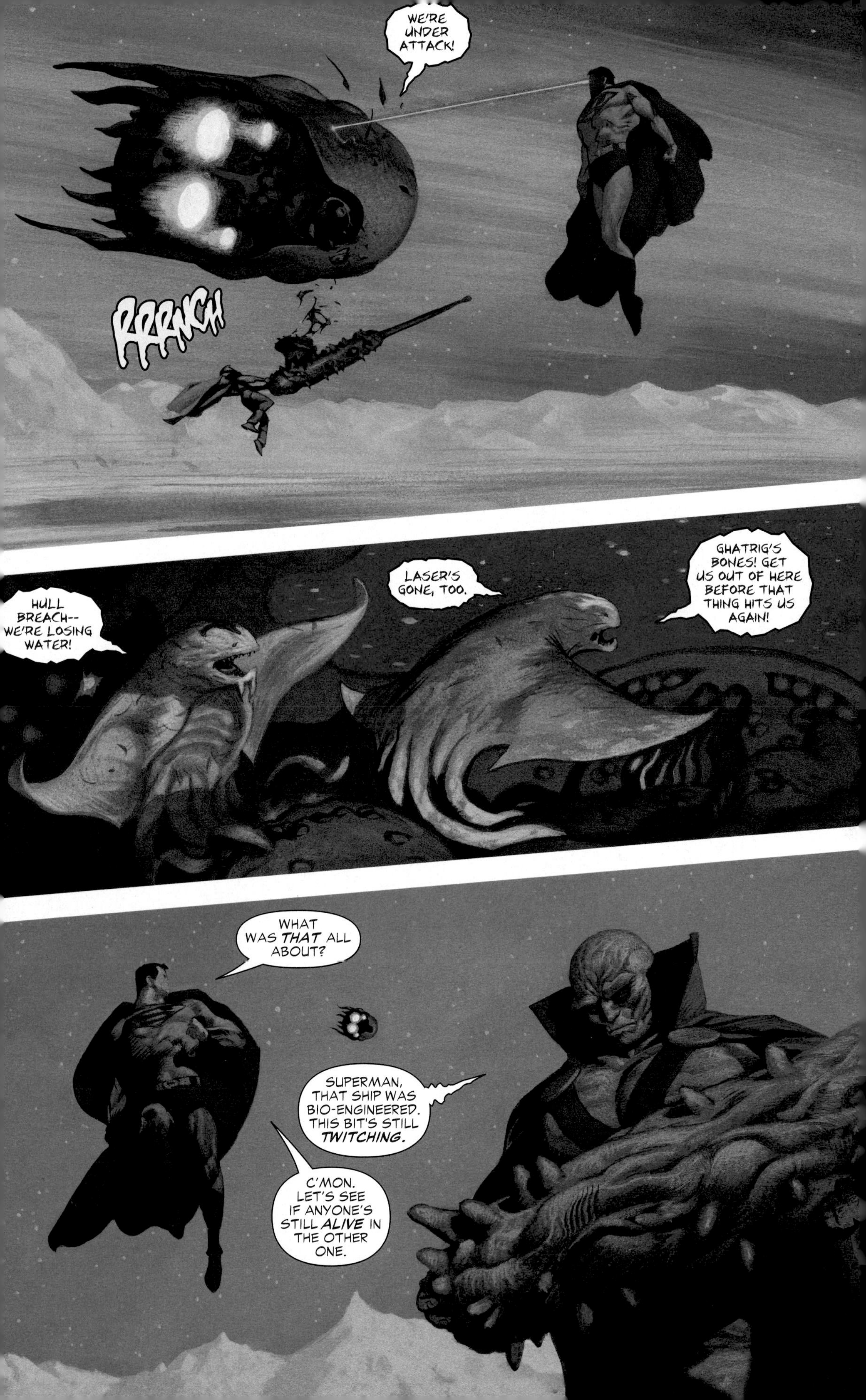
WE'RE UNDER ATTACK!
RRRNCH
HULL BREACH-- WE'RE LOSING WATER!
LASER'S GONE, TOO.
GHATRIG'S BONES! GET US OUT OF HERE BEFORE THAT THING HITS US AGAIN!
WHAT WAS THAT ALL ABOUT?
SUPERMAN, THAT SHIP WAS BIO-ENGINEERED. THIS BIT'S STILL TWITCHING.
C'MON. LET'S SEE IF ANYONE'S STILL ALIVE IN THE OTHER ONE.

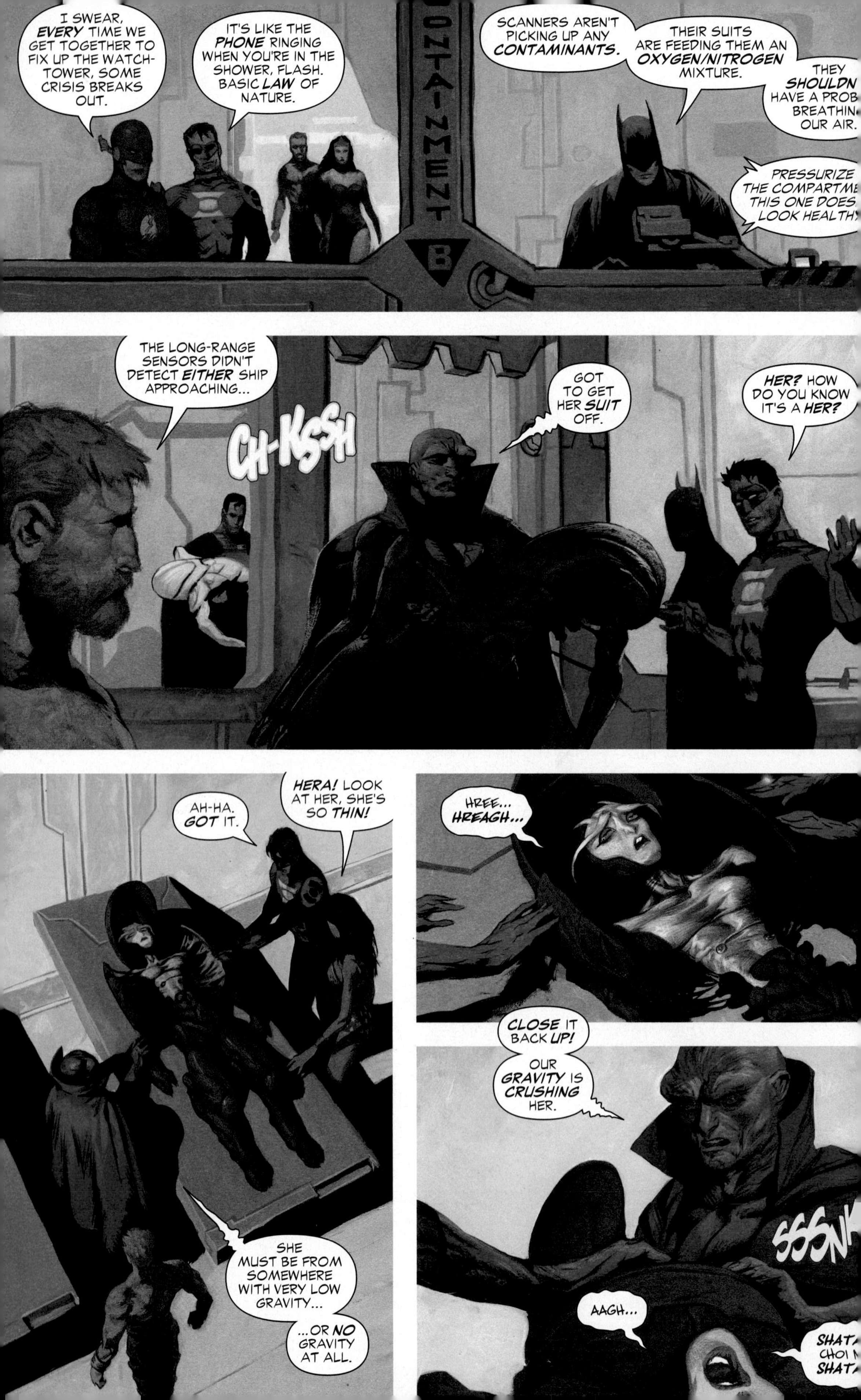
I SWEAR, EVERY TIME WE GET TOGETHER TO FIX UP THE WATCH-TOWER, SOME CRISIS BREAKS OUT.
IT'S LIKE THE PHONE RINGING WHEN YOU'RE IN THE SHOWER, FLASH. BASIC LAW OF NATURE.
CONTAINMENT B
SCANNERS AREN'T PICKING UP ANY CONTAMINANTS.
THEIR SUITS ARE FEEDING THEM AN OXYGEN/NITROGEN MIXTURE.
THEY SHOULDN HAVE A PROB BREATHIN OUR AIR.
PRESSURIZE THE COMPARTME THIS ONE DOES LOOK HEALTHY
THE LONG-RANGE SENSORS DIDN'T DETECT EITHER SHIP APPROACHING...
CH-KSSH
GOT TO GET HER SUIT OFF.
HER? HOW DO YOU KNOW IT'S A HER?
AH-HA. GOT IT.
HERA! LOOK AT HER, SHE'S SO THIN!
SHE MUST BE FROM SOMEWHERE WITH VERY LOW GRAVITY...
...OR NO GRAVITY AT ALL.
HREE... HREAGH...
CLOSE IT BACK UP!
OUR GRAVITY IS CRUSHING HER.
SSSNK
AAGH...

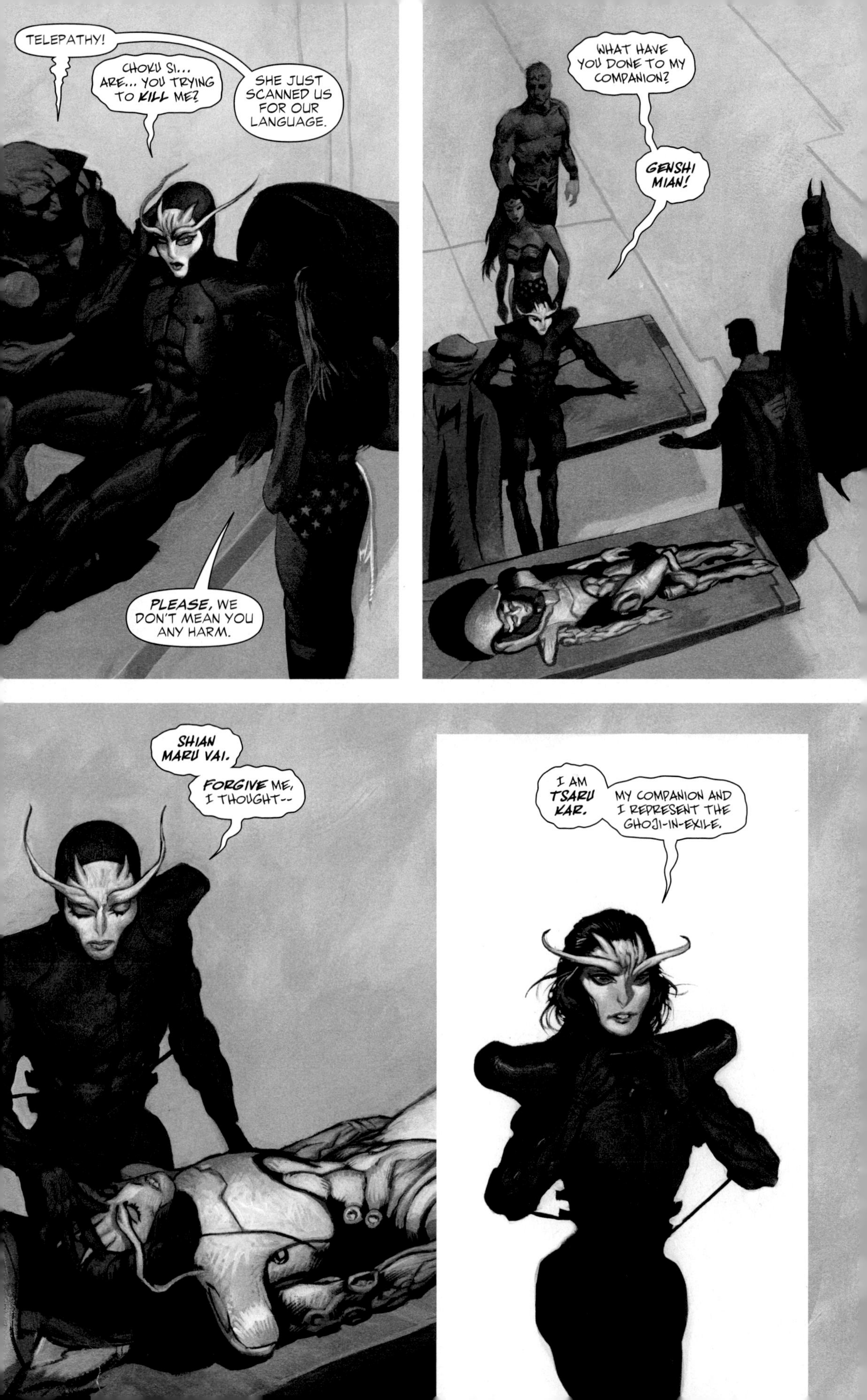
TELEPATHY!
CHOKU SI... ARE... YOU TRYING TO KILL ME?
SHE JUST SCANNED US FOR OUR LANGUAGE.
PLEASE, WE DON'T MEAN YOU ANY HARM.
WHAT HAVE YOU DONE TO MY COMPANION?
GENSHI MIAN!
SHIAN MARU VAI.
FORGIVE ME, I THOUGHT--
I AM TSARU KAR.
MY COMPANION AND I REPRESENT THE GHOJI-IN-EXILE.

WATER-BREATHING **FILTH**?

I DON'T SUPPOSE Y PROVOKE THEM... MA WAR ON THEM...

LET ME BE CLEAR. FOR **MY** PART, I DO NOT **WANT** YOUR HELP. I BELIEVE IN MY **OWN** PEOPLE.

HOWEVER, I REQUEST YOUR AID IN COUNCILMAN **GENSHI MIAN'S** NAME. HE ORGANIZED THIS EXPEDITION.

FAIR ENOUGH. WHY DOES YOUR **FRIEND** WANT OUR HELP?

BECAUSE OF THE **VORUK**--

--THE WATER-BREATHING **FILTH** THAT WRECKED MY CRUISER.

NEARLY A **GENERATION** AGO, THEIR WARSHIPS DESCENDED INTO OUR **OCEANS.** SUFFICE IT TO SAY, IT WAS NOT A DIPLOMATIC VISIT.

WE ARE A PEACEFUL, **CIVILIZED** PEOPLE, AQUAMAN. WE DO **NOT** "MAKE WAR."

"BUT, NEITHER DO WE **SUBMIT** TO OPPRESSION.

"WHEN THEIR GENETIC BEASTS ROSE FROM THE SEA, SEEKING SLAVES TO HELP BUILD THEIR COLONY, WE **RESISTED.**

"THEY **TORTURED** US, SET OUR CITIES ABLAZE. **THOUSANDS** DIED... FLAMI MARTYRS, REMEMBERED FOREVER IN SONG--

"--BUT THE VOR GOT NO **LABO** OUT OF US.

"THEN, AFTER THREE YEARS OF FIRE, MURDER AND BUTCHERY, THEY LEFT AS SUDDENLY AS THEY HAD ARRIVED.

"MANY OF US FLED ON STARSHIPS HIDDEN AWAY DURING THE INVASION, FEARING WORSE WAS TO COME.

"MINE WAS JUST LIFTING OFF WHEN IT ARRIVED. THEIR TERRIBLE WEAPON--

"--THE THING THEY NAMED 'INFINITY COIL'. MY WORLD'S DOOM.

"IT HUNG OVER US, THREATENING AND ENORMOUS, BEFORE WE SLIPPED PAST.

"THE BLAST CAME LATER. THE STRANGLING WAVE OF FORCE.

"AND PENUMBRA FROZE.

"SINCE THAT MOMENT, NOTHING HAS MOVED ON PENUMBRA. NOTHING AGED. NOTHING DIED.

"SOME OF US HAVE GONE BACK... TO DESTROY THE COIL. TO FREE OUR PEOPLE. ONE OF YOUR GREEN LANTERNS EVEN TRIED--

WHAT?

WHAT DID YOU SAY?

--SHE DIDN'T COME BACK. NO ONE HAS EVER COME BACK.

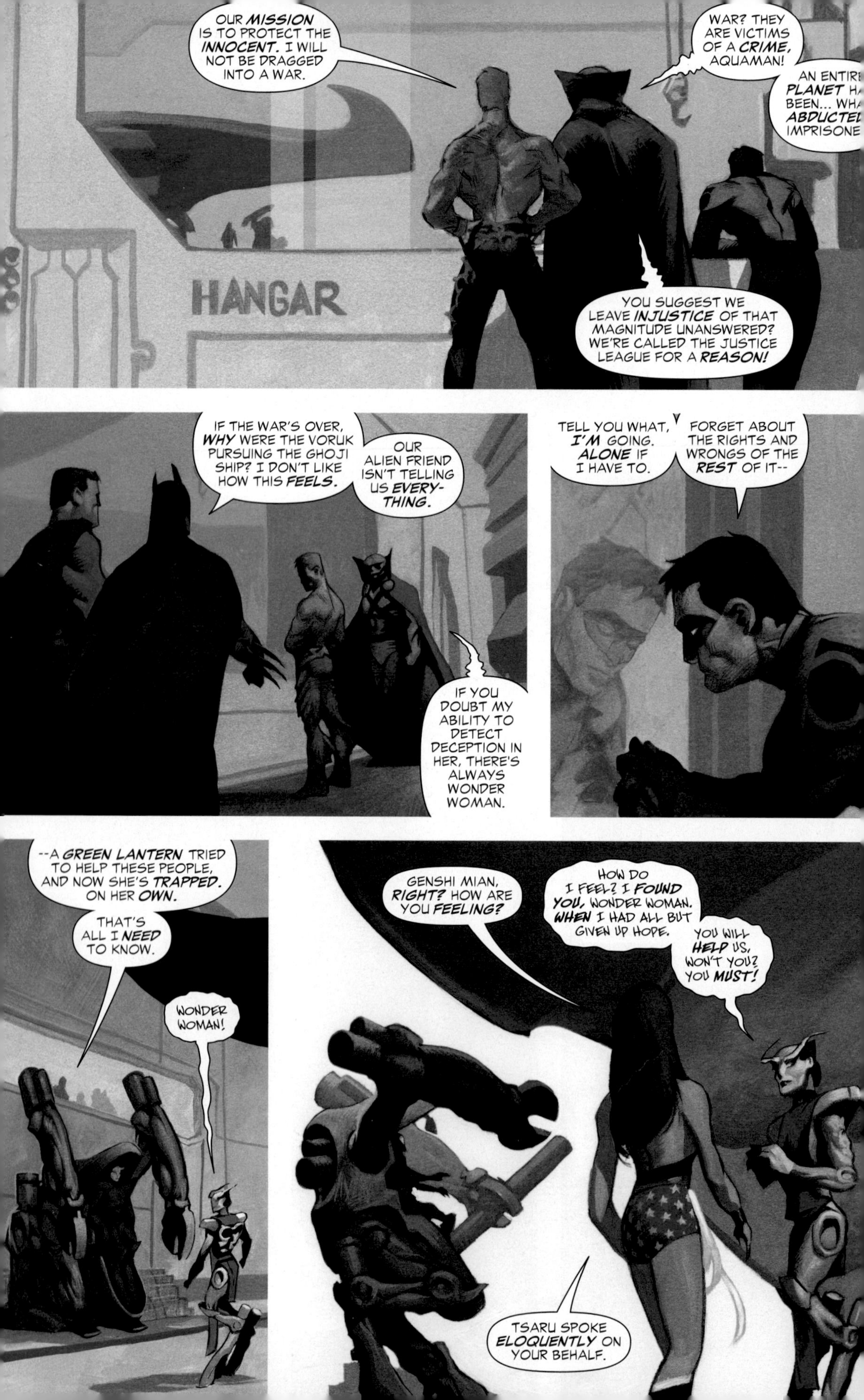
OUR MISSION IS TO PROTECT THE INNOCENT. I WILL NOT BE DRAGGED INTO A WAR.
WAR? THEY ARE VICTIMS OF A CRIME, AQUAMAN!
AN ENTIR PLANET HA BEEN... WHA ABDUCTEL IMPRISONE
HANGAR
YOU SUGGEST WE LEAVE INJUSTICE OF THAT MAGNITUDE UNANSWERED? WE'RE CALLED THE JUSTICE LEAGUE FOR A REASON!
IF THE WAR'S OVER, WHY WERE THE VORUK PURSUING THE GHOJI SHIP? I DON'T LIKE HOW THIS FEELS.
OUR ALIEN FRIEND ISN'T TELLING US EVERY-THING.
IF YOU DOUBT MY ABILITY TO DETECT DECEPTION IN HER, THERE'S ALWAYS WONDER WOMAN.
TELL YOU WHAT, I'M GOING. ALONE IF I HAVE TO.
FORGET ABOUT THE RIGHTS AND WRONGS OF THE REST OF IT--
--A GREEN LANTERN TRIED TO HELP THESE PEOPLE, AND NOW SHE'S TRAPPED. ON HER OWN.
THAT'S ALL I NEED TO KNOW.
WONDER WOMAN!
GENSHI MIAN, RIGHT? HOW ARE YOU FEELING?
HOW DO I FEEL? I FOUND YOU, WONDER WOMAN. WHEN I HAD ALL BUT GIVEN UP HOPE.
YOU WILL HELP US, WON'T YOU? YOU MUST!
TSARU SPOKE ELOQUENTLY ON YOUR BEHALF.

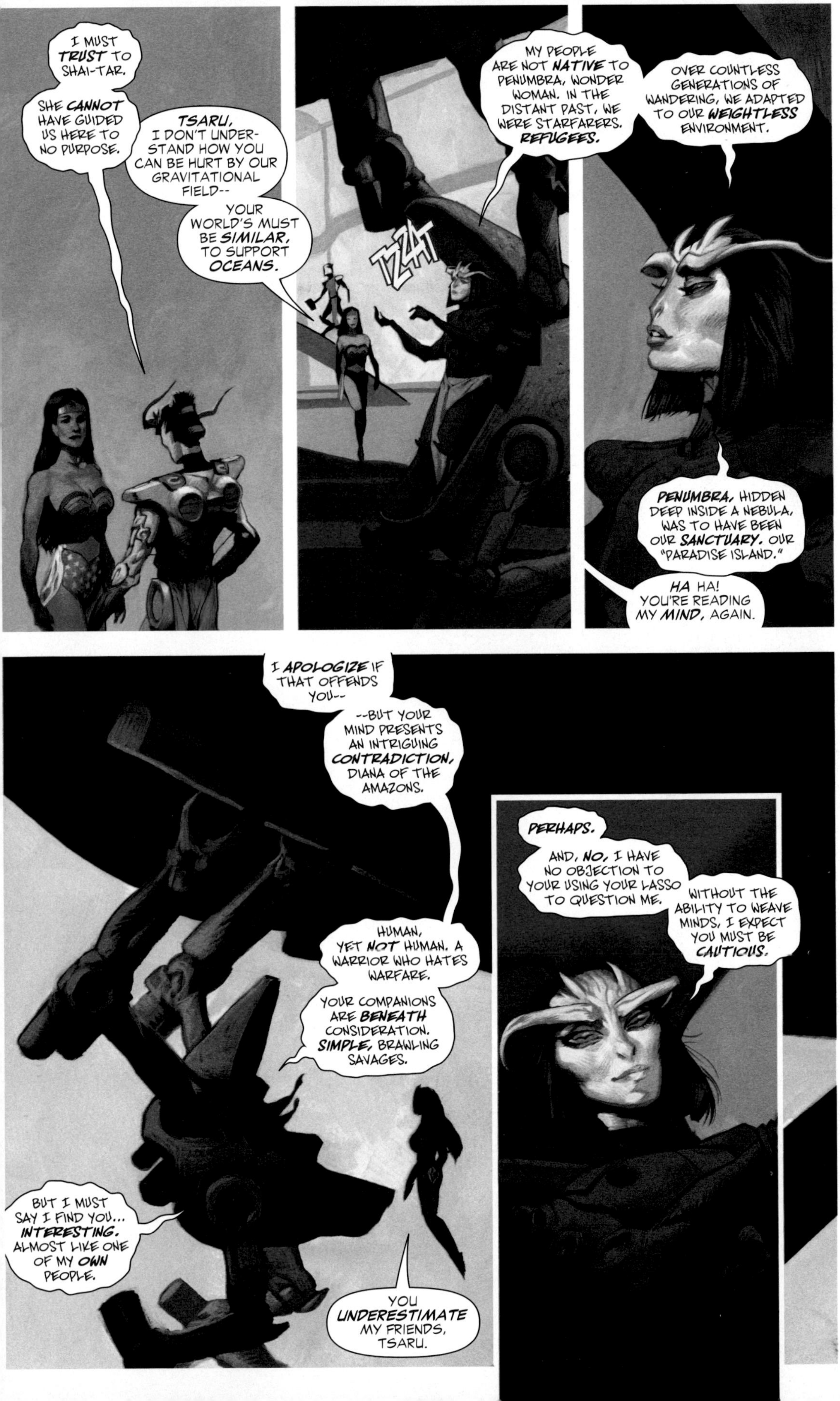
I MUST TRUST TO SHAI-TAR.
SHE CANNOT HAVE GUIDED US HERE TO NO PURPOSE.
TSARU, I DON'T UNDERSTAND HOW YOU CAN BE HURT BY OUR GRAVITATIONAL FIELD--
YOUR WORLD'S MUST BE SIMILAR, TO SUPPORT OCEANS.
MY PEOPLE ARE NOT NATIVE TO PENUMBRA, WONDER WOMAN. IN THE DISTANT PAST, WE WERE STARFARERS. REFUGEES.
TZZAT
OVER COUNTLESS GENERATIONS OF WANDERING, WE ADAPTED TO OUR WEIGHTLESS ENVIRONMENT.
PENUMBRA, HIDDEN DEEP INSIDE A NEBULA, WAS TO HAVE BEEN OUR SANCTUARY. OUR "PARADISE ISLAND."
HA HA! YOU'RE READING MY MIND, AGAIN.
I APOLOGIZE IF THAT OFFENDS YOU--
--BUT YOUR MIND PRESENTS AN INTRIGUING CONTRADICTION, DIANA OF THE AMAZONS.
HUMAN, YET NOT HUMAN. A WARRIOR WHO HATES WARFARE.
YOUR COMPANIONS ARE BENEATH CONSIDERATION. SIMPLE, BRAWLING SAVAGES.
BUT I MUST SAY I FIND YOU... INTERESTING. ALMOST LIKE ONE OF MY OWN PEOPLE.
YOU UNDERESTIMATE MY FRIENDS, TSARU.
PERHAPS.
AND, NO, I HAVE NO OBJECTION TO YOUR USING YOUR LASSO TO QUESTION ME.
WITHOUT THE ABILITY TO WEAVE MINDS, I EXPECT YOU MUST BE CAUTIOUS.

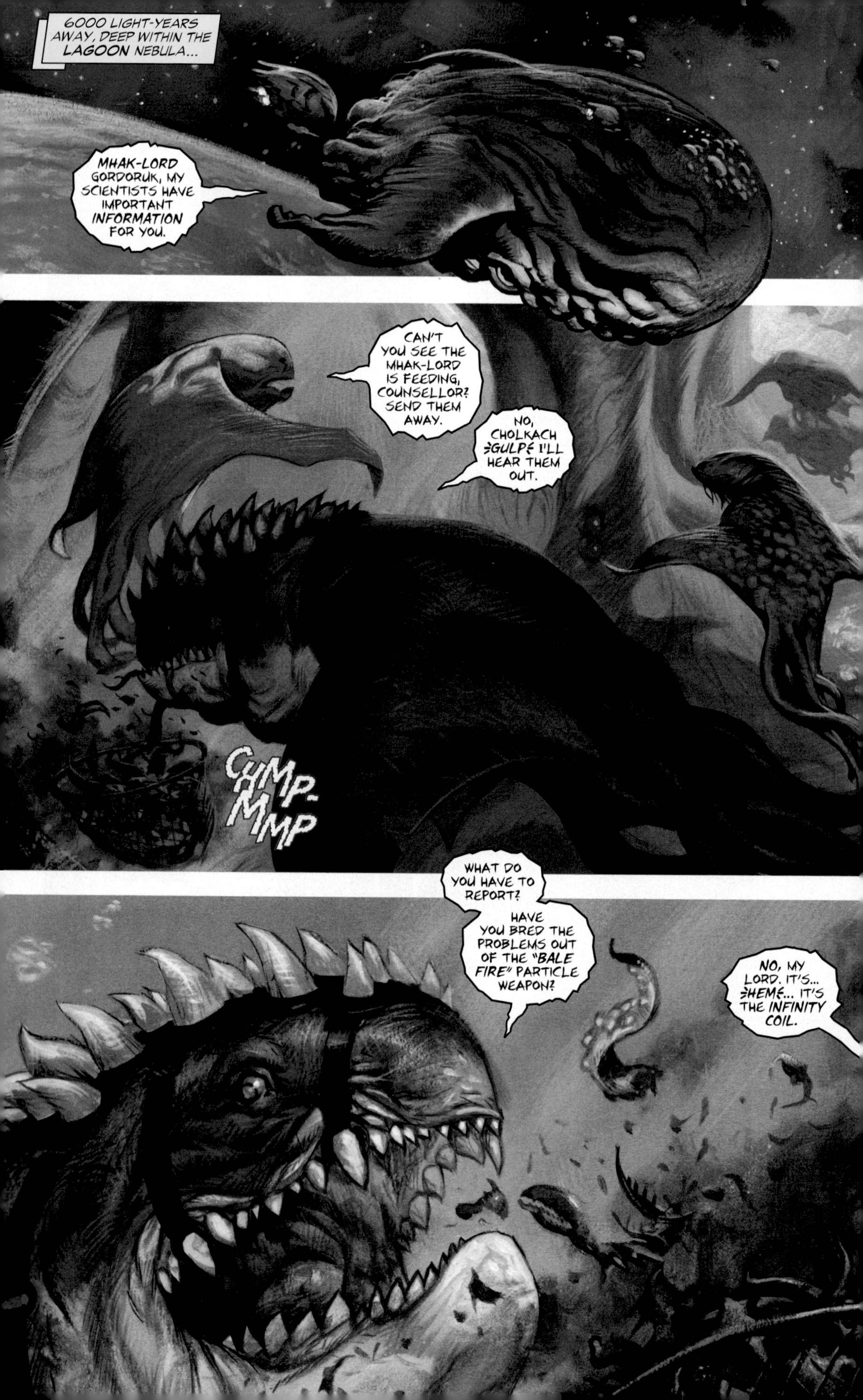
6000 LIGHT-YEARS AWAY, DEEP WITHIN THE LAGOON NEBULA...
MHAK-LORD GORDORUK, MY SCIENTISTS HAVE IMPORTANT INFORMATION FOR YOU.
CAN'T YOU SEE THE MHAK-LORD IS FEEDING, COUNSELLOR? SEND THEM AWAY.
NO, CHOLKACH *GULP* I'LL HEAR THEM OUT.
CHMP-MMP
WHAT DO YOU HAVE TO REPORT?
HAVE YOU BRED THE PROBLEMS OUT OF THE "BALE FIRE" PARTICLE WEAPON?
NO, MY LORD. IT'S... *HEM*... IT'S THE INFINITY COIL.

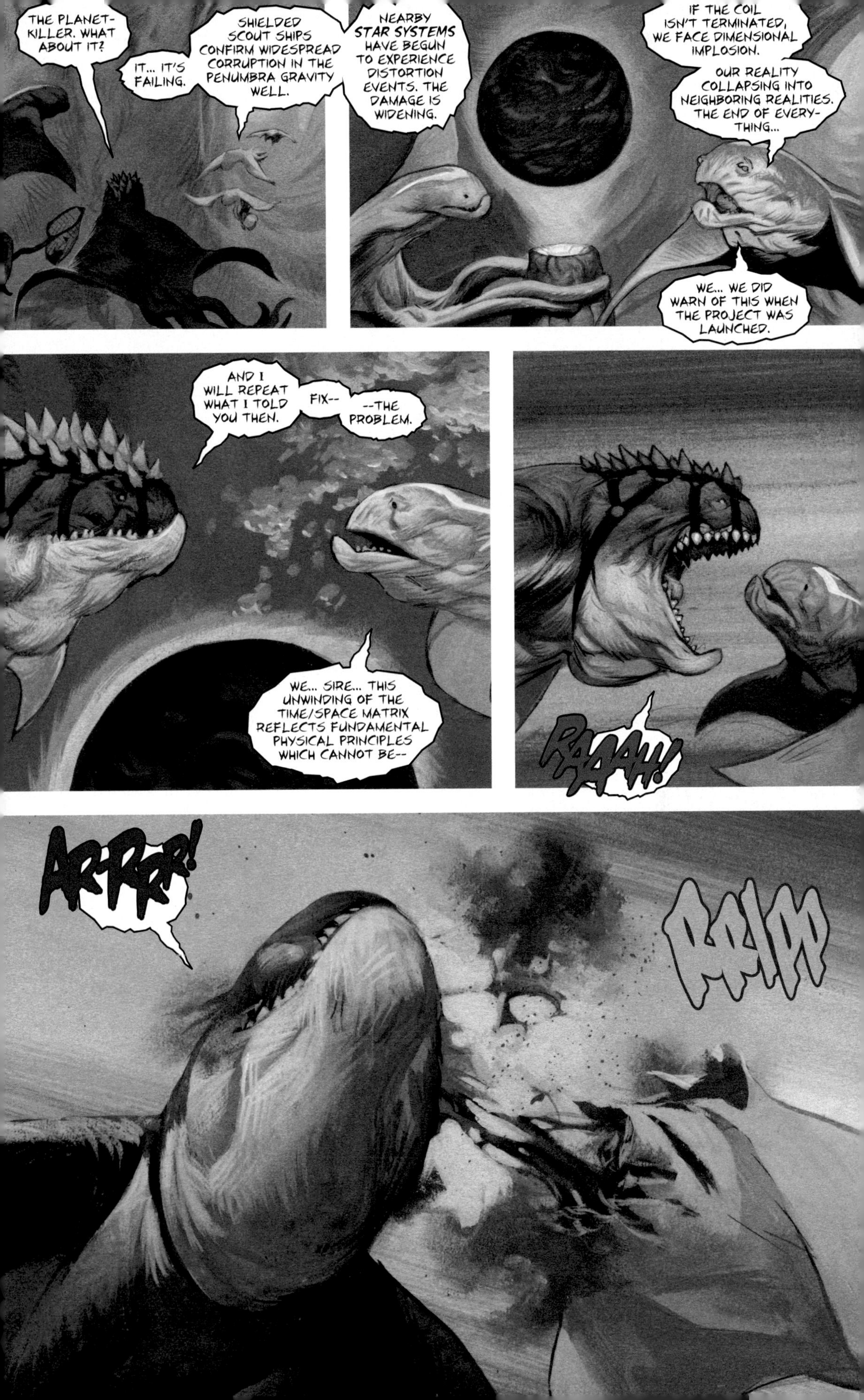
THE PLANET-KILLER. WHAT ABOUT IT?
IT... IT'S FAILING.
SHIELDED SCOUT SHIPS CONFIRM WIDESPREAD CORRUPTION IN THE PENUMBRA GRAVITY WELL.
NEARBY STAR SYSTEMS HAVE BEGUN TO EXPERIENCE DISTORTION EVENTS. THE DAMAGE IS WIDENING.
IF THE COIL ISN'T TERMINATED, WE FACE DIMENSIONAL IMPLOSION.
OUR REALITY COLLAPSING INTO NEIGHBORING REALITIES. THE END OF EVERY-THING...
WE... WE DID WARN OF THIS WHEN THE PROJECT WAS LAUNCHED.
AND I WILL REPEAT WHAT I TOLD YOU THEN.
FIX--
--THE PROBLEM.
WE... SIRE... THIS UNWINDING OF THE TIME/SPACE MATRIX REFLECTS FUNDAMENTAL PHYSICAL PRINCIPLES WHICH CANNOT BE--
RAAAH!
AR-RGR!
RRIPP

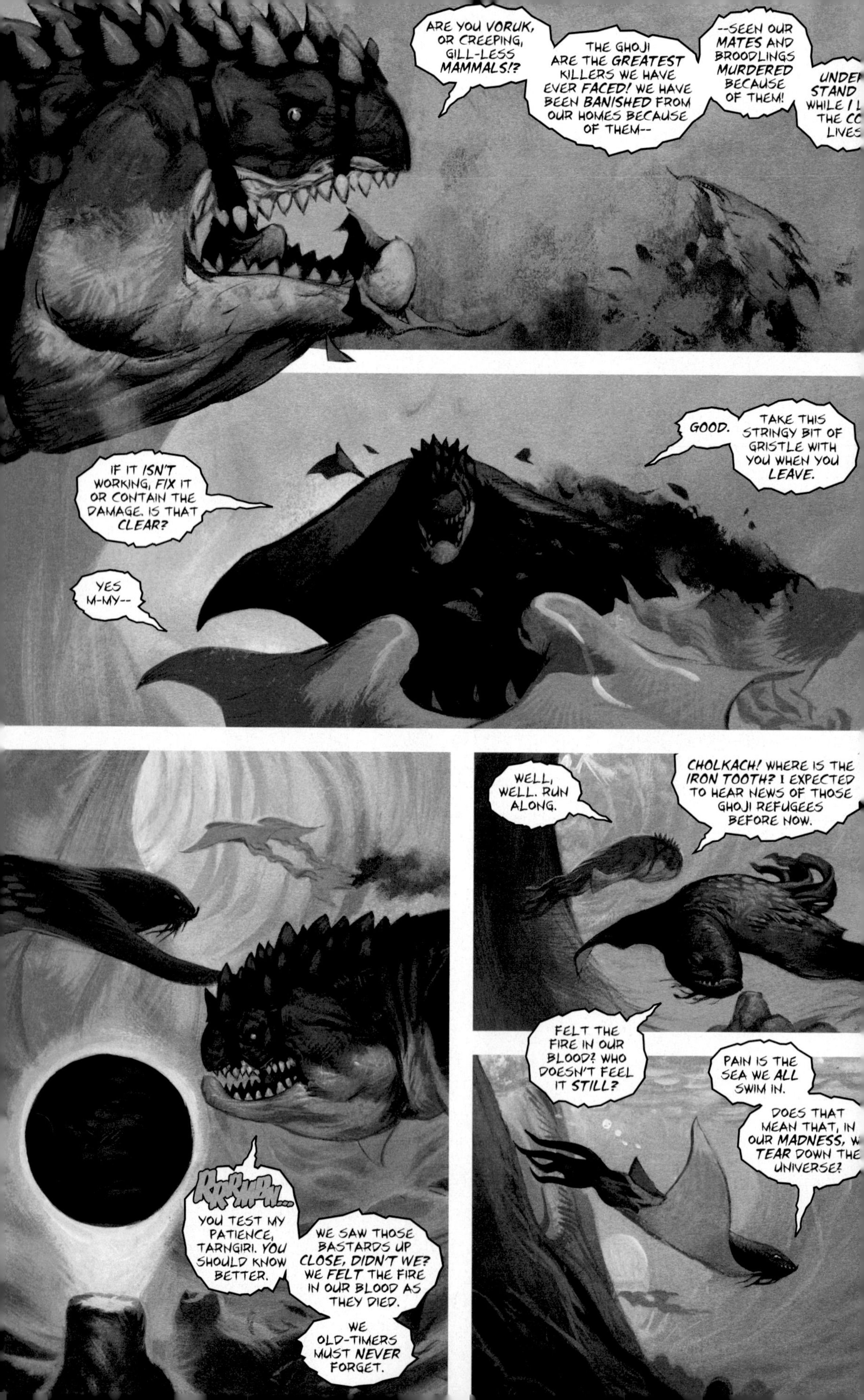

ARE YOU VORUK, OR CREEPING, GILL-LESS MAMMALS!?
THE GHOJI ARE THE GREATEST KILLERS WE HAVE EVER FACED! WE HAVE BEEN BANISHED FROM OUR HOMES BECAUSE OF THEM--
--SEEN OUR MATES AND BROODLINGS MURDERED BECAUSE OF THEM!
UNDER STAND WHILE I L THE CO LIVES
IF IT ISN'T WORKING, FIX IT OR CONTAIN THE DAMAGE. IS THAT CLEAR?
YES M-MY--
GOOD.
TAKE THIS STRINGY BIT OF GRISTLE WITH YOU WHEN YOU LEAVE.
YOU TEST MY PATIENCE, TARNGIRI. YOU SHOULD KNOW BETTER.
WE SAW THOSE BASTARDS UP CLOSE, DIDN'T WE? WE FELT THE FIRE IN OUR BLOOD AS THEY DIED.
WE OLD-TIMERS MUST NEVER FORGET.
WELL, WELL. RUN ALONG.
CHOLKACH! WHERE IS THE IRON TOOTH? I EXPECTED TO HEAR NEWS OF THOSE GHOJI REFUGEES BEFORE NOW.
FELT THE FIRE IN OUR BLOOD? WHO DOESN'T FEEL IT STILL?
PAIN IS THE SEA WE ALL SWIM IN.
DOES THAT MEAN THAT, IN OUR MADNESS, WE TEAR DOWN THE UNIVERSE?

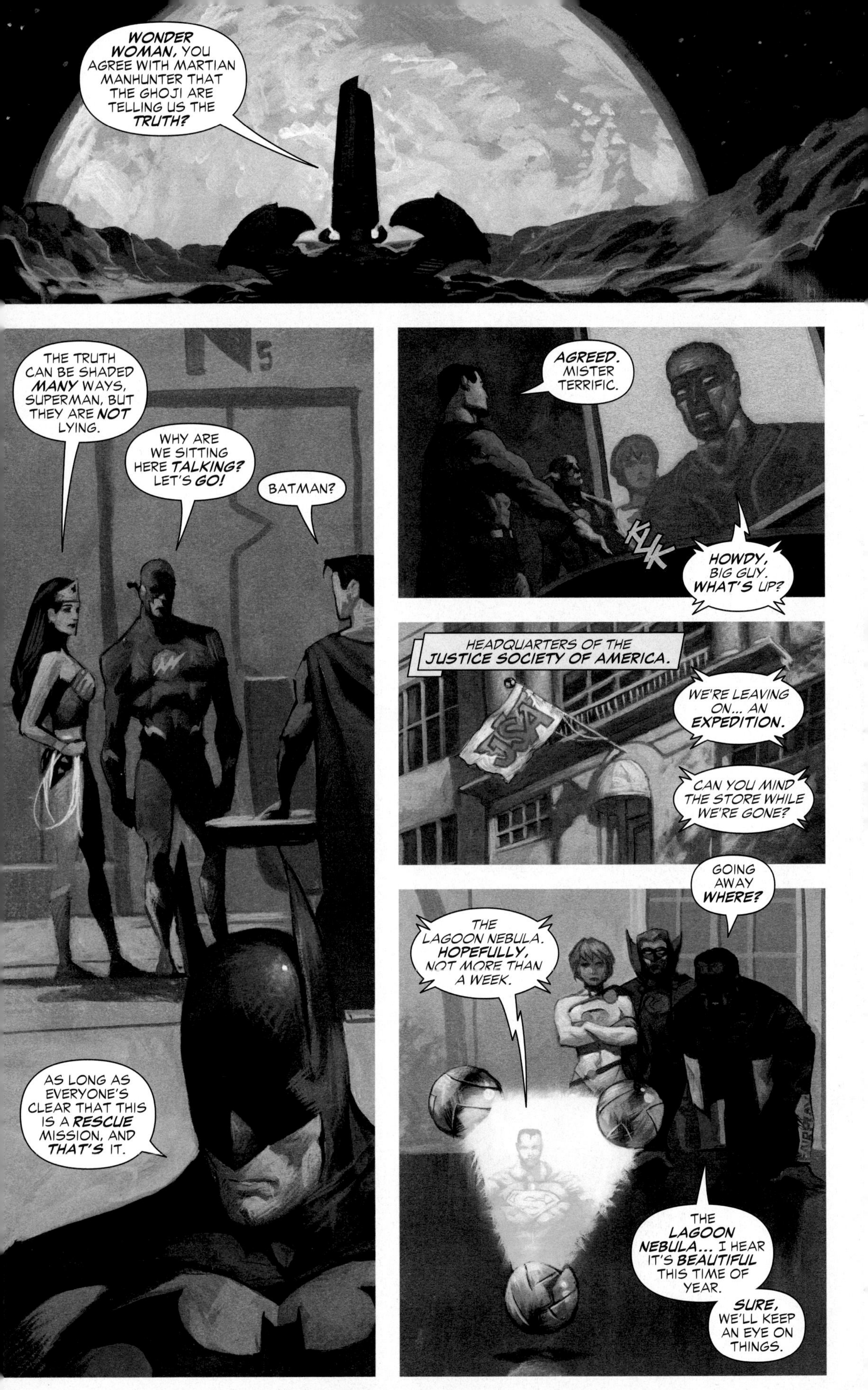
WONDER WOMAN, YOU AGREE WITH MARTIAN MANHUNTER THAT THE GHOJI ARE TELLING US THE TRUTH?
THE TRUTH CAN BE SHADED MANY WAYS, SUPERMAN, BUT THEY ARE NOT LYING.
WHY ARE WE SITTING HERE TALKING? LET'S GO!
BATMAN?
AS LONG AS EVERYONE'S CLEAR THAT THIS IS A RESCUE MISSION, AND THAT'S IT.
AGREED. MISTER TERRIFIC.
KLIK
HOWDY, BIG GUY. WHAT'S UP?
HEADQUARTERS OF THE JUSTICE SOCIETY OF AMERICA.
WE'RE LEAVING ON... AN EXPEDITION.
CAN YOU MIND THE STORE WHILE WE'RE GONE?
GOING AWAY WHERE?
THE LAGOON NEBULA. HOPEFULLY, NOT MORE THAN A WEEK.
THE LAGOON NEBULA... I HEAR IT'S BEAUTIFUL THIS TIME OF YEAR.
SURE, WE'LL KEEP AN EYE ON THINGS.

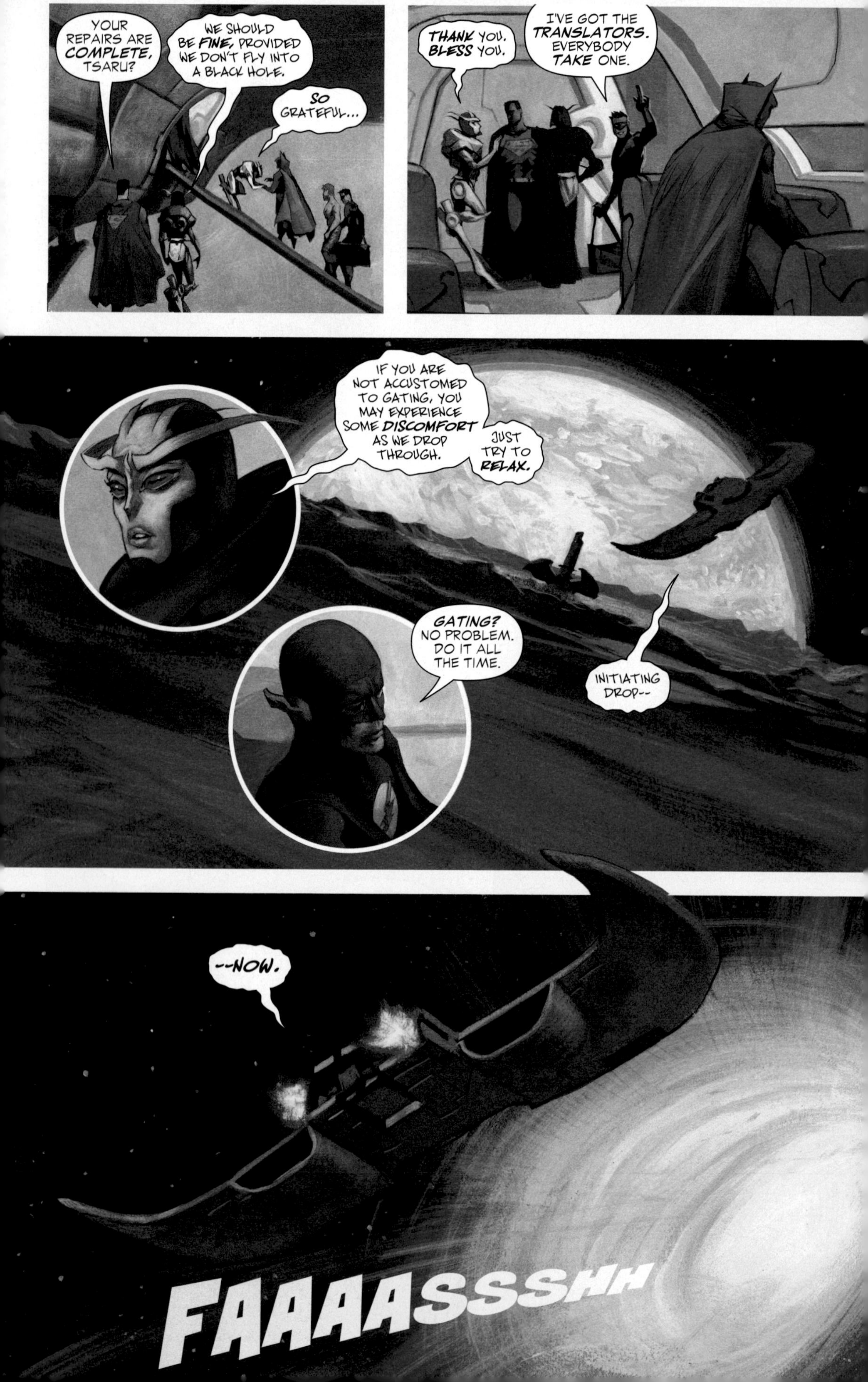
YOUR REPAIRS ARE COMPLETE, TSARU?
WE SHOULD BE FINE, PROVIDED WE DON'T FLY INTO A BLACK HOLE.
SO GRATEFUL...
THANK YOU. BLESS YOU.
I'VE GOT THE TRANSLATORS. EVERYBODY TAKE ONE.
IF YOU ARE NOT ACCUSTOMED TO GATING, YOU MAY EXPERIENCE SOME DISCOMFORT AS WE DROP THROUGH.
JUST TRY TO RELAX.
GATING? NO PROBLEM. DO IT ALL THE TIME.
INITIATING DROP--
--NOW.
FAAAASSSHH

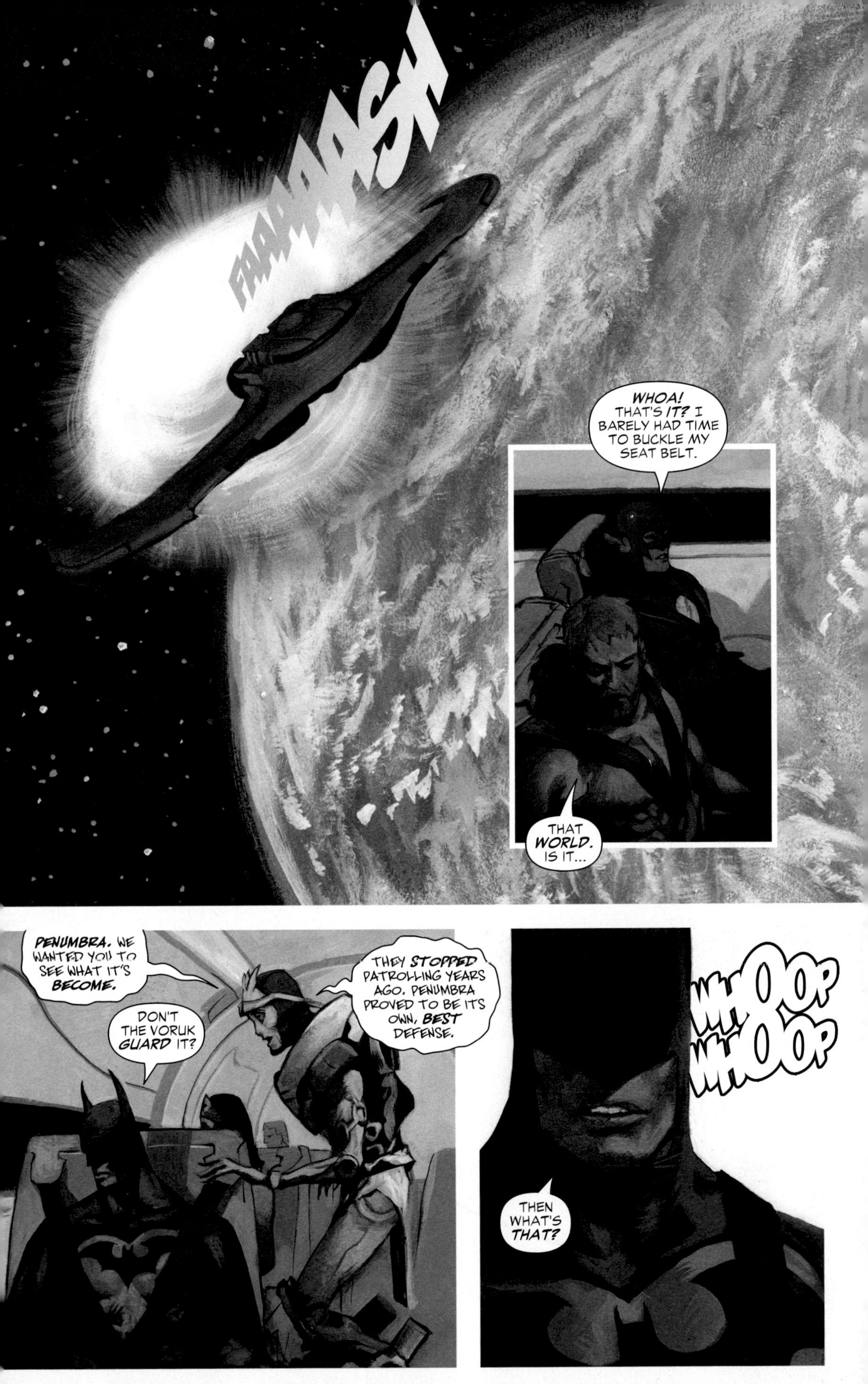
FAAARASH
WHOA! THAT'S IT? I BARELY HAD TIME TO BUCKLE MY SEAT BELT.
THAT WORLD. IS IT...
PENUMBRA. WE WANTED YOU TO SEE WHAT IT'S BECOME.
DON'T THE VORUK GUARD IT?
THEY STOPPED PATROLLING YEARS AGO. PENUMBRA PROVED TO BE ITS OWN, BEST DEFENSE.
WHOOP WHOOP
THEN WHAT'S THAT?

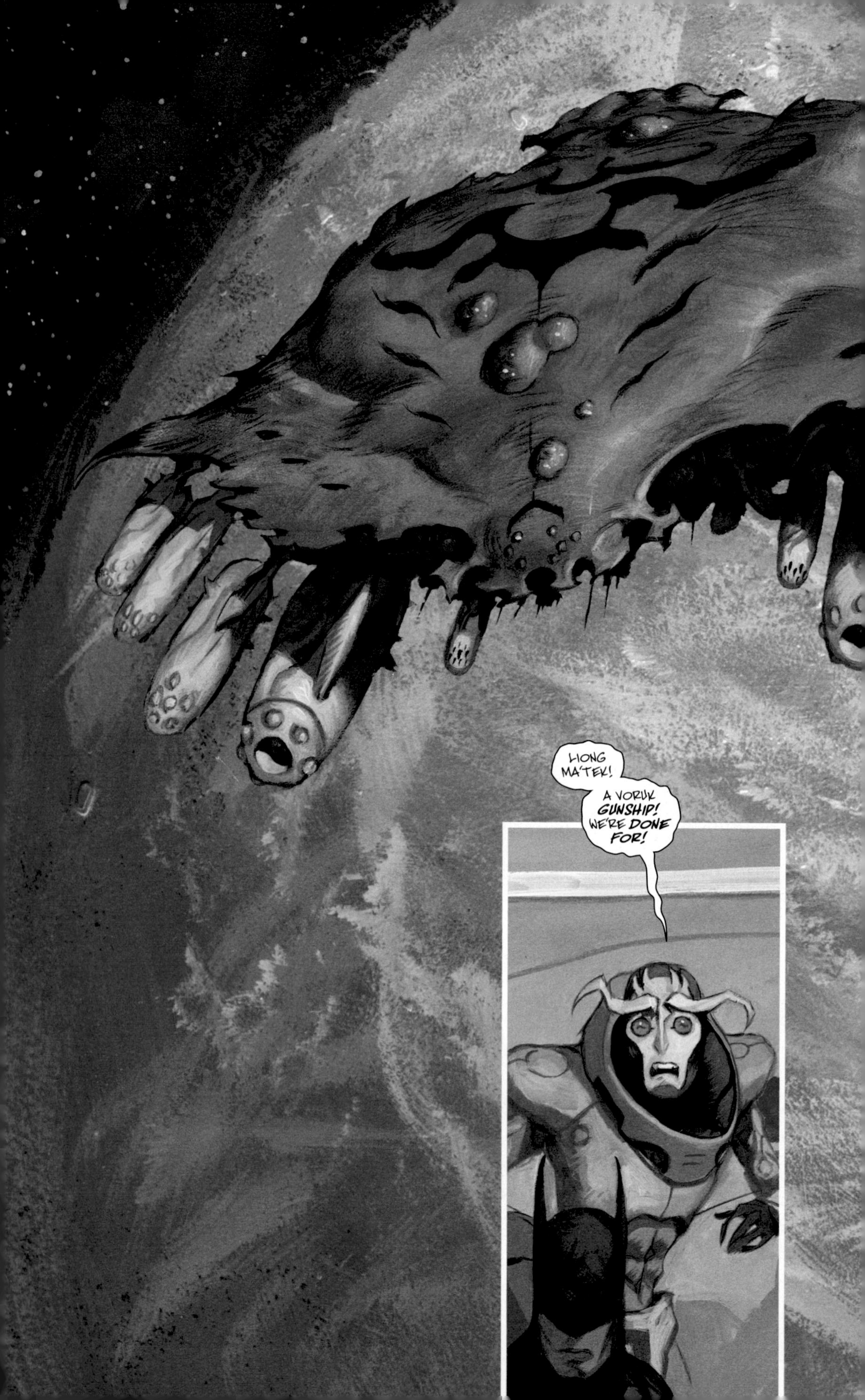
LIONG MA'TEK!
A VORUK GUNSHIP! WE'RE DONE FOR!

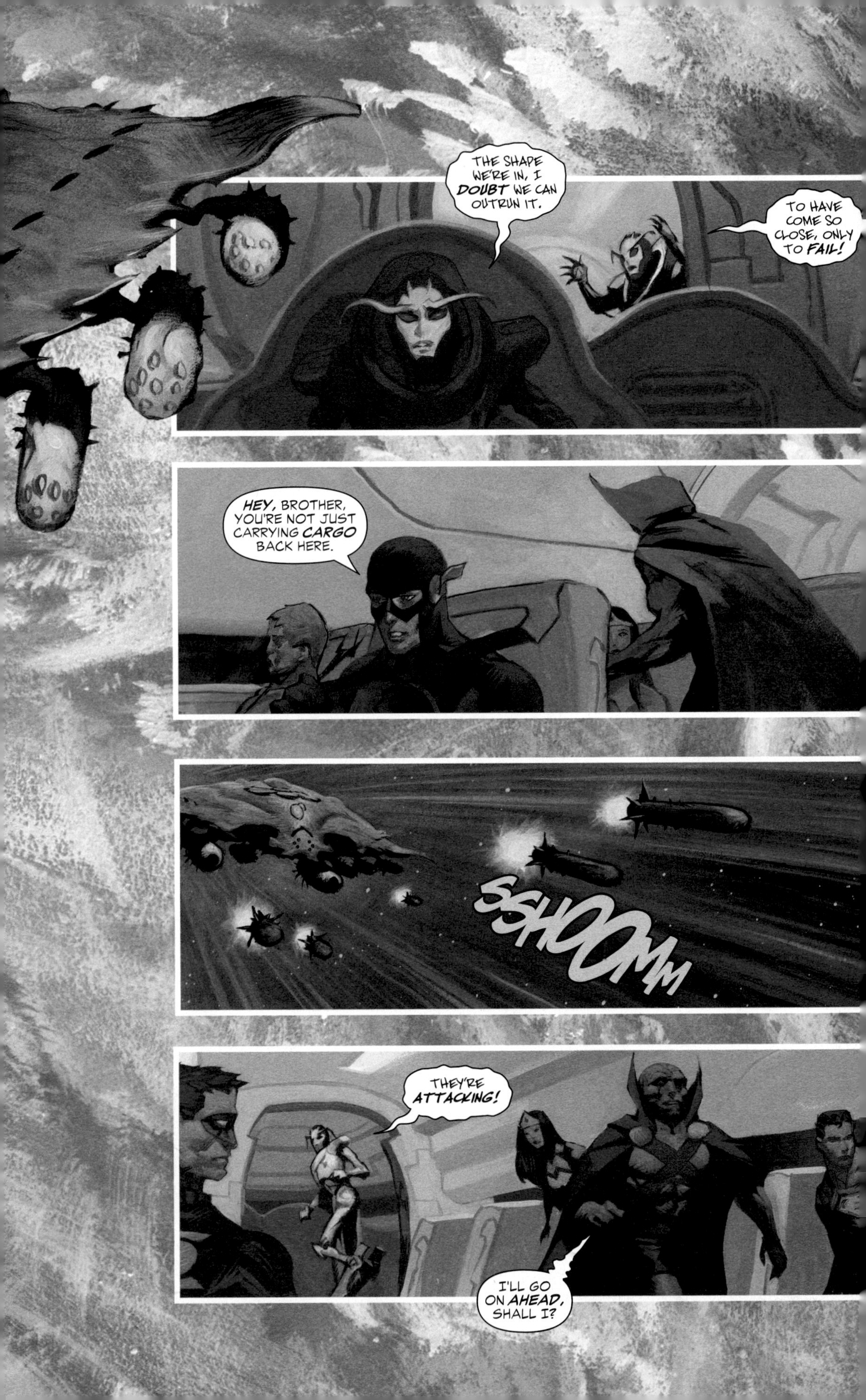
THE SHAPE WE'RE IN, I DOUBT WE CAN OUTRUN IT.
TO HAVE COME SO CLOSE, ONLY TO FAIL!
HEY, BROTHER, YOU'RE NOT JUST CARRYING CARGO BACK HERE.
SSHOOMM
THEY'RE ATTACKING!
I'LL GO ON AHEAD, SHALL I?

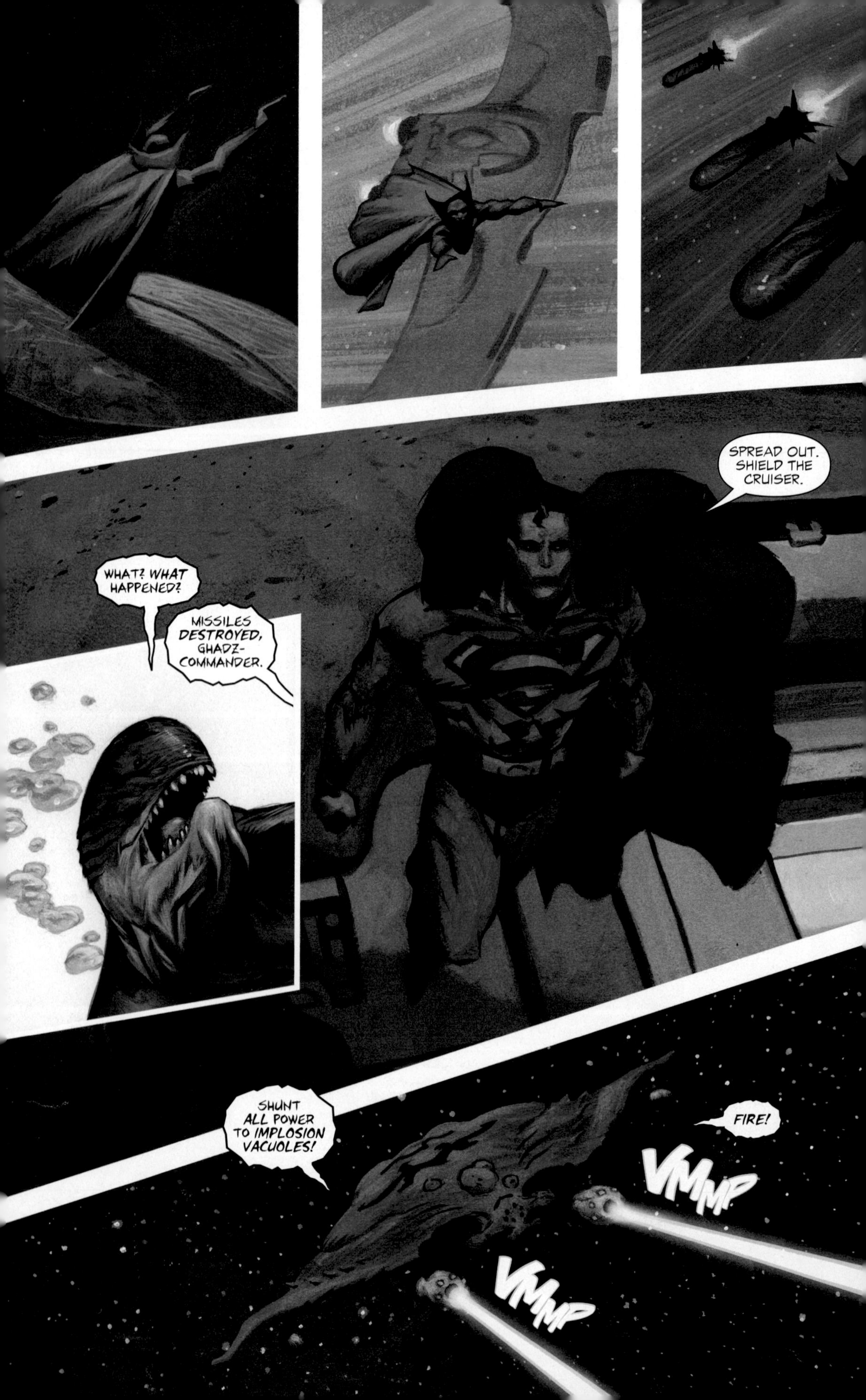
SPREAD OUT. SHIELD THE CRUISER.
WHAT? WHAT HAPPENED?
MISSILES DESTROYED, GHADZ-COMMANDER.
SHUNT ALL POWER TO IMPLOSION VACUOLES!
FIRE!
VMMP
VMMP

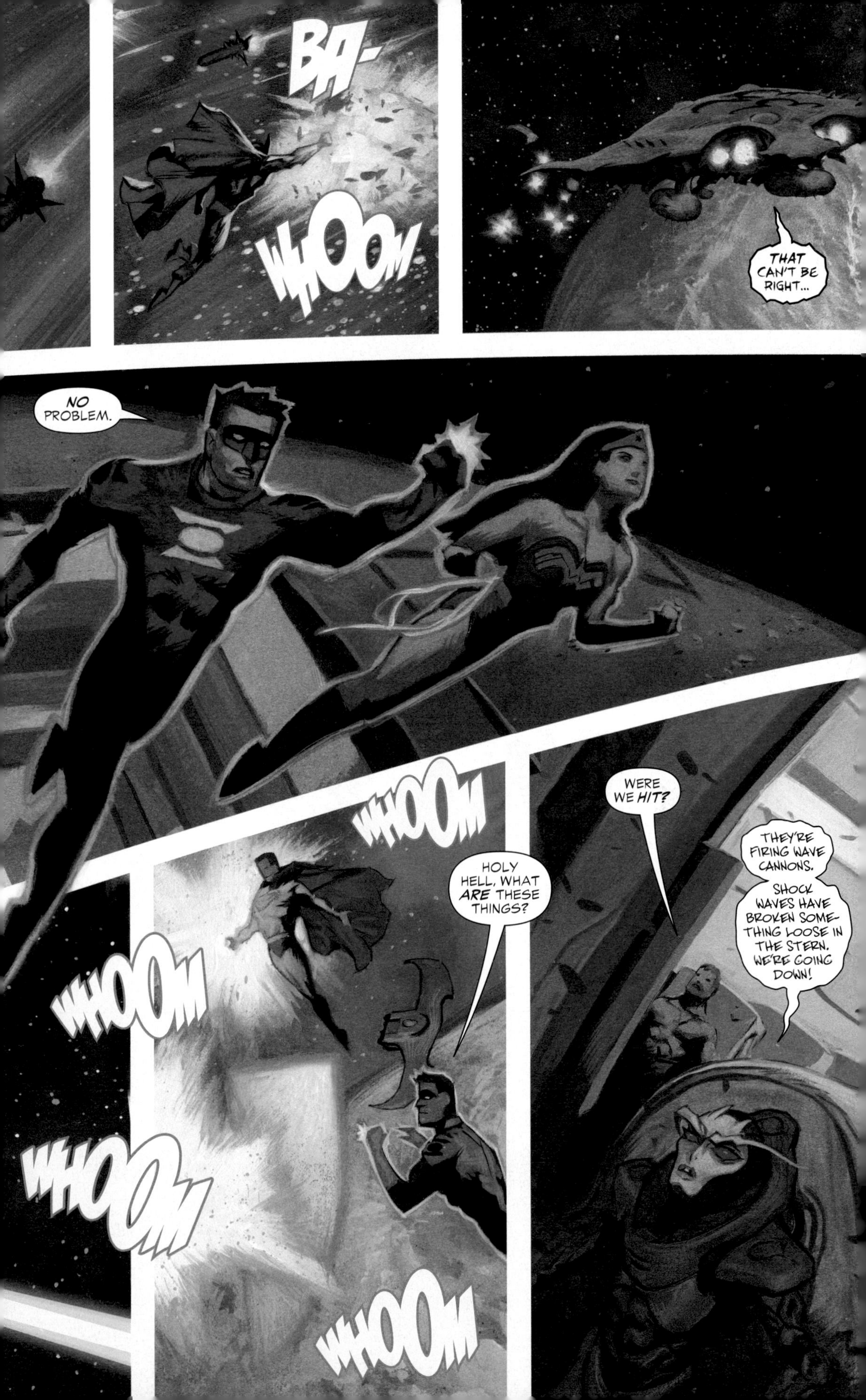
BA-
WHOOM
THAT CAN'T BE RIGHT...
NO PROBLEM.
WHOOM
WHOOM
HOLY HELL, WHAT ARE THESE THINGS?
WHOOM
WHOOM
WERE WE HIT?
THEY'RE FIRING WAVE CANNONS.
SHOCK WAVES HAVE BROKEN SOME-THING LOOSE IN THE STERN. WE'RE GOING DOWN!

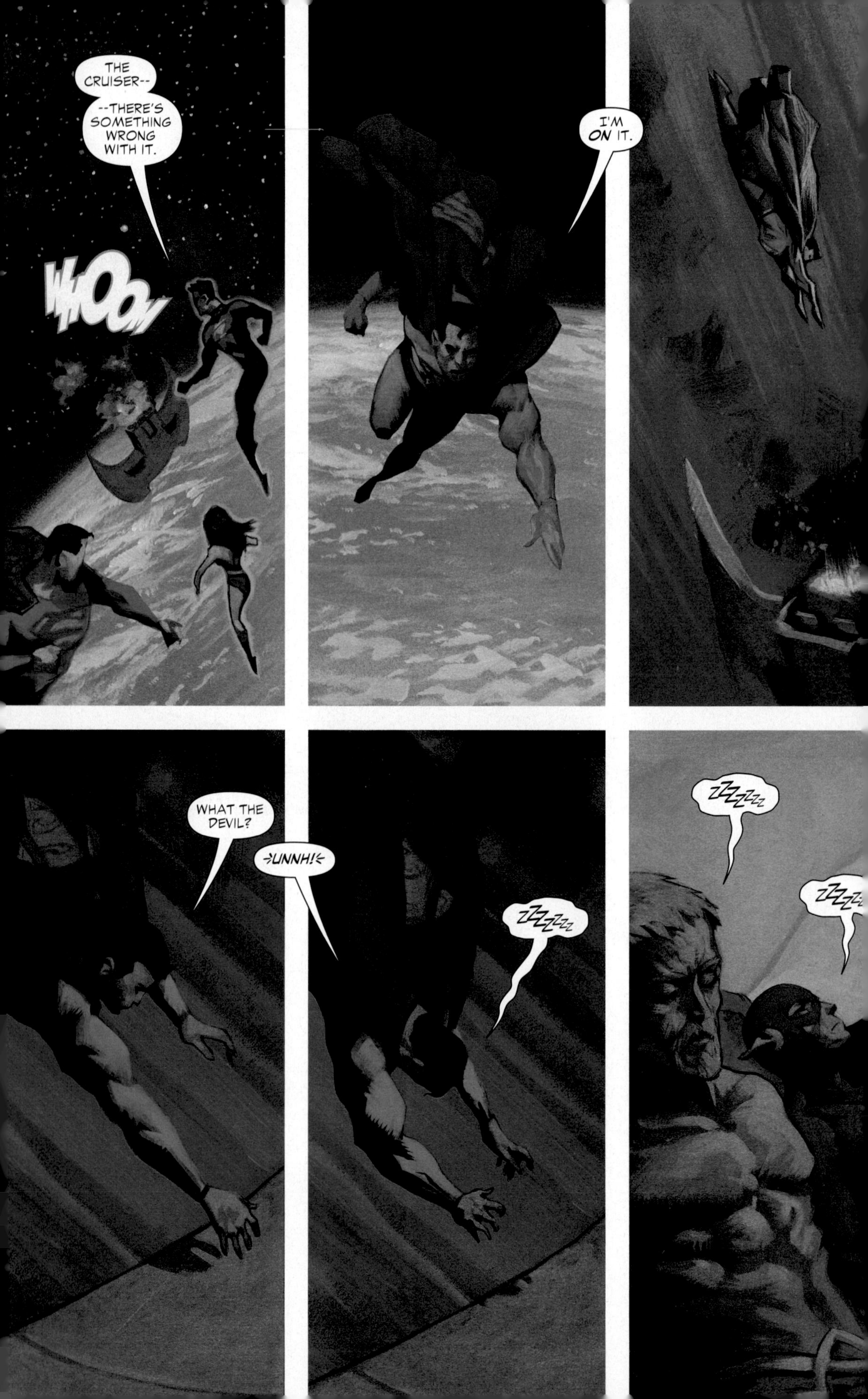
THE CRUISER--
--THERE'S SOMETHING WRONG WITH IT.
WHOOOM
I'M ON IT.
WHAT THE DEVIL?
UNNH!
ZZZZZZZ
ZZZZZZZ
ZZZZ

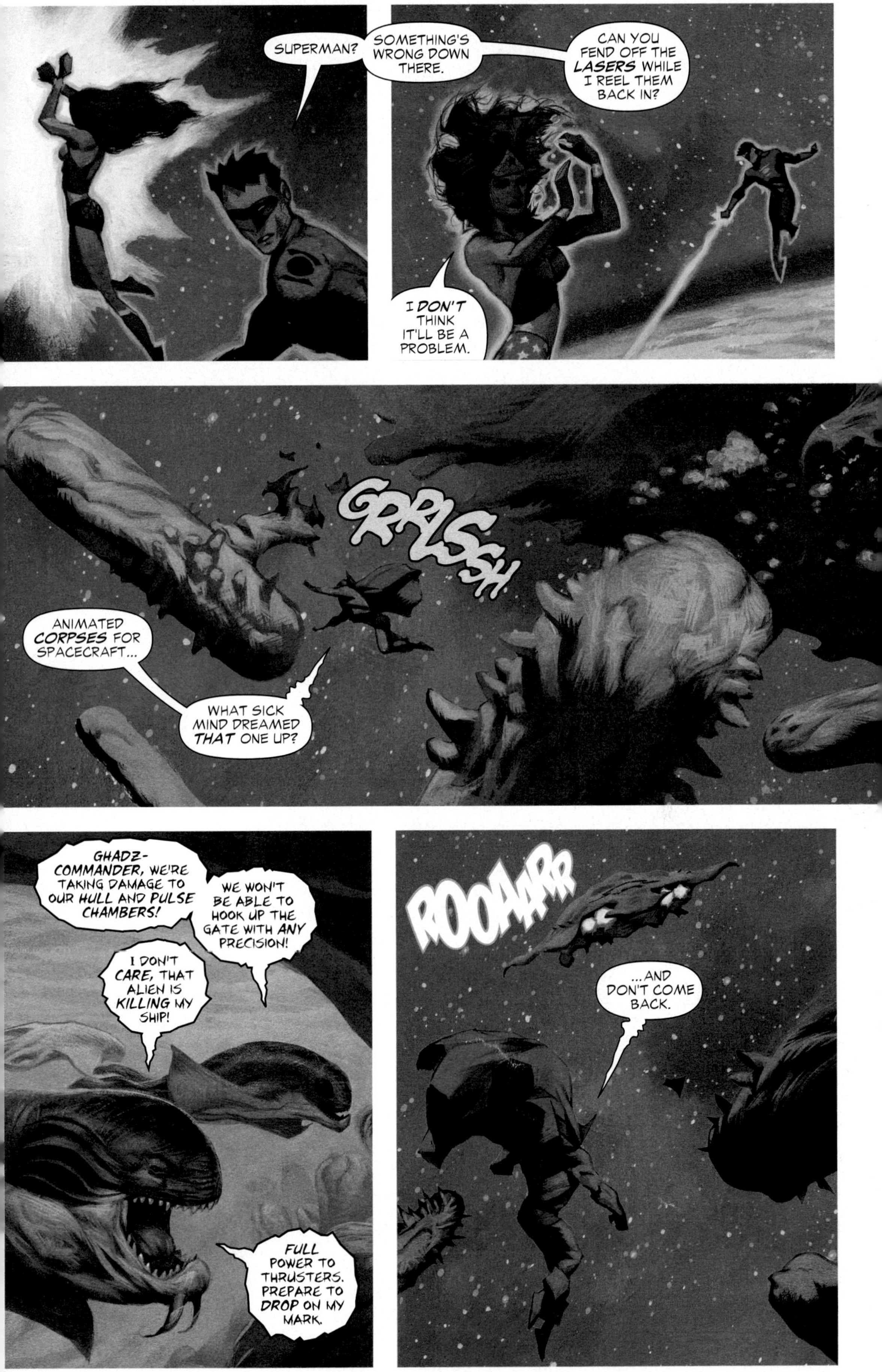
SUPERMAN?
SOMETHING'S WRONG DOWN THERE.
CAN YOU FEND OFF THE LASERS WHILE I REEL THEM BACK IN?
I DON'T THINK IT'LL BE A PROBLEM.
GRRLSSH
ANIMATED CORPSES FOR SPACECRAFT...
WHAT SICK MIND DREAMED THAT ONE UP?
GHADZ-COMMANDER, WE'RE TAKING DAMAGE TO OUR HULL AND PULSE CHAMBERS!
WE WON'T BE ABLE TO HOOK UP THE GATE WITH ANY PRECISION!
I DON'T CARE, THAT ALIEN IS KILLING MY SHIP!
FULL POWER TO THRUSTERS. PREPARE TO DROP ON MY MARK.
ROOAARR
...AND DON'T COME BACK.

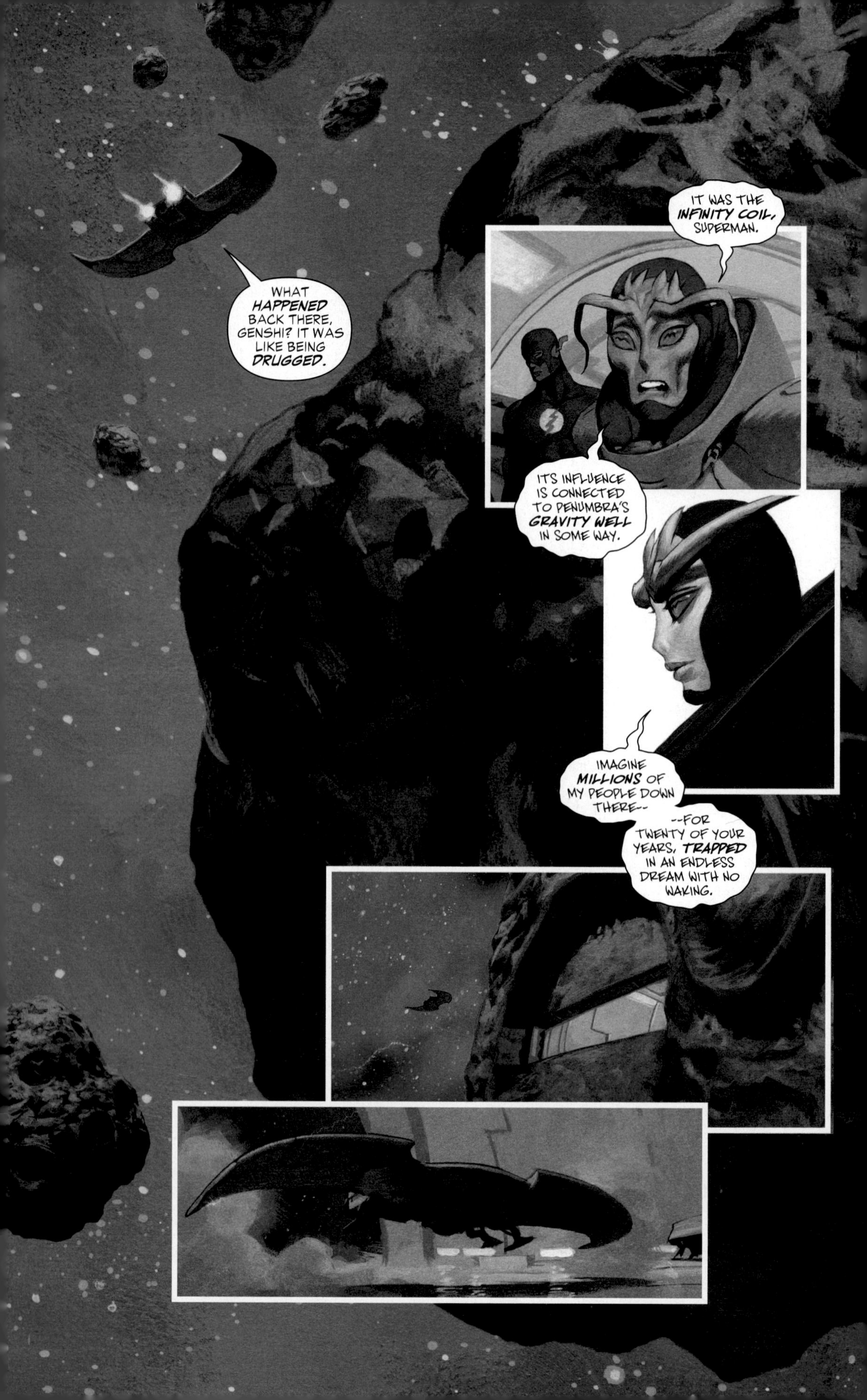
WHAT HAPPENED BACK THERE, GENSHI? IT WAS LIKE BEING DRUGGED.
IT WAS THE INFINITY COIL, SUPERMAN.
ITS INFLUENCE IS CONNECTED TO PENUMBRA'S GRAVITY WELL IN SOME WAY.
IMAGINE MILLIONS OF MY PEOPLE DOWN THERE--
--FOR TWENTY OF YOUR YEARS, TRAPPED IN AN ENDLESS DREAM WITH NO WAKING.

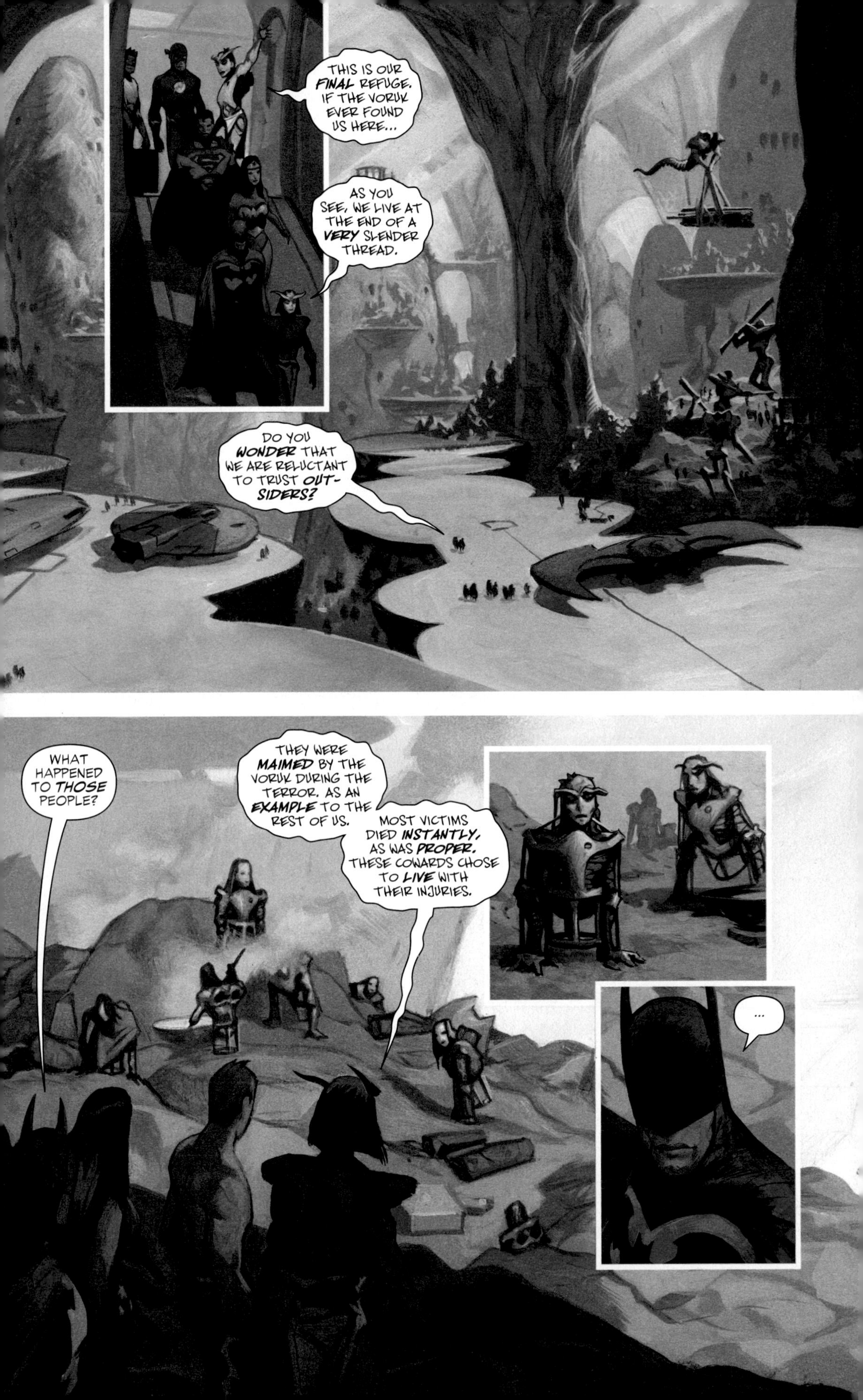
THIS IS OUR FINAL REFUGE. IF THE VORUK EVER FOUND US HERE...
AS YOU SEE, WE LIVE AT THE END OF A VERY SLENDER THREAD.
DO YOU WONDER THAT WE ARE RELUCTANT TO TRUST OUT-SIDERS?
WHAT HAPPENED TO THOSE PEOPLE?
THEY WERE MAIMED BY THE VORUK DURING THE TERROR. AS AN EXAMPLE TO THE REST OF US.
MOST VICTIMS DIED INSTANTLY, AS WAS PROPER. THESE COWARDS CHOSE TO LIVE WITH THEIR INJURIES.
...

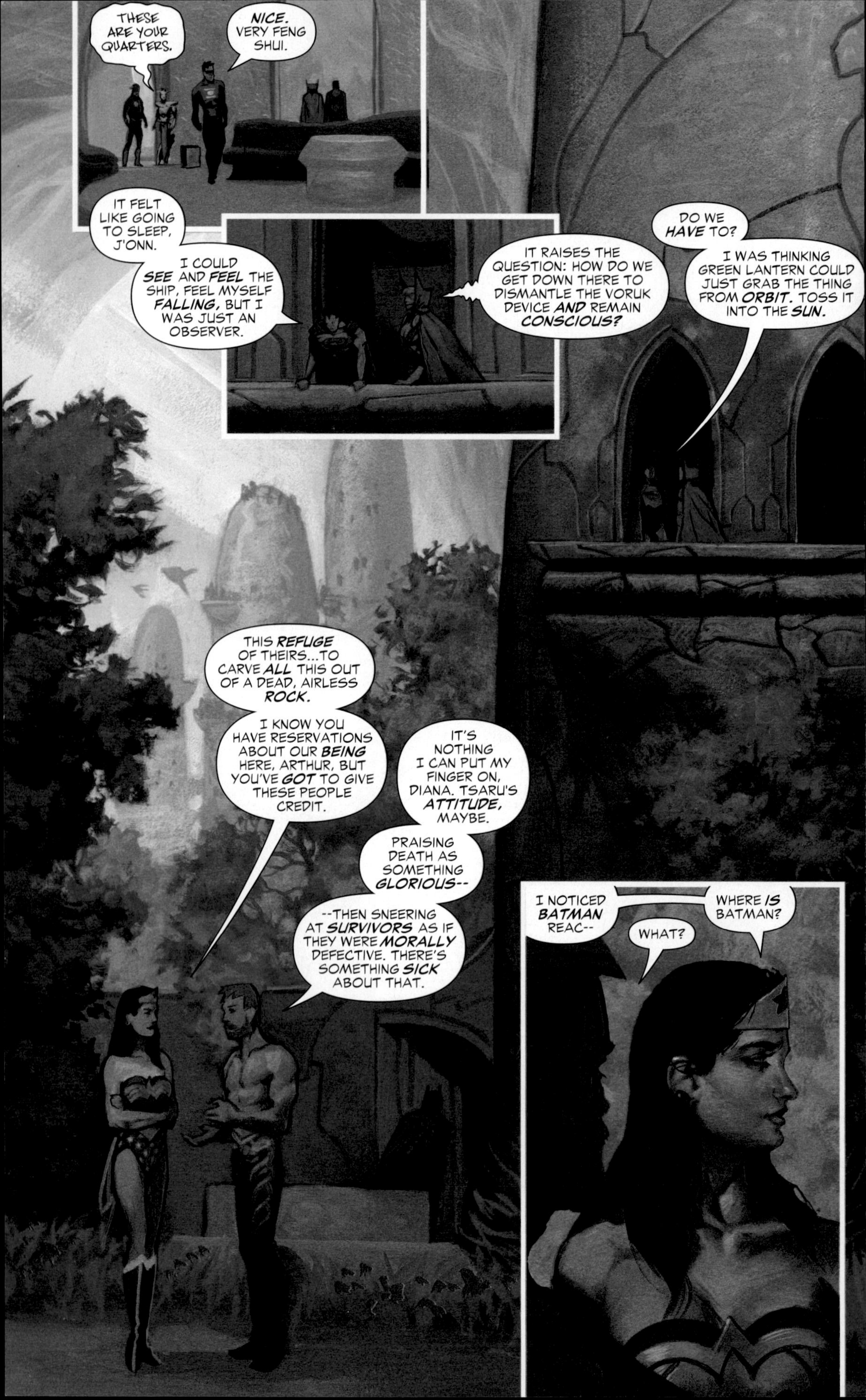
THESE ARE YOUR QUARTERS.
NICE. VERY FENG SHUI.
IT FELT LIKE GOING TO SLEEP, J'ONN.
I COULD SEE AND FEEL THE SHIP, FEEL MYSELF FALLING, BUT I WAS JUST AN OBSERVER.
IT RAISES THE QUESTION: HOW DO WE GET DOWN THERE TO DISMANTLE THE VORUK DEVICE AND REMAIN CONSCIOUS?
DO WE HAVE TO?
I WAS THINKING GREEN LANTERN COULD JUST GRAB THE THING FROM ORBIT. TOSS IT INTO THE SUN.
THIS REFUGE OF THEIRS...TO CARVE ALL THIS OUT OF A DEAD, AIRLESS ROCK.
I KNOW YOU HAVE RESERVATIONS ABOUT OUR BEING HERE, ARTHUR, BUT YOU'VE GOT TO GIVE THESE PEOPLE CREDIT.
IT'S NOTHING I CAN PUT MY FINGER ON, DIANA. TSARU'S ATTITUDE, MAYBE.
PRAISING DEATH AS SOMETHING GLORIOUS--
--THEN SNEERING AT SURVIVORS AS IF THEY WERE MORALLY DEFECTIVE. THERE'S SOMETHING SICK ABOUT THAT.
I NOTICED BATMAN REAC--
WHERE IS BATMAN?
WHAT?

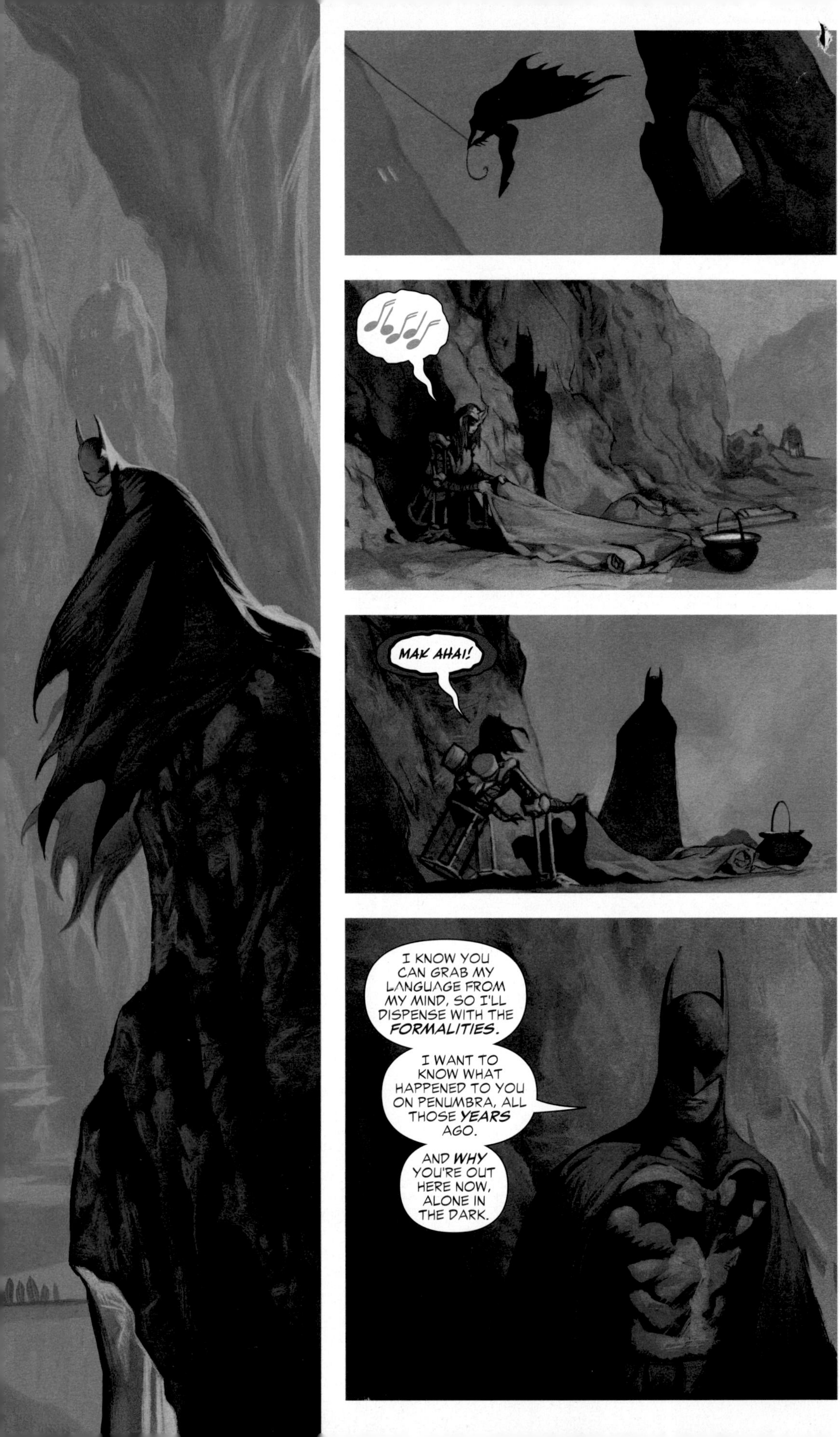
MAK AHAI!
I KNOW YOU CAN GRAB MY LANGUAGE FROM MY MIND, SO I'LL DISPENSE WITH THE FORMALITIES.
I WANT TO KNOW WHAT HAPPENED TO YOU ON PENUMBRA, ALL THOSE YEARS AGO.
AND WHY YOU'RE OUT HERE NOW, ALONE IN THE DARK.

SOMEWHERE IN DEEP SPACE.
BANISHED-SQUADRON GUNSHIP SLASHER.
WELL? WHERE ARE WE!?
THE SHIP'S RETICULAR MEMBRANES WERE DAMAGED IN THE BATTLE, GHADZ-COMMANDER.
WE'RE HAVING TO MAKE OUR STAR POSITIONS MANUALLY.
ZZZTT
ZZZAP
GRRRR I MUST GET WORD BACK TO MHAK-LORD GORDORUK. HE'LL CRUSH THOSE FILTHY AIR BREATHERS.
HOW LONG BEFORE WE CAN OPEN AN ACCURATE GATE?
UNKNOWN, SIR. MIGHT BE AS LONG AS A DAY OR TWO...
GGG GGGH

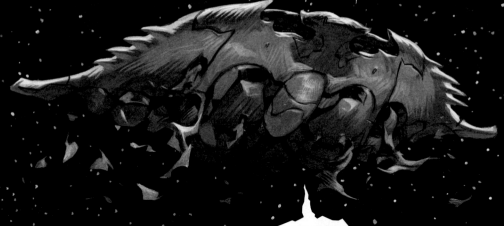

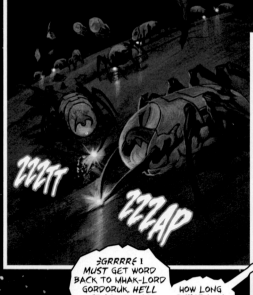

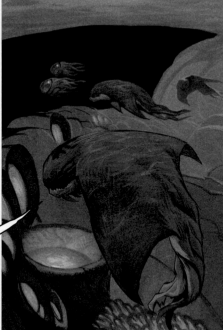

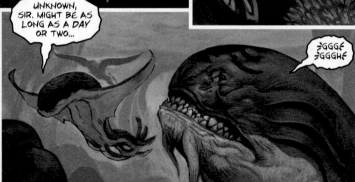

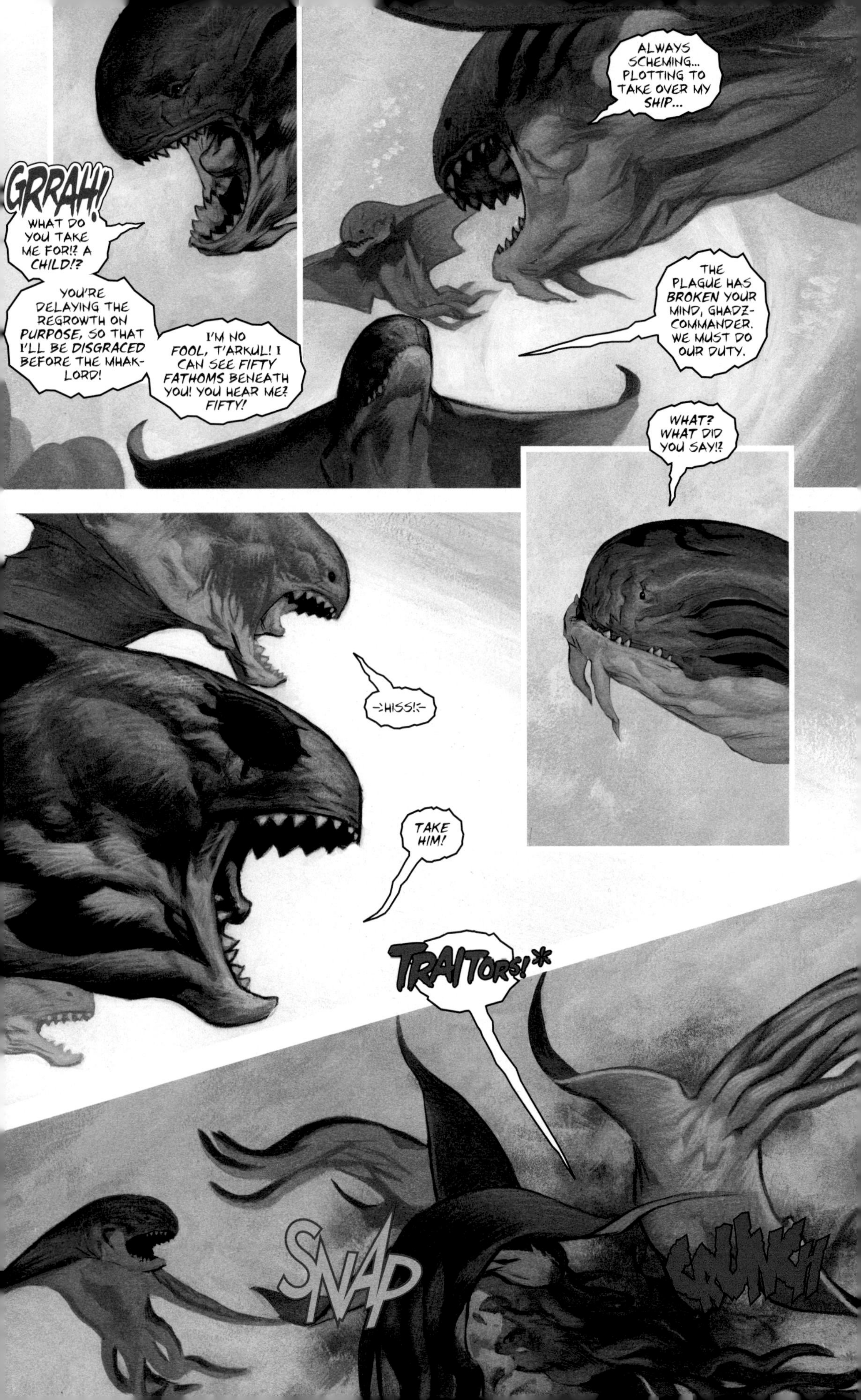
GRRAH!
WHAT DO YOU TAKE ME FOR!? A CHILD!?
YOU'RE DELAYING THE REGROWTH ON PURPOSE, SO THAT I'LL BE DISGRACED BEFORE THE MHAK-LORD!
I'M NO FOOL, T'ARKUL! I CAN SEE FIFTY FATHOMS BENEATH YOU! YOU HEAR ME? FIFTY!
ALWAYS SCHEMING... PLOTTING TO TAKE OVER MY SHIP...
THE PLAGUE HAS BROKEN YOUR MIND, GHADZ-COMMANDER. WE MUST DO OUR DUTY.
WHAT? WHAT DID YOU SAY!?
-HISS!-
TAKE HIM!
TRAITORS!*
SNAP
CRUNCH

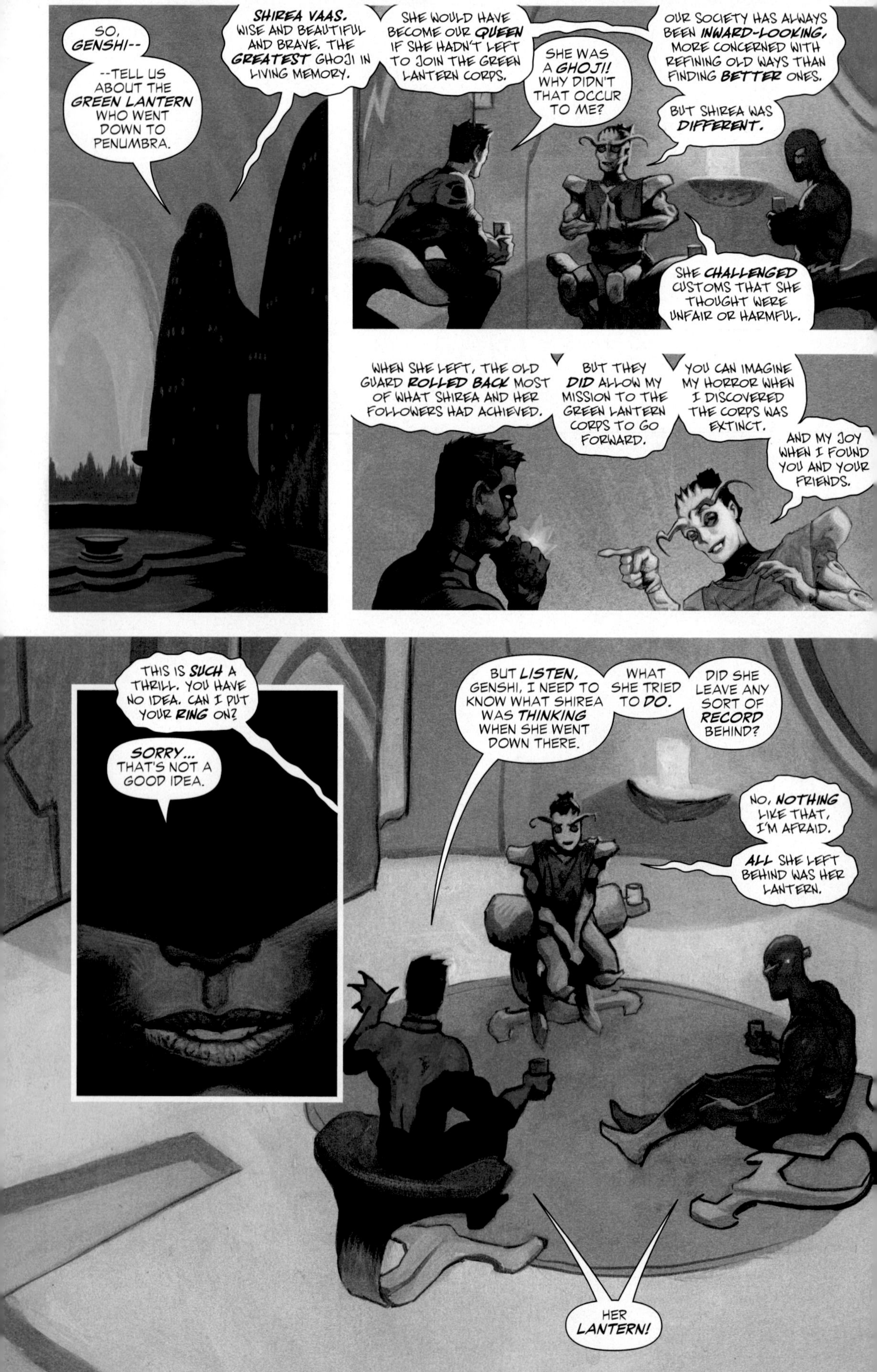
SO, GENSHI--
--TELL US ABOUT THE GREEN LANTERN WHO WENT DOWN TO PENUMBRA.
SHIREA VAAS. WISE AND BEAUTIFUL AND BRAVE. THE GREATEST GHOJI IN LIVING MEMORY.
SHE WOULD HAVE BECOME OUR QUEEN IF SHE HADN'T LEFT TO JOIN THE GREEN LANTERN CORPS.
SHE WAS A GHOJI! WHY DIDN'T THAT OCCUR TO ME?
OUR SOCIETY HAS ALWAYS BEEN INWARD-LOOKING, MORE CONCERNED WITH REFINING OLD WAYS THAN FINDING BETTER ONES.
BUT SHIREA WAS DIFFERENT.
SHE CHALLENGED CUSTOMS THAT SHE THOUGHT WERE UNFAIR OR HARMFUL.
WHEN SHE LEFT, THE OLD GUARD ROLLED BACK MOST OF WHAT SHIREA AND HER FOLLOWERS HAD ACHIEVED.
BUT THEY DID ALLOW MY MISSION TO THE GREEN LANTERN CORPS TO GO FORWARD.
YOU CAN IMAGINE MY HORROR WHEN I DISCOVERED THE CORPS WAS EXTINCT.
AND MY JOY WHEN I FOUND YOU AND YOUR FRIENDS.
THIS IS SUCH A THRILL. YOU HAVE NO IDEA. CAN I PUT YOUR RING ON?
SORRY... THAT'S NOT A GOOD IDEA.
BUT LISTEN, GENSHI, I NEED TO KNOW WHAT SHIREA WAS THINKING WHEN SHE WENT DOWN THERE.
WHAT SHE TRIED TO DO.
DID SHE LEAVE ANY SORT OF RECORD BEHIND?
NO, NOTHING LIKE THAT, I'M AFRAID.
ALL SHE LEFT BEHIND WAS HER LANTERN.
HER LANTERN!

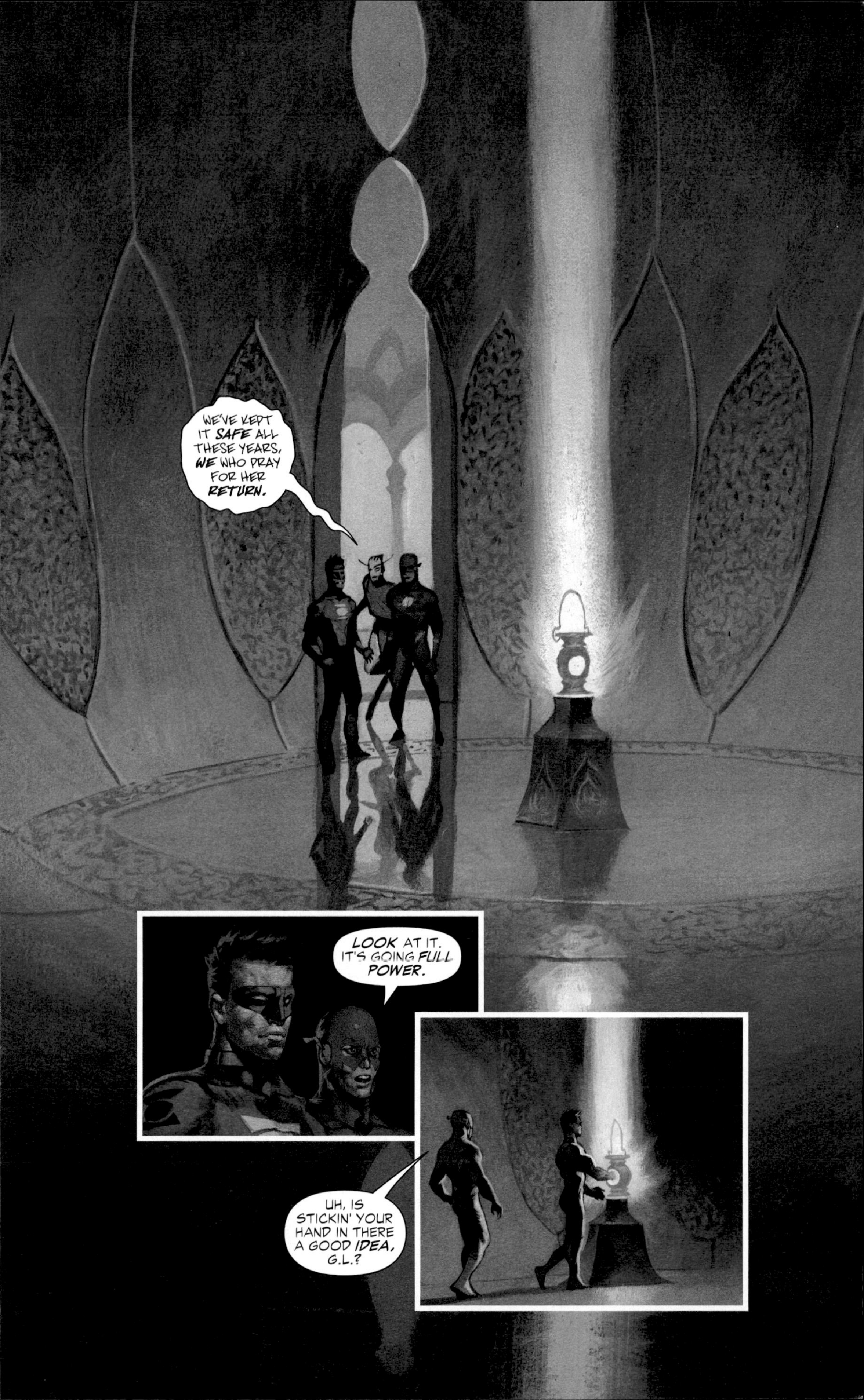
WE'VE KEPT IT SAFE ALL THESE YEARS, WE WHO PRAY FOR HER RETURN.
LOOK AT IT. IT'S GOING FULL POWER.
UH, IS STICKIN' YOUR HAND IN THERE A GOOD IDEA, G.L.?

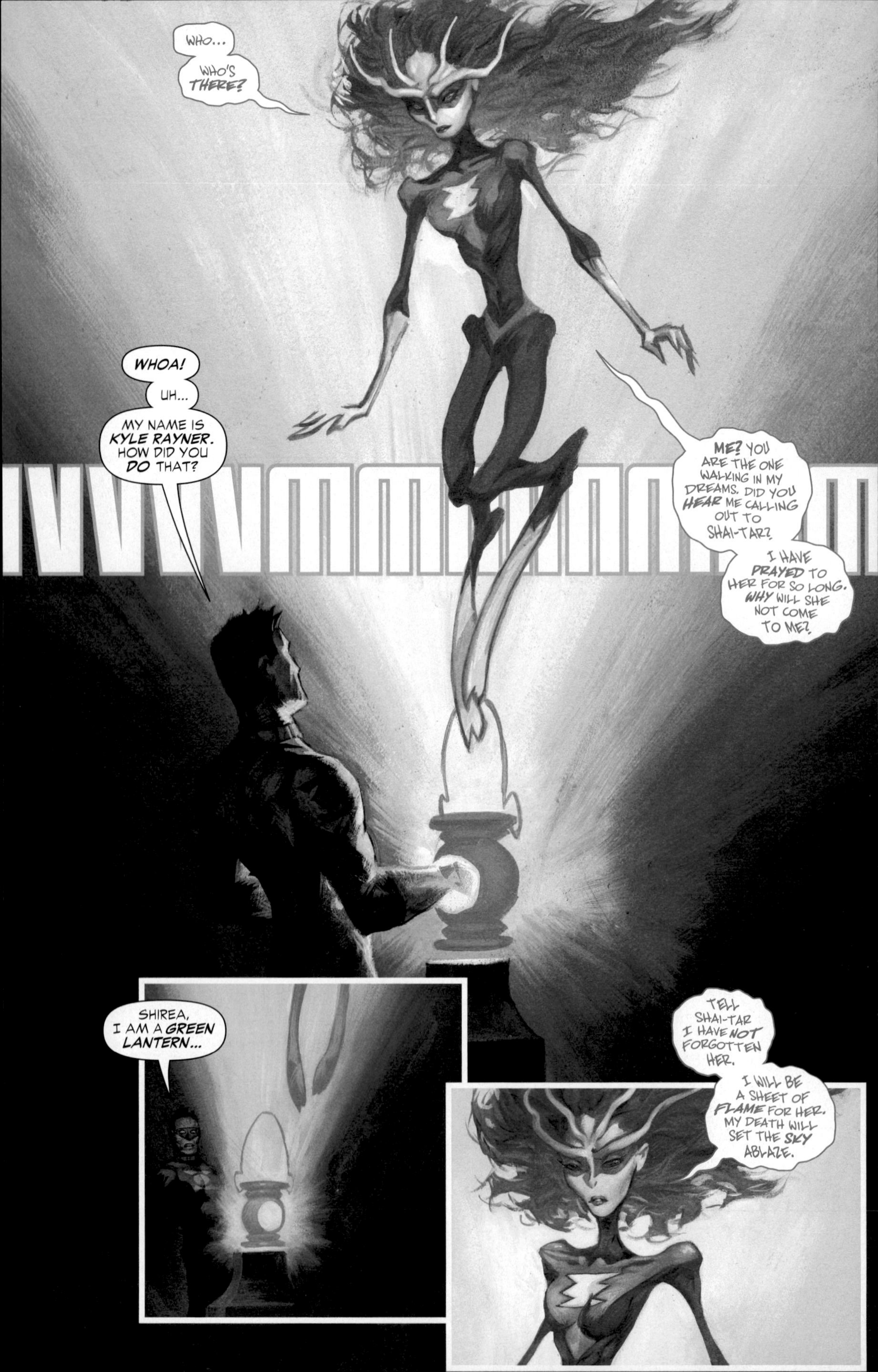
WHO...
WHO'S THERE?
WHOA!
UH...
MY NAME IS KYLE RAYNER. HOW DID YOU DO THAT?
ME? YOU ARE THE ONE WALKING IN MY DREAMS. DID YOU HEAR ME CALLING OUT TO SHAI-TAR?
I HAVE PRAYED TO HER FOR SO LONG. WHY WILL SHE NOT COME TO ME?
SHIREA, I AM A GREEN LANTERN...
TELL SHAI-TAR I HAVE NOT FORGOTTEN HER.
I WILL BE A SHEET OF FLAME FOR HER. MY DEATH WILL SET THE SKY ABLAZE.

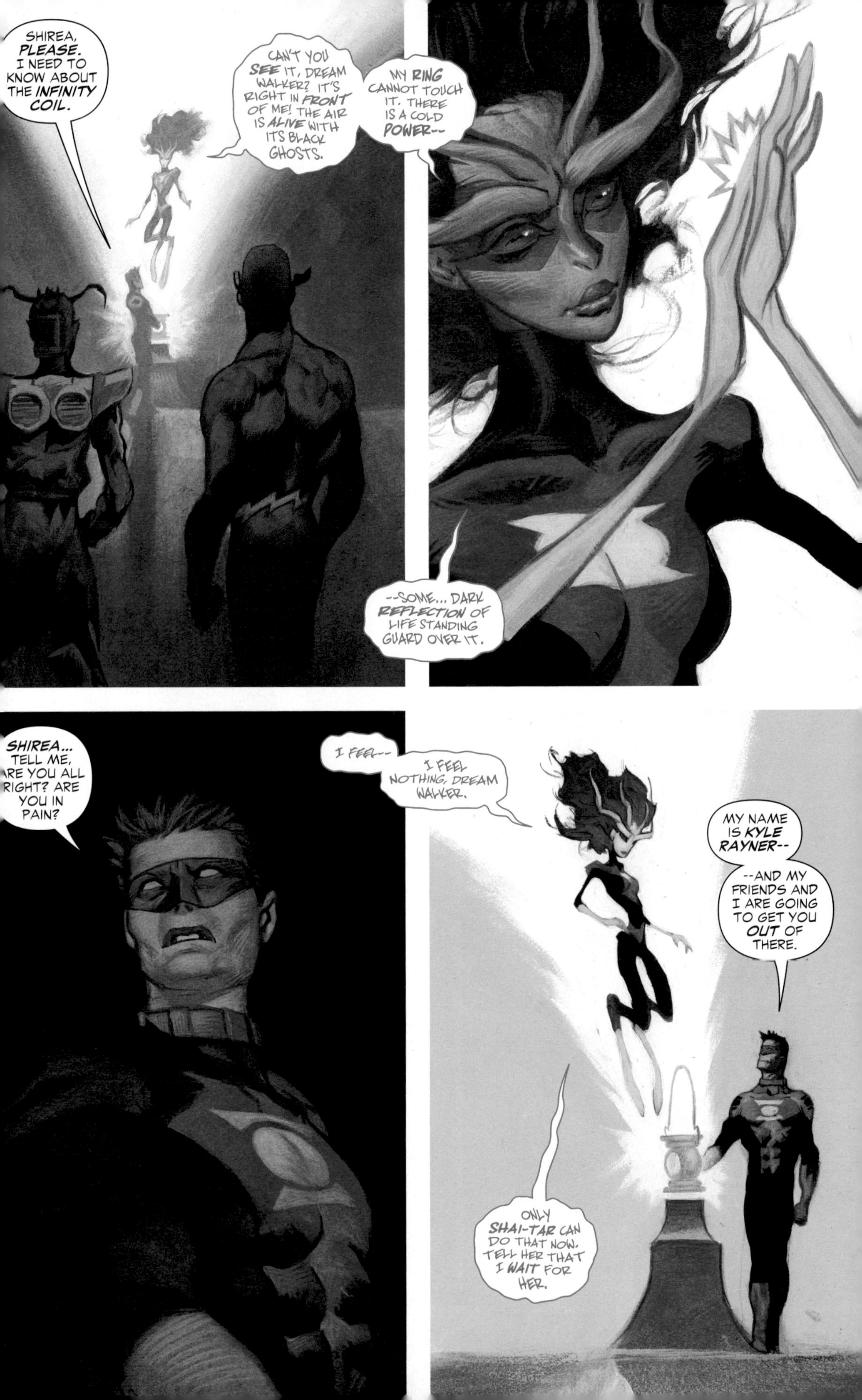
SHIREA, PLEASE. I NEED TO KNOW ABOUT THE INFINITY COIL.
CAN'T YOU SEE IT, DREAM WALKER? IT'S RIGHT IN FRONT OF ME! THE AIR IS ALIVE WITH ITS BLACK GHOSTS.
MY RING CANNOT TOUCH IT. THERE IS A COLD POWER--
--SOME... DARK REFLECTION OF LIFE STANDING GUARD OVER IT.
SHIREA... TELL ME, ARE YOU ALL RIGHT? ARE YOU IN PAIN?
I FEEL--
I FEEL NOTHING, DREAM WALKER.
MY NAME IS KYLE RAYNER--
--AND MY FRIENDS AND I ARE GOING TO GET YOU OUT OF THERE.
ONLY SHAI-TAR CAN DO THAT NOW. TELL HER THAT I WAIT FOR HER.

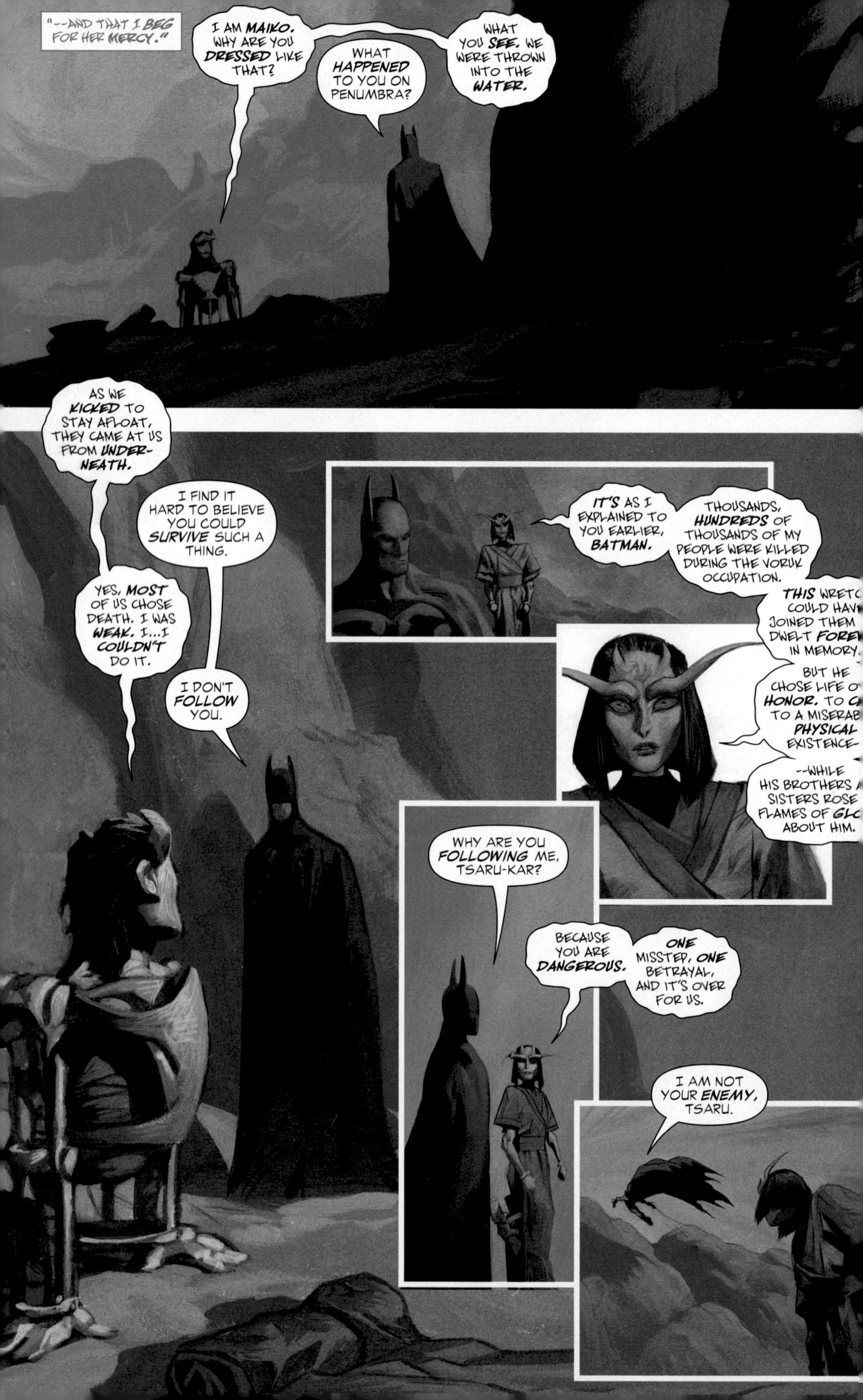
"--AND THAT I BEG FOR HER MERCY."
I AM MAIKO. WHY ARE YOU DRESSED LIKE THAT?
WHAT HAPPENED TO YOU ON PENUMBRA?
WHAT YOU SEE. WE WERE THROWN INTO THE WATER.
AS WE KICKED TO STAY AFLOAT, THEY CAME AT US FROM UNDER-NEATH.
I FIND IT HARD TO BELIEVE YOU COULD SURVIVE SUCH A THING.
YES, MOST OF US CHOSE DEATH. I WAS WEAK. I...I COULDN'T DO IT.
I DON'T FOLLOW YOU.
IT'S AS I EXPLAINED TO YOU EARLIER, BATMAN.
THOUSANDS, HUNDREDS OF THOUSANDS OF MY PEOPLE WERE KILLED DURING THE VORUK OCCUPATION.
THIS WRETC COULD HAV JOINED THEM DWELT FORE IN MEMORY.
BUT HE CHOSE LIFE O HONOR. TO C TO A MISERAB PHYSICAL EXISTENCE-
--WHILE HIS BROTHERS SISTERS ROSE FLAMES OF GL ABOUT HIM.
WHY ARE YOU FOLLOWING ME, TSARU-KAR?
BECAUSE YOU ARE DANGEROUS.
ONE MISSTEP, ONE BETRAYAL, AND IT'S OVER FOR US.
I AM NOT YOUR ENEMY, TSARU.

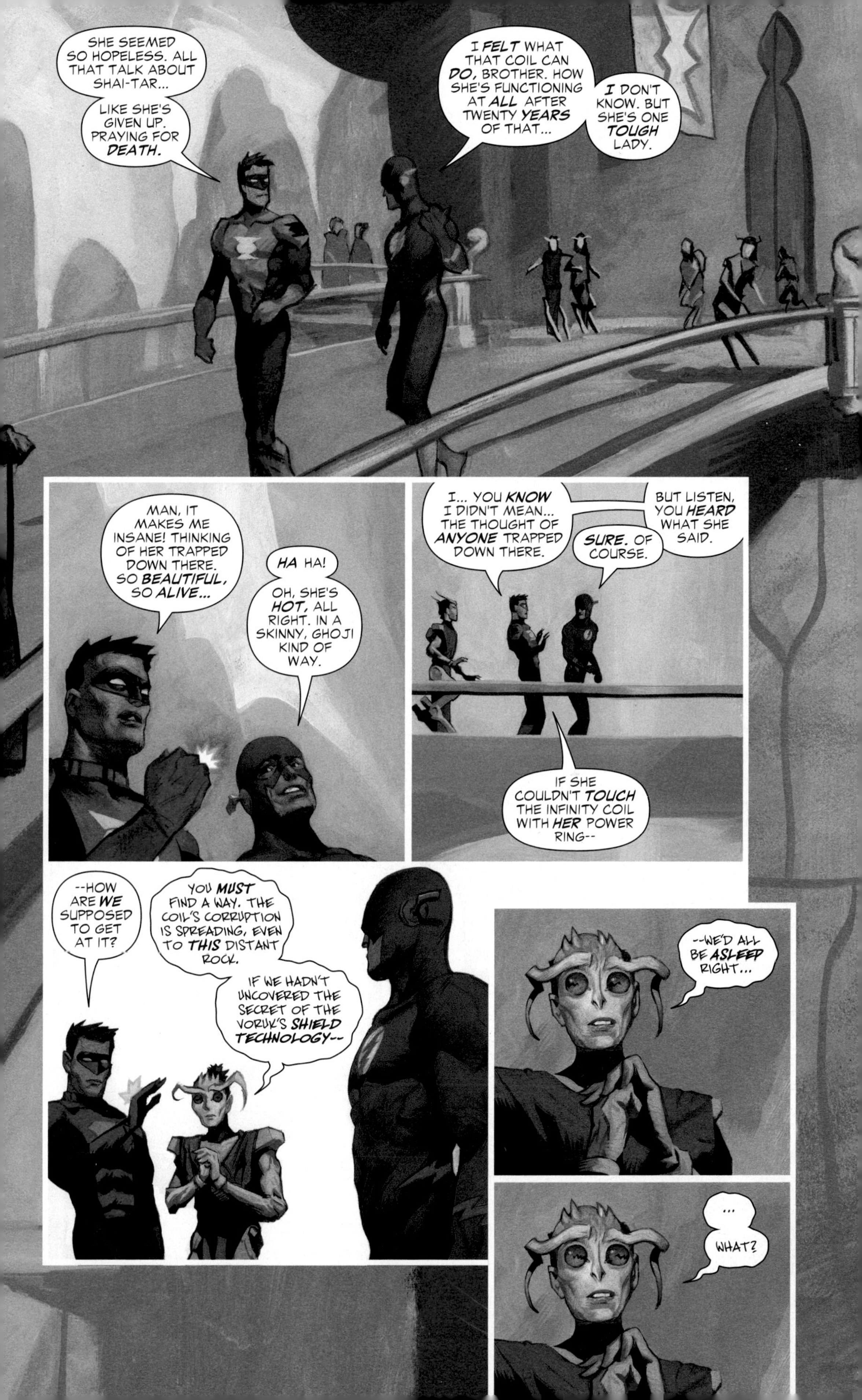
SHE SEEMED SO HOPELESS. ALL THAT TALK ABOUT SHAI-TAR...
LIKE SHE'S GIVEN UP. PRAYING FOR DEATH.
I FELT WHAT THAT COIL CAN DO, BROTHER. HOW SHE'S FUNCTIONING AT ALL AFTER TWENTY YEARS OF THAT...
I DON'T KNOW. BUT SHE'S ONE TOUGH LADY.
MAN, IT MAKES ME INSANE! THINKING OF HER TRAPPED DOWN THERE. SO BEAUTIFUL, SO ALIVE...
HA HA!
OH, SHE'S HOT, ALL RIGHT. IN A SKINNY, GHOJI KIND OF WAY.
I... YOU KNOW I DIDN'T MEAN... THE THOUGHT OF ANYONE TRAPPED DOWN THERE.
SURE. OF COURSE.
BUT LISTEN, YOU HEARD WHAT SHE SAID.
IF SHE COULDN'T TOUCH THE INFINITY COIL WITH HER POWER RING--
--HOW ARE WE SUPPOSED TO GET AT IT?
YOU MUST FIND A WAY. THE COIL'S CORRUPTION IS SPREADING, EVEN TO THIS DISTANT ROCK.
IF WE HADN'T UNCOVERED THE SECRET OF THE VORUK'S SHIELD TECHNOLOGY--
--WE'D ALL BE ASLEEP RIGHT...
...
WHAT?

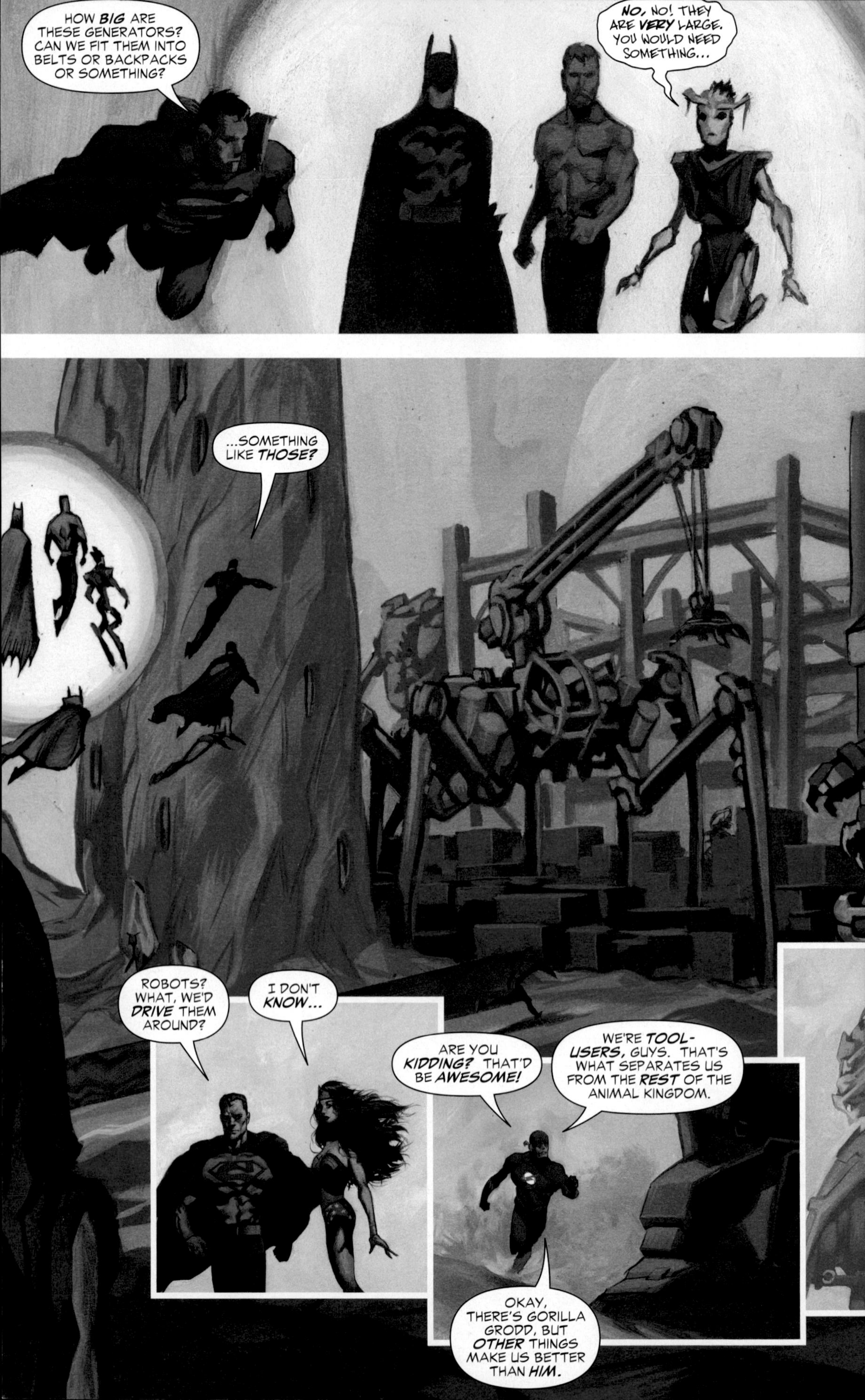
HOW BIG ARE THESE GENERATORS? CAN WE FIT THEM INTO BELTS OR BACKPACKS OR SOMETHING?
NO, NO! THEY ARE VERY LARGE. YOU WOULD NEED SOMETHING...
...SOMETHING LIKE THOSE?
ROBOTS? WHAT, WE'D DRIVE THEM AROUND?
I DON'T KNOW...
ARE YOU KIDDING? THAT'D BE AWESOME!
WE'RE TOOL-USERS, GUYS. THAT'S WHAT SEPARATES US FROM THE REST OF THE ANIMAL KINGDOM.
OKAY, THERE'S GORILLA GRODD, BUT OTHER THINGS MAKE US BETTER THAN HIM.

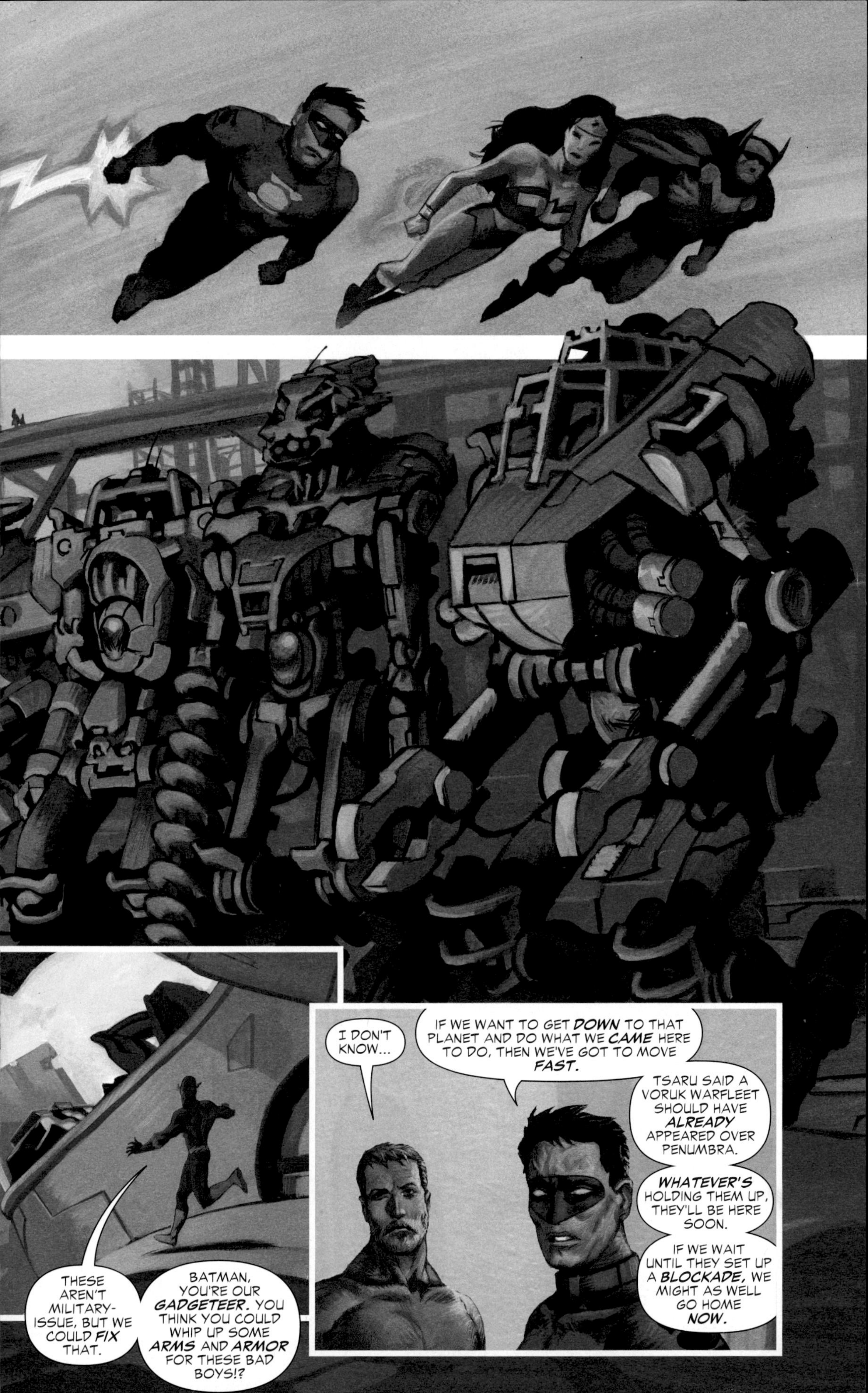
THESE AREN'T MILITARY-ISSUE, BUT WE COULD *FIX* THAT.
BATMAN, YOU'RE OUR *GADGETEER.* YOU THINK YOU COULD WHIP UP SOME *ARMS* AND *ARMOR* FOR THESE BAD BOYS!?
I DON'T KNOW...
IF WE WANT TO GET *DOWN* TO THAT PLANET AND DO WHAT WE *CAME* HERE TO DO, THEN WE'VE GOT TO MOVE *FAST.*
TSARU SAID A VORUK WARFLEET SHOULD HAVE *ALREADY* APPEARED OVER PENUMBRA.
WHATEVER'S HOLDING THEM UP, THEY'LL BE HERE SOON.
IF WE WAIT UNTIL THEY SET UP A *BLOCKADE,* WE MIGHT AS WELL GO HOME *NOW.*

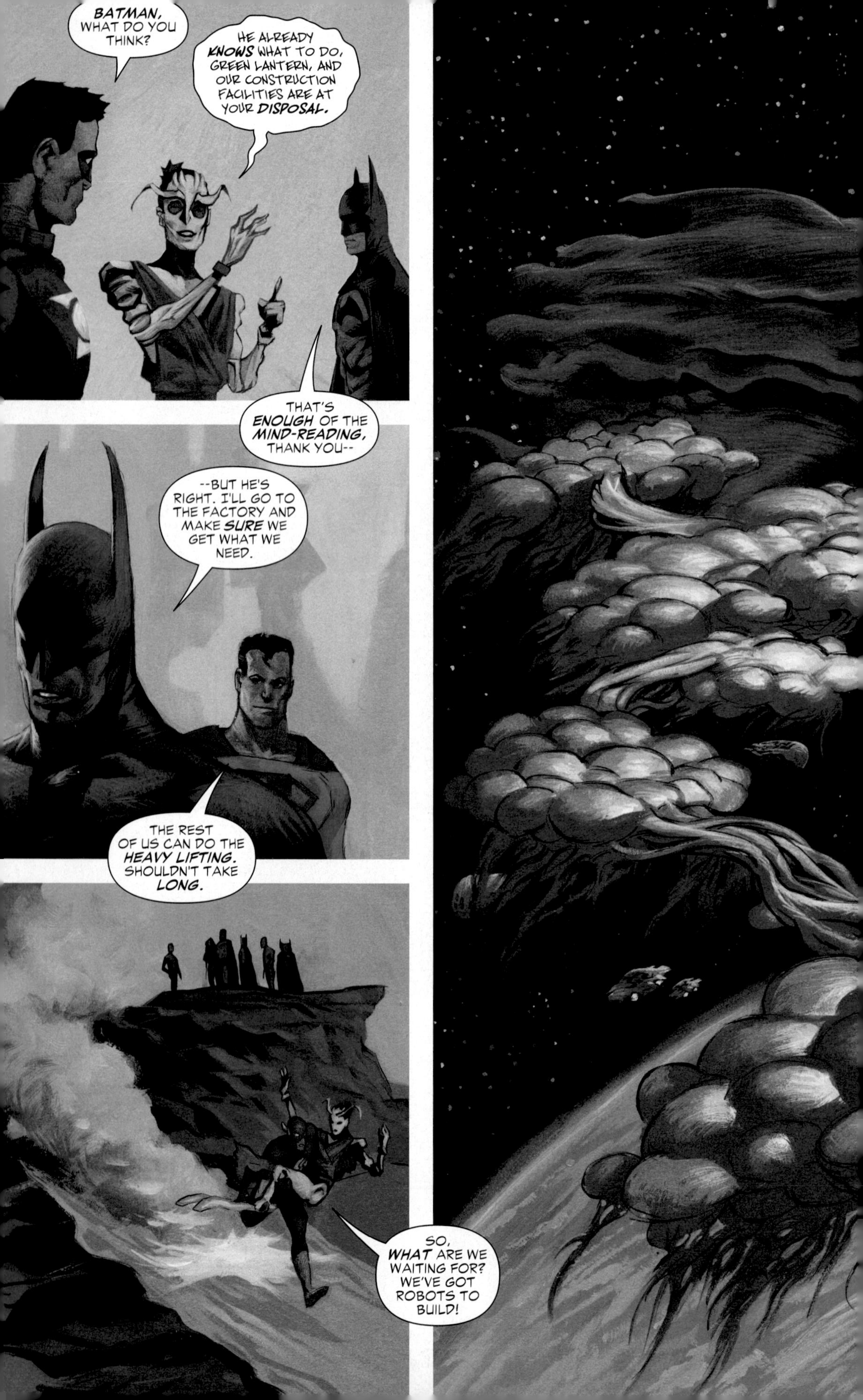
BATMAN, WHAT DO YOU THINK?
HE ALREADY KNOWS WHAT TO DO, GREEN LANTERN, AND OUR CONSTRUCTION FACILITIES ARE AT YOUR DISPOSAL.
THAT'S ENOUGH OF THE MIND-READING, THANK YOU--
--BUT HE'S RIGHT. I'LL GO TO THE FACTORY AND MAKE SURE WE GET WHAT WE NEED.
THE REST OF US CAN DO THE HEAVY LIFTING. SHOULDN'T TAKE LONG.
SO, WHAT ARE WE WAITING FOR? WE'VE GOT ROBOTS TO BUILD!

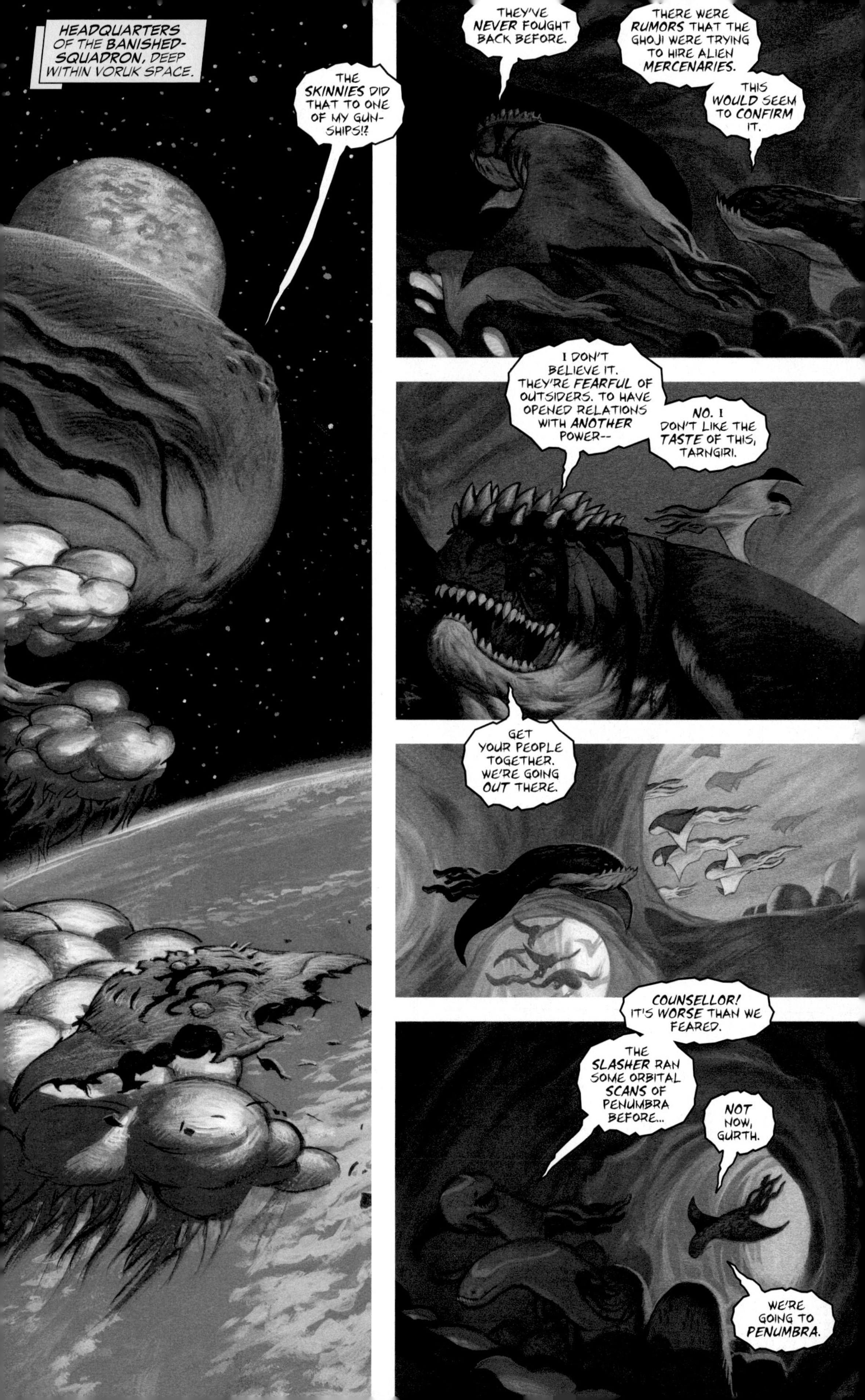
HEADQUARTERS OF THE BANISHED-SQUADRON, DEEP WITHIN VORUK SPACE.
THE SKINNIES DID THAT TO ONE OF MY GUN-SHIPS!?
THEY'VE NEVER FOUGHT BACK BEFORE.
THERE WERE RUMORS THAT THE GHOJI WERE TRYING TO HIRE ALIEN MERCENARIES.
THIS WOULD SEEM TO CONFIRM IT.
I DON'T BELIEVE IT. THEY'RE FEARFUL OF OUTSIDERS. TO HAVE OPENED RELATIONS WITH ANOTHER POWER--
NO. I DON'T LIKE THE TASTE OF THIS, TARNGIRI.
GET YOUR PEOPLE TOGETHER. WE'RE GOING OUT THERE.
COUNSELLOR! IT'S WORSE THAN WE FEARED.
THE SLASHER RAN SOME ORBITAL SCANS OF PENUMBRA BEFORE...
NOT NOW, GURTH.
WE'RE GOING TO PENUMBRA.

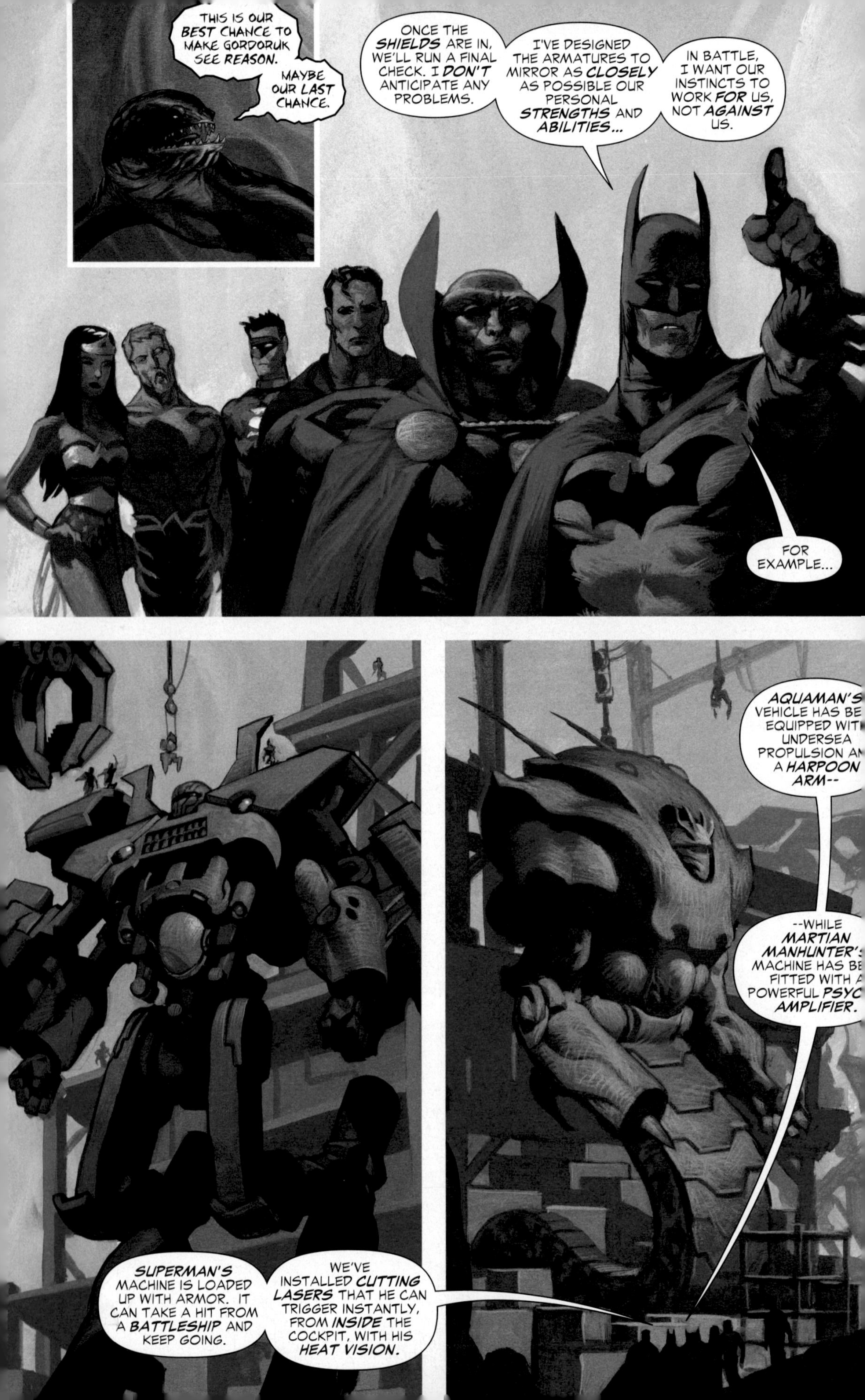
THIS IS OUR BEST CHANCE TO MAKE GORDORUK SEE REASON.
MAYBE OUR LAST CHANCE.
ONCE THE SHIELDS ARE IN, WE'LL RUN A FINAL CHECK. I DON'T ANTICIPATE ANY PROBLEMS.
I'VE DESIGNED THE ARMATURES TO MIRROR AS CLOSELY AS POSSIBLE OUR PERSONAL STRENGTHS AND ABILITIES...
IN BATTLE, I WANT OUR INSTINCTS TO WORK FOR US, NOT AGAINST US.
FOR EXAMPLE...
SUPERMAN'S MACHINE IS LOADED UP WITH ARMOR. IT CAN TAKE A HIT FROM A BATTLESHIP AND KEEP GOING.
WE'VE INSTALLED CUTTING LASERS THAT HE CAN TRIGGER INSTANTLY, FROM INSIDE THE COCKPIT, WITH HIS HEAT VISION.
AQUAMAN'S VEHICLE HAS BE EQUIPPED WIT UNDERSEA PROPULSION A A HARPOON ARM--
--WHILE MARTIAN MANHUNTER' MACHINE HAS BE FITTED WITH A POWERFUL PSYC AMPLIFIER.

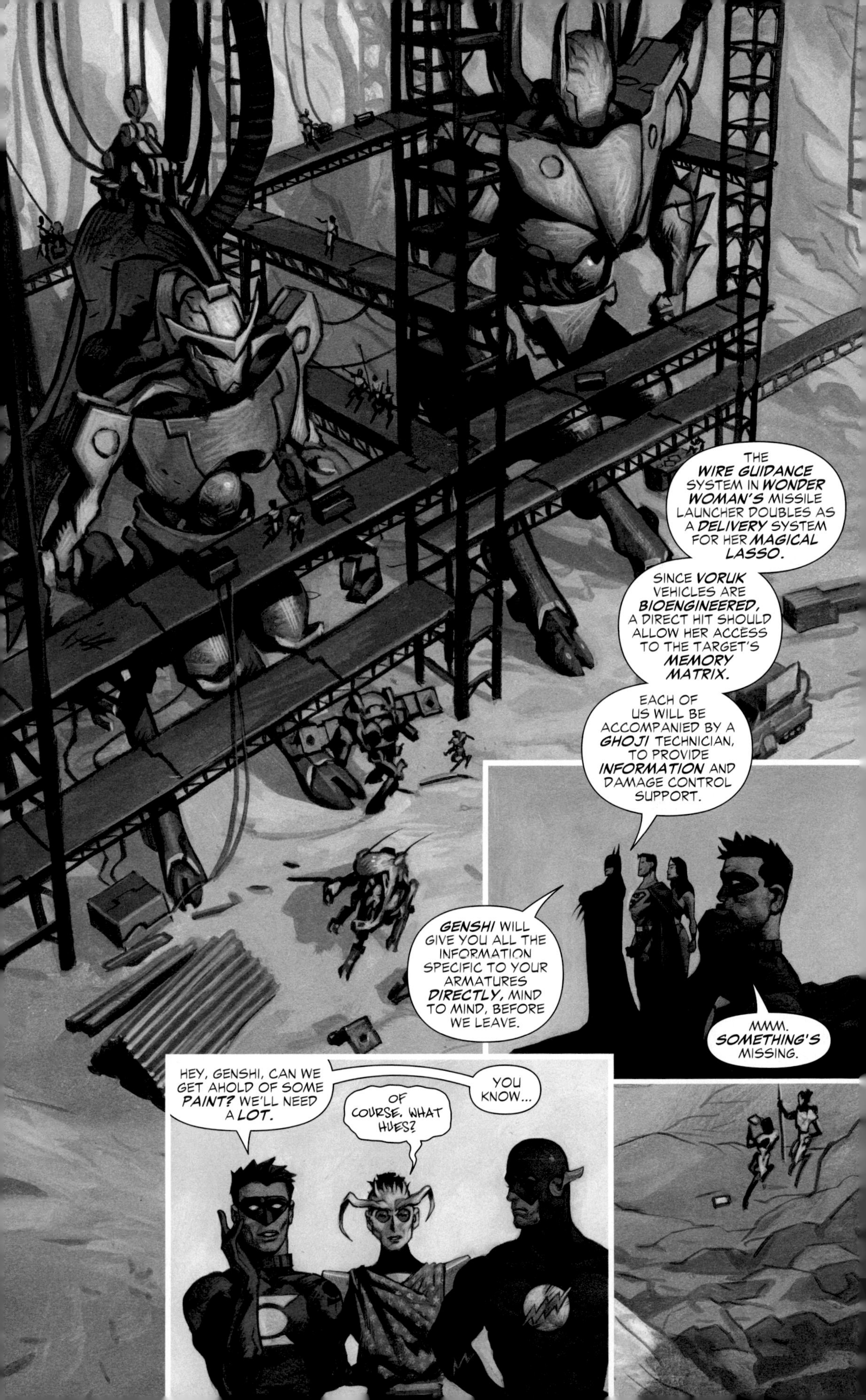
THE WIRE GUIDANCE SYSTEM IN WONDER WOMAN'S MISSILE LAUNCHER DOUBLES AS A DELIVERY SYSTEM FOR HER MAGICAL LASSO.
SINCE VORUK VEHICLES ARE BIOENGINEERED, A DIRECT HIT SHOULD ALLOW HER ACCESS TO THE TARGET'S MEMORY MATRIX.
EACH OF US WILL BE ACCOMPANIED BY A GHOJI TECHNICIAN, TO PROVIDE INFORMATION AND DAMAGE CONTROL SUPPORT.
GENSHI WILL GIVE YOU ALL THE INFORMATION SPECIFIC TO YOUR ARMATURES DIRECTLY, MIND TO MIND, BEFORE WE LEAVE.
MMM. SOMETHING'S MISSING.
YOU KNOW...
HEY, GENSHI, CAN WE GET AHOLD OF SOME PAINT? WE'LL NEED A LOT.
OF COURSE. WHAT HUES?

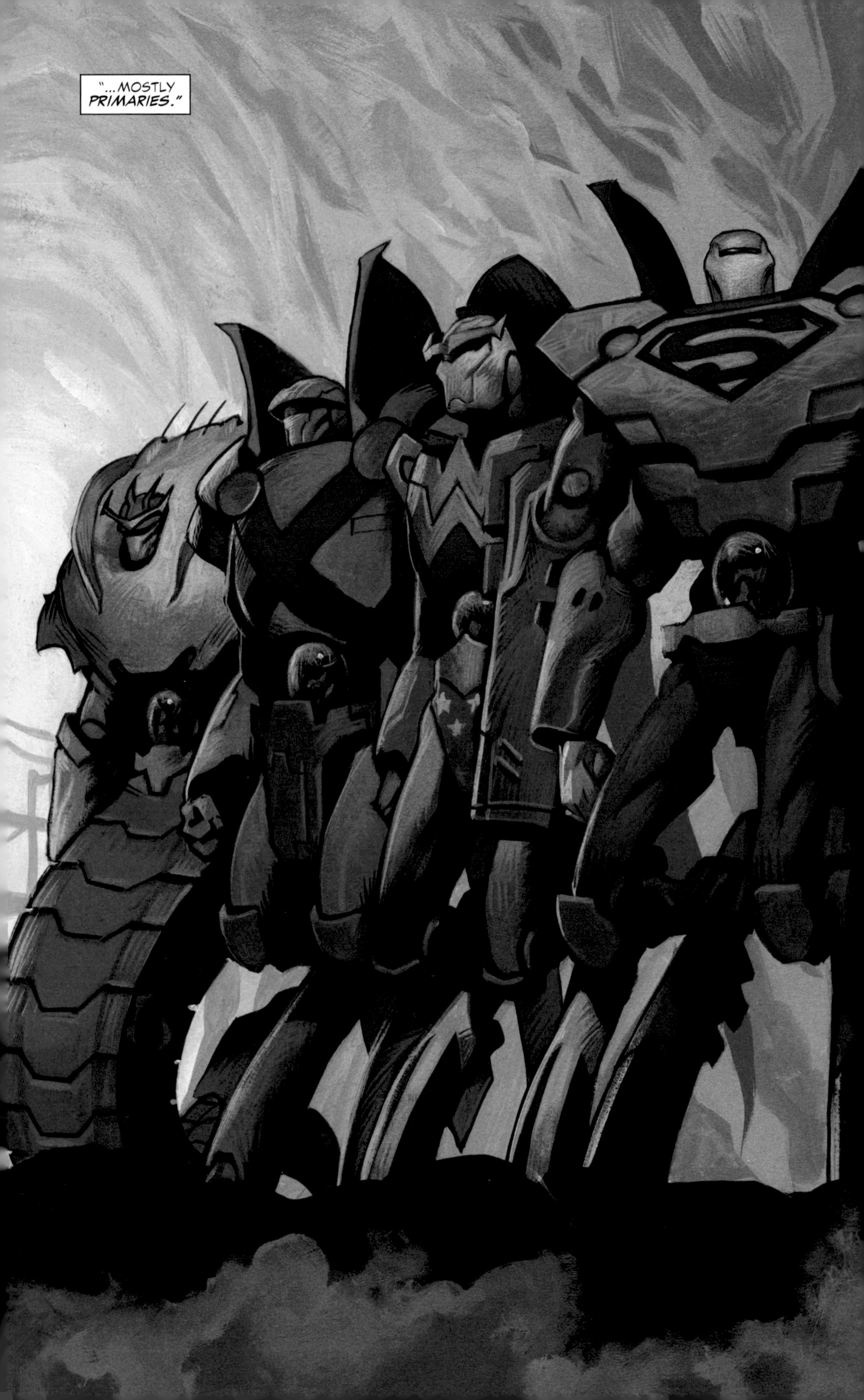
"...MOSTLY PRIMARIES."

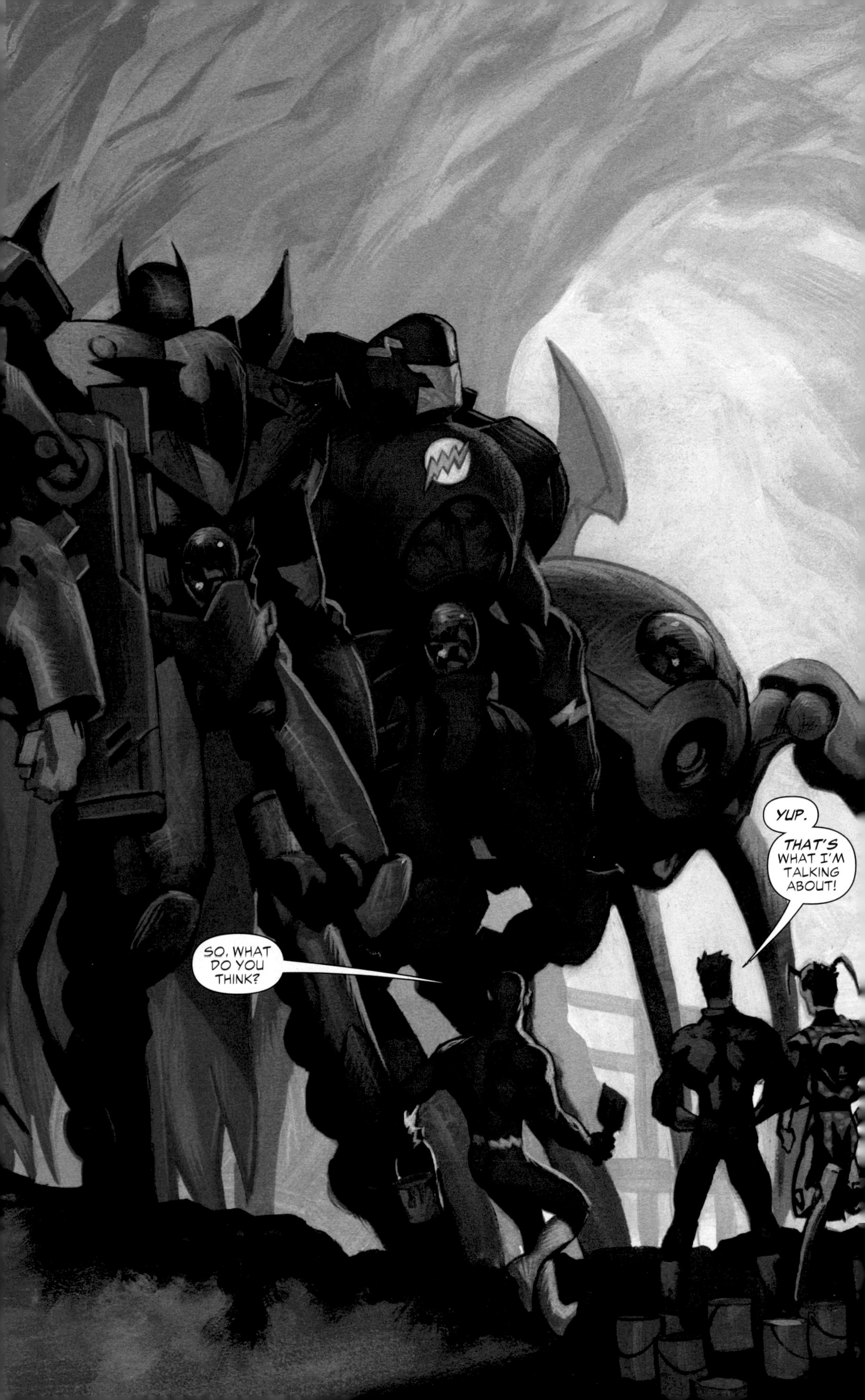
So, what do you think?
Yup.
That's what I'm talking about!

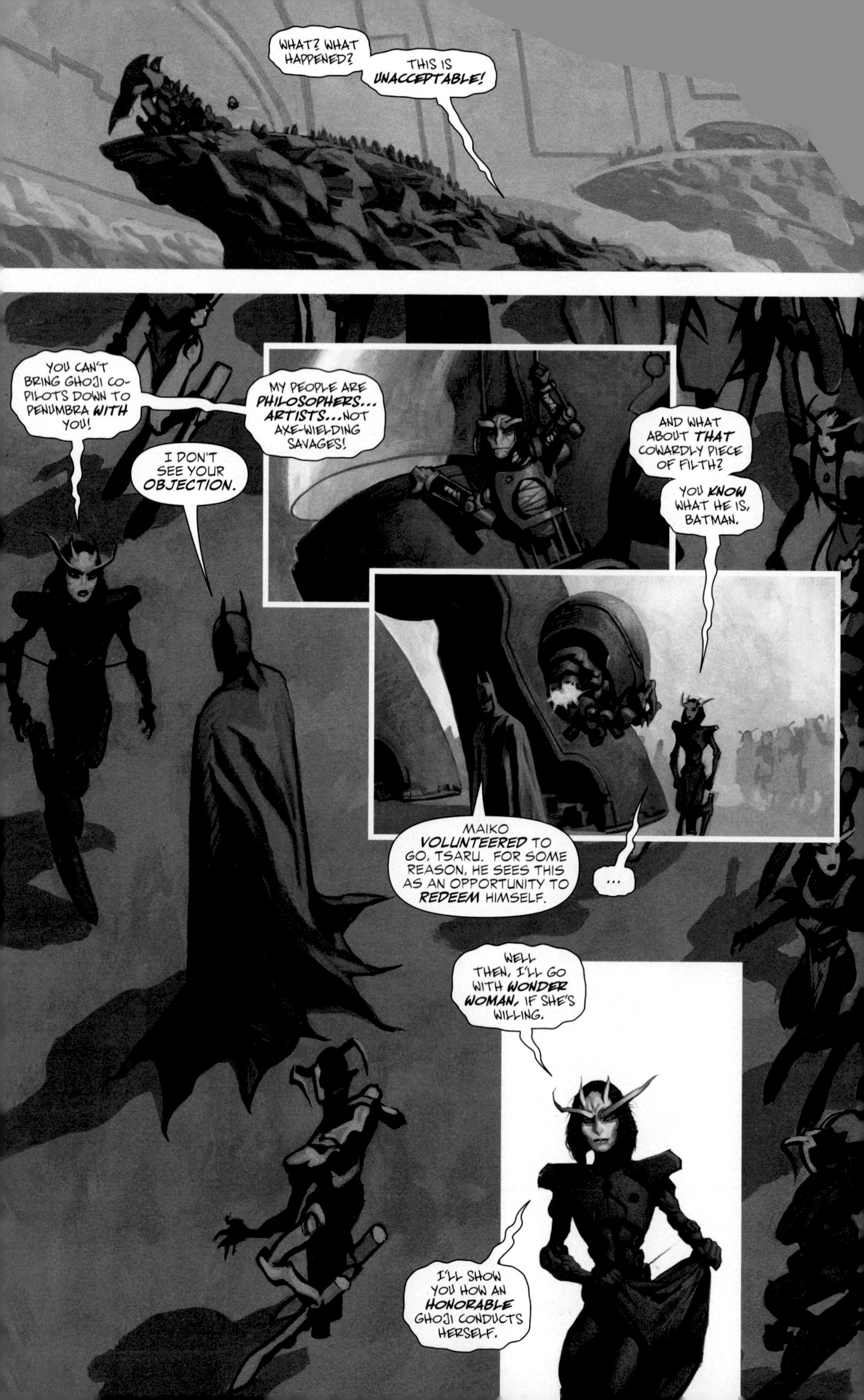
WHAT? WHAT HAPPENED?
THIS IS UNACCEPTABLE!
YOU CAN'T BRING GHOJI CO-PILOTS DOWN TO PENUMBRA WITH YOU!
MY PEOPLE ARE PHILOSOPHERS... ARTISTS...NOT AXE-WIELDING SAVAGES!
I DON'T SEE YOUR OBJECTION.
AND WHAT ABOUT THAT COWARDLY PIECE OF FILTH?
YOU KNOW WHAT HE IS, BATMAN.
MAIKO VOLUNTEERED TO GO, TSARU. FOR SOME REASON, HE SEES THIS AS AN OPPORTUNITY TO REDEEM HIMSELF.
...
WELL THEN, I'LL GO WITH WONDER WOMAN, IF SHE'S WILLING.
I'LL SHOW YOU HOW AN HONORABLE GHOJI CONDUCTS HERSELF.

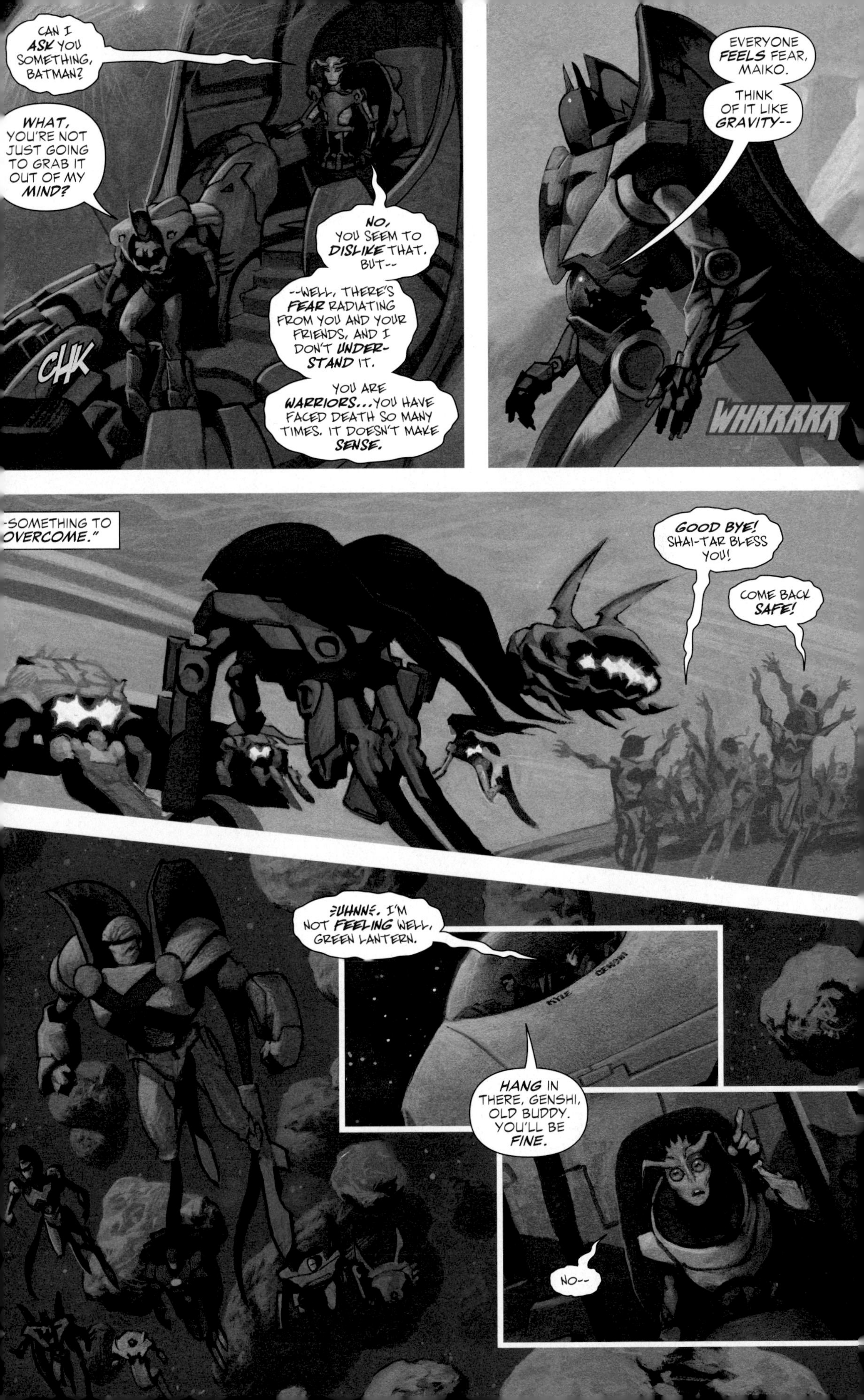
CAN I ASK YOU SOMETHING, BATMAN?
WHAT, YOU'RE NOT JUST GOING TO GRAB IT OUT OF MY MIND?
NO, YOU SEEM TO DISLIKE THAT. BUT--
--WELL, THERE'S FEAR RADIATING FROM YOU AND YOUR FRIENDS, AND I DON'T UNDER-STAND IT.
YOU ARE WARRIORS...YOU HAVE FACED DEATH SO MANY TIMES. IT DOESN'T MAKE SENSE.
CHK
EVERYONE FEELS FEAR, MAIKO.
THINK OF IT LIKE GRAVITY--
WHRRRRR
-SOMETHING TO OVERCOME."
GOOD BYE! SHAI-TAR BLESS YOU!
COME BACK SAFE!
UHNN. I'M NOT FEELING WELL, GREEN LANTERN.
KYLE
GENSHI
HANG IN THERE, GENSHI, OLD BUDDY. YOU'LL BE FINE.
NO--

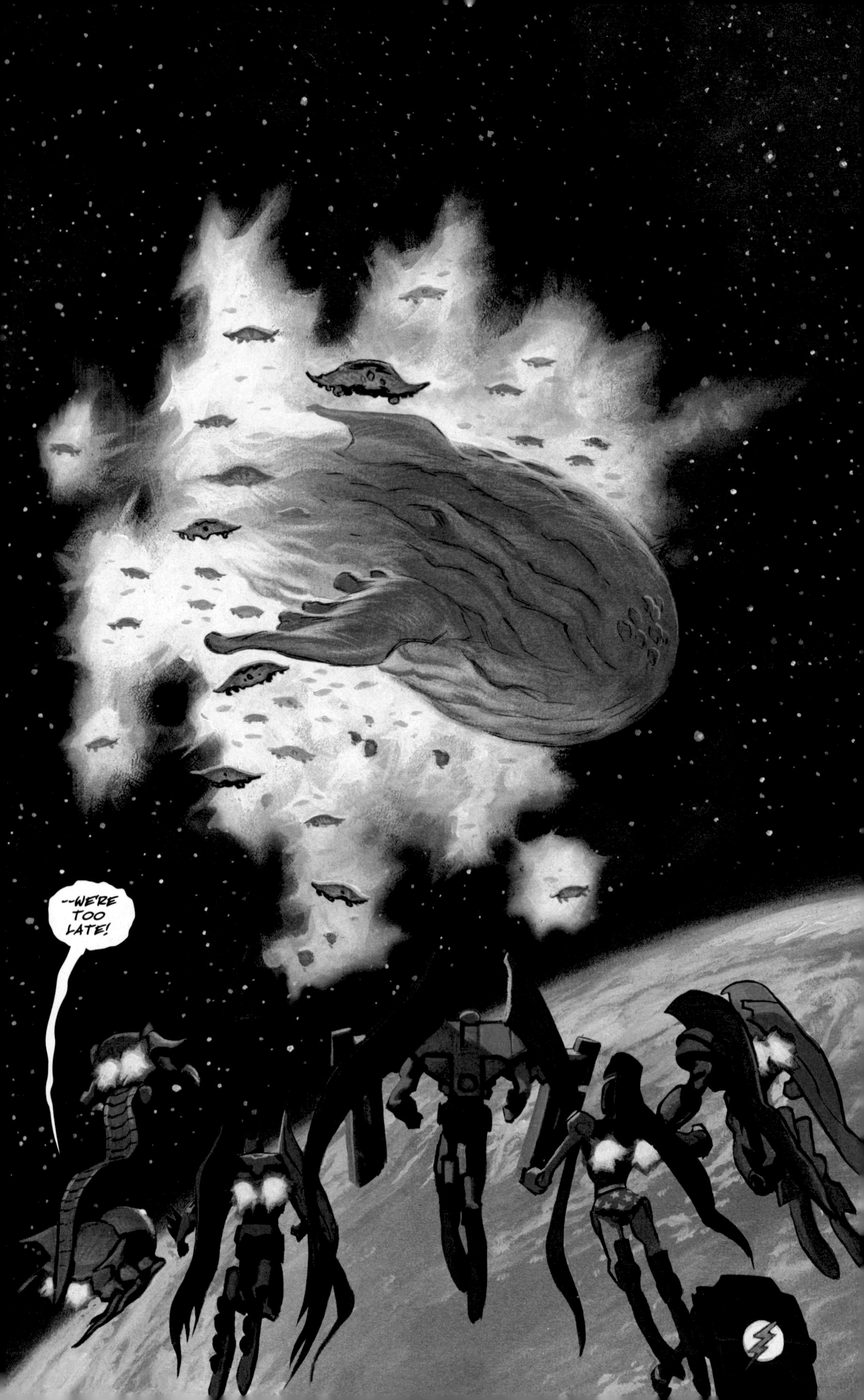
--WE'RE TOO LATE!

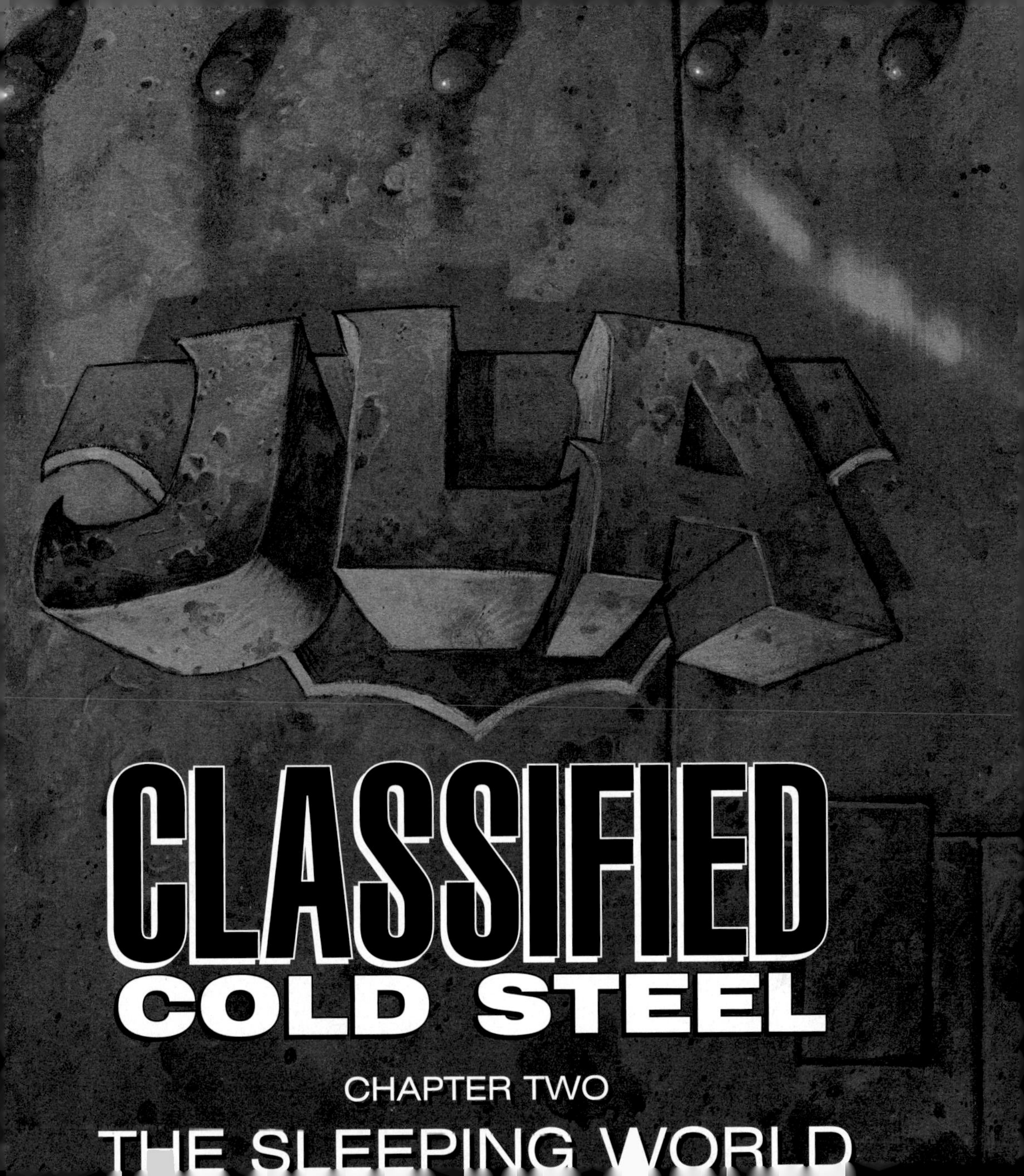
JLA
CLASSIFIED
COLD STEEL
CHAPTER TWO
THE SLEEPING WORLD

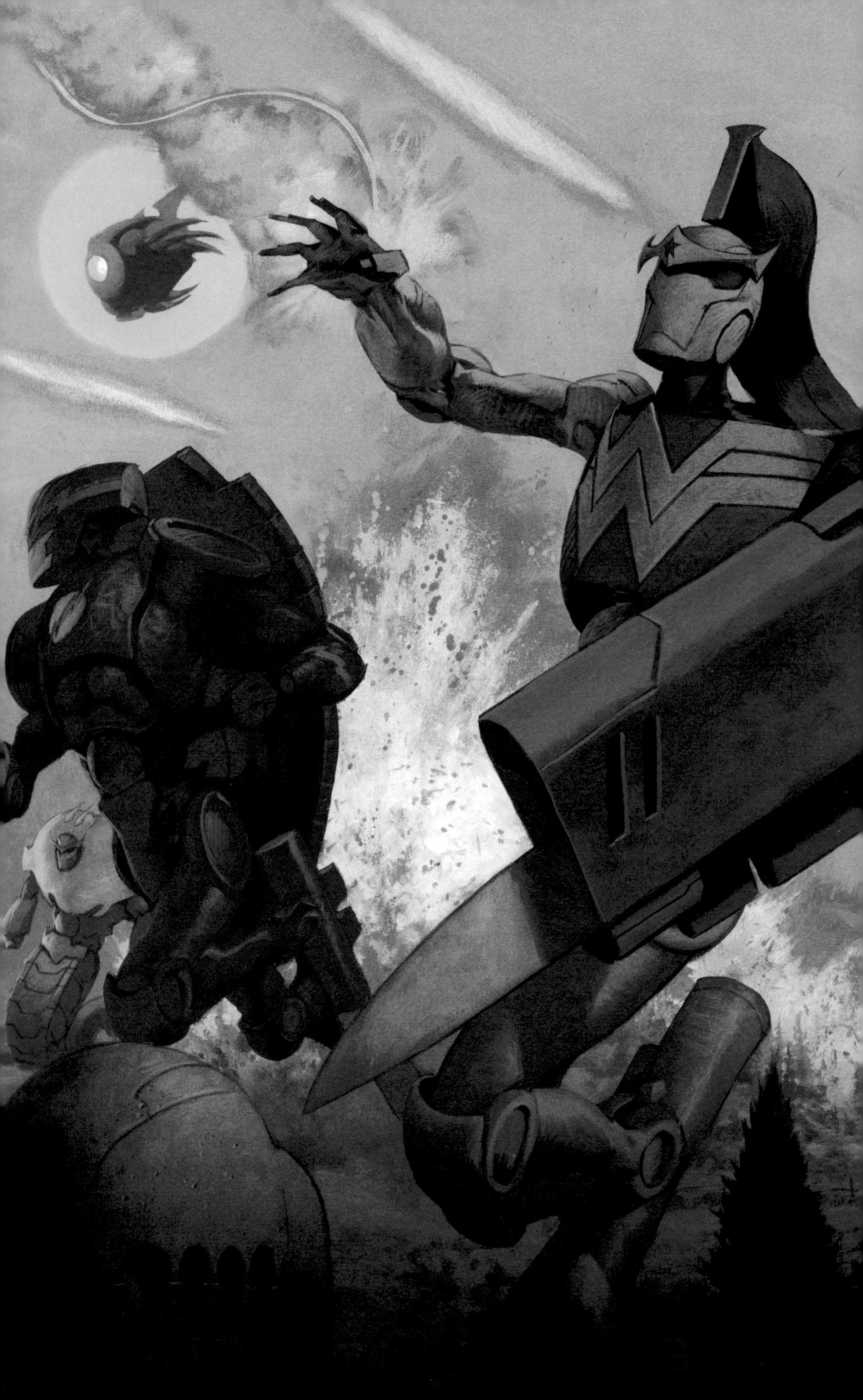

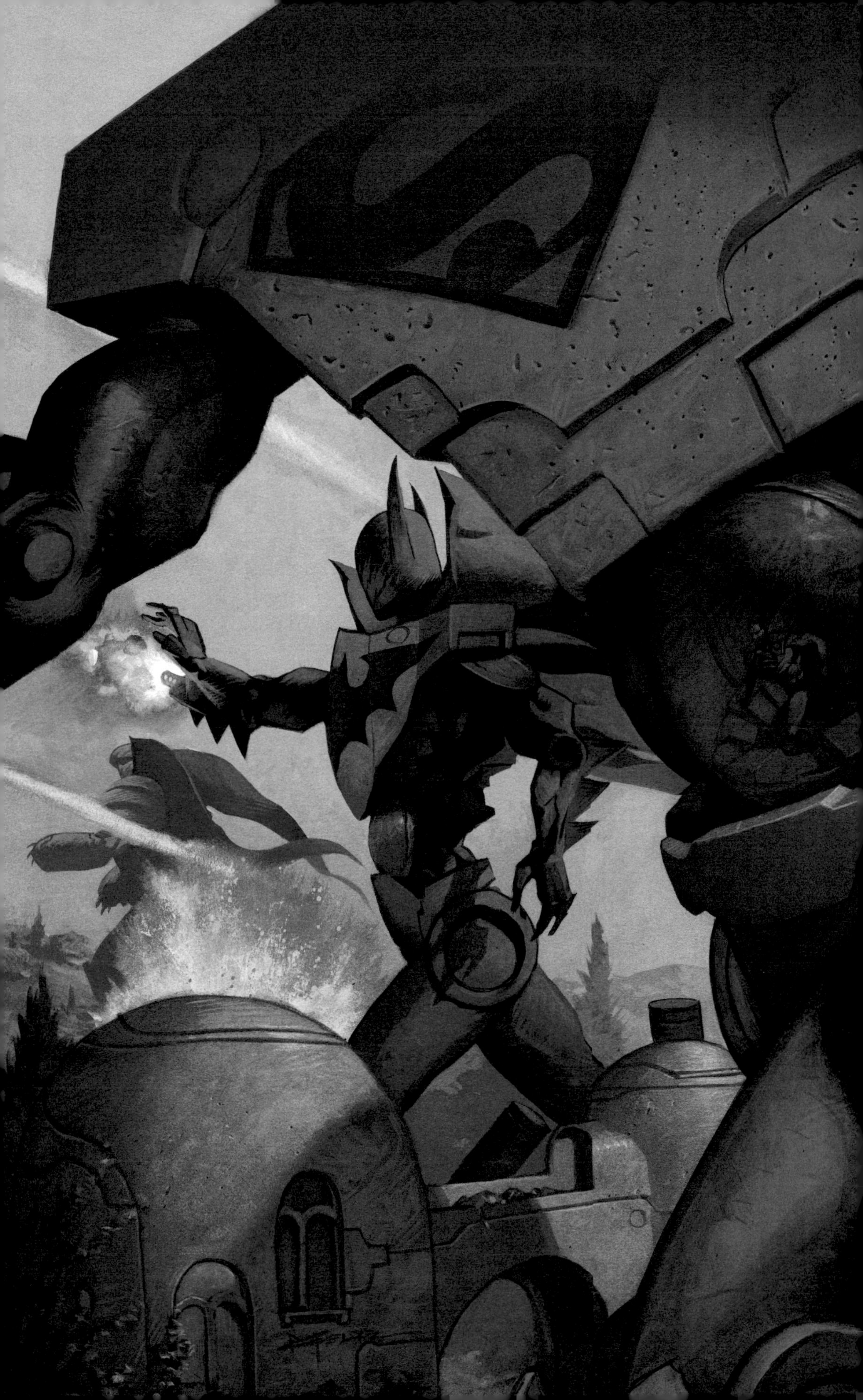

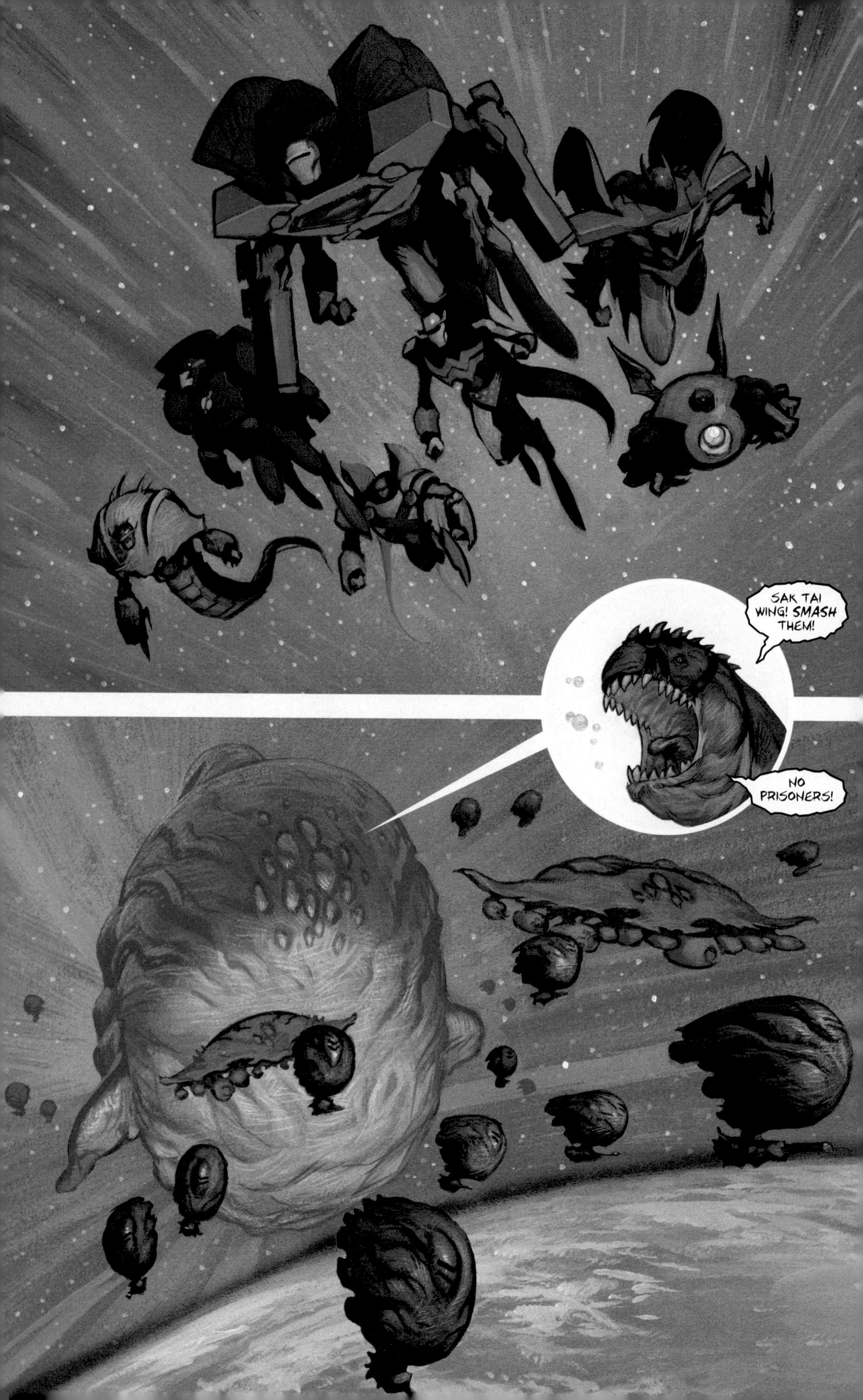
SAK TAI WING! SMASH THEM!
NO PRISONERS!

RAK

I DON'T WANT TO BE A *DEFEATIST* HERE, BUT THERE ARE AN AWFUL LOT OF THEM.

PROTECT YOUR *SHIELDS!*

AT *SOME* POINT, THEY'RE GONNA HIT WHAT THEY *WANT* TO HIT.

KANG

GODS! GREEN LANTERN! CAN'T YOU THROW UP A *SHIELD* OR SOME-THING?

I CAN FEND THESE BOZOS OFF, AQUAMAN, AS LONG AS YOU *WANT*--

--BUT THE LONGER WE SPEND *DOGFIGHTING,* THE *CLOSER* THOSE BIG SHIPS AND THEIR BIG *GUNS* ARE GONNA GET.

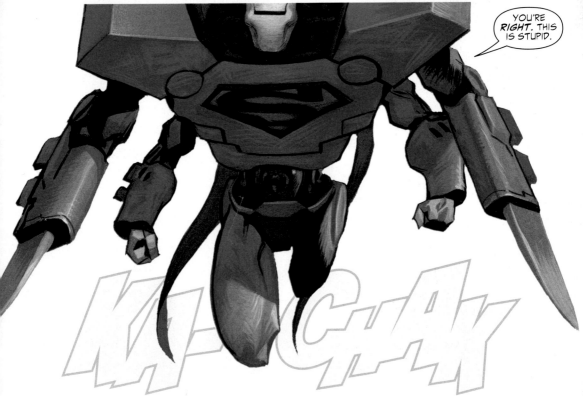

YOU'RE *RIGHT.* THIS IS STUPID.

KA-C-AK

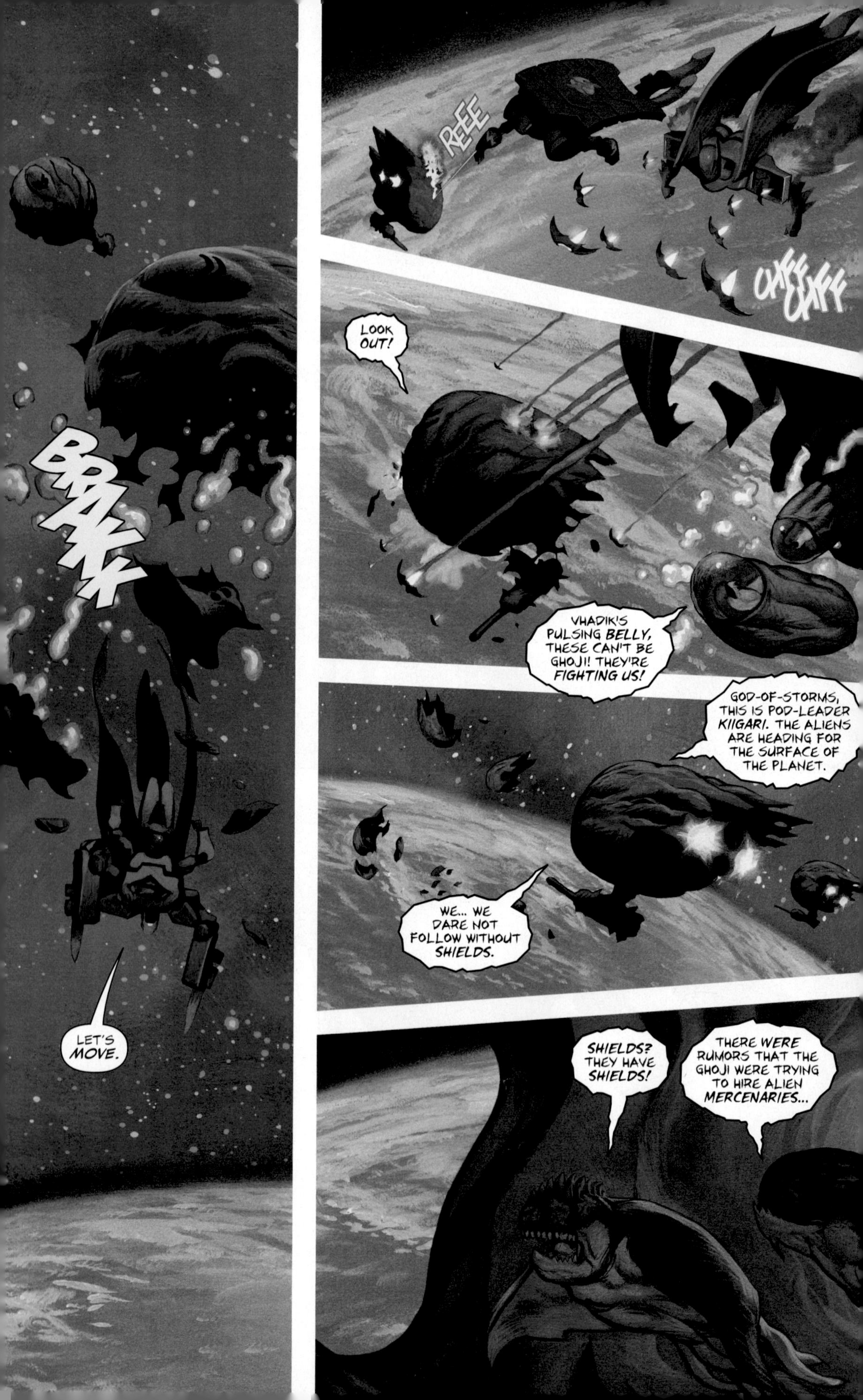
BRAKK
LET'S MOVE.
REEE
CHFF CHFF
LOOK OUT!
VHADIK'S PULSING BELLY, THESE CAN'T BE GHOJI! THEY'RE FIGHTING US!
GOD-OF-STORMS, THIS IS POD-LEADER KIIGARI. THE ALIENS ARE HEADING FOR THE SURFACE OF THE PLANET.
WE... WE DARE NOT FOLLOW WITHOUT SHIELDS.
SHIELDS? THEY HAVE SHIELDS!
THERE WERE RUMORS THAT THE GHOJI WERE TRYING TO HIRE ALIEN MERCENARIES...

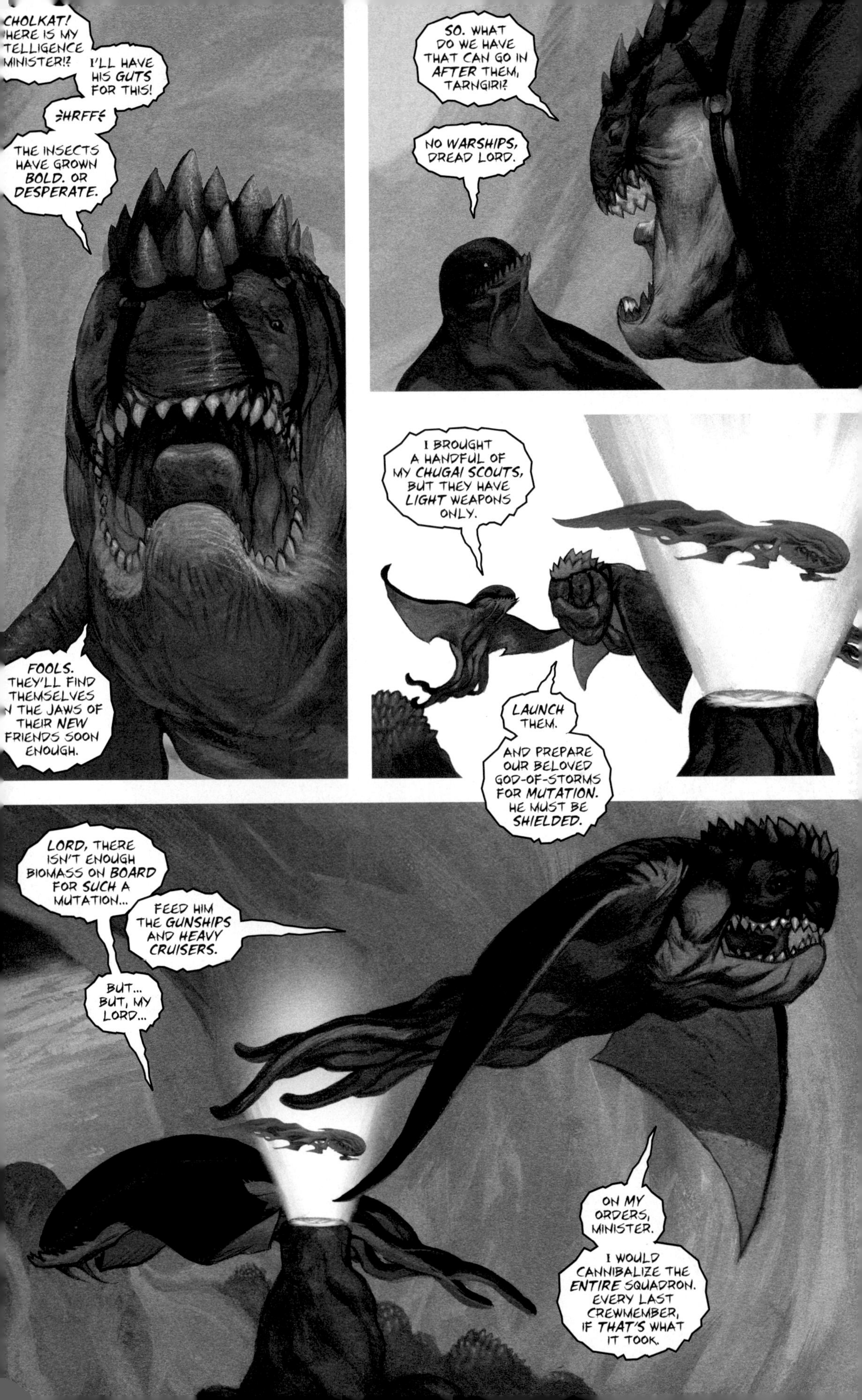
CHOLKAT! WHERE IS MY INTELLIGENCE MINISTER!?
I'LL HAVE HIS GUTS FOR THIS!
SHRFF
THE INSECTS HAVE GROWN BOLD. OR DESPERATE.
SO. WHAT DO WE HAVE THAT CAN GO IN AFTER THEM, TARNGIRI?
NO WARSHIPS, DREAD LORD.
FOOLS. THEY'LL FIND THEMSELVES IN THE JAWS OF THEIR NEW FRIENDS SOON ENOUGH.
I BROUGHT A HANDFUL OF MY CHUGAI SCOUTS, BUT THEY HAVE LIGHT WEAPONS ONLY.
LAUNCH THEM.
AND PREPARE OUR BELOVED GOD-OF-STORMS FOR MUTATION. HE MUST BE SHIELDED.
LORD, THERE ISN'T ENOUGH BIOMASS ON BOARD FOR SUCH A MUTATION...
FEED HIM THE GUNSHIPS AND HEAVY CRUISERS.
BUT... BUT, MY LORD...
ON MY ORDERS, MINISTER.
I WOULD CANNIBALIZE THE ENTIRE SQUADRON. EVERY LAST CREWMEMBER, IF THAT'S WHAT IT TOOK.

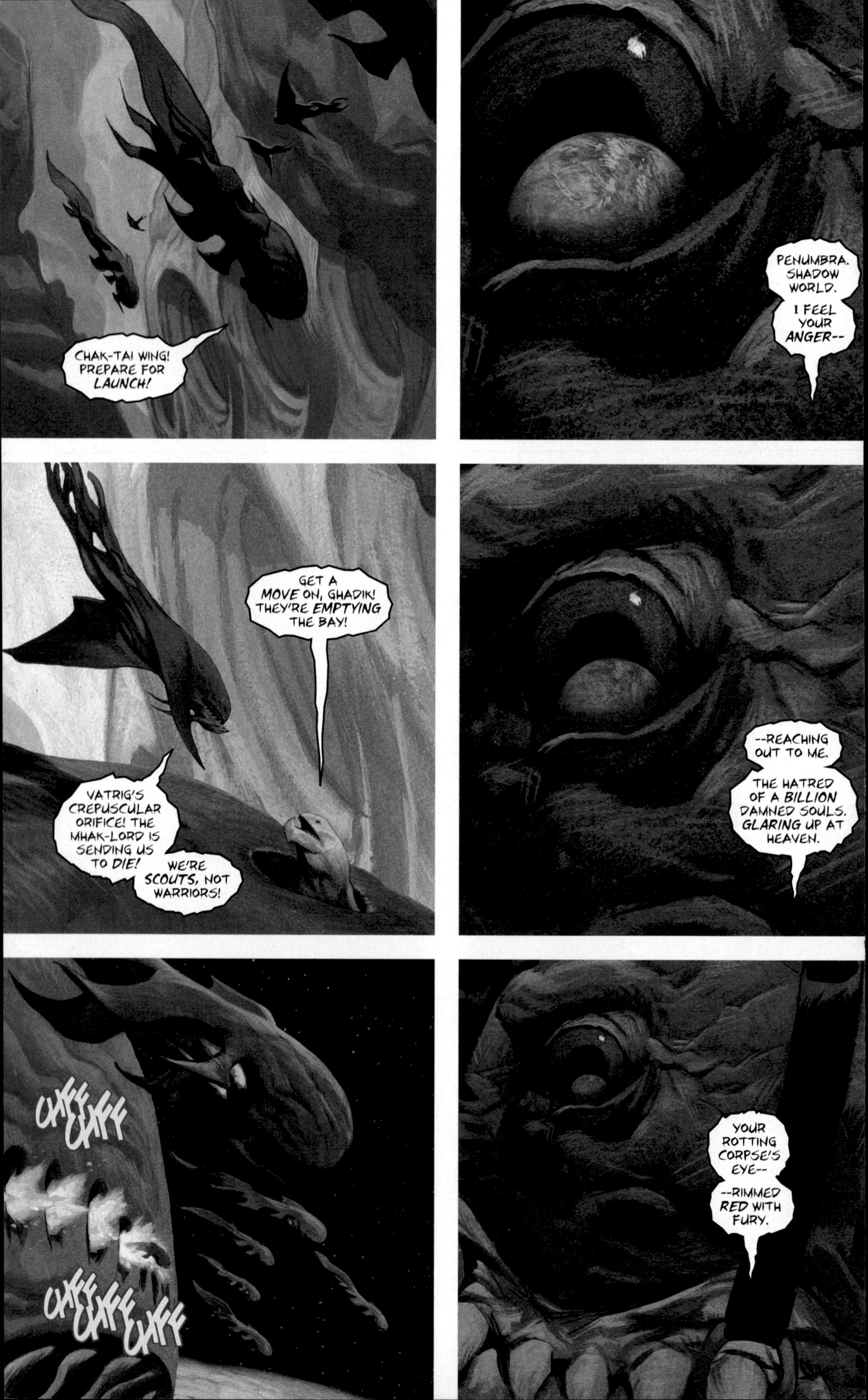
CHAK-TAI WING! PREPARE FOR LAUNCH!
PENUMBRA. SHADOW WORLD.
I FEEL YOUR ANGER--
GET A MOVE ON, GHADIK! THEY'RE EMPTYING THE BAY!
VATRIG'S CREPUSCULAR ORIFICE! THE MHAK-LORD IS SENDING US TO DIE!
WE'RE SCOUTS, NOT WARRIORS!
--REACHING OUT TO ME.
THE HATRED OF A BILLION DAMNED SOULS. GLARING UP AT HEAVEN.
CHFF CHFF
CHFF CHFF CHFF
YOUR ROTTING CORPSE'S EYE--
--RIMMED RED WITH FURY.

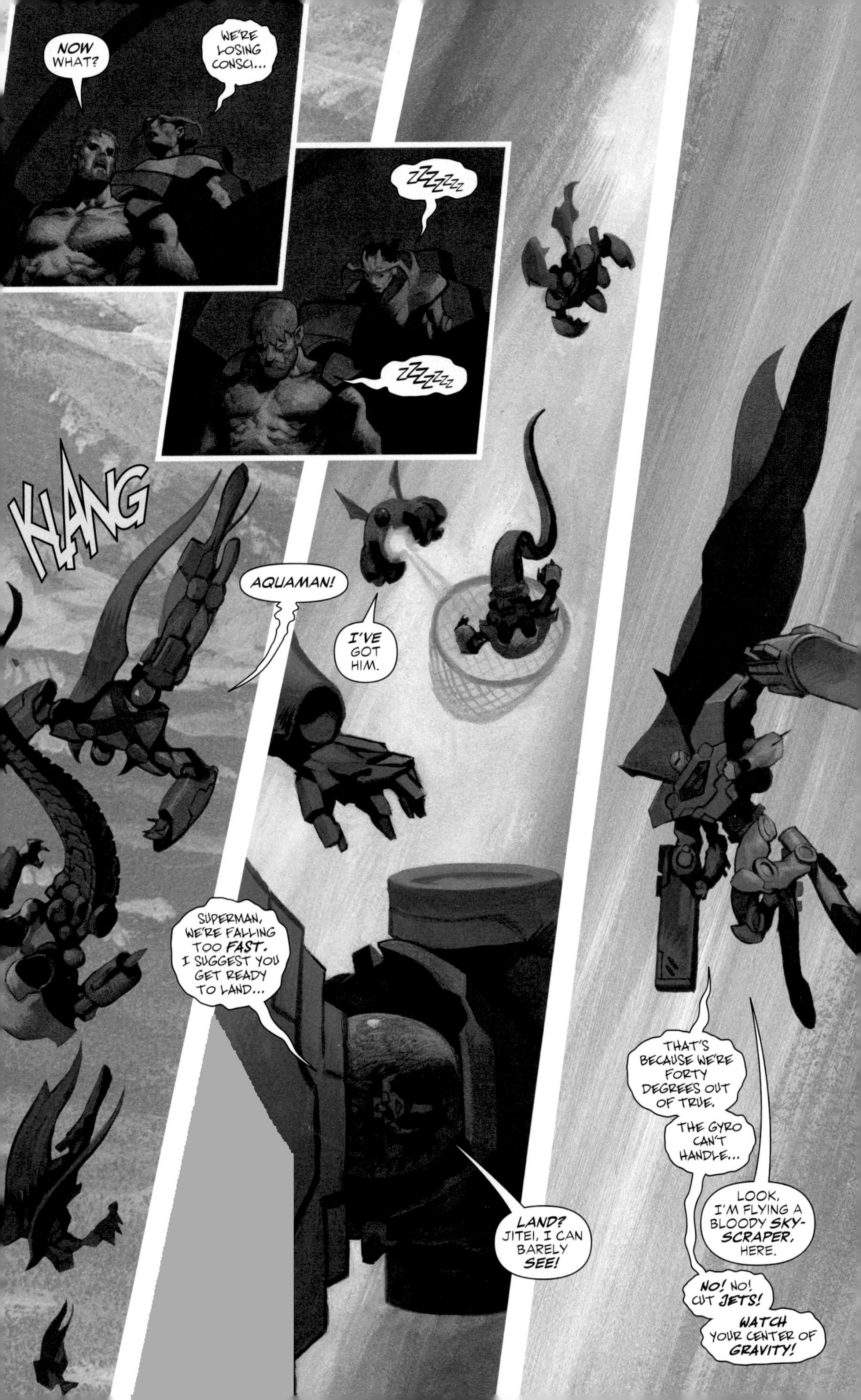
NOW WHAT?
WE'RE LOSING CONSCI...
ZZZZZZZ
ZZZZZZZ
KLANG
AQUAMAN!
I'VE GOT HIM.
SUPERMAN, WE'RE FALLING TOO FAST. I SUGGEST YOU GET READY TO LAND...
LAND? JITEI, I CAN BARELY SEE!
THAT'S BECAUSE WE'RE FORTY DEGREES OUT OF TRUE.
THE GYRO CAN'T HANDLE...
LOOK, I'M FLYING A BLOODY SKY-SCRAPER, HERE.
NO! NO! CUT JETS!
WATCH YOUR CENTER OF GRAVITY!

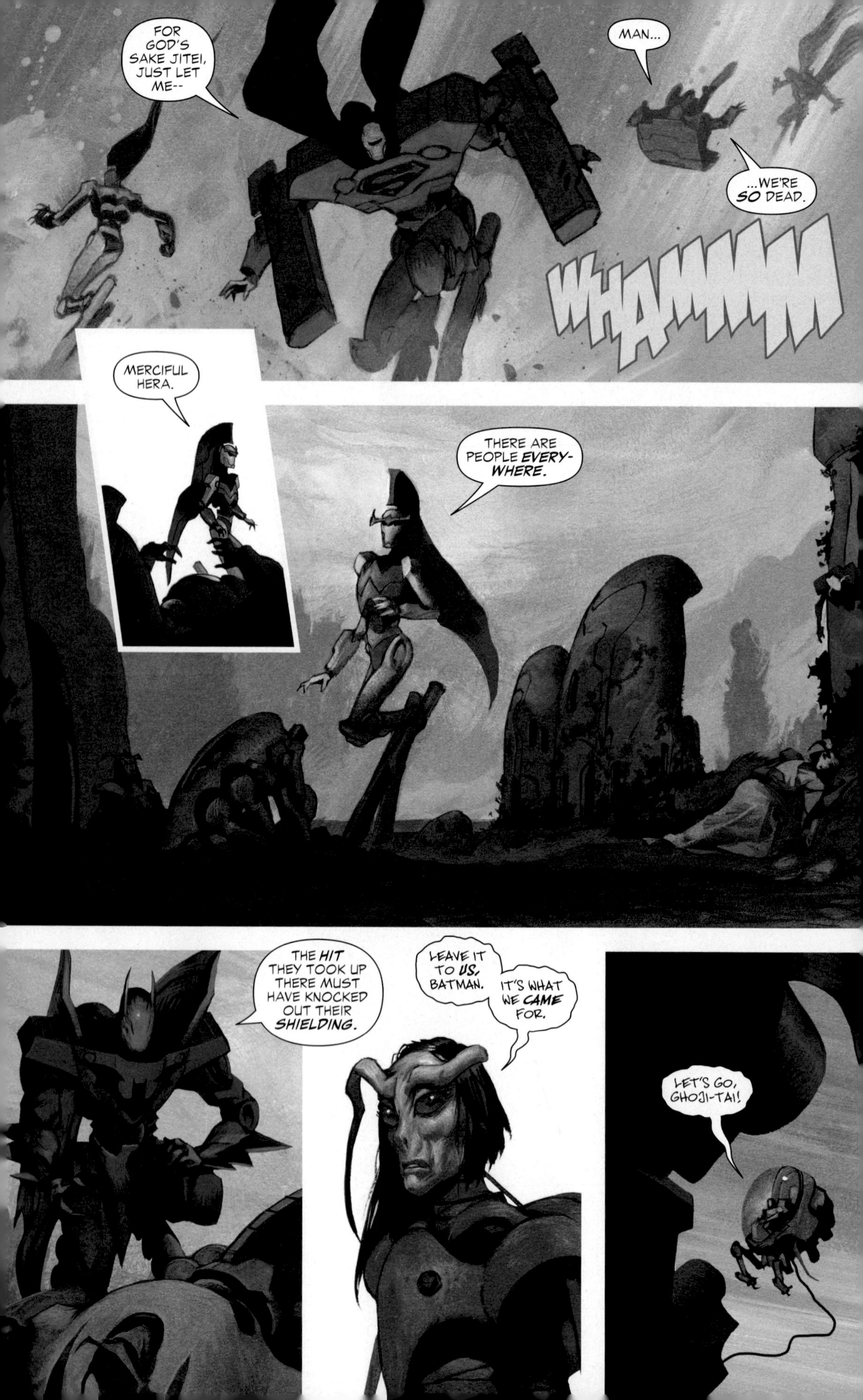
FOR GOD'S SAKE JITEI, JUST LET ME--
MAN...
...WE'RE SO DEAD.
WHAMMMM
MERCIFUL HERA.
THERE ARE PEOPLE EVERY-WHERE.
THE HIT THEY TOOK UP THERE MUST HAVE KNOCKED OUT THEIR SHIELDING.
LEAVE IT TO US, BATMAN.
IT'S WHAT WE CAME FOR.
LET'S GO, GHOJI-TAI!

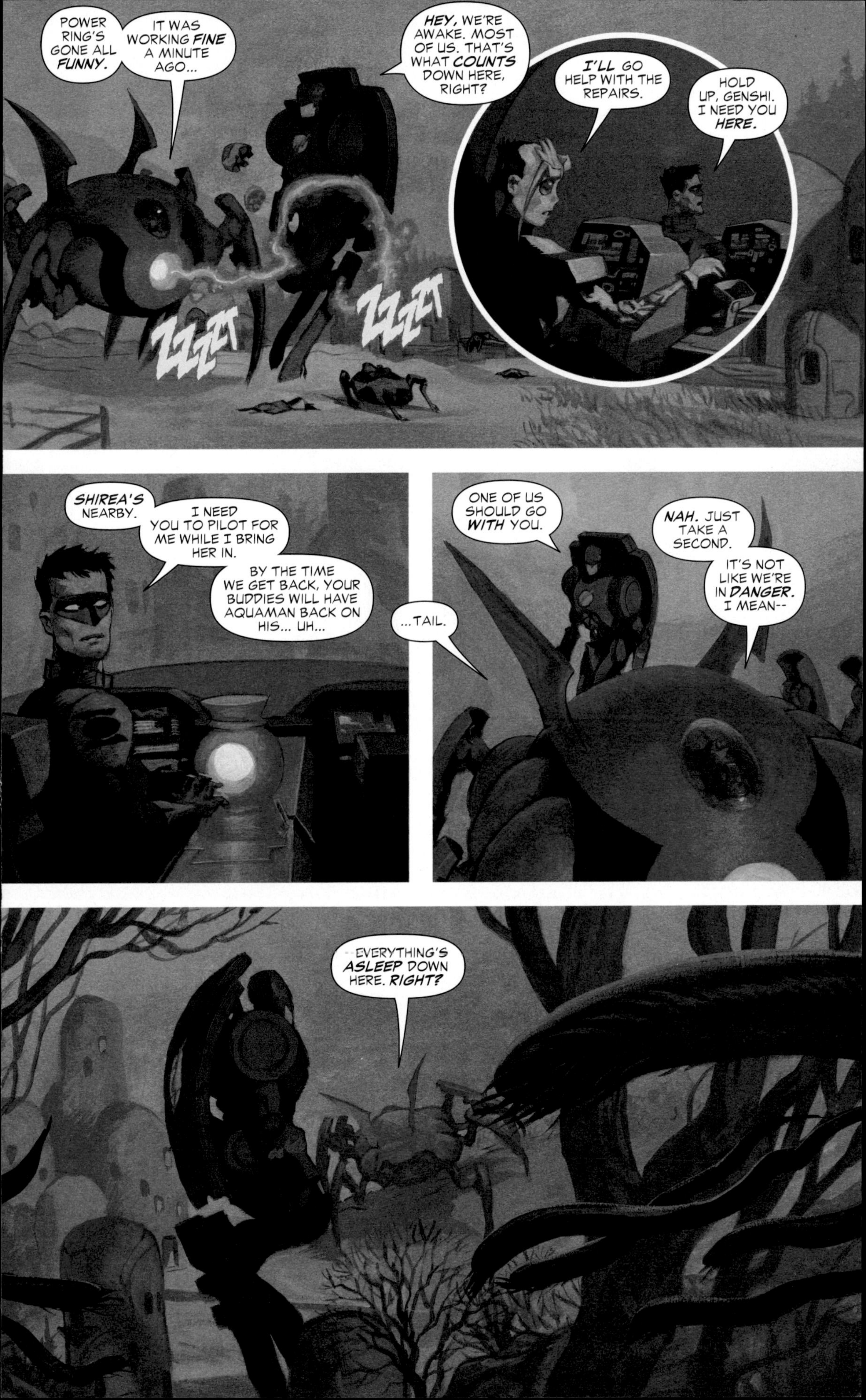
POWER RING'S GONE ALL FUNNY.
IT WAS WORKING FINE A MINUTE AGO...
HEY, WE'RE AWAKE. MOST OF US. THAT'S WHAT COUNTS DOWN HERE, RIGHT?
I'LL GO HELP WITH THE REPAIRS.
HOLD UP, GENSHI. I NEED YOU HERE.
ZZZZZT
ZZZZZT
SHIREA'S NEARBY.
I NEED YOU TO PILOT FOR ME WHILE I BRING HER IN.
BY THE TIME WE GET BACK, YOUR BUDDIES WILL HAVE AQUAMAN BACK ON HIS... UH...
...TAIL.
ONE OF US SHOULD GO WITH YOU.
NAH. JUST TAKE A SECOND.
IT'S NOT LIKE WE'RE IN DANGER. I MEAN--
--EVERYTHING'S ASLEEP DOWN HERE. RIGHT?

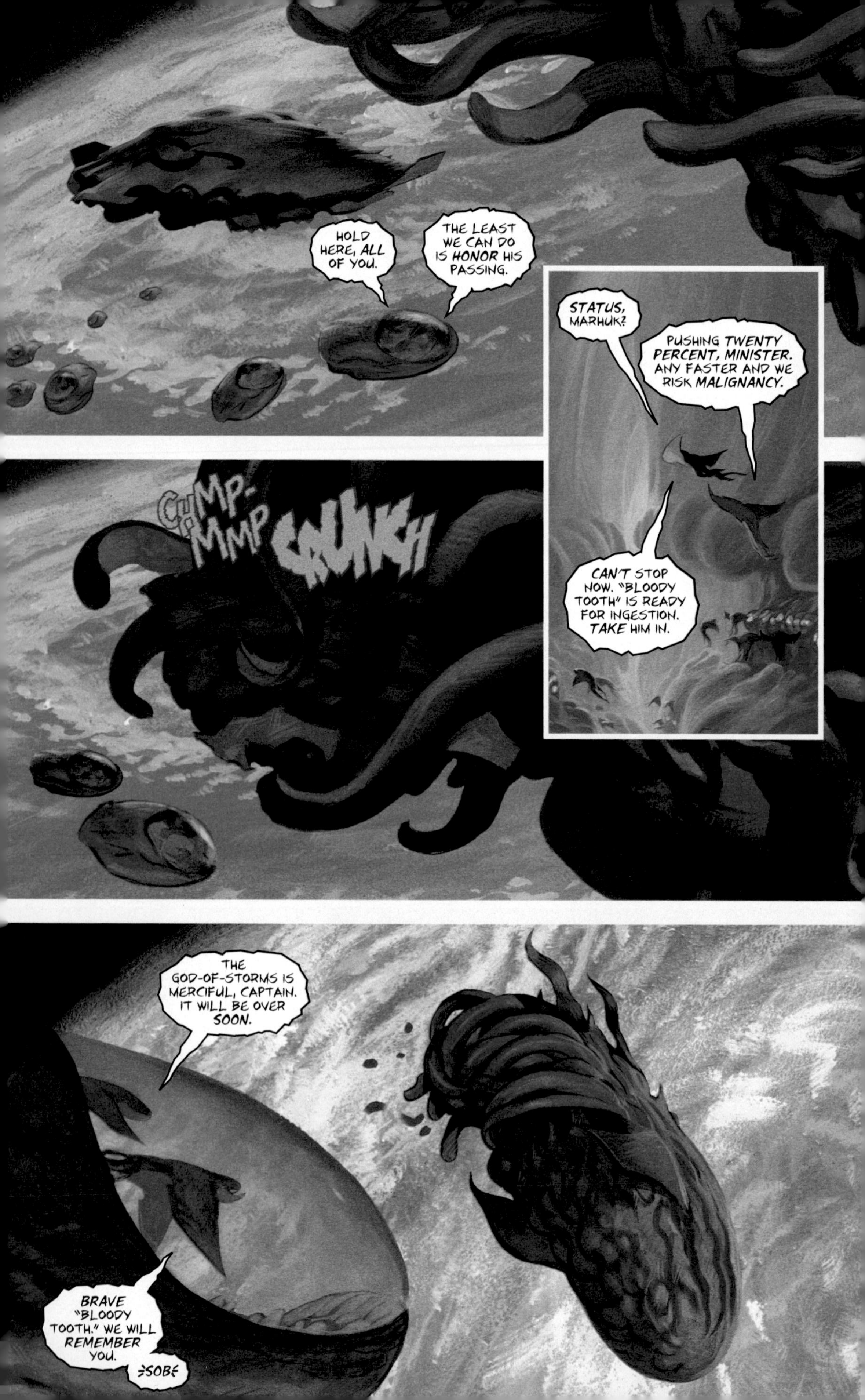
HOLD HERE, ALL OF YOU.
THE LEAST WE CAN DO IS HONOR HIS PASSING.
STATUS, MARHUK?
PUSHING TWENTY PERCENT, MINISTER. ANY FASTER AND WE RISK MALIGNANCY.
CAN'T STOP NOW. "BLOODY TOOTH" IS READY FOR INGESTION. TAKE HIM IN.
CHMP-MMP
CRUNCH
THE GOD-OF-STORMS IS MERCIFUL, CAPTAIN. IT WILL BE OVER SOON.
BRAVE "BLOODY TOOTH." WE WILL REMEMBER YOU.
SOB

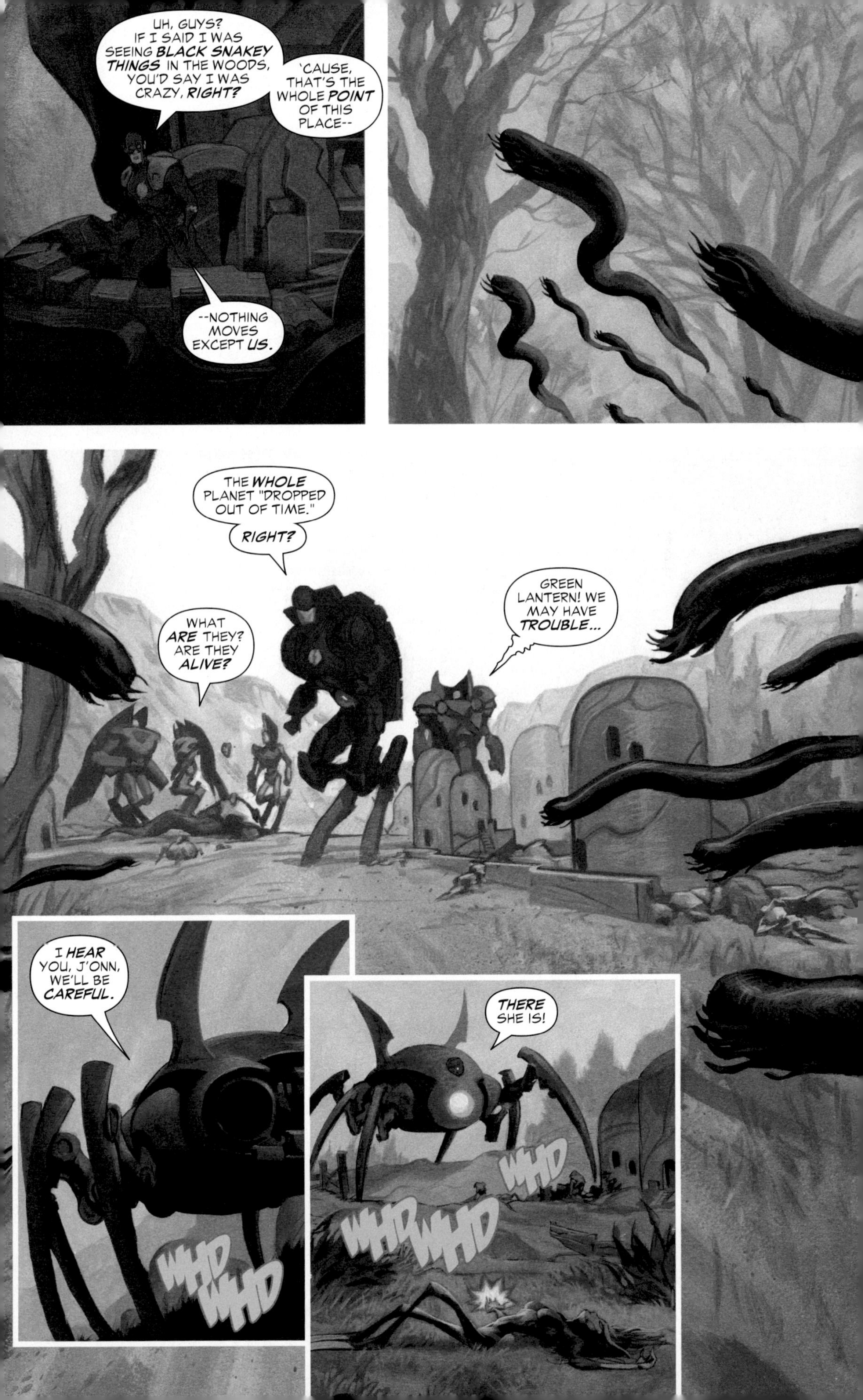
UH, GUYS? IF I SAID I WAS SEEING BLACK SNAKEY THINGS IN THE WOODS, YOU'D SAY I WAS CRAZY, RIGHT?
'CAUSE, THAT'S THE WHOLE POINT OF THIS PLACE--
--NOTHING MOVES EXCEPT US.
THE WHOLE PLANET "DROPPED OUT OF TIME."
RIGHT?
WHAT ARE THEY? ARE THEY ALIVE?
GREEN LANTERN! WE MAY HAVE TROUBLE...
I HEAR YOU, J'ONN, WE'LL BE CAREFUL.
WHD WHD
THERE SHE IS!
WHD WHD WHD

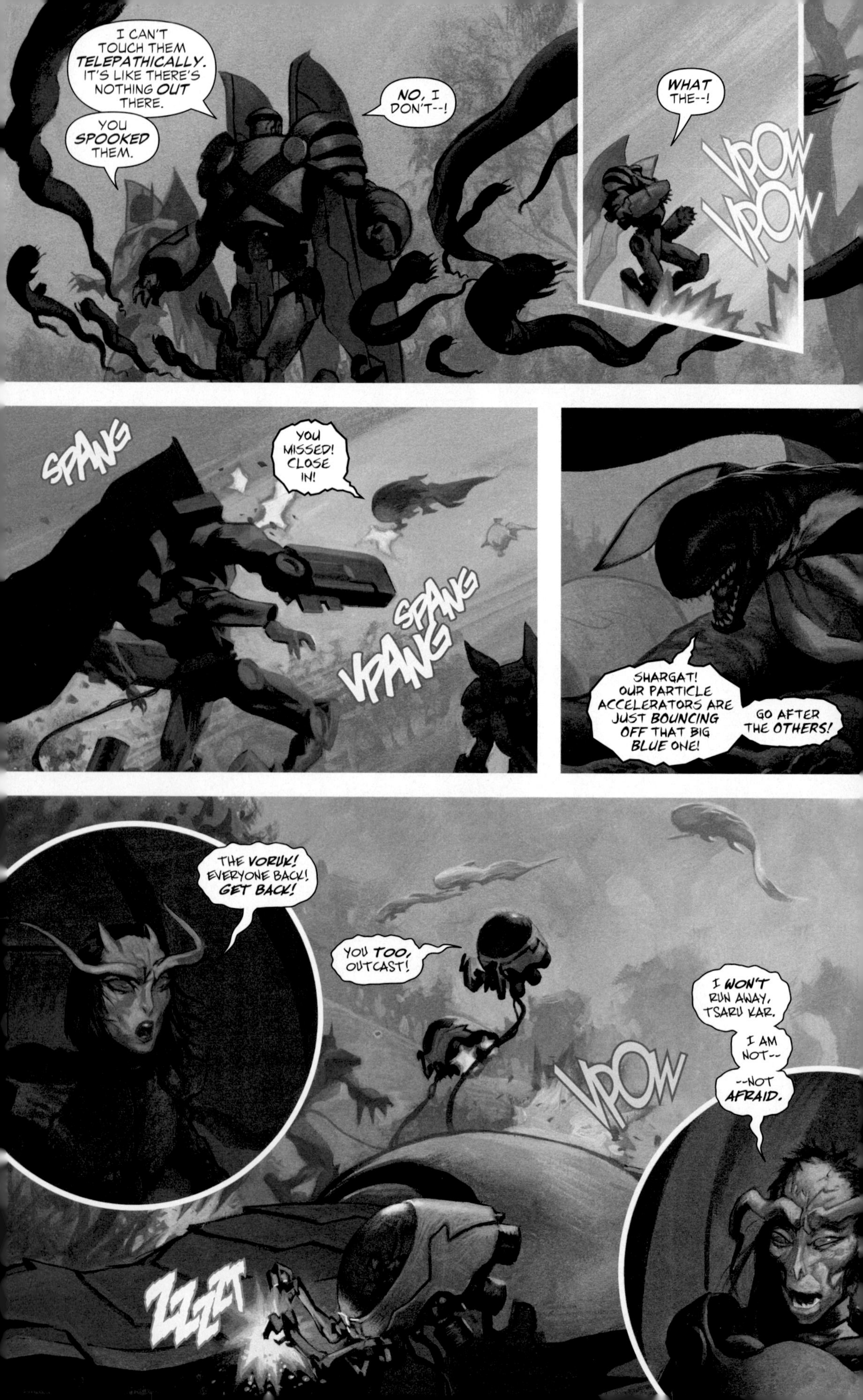
I CAN'T TOUCH THEM TELEPATHICALLY. IT'S LIKE THERE'S NOTHING OUT THERE.
YOU SPOOKED THEM.
NO, I DON'T--!
WHAT THE--!
VPOW VPOW
SPANG
YOU MISSED! CLOSE IN!
SPANG VPANG
SHARGAT! OUR PARTICLE ACCELERATORS ARE JUST BOUNCING OFF THAT BIG BLUE ONE!
GO AFTER THE OTHERS!
THE VORUK! EVERYONE BACK! GET BACK!
YOU TOO, OUTCAST!
I WON'T RUN AWAY, TSARU KAR.
I AM NOT--
--NOT AFRAID.
VPOW
ZZZZZT

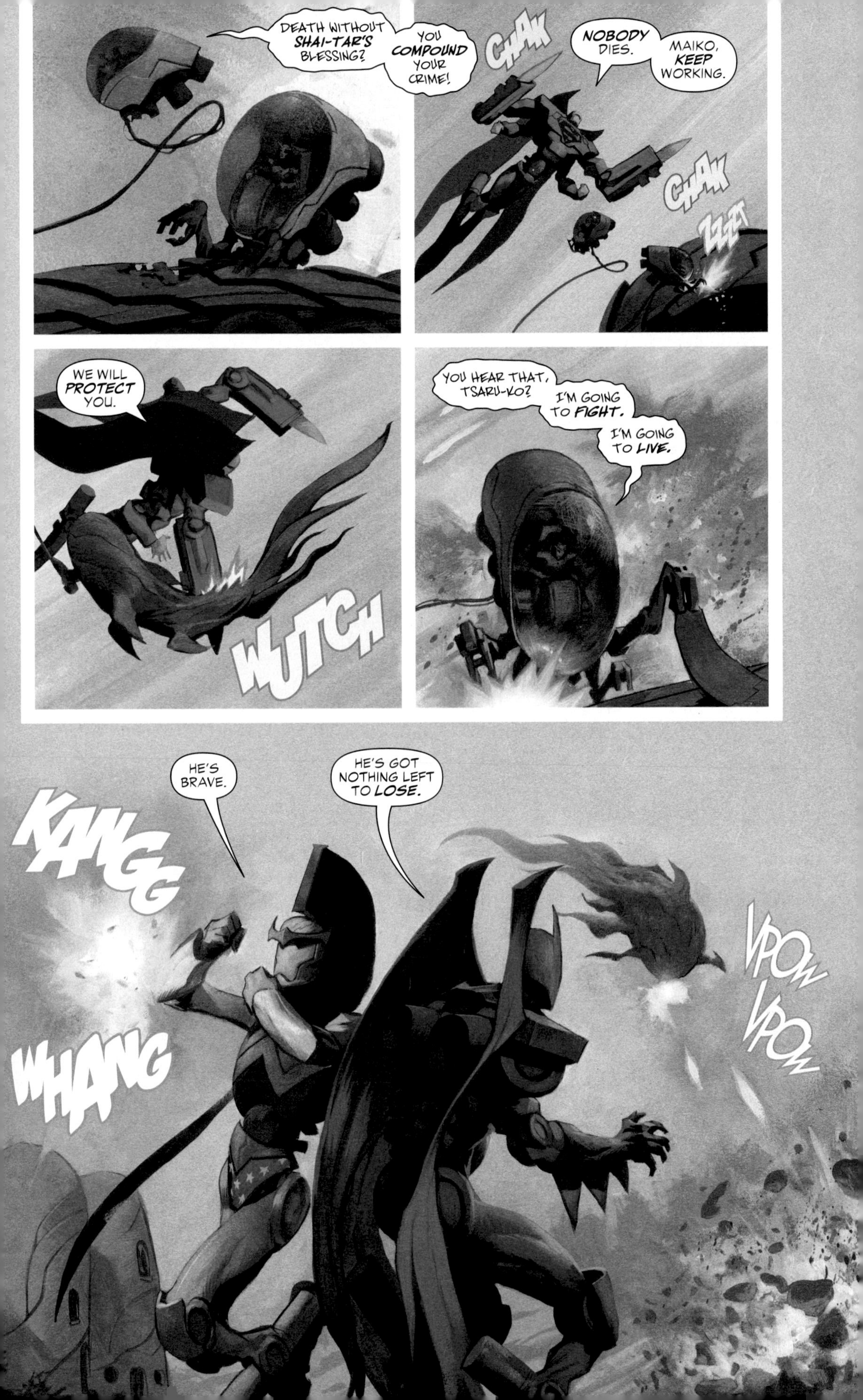
DEATH WITHOUT SHAI-TAR'S BLESSING?
YOU COMPOUND YOUR CRIME!
CHAK
NOBODY DIES.
MAIKO, KEEP WORKING.
CHAK
ZZZZT
WE WILL PROTECT YOU.
WUTCH
YOU HEAR THAT, TSARU-KO?
I'M GOING TO FIGHT.
I'M GOING TO LIVE.
HE'S BRAVE.
HE'S GOT NOTHING LEFT TO LOSE.
KANGG
WHANG
VPOW VPOW

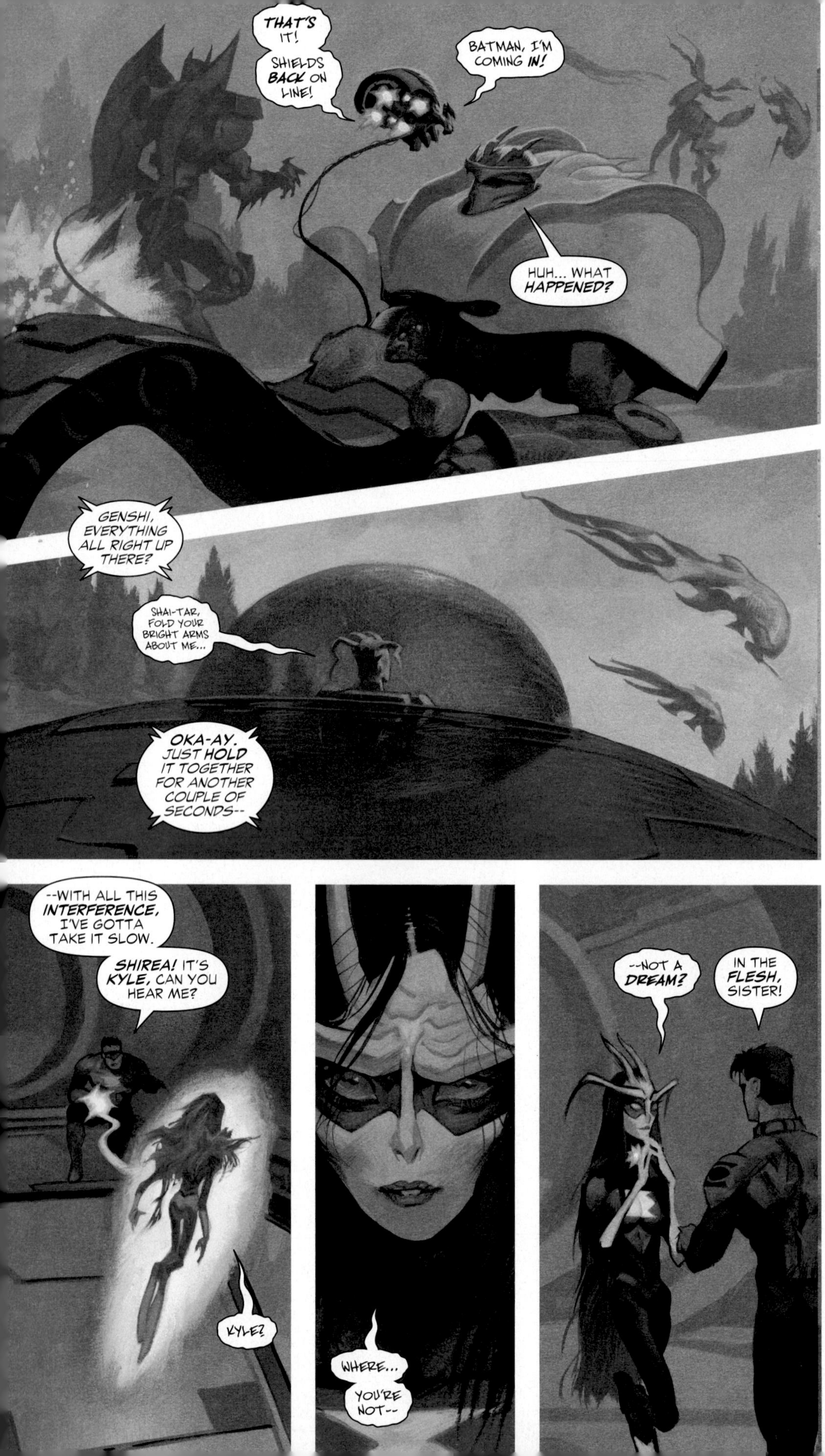
THAT'S IT! SHIELDS BACK ON LINE!
BATMAN, I'M COMING IN!
HUH... WHAT HAPPENED?
GENSHI, EVERYTHING ALL RIGHT UP THERE?
SHAI-TAR, FOLD YOUR BRIGHT ARMS ABOUT ME...
OKA-AY. JUST HOLD IT TOGETHER FOR ANOTHER COUPLE OF SECONDS--
--WITH ALL THIS INTERFERENCE, I'VE GOTTA TAKE IT SLOW.
SHIREA! IT'S KYLE, CAN YOU HEAR ME?
KYLE?
WHERE... YOU'RE NOT--
--NOT A DREAM?
IN THE FLESH, SISTER!

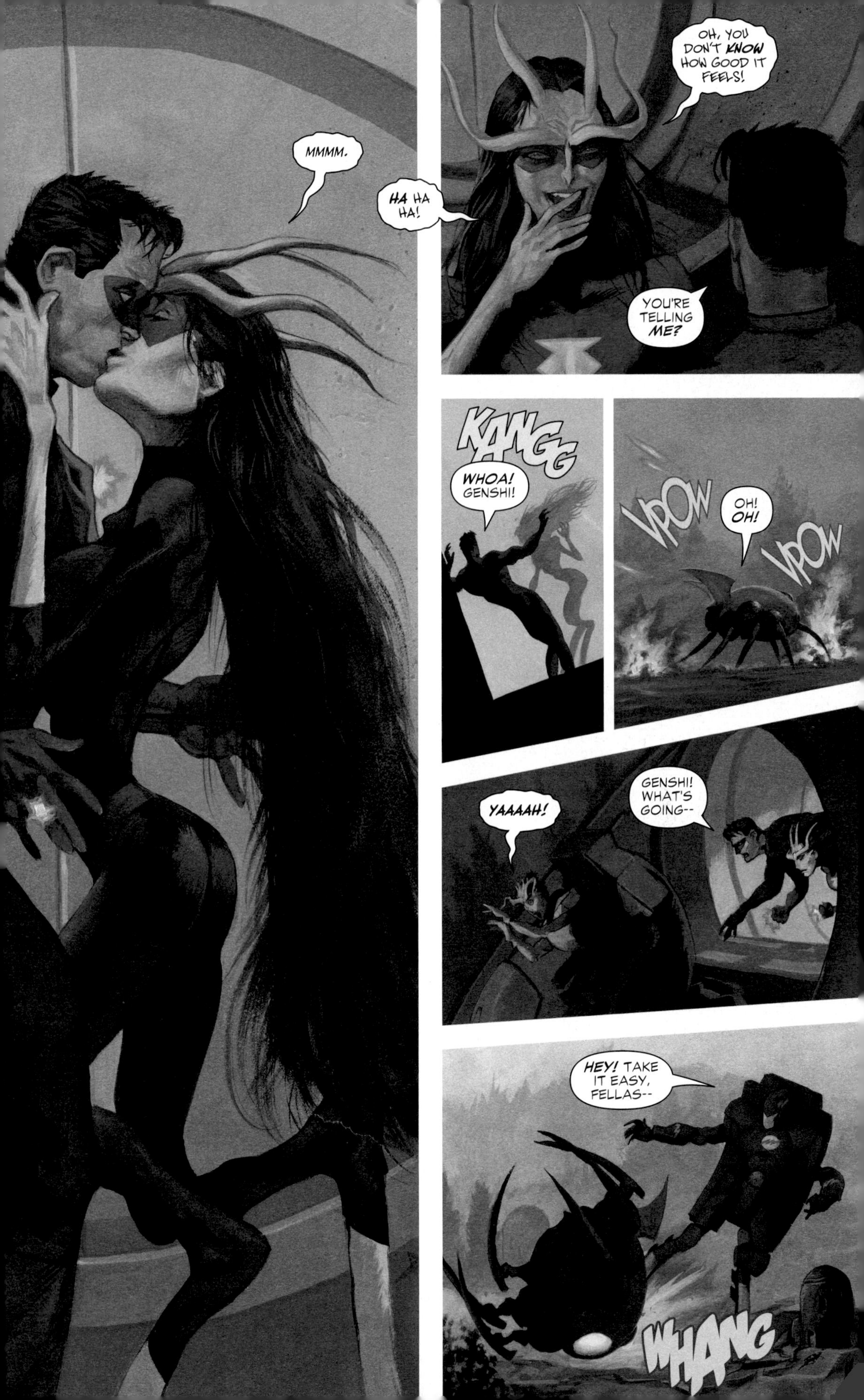
MMMM.
HA HA HA!
OH, YOU DON'T KNOW HOW GOOD IT FEELS!
YOU'RE TELLING ME?
KANGG
WHOA! GENSHI!
VPOW
OH! OH!
VPOW
YAAAAH!
GENSHI! WHAT'S GOING--
HEY! TAKE IT EASY, FELLAS--
WHANG

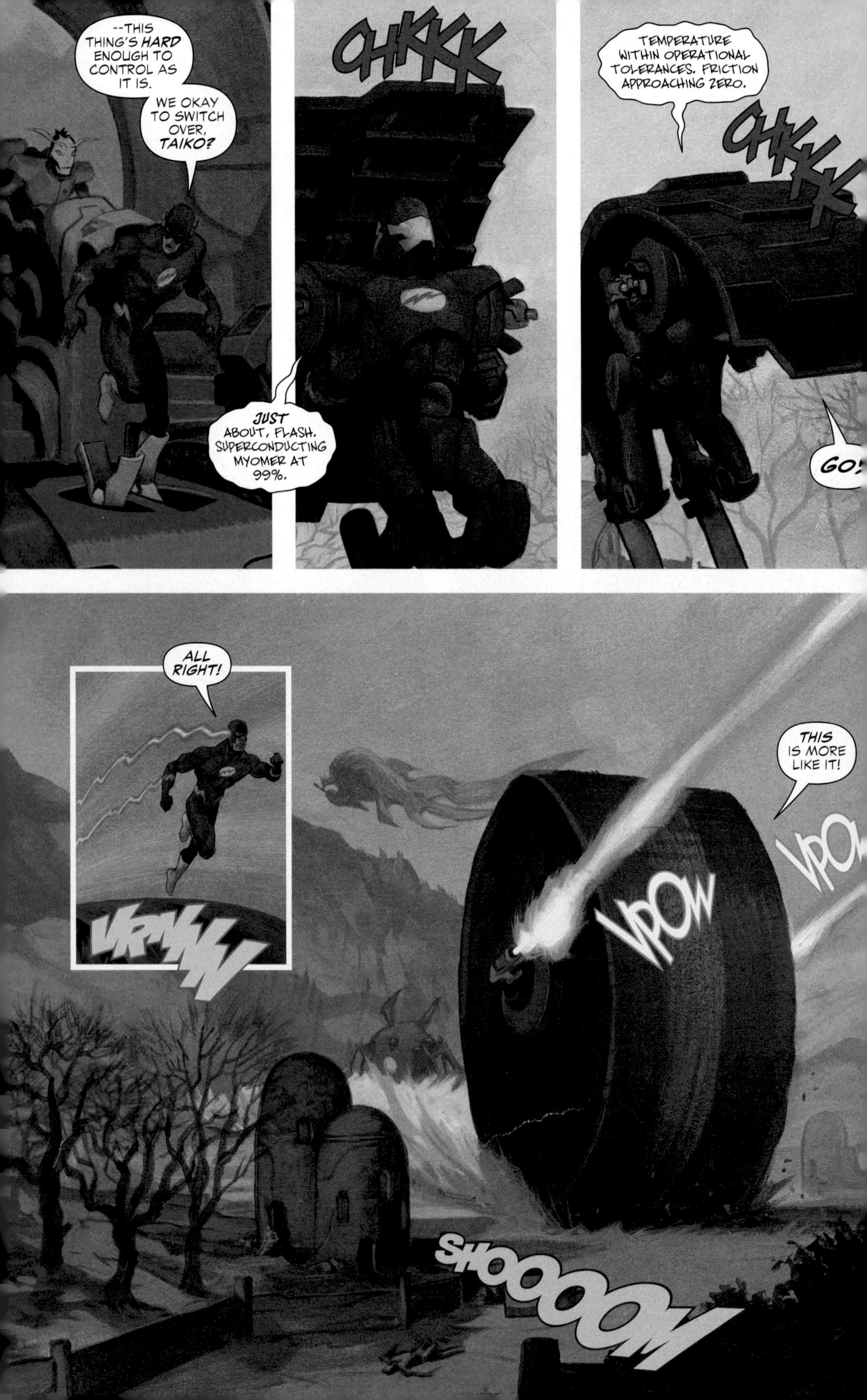
--THIS THING'S HARD ENOUGH TO CONTROL AS IT IS.
WE OKAY TO SWITCH OVER, TAIKO?
OHKKK
JUST ABOUT, FLASH. SUPERCONDUCTING MYOMER AT 99%.
TEMPERATURE WITHIN OPERATIONAL TOLERANCES. FRICTION APPROACHING ZERO.
OHKKK
GO!
ALL RIGHT!
URMMM
THIS IS MORE LIKE IT!
VPOW
VPO
SHOOOOM

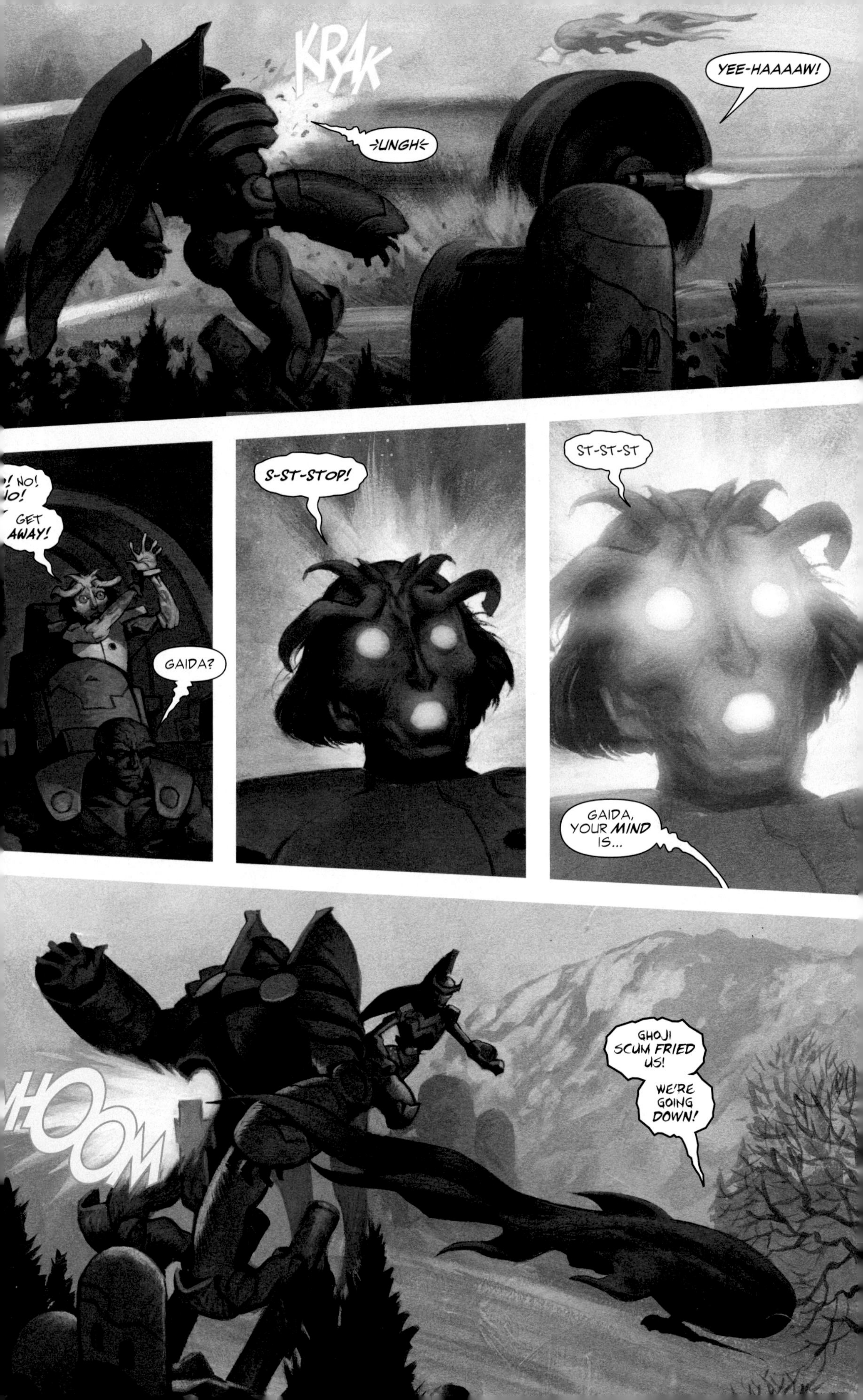
KRAK
UNGH
YEE-HAAAAW!
NO!
GET AWAY!
GAIDA?
S-ST-STOP!
ST-ST-ST
GAIDA, YOUR MIND IS...
GHOJI SCUM FRIED US!
WE'RE GOING DOWN!

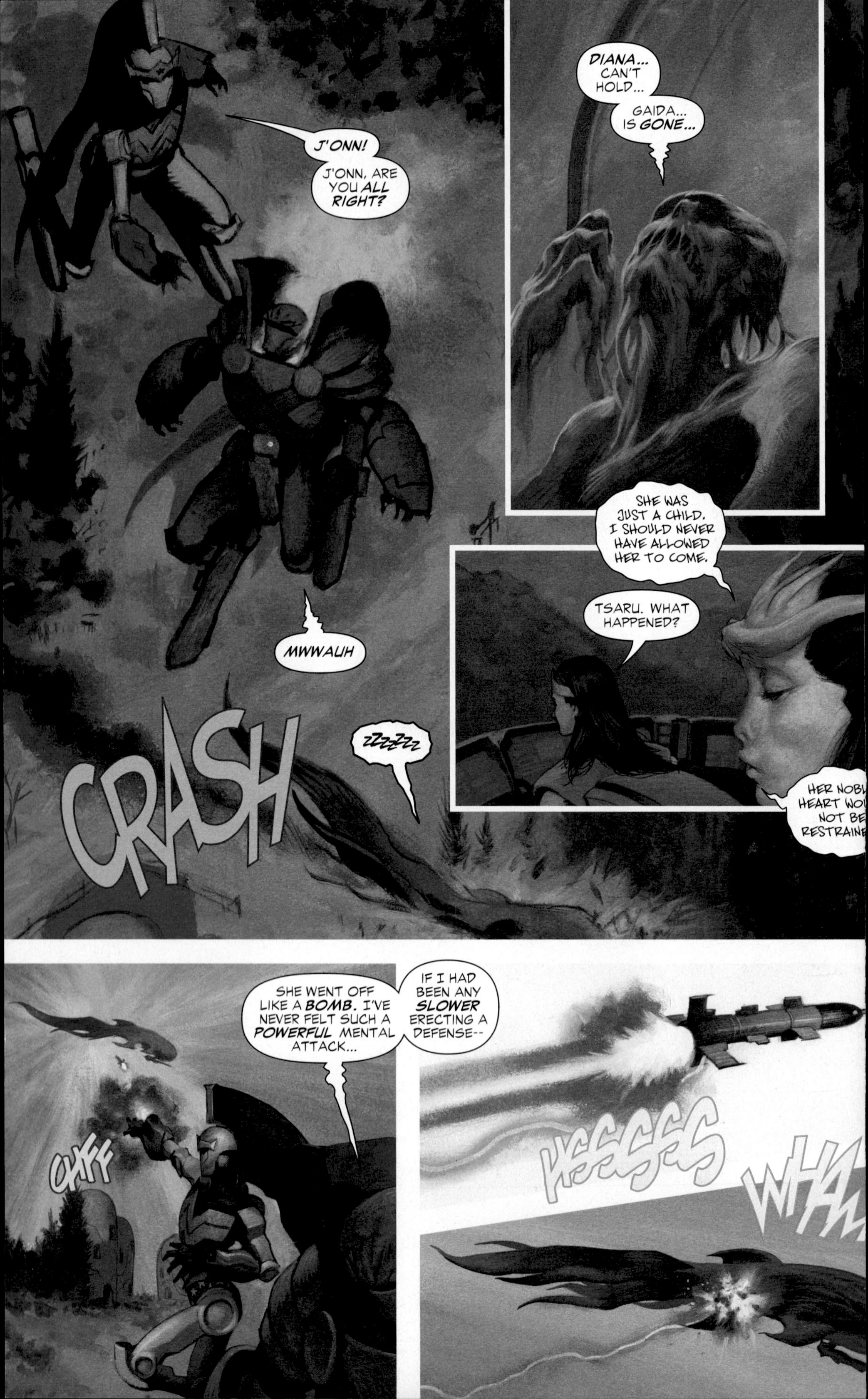
J'ONN!
J'ONN, ARE YOU ALL RIGHT?
DIANA... CAN'T HOLD...
GAIDA... IS GONE...
MWWAUH
CRASH
ZZZZZZZ
SHE WAS JUST A CHILD. I SHOULD NEVER HAVE ALLOWED HER TO COME.
TSARU. WHAT HAPPENED?
HER NOBL HEART WO NOT BE RESTRAINE
SHE WENT OFF LIKE A BOMB. I'VE NEVER FELT SUCH A POWERFUL MENTAL ATTACK...
IF I HAD BEEN ANY SLOWER ERECTING A DEFENSE--
OFFF
HSSSSS
WHA

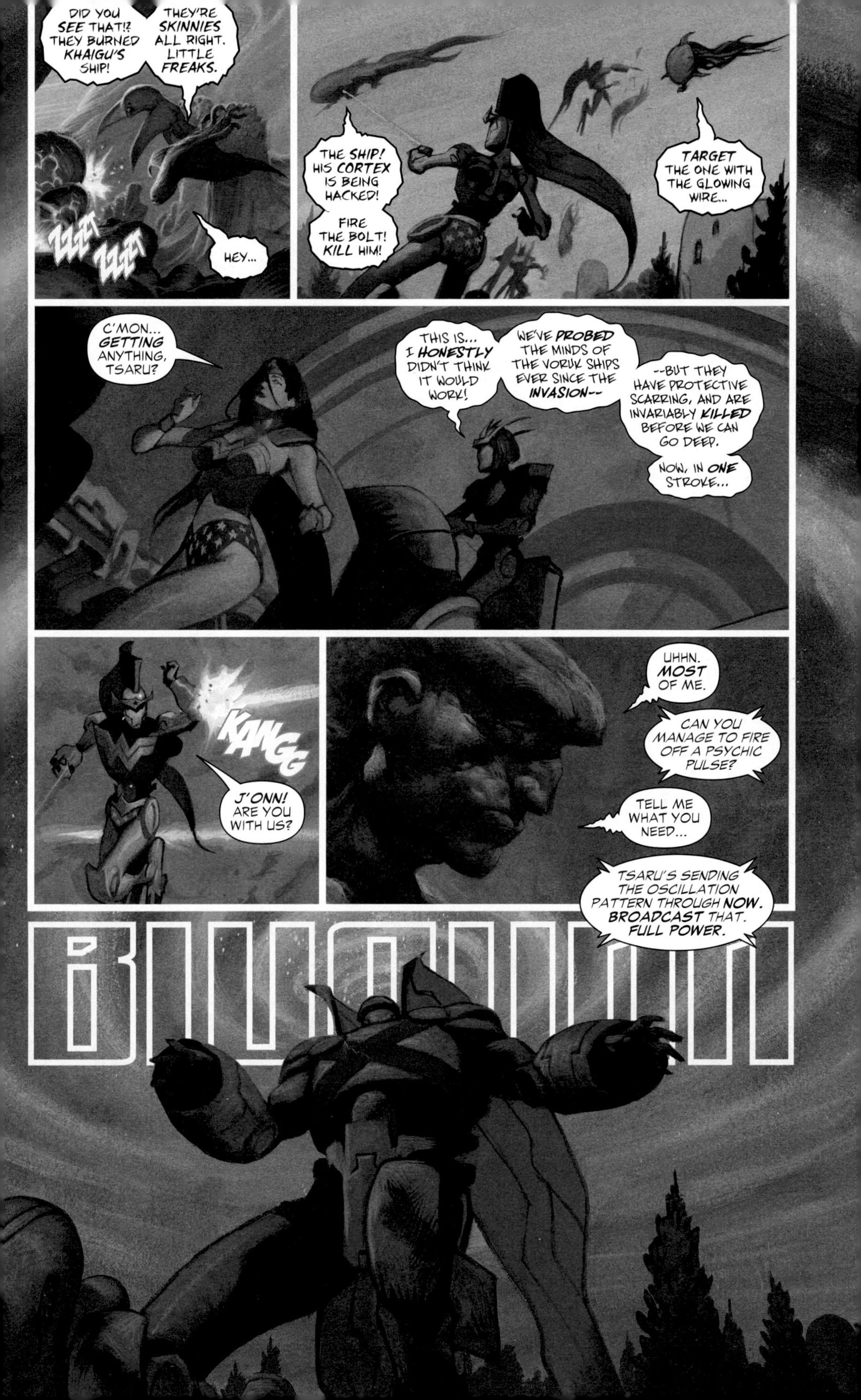

DID YOU SEE THAT!? THEY BURNED KHAIGU'S SHIP!
THEY'RE SKINNIES ALL RIGHT. LITTLE FREAKS.
HEY...
THE SHIP! HIS CORTEX IS BEING HACKED!
FIRE THE BOLT! KILL HIM!
TARGET THE ONE WITH THE GLOWING WIRE...
C'MON... GETTING ANYTHING, TSARU?
THIS IS... I HONESTLY DIDN'T THINK IT WOULD WORK!
WE'VE PROBED THE MINDS OF THE VORUK SHIPS EVER SINCE THE INVASION--
--BUT THEY HAVE PROTECTIVE SCARRING, AND ARE INVARIABLY KILLED BEFORE WE CAN GO DEEP.
NOW, IN ONE STROKE...
KANGG
J'ONN! ARE YOU WITH US?
UHHN. MOST OF ME.
CAN YOU MANAGE TO FIRE OFF A PSYCHIC PULSE?
TELL ME WHAT YOU NEED...
TSARU'S SENDING THE OSCILLATION PATTERN THROUGH NOW. BROADCAST THAT. FULL POWER.

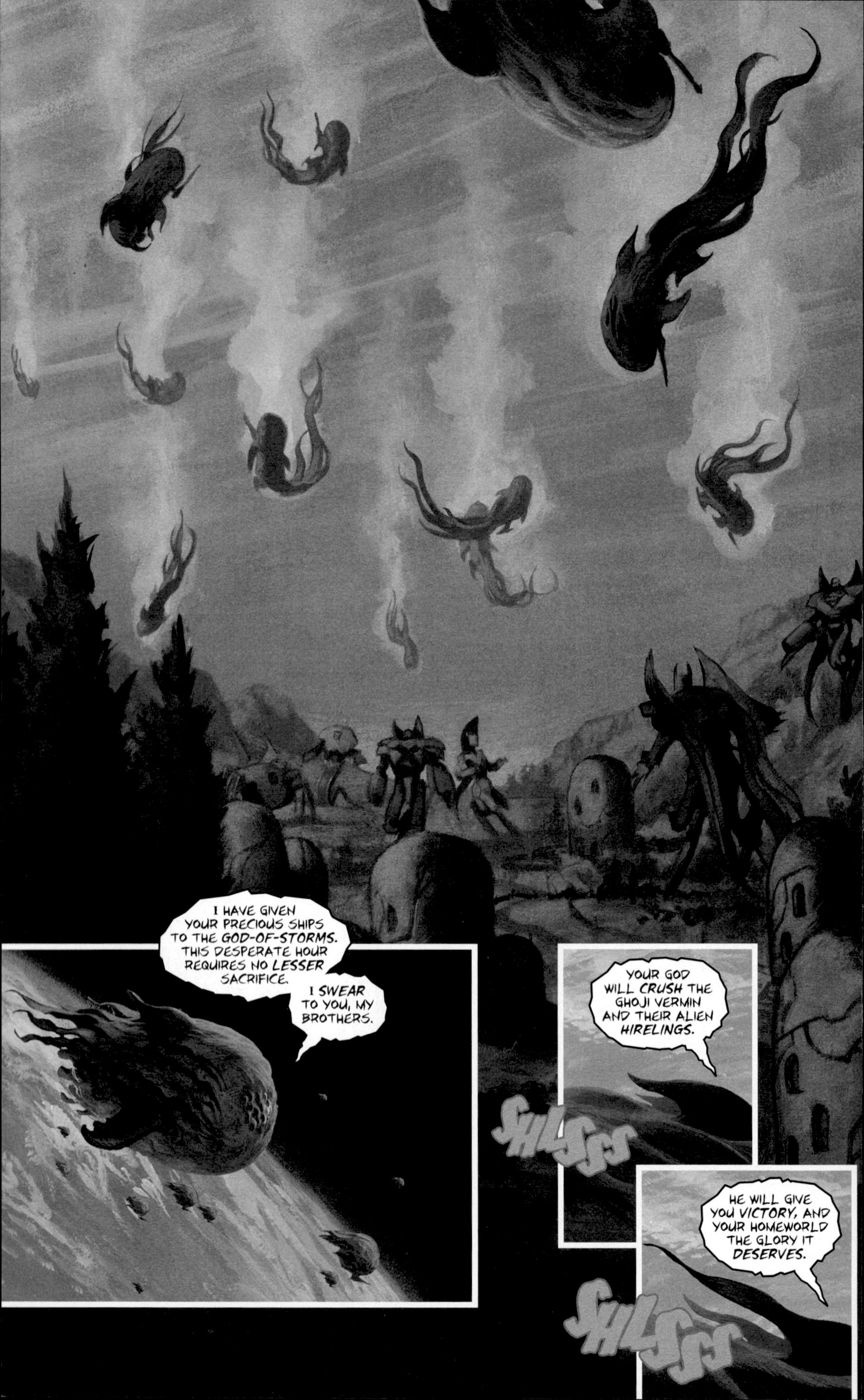
I HAVE GIVEN YOUR PRECIOUS SHIPS TO THE GOD-OF-STORMS. THIS DESPERATE HOUR REQUIRES NO LESSER SACRIFICE.
I SWEAR TO YOU, MY BROTHERS.
YOUR GOD WILL CRUSH THE GHOJI VERMIN AND THEIR ALIEN HIRELINGS.
SHLSSSS
HE WILL GIVE YOU VICTORY, AND YOUR HOMEWORLD THE GLORY IT DESERVES.
SHLSSSS

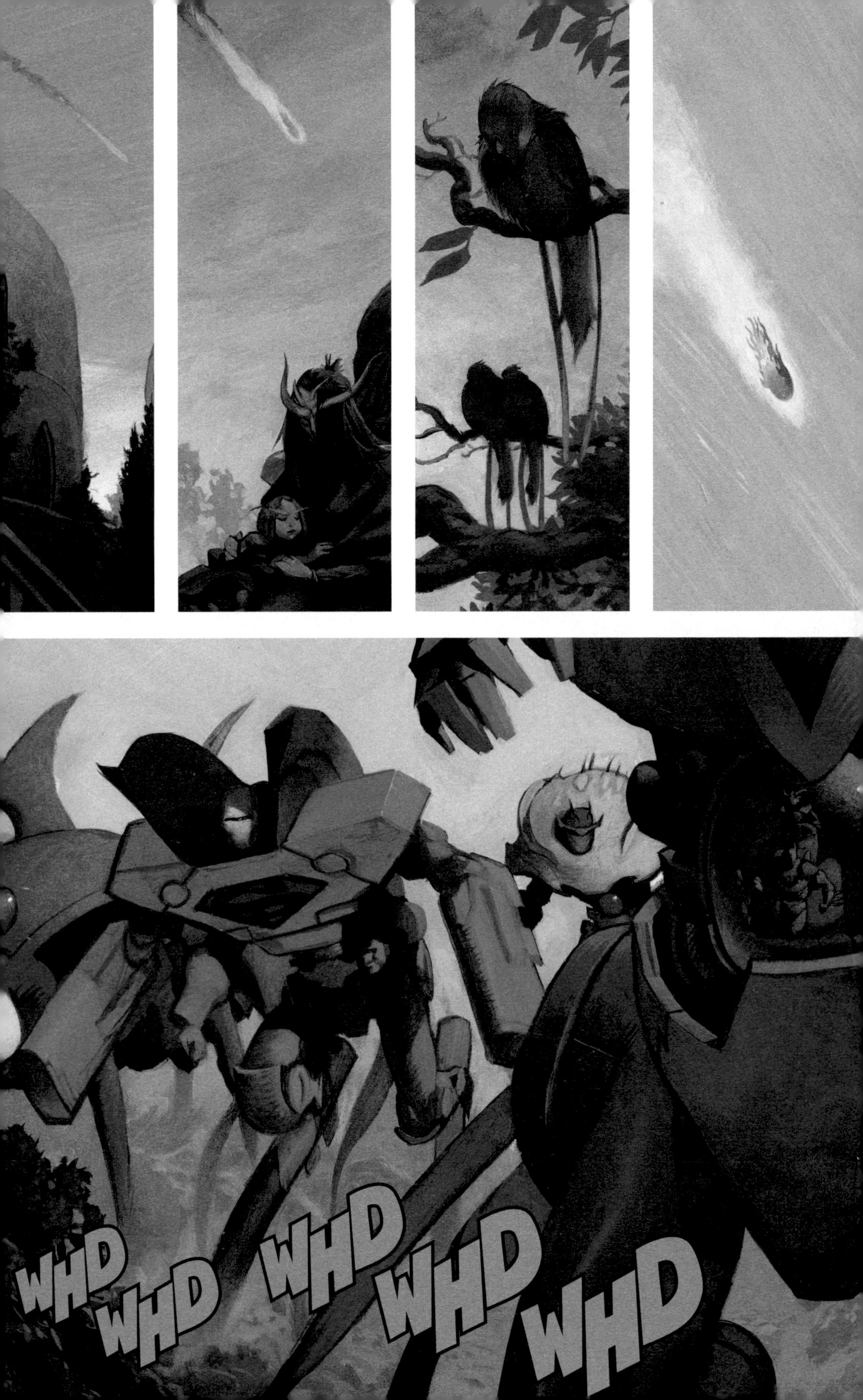
WHD
WHD
WHD
WHD
WHD

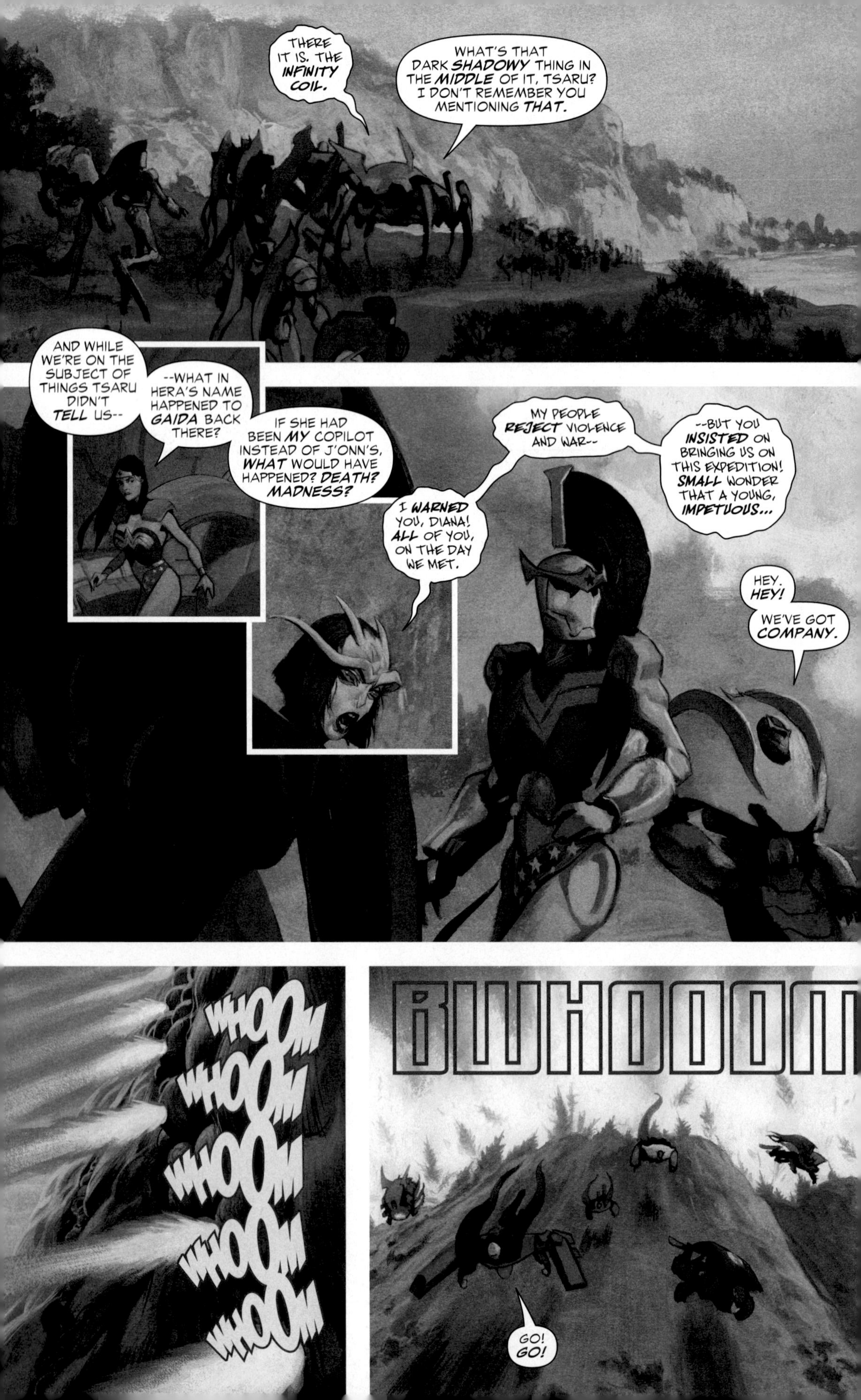
THERE IT IS. THE INFINITY COIL.
WHAT'S THAT DARK SHADOWY THING IN THE MIDDLE OF IT, TSARU? I DON'T REMEMBER YOU MENTIONING THAT.
AND WHILE WE'RE ON THE SUBJECT OF THINGS TSARU DIDN'T TELL US--
--WHAT IN HERA'S NAME HAPPENED TO GAIDA BACK THERE?
IF SHE HAD BEEN MY COPILOT INSTEAD OF J'ONN'S, WHAT WOULD HAVE HAPPENED? DEATH? MADNESS?
I WARNED YOU, DIANA! ALL OF YOU, ON THE DAY WE MET.
MY PEOPLE REJECT VIOLENCE AND WAR--
--BUT YOU INSISTED ON BRINGING US ON THIS EXPEDITION! SMALL WONDER THAT A YOUNG, IMPETUOUS...
HEY. HEY!
WE'VE GOT COMPANY.
WHOOM WHOOM WHOOM WHOOM WHOOM
BWHOOOM
GO! GO!

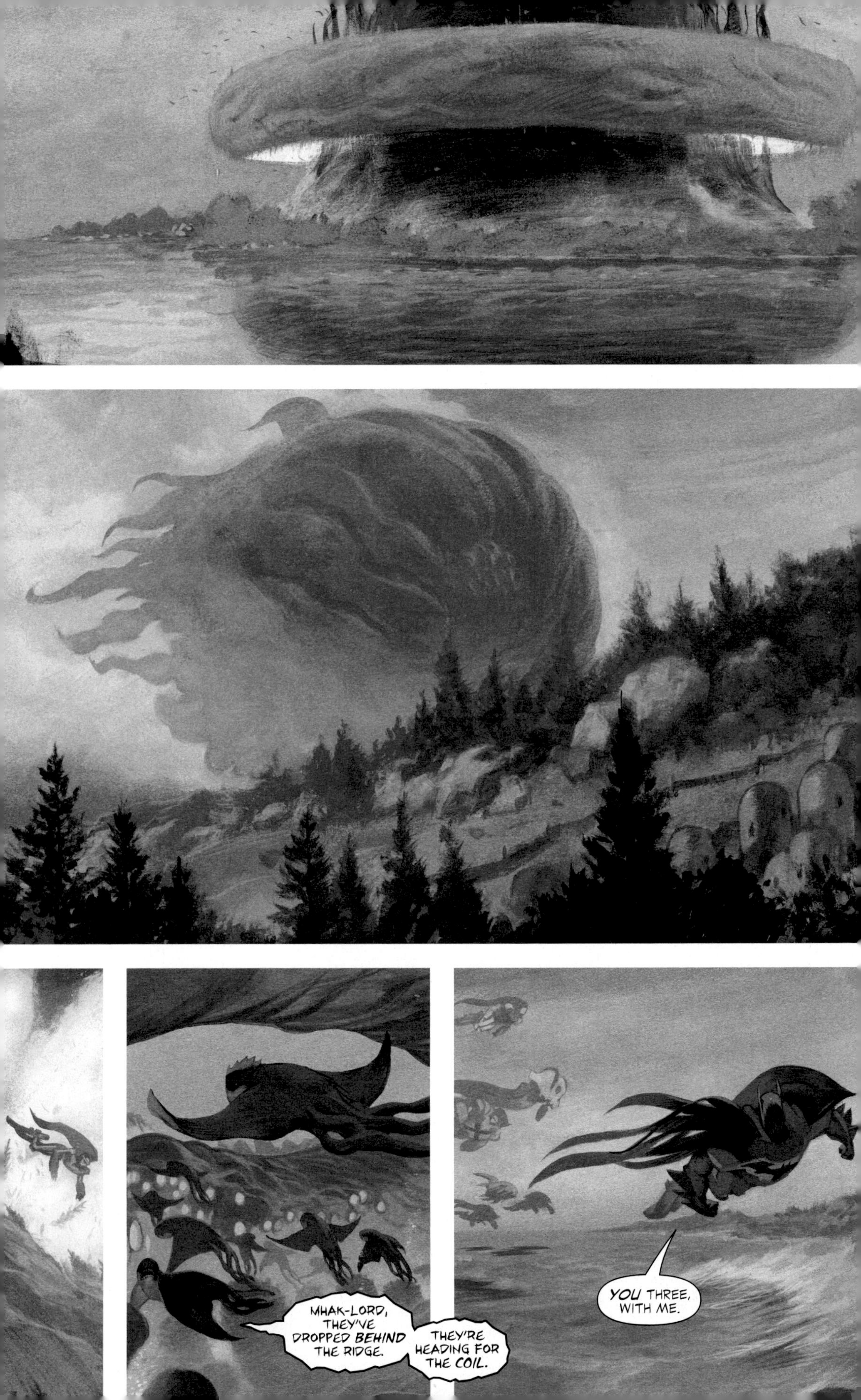
MHAK-LORD, THEY'VE DROPPED BEHIND THE RIDGE.
THEY'RE HEADING FOR THE COIL.
YOU THREE, WITH ME.

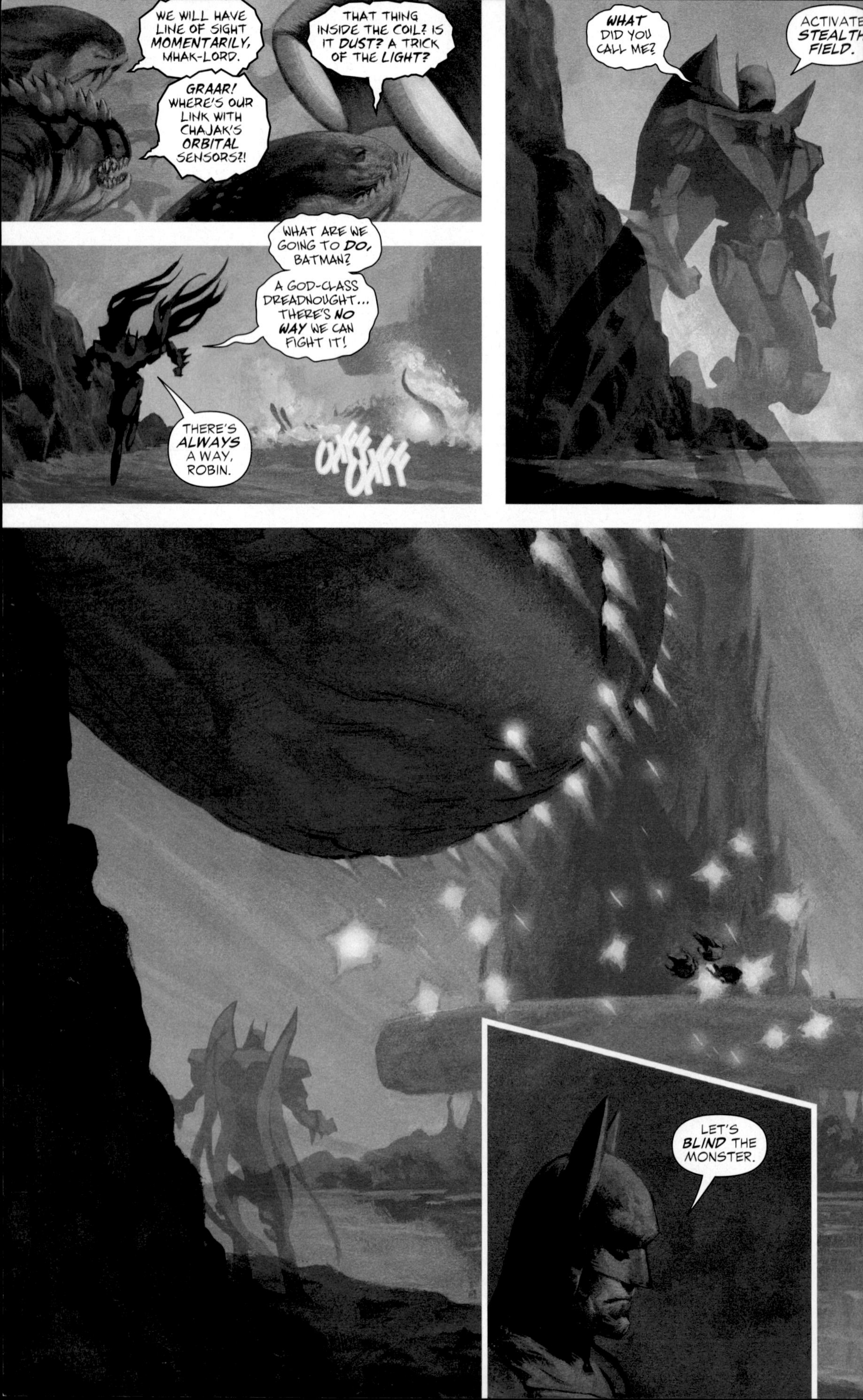

WE WILL HAVE LINE OF SIGHT MOMENTARILY, MHAK-LORD.
GRAAR! WHERE'S OUR LINK WITH CHAJAK'S ORBITAL SENSORS?!
THAT THING INSIDE THE COIL? IS IT DUST? A TRICK OF THE LIGHT?
WHAT ARE WE GOING TO DO, BATMAN?
A GOD-CLASS DREADNOUGHT... THERE'S NO WAY WE CAN FIGHT IT!
THERE'S ALWAYS A WAY, ROBIN.
WHAT DID YOU CALL ME?
ACTIVATE STEALTH FIELD.
LET'S BLIND THE MONSTER.

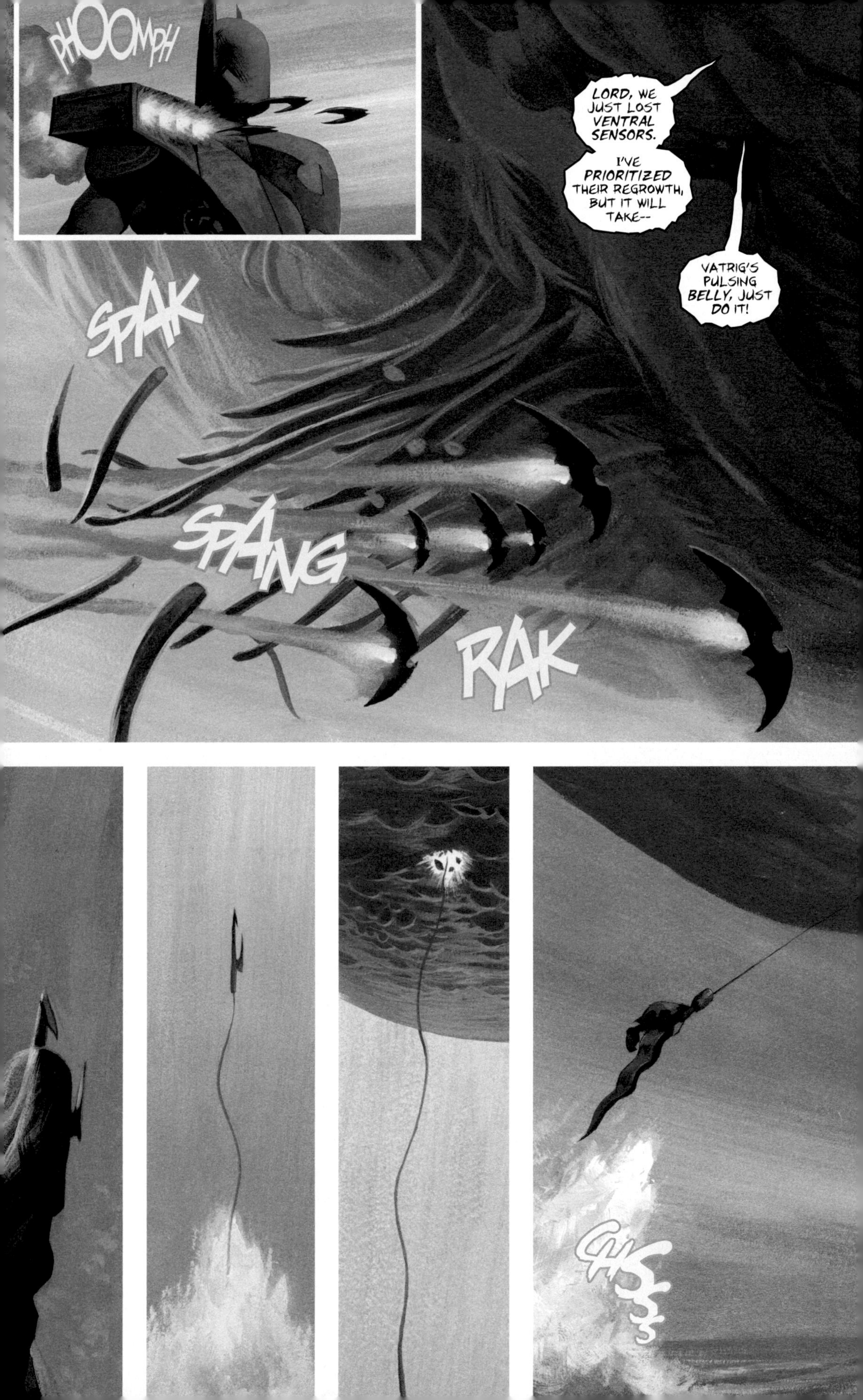
PHOOMPH
LORD, WE JUST LOST VENTRAL SENSORS.
I'VE PRIORITIZED THEIR REGROWTH, BUT IT WILL TAKE--
VATRIG'S PULSING BELLY, JUST DO IT!
SPAK
SPANG
RAK
CHSSS

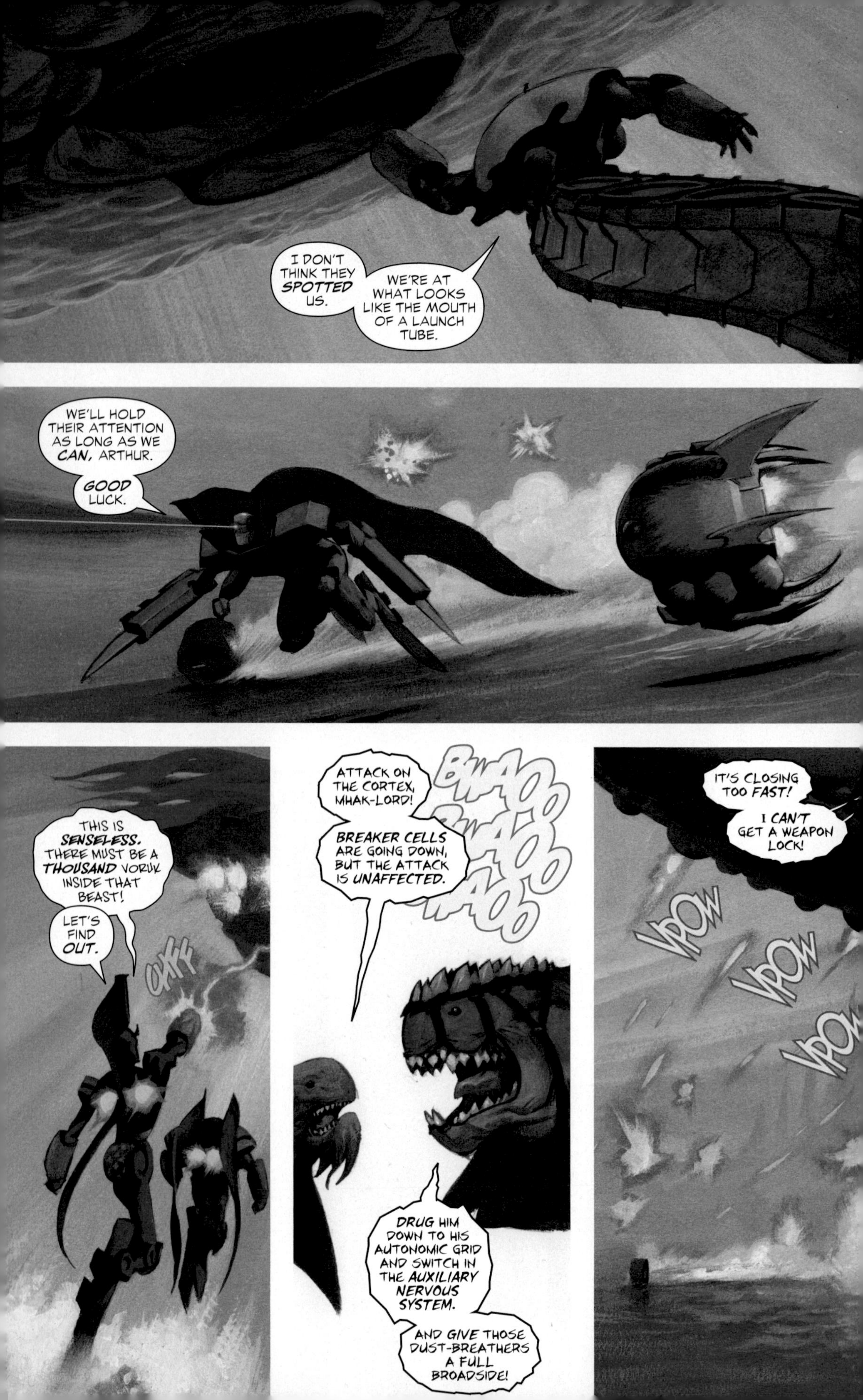
I DON'T THINK THEY *SPOTTED* US.
WE'RE AT WHAT LOOKS LIKE THE MOUTH OF A LAUNCH TUBE.
WE'LL HOLD THEIR ATTENTION AS LONG AS WE *CAN*, ARTHUR.
GOOD LUCK.
THIS IS *SENSELESS.* THERE MUST BE A *THOUSAND* VORUK INSIDE THAT BEAST!
LET'S FIND *OUT*.
ATTACK ON THE CORTEX, MHAK-LORD!
BREAKER CELLS ARE GOING DOWN, BUT THE ATTACK IS *UNAFFECTED*.
BWAOOO
DRUG HIM DOWN TO HIS AUTONOMIC GRID AND SWITCH IN THE *AUXILIARY NERVOUS SYSTEM*.
AND *GIVE* THOSE DUST-BREATHERS A FULL BROADSIDE!
IT'S CLOSING TOO *FAST!*
I *CAN'T* GET A WEAPON LOCK!
VPOW
VPOW
VPOW

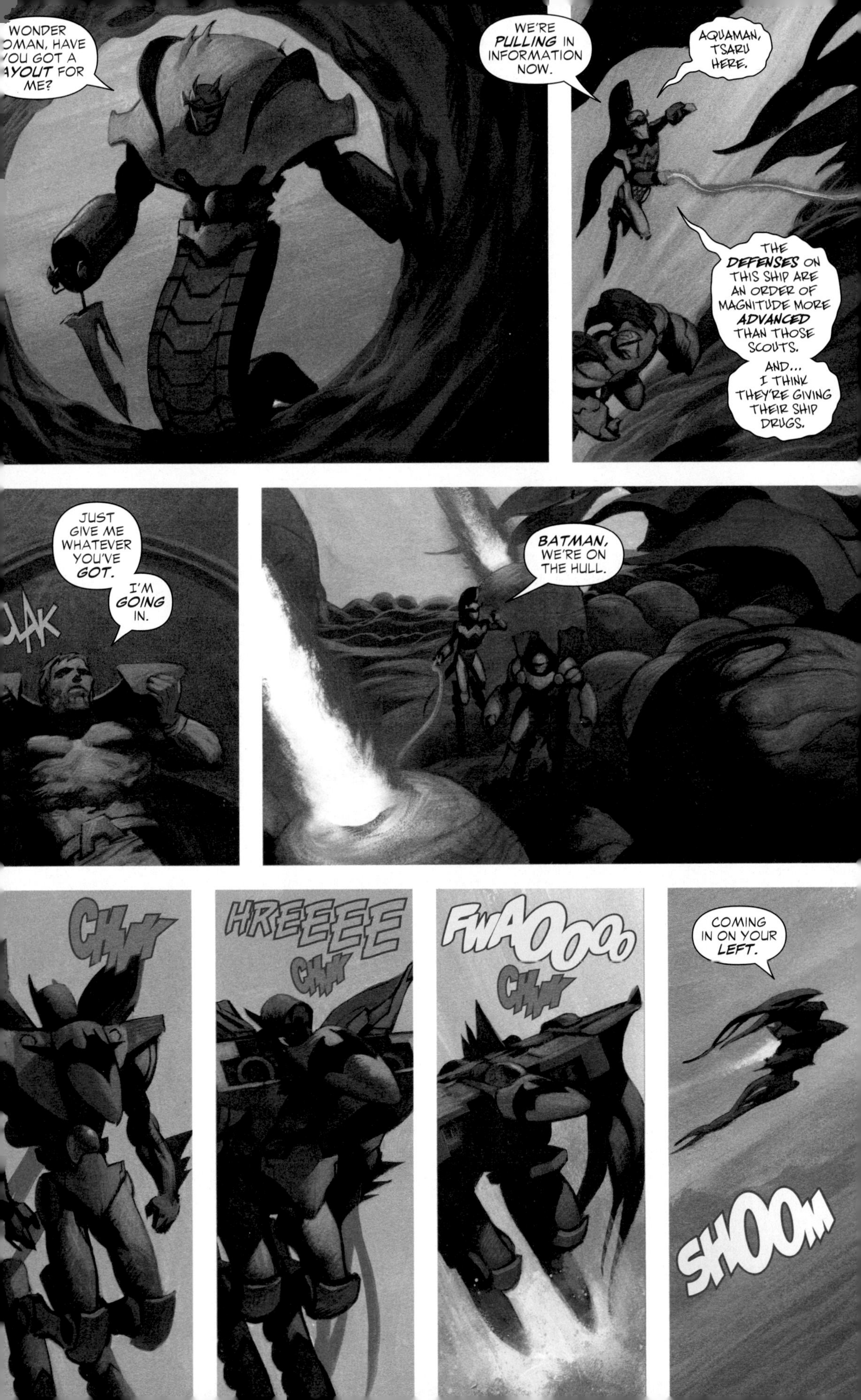
WONDER
OMAN, HAVE
YOU GOT A
AYOUT FOR
ME?
WE'RE
PULLING IN
INFORMATION
NOW.
AQUAMAN,
TSARU
HERE.
THE
DEFENSES ON
THIS SHIP ARE
AN ORDER OF
MAGNITUDE MORE
ADVANCED
THAN THOSE
SCOUTS.
AND...
I THINK
THEY'RE GIVING
THEIR SHIP
DRUGS.
JUST
GIVE ME
WHATEVER
YOU'VE
GOT.
I'M
GOING
IN.
JAK
BATMAN,
WE'RE ON
THE HULL.
CHAK
HREEEEE
CHAK
FWAOOOOO
CHAK
COMING
IN ON YOUR
LEFT.
SHOOM

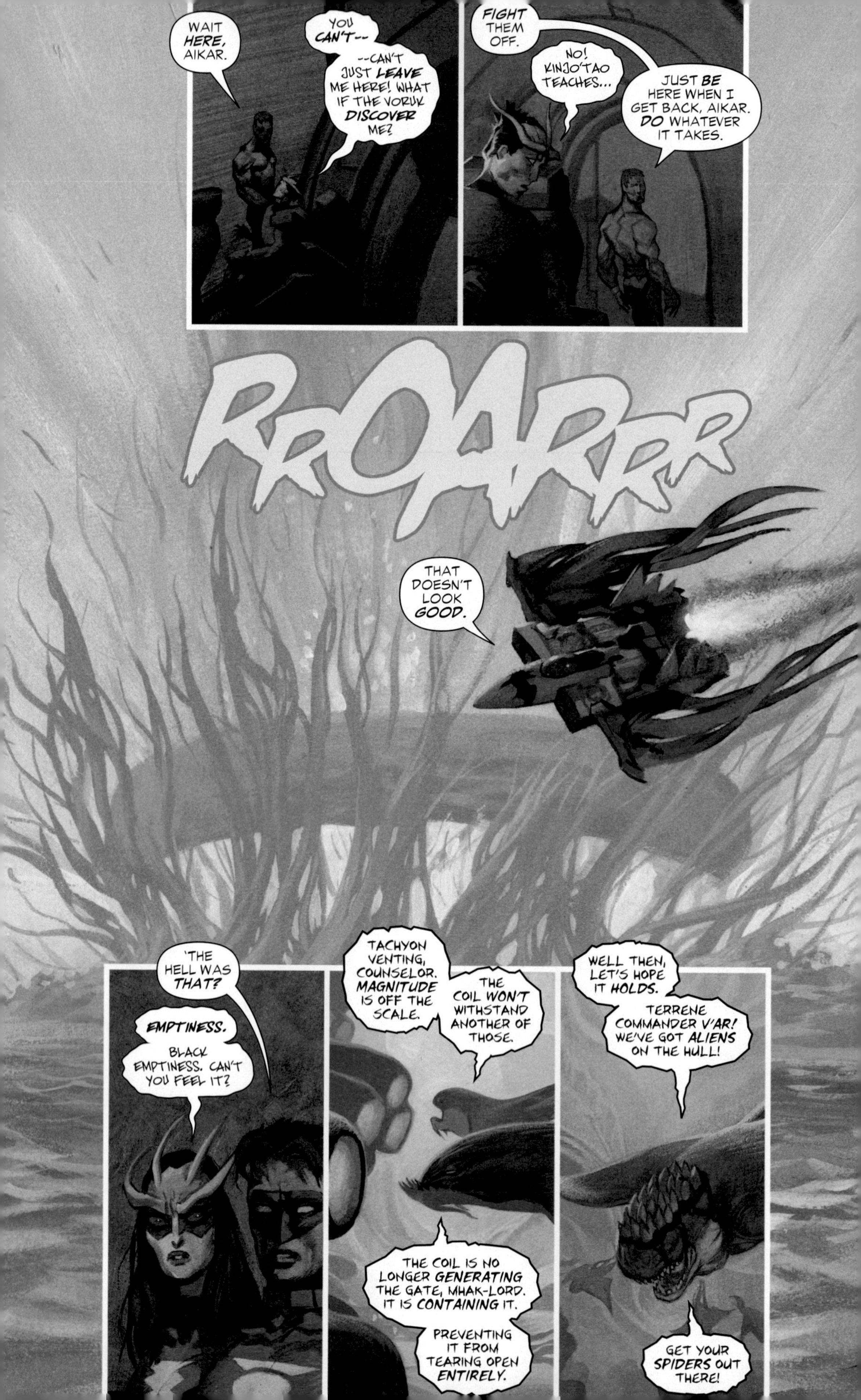
WAIT HERE, AIKAR.
YOU CAN'T--
--CAN'T JUST LEAVE ME HERE! WHAT IF THE VORUK DISCOVER ME?
FIGHT THEM OFF.
NO! KINJO'TAO TEACHES...
JUST BE HERE WHEN I GET BACK, AIKAR. DO WHATEVER IT TAKES.
RROARRR
THAT DOESN'T LOOK GOOD.
'THE HELL WAS THAT?
EMPTINESS.
BLACK EMPTINESS. CAN'T YOU FEEL IT?
TACHYON VENTING, COUNSELOR. MAGNITUDE IS OFF THE SCALE.
THE COIL WON'T WITHSTAND ANOTHER OF THOSE.
THE COIL IS NO LONGER GENERATING THE GATE, MHAK-LORD. IT IS CONTAINING IT.
PREVENTING IT FROM TEARING OPEN ENTIRELY.
WELL THEN, LET'S HOPE IT HOLDS.
TERRENE COMMANDER V'AR! WE'VE GOT ALIENS ON THE HULL!
GET YOUR SPIDERS OUT THERE!

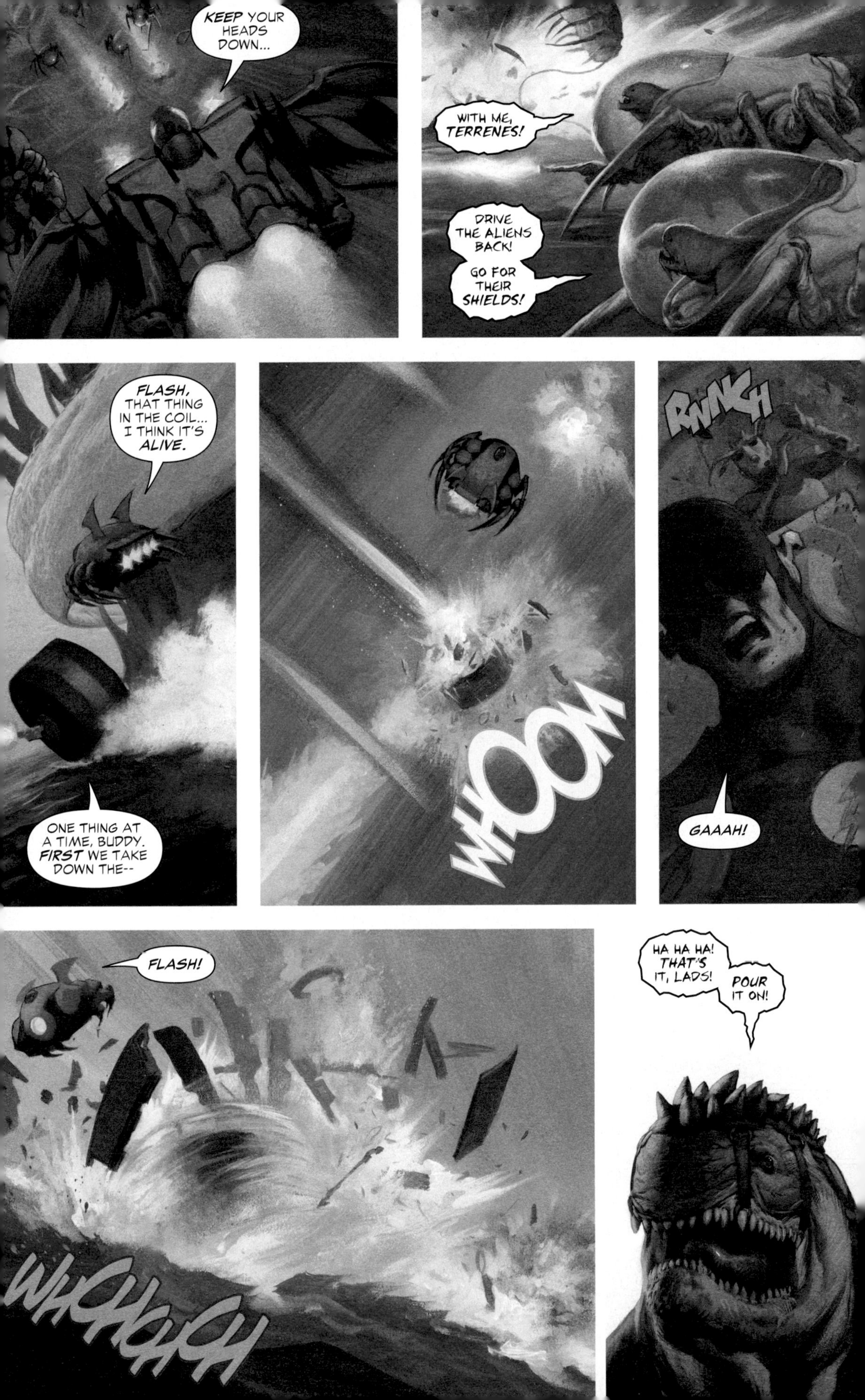
KEEP YOUR HEADS DOWN...
WITH ME, TERRENES!
DRIVE THE ALIENS BACK!
GO FOR THEIR SHIELDS!
FLASH, THAT THING IN THE COIL... I THINK IT'S ALIVE.
ONE THING AT A TIME, BUDDY. FIRST WE TAKE DOWN THE--
WHOOM
RNNCH
GAAAH!
FLASH!
WHOOOSH
HA HA HA! THAT'S IT, LADS!
POUR IT ON!

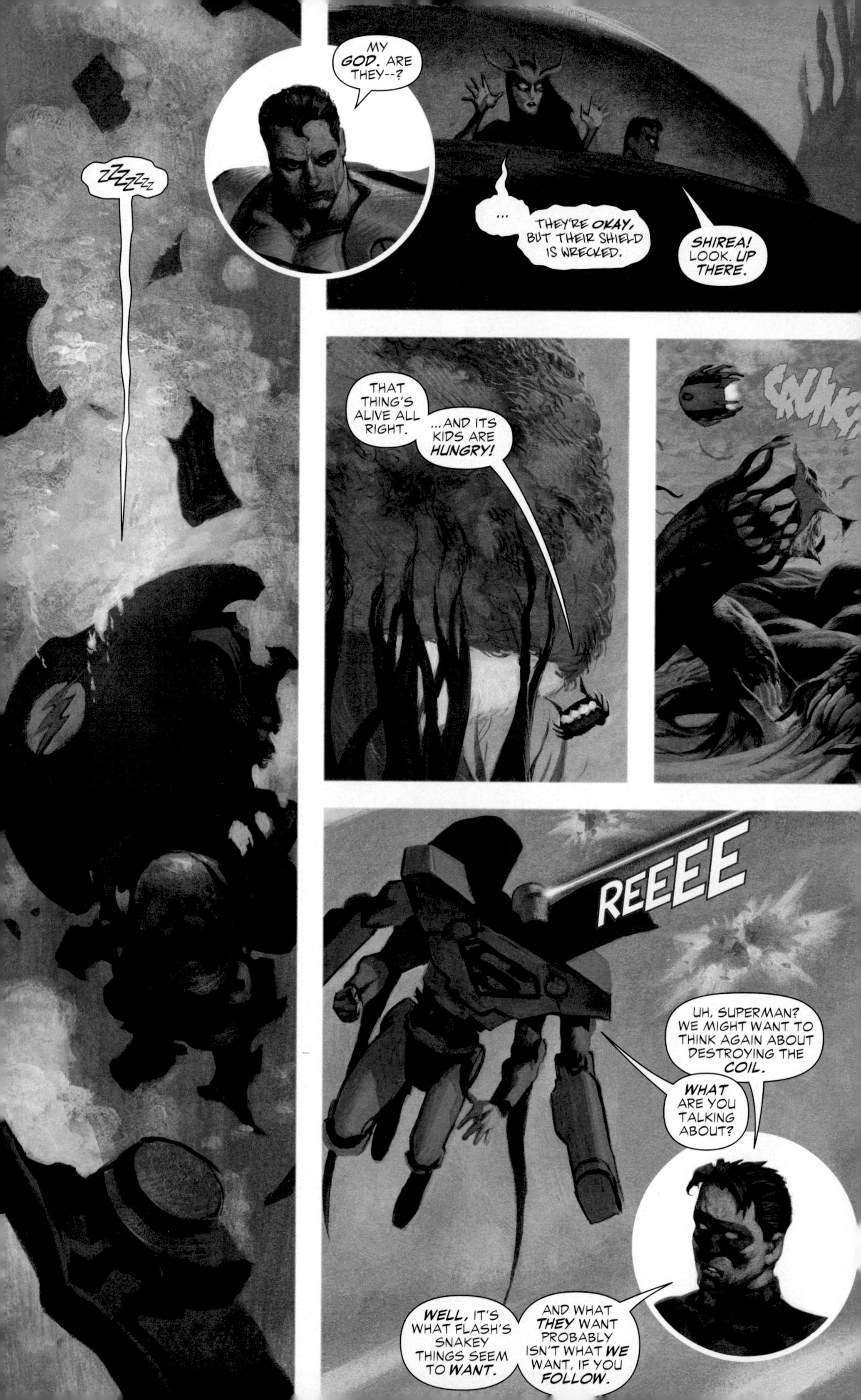
ZZZZZZZ
MY GOD. ARE THEY--?
...
THEY'RE OKAY, BUT THEIR SHIELD IS WRECKED.
SHIREA! LOOK. UP THERE.
THAT THING'S ALIVE ALL RIGHT.
...AND ITS KIDS ARE HUNGRY!
REEEE
UH, SUPERMAN? WE MIGHT WANT TO THINK AGAIN ABOUT DESTROYING THE COIL.
WHAT ARE YOU TALKING ABOUT?
WELL, IT'S WHAT FLASH'S SNAKEY THINGS SEEM TO WANT.
AND WHAT THEY WANT PROBABLY ISN'T WHAT WE WANT, IF YOU FOLLOW.

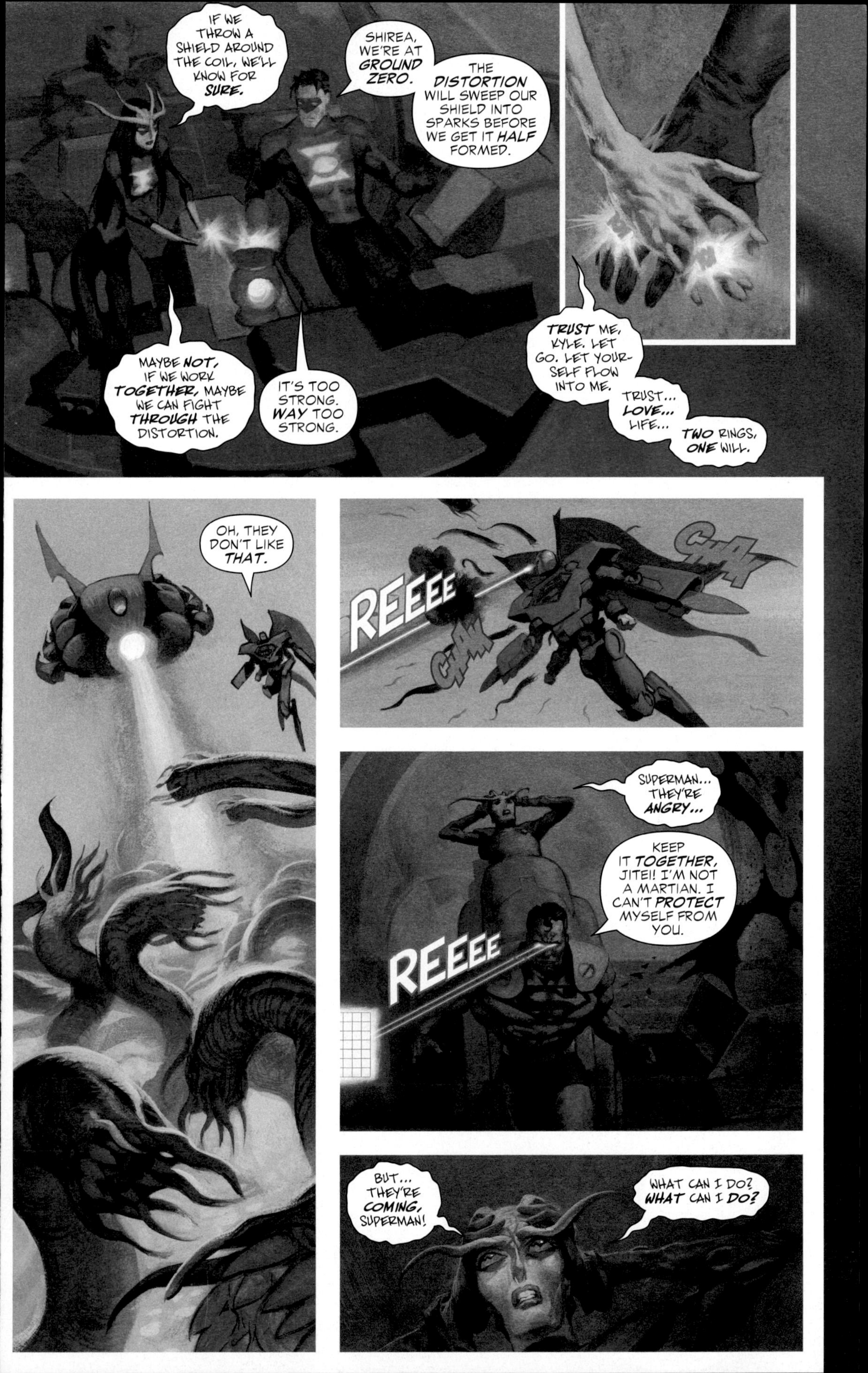

IF WE THROW A SHIELD AROUND THE COIL, WE'LL KNOW FOR SURE.
SHIREA, WE'RE AT GROUND ZERO.
THE DISTORTION WILL SWEEP OUR SHIELD INTO SPARKS BEFORE WE GET IT HALF FORMED.
MAYBE NOT, IF WE WORK TOGETHER, MAYBE WE CAN FIGHT THROUGH THE DISTORTION.
IT'S TOO STRONG. WAY TOO STRONG.
TRUST ME, KYLE. LET GO. LET YOURSELF FLOW INTO ME.
TRUST... LOVE... LIFE...
TWO RINGS, ONE WILL.
OH, THEY DON'T LIKE THAT.
REEEE
SUPERMAN... THEY'RE ANGRY...
KEEP IT TOGETHER, JITEI! I'M NOT A MARTIAN. I CAN'T PROTECT MYSELF FROM YOU.
REEEE
BUT... THEY'RE COMING, SUPERMAN!
WHAT CAN I DO? WHAT CAN I DO?

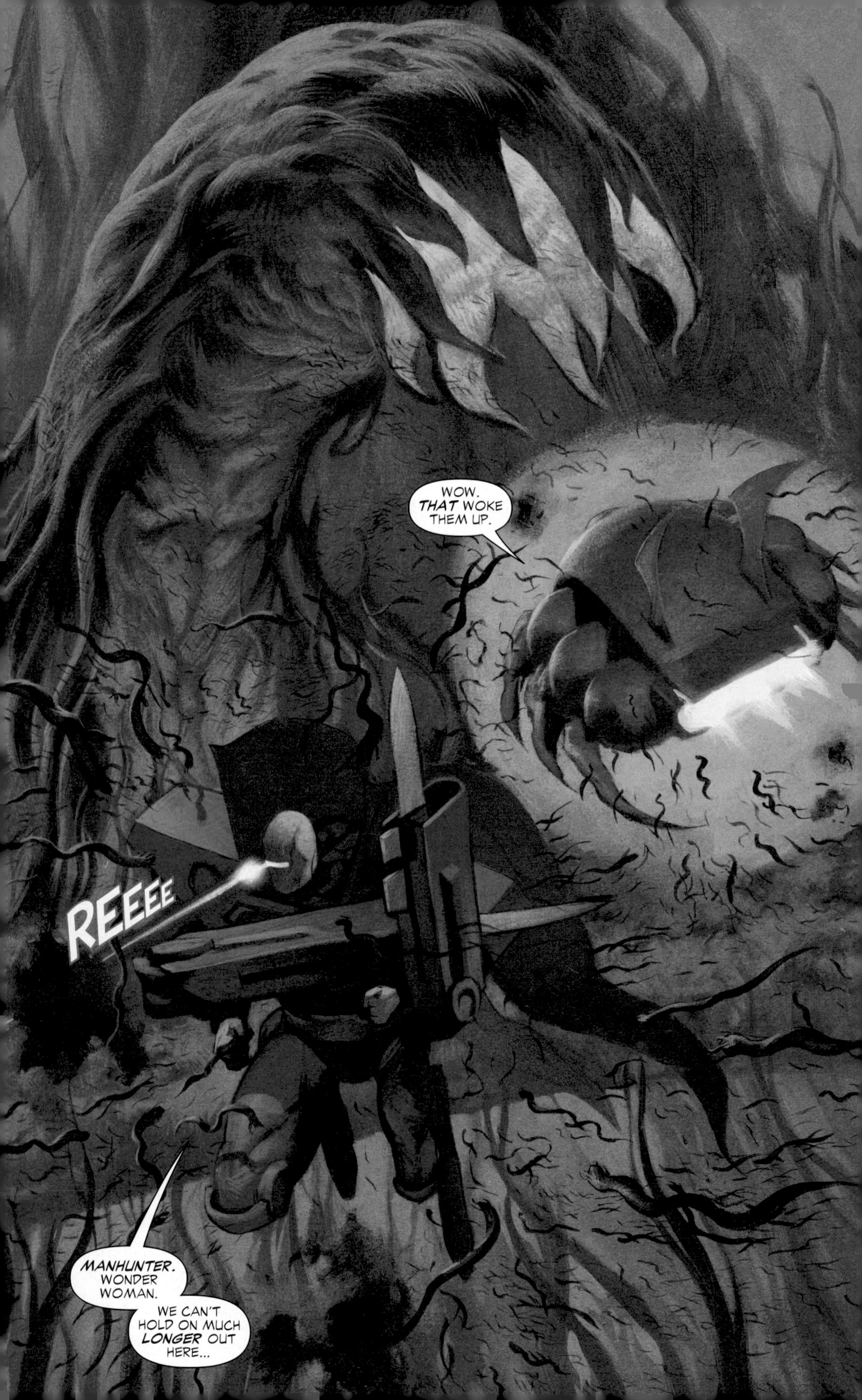
WOW. THAT WOKE THEM UP.
REEEEE
MANHUNTER. WONDER WOMAN.
WE CAN'T HOLD ON MUCH LONGER OUT HERE...

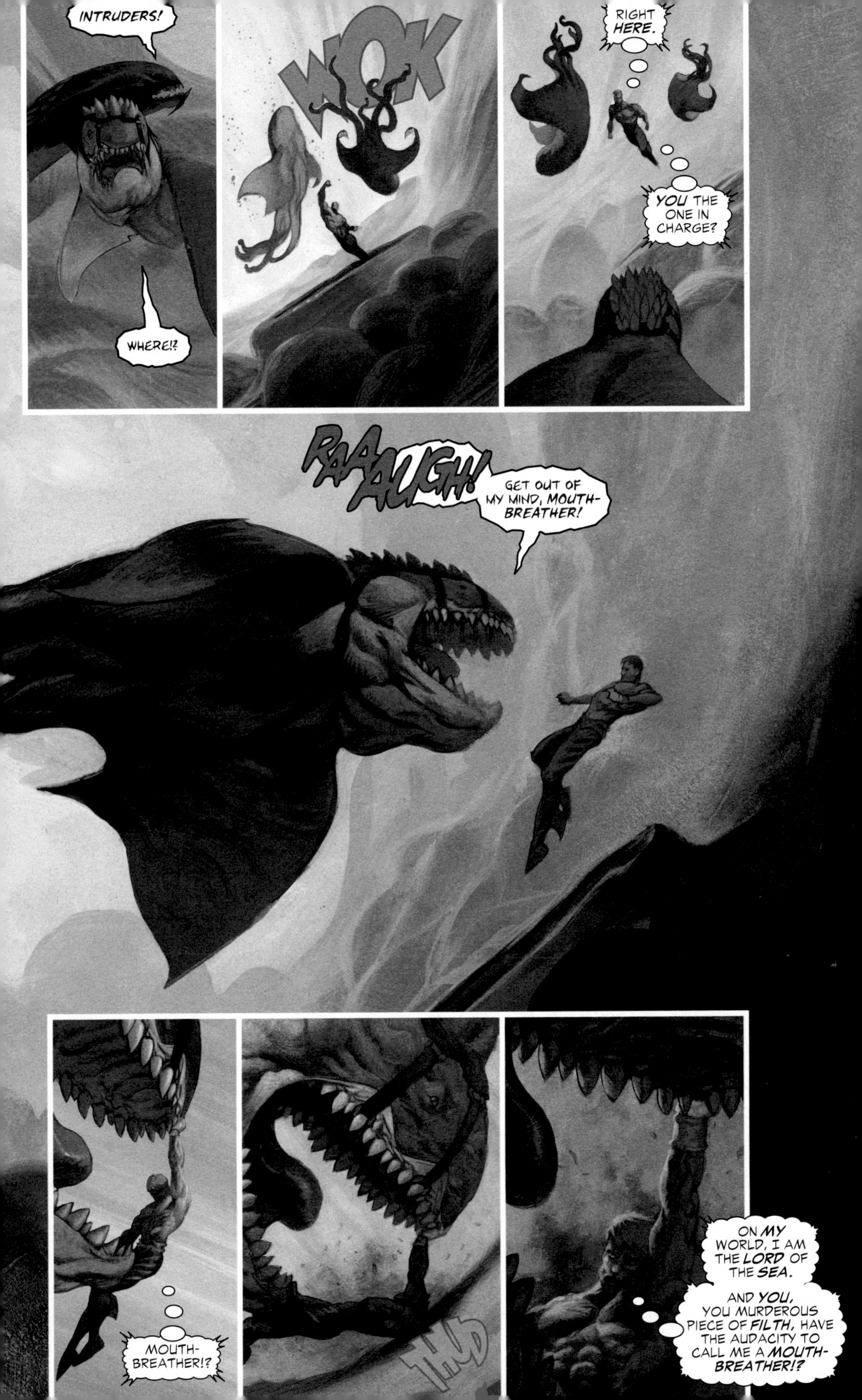
INTRUDERS!
WHERE!?
WOK
RIGHT HERE.
YOU THE ONE IN CHARGE?
RAAAAUGH!
GET OUT OF MY MIND, MOUTH-BREATHER!
MOUTH-BREATHER!?
THUD
ON MY WORLD, I AM THE LORD OF THE SEA.
AND YOU, YOU MURDEROUS PIECE OF FILTH, HAVE THE AUDACITY TO CALL ME A MOUTH-BREATHER!?

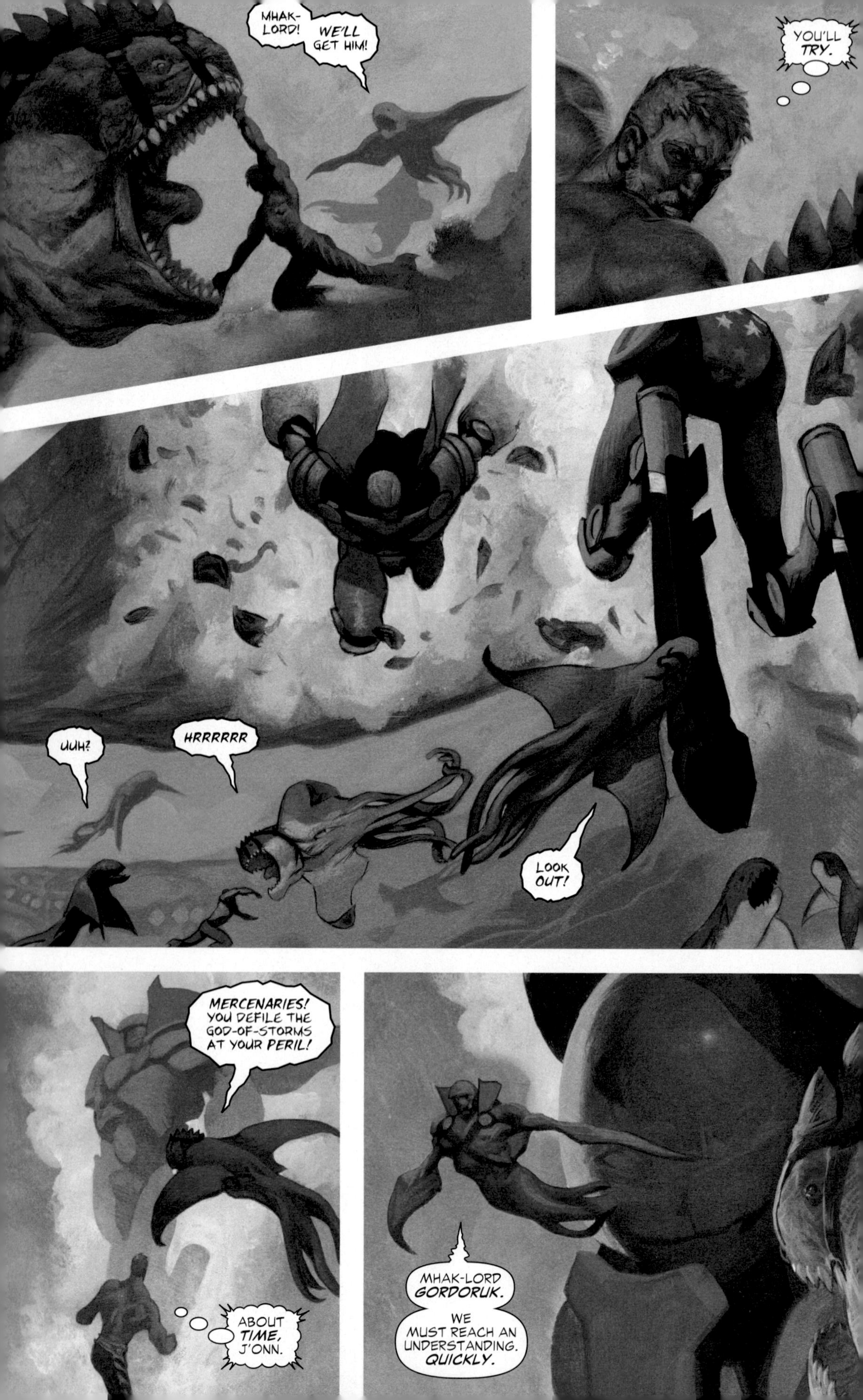
MHAK-LORD! WE'LL GET HIM!
YOU'LL TRY.
UUH?
HRRRRRR
LOOK OUT!
MERCENARIES! YOU DEFILE THE GOD-OF-STORMS AT YOUR PERIL!
ABOUT TIME, J'ONN.
MHAK-LORD GORDORUK.
WE MUST REACH AN UNDERSTANDING. QUICKLY.

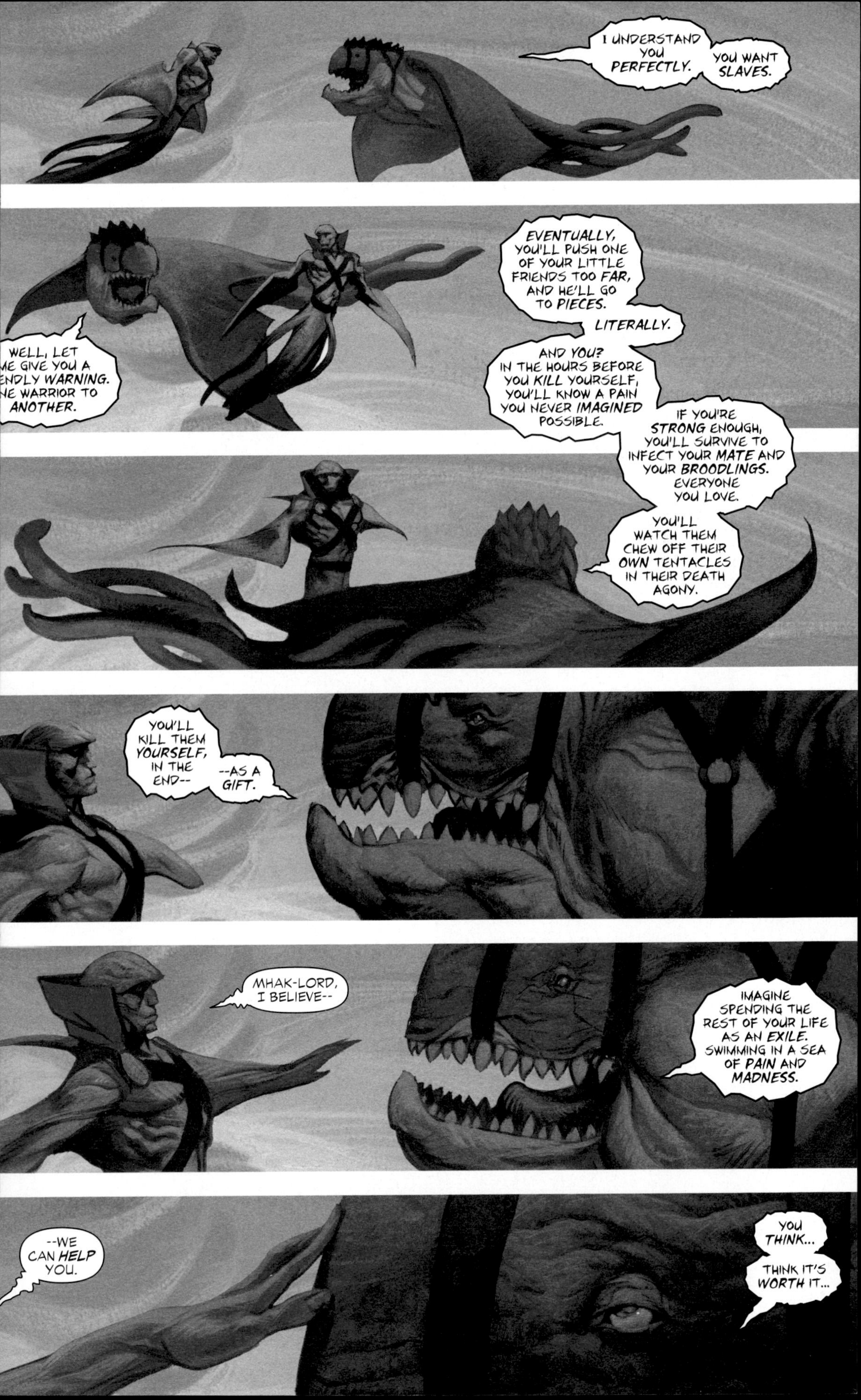
I UNDERSTAND YOU PERFECTLY.
YOU WANT SLAVES.
WELL, LET ME GIVE YOU A ENDLY WARNING. NE WARRIOR TO ANOTHER.
EVENTUALLY, YOU'LL PUSH ONE OF YOUR LITTLE FRIENDS TOO FAR, AND HE'LL GO TO PIECES.
LITERALLY.
AND YOU? IN THE HOURS BEFORE YOU KILL YOURSELF, YOU'LL KNOW A PAIN YOU NEVER IMAGINED POSSIBLE.
IF YOU'RE STRONG ENOUGH, YOU'LL SURVIVE TO INFECT YOUR MATE AND YOUR BROODLINGS. EVERYONE YOU LOVE.
YOU'LL WATCH THEM CHEW OFF THEIR OWN TENTACLES IN THEIR DEATH AGONY.
YOU'LL KILL THEM YOURSELF, IN THE END--
--AS A GIFT.
MHAK-LORD, I BELIEVE--
IMAGINE SPENDING THE REST OF YOUR LIFE AS AN EXILE. SWIMMING IN A SEA OF PAIN AND MADNESS.
--WE CAN HELP YOU.
YOU THINK...
THINK IT'S WORTH IT...

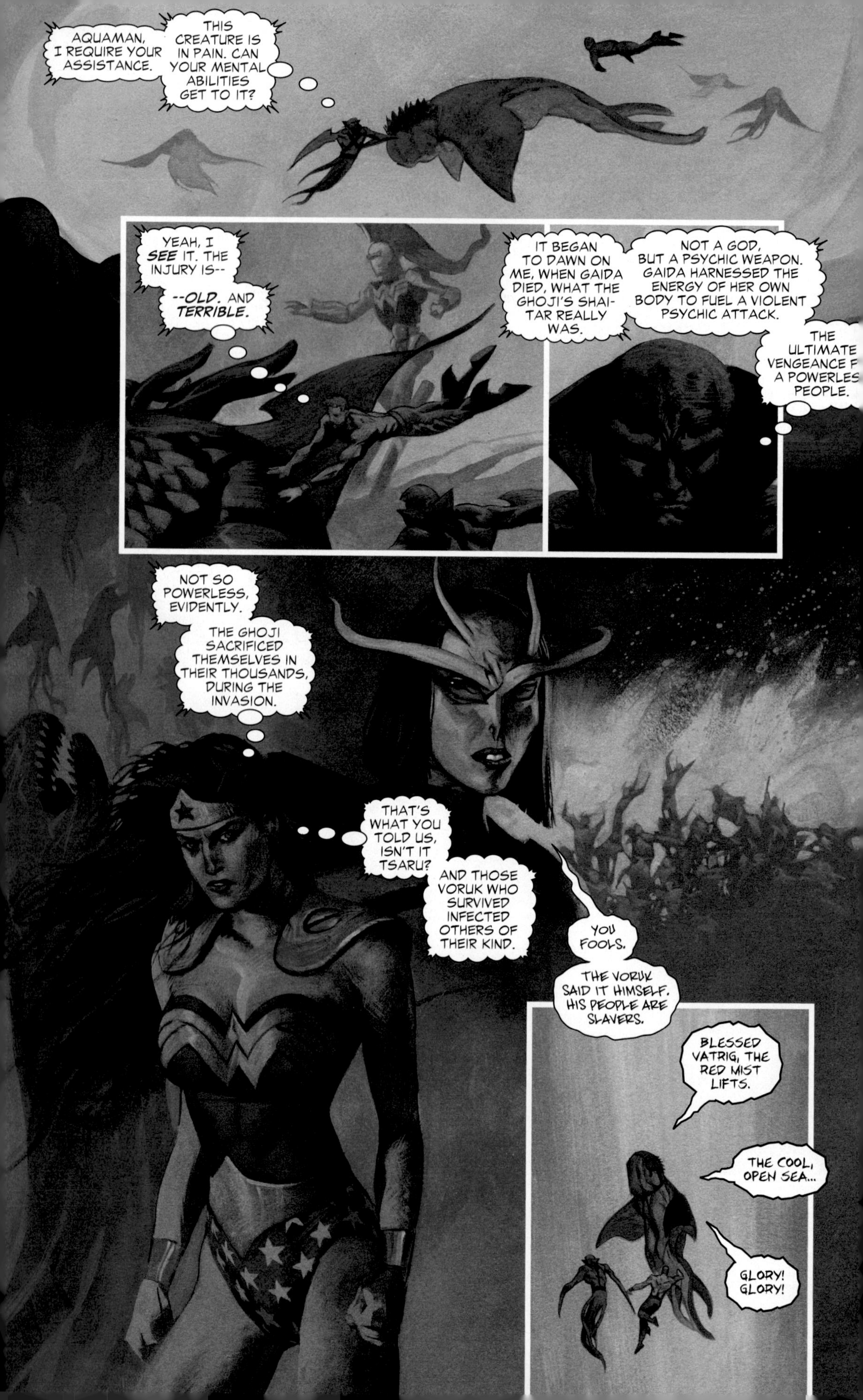
AQUAMAN, I REQUIRE YOUR ASSISTANCE.
THIS CREATURE IS IN PAIN. CAN YOUR MENTAL ABILITIES GET TO IT?
YEAH, I *SEE* IT. THE INJURY IS--
--*OLD.* AND *TERRIBLE.*
IT BEGAN TO DAWN ON ME, WHEN GAIDA DIED, WHAT THE GHOJI'S SHAI-TAR REALLY WAS.
NOT A GOD, BUT A PSYCHIC WEAPON. GAIDA HARNESSED THE ENERGY OF HER OWN BODY TO FUEL A VIOLENT PSYCHIC ATTACK.
THE ULTIMATE VENGEANCE F A POWERLES PEOPLE.
NOT SO POWERLESS, EVIDENTLY.
THE GHOJI SACRIFICED THEMSELVES IN THEIR THOUSANDS, DURING THE INVASION.
THAT'S WHAT YOU TOLD US, ISN'T IT TSARU?
AND THOSE VORUK WHO SURVIVED INFECTED OTHERS OF THEIR KIND.
YOU FOOLS.
THE VORUK SAID IT HIMSELF. HIS PEOPLE ARE SLAVERS.
BLESSED VATRIG, THE RED MIST LIFTS.
THE COOL, OPEN SEA...
GLORY! GLORY!

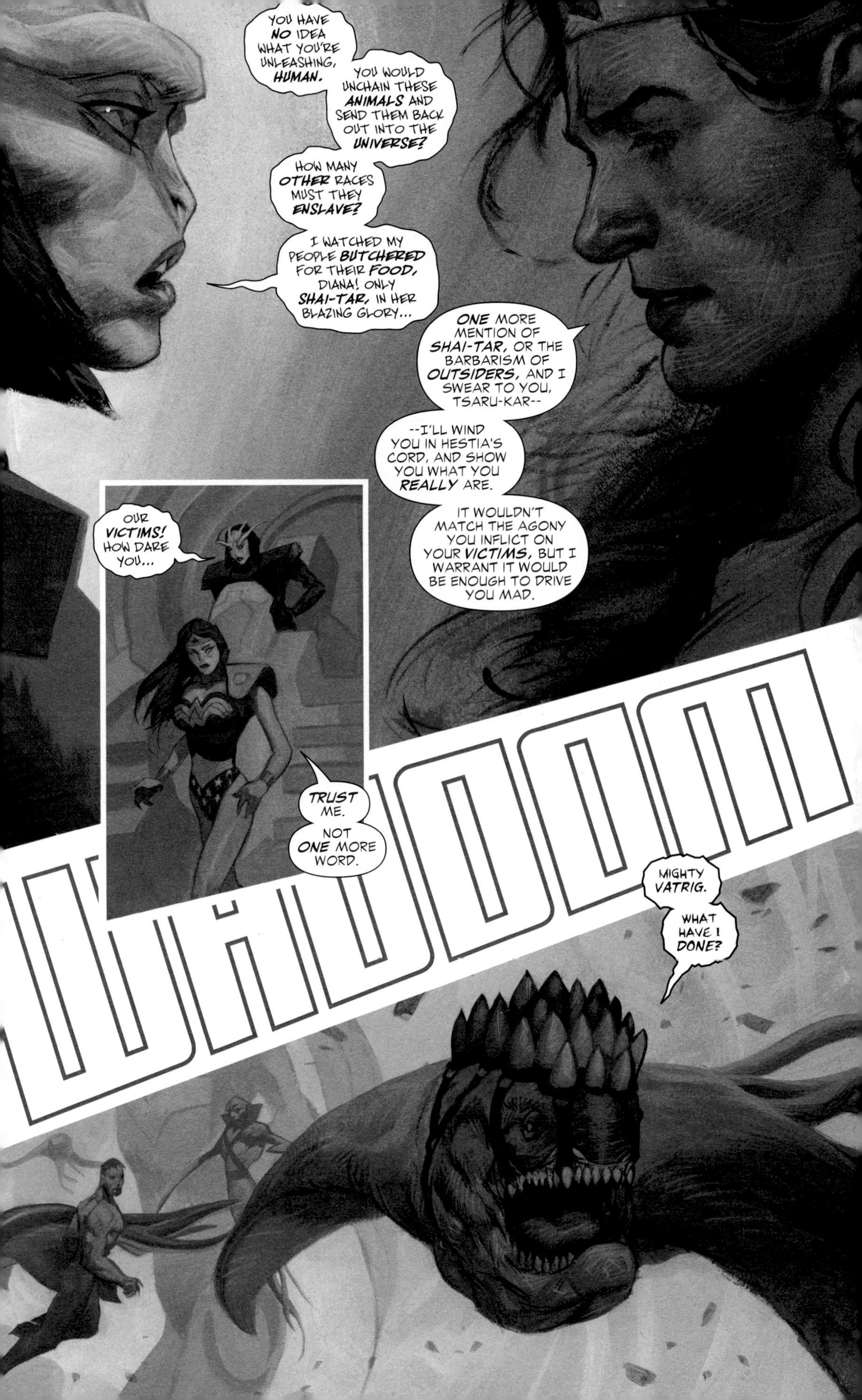
YOU HAVE NO IDEA WHAT YOU'RE UNLEASHING, HUMAN.
YOU WOULD UNCHAIN THESE ANIMALS AND SEND THEM BACK OUT INTO THE UNIVERSE?
HOW MANY OTHER RACES MUST THEY ENSLAVE?
I WATCHED MY PEOPLE BUTCHERED FOR THEIR FOOD, DIANA! ONLY SHAI-TAR, IN HER BLAZING GLORY...
ONE MORE MENTION OF SHAI-TAR, OR THE BARBARISM OF OUTSIDERS, AND I SWEAR TO YOU, TSARU-KAR--
--I'LL WIND YOU IN HESTIA'S CORD, AND SHOW YOU WHAT YOU REALLY ARE.
IT WOULDN'T MATCH THE AGONY YOU INFLICT ON YOUR VICTIMS, BUT I WARRANT IT WOULD BE ENOUGH TO DRIVE YOU MAD.
OUR VICTIMS! HOW DARE YOU...
TRUST ME.
NOT ONE MORE WORD.
WHOOOOM
MIGHTY VATRIG.
WHAT HAVE I DONE?

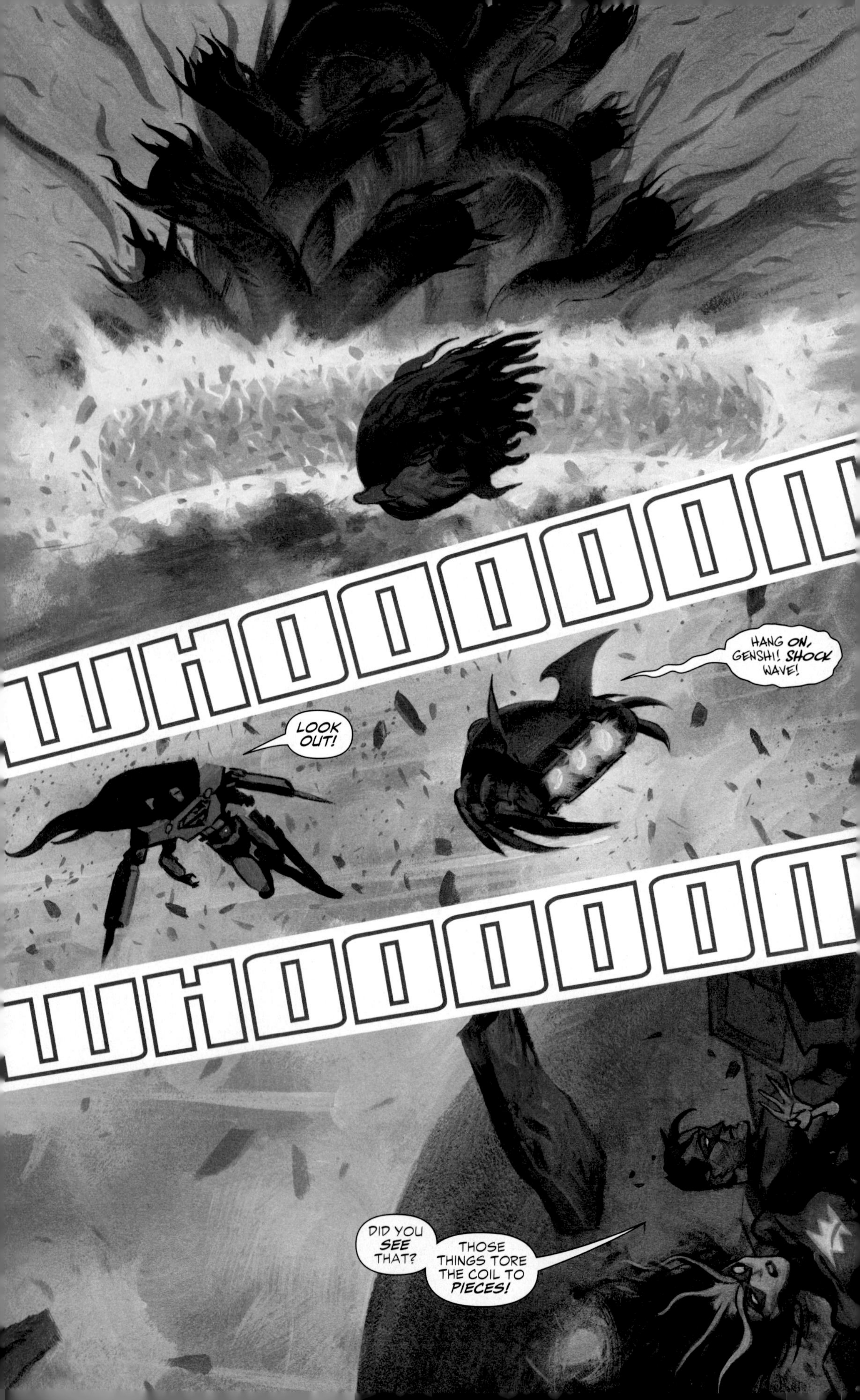
WHOOOOOOM
HANG ON, GENSHI! SHOCK WAVE!
LOOK OUT!
WHOOOOOOM
DID YOU SEE THAT?
THOSE THINGS TORE THE COIL TO PIECES!

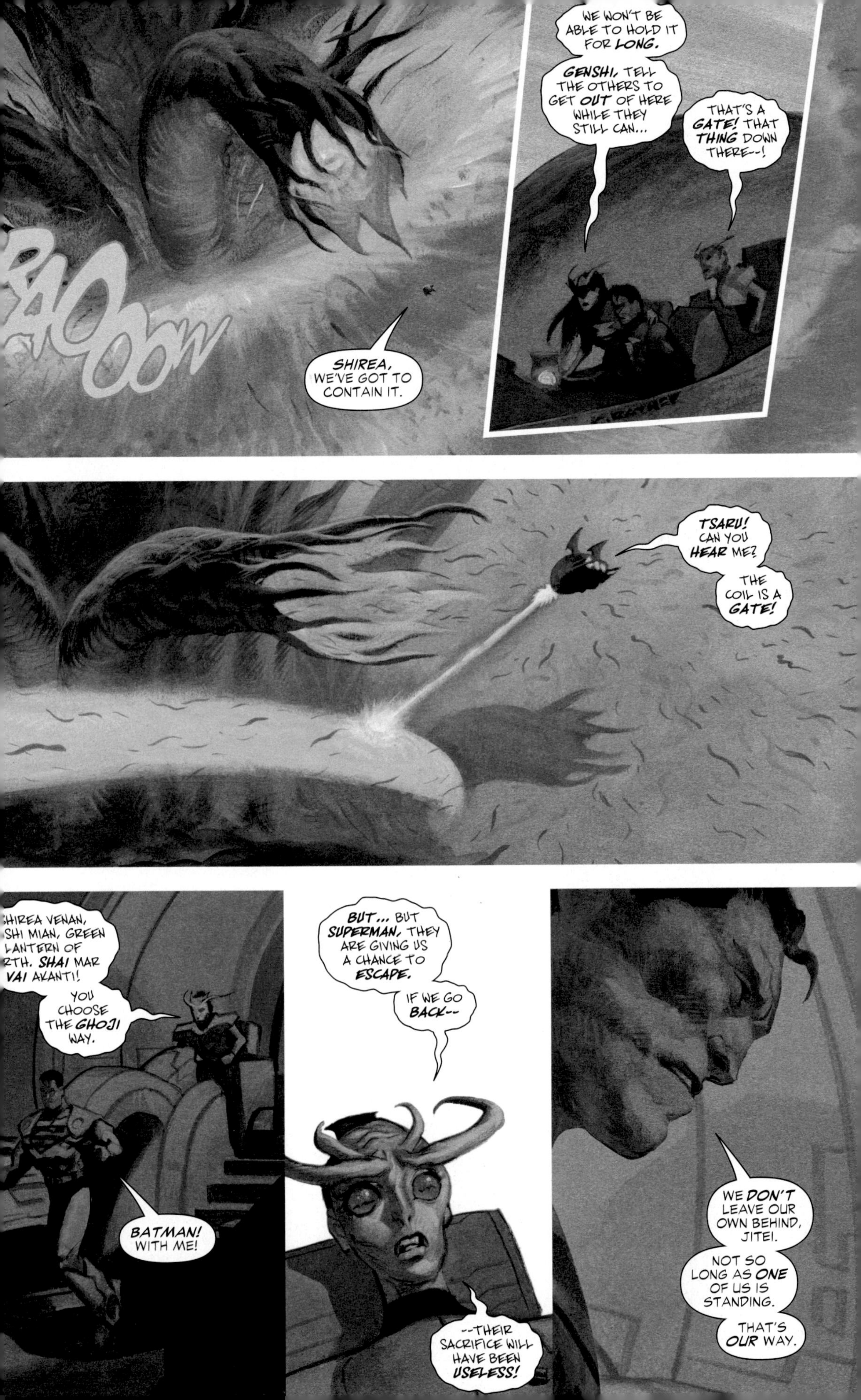

BRAOOOOW
SHIREA, WE'VE GOT TO CONTAIN IT.
WE WON'T BE ABLE TO HOLD IT FOR LONG.
GENSHI, TELL THE OTHERS TO GET OUT OF HERE WHILE THEY STILL CAN...
THAT'S A GATE! THAT THING DOWN THERE--!
TSARU! CAN YOU HEAR ME?
THE COIL IS A GATE!
SHI MIAN, GREEN LANTERN OF
SHAI MAR VAI AKANTI!
YOU CHOOSE THE GHOJI WAY.
BATMAN! WITH ME!
BUT... BUT SUPERMAN, THEY ARE GIVING US A CHANCE TO ESCAPE.
IF WE GO BACK--
--THEIR SACRIFICE WILL HAVE BEEN USELESS!
WE DON'T LEAVE OUR OWN BEHIND, JITEI.
NOT SO LONG AS ONE OF US IS STANDING.
THAT'S OUR WAY.

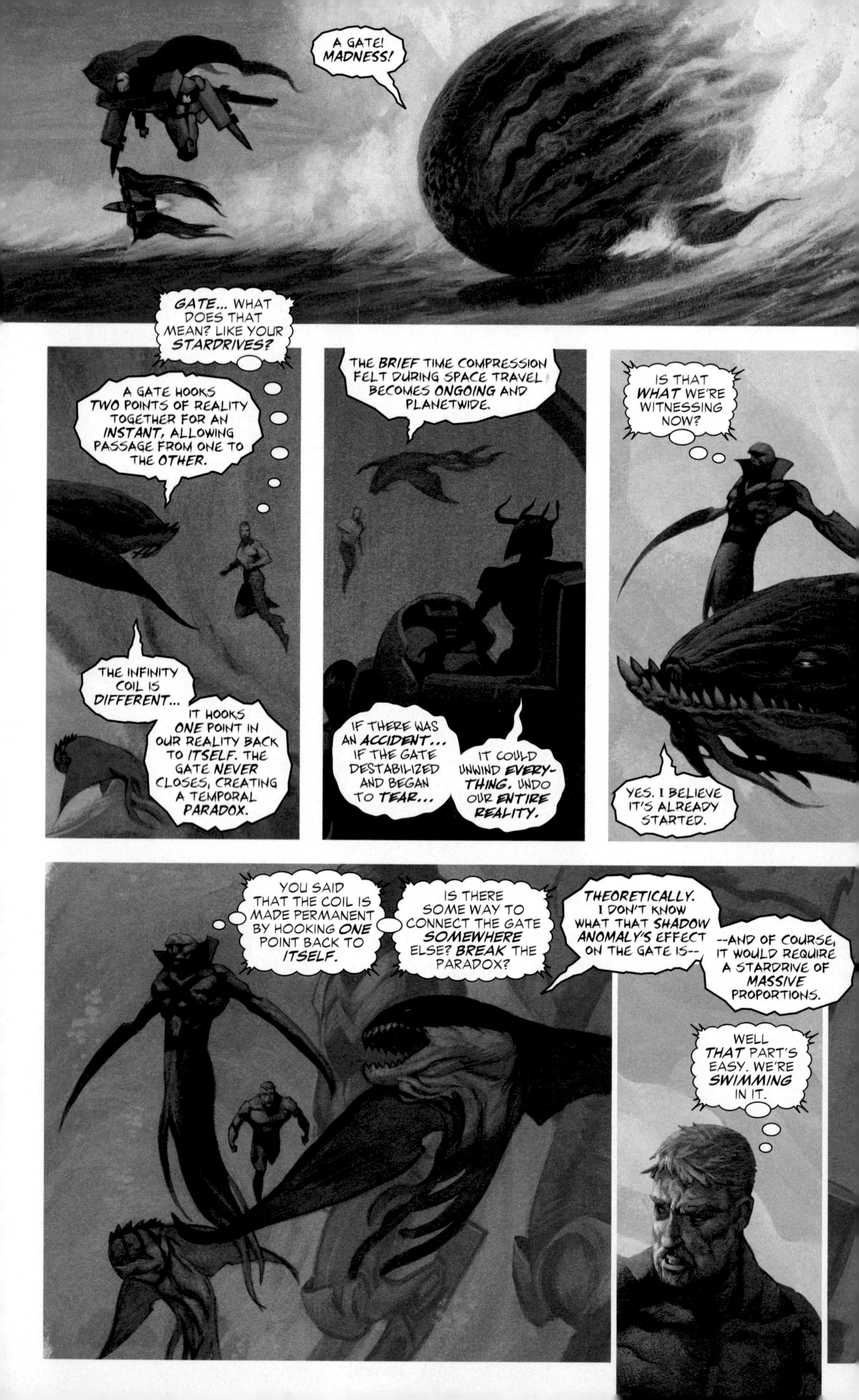
A GATE! MADNESS!
GATE... WHAT DOES THAT MEAN? LIKE YOUR STARDRIVES?
A GATE HOOKS TWO POINTS OF REALITY TOGETHER FOR AN INSTANT, ALLOWING PASSAGE FROM ONE TO THE OTHER.
THE INFINITY COIL IS DIFFERENT...
IT HOOKS ONE POINT IN OUR REALITY BACK TO ITSELF. THE GATE NEVER CLOSES, CREATING A TEMPORAL PARADOX.
THE BRIEF TIME COMPRESSION FELT DURING SPACE TRAVEL BECOMES ONGOING AND PLANETWIDE.
IF THERE WAS AN ACCIDENT... IF THE GATE DESTABILIZED AND BEGAN TO TEAR...
IT COULD UNWIND EVERYTHING. UNDO OUR ENTIRE REALITY.
IS THAT WHAT WE'RE WITNESSING NOW?
YES. I BELIEVE IT'S ALREADY STARTED.
YOU SAID THAT THE COIL IS MADE PERMANENT BY HOOKING ONE POINT BACK TO ITSELF.
IS THERE SOME WAY TO CONNECT THE GATE SOMEWHERE ELSE? BREAK THE PARADOX?
THEORETICALLY. I DON'T KNOW WHAT THAT SHADOW ANOMALY'S EFFECT ON THE GATE IS--
--AND OF COURSE, IT WOULD REQUIRE A STARDRIVE OF MASSIVE PROPORTIONS.
WELL THAT PART'S EASY. WE'RE SWIMMING IN IT.

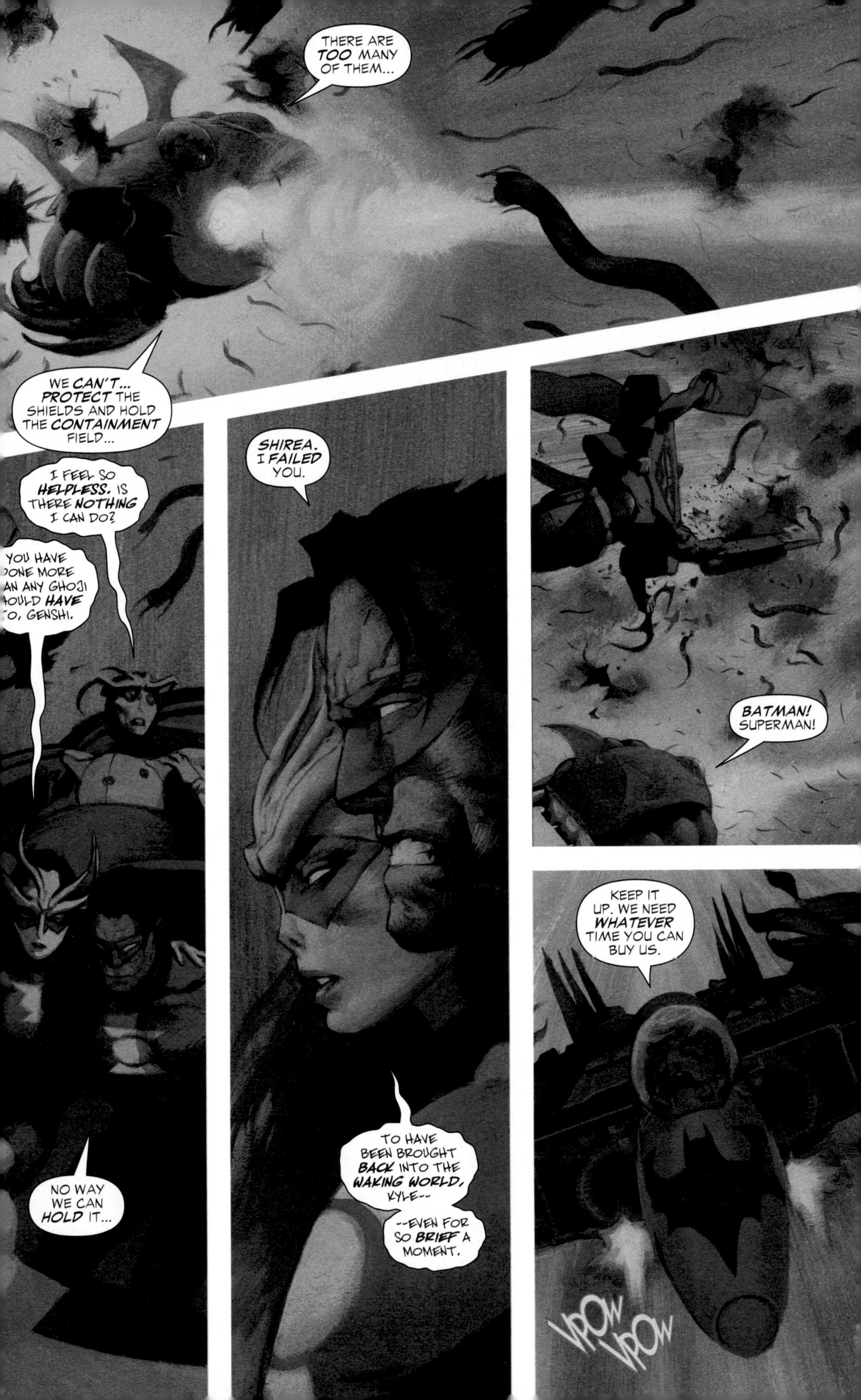
THERE ARE TOO MANY OF THEM...
WE CAN'T... PROTECT THE SHIELDS AND HOLD THE CONTAINMENT FIELD...
SHIREA. I FAILED YOU.
I FEEL SO HELPLESS. IS THERE NOTHING I CAN DO?
NO WAY WE CAN HOLD IT...
TO HAVE BEEN BROUGHT BACK INTO THE WAKING WORLD, KYLE--
--EVEN FOR SO BRIEF A MOMENT.
BATMAN! SUPERMAN!
KEEP IT UP. WE NEED WHATEVER TIME YOU CAN BUY US.
VROW VROW

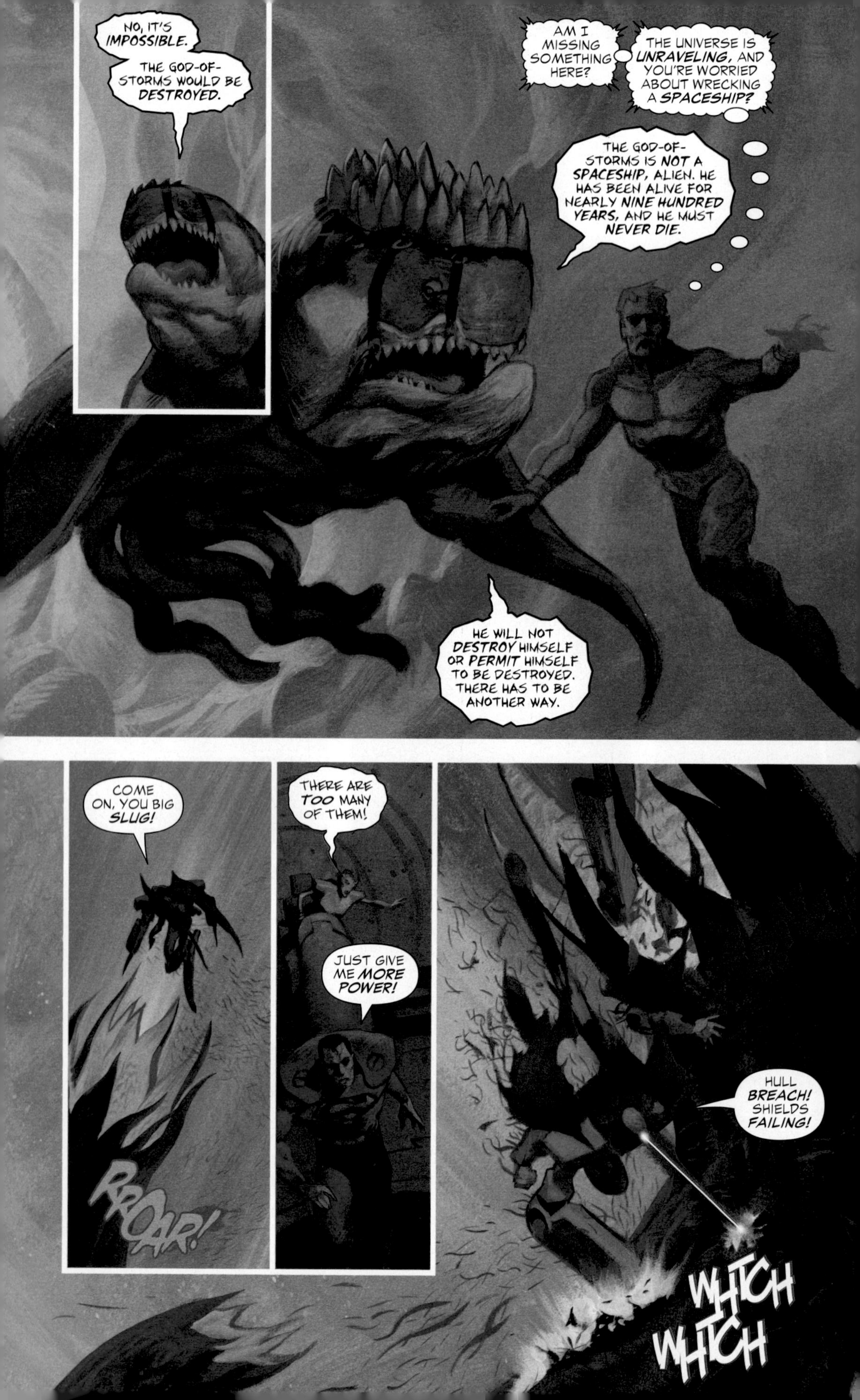
NO, IT'S IMPOSSIBLE.
THE GOD-OF-STORMS WOULD BE DESTROYED.
AM I MISSING SOMETHING HERE?
THE UNIVERSE IS UNRAVELING, AND YOU'RE WORRIED ABOUT WRECKING A SPACESHIP?
THE GOD-OF-STORMS IS NOT A SPACESHIP, ALIEN. HE HAS BEEN ALIVE FOR NEARLY NINE HUNDRED YEARS, AND HE MUST NEVER DIE.
HE WILL NOT DESTROY HIMSELF OR PERMIT HIMSELF TO BE DESTROYED. THERE HAS TO BE ANOTHER WAY.
COME ON, YOU BIG SLUG!
RROAR!
THERE ARE TOO MANY OF THEM!
JUST GIVE ME MORE POWER!
HULL BREACH! SHIELDS FAILING!
WHTCH
WHTCH

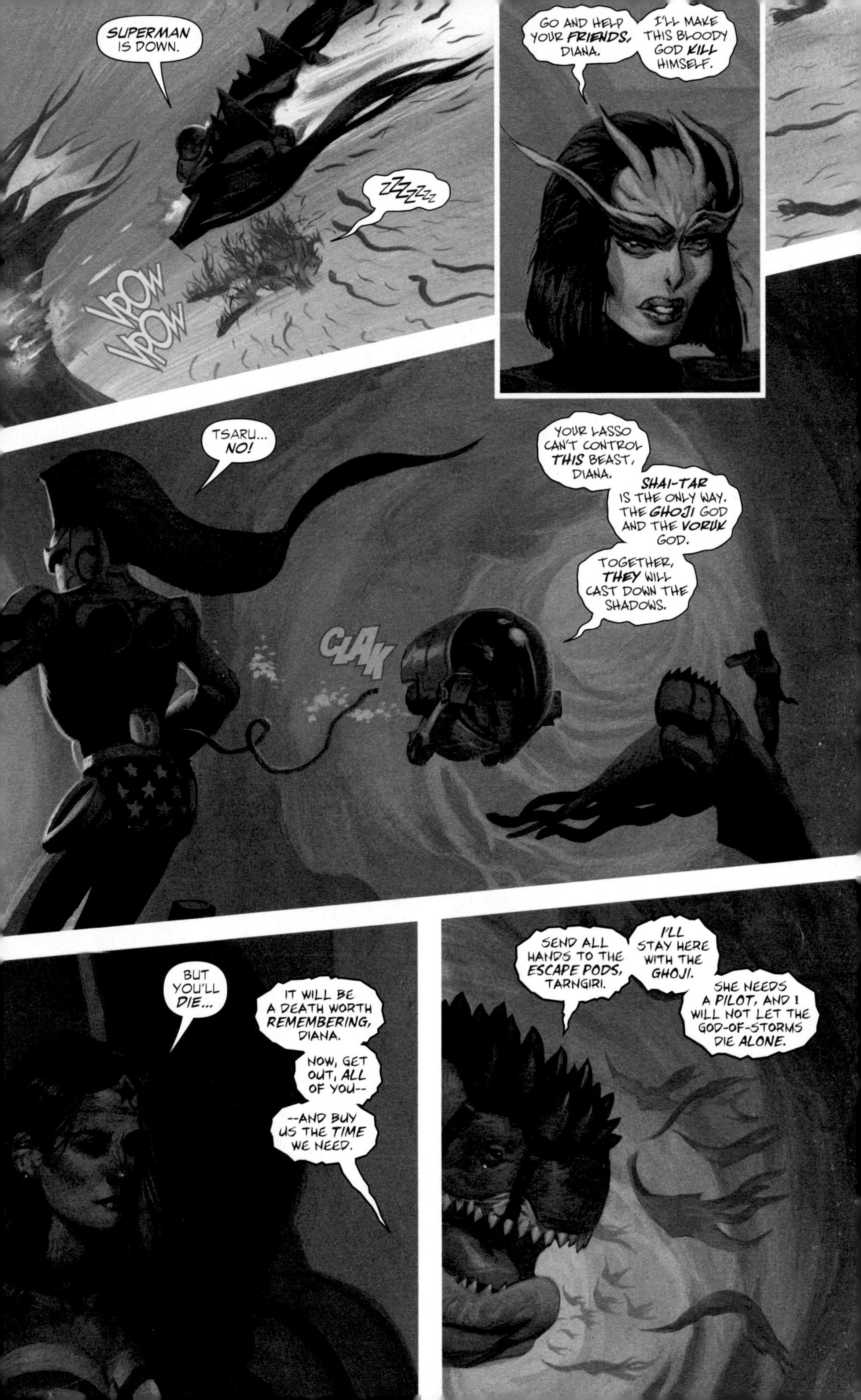
SUPERMAN IS DOWN.
ZZZZZZZ
VPOW VPOW
GO AND HELP YOUR FRIENDS, DIANA.
I'LL MAKE THIS BLOODY GOD KILL HIMSELF.
TSARU... NO!
YOUR LASSO CAN'T CONTROL THIS BEAST, DIANA.
SHAI-TAR IS THE ONLY WAY. THE GHOJI GOD AND THE VORUK GOD.
TOGETHER, THEY WILL CAST DOWN THE SHADOWS.
CLAK
BUT YOU'LL DIE...
IT WILL BE A DEATH WORTH REMEMBERING, DIANA.
NOW, GET OUT, ALL OF YOU--
--AND BUY US THE TIME WE NEED.
SEND ALL HANDS TO THE ESCAPE PODS, TARNGIRI.
I'LL STAY HERE WITH THE GHOJI.
SHE NEEDS A PILOT, AND I WILL NOT LET THE GOD-OF-STORMS DIE ALONE.

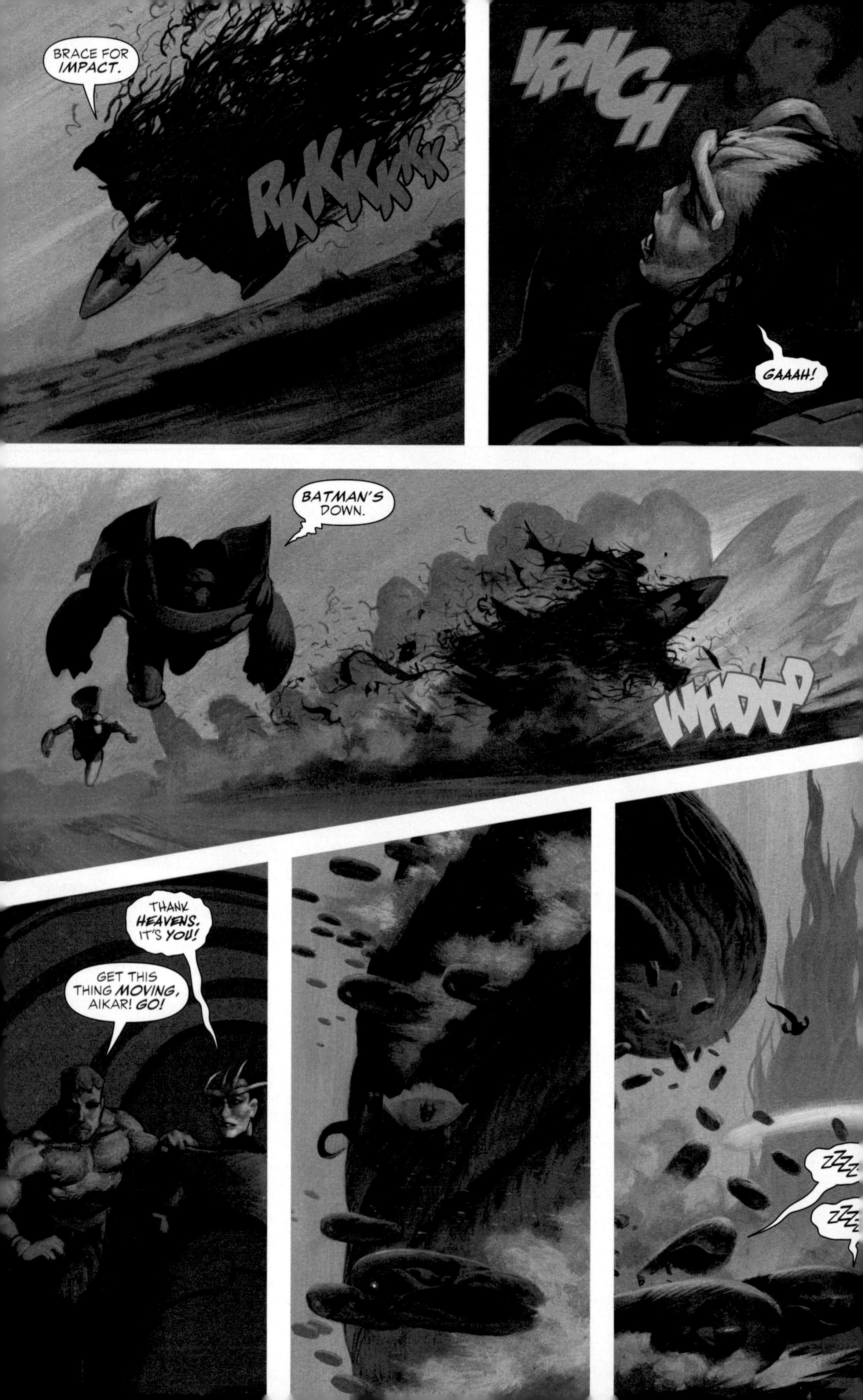
BRACE FOR *IMPACT.*
RKKKKKKK
KRNCH
GAAAH!
BATMAN'S DOWN.
WHOOP
THANK *HEAVENS.* IT'S *YOU!*
GET THIS THING *MOVING,* AIKAR! *GO!*
ZZZZ
ZZZZ

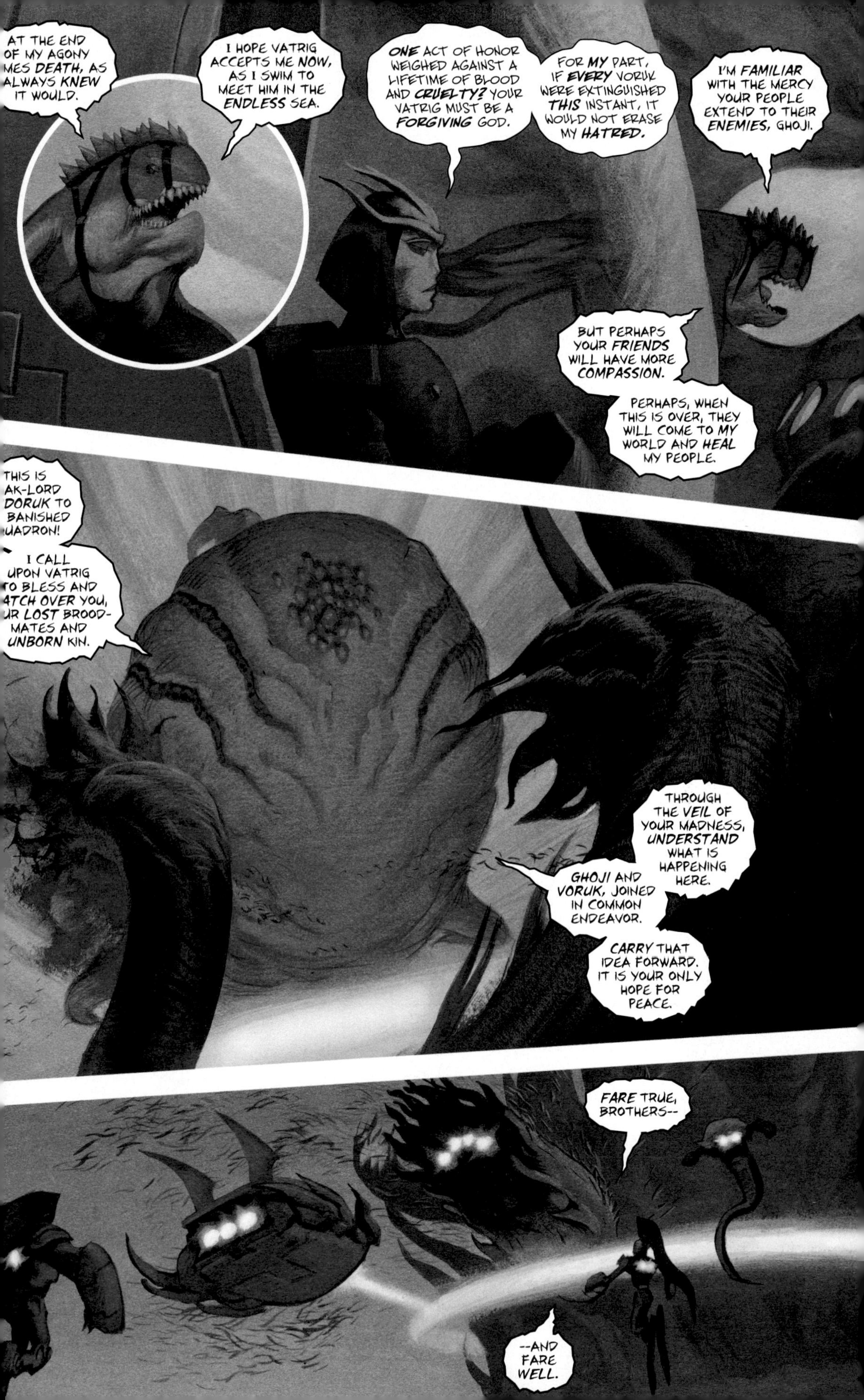
AT THE END OF MY AGONY MES DEATH, AS ALWAYS KNEW IT WOULD.
I HOPE VATRIG ACCEPTS ME NOW, AS I SWIM TO MEET HIM IN THE ENDLESS SEA.
ONE ACT OF HONOR WEIGHED AGAINST A LIFETIME OF BLOOD AND CRUELTY? YOUR VATRIG MUST BE A FORGIVING GOD.
FOR MY PART, IF EVERY VORUK WERE EXTINGUISHED THIS INSTANT, IT WOULD NOT ERASE MY HATRED.
I'M FAMILIAR WITH THE MERCY YOUR PEOPLE EXTEND TO THEIR ENEMIES, GHOJI.
BUT PERHAPS YOUR FRIENDS WILL HAVE MORE COMPASSION.
PERHAPS, WHEN THIS IS OVER, THEY WILL COME TO MY WORLD AND HEAL MY PEOPLE.
THIS IS AK-LORD DORUK TO BANISHED UADRON!
I CALL UPON VATRIG TO BLESS AND ATCH OVER YOU, UR LOST BROOD-MATES AND UNBORN KIN.
THROUGH THE VEIL OF YOUR MADNESS, UNDERSTAND WHAT IS HAPPENING HERE.
GHOJI AND VORUK, JOINED IN COMMON ENDEAVOR.
CARRY THAT IDEA FORWARD. IT IS YOUR ONLY HOPE FOR PEACE.
FARE TRUE, BROTHERS--
--AND FARE WELL.

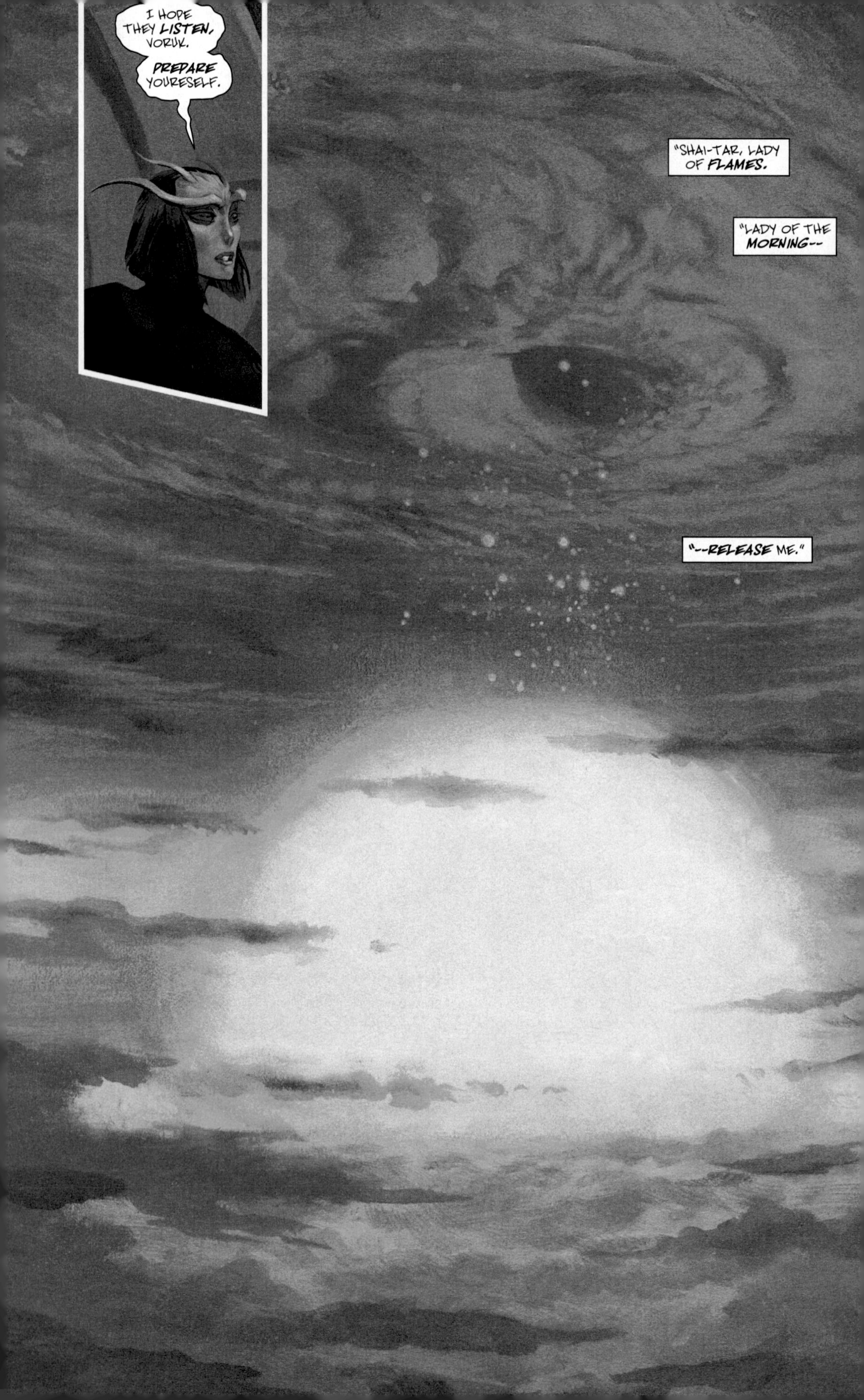
I HOPE THEY LISTEN, VORUK.
PREPARE YOURESELF.
"SHAI-TAR, LADY OF FLAMES.
"LADY OF THE MORNING--
"--RELEASE ME."

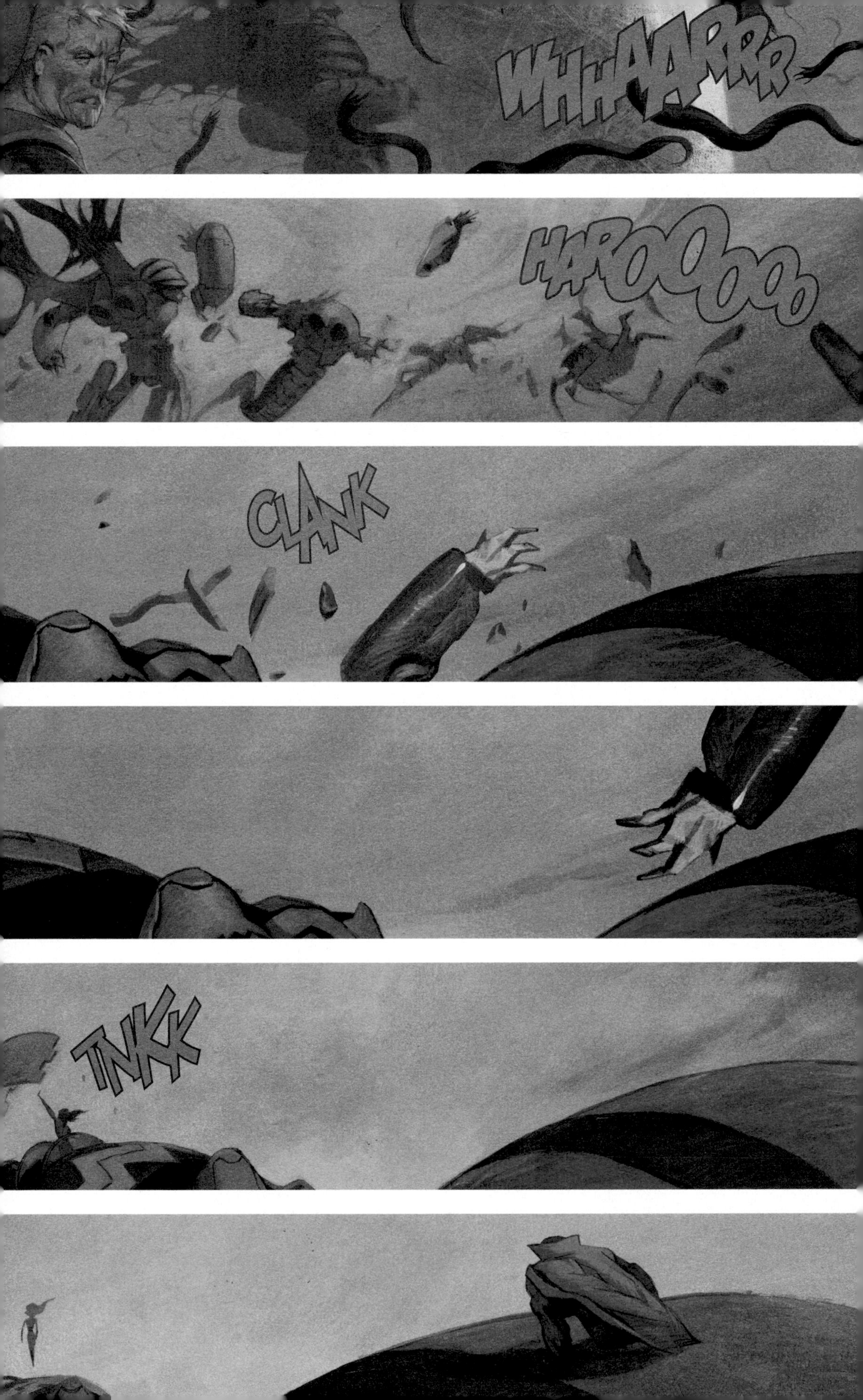
WHHAARRR
HAROOOOO
CLANK
TNKK

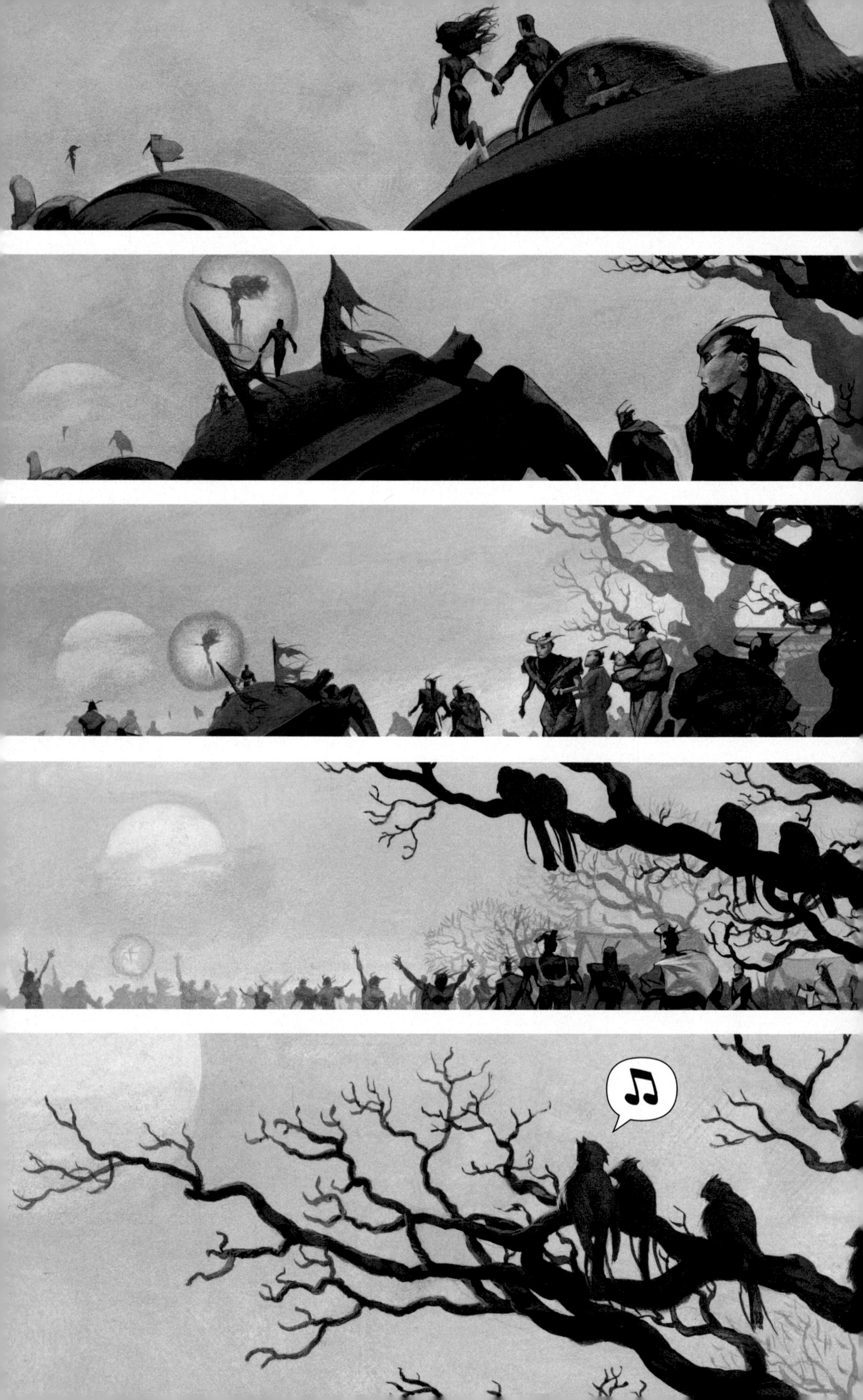

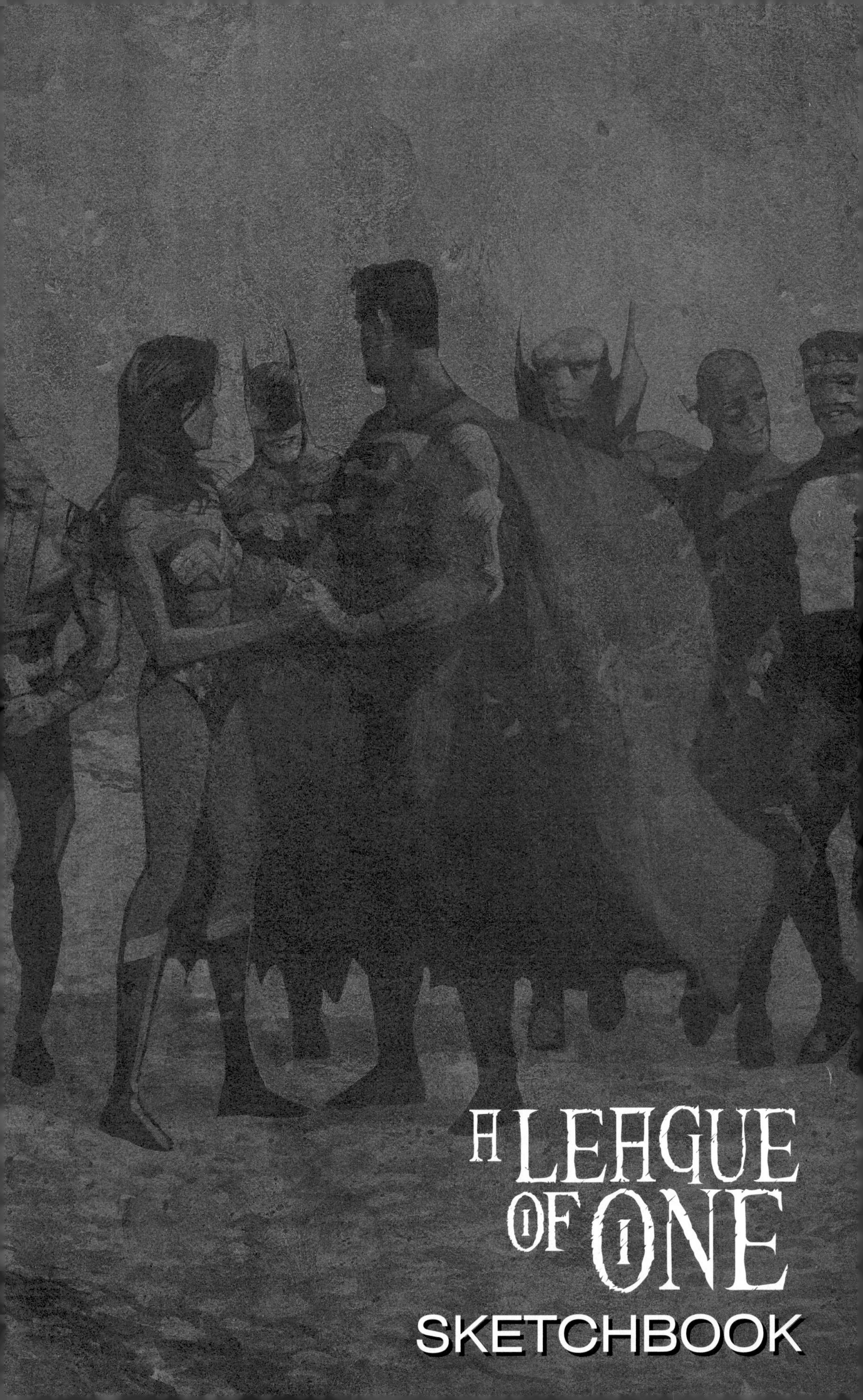

A LEAGUE OF ONE SKETCHBOOK

Lasso & Hair —
expressive/de[...]
element[...]

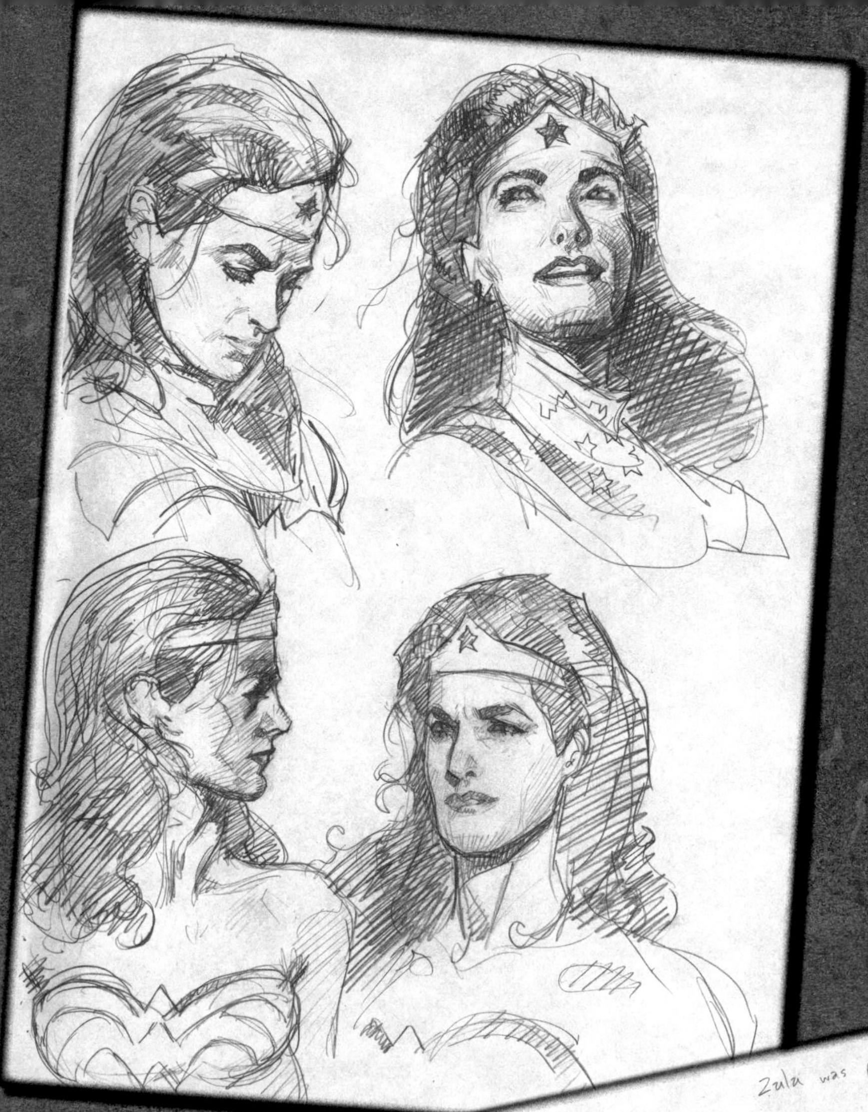

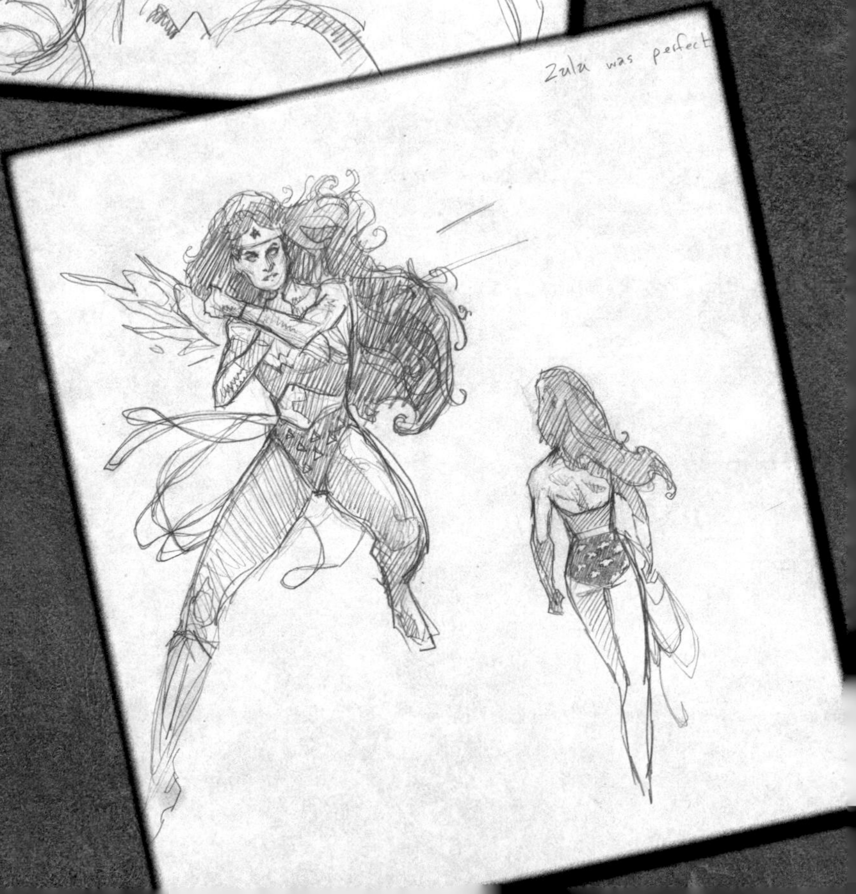
Zula was perfect

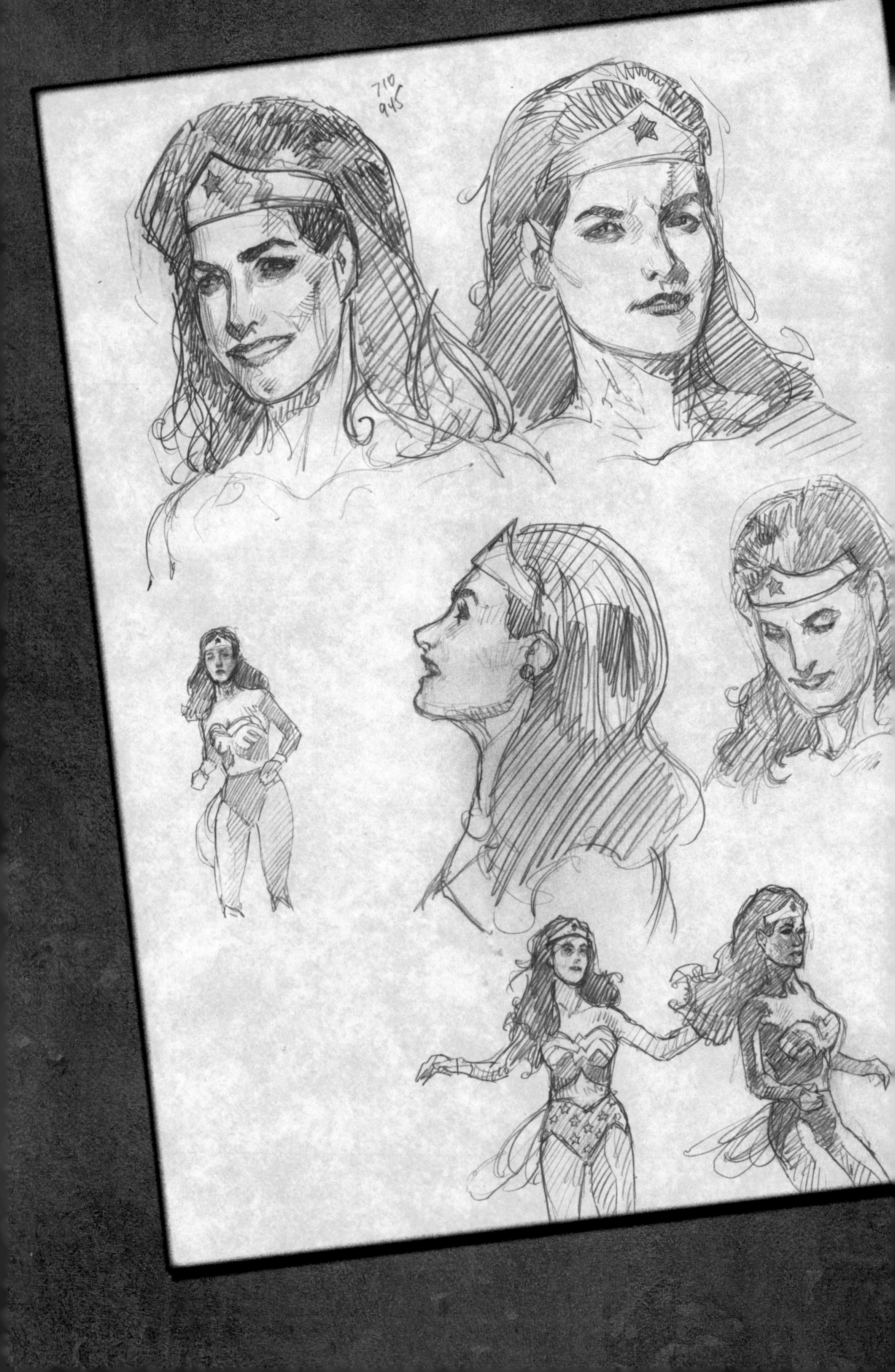
710
945

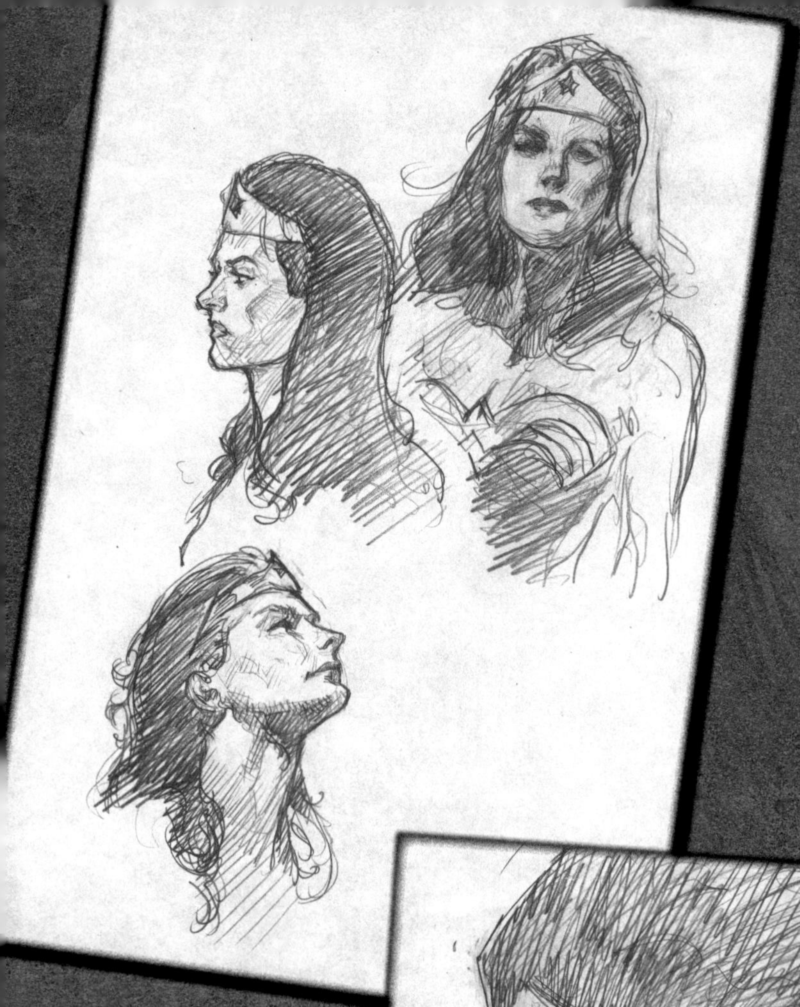

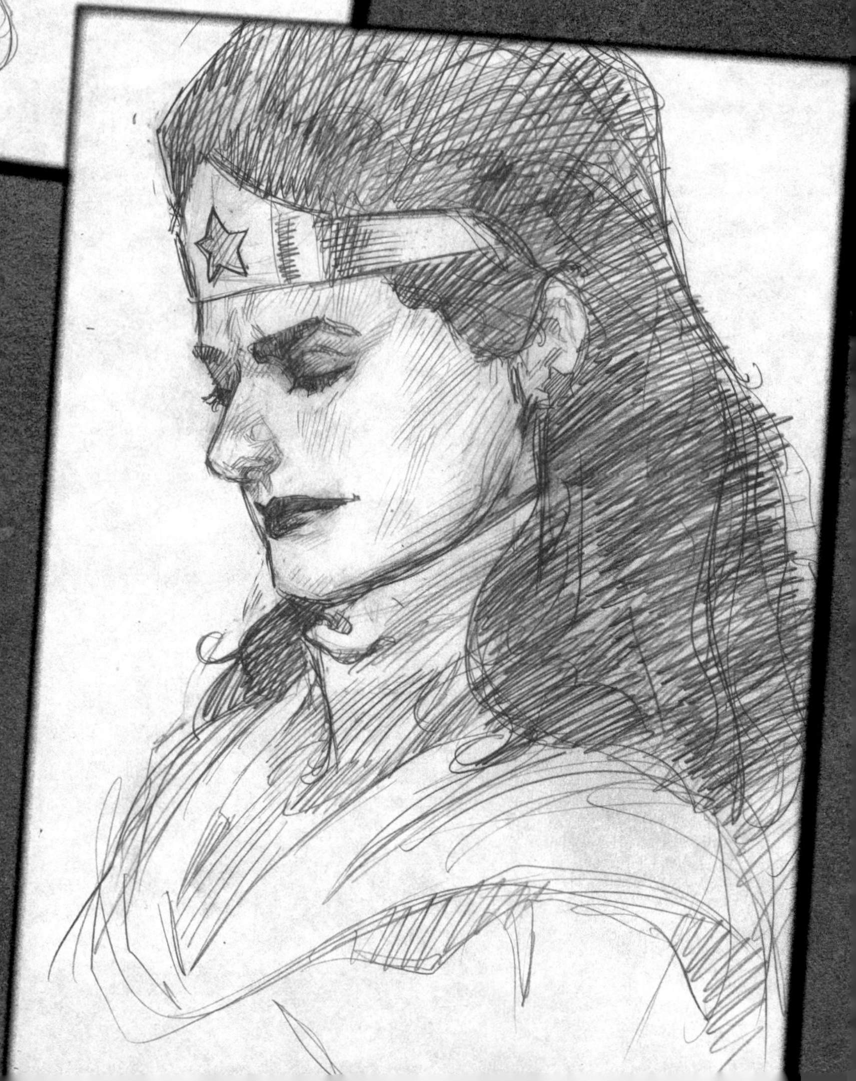

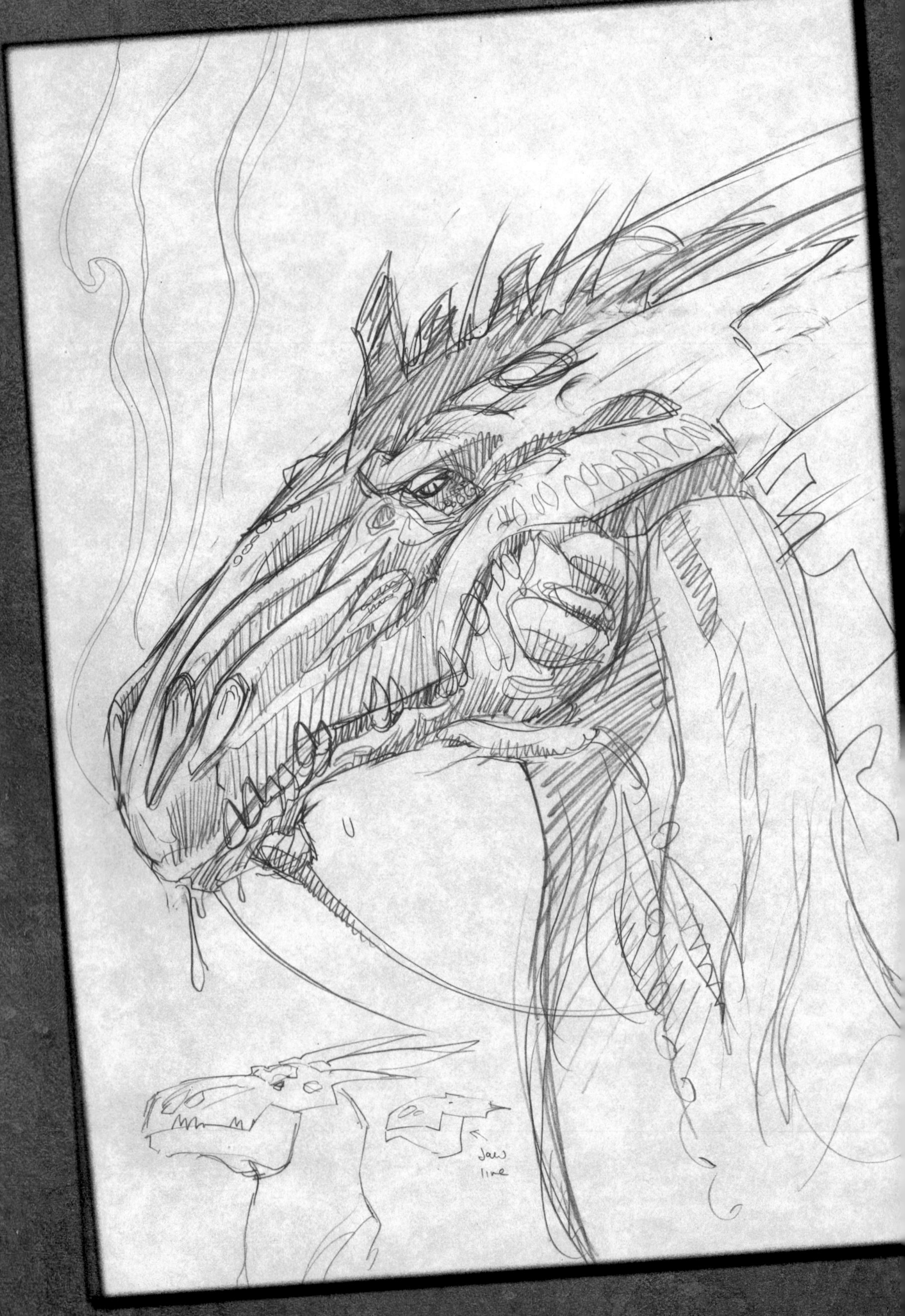
Jaw line

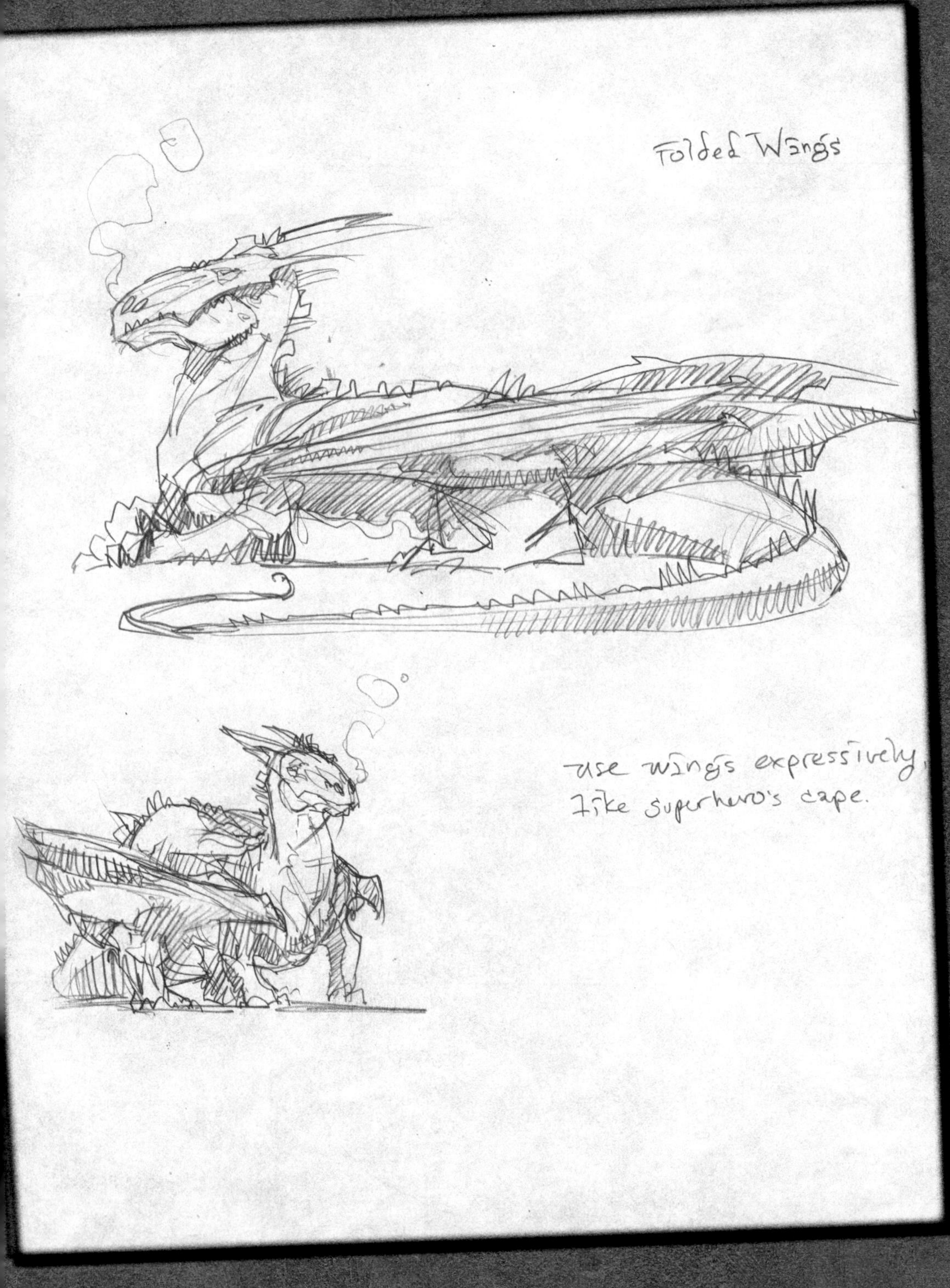
Folded Wings
use wings expressively,
like superhero's cape.

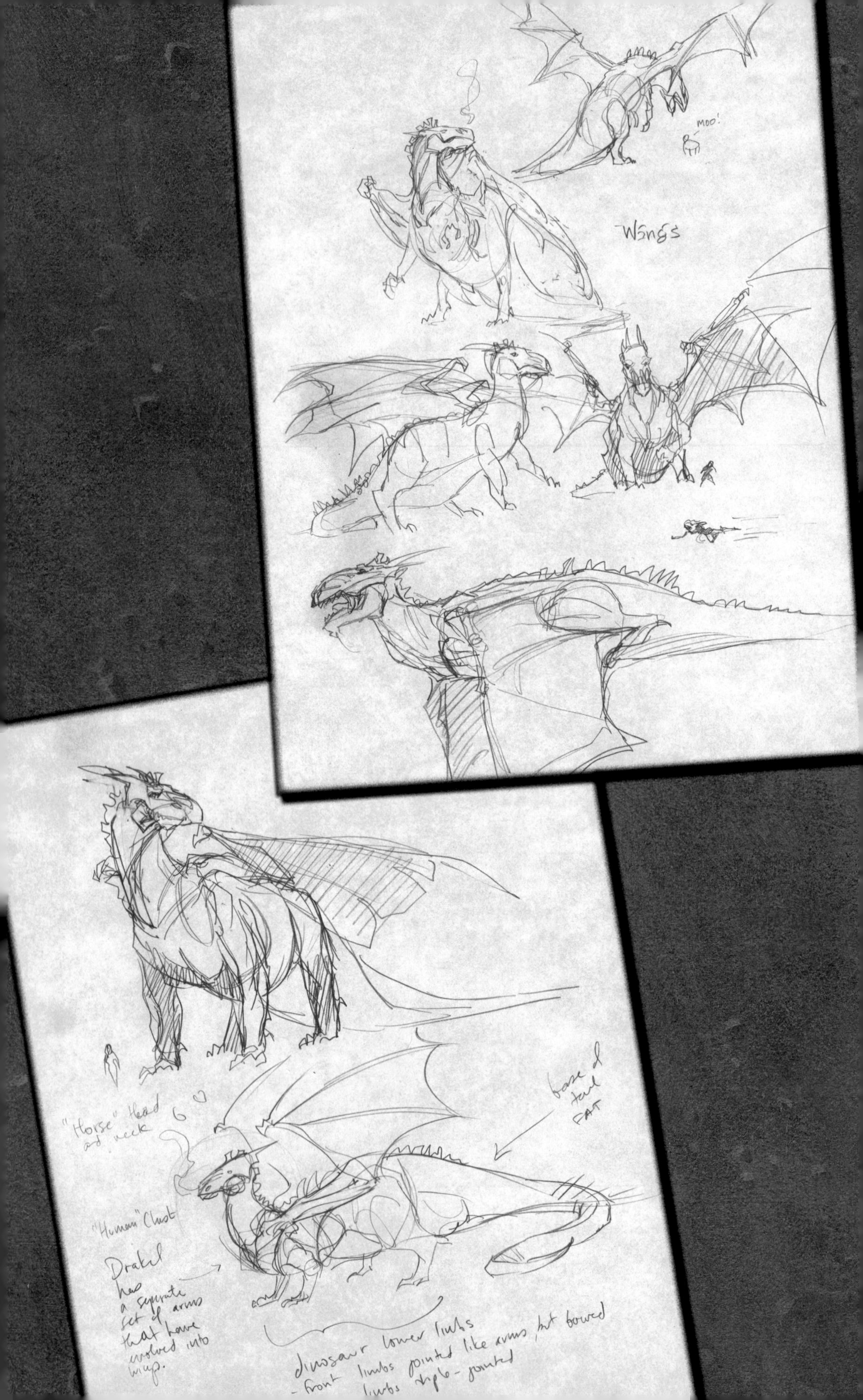
MOO!
Wings
"Horse" Head and neck
base of tail FAT
"Human" Chest
Drakel has a separate set of arms that have evolved into wings.
dinosaur lower limbs
- front limbs jointed like arms, but bowed limbs triple-jointed

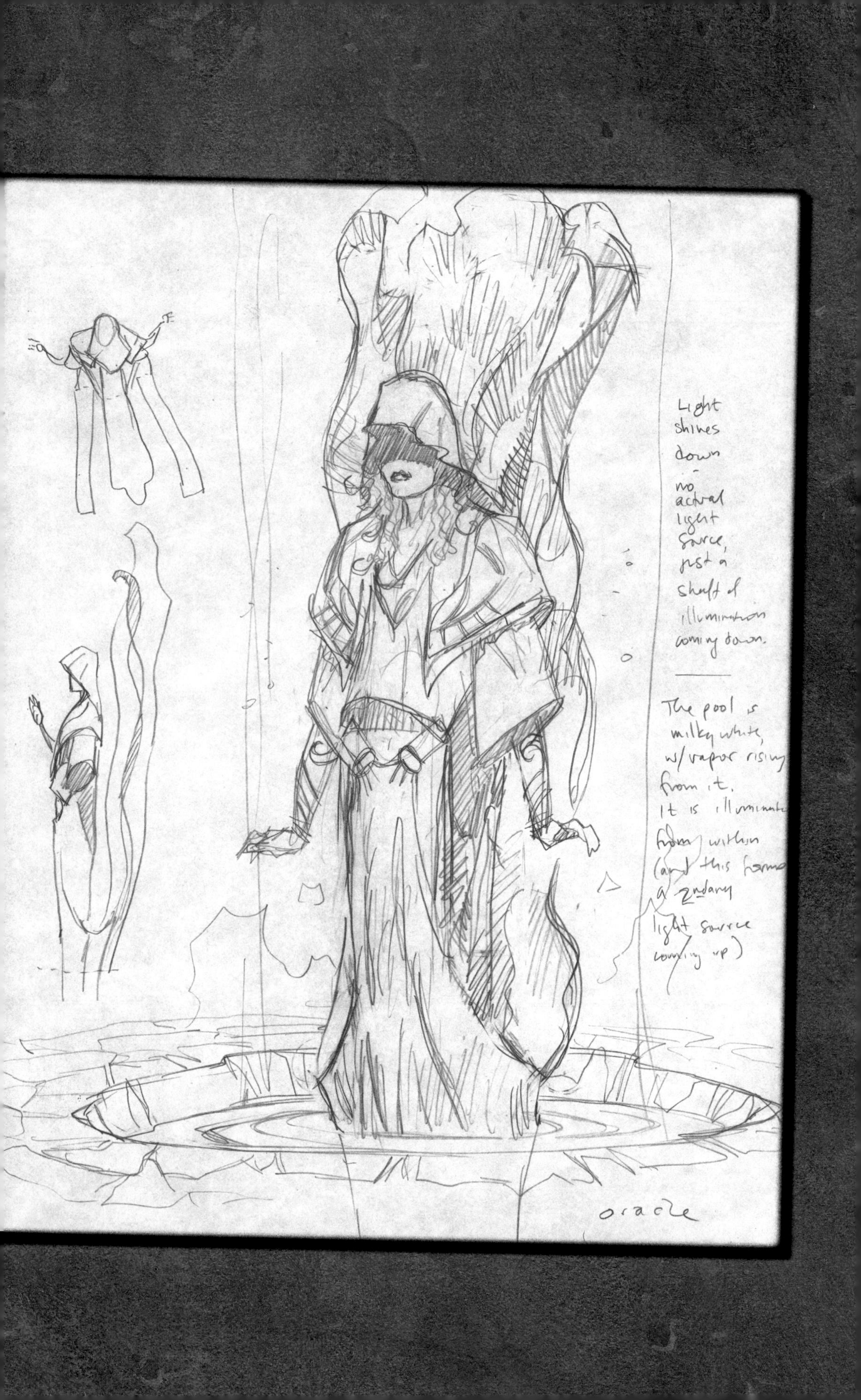

Light shines down - no actual light source, just a shaft of illumination coming down.
The pool is milky white, w/vapor rising from it. It is illuminate from within (and this forms a 2ndary light source coming up)
oracle

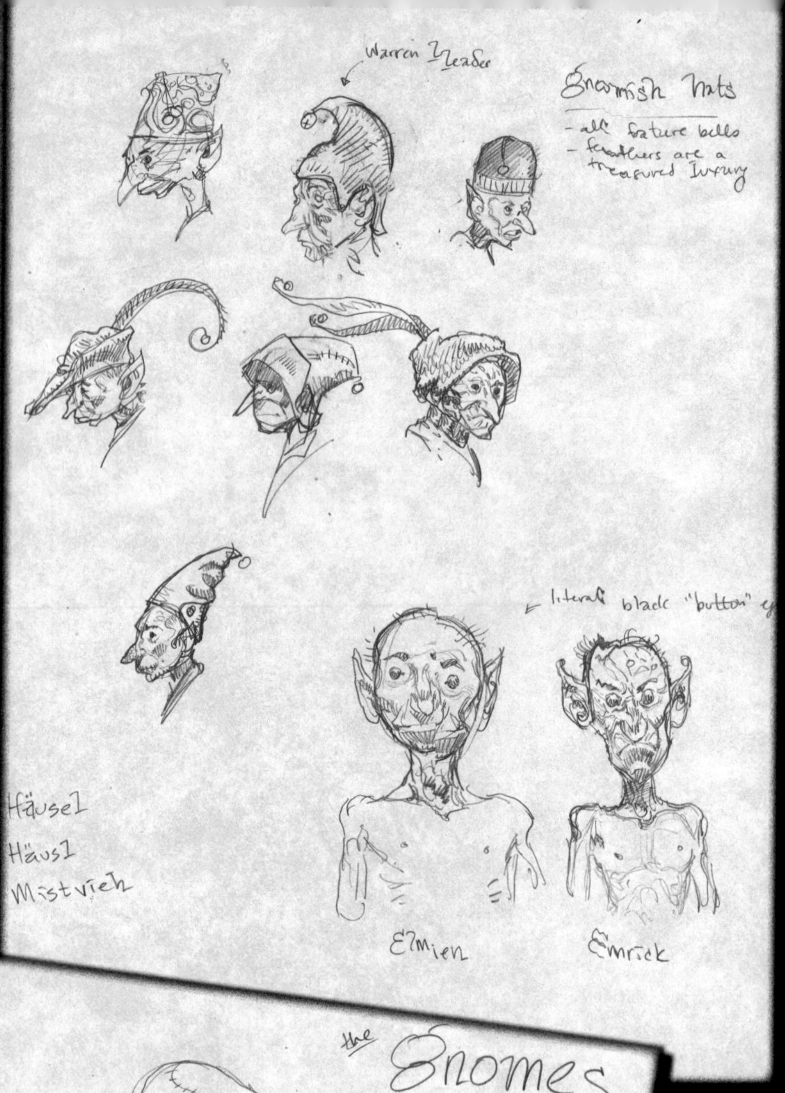
Warren Leader
Gnomish Hats
- all feature bells
- feathers are a treasured luxury
literal black "button"
Häusel
Häusl
Mistvieh
Elmien
Emrick

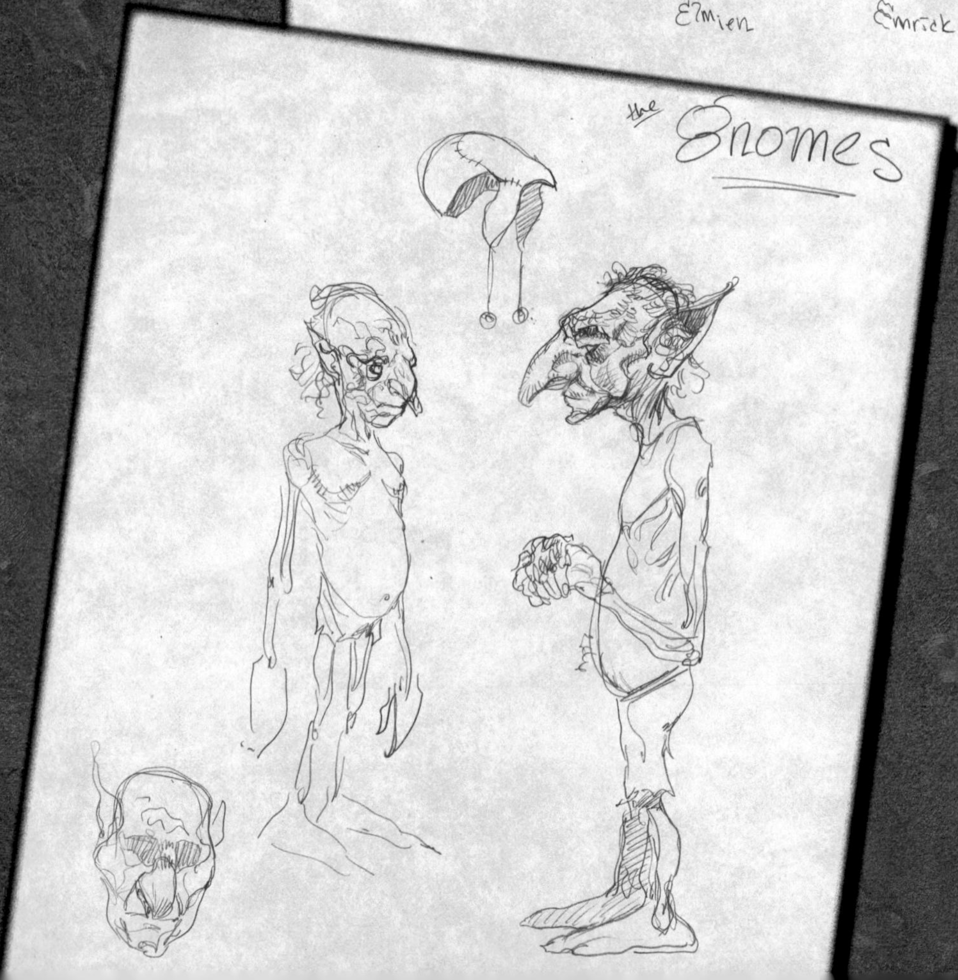
the Gnomes

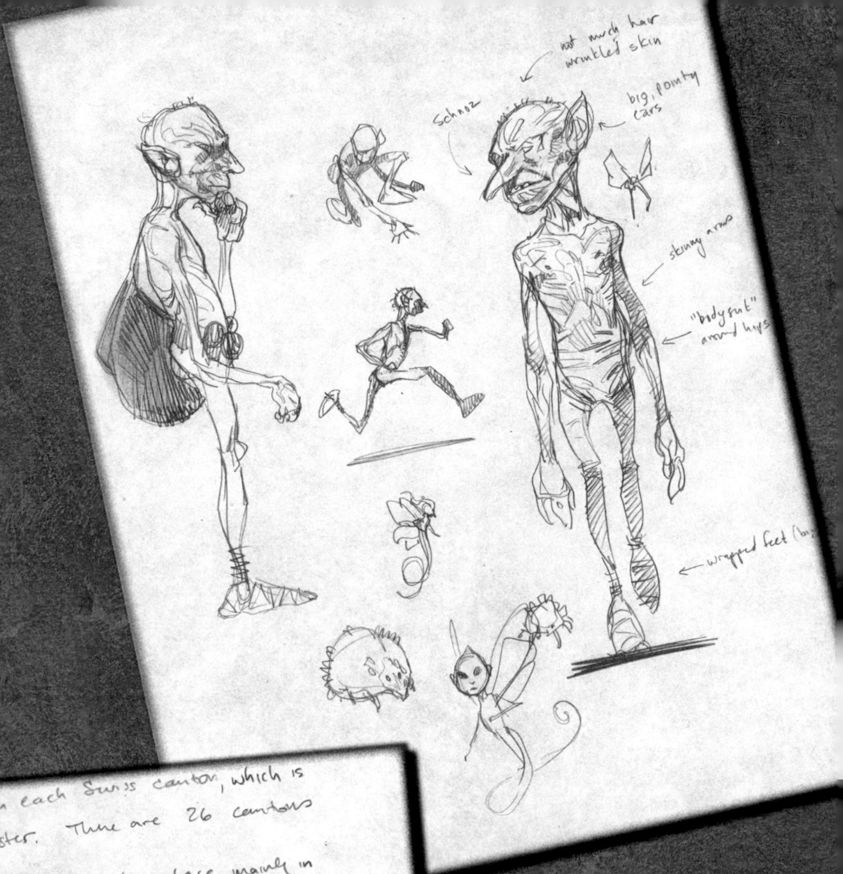

not much hair
wrinkled skin
Schnoz
big, pointy ears
skinny arms
"bodysuit" around hips
wrapped feet

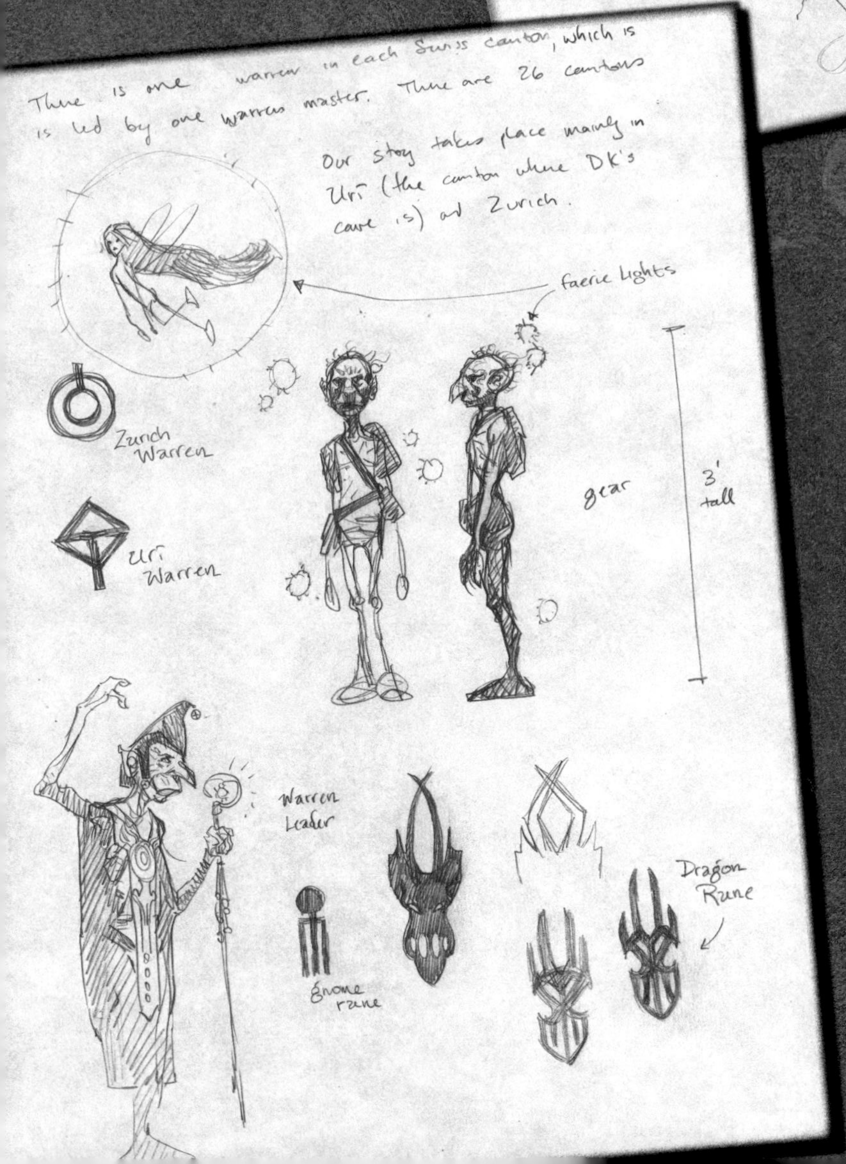

There is one warren in each Swiss canton, which is
is led by one warren master. There are 26 cantons
Our story takes place mainly in Uri (the canton where DK's cave is) and Zurich.
faerie lights
Zurich Warren
Uri Warren
gear
3' tall
Warren Leader
gnome rune
Dragon Rune

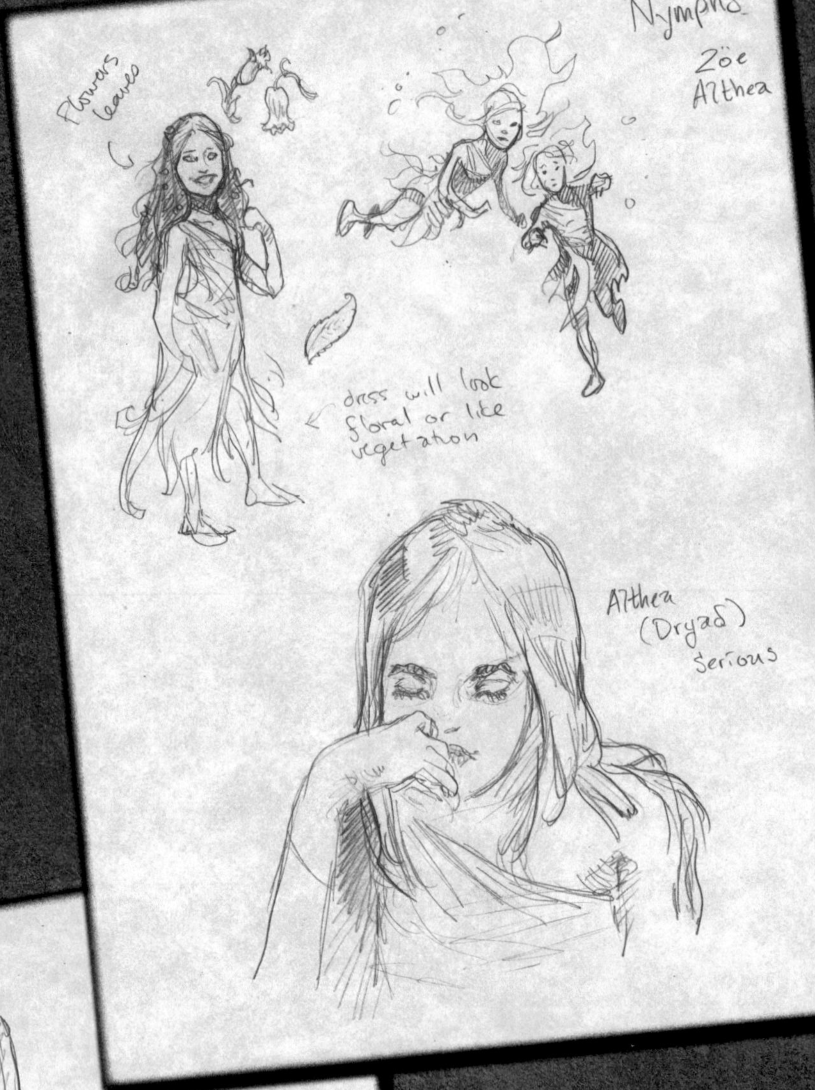
Nymphs
Zöe
Althea
Flowers leaves
dress will look floral or like vegetation
Althea (Dryad) serious

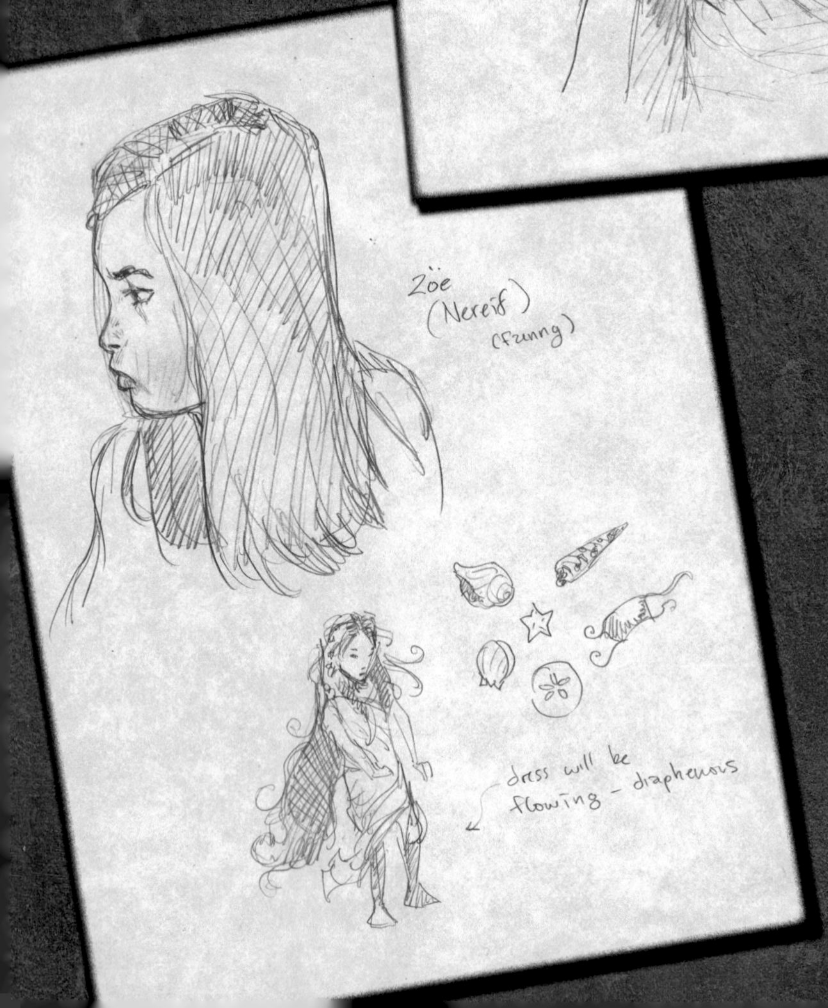
Zöe (Nereid) (Funny)
dress will be flowing - diaphenous

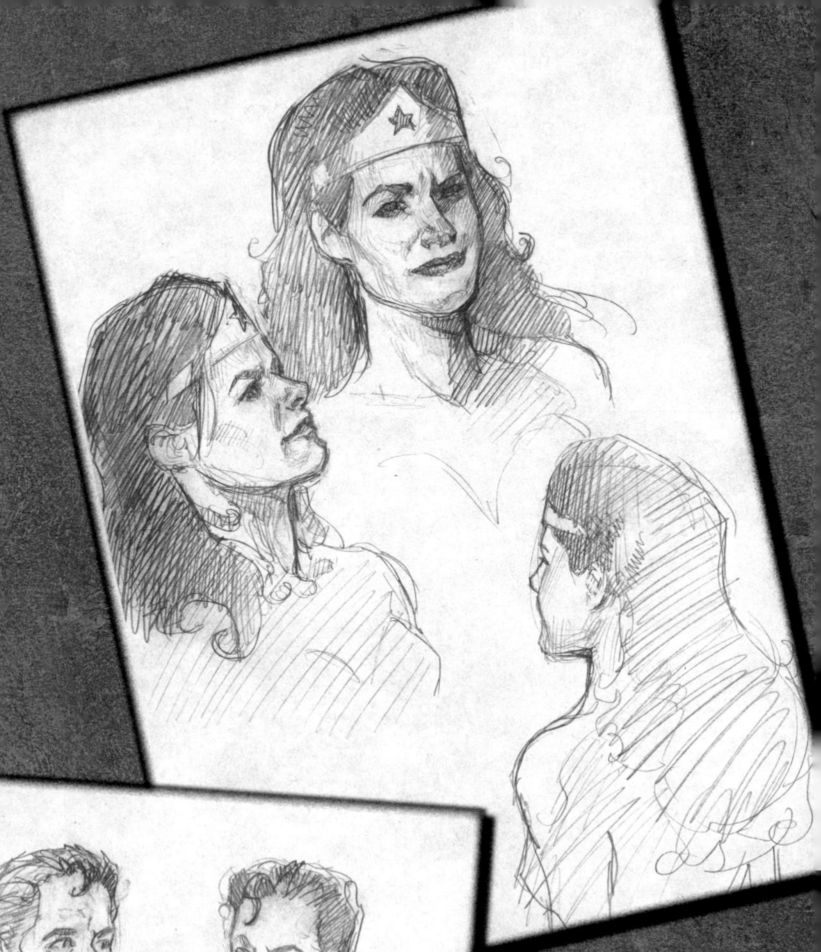

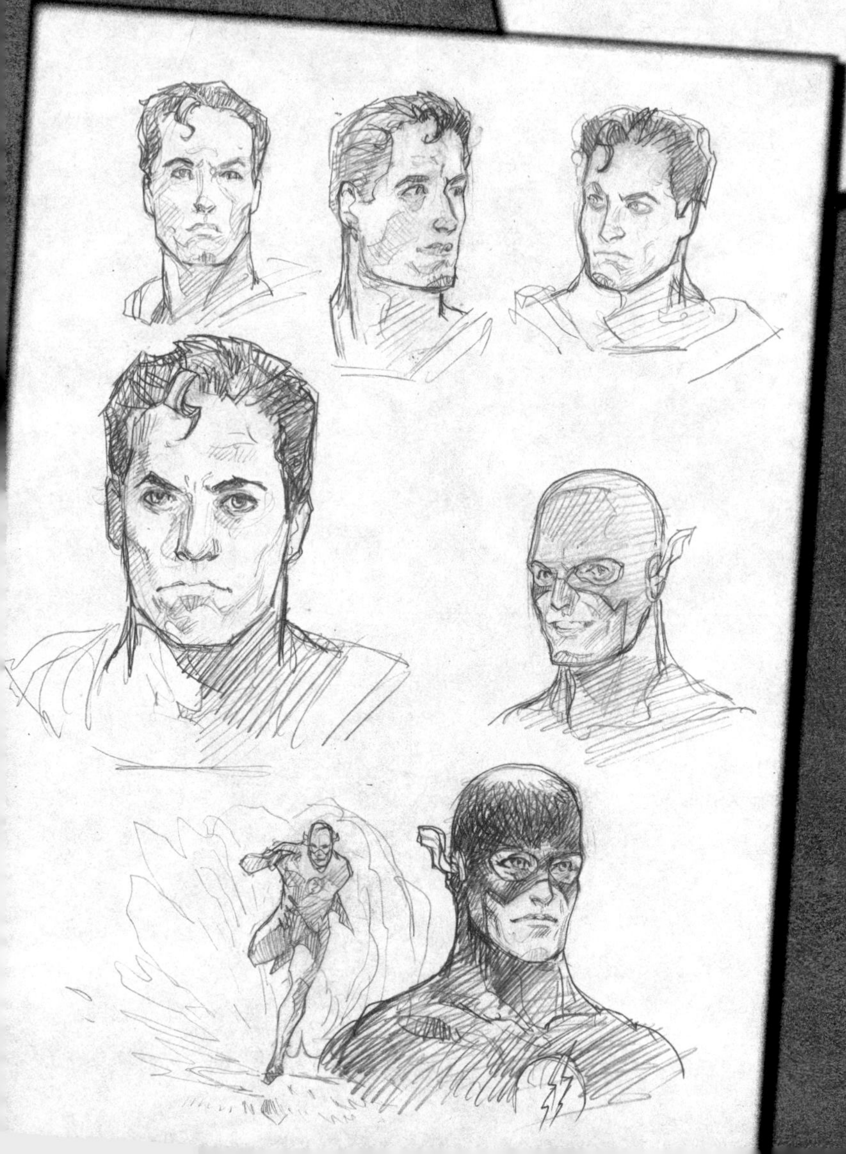

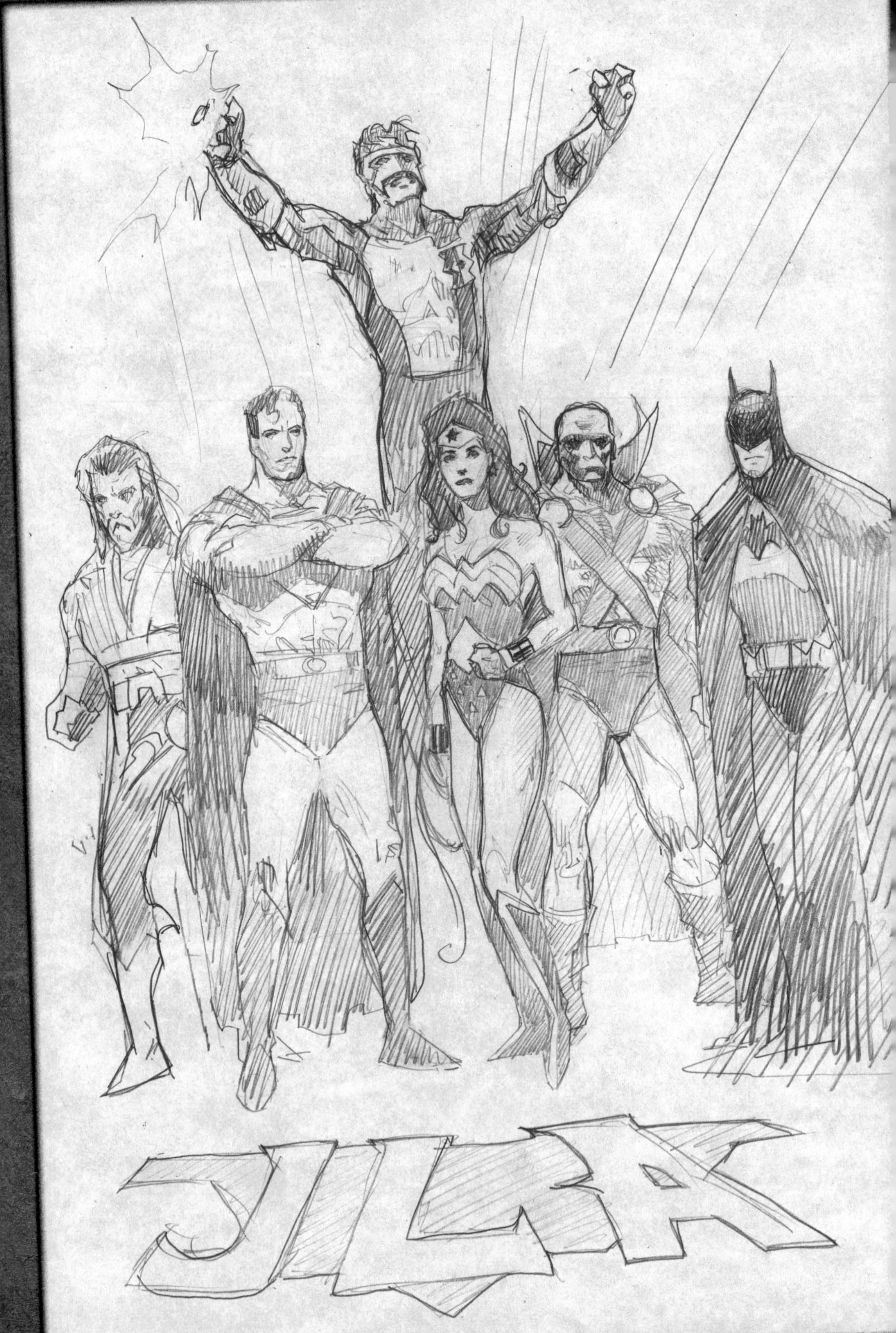
JLA

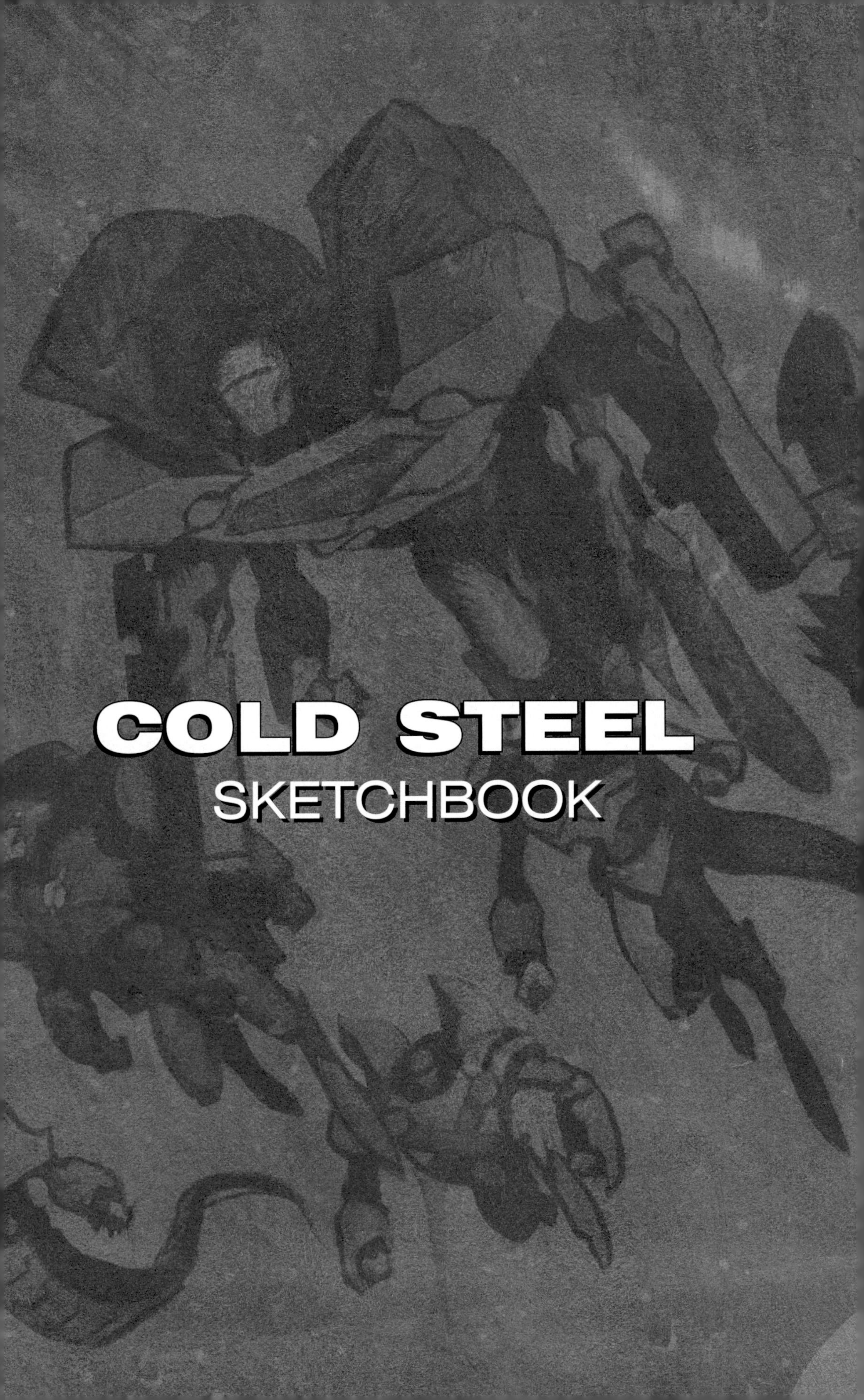

COLD STEEL

SKETCHBOOK

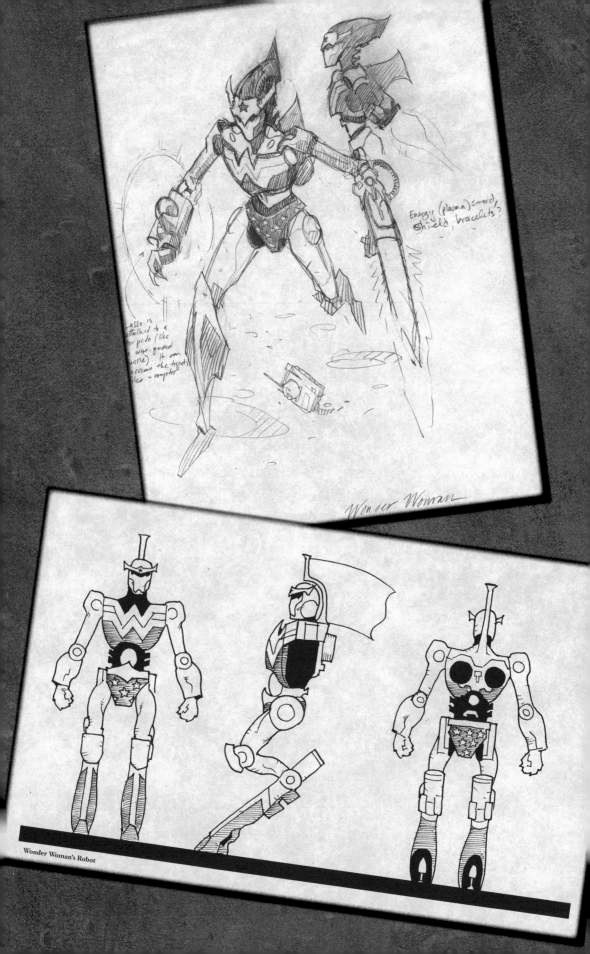

Energy (plasma) snword/
shield, bracelets?

Lasso is
attached to a
[...] torpedo (like
a wire-guided
missile). It can
access the target's
[...] computer

Wonder Woman

Wonder Woman's Robot

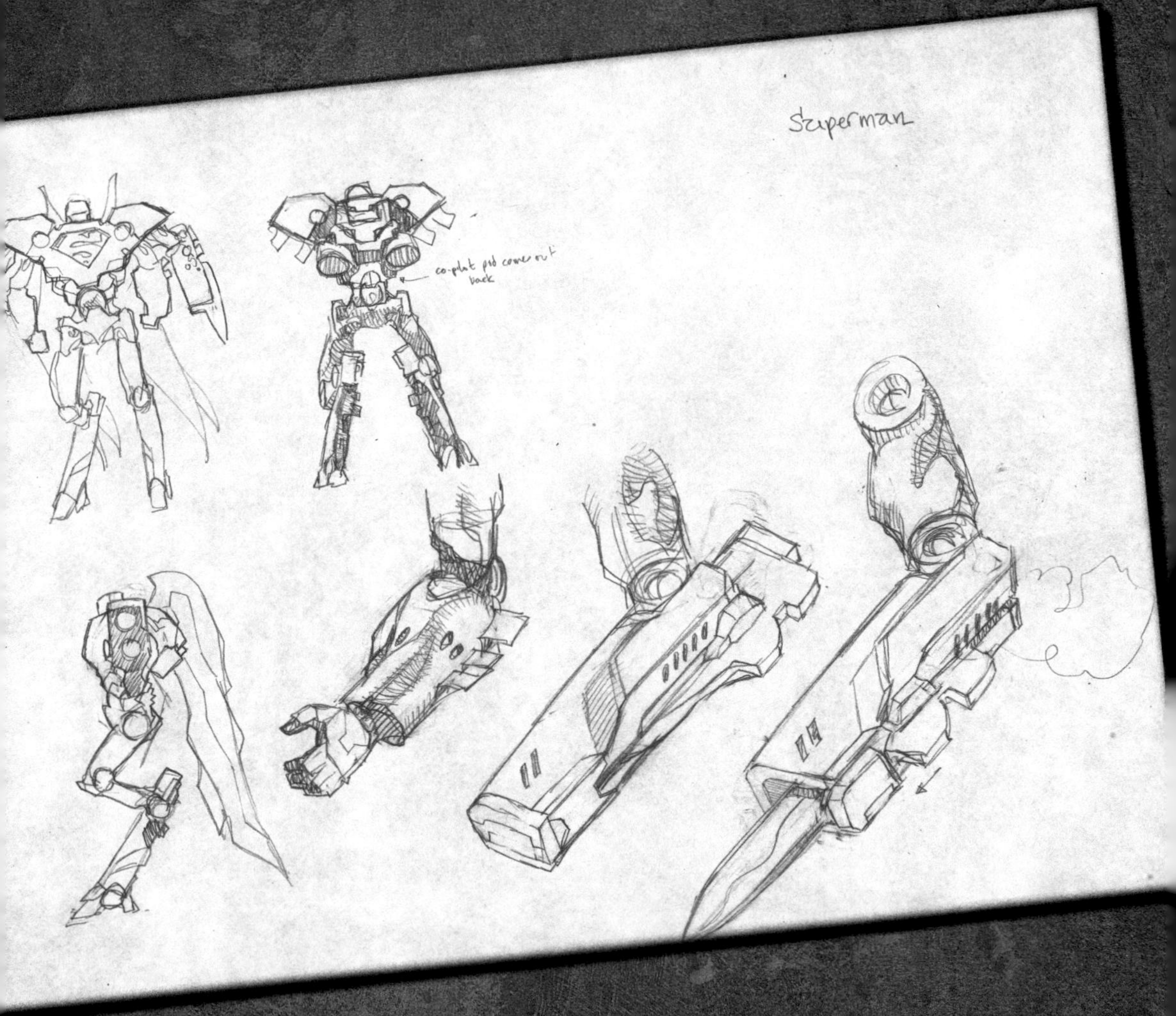
Superman
co-pilot pod comes out back

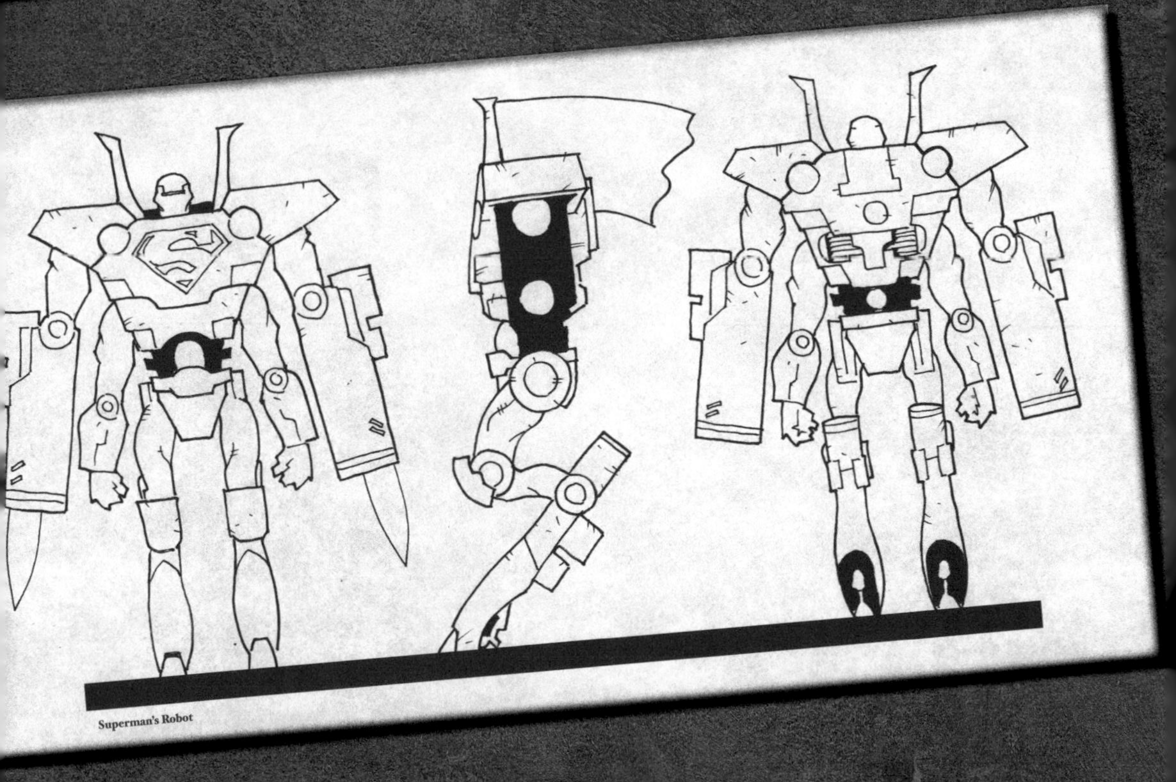

Superman's Robot

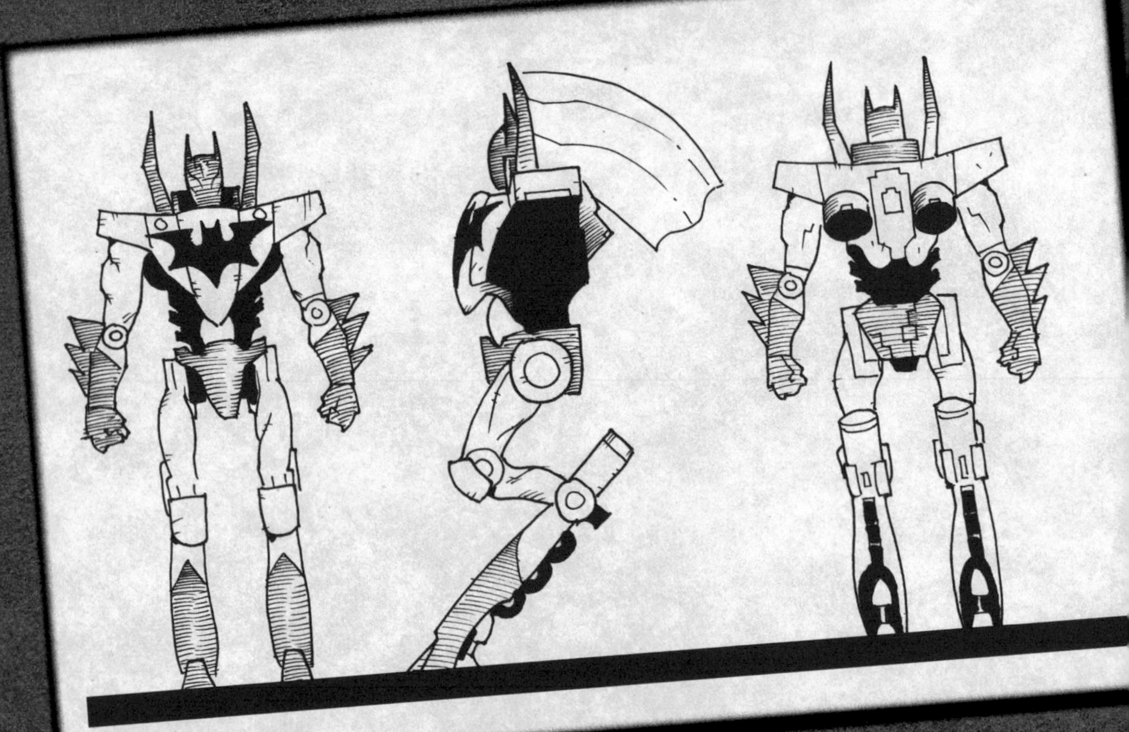

Batman's Robot

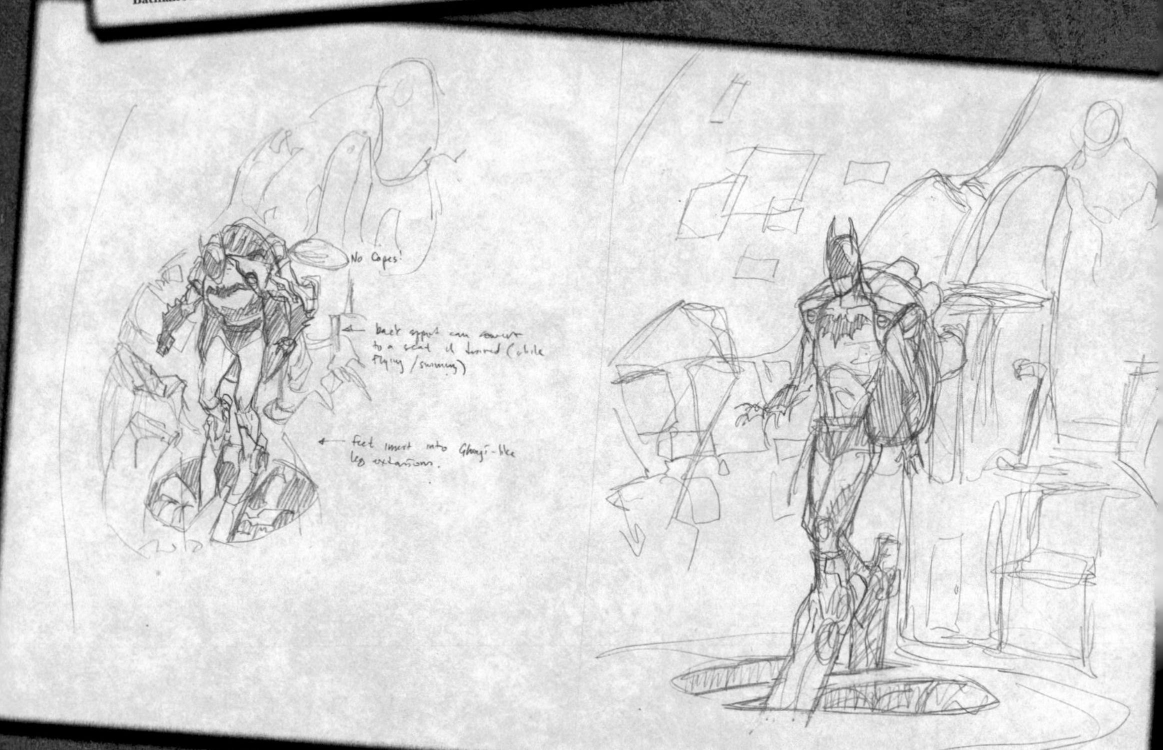
No Capes!
back support can convert to a seat if desired (while flying/swimming)
feet insert into Ghogi-like leg extensions.

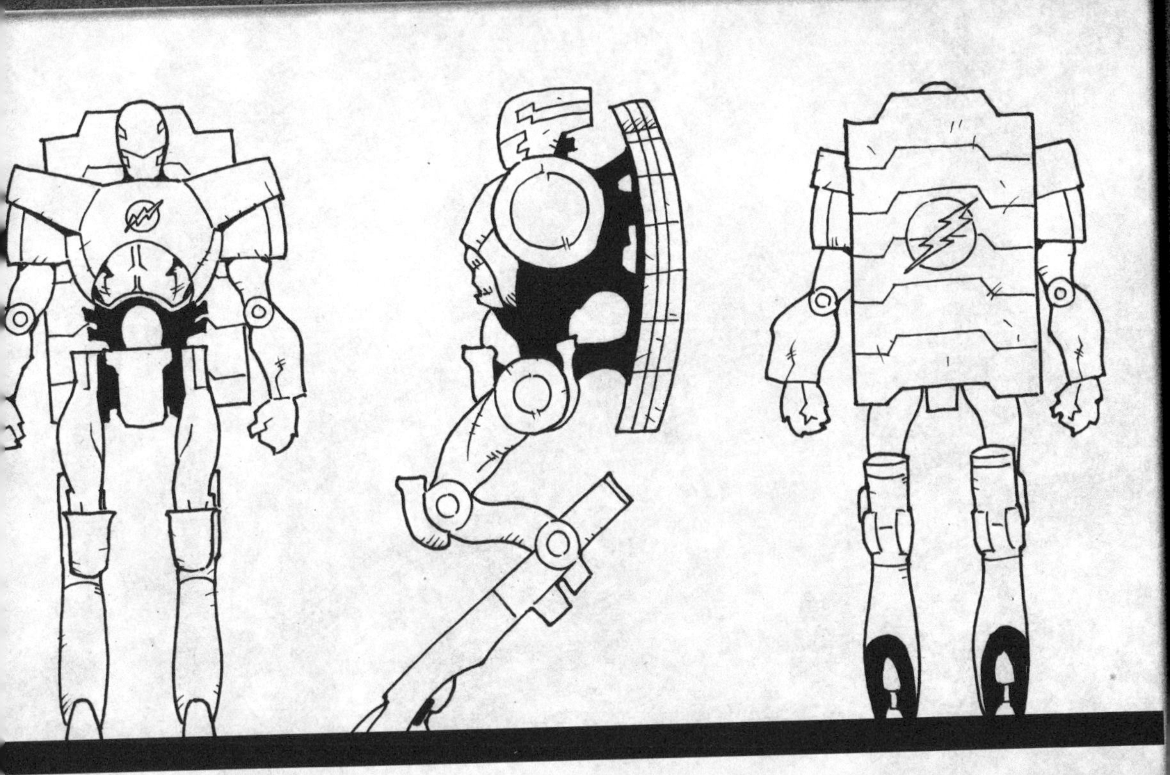

ash's Robot

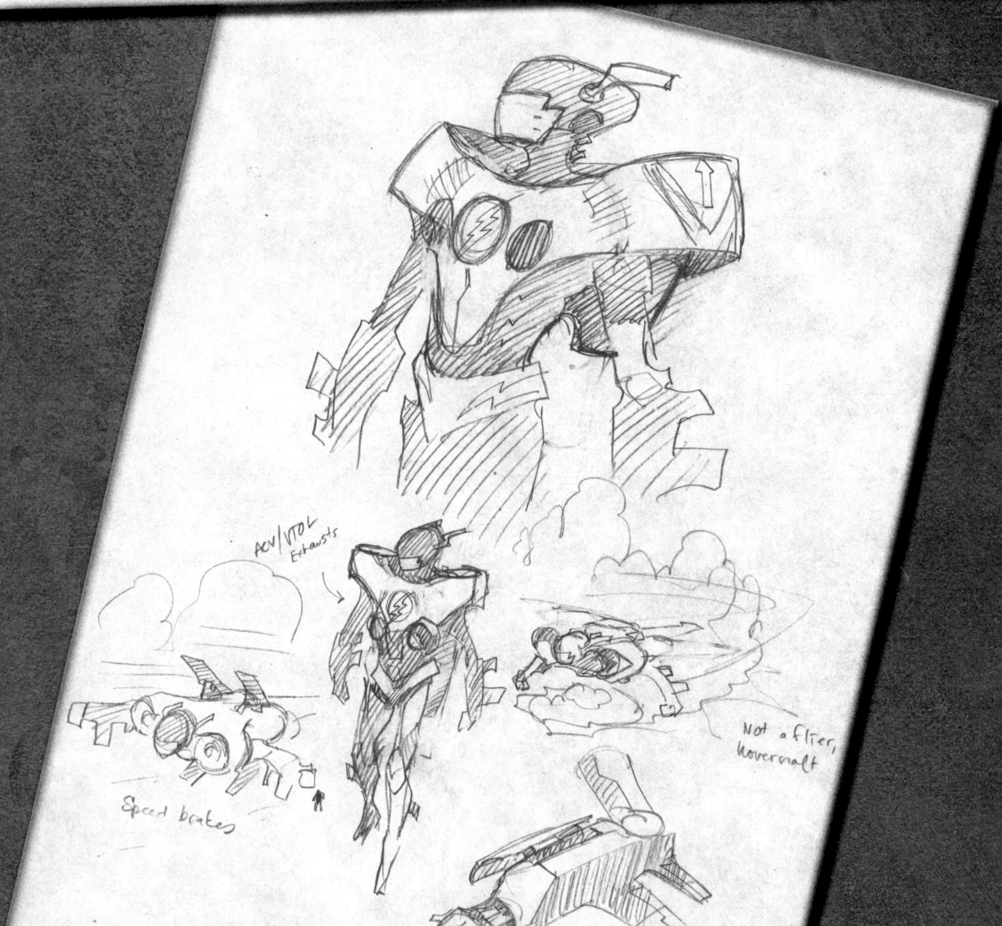
ACV/VTOL Exhausts
Speed brakes
Not a flier, hovercraft
Control surfaces on arms

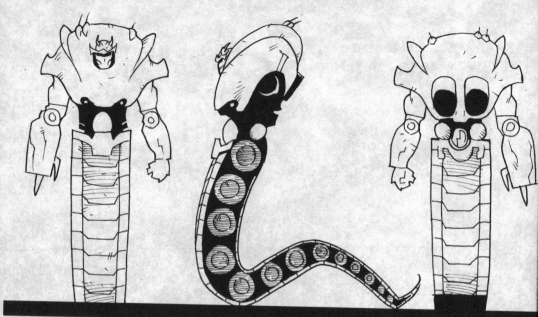

Aquaman's Robot

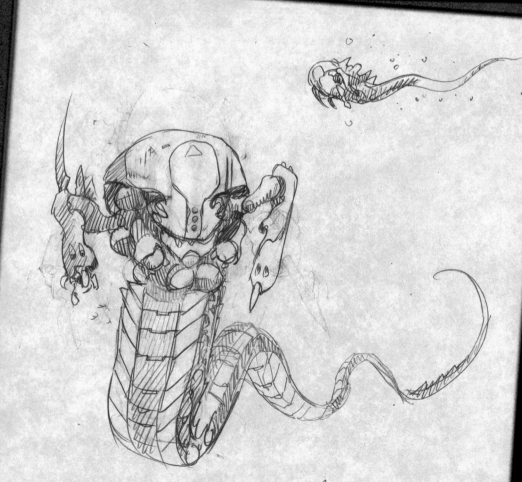

Aquaman

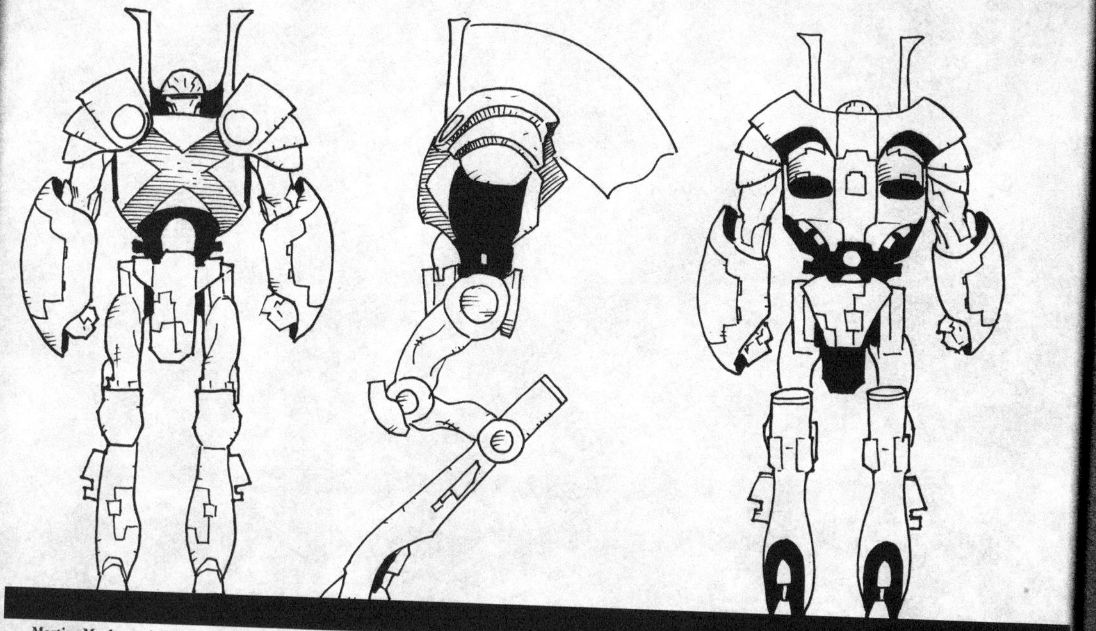

Martian Manhunter's Robot

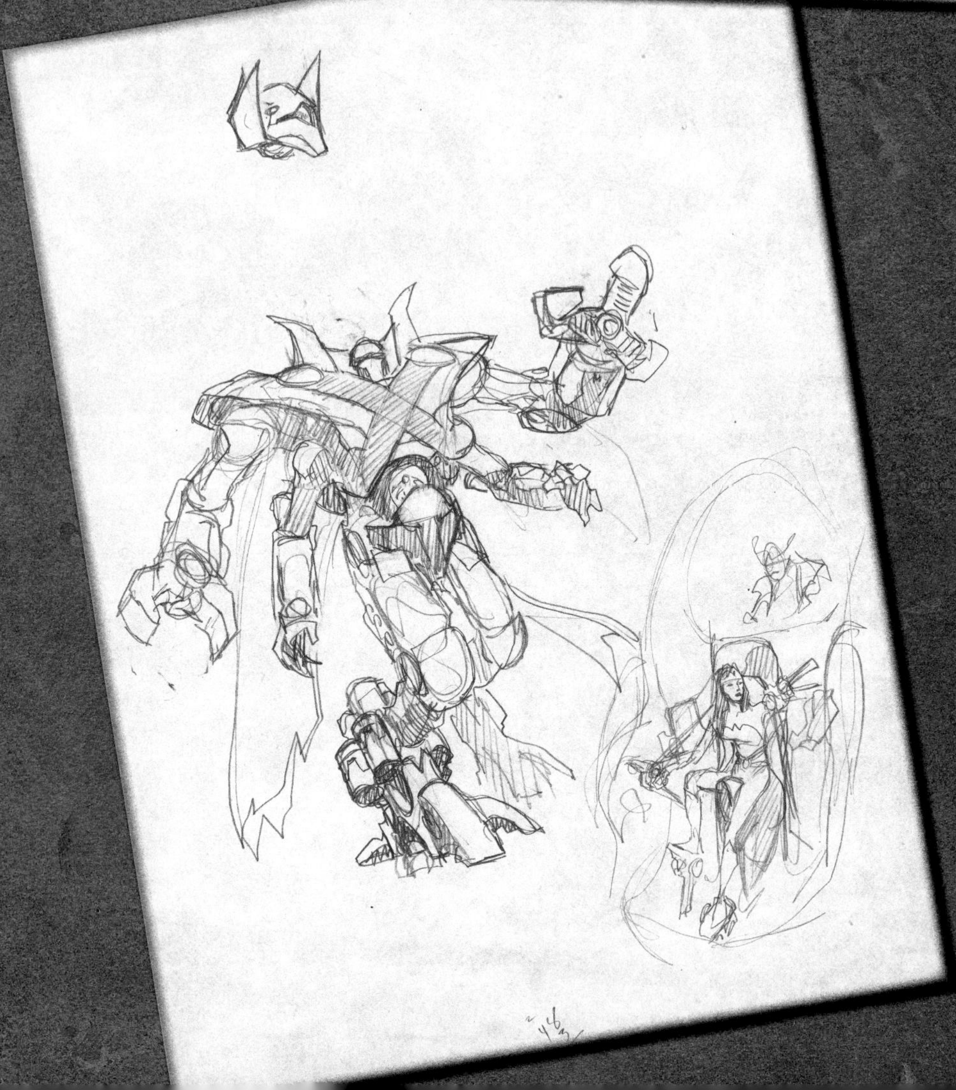

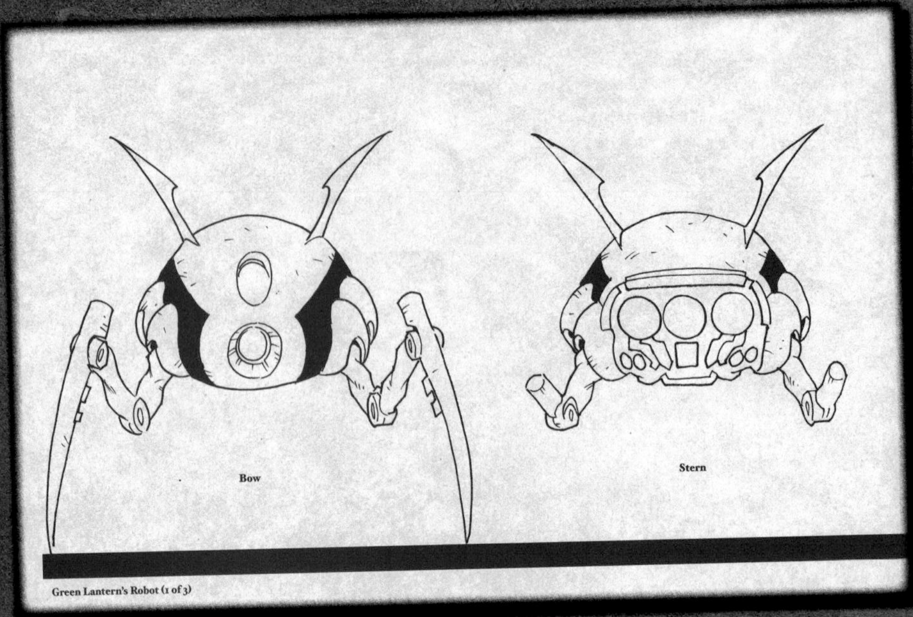
Bow
Stern

Green Lantern's Robot (1 of 3)

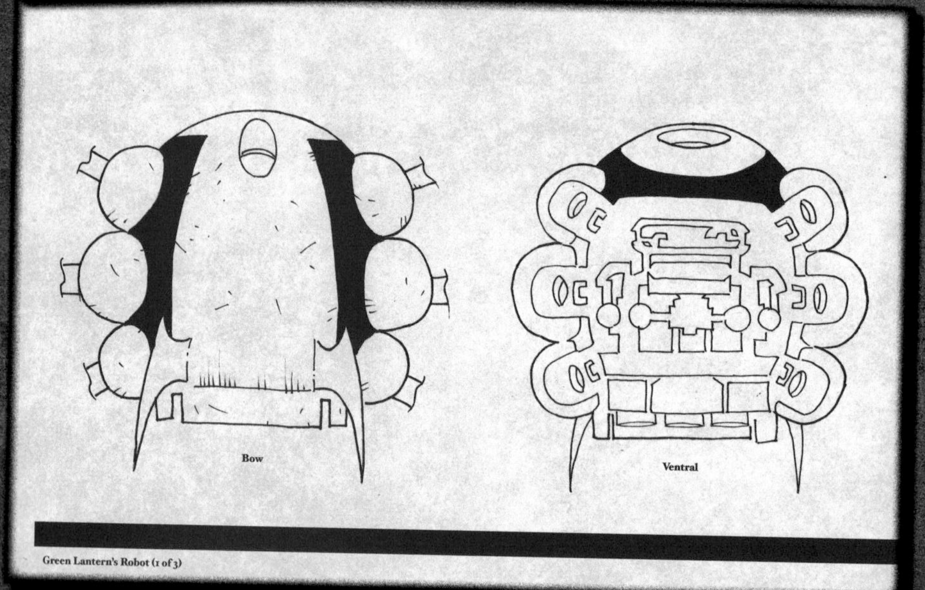
Bow
Ventral

Green Lantern's Robot (1 of 3)

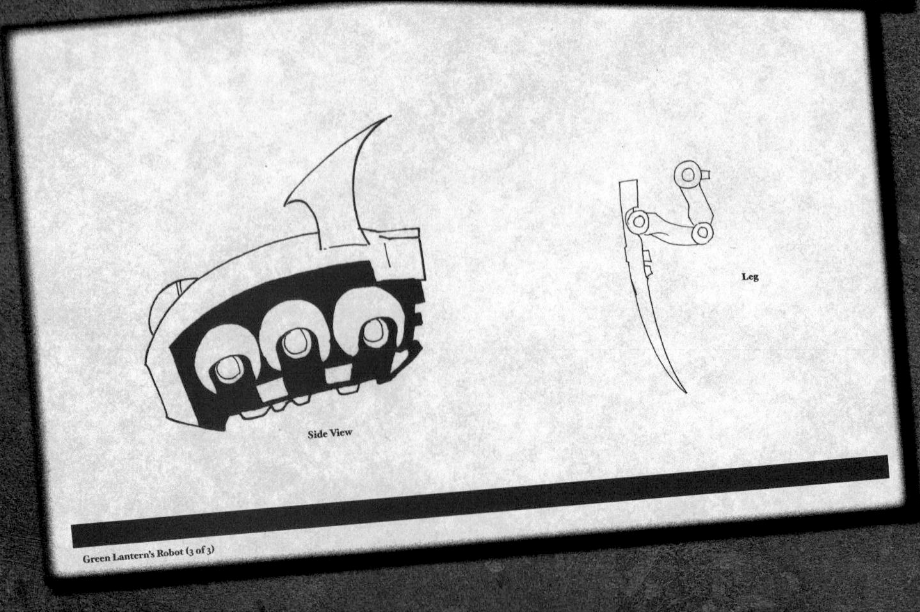
Side View
Leg

Green Lantern's Robot (3 of 3)

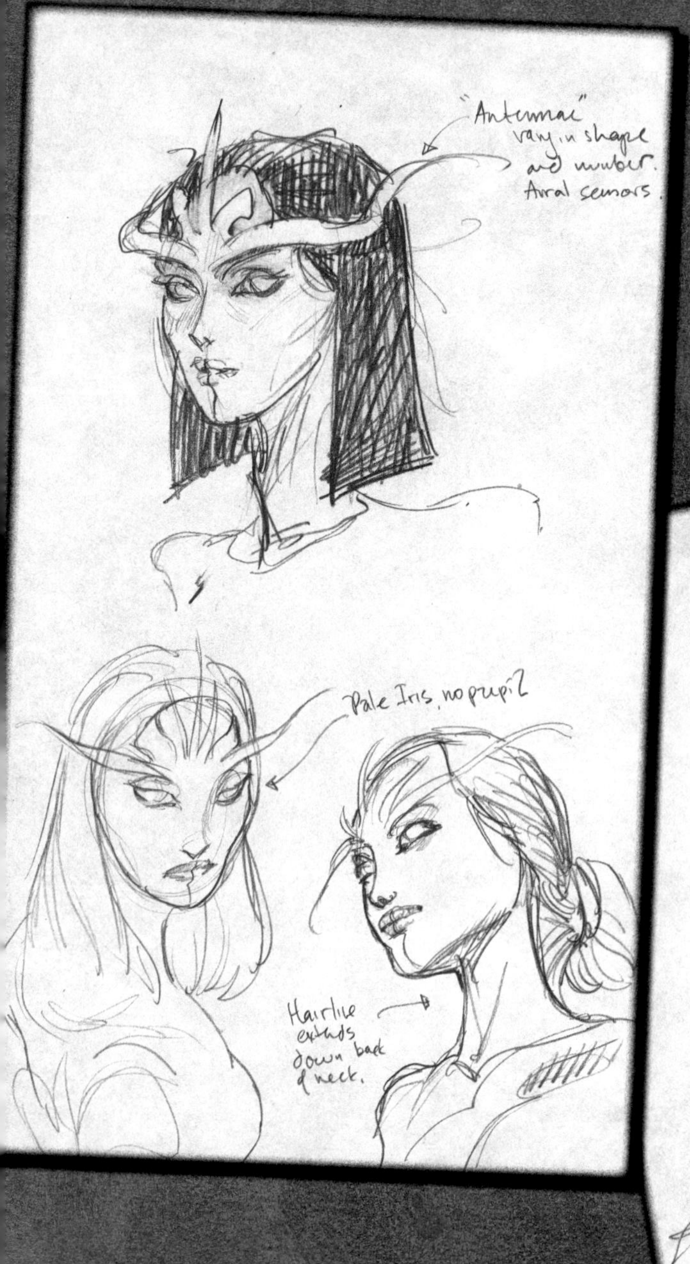
"Antennae" vary in shape and number. Aural sensors.
Pale Iris, no pupil
Hairline extends down back of neck.
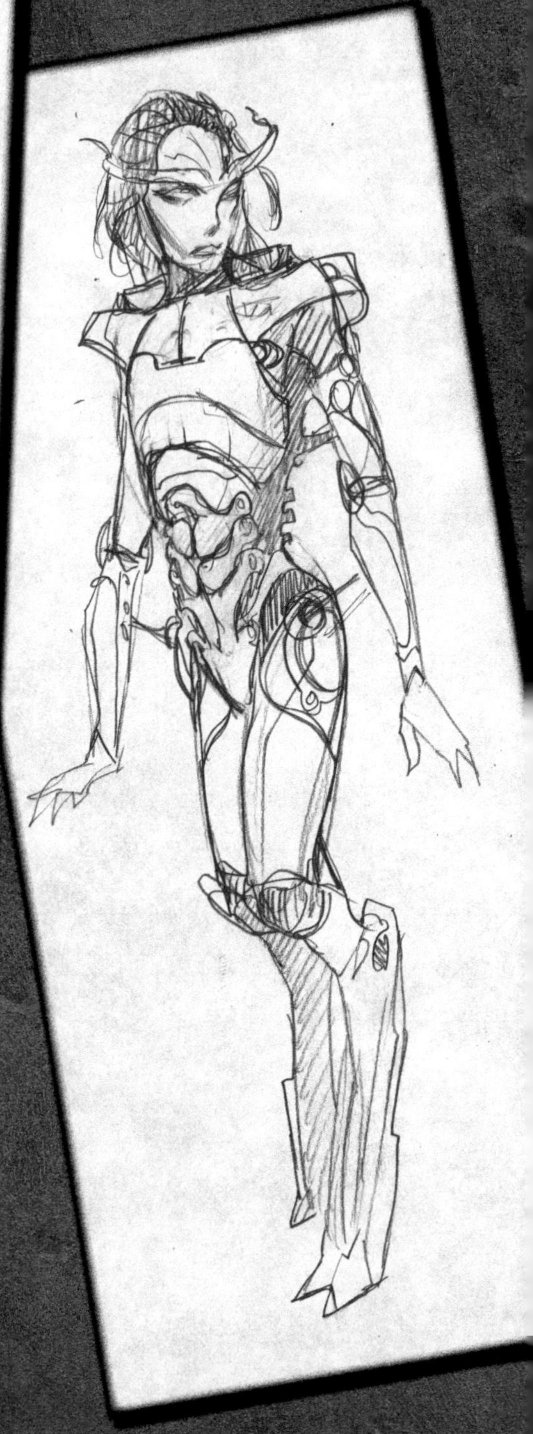

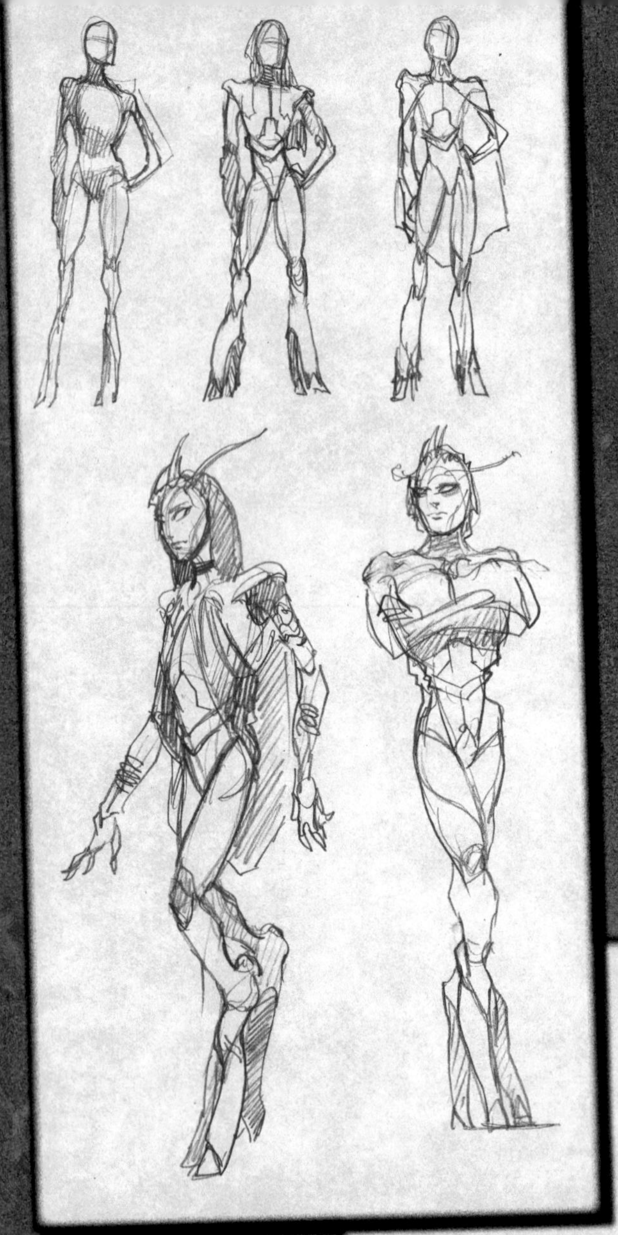

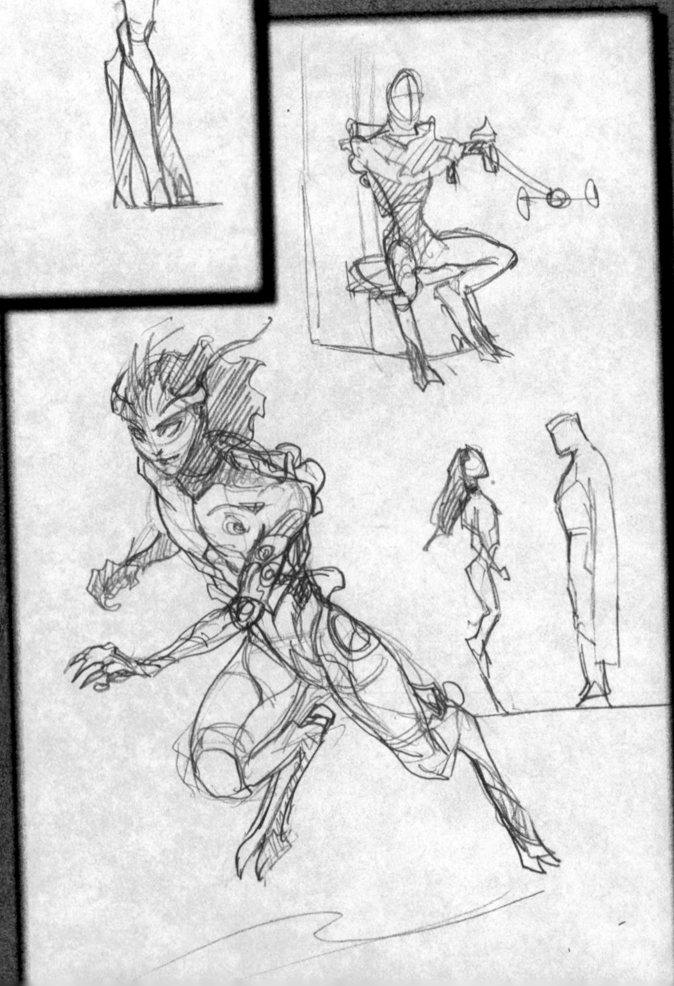

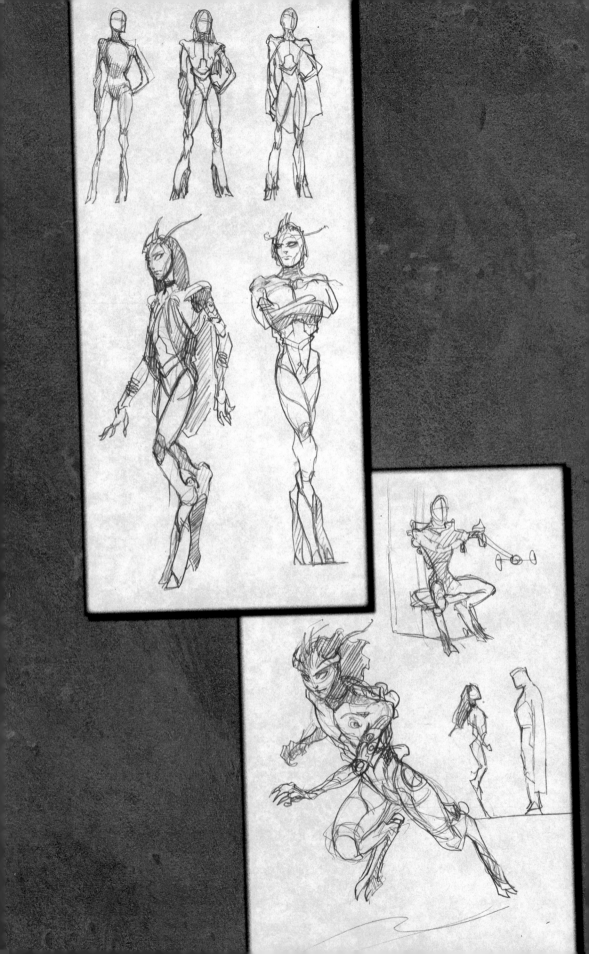

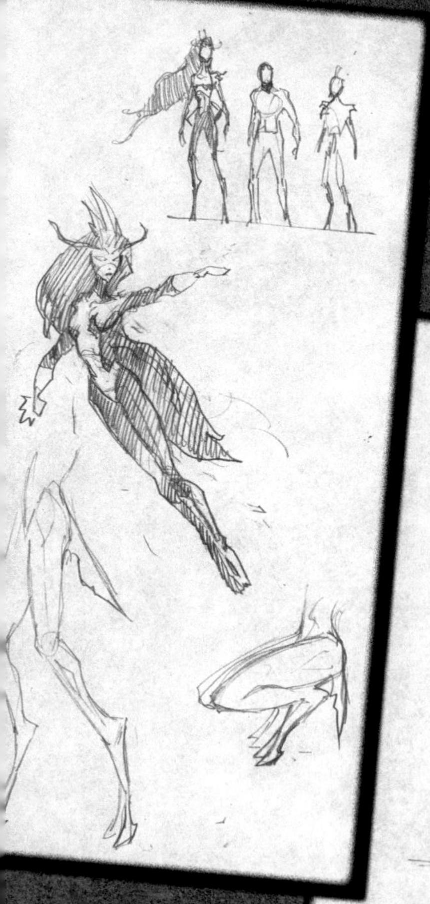

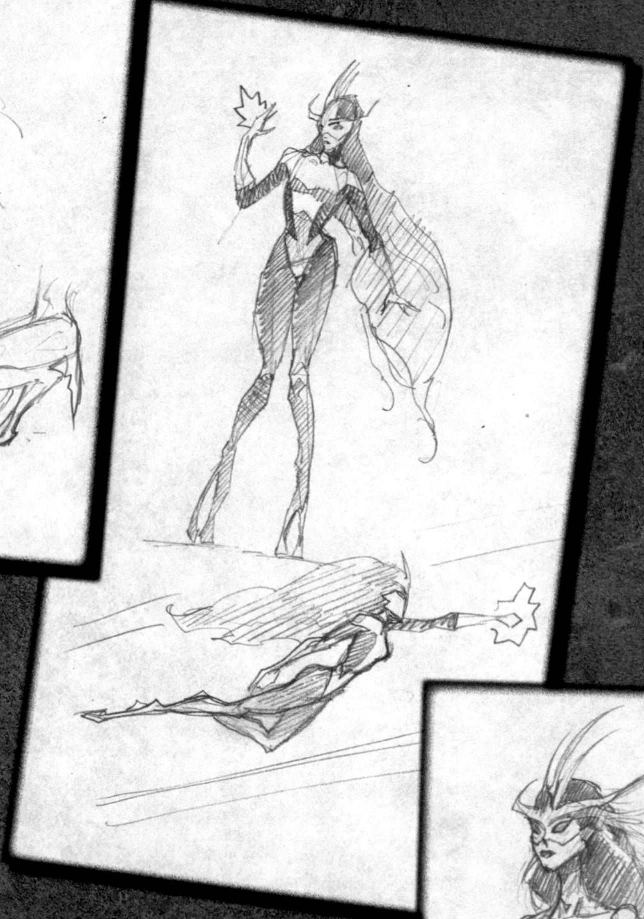

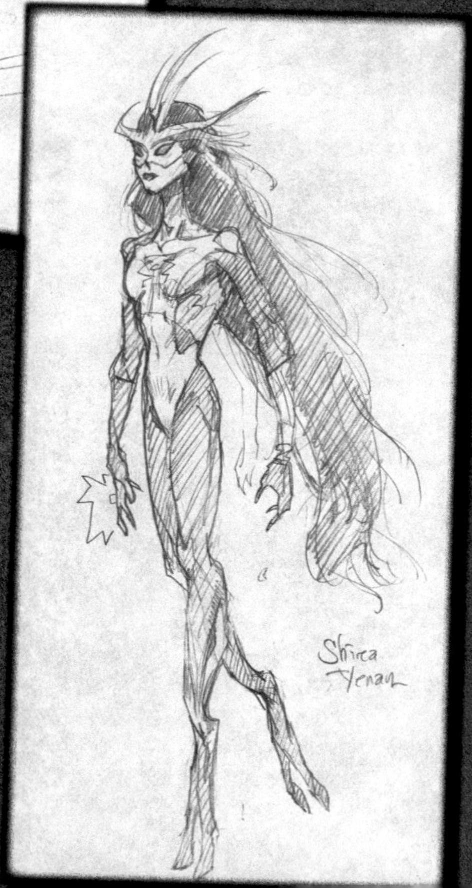

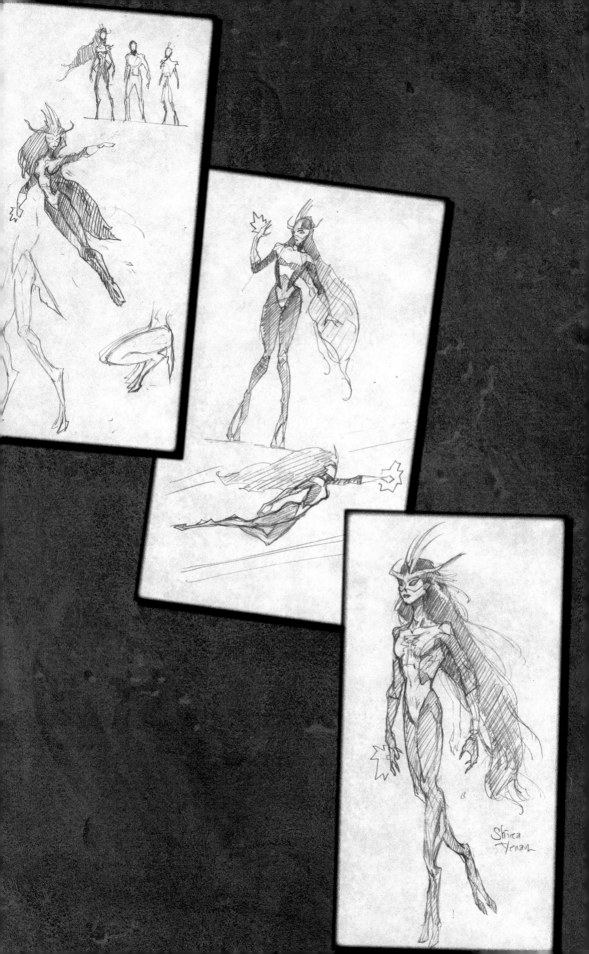

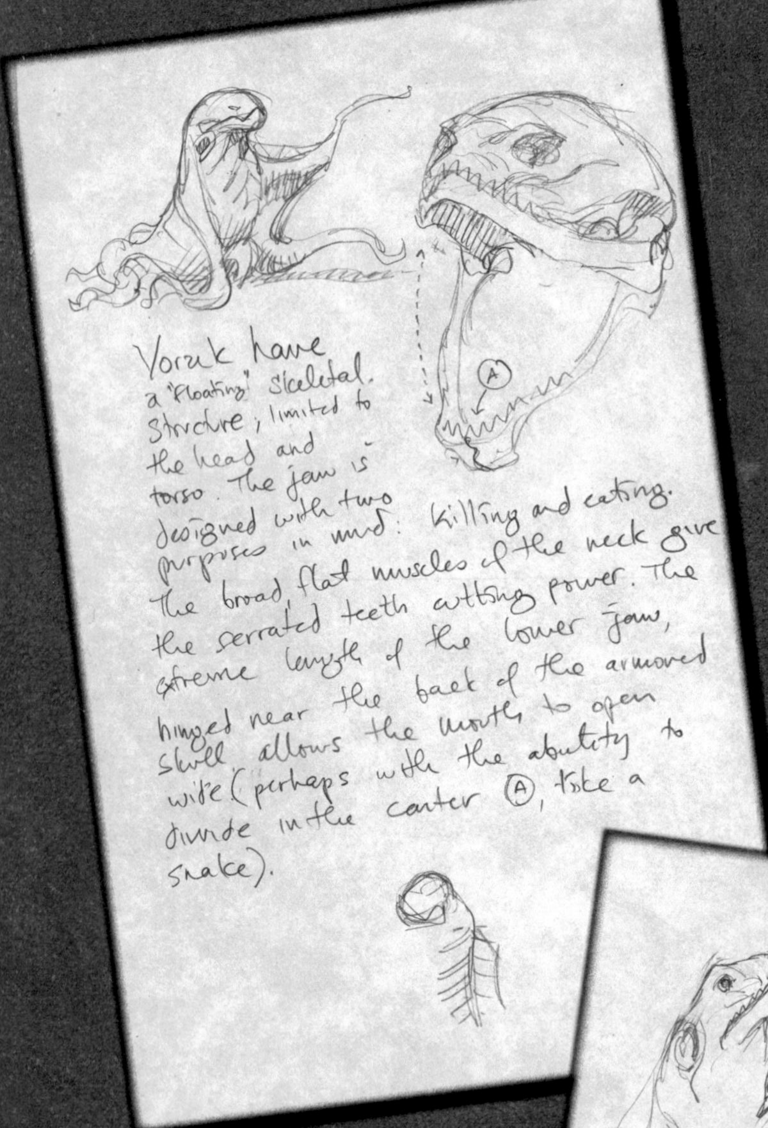
A
Voruk have a "Floating" skeletal structure; limited to the head and torso. The jaw is designed with two purposes in mind: killing and eating. The broad, flat muscles of the neck give the serrated teeth cutting power. The extreme length of the lower jaw, hinged near the back of the armored skull allows the mouth to open wide (perhaps with the ability to divide in the center Ⓐ, like a snake).

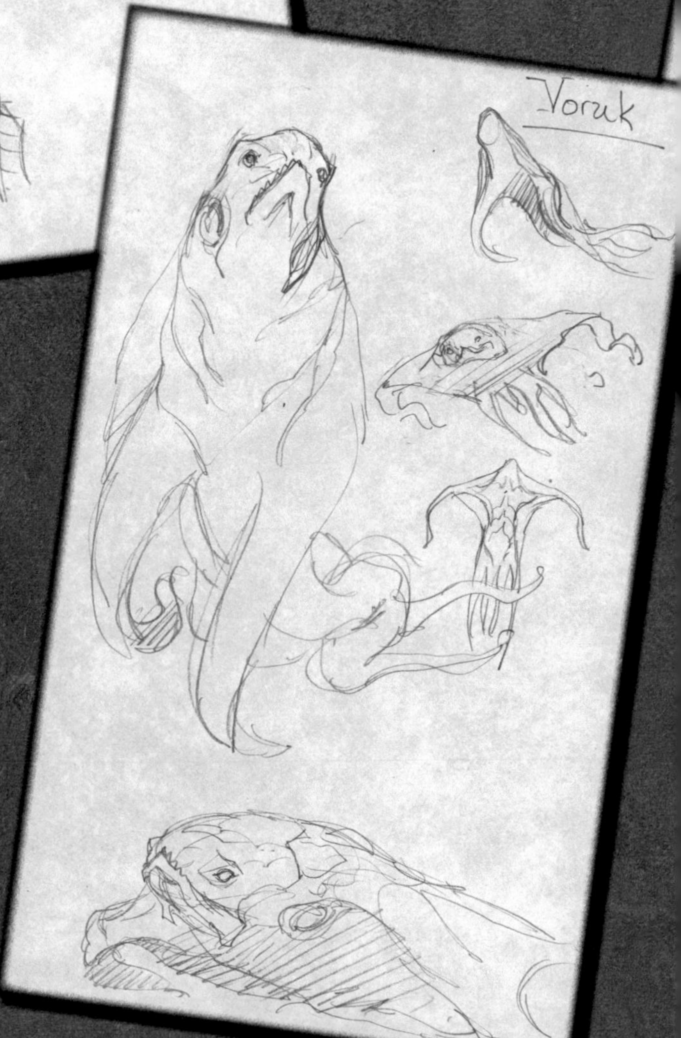
Voruk

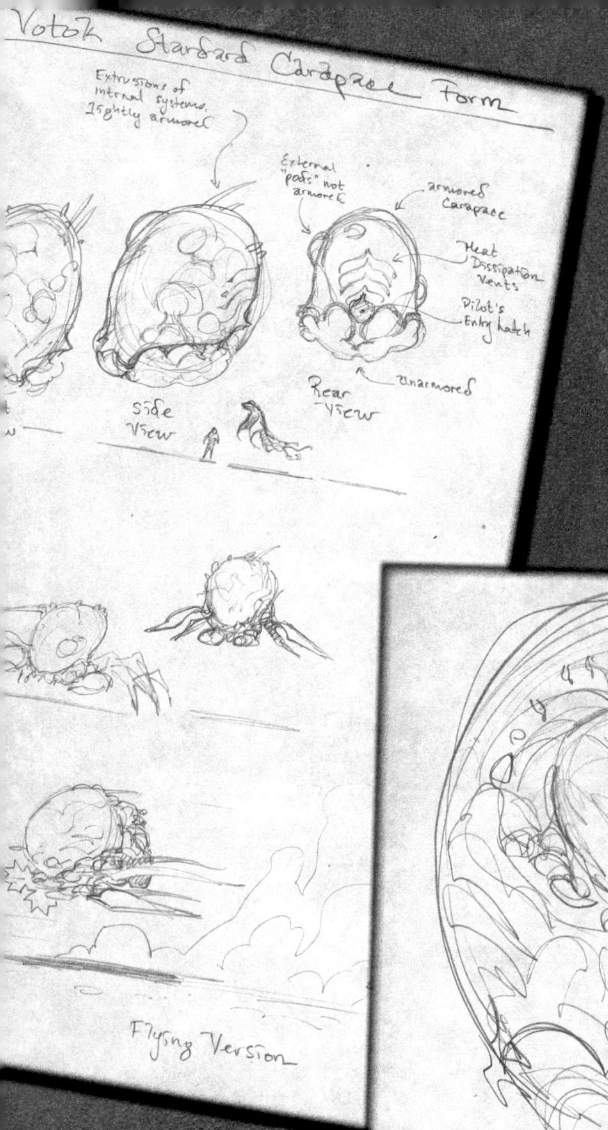

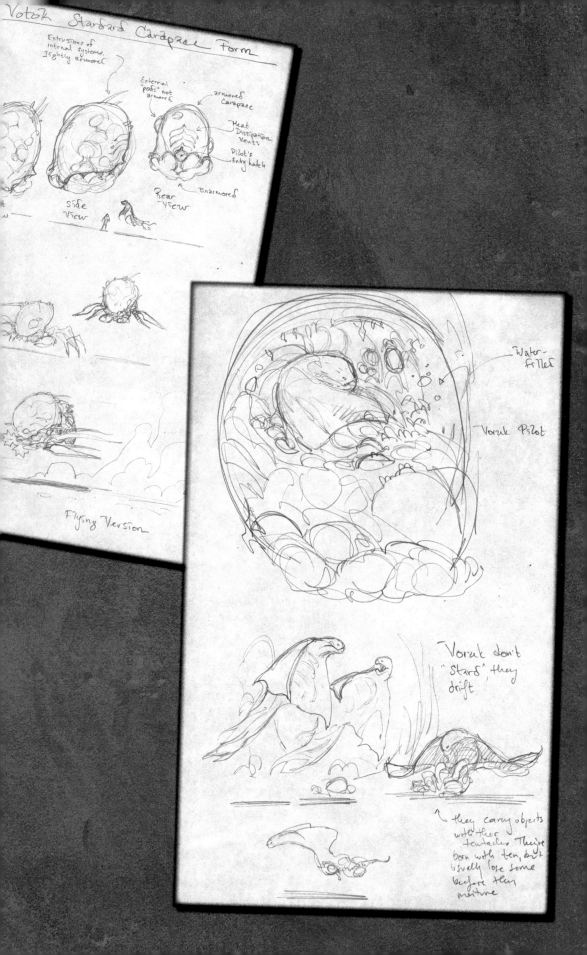

Votok Standard Carapace Form
Extrusions of internal systems, lightly armored
External "pods" not armored
armored Carapace
Heat Dissipation Vents
Pilot's Entry hatch
unarmored
Side View
Rear View
Flying Version

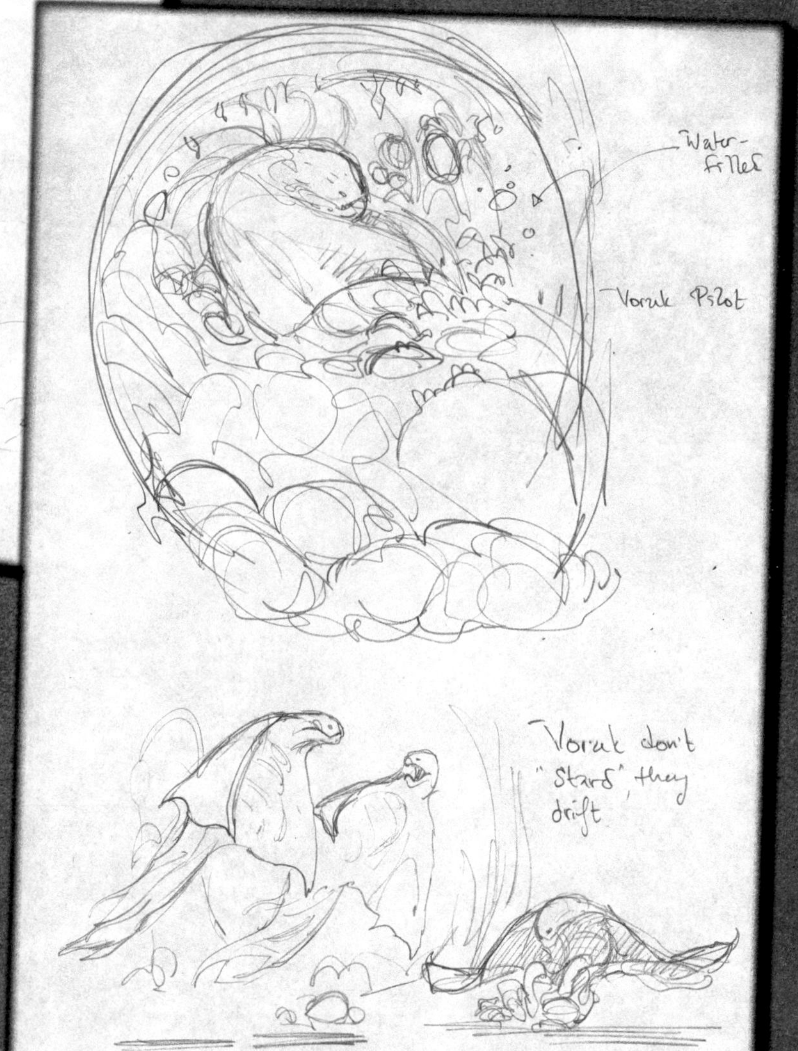

Water-filled
Vorak Pilot
Vorak don't "stand", they drift
they carry objects with their tentacles. They're born with ten, but usually lose some before they mature

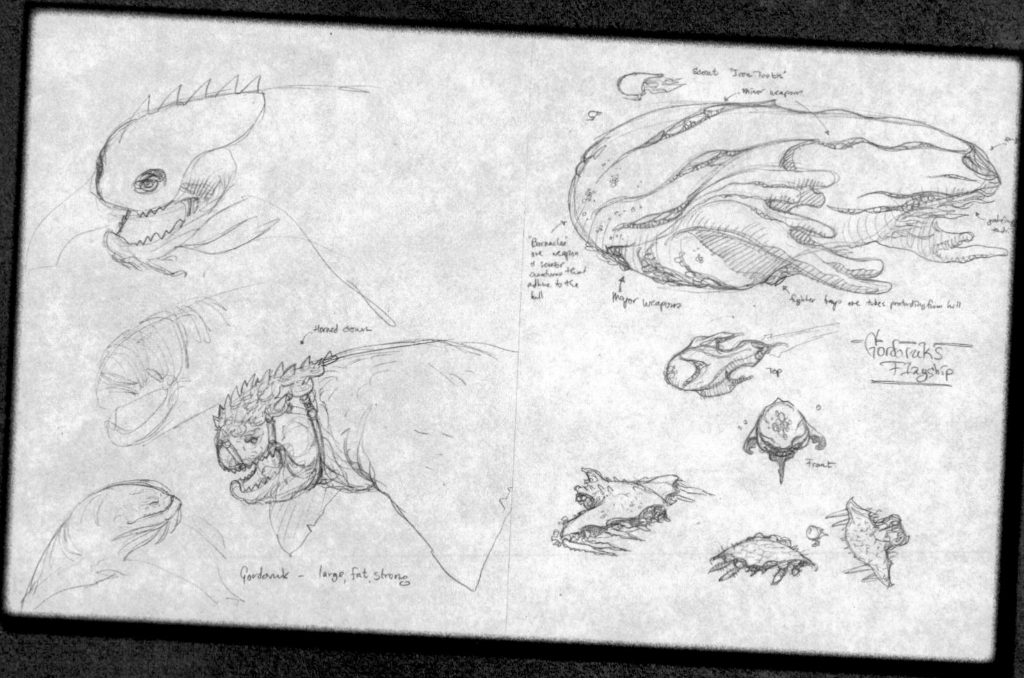

Horned crown
Gordorak - large, fat, strong
Scout "Iron Tooth"
Minor weapons
"Barnacles" are weapons & scavenger creatures that adhere to the hull
Major weapons
fighter bays are tubes protruding from hull
Gordorak's Flagship
Top
Front

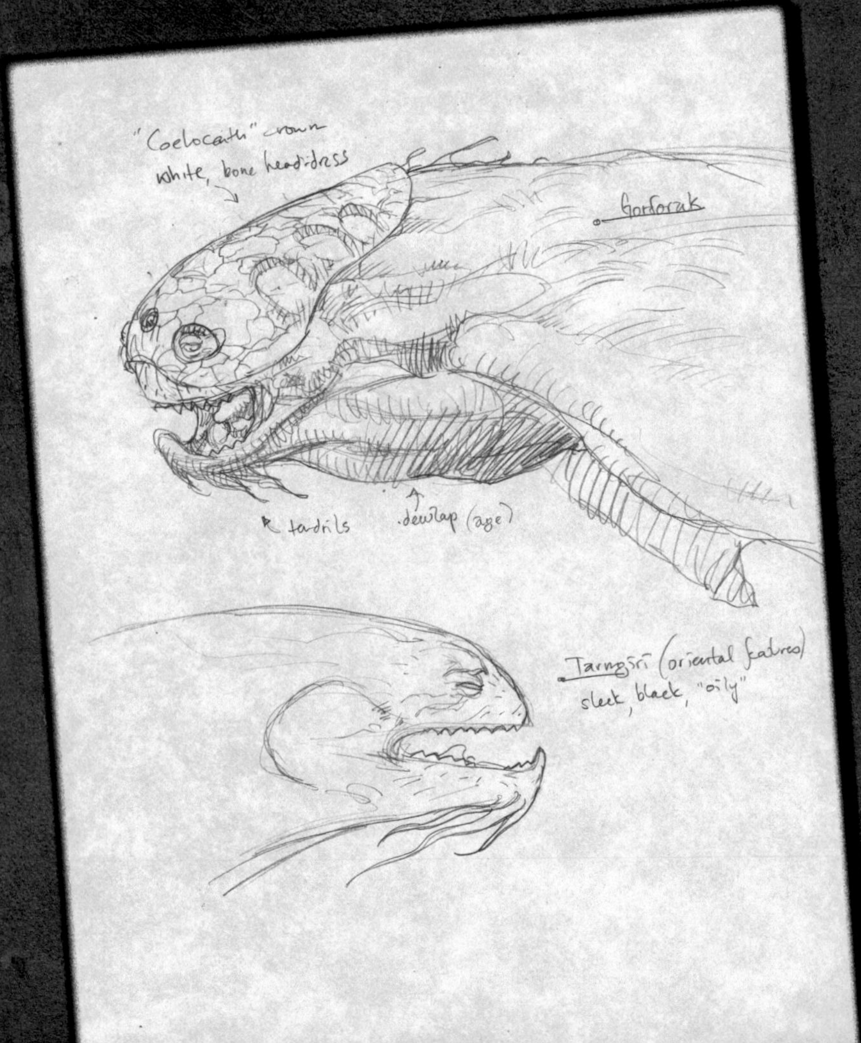

"Coelocanth" crown
white, bone headdress
Gorforak
tendrils
dewlap (age)
Tarngsri (oriental features)
sleek, black, "oily"

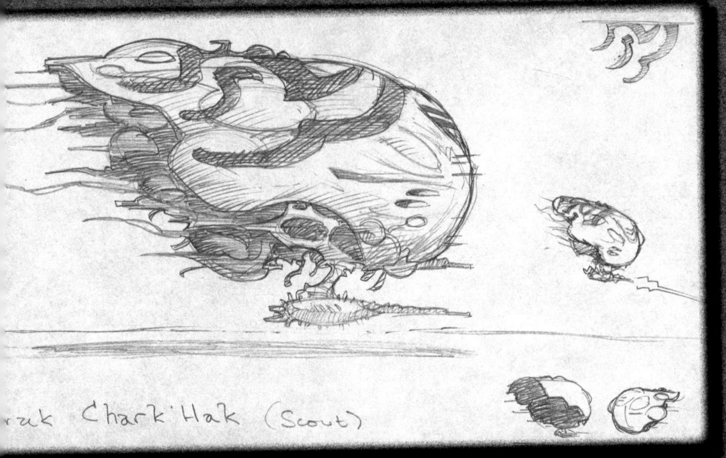
ruk Chark'Hak (Scout)

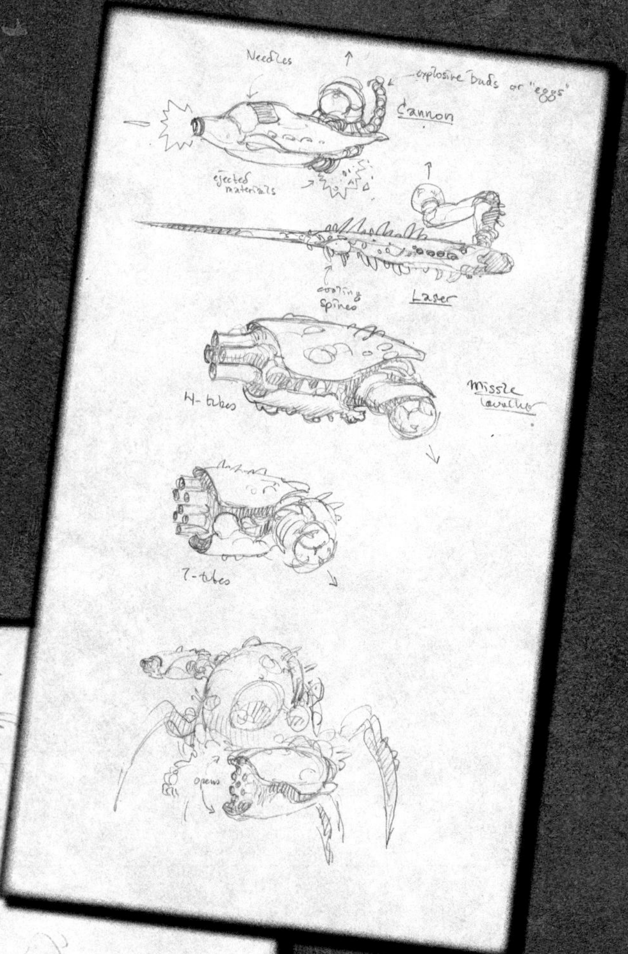
Needles
explosive buds or "eggs"
Cannon
ejected materials
cooling spines
Laser
4-tubes
Missle launcher
7-tubes
opens

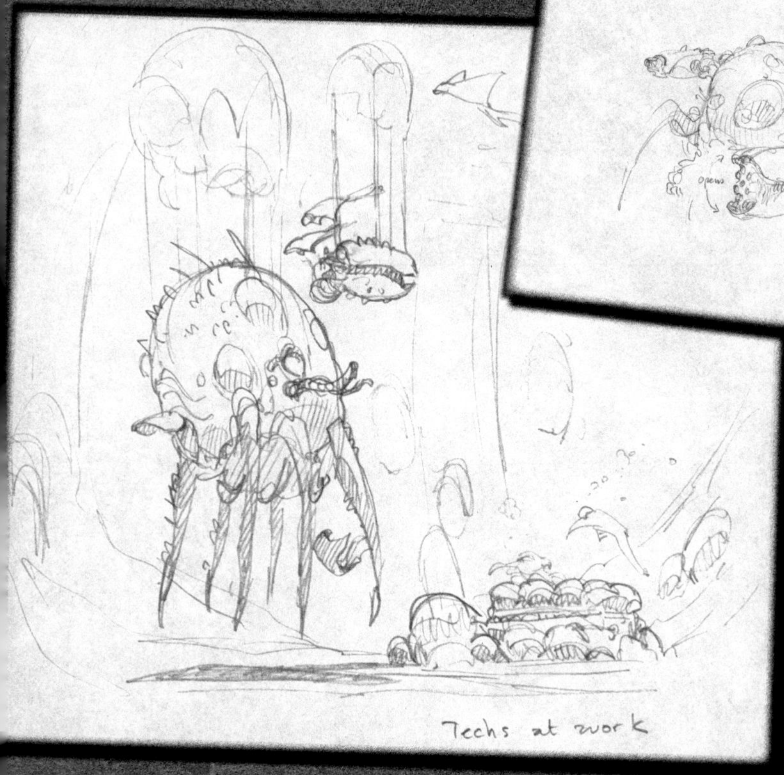
Techs at work

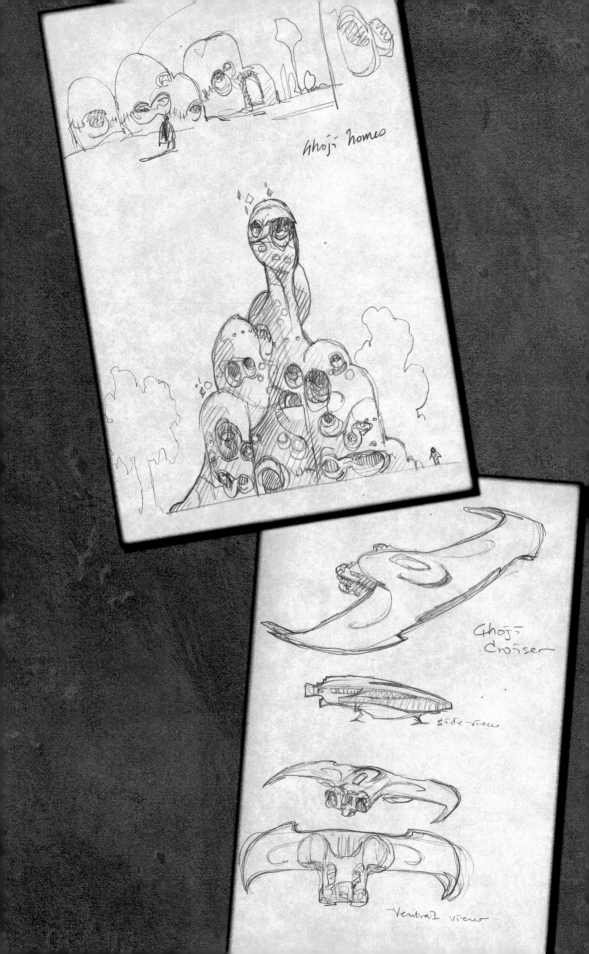

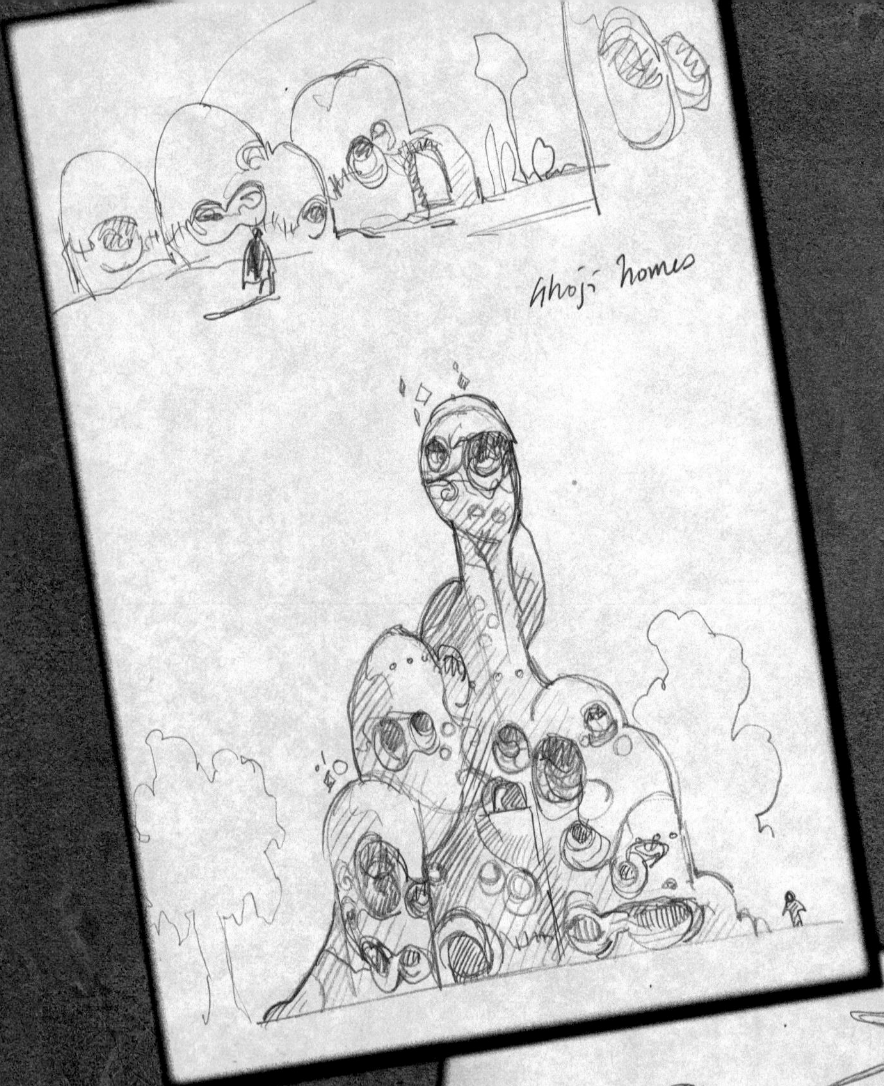
Ghoji homes

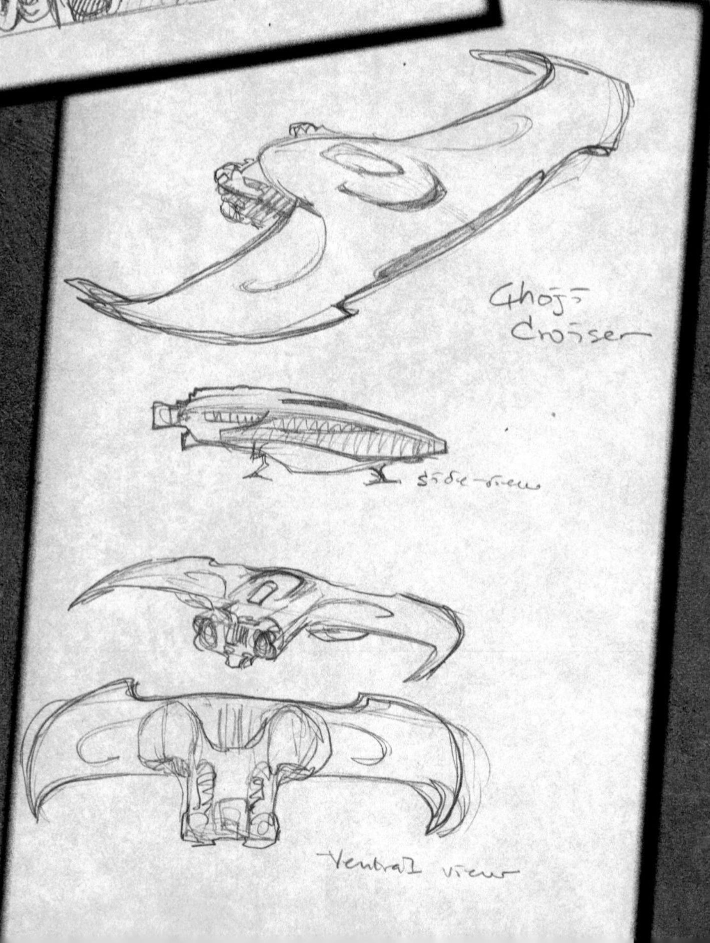
Ghoji
Cruiser
side view
Ventral view

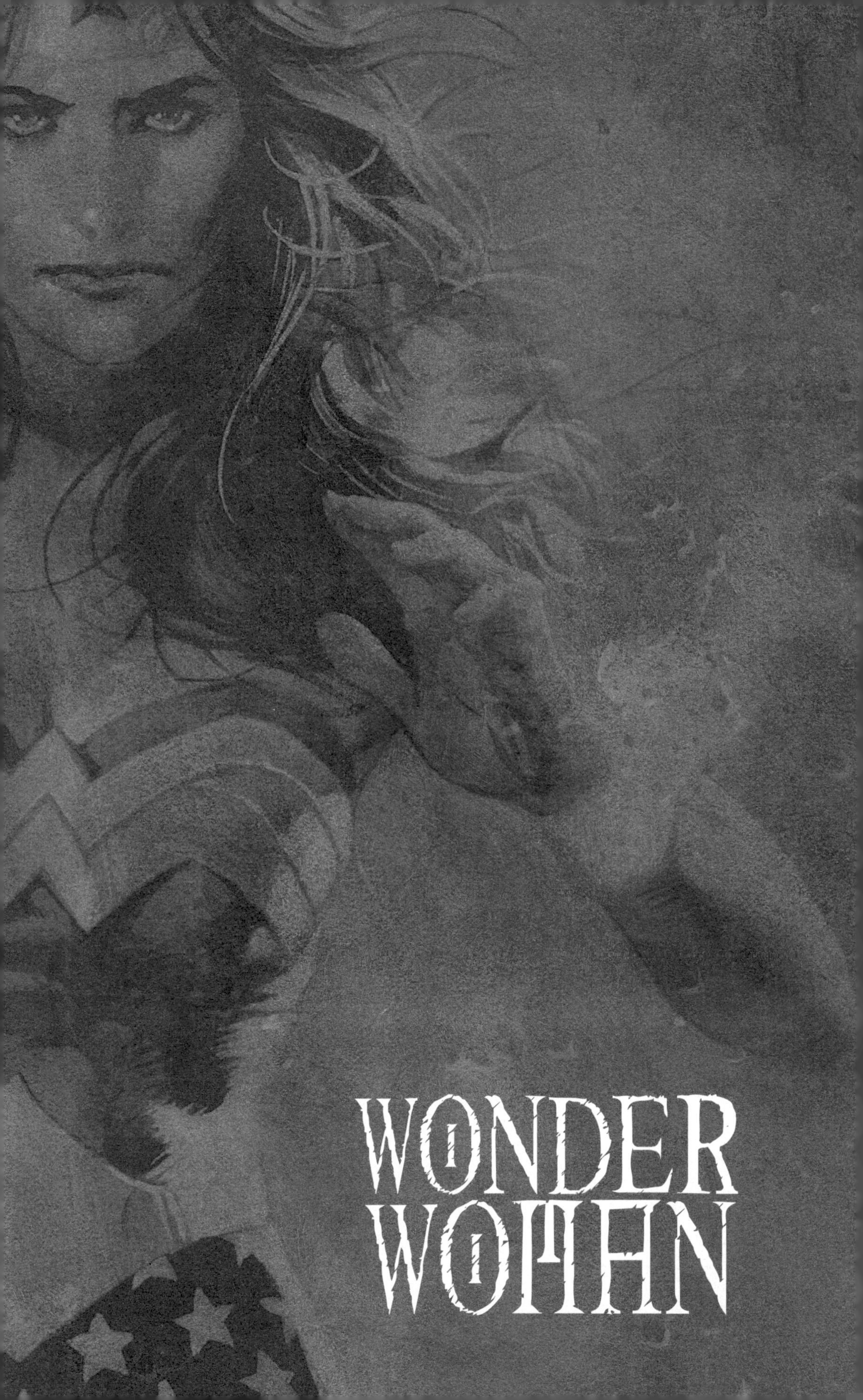
WONDER
WOMAN

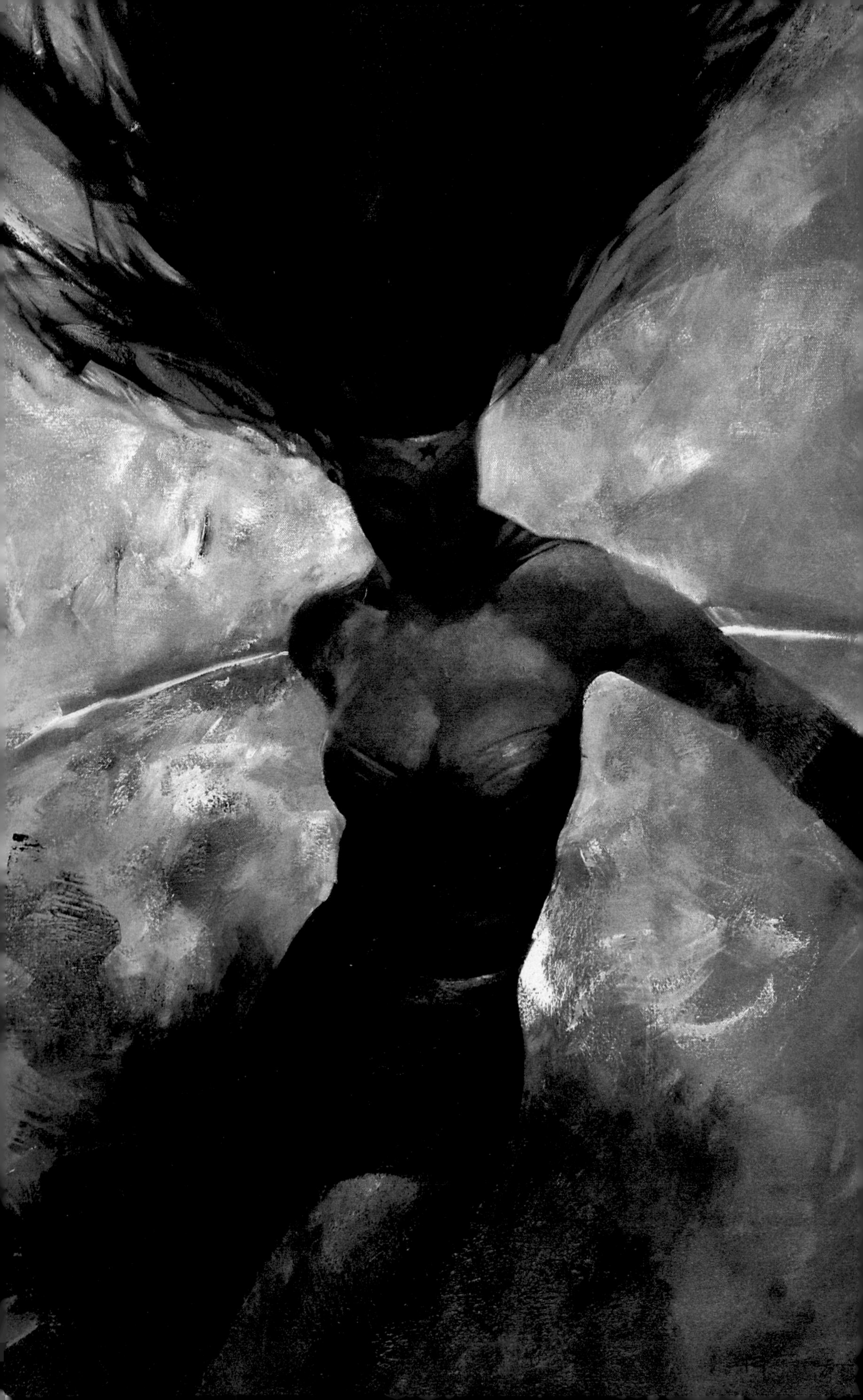

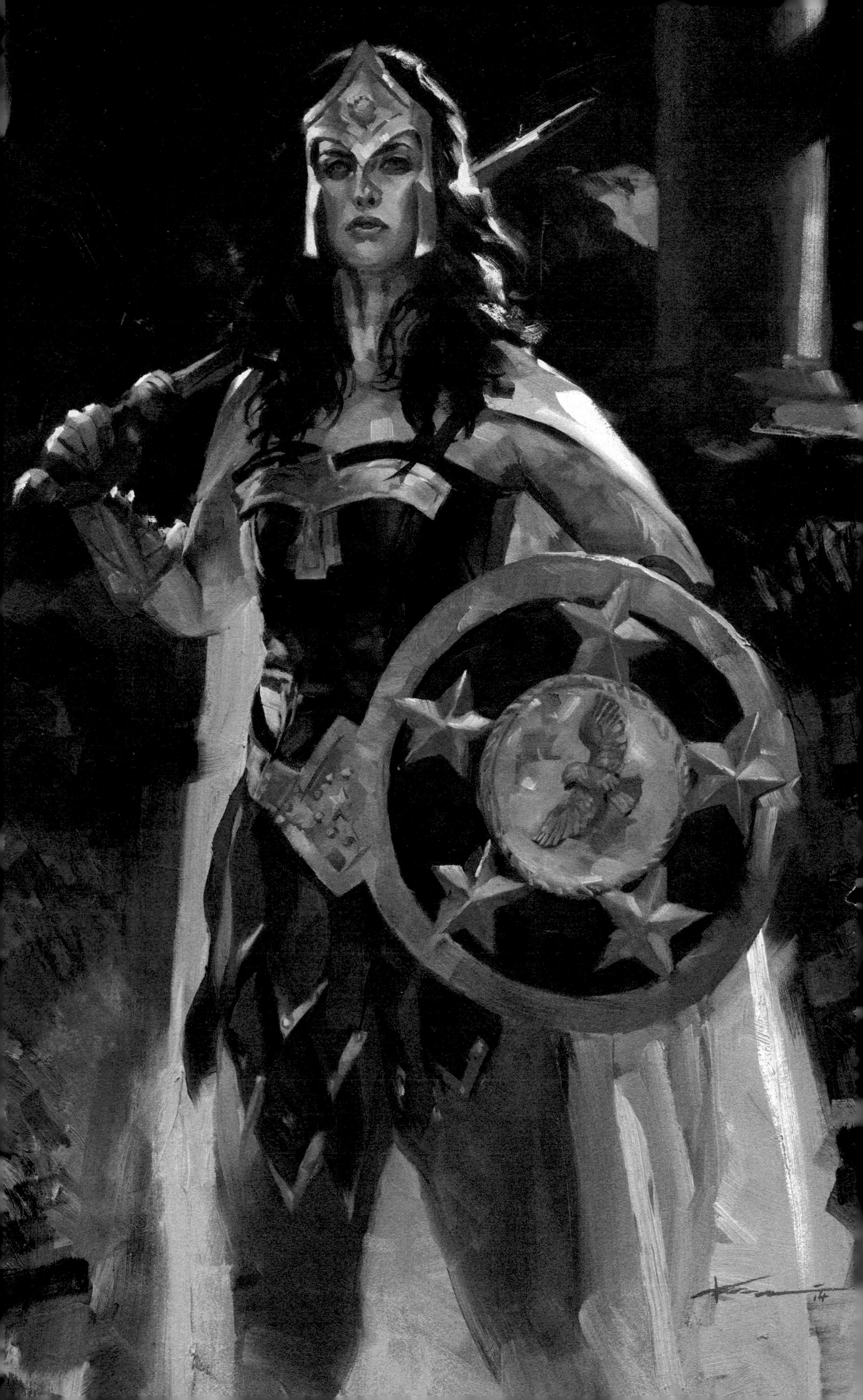

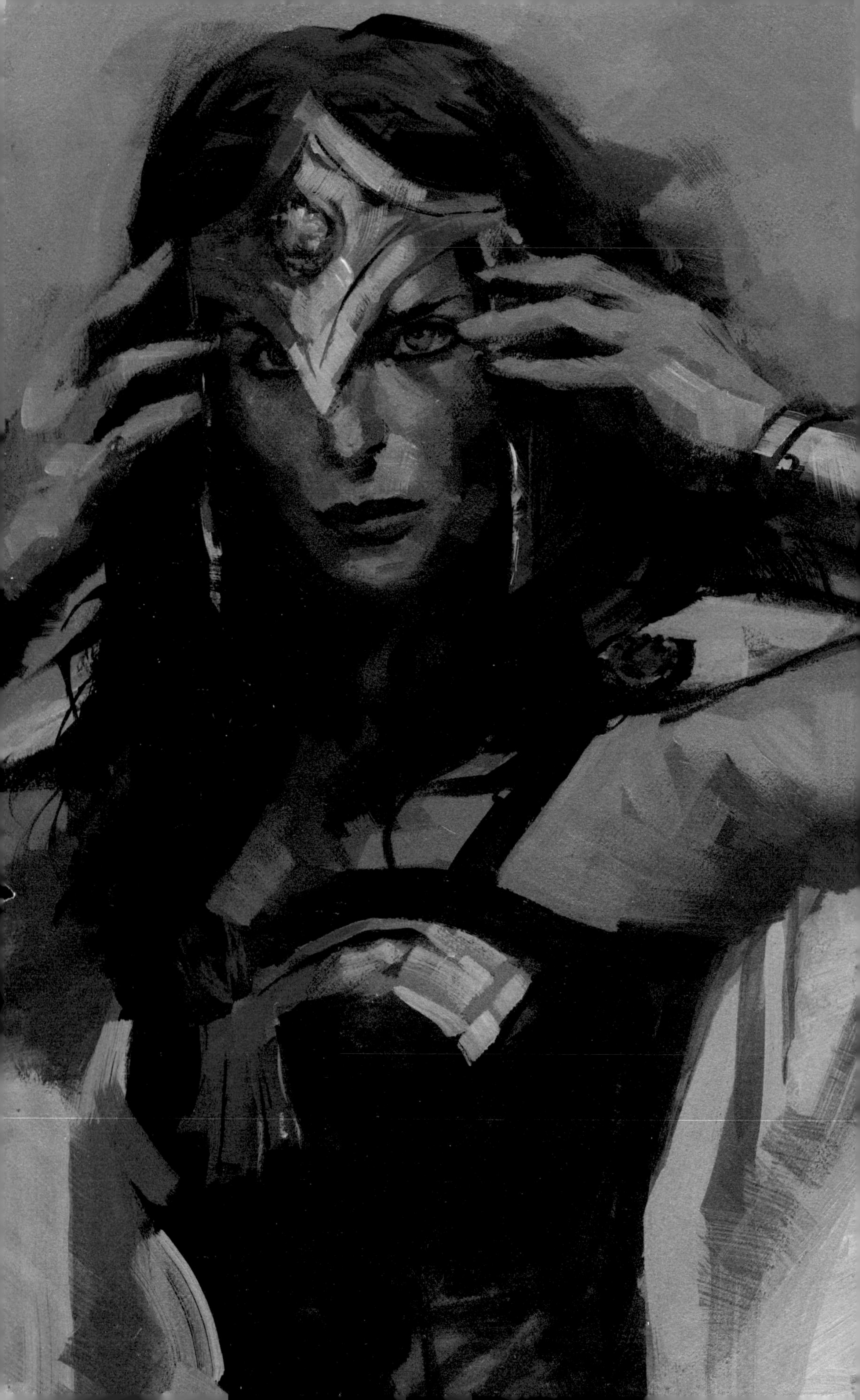